San Francisco Deaths 1865 - 1905

Volume II
Surnames
Starting with
E - K

Abstracts from
Surviving Civil Records

Compiled by
Barbara Ross Close
Vernon A. Deubler

Library of Congress Control Number 2009940489
ISBN (vol. ɪɪ) 978-0-9785694-2-6

Published by
California Genealogical Society
California Genealogical Society and Library
2201 Broadway, Suite LL2
Oakland, California 94612-3031

Telephone: 510-663-1358 – Fax: 510-662-1596
Website: *CaliforniaAncestors.org*

ACKNOWLEDGEMENTS

California Genealogical Society acknowledges with gratitude the many people who contributed to this publication, including Kay Arnold, Bob Bly, John Callan, Vernon Deubler, Joyce Dye, George Field, Wilbur Frye, Tom Gesner, Susan Goldstein, Marjorie Kelt, Judith C. Kettwig, Elizabeth G. Kot, Lynne Fisher, Lisa Lee, Eileen Lennon, Esther W. Mott, Eugene H. Peck, Mark Pierce, Michelle Reeder, Bev Schroder, Philip B. Seelinger, Nancy Hart Servin, Rick Sherman, Marilyn Tanner, Shirley Pugh Thomson, Terry Toomey, Judy Velardi, Lorna Wallace, Marjorie Wyatt, Sharon M. Yost, and Judy Zelver.

In addition, the society extends special thanks to:

Barbara Close, Jerry McGovern and Cathy Paris for transforming and publishing the index as reference books;

Susan Goldstein, City Archivist, San Francisco Public Library for arranging the transfer of early San Francisco Death indexes from the Department of Public health in San Francisco and holding and providing work space in the Library so they could be photographed and proofread; and

Eugene H. Peck for his weekly BART trip to proofread those volumes of old death indexes at the library.

INTRODUCTION

About The Records in This Index

This four volume set of books, with over 96,000 records, provides an index to all civil records of death known to have survived the San Francisco earthquake and fire of 1906. The sources for this information are several ledgers containing death registers and indexes to death registers, six months of death certificates and a coroner's register. The original ledgers are housed at the San Francisco Department of Public Health.

The Genealogical Society of Utah filmed all but two of the ledgers, and volunteers of the California Genealogical Society (CGS) indexed the records. The films of these records are available at CGS's Library, the San Francisco Public Library, and the Salt Lake City Family History Library. Photocopies of these records may be ordered from CGS.

Volunteers of the California Genealogical Society photographed and indexed the two ledgers not filmed by the Genealogical Society of Utah. CGS did not retain the photographs of the records.

To make it easier for readers to find needed information, all the indexes have been merged into a single index, presented alphabetically by surname and then first name, across this four volume set of books.

How to Use the Index

Entries are recorded as shown in the original records. All are computer sorted; thus, McCarthy and Mc Carthy may sort differently. Readers should also remember that the original records were handwritten and legibility therefore varied considerably. It was often difficult, for instance, to distinguish among the capitals L, S and T. A researcher might find Simmons rather than Timmons or Landers/Sanders. Do check alternate spellings.

A Set of Four Volumes

The index is published in four volumes as follows:

Volume I, surnames starting with A-D   Volume III, surnames starting with L-P
Volume II, surnames starting with E-K   Volume IV, surnames starting with Q-Z

What the Records Contain

Most records contain a wealth of genealogical information: sex, age (often in years, months and days), occupation, place of birth (sometimes very specific information, including, for instance, county of birth in Ireland), marital condition (married, single, widow or widower), date and cause of death, residence at time of death, place of burial, physician, undertaker and additional remarks. This collection includes records for many people who were not necessarily San Francisco residents, including the following:

- o   those who died in San Francisco,
- o   those who died at sea for whom San Francisco was the next port of call,
- o   military personnel who died in the Spanish-American War and whose bodies were returned to the Port of San Francisco,
- o   those who died abroad and whose bodies were returned to San Francisco,
- o   those whose bodies were to be re-interred, and
- o   those whose bodies were sent to San Francisco for forensic or other investigation.

Important Details about the Records

- The records are not entirely complete, they are not consistent in format, and there are gaps.
- The records from April 1, 1882 to June 30, 1889 are coroner's cases only, so there are no other death records for those years.
- Unnamed children are shown under the surname with "-----" or "c/o" which stands for "child of."
- Records for July 1898 to 16 March 1900 show **only** the year and month of death. Please do not request these records as all information available is listed in this index.
- The letters "a" and "b" which follow some of the certificate numbers are important as in some years the numbering began again on July 1, giving two records the same certificate number.
- The letter "c" indicates the source document is a death certificate.
- Beginning 1 July 1905, California death records were filed with the State Registrar of Vital Statistics in Sacramento and are available from that source or from the San Francisco Department of Public Health.

How to Obtain a Copy of a Record

Generally the original record contains more information than is included in this book. To order a photocopy of an original record as it appears in the old ledgers, use the Lookups feature on the society's website, *CaliforniaAncestors.org*. If you prefer to place your order by regular mail, please use a copy of the order form included at the back of this book.

FHL Film Numbers for Surviving San Francisco City and County Death Records

Researchers wishing to view the original records may consult these films held by the Family History Library in Salt Lake City, Utah.

Record Name	Inclusive Dates	Type of Record	Film No.
Death records, v.1	8 November – 1865 – 30 September 1869	death register, no index	975,830
Death records, v.2	October 1869 – 30 April 1873	death register, no index	975,830
Death records, v.3	1 April 1882 – 30 June 1889	coroner's cases and index	975,831
Death records, v.M	1 August 1894 – 30 June 1896	death register and index	975,832
Death records, v.O	1 July 1898 – 16 March 1900	index to death register	not filmed
Death records, v.P	17 March 1900 – 22 October 1901	death register and index	975, 833
Death records, v.Q	23 October 1901 – 30 June 1903	death register and index	974, 834
Death records, v.R	1 July 1903 – 30 June 1904	death register and index	975, 835
Death certificates	1 July 1904 – 1 December 1904	death certificates	975,839 - 47
Death records, last book	1 July 1904 – 31 January 1905	index to death register	not filmed

GEOGRAPHIC ABBREVIATIONS

U.S. State & Territories

AK	Alaska
AL	Alabama
AR	Arkansas
AZ	Arizona
CA	California
CO	Colorado
CT	Connecticut
DA	Dakota
DC	District of Columbia
DE	Delaware
FL	Florida
GA	Georgia
HI	Hawaii
IA	Iowa
ID	Idaho
IL	Illinois
IN	Indiana
KS	Kansas
KY	Kentucky
LA	Louisiana
MA	Massachusetts
MD	Maryland
ME	Maine
MI	Michigan
MN	Minnesota
MO	Missouri
MS	Mississippi
MT	Montana
NC	North Carolina
ND	North Dakota
NE	Nebraska
NH	New Hampshire
NJ	New Jersey
NM	New Mexico
NV	Nevada
NY	New York
OH	Ohio
OK	Oklahoma
OR	Oregon
PA	Pennsylvania
RI	Rhode Island
SC	South Carolina
SD	South Dakota
SF	San Francisco
TN	Tennessee
TX	Texas
UT	Utah
VA	Virginia
VT	Vermont
WA	Washington
WI	Wisconsin
WV	West Virginia
WT	Washington Territory
WY	Wyoming
YT	Yukon Territory

Canadian Provinces

AB	Alberta
BC	Brit. Columbia
MB	Manitoba
NB	New Brunswick
NF	Newfoundland
NS	Nova Scotia
ON	Ontario
PE	Prince Edward Island
QU	Quebec
SK	Saskatchewan

Countries and Other

AFR	Africa
ALG	Algiers
ALS	Alsace
AME	America
ARA	Arabia
ARG	Argentina
ASC	Ascension Island
AUS	Austria
AUT	Australia
AZO	Azores
BAH	Bahama Islands
BAL	Baltic
BAV	Bavaria
BEL	Belgium
BER	Bermuda
BHN	British Honduras
BOH	Bohemia
BRA	Brazil
BRH	British Honduras
CAI	Canary Islands
CAM	Central America
CAN	Canada
CHI	Chile
CHN	China
CLB	Colombia
COR	Costa Rica
CUB	Cuba
CVI	Cape Verde Islands
DAL	Dalmatia
DEN	Denmark
DOM	Dominican Republic
ECU	Ecuador
EIN	East Indies
ENG	England
ESP	Spain
FIJ	Fiji Island
FIN	Finland
FIS	French Islands
FRA	France
GER	Germany
GIB	Gibralter
GRE	Greece
GUA	Guatemala
GUM	Guam
HAI	Haiti
HAN	Hanover

HOL	Holland	NSW	New South Wales	SLA	Slavonia
HUN	Hungary	NZD	New Zealand	SLE	Sierra Leone
ICE	Iceland	PAN	Panama	SLO	Slovakia
IND	India	PER	Peru	SMA	Samoa
IOJ	Isle of Jersey	PHI	Philippines	SOA	South Africa
IOM	Isle of Man	POC	Pacific Ocean	SSI	South Sea Islands
IOW	Isle of Wight	POL	Poland	SVI	St. Vincent Island
IRL	Ireland	POR	Portugal	SWA	South Wales
ISI	Isle of St. Iago	PRU	Prussia	SWE	Sweden
ITA	Italy	PUR	Puerto Rico	SWT	Switzerland
JAM	Jamaica	RAM	Russian America	SYR	Syria
JPN	Japan	ROM	Romania	TAB	Taboga, South America
JAV	Java	RUS	Russia		
JER	Jerusalem	SAF	South Africa	TAH	Tahiti
KOR	Korea	SAM	South America	TAS	Tasmania
LAD	Ladrones Islands	SAN	Sandwich Islands	TON	Tonga
LIB	Liberia	SAX	Saxony	TUR	Turkey
LUX	Luxemberg	SCA	Scandinavia	URU	Uruguay
MAL	Malta	SCH	Schleswig	USA	United States
MAU	Mauritius	SCT	Scotland	VEN	Venezuela
MEX	Mexico	SDO	Santa Domingo	WAL	Wales
NAS	Nassau	SEA	At Sea	WIN	West Indies
NGR	New Granada	SGI	St. George Island	WIS	Western Isles
NIC	Nicaragua	SHI	St. Helena Island	WUR	Würtemberg
NOR	Norway	SIN	Singapore	YUG	Yugoslavia

NAME	AGE OR YOB.	BIRTH PLACE	CERT. NO	ID	DEATH YEAR	NAME	AGE OR YOB.	BIRTH PLACE	CERT. NO	ID	DEATH YEAR
EABOEM						Thomas	40	MA	1199		1900
Joseph	70	FRA	5189a		1895	Wm.	65	IRL	4859a		1895
						EAGAR					
EACHMAN						Thomas	70	NY	2412		1900
Herrelt	78	ME	2304		1894	Walter S.	32	CA	1157		1903
EACHUS						**E**AGEN					
W. A.	71	VA	7391		1902	James	<1	SF	8678		1868
EADE						**E**AGER					
Lena Ellen	1	SF	3683		1903	Daniel	52	IL	5909		1903
EADES						E. T.	11	MA	E29		1885
Mary Jane	<1	SF	2333a		1872	George L.	<1	SF	2474		1866
Robert R.	35	NSW	E44		1887	Sarah	48		1700		1902
William	49	ENG	1660b		1871						
						EAGETT					
EADIE						Geo. E.				Mar	1900
Jane B.	54	SCT	4568		1904						
						EAGLE					
EADON						Thomas B.	54	OH	708b		1895
Caroline	3	SF	9572		1868						
John C.	23	CAN	3301		1866	**E**AGLES					
						R. W.	40	NS	2729		1900
EAGAN											
——		SF	915		1870	**E**AGLESON					
——			5481		1867	Erastes	76	VA	6861		1895
Annie	2	SF	2604		1873	**E**AGON					
Bridget	1	SF	534b		1871	James Lawrence	76	VA	6110	Jan	1901
Catharine	<1	SF	1377		1869						
Edward	19	MA	2885a		1872	**E**AKEL					
Ellen	<1	SF	2603		1873	Bernhardina	77	GER	558		1900
Ellen	50	IRL	E20		1885	**E**AKIN					
James	52	IRL	E31		1886	Mary	30	MA	3550		1870
James E.	44	NY	2231		1901	**E**AKINS					
Jennie E.	45	NY	3277		1873	Isaiah O.	46		8914		1868
Jno. J.	70	IRL	6656a		1895	John J	26	KS	7034		1902
John				Oct	1899	**E**AKLE					
Lillie	13	SF	6933	Feb	1901	Irene Callaway	21	CA	32		1903
Michael		IRL	E38		1887	**E**ALING					
Michael	52	IRE	3196		1903	Leonard J. (soldier)			6929		1900

Key: a = 1st part of year; b = 2nd part of year; c = death certificate copy; c/o = child of

NAME	AGE OR YOB.	BIRTH PLACE	CERT. NO	ID	DEATH YEAR	NAME	AGE OR YOB.	BIRTH PLACE	CERT. NO	ID	DEATH YEAR
EALON						Frank L.				Mar	1900
Theresa	26	CA	8344		1900	Rose	39	CA	5230		1903
EAMES						**EARNEST**					
Helen	<1	SF	354		1902	Henry	17	NJ	7018		1868
EAMIS						Joseph T.				Aug	1898
Mary Frances	1	MO	3228		1873	**EARON**					
EANER						William	22	CA	E28		1885
Ralph Henry	13	CA	439		1900	**EARP**					
EANS						Kitty	39	MN	5926	Jan	1901
Lottie	33	GER	8001		1900	**EASDALE**					
EARL						Jane W.	37	IRE	7408		1902
Ida E.	40	MI	5244a		1896	**EASLEY**					
John O.				Jan	1900	Charles F. (soldier)			7744		1901
EARLE						**EASSON**					
Cecil	21	CA	5443a		1895	Margaret				Jan	1900
Elizabeth Barker	76	MA	378b		1895	**EAST**					
George H.	48	NY	1916		1900	Bertha	28	CA	1628		1903
Halford	92	VT	5341		1904	Wm.	36	WIN	1534b		1872
John Clay	37	NJ	9882		1868	**EASTABROOK**					
Mary	61	IRL	5659	Jan	1901	James A.	49	MA	2984		1866
Mary S.				Feb	1899	Margaret R.	40	NH	6442		1867
EARLEY						**EASTER**					
James , c/o		SF	2368a		1872	Elizabeth	1826	ENG	1591c		1904
James E.	62	IRL	2798		1895	Harry A. (soldier)			5687	Jan	1901
Ollie	11	PA	4043		1902	**EASTERBY**					
EARLINGTON						Agnes	66	ENG	5891a		1895
Maud, c/o		CA	1062		1900	**EASTERLY**					
EARLL						Jas. E. (soldier)			1177		1901
Cornelia Ann	84	NY	2336		1903	**EASTERN**					
EARLSTEN						Susan	73	NF	E9		1883
Beulah	23	NY	8743		1904	**EASTHAM**					
EARLY						Henry Sherman	66	MA	4279		1900
Edward	24	NY	4437		1867						
Ernest (ex soldier)	35		6342		1904						

NAME	AGE OR YOB.	BIRTH PLACE	CERT. NO	ID	DEATH YEAR	NAME	AGE OR YOB.	BIRTH PLACE	CERT. NO	ID	DEATH YEAR
EASTING						Mary F.				Apr	1899
Bartholomew				Jan	1900	Samuel Edward	1	SF	2409		1903
EASTLAND						**EASTWOOK**					
J. G., c/o	<1	NY	11b		1872	Mary Hannah	1864	ENG	1958c		1904
Val Leer	57	PA	1308		1894	**EATON**					
EASTMAN						——			4478		1867
Annette O.	26	CA	2128		1903	Agnes	36	CA	215		1901
Catherine	55	NY	5831		1902	Almira	86	MA	3974		1902
Florence M.	1	SF	5359		1896	Arthur Holland				Aug	1898
Galen				Jan	1899	Charles C.	52	OH	8494		1903
Iva M.	11	CA	9806		1868	Charles S.	58	NH	4455		1896
James Iva M.			9560		1868	Francis G.	46	ENG	5291		1896
John (soldier)			8774		1901	Frank G.				Apr	1899
Lottie	22	CA	7362		1902	Frederick	66	ENG	355		1902
Loucretia M.	78	TN	8308		1903	Helen A.	26	CA	1500		1903
Luke F.	<1	SF	5598	Jan	1901	Isabella M.	64	SCT	6165a		1895
Mary L. F.	66	MI	8384		1903	J. Ward	48	NY	2436		1866
Mattie M.	27	LA	3114	Oct	1901	James	30	NY	9909		1868
Ruby	20	CA	6523		1902	Mary A.	49	MA	51		1870
Sophia	80	NH	270		1903	Reuben Lloyd	1870	CA	246c		1904
William H.				Jan	1900	William				Jul	1898
EASTON						**EATWELL**					
Ansel I.	49	MA	8691		1868	Charles				Jul	1899
Charles	71	SCT	6494		1902	**EAU**					
Charlie	35	MA	8162		1868	Ah Song					1899
Elizabeth	<1	SF	3436b		1870	**EAVES**					
Harry	33	WI	6755		1903	Jane	42	IRL	617b		1871
John	78	SCT	6943		1904	**EAYRS**					
EASTWOOD						George Alfred	9	SF	2247		1902
Barr/Jessie, c/o		SF	1493		1900	George/Mary, c/o	<1	SF	7935		1900
Charles Edward	1	SF	1263		1869	Harry E.	22	MA	374b		1871
Gertrude J.	76	HOL	6767		1900	Jannie W.	67	MA	73b		1895
Henry	<1	SF	2085		1873	Mary Ellen	28	SF	6594		1903
Herbert	65	ENG	5499	Jan	1901						
Leurs D.				Mar	1900						

Key: a = 1st part of year; b = 2nd part of year;
c = death certificate copy; c/o = child of

NAME	AGE OR YOB.	BIRTH PLACE	CERT. NO	ID	DEATH YEAR	NAME	AGE OR YOB.	BIRTH PLACE	CERT. NO	ID	DEATH YEAR
EBARRA						Maria	39	GER	3318		1900
Felix	<1	SF	4839		1902	**EBERLE**					
EBBECK						Ardis Mervin	2	SF	417		1902
Freda, c/o	<1	CA	6378		1904	Christian				Nov	1898
EBBENGHAUSEN						Clifford	4	CA	519		1902
George	24	GER	8996		1868	Edmond	7	SF	6014		1903
EBBETS						Leo	73	GER	2819		1903
Daniel	15	SF	58a		1871	Walburga	63	GER	930		1903
EBBINGHAUSAN						**EBERT**					
Henry	<1	SF	8826		1868	Bertha A.	<1	SF	2862		1894
EBBINGHAUSEN						Jacob				Feb	1899
Annie	30	GER	3040		1873	John				Feb	1900
Edward L. E.	30	CA	5823		1904	Louisa				Aug	1899
Henry	60	GER	2567		1900	**EBERWEIN**					
EBEL						Teresa	26	IRE	3325		1903
Nannie B.	27	CA	1604		1903	**EBIG**					
EBELING						Edward A. (soldier)			2045		1901
Anna Maria	35	GER	1278a		1871	**EBNER**					
EBELOE						Charles M.	44	GER	6883		1868
Martin	48	DEN	3014		1900	Paul Jerome	<1	SF	2818		1902
EBEMEIN						**EBRARD**					
Walter J.	<1	SF	8160		1903	John	39	FRA	2929		1902
EBENHACK						**EBY**					
Frank			8131		1904	Clara Francis	19	MO	452		1866
EBER						Eleanor Montague	61	PA	7643		1904
Paul/Julia, c/o		SF	1547		1901	L.	1882	MN	3319c		1904
EBERHARD						**ECCLES**					
Joseph C.	2	BC	1131		1866	Alice	50	IRE	7340		1902
EBERHARDT						Cath	<1	SF	3591		1867
——		SF	1064		1870	Chas.		SF	2291b		1895
Caroline E.	<1	SF	1287		1869	Francis	15	NY	8766		1868
EBERHART						Robert	77	IRE	860		1903
C.	37	GER	3919		1902	**ECELSEN**					
						Charles	43	DEN	6298		1900

*Key: a = 1st part of year; b = 2nd part of year;
c = death certificate copy; c/o = child of*

NAME	AGE OR YOB.	BIRTH PLACE	CERT. NO	ID	DEATH YEAR	NAME	AGE OR YOB.	BIRTH PLACE	CERT. NO	ID	DEATH YEAR
ECHARD						**ECKENRATH**					
Maria Elizth	<1	SF	5885		1867	Rosa	2	SF	4250		1867
ECHERT						**ECKENROTH**					
George M.	30	MO	1132		1870	Frank Henry	45	SF	4840		1902
ECHEVERRIA						**ECKER**					
Dolores				Mar	1899	Margaret Ann				Jan	1900
Frank	1866	URU	3005c		1904	**ECKERMANN**					
John Albert				Mar	1899	Charles	78	GER	3697		1900
ECHFELDT						**ECKERS**					
Fannie	6	SF	2983		1866	Christina	79	GER	1065		1869
ECHGELMEIER						**ECKERT**					
——		SF	874		1870	Ignatius	55	NY	E1		1882
						Josephine				Jun	1899
ECHLMAIER						Peter J. (soldier)			8776		1901
Joseph	50	BAV	1060		1870	**ECKFELDT**					
ECHOLDT						William Henry	12	CA	3384		1900
Charles	16	GER	9615		1868	**ECKHARDT**					
ECHTER						Barbara				Jul	1898
Margaret	42	FRA	1323b		1872	Barbara Ann				Oct	1898
ECK						Conrad	53	GER	1743		1894
Adam Joseph	81	GER	6599	Feb	1901	Fred	68	GER	5663		1896
John	57	LA	7036		1903	Joseph Leslie	<1	SF	5784		1903
ECKART						Louis (soldier)			1812		1900
Anton P.				Oct	1898	Robert J.	1	CA	6871		1903
Augusta	6	SF	3835		1902	**ECKHART**					
Chas. F./M. B., c/o				Jan	1900	John F.	<1	SF	116b		1871
Elizabeth	63	GER	8371		1904	**ECKHOFF**					
John D.					1898	William T.	52	GER	4364		1896
May Tichner				Feb	1900	**ECKLAND**					
ECKEL						John/Rebecca, c/o	1	SF	672		1903
John Nicholas	78	BAV	6479	Feb	1901	Nelse/Mary, c/o		SF	1278		1895
ECKELMANN						**ECKLES**					
Otto	78	GER	6646		1903	Elsie Evelyn	1	SF	256		1903
						Robert E.	65	IL	7324		1900

Key: a = 1st part of year; b = 2nd part of year;
c = death certificate copy; c/o = child of

NAME	AGE OR YOB.	BIRTH PLACE	CERT. NO	ID	DEATH YEAR
ECKLEY					
John Lowell					1898
Sarah E.	69	MA	5279		1903
ECKLUND					
Caroline Elizabeth	8	SF	3926		1900
ECKMAN					
Amanda C.	28	SWE	5502		1904
Mattie George	55	PA	4627		1903
Oscar/Lillian, c/o		SF	1718		1901
Sarah Avery	51	NY	5633		1902
ECKMANN					
Harry	5	CA	E33		1886
ECKOWICZ					
Alec/Yette, c/o		SF	790		1895
ECKS					
Adam, c/o	<1	SF	2135a		1872
ECKSTEIN					
Mary E.	51	OH	7252		1902
EDARDS					
Jno. Sidney	61	ENG	2231		1894
EDBERG					
Magnus	74	SWE	1936		1900
EDDINGTON					
James	33	NY	1226b		1871
EDDY					
Charles John	14	SF	5154		1867
Elizabeth	81	ENG	6722Feb		1901
Hetty Rebecca	11	SF	3224		1900
Isabelle	61	LA	2557		1895
Laura	63	CAN	1352b		1895
Mathew T.	29	NE	E30		1886
Maude Lillian					1899
Morton	33	NY	1220		1869
Nellie L.	<1	SF	4067		1896

NAME	AGE OR YOB.	BIRTH PLACE	CERT. NO	ID	DEATH YEAR
Rosina	45	ENG	8803		1904
EDE					
H. P./I., c/o	<1	SF	4185		1895
Nettie E.	4	SF	797b		1871
Walter	65	ENG	7481		1901
William					Oct 1898
Wm./C., c/o		SF	1371b		1872
EDEL					
August	23	GER	3826Nov		1901
EDELMANN					
Carl	24	CA	7857		1901
George W.	76	GER	6401		1902
Louisa		SF	4228b		1870
M. A., c/o		SF	1178b		1872
Sibilla	23	GER	1416		1869
EDELSTEIN					
Annie	<1	SF	1297		1869
EDELSTEN					
Ernest (soldier)			1544		1900
Maggie	32	IL	4019		1903
EDEN					
Bessie	<1	SF	5423a		1895
Henry Wm.	<1	SF	1561		1866
John	<1	SF	8878		1868
Menne	51	GER	7840		1900
(twins)			5480		1867
EDGAN					
Thomas	33	IRE	7719		1903
EDGAR					
Daniel J.	68	MA	7447		1902
David	61	SCT	2987		1895
George	31	OR	8892		1901
James					Aug 1898
John					Jan 1899

Key: a = 1st part of year; b = 2nd part of year; c = death certificate copy; c/o = child of

NAME	AGE OR YOB.	BIRTH PLACE	CERT. NO	ID	DEATH YEAR	NAME	AGE OR YOB.	BIRTH PLACE	CERT. NO	ID	DEATH YEAR
Philip Blain	<1	SF	1615b		1872	Margaret	86	IRL	3998a		1895
Robert W.	54	ENG	2502		1900	Sophia	65	IRL	2856a		1872
Will F.	46	IA	5026		1902	Stephen	1839	IRE	2849c		1904
EDGERLY						William, Mrs.	31	ENG	4828		1896
Henry F.	38	NH	7031		1868	**EDMONDSON**					
EDGERTON						Mary Jane	50	ENG	6481		1903
Arthur J. (soldier)			4583		1901	Sarah Jane	59	NH	866		1900
Frances B.	58	MD	5520		1902	**EDMONSON**					
N. J./M., c/o				Dec	1899	Holt	51	ENG	2170		1900
Walter	33	PA	5656		1903	Johnathan					1899
EDINGER						**EDMONSTON**					
Achilles				Jan	1899	B. B.	62	MD	E36		1886
EDISON						Martha A.	41	DC	1065		1869
Emma	28	IRL	838		1870	Raphael A. (soldier)			366		1900
EDITH						**EDMUNDS**					
——	<1	SF	855		1894	Evan	60	WAL	3906a		1895
EDLEFSON						Margaret	<1	SF	984a		1871
M.					1899	Mary E.				Jul	1899
EDLIN						**EDSALL**					
Lena	15	CA	6108		1902	Edmund P.					1898
EDLUND						**EDSELL**					
Gustaf E.				Feb	1900	Jacob W.	40	NY	4204		1900
EDMESTER						**EDSEN**					
Frank J.	<1	SF	2912		1894	Charles H./Anna, c/o	<1	SF	6699		1896
EDMINISTER						**EDSON**					
Newton/Annie, c/o		SF	5729		1902	Albert	60	NOR	1375		1900
EDMINSTER						**EDSTROM**					
Violet Etta				Mar	1900	Thomas	78	PE	927		1900
EDMOND						**EDSTRON**					
Louis	75	FRA	3148		1895	Anna	89	IRE	2560		1902
EDMONDS						**EDWARD**					
Anson (soldier)	21	IL	2464		1900	——	<1	SF	3810		1870
Henry	1865	CA	1928c		1904	Clarence				Jun	1899
						Harry	29	IL	5681		1896

NAME	AGE OR YOB.	BIRTH PLACE	CERT. NO	ID	DEATH YEAR	NAME	AGE OR YOB.	BIRTH PLACE	CERT. NO	ID	DEATH YEAR
John	40	ENG	E45		1887	Frank G.	75	ENG	7731		1900
John	52	ITA	9326		1868	Frank H. (soldier)			132		1901
Joseph				May	1899	Frederick	12	CA	33		1870
EDWARDS						George C.	23	IN	1441		1902
Adelia Elizabeth	53	IRE	6015		1903	George F. (soldier)			3031	Oct	1901
Adeline F.	59	MA	2765		1900	George Washington	<1	SF	9125		1901
Alberto Florence	1904	SF	1483c		1904	H. H.	40	VT	632b		1895
Alton	<1	SF	79		1901	Harry S.	52	ENG	1892b		1872
Ann	69	WAL	1866		1901	Henry	68	MA	3371		1896
Anne				Mar	1899	Hyman/Eva, c/o		SF	5110		1901
Augustus					1898	Isabella	14		1046		1870
Axle	33	SWE	3297		1895	James	80	OH	4892		1903
Belle M.	44	SF	2827		1902	James	84	ENG	1572		1900
c/o	<1	SF	2497a		1872	James				Mar	1899
Carl	<1	SF	5892a		1895	John	28	ENG	1480b		1872
Carrie Lucille	15	CA	5163		1904	John	32	OR	7363		1901
Charles	<1	SF	6052		1867	John	68	ENG	6944		1904
Chas. W. (soldier)			6811		1900	John Daniel	37	WAL	4860		1896
Daisy Blondina	20	OR	9078		1901	John G.					1898
Dennis	<1	SF	2703		1894	John Henry	23	CA	6208		1902
Dollie				Jul	1899	John/Anna, c/o	1904	SF	1735		1904
Douglas F.				Oct	1898	Joseph Leslie				Jun	1899
Edward	73	NY	2491		1901	Josephine	<1	SF	7471		1900
Edward H.	40	ENG	981		1870	Justus Huff	69	VT	5829		1896
Edwin C.	33	NC	8754		1903	Kittie	27	CAN	633b		1895
Elaine	<1	CA	7149		1903	Leah	1	CA	634b		1895
Elihu	23	NC	9611		1901	Louis	61	NY	9213		1868
Ellen	3	SF	3686		1870	Lulu	28	SF	5369		1902
Emelia	<1	SF	1006		1868	Maggie	31	MD	5104		1903
Ernest	26	ENG	3448		1903	Margaret	<1	SF	5210		1902
Etta	1	SF	4137		1903	Margaret Ann	22	CA	7288		1902
Eugene Samuel	36	CA	1501		1903	Margaret M.	37	NY	1358b		1871
Everett John David	6	SF	1608		1901	Mary Ann	54	ENG	1171		1894
Fay	<1	CA	1211		1902	Mary E.	31	CA	3390		1903
Frank	1831	SCT	1896c		1904	Mary E.				Jun	1899
Frank	18	OH	5657		1903	Mary Elizabeth	81	ENG	2379		1900

Key: a = 1st part of year; b = 2nd part of year; c = death certificate copy; c/o = child of

NAME	AGE OR YOB.	BIRTH PLACE	CERT. NO	ID	DEATH YEAR
Mary Jane	<1	SF	1266		1869
Nellie W.	45	RI	6370		1902
R. M.	70	ENG	6483		1896
Rosanna	69	IRE	356		1902
Rowena M.	<1	SF	3458		1870
Russell Francis	<1	SF	7455		1904
Samuel	27	CAN	445b		1895
Sarah Grace					Apr 1899
Shirley	<1	CA	6290a		1895
Teresa	<1	SF	2584		1894
Thomas	45	MO	8805		1901
Thomas C.	4	SF	8396		1868
Thomas M.	58	NY	3647		1896
Thomas R. (soldier)			7298		1901
Vermy J. (soldier)			135		1901
Wilhelm	29	PA	5006		1901
William					1898
William Thomas	57	ENG	7392		1902
Wm. D.					Nov 1898

EDWARDSEN

NAME	AGE OR YOB.	BIRTH PLACE	CERT. NO	ID	DEATH YEAR
Hanna S.					Aug 1898

EDWIN

NAME	AGE OR YOB.	BIRTH PLACE	CERT. NO	ID	DEATH YEAR
Willie	<1	SF	5339		1896

EELLS

NAME	AGE OR YOB.	BIRTH PLACE	CERT. NO	ID	DEATH YEAR
Allan M.	71	NY	413b		1871
James J. (soldier)	29	IL	1583		1900

EFFINGER

NAME	AGE OR YOB.	BIRTH PLACE	CERT. NO	ID	DEATH YEAR
Christen	70	GER	2668		1903

EFFORS

NAME	AGE OR YOB.	BIRTH PLACE	CERT. NO	ID	DEATH YEAR
Frank	65	RUS	3874		1903

EGAN

NAME	AGE OR YOB.	BIRTH PLACE	CERT. NO	ID	DEATH YEAR
Annie E.	50	CT	6016		1903
Bridget	<1	NY	456		1870
Bridget					Jan 1900
Catherine	<1	SF	1285		1869

NAME	AGE OR YOB.	BIRTH PLACE	CERT. NO	ID	DEATH YEAR
Daniel V.	34	SF	1172		1903
Eugene/Lulu, c/o		SF	533		1902
Frank	38	IRL	165b		1871
Frank J.	37	SF	56		1902
George D.	59	IRE	8385		1903
Henry	75	IRL	4078		1900
James	33	IRL	3128a		1872
James	36	MA	2793		1866
Jane	49	SF	4303		1903
John	<1	SF	2813a		1872
John	32	IRL	2093		1902
John	89	IRL	5442a		1895
John	68	IRL	5267		1896
John Henry					Jun 1899
John W.	66	IRL	8689		1900
Katie Agnes	14	SF	8324		1903
Lena Bernice	20	SF	2669		1903
Margaret	75	NY	6777	Feb	1901
Maria	26	IRE	8942		1903
Mary	4	SF	4326		1867
Mary	67	IRL	5091		1901
Mary Clement	20	CA	5210		1903
Mary Francis	6	MA	7109		1904
Mary M.	<1	SF	1522a		1871
Mary Mechhilda	40	IRE	7076		1904
Michael	78	IRL	2661		1894
Michael	72	IRL	6147a		1895
Michael J.	1867	IRE	747c		1904
Minnie Lake	27		9058		1901
Nellie					Feb 1900
P. J.	60	IRL	E34		1886
Rose	39	MA	7206		1903
Sarah Ann	<1	SF	729b		1872
Thomas	<1	SF	1390		1870
Thomas	1858	MA	190c		1904
Thomas					Jan 1900

Key: a = 1st part of year; b = 2nd part of year;
c = death certificate copy; c/o = child of

NAME	AGE OR YOB.	BIRTH PLACE	CERT. NO	ID	DEATH YEAR	NAME	AGE OR YOB.	BIRTH PLACE	CERT. NO	ID	DEATH YEAR
Thomas (soldier)			257		1901	**EGGERS**					
Thos. F.	27	IRL	1433b		1872	Ferdinand	42	GER	1072		1869
Thos./Theresa, c/o		SF	4110		1902	George H.	76	GER	6043		1896
William Matthew	<1	SF	5384		1901	H. Fred	69	GER	880		1900
William Vincent	28	SF	3909		1903	Harry	30	GER	E21		1885
EGAR						Harry	35	GER	E22		1885
Fanny	49	GER	2699		1902	Minna				Jan	1900
EGBERT						**EGGERT**					
Edward	72	GER	6402		1902	Chas	40		6141		1900
Harry C.				May	1899	Louise L.	77	GER	1560		1902
EGEBERG						William	50	GER	3449		1903
Annie	1856	GER	463c		1904	**EGGERTSON**					
EGEN						Jacob				Mar	1899
George	12	SF	6316		1867	**EGGLESTON**					
EGER						John D. (soldier)			872		1902
Justine				Nov	1898	**EGGLETON**					
Lucien	38	SF	2922		1895	Lilley	5	SF	9985		1868
EGERTON						Rasina	10	SF	1129		1869
Tom	<1	SF	8965		1901	**EGGRLING**					
EGETT						Hilda	1	SF	1858		1894
Raymond				Jan	1899	**EGHMEY**					
EGG						William J.	27	NY	3855		1870
Ar	25	CHN	1420		1869	**EGING**					
EGGELING						Christian					1898
Charles	59	GER	1256b		1895	**EGLE**					
EGGELTON						Leo (baker)			2288c		1904
Mary Ann	65	ENG	4220		1902	**EGLESTON**					
EGGENBERGER						Arthur	21	CAN	E37		1886
Ann				Feb	1900	Lillian B.	32	MA	8158		1901
EGGER						**EGLING**					
Mary	6	CA	2195b		1895	Rosa	4	NY	4749		1901
EGGERDINGER						**EGLUND**					
G. F.	35	OH	6749		1902	Emil	68	DEN	3335		1902

Key: a = 1st part of year; b = 2nd part of year;
c = death certificate copy; c/o = child of

NAME	AGE OR YOB.	BIRTH PLACE	CERT. NO	ID	DEATH YEAR	NAME	AGE OR YOB.	BIRTH PLACE	CERT. NO	ID	DEATH YEAR
EGRY						**E**HREICHFORT					
Paul	42	HUN	5211		1903	Carl A.	68	GER	5139		1867
EGUARD						**E**HRENFFORT					
Eliza	43	FRA	E10		1883	Fredrike	24	GER	4357		1867
EGUREN						Tito	57	HUN	838		1894
Maura	19	MEX	1729		1866	**E**HRENPFORT					
EHINGER						Edward					Nov 1898
Rudolph					Nov 1899	**E**HRENWERTH					
EHLART						Oswald	14	SF	7766		1901
Charles	44	GER	3516		1903	**E**HRET					
EHLBREK						Albert	66	GER	1859		1903
——	<1	SF	9725		1868	Eugenie	31	FRA	782		1901
EHLE						**E**HRHARDT					
Oscar	30	MA	1312		1866	Adam	64	GER	356b		1895
EHLERS						Chas.	50	GER	E14		1884
Betty	<1	SF	1361		1869	**E**HRHART					
Charles G.	1895	SF	3061c		1904	Anna Josephine	4	SF	6700		1896
F.	43	GER	1617b		1872	**E**HRHEART					
Henry	2	SF	94		1865	Thomas A. (soldier)			7990		1900
Richard A. J.	32	NY	1443		1903	**E**HRHOM					
Wm.	1	SF	1000b		1871	Paul Adolph	47	GER	2557		1873
EHLERT						**E**HRICH					
Jennie	41	AUT	931		1903	Herman (soldier)			7764		1902
John (soldier)	25	KS	3369		1903	**E**HRICHS					
Robert					Jan 1900	Helene					May 1899
EHM						**E**HRICHZ					
Charles Arthur	15	ENG	2568		1900	Johann E.	3	SF	117		1870
Rosalie	38	GER	4504		1901	**E**HRLICH					
EHMAN						——	<1	SF	5378		1867
George E.	45	GER	1499b		1872	Fanny	<1	SF	1003		1868
EHNERT						Herman	1864	GER	2888c		1904
August	46	AUS	2864		1902	**E**HRLICHE					
						Isaac	1	SF	1492		1866

Key: a = 1st part of year; b = 2nd part of year;
c = death certificate copy; c/o = child of

NAME	AGE OR YOB.	BIRTH PLACE	CERT. NO	ID	DEATH YEAR	NAME	AGE OR YOB.	BIRTH PLACE	CERT. NO	ID	DEATH YEAR
EHRMAN						**EICHLAMER**					
Herman	52	GER	1161		1902	Geo. (soldier)			6176		1900
M./F., c/o	<1	SF	1309		1869	**EICHLBERGER**					
May	1	SF	2494		1873	Charley	29	GER	1832b		1895
EHRMANN						**EICHNER**					
Anton	<1	SF	3880		1867	John Jr.	42	OH	2071		1902
Frank/Maggie, c/o	<1	CA	7882		1901	June				Oct	1899
Martin	72	GER	2956		1900	**EICHOLZER**					
Max		GER	1403		1869	Margaret	49	IRL	2091		1900
Valentine					1899	**EICHORN**					
EHRNK						E. F.	42	GER	1205		1869
Willie P. T.	<1	SF	107b		1895	Mathias				Feb	1899
EHRTICK						**EICHS**					
Louis, c/o	<1	SF	2980		1866	Jacob	40	GER	641b		1871
EHRU						**EICKELROTH**					
George H					1898	Paul	27	CA	7241		1903
EIBEN						**EICKHOFF**					
Edgard Henry	1	SF	2411		1900	Lula				Nov	1898
EICH						**EICKHOLT**					
Jacob				Jan	1899	Frank	<1	SF	7888		1904
EICHEL						**EICKHOLTZ**					
Christian	37	GER	2156		1873	Levi E. (soldier)			7135		1901
Lizzie	6	SF	9254		1868	**EIDENMULLER**					
EICHELITE						Candida	32	ITA	6865	Feb	1901
Virginia				Mar	1900	Fredrick A.	<1	SF	1992		1866
EICHEN						George	41	GER	1296a		1871
Cecelia B.				Jan	1899	**EIDINGER**					
EICHENBERG						Edward	66	GER	5872		1903
Alma Elizabeth	53	OH	3260	Nov	1901	**EIDSNER**					
EICHERMAN						Cesket O.				Mar	1900
A.	38	GER	9092		1868	**EIDSNESS**					
EICHHOLZ						Ashel O. (soldier)			6254		1900
Louis Arthur	2	SF	9145		1901						

Key: *a = 1st part of year; b = 2nd part of year;*
c = death certificate copy; c/o = child of

NAME	AGE OR YOB.	BIRTH PLACE	CERT. NO	ID	DEATH YEAR	NAME	AGE OR YOB.	BIRTH PLACE	CERT. NO	ID	DEATH YEAR
EIFGANG						**EISELEU**					
Gottfried (soldier)			6928		1900	Oscar James	1875	CA	2978c		1904
EIGASIER						**EISEN**					
Joseph	50	FRA	1110		1870	Adelaida	58	MEX	2012		1894
EILGELMAN						Augustus F.	48	SWE	2399		1873
Mary		SF	1432		1900	Babette	76	GER	7524		1901
						Francis J.	69	SWE	6678a		1895
EINCELEN						George	43	GER	1080		1870
Juanita	<1	SF	1690		1900	Peter	61	GER	1862		1900
EINFELD						**EISENACH**					
Frederick				Aug	1899	Richard (soldier)			131		1901
EINFELDT						**EISENBACH**					
Christ	37	GER	7491		1903	Adolph				Jul	1899
EINSELEN						Adolph				May	1899
Augusta G.				Jan	1899	**EISENBEIS**					
Ernst J.				Mar	1899	Gustave	1877	CA	510c		1904
Friedericke	77	GER	4471		1901						
Henry W.	37	GER	8705		1903	**EISENBERG**					
						Eugene	<1	SF	3181		1895
EINSFELD						Jennie	<1	SF	4087		1902
Peter	55	GER	5802		1896	Sara	3	CA	E42		1887
EINSTEIN						**EISENBERS**					
Ellen	41	IL	2429		1901	Gustave	1877	CA	510c		1904
Jacob	76	GER	2298		1903						
Morris				Jan	1900	**EISENHARDT**					
						John				Jan	1899
EIS						**EISENHAUER**					
Hildegard, Mrs.	27	GER	2597		1901	Clayton	12	SF	6443a		1895
EISEL						Margerette	75	PA	62		1903
Carl	<1	AUT	1366		1869	**EISENMANN**					
Carl William	66	GER	2092		1900	Christina	75	GER	805		1902
EISELE						Lena	34	PA	7977		1903
Anna L.	1	SF	1547		1894	Peter	32	MO	6830		1903
Fritz	44	GER	8657		1904	**EISENSCHIMEL**					
EISELEN						Edward C.	21	SF	2577		1901
Alfred Julius	55	GER	5782	Jan	1901						

NAME	AGE OR YOB.	BIRTH PLACE	CERT. NO	ID	DEATH YEAR
EISENZOPF					
Gertrude H.				Feb	1900
EISFELDER					
Caroline	<1	SF	5639		1867
Samuel D.	27	CA	747b		1895
EISLER					
John	70	BOH	5783a		1895
EISMANN					
Marie	20	GER	5893		1896
EISNER					
Daniel	50	BOH	1747b		1872
Johanna	32	GER	2187		1902
Joseph	46	BOH	6396		1867
Mark	45	CA	4801		1903
Nathan/Solate, c/o	<1	SF	8300		1903
EISSELDEN					
——			6333		1867
EITZEN					
Carolina	48	GER	4183		1900
EK					
Mary				Nov	1898
EKBERG					
Charles					1898
Marie E.	23	IL	3189		1895
Otto M.	27	IL	3431	Nov	1901
EKBLOM					
Charles	24	OR	5394		1904
EKHARDT					
Henry	42	OH	2506a		1872
EKLUND					
Gustave (soldier)			3032	Oct	1901
John P.	50	SWE	1185b		1895
Marie				Feb	1899

NAME	AGE OR YOB.	BIRTH PLACE	CERT. NO	ID	DEATH YEAR
EKMAN					
Carl	35	SWE	6232		1896
EKOLA					
Mathew (soldier)			8773		1901
EKOOS					
Tom/Martine, c/o	<1	SF	3687		1901
EKSTROM					
Augusta	54	SWE	1165b		1871
Charles Andrew	74	SWE	2777		1902
William	3	JAV	9665		1868
William Charles	18	CA	3584		1902
EL					
Hin Wo				Oct	1899
ELAM					
Robert H.	8	SF	1246		1866
ELBERLING					
Flora	20	WI	6382		1903
Johanna	33	GER	2192		1873
ELBERT					
Otto (soldier)	24	GER	3085	Oct	1901
ELBERTO					
Joseph	45	IRL	1148		1900
ELBERTY					
George W.	65	PA	8346		1904
ELDEN					
William H.	29	ENG	1594		1866
ELDER					
Alvin E.				Mar	1900
Charles N.	35	ME	424		1865
Elizabeth	4	CA	7792		1868
Frank F.	22	WA	8893		1901
George W. (soldier)			2046		1901
Suviah L.	75	MA	6526		1903

Key: a = 1st part of year; b = 2nd part of year; c = death certificate copy; c/o = child of

NAME	AGE OR YOB.	BIRTH PLACE	CERT. NO	ID	DEATH YEAR	NAME	AGE OR YOB.	BIRTH PLACE	CERT. NO	ID	DEATH YEAR
ELDRACHER						**ELGG**					
Peter					Apr 1899	Augusta					1899
Peter/H., c/o					Aug 1898	**ELHEREN**					
ELDRED						Ellen Elizabeth	4	SF	1218		1869
Mary E.	42	IA	3399		Nov 1901	**ELHERLING**					
Roland/Lily, c/o	<1	CA	6422		1903	Herman	<1	SF	1617b		1871
ELDRIDGE						**ELHERS**					
Boyardus					Nov 1899	Catherine A.	3	GER	630		1866
Carrie	43	SWE	1528b		1895	**ELIA**					
Clara	<1	SF	9916		1868	――	27	HI	1418		1869
Clark H.	36	MI	2137b		1895	**ELIAS**					
Cornelia	<1	SF	6118		1867	Jenny	52	NY	1639		1901
Eliza	48	MA	9448		1901	Joseph		SF	2053		1870
Harold Emmett	3	CA	6451		1903	Lipman	70	GER	4404		Dec 1901
Mary O.	34	CHI	2950		1873	Louis	19	SF	8964		1901
Oliver	84	MA	4061		1902	Morris		SF	778b		1871
Sarah E.	59	IRL	5799a		1895	Rosa					1899
Sylvester Allen					Mar 1899	Rose					Aug 1898
Truman	54	NY	2248		1903	**ELIASER**					
ELEDGE						Abraham	76	AUT	5520		1896
Mary Jane	30	NY	9477		1868	**ELIE**					
ELFELT						Joseph	1867	WIN	771c		1904
Joseph	65	PA	9645		1901	**ELIOPOLUS**					
ELFERD						Louis	1856	GRE	2127c		1904
――		SF	1163		1869	**ELIOT**					
ELFERS						Robert, Jr.	41	WI	7956		1903
Rebecca	1	SF	1117		1869	**ELIOTT**					
ELFORD						Wm.					1899
Harry	56	ENG	7067		1900	**ELISON**					
ELFORS						Hans	40	NOR	8019		1901
Frank	65	RUS	3874		1903	**ELIZABETH**					
ELGER						――	1	CA	3684		1903
Wenzel	70	AUT	2492		1901	――	<1	SF	2324		1902

NAME	AGE OR YOB.	BIRTH PLACE	CERT. NO	ID	DEATH YEAR	NAME	AGE OR YOB.	BIRTH PLACE	CERT. NO	ID	DEATH YEAR
Hilda	<1	SF	231b		1895	Minnie W.				Jun	1899
Mary	<1	SF	1440		1869	William	47	GER	8323		1903
ELIZALDE						**ELLERY**					
Julious G.	24	CA	5726		1904	Jessie	34	CA	3577		1900
ELIZEL						John (soldier)			7136		1901
Jno.	54	GER	E16		1884	Sarah	47	ENG	4264		1901
ELIZENDY						**ELLESSEN**					
Frank	2	SF	7364		1901	Olof A./Carrie, c/o	<1	CA	8534		1903
ELKINS						**ELLESSON**					
Adeline M/				Nov	1899	Oluf/Carrie, c/o	<1	SF	8676		1900
Frank E. /Alice M., c/o	<1	SF	6672		1902	**ELLESWORTH**					
ELKUS						Martha				Jan	1899
Louis	76	GER	5953		1904	**ELLETT**					
ELLABROCK						Duther M.				Mar	1900
Mercados	14	SF	3041		1903	William S. (soldier)			2469		1901
ELLARD						**ELLIAN**					
Enea M.	5	CT	1196		1869	Y./A. M., c/o	<1	SF	3797		1895
ELLEDGE						**ELLIAS**					
Charles W.	30	IL	6513		1902	Cornelius				Jul	1899
ELLENBERGER						**ELLICH**					
Cyrus	36	PA	6734		1900	Caleb G.	38	NC	1028		1868
ELLENBURG						Chris	35	AUT	E24		1885
Robert	23	KS	8327		1904	**ELLICOT**					
ELLER						Thomas	69	IRL	148		1900
Mary L.	44	NY	8136		1903	**ELLIES**					
ELLERD						Solomon	1	SF	1620a		1871
Catherine Theresa				Nov	1898	**ELLINGER**					
Thomas	51	IRL	8966		1901	G./S., c/o				May	1899
ELLERT						Theresa				Jul	1898
John	56	SWE	4452		1867	**ELLINGHEM**					
John A.	56	USA	4042	Dec	1901	John J.	1841	CO	887c		1904
Levi Richard	44	SF	643		1901	**ELLINGHOUSE**					
Ligviaz	40	GER	1052a		1871	Alfred	38	CA	986		1902

Key: a = 1st part of year; b = 2nd part of year;
c = death certificate copy; c/o = child of

NAME	AGE OR YOB.	BIRTH PLACE	CERT. NO	ID	DEATH YEAR
Bertha	67	GER	5701		1903
ELLINGSEN					
Leverine Catherine	<1	SF	2647		1894
ELLINGWOOD					
Fannie	30	MA	E15		1884
Mary R.	2	CA	1861a		1872
ELLIOT					
A./Beatrice, c/o		SF	6778		1901
Elizabeth	22	IRE	5947		1867
George/Grace, c/o	1904	SF	2406		1904
Russell T. (soldier)			8777		1901
ELLIOTT					
A. May, c/o		SF	6153		1900
Abel/May, c/o	<1	SF	6246		1902
Archie (soldier)			3678		1900
Clarence H.	4	SF	202		1870
Edward				Aug	1899
Emily	47	ENG	2721		1900
George H.				Aug	1898
Herbert Sherwin	23	SF	2881		1895
James	32	SCT	3720		1903
John B. (soldier)			6393		1900
Joseph	28	IRE	1235		1866
Joseph	1	SF	2500		1903
Joseph				Jan	1899
Kate Alice	35	CA	211		1903
LLoyd	<1	SF	6145		1902
Luther B.	32	IL	8627		1904
Maria E.	50	PA	3249		1902
Marria F.	53	IRE	4872		1902
Mary	65	NJ	1170		1870
Mary Jane	38	ENG	1099		1902
Mary S.	74	ME	5132a		1895
Nellie R.	1	SF	2757		1866
Randle			2778		1902

NAME	AGE OR YOB.	BIRTH PLACE	CERT. NO	ID	DEATH YEAR
Rev. Wm.					1899
Richard E.				Oct	1899
Rupert	<1	SF	6524		1902
Sarah Temperance	58	MO	3167		1900
Thomas	36	IRL	455a		1871
Thomas	35	IRL	3660	Nov	1901
Thomas	79	ENG	7765		1901
Thos.	58	NY	1604		1901
Valerie Biddle	71	NC	7732		1900
Verginia	20	CA	5619a		1895
William Wallace				Aug	1898
Wm.	35	MO	2646		1894
ELLIS					
Albert	60	RI	E19		1885
Andrew	3	SF	1169		1869
Anna	65	IL	1140b		1871
Arden	42	ME	3281a		1872
Ardin	1	SF	1179		1869
Arthur E.	27	ENG	E35		1886
Arthur J. (soldier)			2155		1901
Augusta	<1	SF	2051		1894
Barbara A.	<1	SF	9351		1868
Bennett	64	POL	6679		1903
Caroline C.	80	ME	4246		1903
Catherine H.	69	IRL	8561		1900
Charles	1864		1484c		1904
Charles	69	NY	3531		1896
Charles A.	72	IRL	1408b		1895
Charles J.	30	CA	5212		1904
Charles P. (soldier)			2156		1901
Clement Brook	41	DC	133		1870
Dorothy	<1	CA	720		1902
Edward	3	SF	4386		1867
Edward	29	PA	2786		1900
Elmer A.	21	SF	5689		1902
Emmett				Feb	1900

Key: a = 1st part of year; b = 2nd part of year;
c = death certificate copy; c/o = child of

NAME	AGE OR YOB.	BIRTH PLACE	CERT. NO	ID	DEATH YEAR
Flora C.	3	SF	2064		1873
Frank	35	PA	1571b		1895
Frankie	<1	SF	3682		1902
George	44	PA	E8		1883
Georgiana	1	SF	2476		1903
Gilbert	42	MA	7618		1903
Herbert E. (soldier)			8771		1901
Howard	<1	SF	3348		1900
Irving	45	NY	1272		1869
Jacob	52	ENG	5785		1896
James J.					1898
Jane					1898
John	74	SC	411		1870
John	61	IRL	7814		1901
John					1898
John A.	29	POR	2798		1866
Joseph	72	GER	7724		1902
Joseph N.	61	MA	2903		1900
Josephine Margaret	44	IL	4095		1903
Leo	18	NY	8436		1904
Lillian	<1	SF	2702		1894
Lizzie Anne	4	SF	606a		1872
Louis W. (soldier)			4584		1901
Lucille/Joseph, c/o		SF	7777		1903
Lucy	57	PA	6221		1900
Lulu H.					Nov 1899
Margarett Jane	8	SF	1157		1869
Mary	64	GER	8386		1903
Mary	38	CA	975		1901
Mary					Oct 1898
Mattie	34	OH	8191		1900
Melvin	17	CA	781		1902
Michael					Nov 1898
Minnie					Mar 1900
Nathan R.					Oct 1898
Nettie	1880	SF	1736c		1904

NAME	AGE OR YOB.	BIRTH PLACE	CERT. NO	ID	DEATH YEAR
Owen	38	WAL	1364		1869
Pesley S.	38	OH	1368		1869
Quinton					1899
Ralph	66	PA	1187b		1895
Sarah					Feb 1899
Thomas W.	37	IL	5328		1904
Tillie					Jan 1899
Valentine	70	IRL	3273a		1872
Walter F.					Aug 1898
William	17	ENG	1876		1866
William H.	16	NY	1004b		1871
Wm. Henry	<1	SF	208b		1895

ELLISEN

NAME	AGE OR YOB.	BIRTH PLACE	CERT. NO	ID	DEATH YEAR
Cathrine	44	IRL	3395		1870

ELLISON

NAME	AGE OR YOB.	BIRTH PLACE	CERT. NO	ID	DEATH YEAR
——			3645		1867
Frederick					Mar 1899
John	2	SF	3389		1870
John	28	ME	E47		1889
Samuel	71	NOR	168		1903

ELLMAN

NAME	AGE OR YOB.	BIRTH PLACE	CERT. NO	ID	DEATH YEAR
Emelia	37	SWE	7207		1903

ELLSBETH

NAME	AGE OR YOB.	BIRTH PLACE	CERT. NO	ID	DEATH YEAR
S./I., c/o					Jun 1899

ELLSWORTH

NAME	AGE OR YOB.	BIRTH PLACE	CERT. NO	ID	DEATH YEAR
Caroline Rankin	20	CA	1533		1901
Charles Eaton					Aug 1899
Harold E.	<1	SF	7289		1902
Johanna					Jun 1899
LeGrand	72	NY	2693		1900
Martin	67	IRL	795		1900

ELLWOOD

NAME	AGE OR YOB.	BIRTH PLACE	CERT. NO	ID	DEATH YEAR
Edward					Jan 1900
Hillard (soldier)			8772		1901

Key: *a = 1st part of year; b = 2nd part of year;*
c = death certificate copy; c/o = child of

NAME	AGE OR YOB.	BIRTH PLACE	CERT. NO	ID	DEATH YEAR	NAME	AGE OR YOB.	BIRTH PLACE	CERT. NO	ID	DEATH YEAR
ELLYSEN						**ELSTON**					
Mary J.	27	MO	1863		1870	Emmet	<1	SF	3653		1902
ELLZEY						George S.				Jan	1900
Robert L./Linda, c/o	<1	SF	873		1902	James	35	MO	755		1902
ELMER						Thomas	67	NB	7548		1902
Peter				Aug	1899	**ELSTONE**					
Ramona	2	SF	8914		1901	Annie	1861	SWE	128c		1904
Rufus	60	VT	84		1870	**ELSWAENDER**					
Walter/Catherine, c/o		SF	1668		1895	Ernest	60	PRU	3164		1866
ELMIGER						**ELSWORTH**					
Leong	42	SWT	3049a		1872	F./Jennie, c/o	<1	CA	1081		1895
ELMORE						Mary Belle	48	IA	6484		1904
M. Gage	60	NY	1269		1894	**ELTO**					
ELMQUIST						Phillip	55	MA	4038a		1895
John M.	78	SWE	2743		1901	**ELURO**					
Julia M.	70	SWE	2264		1903	Peter	16	CA	714		1894
ELMWOOD						**ELVER**					
John				Jul	1899	Max	25	GER	8361		1903
ELOESSER						**ELVICK**					
Ida	74	GER	7052		1903	Martin				Apr	1899
Leo	86	GER	4448		1902	**ELVIN**					
ELRIECHE						H.	50	FIN	E40		1887
Rosemund Catherine				Feb	1899	**ELVIS**					
ELSASSER						Gurmendez	48	ARG	1344a		1871
Charles	56	GER	1007b		1895	**ELVISO**					
Fred	1877	CA	641c		1904	Juan Jose	63	MEX	6668a		1895
ELSDATE						**ELWELL**					
Henry				Feb	1900	Harriet B.	37	NY	942b		1872
ELSENLATE						**ELWERT**					
Juan	<1	SF	820		1866	Henry	1831	GER	1080c		1904
ELSNER						**ELWIN**					
Edward	46	AUT	3403a		1872	Martha	<1	CA	483b		1895
Henry	63	GER	4978		1903						

Key: a = 1st part of year; b = 2nd part of year;
c = death certificate copy; c/o = child of

NAME	AGE OR YOB.	BIRTH PLACE	CERT. NO	ID	DEATH YEAR	NAME	AGE OR YOB.	BIRTH PLACE	CERT. NO	ID	DEATH YEAR
ELWYN						EMERINE					
Clara	27	IRE	1099		1866	Edith Rose	20	CA	6452		1904
ELY						EMERSON					
Benjamin	34	CT	3559		1867	Alice	55	IRL	3044		1900
George				Jul	1898	Charles F.	4	SF	7309		1902
Jonas, M. D.	45	PA	2430		1900	E. W.	24	CA	E26		1885
Mary	61	IRL	2023		1901	Eleanor H.	70	NB	6335	Feb	1901
Ralph A.	1861	OH	1737c		1904	Eliza	31	ENG	5351		1867
Sarah	48	ENG	2226		1900	Emeralda A.					1899
Sarah D.				Feb	1899	F. W.	45		8203		1903
Vivienne	23	CA	8052		1903	Geo. D.	26	CA	6520a		1895
ELYE						George T.	68	MA	5717		1896
Charles	51	GER	1199		1869	George W.	54	MA	3583		1896
ELZY						Henry C.	2	WA	5521		1896
E. J.	74	OH	1678		1900	John A.					1899
						John Thomas	77	ENG	1648		1900
EMALA						Louise	<1	SF	1063		1900
Elizabeth				Mar	1900	May	23	FRA	1477b		1895
EMANDES						Polly	90	NY	5277		1902
Florentine	26	MEX	142b		1871	Rebecca	<1		5858		1867
EMANUEL						Richard	79	NH	2344		1902
Emanuel				Apr	1899	Sarah W.	28	ME	9506		1868
Julia	26	SF	2305		1894	Wm.	60	ME	E13		1884
Thomas				Feb	1900	EMERTON					
EMANURELI						Margaret	1845	IRE	76c		1904
Vittorio	37	ITA	5584a		1895	Mary Elvira	2	SF	1405		1869
EMARSON						EMERY					
Marian	1904		2479c		1904	Annie J.				May	1899
EMBER						Augustine H.	64	VT	5284		1904
Nova	<1	SF	2923		1900	Catherine				Feb	1899
EMELUND						Charles Sibly	2	MA	1194		1869
Anton L.	45	SWE	6558		1902	Eugene	53	MA	6276		1900
EMERIC						Frank				Aug	1898
Harry T,				Aug	1899	Fred/Hester, c/o	1904	SF	2331		1904
						George T.				Jan	1899

Key: a = 1st part of year; b = 2nd part of year;
c = death certificate copy; c/o = child of

NAME	AGE OR YOB.	BIRTH PLACE	CERT. NO	ID	DEATH YEAR
Henry Tilton	60	ME	2525		1900
Imogene	<1	SF	6330a		1895
Lillie	<1	SF	6252a		1895
Mary A.	2	SF	6384		1900
Mary J.	79	NJ	6432		1904
Olive C.	74	ME	3699a		1895
Pauline	<1	SF	2924		1900
Richard	53	ME	7916		1900
Rose	27	SCT	29b		1895
Rufus Choate	59	MA	4762		1903
Susan S.				Apr	1899
Thatcher G.	63	ME	2345		1902
W. E.				Jul	1898
EMHOFF					
Joseph	42	SWT	1420		1894
EMIL					
——	58	BEL	2230		1903
EMILY					
——	<1	CA	8347		1904
EMINEL					
Conrad				Mar	1900
EMLET					
David	38	WV	6195a		1895
EMMA					
Mary	20	CA	8147		1868
EMMAL					
Joseph Burt	46	CA	8704		1903
EMMARICK					
Mary	38	GER	646		1866
EMMAS					
Gertrude	9	SF	355b		1895
EMMENS					
Mary	38	NJ	4944		1901

NAME	AGE OR YOB.	BIRTH PLACE	CERT. NO	ID	DEATH YEAR
EMMERSON					
Ida	23	CAN	1158		1903
John	45	CA	4539		1904
John	41	ENG	1222		1900
EMMERTON					
Edward	45	ENG	5059a		1895
EMMET					
Annie	14	CA	500		1900
Robert	<1	CA	446b		1895
EMMETT					
George	1832	IRE	1783c		1904
John	28	ENG	1154		1866
Michael				Feb	1900
Robert (soldier)			6845	Feb	1901
William					1899
EMMITT					
John Franklin	1854	OR	191c		1904
EMMONS					
Bert J.	30	KS	3195		1900
Elmer Stillman	51	MA	2265		1903
Sybil Sherwood	29	NY	5387		1903
William B.	21	IL	6478	Feb	1901
EMPEY					
Arther M.	<1	AUS	109		1870
Edward F.	22	SF	8621		1900
George Ferrell	<1	SF	4968		1896
Janet	59	CAN	6334	Feb	1901
William Fletcher	1852	AUT	2889c		1904
EMPSY					
Alfred Frank M.	<1	SF	1533a		1871
EMPTAGE					
Kate				Mar	1899
EN					
Gow Kong					1899

Key: a = 1st part of year; b = 2nd part of year;
c = death certificate copy; c/o = child of

NAME	AGE OR YOB.	BIRTH PLACE	CERT. NO	ID	DEATH YEAR	NAME	AGE OR YOB.	BIRTH PLACE	CERT. NO	ID	DEATH YEAR
ENABURG						**ENGDAHL**					
Martin	60	IRL	5033a		1895	Arthur W.	<1	CA	4618		1901
ENANS						**ENGDAL**					
Minna C.	13	SF	9386		1868	Arthur H.				Oct	1898
ENBANLES						**ENGEL**					
Elizabeth				Jul	1899	Bernard				Jan	1899
ENBOOM						Edna Emma	1904	SF	2183c		1904
Emanuel	50	SWE	E25		1885	George Nelson	45	SF	6270		1903
ENCISCO						John George	63	GER	7541		1903
Lewis	<1	SF	1036		1868	**ENGELBERG**					
ENDEAN						Elizabeth Annie	1867	CA	2356c		1904
John	56	ENG	2518a		1872	Tillie	36	CA	5365a		1895
ENDERLE						**ENGELHARDT**					
Theodore	42	GER	6888Feb		1901	Charles	4	SF	9187		1868
ENDERS						F. B.	47	GER	1385		1869
Robert M. (soldier)			293		1903	Henrietta	76	GER	6146		1902
ENDORF						John	72	GER	1457		1903
Peter	35	PRU	5866		1867	Mary				Jan	1900
ENDRES						**ENGELKE**					
Ernst	44	GER	2804a		1872	August	55	GER	6277		1900
Henry W.	<1	SF	1564		1866	August				Oct	1898
Wilhelmina	<1	SF	1632b		1871	**ENGELKEN**					
ENEIX						Frederick W.	33	GER	1236		1870
Addison L. (soldier)			2047		1901	**ENGELS**					
ENFREY						Bernard				Oct	1899
Victoria	60	FRA	969a		1871	**ENGELSTEIN**					
ENG						Charles	1836	GER	1217c		1904
Sing	55	CHN	6578		1900	**ENGESTROM**					
ENGARD						Elizabeth	81	SWE	539		1903
William S. (soldier)			2546		1902	Svante Ulysess	1	SF	1032		1870
ENGBLOM						**ENGINER**					
E. E.	26	FIN	9029		1901	Arthur Washington	1880	SF	26c		1904
						ENGIVECHT					
						Theresa E.	<1	SF	527		1900

Key: a = 1st part of year; b = 2nd part of year; c = death certificate copy; c/o = child of

NAME	AGE OR YOB.	BIRTH PLACE	CERT. NO	ID	DEATH YEAR
ENGLAND					
Berton (soldier)			1176		1901
Edward C. (soldier)			921		1902
Isaac Newton	34	CA	5395		1904
John (soldier)			7137		1901
Thomas	46	IRE	1381		1869
ENGLANDEN					
Joseph	2	SF	2880		1873
ENGLANDER					
——	<1	SF	1322		1869
Esther	<1	SF	9264		1868
Frank Emil					Jan 1900
ENGLE					
Charles Elmer					Jul 1899
Emma E.	1	SF	6787		1868
Frank					1898
George					1898
Mary Ellen					1898
Maurice J.	36	WI	8348		1904
V. J.	60		5640		1904
ENGLEDON					
Louisa					Oct 1899
ENGLEHARDT					
John (soldier)			133		1901
Josephine	44	AUT	5184a		1896
Willie D.	4	SF	4562		1901
ENGLEKE					
Louis	55	GER	3721		1903
ENGLER					
Anna T.	19	SF	4908		1901
ENGLISH					
Alice	1	SF	2623		1900
Anne	80	IRL	4079		1900
Bill	48		4136		1902
Daniel	46	NY	4043		Dec 1901
Emma	<1	SF	8985		1868
George A.	38	ENG	1111		1869
Jacob (sailor)		GER	5991		Jan 1901
James W.	63	MA	E7		1883
Jerome	1850	MA	3469c		1904
Jerome A.	54	MA	706b		1872
John C.	<1	SF	3148		1870
John Francis	58	IN	8157		1901
Lucia	3	PA	4304		1903
Mary	43	NOR	5597		Jan 1901
Melville	2	SF	2874		1900
Mowren Margaret					Jul 1899
Sarah C.	56	NJ	5366a		1895
Thomas	1	NY	5029		1867
William	78	IRL	619		1900
William B. (soldier)			134		1901
William Pope	31	IL	2925		1900
ENGSTROM					
Engborg	2	SF	609b		1895
Richard (soldier)			748		1900
ENGWER					
William A.	61	POL	3861		1896
ENKLE					
Herman	50	NY	1365		1903
Jacob	46	NY	1654b		1895
ENLERT					
Frederick					May 1899
ENNIS					
Catherine	<1	SF	295b		1871
Ellen	70	IRL	1370a		1871
John D.	1855	NY	2480c		1904
Kittie	24	SF	3798a		1895
Lawrence	54	IRE	2729		1903
Loretta	17	SF	1478b		1895

Key: a = 1st part of year; b = 2nd part of year; c = death certificate copy; c/o = child of

NAME	AGE OR YOB.	BIRTH PLACE	CERT. NO	ID	DEATH YEAR	NAME	AGE OR YOB.	BIRTH PLACE	CERT. NO	ID	DEATH YEAR
Margaret	30	SCT	6206		1903	Elizabeth	24	IRE	9454		1868
Martin	39	IRL	2299		1873	Genevieve C.	<1	SF	3278		1894
Mary	<1	CA	3296		1894	John				Feb	1899
Mary A.	80	IRE	6383		1903	John				Jul	1899
Richard		SF	943b		1871	Loretta M.	<1	SF	3482a		1895
ENNO						Mary E.	74	IRE	6452		1903
John	22	FIN	2545		1894	Patrick	45	IRL	3734		1896
ENO						Patrick J. (soldier)			130		1901
Joseph				Feb	1900	Thomas	75	IRL	9057		1901
ENOKSEN						Timothy				Feb	1900
Inga	<1	SF	5676		1903	**ENRITGHT**					
Thelma M.	1	SF	4247		1903	Annie				Aug	1899
ENOS						**ENSEN**					
A. T., c/o		SF	3027a		1872	Ling	27	CHN	2995a		1872
Arthur Francis	<1	SF	5801		1896	**ENSEY**					
Elizabeth	49	NY	1578b		1872	Sarah J.	10	CA	1242		1869
Ellen	55	AUT	7424		1904	**ENSIGN**					
George F.				Oct	1898	George H.	49	NY	902b		1871
Joe	<1	CA	8328		1904	William T.	70	NY	7094		1901
Joseph				Jan	1899	**ENSINGER**					
Marie	32	CA	3762		1903	Carl H.	50	GER	7195		1900
Mary	2	SF	1691		1903	**ENSTROM**					
ENPHRAT						Peter	53	SWE	5092		1901
Seedurg				Jul	1899	**ENTENMAN**					
ENQUIST						Christine	46	GER	8792		1900
Charles	38	FIN	903b		1895	**ENTOINE**					
ENRIGHT						Eugene	54	FRA	2054a		1872
Ann	60	IRL	1155a		1871	H. Eugenia	<1	SF	1415b		1871
Bartholomew				Apr	1899	**ENTORFF**					
Bridget	89	IRL	7688		1900	Rosa	20	MO	E27		1885
Cornelius	65	IRE	2377		1902	**ENTRADA**					
Cornelius	55	IRL	4280		1900	Sebrians	55	MEX	2167		1866
Daniel	<1	CA	E48		1889	**ENTZMINGER**					
Elizabeth	67	IRL	1544		1870	Lizzie	44	GER	4757		1902

NAME	AGE OR YOB.	BIRTH PLACE	CERT. NO	ID	DEATH YEAR	NAME	AGE OR YOB.	BIRTH PLACE	CERT. NO	ID	DEATH YEAR
ENWRIGHT						Annie					Apr 1899
Edward P.		SF	4115b		1870	Louis	1	SF	650b		1871
James E.	<1	SF	9750		1868	**EPPS**					
Jeremiah (soldier)			3077		1903	Charles	90	LA	5291		1902
Mary	55	IRL	1386b		1872	**EPPSTEIN**					
ENYART						Herman	3	SF	3875		1903
Lissie G.	35	OR	1567		1900	**EPSTEIN**					
ENYMON						David	52	GER	8619		1903
William	38	ENG	3008		1902	Jacob M.	33	POL	7339		1904
ENZ						Morris	30	BOH	930b		1871
Josephine					Oct 1899	**EPTING**					
EOCH						Henry	75	GER	5566		1902
Wm., c/o		SF	2767		1873	Maria S. K.	<1	SF	5784		1867
EOFF						Sophia Maria	<1	SF	1576b		1871
Calvin H. (soldier)			7765		1902	**ERANCHY**					
Samuel	60	NJ	368b		1871	Ernst	32	GER	9409		1868
EOMOTH						**ERASMY**					
Saphia	49	GER	189b		1895	Fritz	7	CA	5308		1896
EONS						**ERB**					
Joseph					1898	Emanuel	65	GER	458		1901
EPHRAIM						Fredericka	54	GER	321		1901
A.B.	48	PRU	801b		1871	**ERBE**					
EPLING						Charles	4	SF	53b		1872
George F.	<1	SF	9204		1868	**ERCEGORICH**					
EPPARD						Christopher					Mar 1899
George William	37	MO	4579		1903	**ERCHEL**					
EPPERSON						Annah	8	SF	9537		1868
Chester H.	1882	NY	2548c		1904	**ERERA**					
EPPERTSHANSEN						Felis	2	SF	1149		1869
Ignatz					Mar 1900	**ERESEUMA**					
EPPLER						Charles A.	<1	SF	1568a		1871
——			1039		1868	**ERESMY**					
A. O./Annie, c/o					Apr 1899	Louis	2	SF	3069		1894

NAME	AGE OR YOB.	BIRTH PLACE	CERT. NO	ID	DEATH YEAR
ERESUMA					
Concepcion	<1	SF	1359		1869
EREVA					
Giovani	35	WI	1129b		1871
ERHART					
Lena	63	GER	2694		1900
ERIANES					
Pasqua	25	CHL	9259		1868
ERICESON					
C. W.	24	SWE	E39		1887
ERICKSEN					
Emil H.	46	NOR	724		1901
ERICKSON					
Alexander					1899
Alfred	<1	CA	6604		1896
Andrew					1899
August M. (soldier)			4585		1901
Axel Olif	30	SWE	4221		1902
Baby				Nov	1899
Carl Gustaf Theodore	28	SWE	5352		1903
Carl Oscar	52	SWE	1607		1901
Caroline	46	SWE	169		1903
Charles	25	SWE	3410		1902
Charles (soldier)			9560		1901
Christian				Feb	1899
Dora E	7	SF	6109		1902
Ellen	1854	IRE	2408c		1904
Erick				Jan	1899
Frank	45	SWE	1655		1900
Fred (soldier)			6470		1900
Frederick L.	2	SF	3192		1866
Ga	33	SWE	760		1894
Henry	57	SWE	7363		1902
John	24	FIN	241		1900

NAME	AGE OR YOB.	BIRTH PLACE	CERT. NO	ID	DEATH YEAR
John				Jan	1899
John				Nov	1899
John R.	27	FIN	2188		1902
Leros	77	SWE	4261		1900
Loretta	9	CA	E11		1883
Martin	Abt	NOR	726		1903
Olaf				Mar	1899
Oscar	44	SWE	1162		1902
Paul	1	CA	9093		1901
Peter A.	2	SF	3526		1870
Simon	35	FIN	E6		1883
Syrena E. S.				Aug	1898
Theresa	1	SF	2535		1873
Thomas				Jul	1899
William	54	SWE	7414		1903
William H.	<1	CA	5698		1896
ERICMAN					
Alfred J.				Jan	1900
ERICOSN					
A./O., c/o		SF	377		1895
ERICSON					
Fred	1	SF	8643		1904
Henry W. (soldier)			2044		1901
ERICSSON					
Sarah	<1	SF	1362		1869
ERIENS					
John H.	<1	SF	1072		1869
ERIGERO					
Eugene/A., c/o				Jul	1898
ERIGERS					
Maria Delfina	<1	SF	2787		1900
ERIKSON					
John O.	52	SWE	4107	Dec	1901

Key: a = 1st part of year; b = 2nd part of year;
c = death certificate copy; c/o = child of

NAME	AGE OR YOB.	BIRTH PLACE	CERT. NO	ID	DEATH YEAR
ERKAUBRECK					
William	21	NY	2151a		1872
ERKENBACH					
Philip	34	NY	4226b		1870
ERLAND					
James	1877	CA	1422c		1904
ERLANDSON					
Henrietta N.	20	CA	1983		1900
ERLEBACH					
Clara	24	CA	6333	Feb	1901
ERLEN					
Annie				Jul	1899
ERLENHUM					
Alexander Walter	24	SF	309		1902
ERLENWEIN					
Lewis				Nov	1899
ERMONT					
L.	65		5456		1896
ERNEST					
Emile M.	24	DEN	3661	Nov	1901
George	35	MA	2618		1902
Jane	48	ENG	E43		1887
Nellie	26	CA	8855		1901
ERNESTON					
Margaret Josep	4	SF	3017		1873
ERNETT					
Edward	<1	SF	6199		1867
ERNHOFF					
Frank	50	SWT	1220		1894
ERNI					
Marg	69	SWT	E5		1883
ERNPY					
Mary					1899

NAME	AGE OR YOB.	BIRTH PLACE	CERT. NO	ID	DEATH YEAR
ERNSER					
Nicholas	47	GER	7159		1902
ERNSHAW					
Walker				Mar	1899
ERNST					
——		SF	1450		1869
Charles Alexander	35	RUS	5521	Jan	1901
Frederick (soldier)			922		1902
George	5	SF	2550		1901
Lulu	42	CA	5283		1904
Martha Amelia Yolton	1820	ENG	1334c		1904
Minnie	10	SF	302		1900
William D./Bessie, c/o	1	SF	402		1903
ERPONISA					
Horingio	48	MEX	9439		1868
ERRATT					
Mary E.				Mar	1899
Musette A.				Feb	1899
ERRECARD					
Marie	<1	SF	3293	Nov	1901
ERRICA					
Bernat	36	FRA	1237		1870
ERRICARD					
Mary Therize	28	FRA	6621		1902
ERRICKSON					
John Edward	1	SF	2768		1873
ERRICSON					
Hans				Nov	1898
ERROR					
See Throvadle (?)				Oct	1898
ERRUTT					
Theresa L.				Jan	1900

Key: *a = 1st part of year; b = 2nd part of year;*
c = death certificate copy; c/o = child of

NAME	AGE OR YOB.	BIRTH PLACE	CERT. NO	ID	DEATH YEAR	NAME	AGE OR YOB.	BIRTH PLACE	CERT. NO	ID	DEATH YEAR
ERSKIN						ESBANSHADE					
John	43	IRE	7837		1868	Mary E.	44	KY	684		1902
ERSKINE						ESBERG					
Ada Malvina	<1	SF	1227b		1871	Mendel	61	GER	4323		1896
Irene M. F.	19	NY	1080		1900	ESBOALEA					
John Bucknor	1839	BHN	996c		1904	Alfonzo	<1	SF	5190a		1895
Mary A.	59	JAM	5727		1904						
Pearl, c/o		SF	1784a		1872	ESCAIG					
Philip Alexander	<1	SF	1315		1869	Jacques/Marie, c/o		SF	7755		1903
ERSON						ESCALANTE					
Ernest (soldier)			1943		1903	E.	22	MEX	770		1870
ERTH						ESCALON					
George				Jul	1899	Bayida	68	CHI	1268		1900
ERTOLA						ESCHARTT					
Antoinetta					1898	Justus	62	GER	4980		1867
Antonietta	<1	SF	3648		1896	ESCHELBACH					
Eleonora	4	SF	8628		1904	George				Feb	1900
Guiseppe	34	ITA	7627		1902	ESCHELS					
ERVAST						Charles				Feb	1900
Matilda				Aug	1899	ESCHER					
ERVIN						John	66	GER	5364a		1895
Clara L.	19	SF	540		1903	ESCOBA					
Hannah	52	IRE	534		1902	Andreas	40	CA	1931		1902
ERWIN						Andreas	40	CA	1941		1902
Agatha	18	CA	257		1903	ESCOBAR					
Ann	52	NY	1438		1869	Bennie	20	CA	6992		1903
Annie	47	NY	8437		1904	Francis	62	MEX	976b		1872
Frank E.			3067		1902	Paul				Jan	1899
Henry J.	62	NY	1186b		1895	Primitava	30	CLB	7713		1868
Leonard S.	22	IL	4177		1902	Ramon	57	COL	340		1870
Margarett G.	35	IRE	1230		1869	ESCOBOZA					
Wm. H. (soldier)			8775		1901	Maria	50	MEX	2410a		1872
ERZGRABER						ESCOUBET					
Robt.	34	GER	E4		1882	Peter	28	FRA	5067		1903

Key: a = 1st part of year; b = 2nd part of year;
c = death certificate copy; c/o = child of

NAME	AGE OR YOB.	BIRTH PLACE	CERT. NO	ID	DEATH YEAR	NAME	AGE OR YOB.	BIRTH PLACE	CERT. NO	ID	DEATH YEAR
ESCOVAL						ESPARZO					
Tomaso	23	MEX	1494		1866	Sandalio	32	SPA	3471		1902
ESCOVYE						ESPEL					
Manuel	35	MEX	1043		1868	Annie	37	GER	6624		1903
ESCUDERO						ESPENSON					
Manuel E.	25	MEX	3111		1873	Hans (soldier)			1128		1900
ESHELMAN						ESPERANCE					
Amos (soldier)			7766		1902	Jean					Nov 1898
ESHLITE						Leonie	<1	SF	404		1900
Julia	<1	SF	64b		1871	ESPEY					
ESLER						Robert J.					Nov 1898
Daughter					Nov 1899	Virginia	40	CA	8806		1901
W. B./Nellie, c/o					Nov 1899	ESPIE					
ESLICK						Augusti					Jan 1899
c/oJoseph H./Caroline, c/o		SF	6642		1901	ESPINODA					
ESMANTT						Juanita	1	SF	3552		1867
——			1897		1870	ESPINOSA					
ESMOND						Aleck	31	PER	7054Feb		1901
Thomas F.	68	IRL	8018		1901	Amieto D.	1	CA	1295		1870
ESNAULD						ESPINOZA					
Louis	25	FRA	1522b		1871	Angelina					Jan 1899
Louise Ellen	<1	SF	2337a		1872	Consusion	<1	SF	1312		1870
ESNAULT						ESPITALLIER					
Rene					1899	Olga	3	SF	5482a		1895
ESPANOLA						ESPY					
Maria G.	1903	SF	2738c		1904	Robert	4	SF	8677		1900
ESPARGA						ESQUEDA					
Victor/Maria, c/o					Apr 1899	Frank/Mary, c/o		SF	6278		1904
ESPARZA						Rose	65	MEX	8302		1900
Gertrudis					Aug 1898	Soledad					Nov 1898
Manuel/Ester, c/o		SF	750		1900	ESQUERRO					
Ramon					Feb 1900	Concha	4	SF	4443a		1895

Key: a = 1st part of year; b = 2nd part of year;
c = death certificate copy; c/o = child of

NAME	AGE OR YOB.	BIRTH PLACE	CERT. NO	ID	DEATH YEAR	NAME	AGE OR YOB.	BIRTH PLACE	CERT. NO	ID	DEATH YEAR
ESQUIVAL						**ESTILL**					
Jacinta	21	MEX	4771		1867	James Rhodes	57	KY	1933		1901
ESQUIVEL						**ESTRADA**					
Merced					Nov 1899	Edward	34	CA	584		1900
						Eligrie	1	CA	2357		1873
ESSATSTROM						Francisca					Apr 1899
Abraham	73	FIN	3079a		1872	John	19	SF	3129		1873
ESSWINE						John J.					Aug 1899
Anna					Mar 1899	Luisa	20	SF	9006		1903
ESTABING						Margaret	<1	CA	1081		1900
Wm. W.	59	NH	1127		1869	Maria I.	1	SF	1597		1866
ESTACIO						Susie					Nov 1899
Franceur M.	20	POR	1019		1868	Tomas	33	MEX	1027		1868
ESTANISLAS						**ESTRADE**					
Gunsolio					Nov 1899	Henry	<1	SF	2136b		1895
ESTEE						**ESTRANGE**					
Herbert Lawrence	32	CA	4788		1903	Patrick L.	48	IRL	198		1870
Morris M.	67	PA	2951		1903	**ESTRELLA**					
ESTELITA						Geo. R.					Aug 1899
Joseph A.	64	POR	1859		1902	Louisa	14	MEX	3059a		1872
Louise	<1	SF	309b		1871	**ESTUDILLA**					
ESTELLA						Antonio (soldier)	30	PHI	5992		1904
Thomas	54	MI	8721		1904	**ESTUDILLO**					
ESTELLE						Charlotte	4	SF	5716		1896
Benjamin	35	IRL	2895		1873	Emma	30	MEX	8101		1900
ESTERBROOK						**ETE**					
Clifton E.					Aug 1898	Ah	24	CHN	1052		1870
ESTES						**ETHELBERT**					
David H.					Oct 1899	Francis	<1	SF	8576		1900
Emily Adelaid	1	SF	7759		1900	**ETHEN**					
W.E./Kate, c/o	1904	SF	723		1904	Louis Aloysius	<1	SF	6185		Jan 1901
William R. (soldier)			7299		1901	**ETHIRE**					
ESTILITA						David/Margaret, c/o	<1	CA	6922		1902
Alexander	18	WIS	493b		1871						

Key: a = 1st part of year; b = 2nd part of year;
c = death certificate copy; c/o = child of

NAME	AGE OR YOB.	BIRTH PLACE	CERT. NO	ID	DEATH YEAR
ETHRIDGE					
Perry G. (soldier)			7138		1901
ETNY					
Augustine	42	FRA	877a		1871
ETSBERG					
Raguhilda	<1	SF	430b		1871
ETTINGER					
B., c/o	<1	CA	3280a		1872
Moritz	75	GER	4416		1902
ETTLIN					
Leonard	41	SWT	3927		1867
ETTLING					
Louisa	19	NY	4197b		1870
ETTLINGER					
Eva	<1	CA	7362		1904
Sarah	54	GER	6697		1900
EU					
Ho				Feb	1900
Long Lung					1899
EUEN					
Magdalene E.	51	GER	7963		1904
EUGASSER					
Mary M.	<1	CA	1073		1869
EUGH					
Harry	45	NOR	2266		1903
EUGINA					
Olga	<1	CA	E41		1887
EULER					
Henry, Sr.	76	GER	2930Oct		1901
Maria Jane	44	NY	1008		1903
EUMETO					
Amada	<1	SF	412		1865
EUNIS					
Frank Nachado Tachura			6621		1902
EUSTACE					
Francis	1	SF	4428b		1870
James	42	IRL	4102b		1870
James	1	SF	860		1866
Mary Jane	<1	SF	9533		1868
Tina	33	AUS	4463		1904
EUSTACHE					
Martial	47	FRA	990b		1872
EUSTASE					
Thomas	3	CA	2707a		1872
EUSTATHEW					
Anna	1844	ROM	1373c		1904
EUSTICE					
Grace E.	2	SF	2526		1900
Lillian	30	CA	3292		1902
EUSTIS					
Edward, c/o		SF	343b		1872
EUTERPE					
Andrea	4	ITA	8720		1904
EVAIN					
Victorine	55	FRA	3497		1896
EVANO					
Jean Marie	74	FRA	6605a		1895
EVANS					
Adolphus M.	45	IA	644		1901
Agnes	30	AK	8943		1903
Alfred W.	12	IA	7467		1868
Amina	59	VT	6866Feb		1901
Anna	58	CAN	E18		1885
Arthur H.	52	IL	5634		1902
Bella	23	CA	618		1902
Benjamin (soldier)			218		1902

Key: a = 1st part of year; b = 2nd part of year;
c = death certificate copy; c/o = child of

NAME	AGE OR YOB.	BIRTH PLACE	CERT. NO	ID	DEATH YEAR
Charles	74	ENG	5309		1903
Charles	29	FRA	1306		1869
Charles J.	15	ME	3189		1870
Charles W.	50	GA	871b		1871
Christopher	71	KY	2580		1902
Clara	<1	SF	3016	Oct	1901
Clara A.	76	OH	1086		1903
David W.	25	WAL	1577b		1871
E. c/o				Apr	1899
Elizabeth	67	ME	2820		1903
Elizabeth Ann	<1	SF	1225		1869
Ella A.	24	CA	6002	Jan	1901
Frank	50	ENG	E46		1889
Frederick J. (soldier)	24	DC	4453		1901
George	<1	CA	3499		1870
George S.	27	CA	8132		1904
George H.	2	SF	308		1865
George H. (soldier)			6050		1904
Grace McLeod	<1	SF	952b		1872
Hannah P.	82	NJ	303		1900
Harry Christmas	35	PA	356		1903
Isaac (USN)			4387		1903
Ivan	30	WAL	1014		1868
Jane	50	WAL	1317a		1871
Jno (alias)		MA	6294a		1895
John	25	IN	1215		1869
John	30	ENG	7551		1904
John	34	SWE	6637a		1895
John	38	ENG	6638a		1895
John (soldier)			2154		1901
John Doe	50		8666		1901
John Erastus	<1	CA	88b		1872
John Frank	34	OR	169		1902
John W.				Mar	1900
John W. (soldier)			2708		1901
Lark	56	DE	505		1902
Lucy M.	22	OH	1182		1869
Maria	33	NY	5287a		1895
Mary	<1	SF	3177		1894
Minnie H.	1867	SF	1986c		1904
Othello Freeman	22	KY	995b		1872
Pearl M.	24	CA	3760		1902
Ralph/Pearl, c/o		SF	3654		1902
Raymond	<1	SF	4397		1902
Richard J.	41	MA	8413		1904
Robert F.	30	NY	4328b		1870
Rose				Aug	1898
Ruth Lavina	<1	SF	6560		1896
S. W.	45	NY	1161a		1871
T. B./Matilda, c/o		SF	6405		1896
Thomas	49	WAL	1406		1869
Thomas	25	CA	824		1902
Thomas	27	PE	4913		1904
Thomas	44	MA	2619		1902
Thomas E.	33	SC	1969		1900
Thomas J./Margaret, c/o		SF	8815		1903
Thomas T.	52	ENG	5621		1903
Thomas V.	23	SF	8658		1904
Thomas/Fannie, c/o		SF	2309		1895
Thos./L., c/o	<1	CA	3122		1894
William	53	ENG	3779	Nov	1901
William Homer				Jan	1900
William J.				May	1899
William R.	45	ENG	2643		1873
Wm.	<1	SF	926		1894
Wm. Henry	25	NB	5904		1904

EVARA

NAME	AGE OR YOB.	BIRTH PLACE	CERT. NO	ID	DEATH YEAR
Michael	1844	CA	700c		1904

EVARCIA

NAME	AGE OR YOB.	BIRTH PLACE	CERT. NO	ID	DEATH YEAR
Margurita Elisa	<1	SF	260b		1871

Key: a = 1st part of year; b = 2nd part of year; c = death certificate copy; c/o = child of

NAME	AGE OR YOB.	BIRTH PLACE	CERT. NO	ID	DEATH YEAR	NAME	AGE OR YOB.	BIRTH PLACE	CERT. NO	ID	DEATH YEAR
EVARETT						Carie Winton	<1	SF	1162		1869
Margaret A.				Jul	1899	Carrie B.	<1	SF	1070		1869
						Cathe	43	GER	E2		1882
EVARTZ						Laurence D.	1	SF	7934		1903
Nellie	26	IA	91		1903	Mabel Estee	24	SF	6577		1900
EVATT						Margaret	29	CA	7353		1900
Fannie		SF	1827		1870	Marjorie Elizabeth	21	CA	3195		1902
EVEGNO						Martin V. B.	40	NY	7a		1871
Giacomo	1885	SAM	2107c		1904	Martin V. B.	40	NY	22a		1871
EVELETH						William	1842	MD	192c		1904
Sarah	77	RI	7668		1904	William M.	35	NY	1802		1866
EVELIA						**EVERHARD**					
Edward H.	32	FRA	1256		1869	Paul E.	<1	SF	6364	Feb	1901
EVELINE						**EVERINGTON**					
Ruth	<1	SF	1371b		1895	Joseph W. (soldier)			3421	Nov	1901
EVELITH						**EVERLEY**					
Dwight	53	NH	1171		1869	Miles	63	SCT	3291		1902
George C.	12	SF	1159		1869	**EVERS**					
EVENS						Catherine				Jul	1898
William F.	72	NY	1860		1902	Edward Rudolph	1	SF	1138		1869
EVENSON						George	45	GER	811b		1872
Herman	<1	SF	55b		1895	Henry	38	GER	E17		1884
Trena	45	NOR	2074b		1895	Herman A.	47	GER	4548b		1870
EVERAERK						Johann J. C.	<1	SF	2420		1866
Felix	53	BEL	E3		1882	Ralph	1904	SF	1239c		1904
EVERDING						Roy	<1	CA	1107b		1895
Cathrine T.	70	GER	1066		1866	William	50	GER	667		1901
Freddy		SF	1110		1869	Wm.	39	GER	E12		1884
Frederick W.	68	GER	8731		1900	**EVERSON**					
George	1	CA	2072		1903	Bridget				Apr	1899
						Charles	63	NOR	5626		1896
EVERETT						Ellen	46	LA	3149		1895
Abijah Pond	75	MA	2181b		1895	Evelyn	4	SF	1606		1901
Alexander Hill	77	MA	3175		1902	George	2	SF	7256		1868
Ann M.	78	NF	6527		1903	George C.	22	SF	2861		1895

Key: a = 1st part of year; b = 2nd part of year;
c = death certificate copy; c/o = child of

NAME	AGE OR YOB.	BIRTH PLACE	CERT. NO	ID	DEATH YEAR	NAME	AGE OR YOB.	BIRTH PLACE	CERT. NO	ID	DEATH YEAR
Mary	70	IRE	5465		1902	Frank L.	2	SF	4685		1867
Swan	34	SWE	3653a		1895	Fred F.					Apr 1899
William	1	SF	8816		1903	Luther J.					Aug 1898
EVERTS						Mary	72	USA	7264		1901
Edward	45	TX	8622		1901	Silvia C.	32	NY	1761b		1872
EVERY						**EWERS**					
Henry Van	84	NY	7702		1901	Dorothy Lois	1	SF	5503		1904
EVES						**EWERT**					
J. W.	44	CAN	3038		1895	John	69	GER	5323		1902
Patrick	36	IRE	1077		1869	**EWIN**					
EVIER						Oliver	51	IRL	3054		1894
Blanche	35	FRA	4365		1896	**EWING**					
EVILSON						Andrew	49	ENG	1124a		1871
Gustave					May 1899	Ann	62	IRE	985		1903
						Calvin	58		917c		1904
EVINS						Charles Gray	63	SCT	5993		1904
Frank	34	MD	4138b		1870	Chesney W.	34	MI	2259		1900
EVISON						Edith Elizabeth					Nov 1899
Emma J.	23		1211		1866	Elmore Ellis, Capt.	60	OH	2397		1900
EVOY						Imogene	50	PA	2219		1902
Susan	18	CA	1159		1869	Isabella	59	PA	4403		1903
EVRAND						James Dewey	3	SF	3688		Nov 1901
James	56	NY	1633a		1871	John A.					Feb 1900
EVSON						Julie	<1	SF	1404		1866
Edward	35	ENG	2196		1866	Louisa	59	CAN	6110		1902
						Margaret A.	4	SF	1470a		1871
EWALD						Mary	69	IRE	4628		1903
Anton	78	GER	6703		1903	Thomas	37	KY	1279		1870
Elizabeth	62	MA	6315		1903	**EXAYOT**					
Frederick	26	GER	5973		1903	Frank	1833	FRA	247c		1904
Fredrich	<1	SF	753		1866	**EXELBY**					
Henry	4	SF	1973a		1872	Ellen F.	20	SF	6559		1896
Jacob	50	GER	1963b		1895						
Josephine	68	GER	5068		1903	**EXNER**					
EWELL						Charles Rudolph	28	RUS	1409b		1895
Eda L.	11	SF	5313		1867						

NAME	AGE OR YOB.	BIRTH PLACE	CERT. NO	ID	DEATH YEAR	NAME	AGE OR YOB.	BIRTH PLACE	CERT. NO	ID	DEATH YEAR
EXPEDITE						**EZEKIEL**					
Joseph		SF	4152		Dec 1901	Edward H./Edith, c/o		SF	7917		1900
EXPERANCE						**EZQUERRA**					
Lucien	1904	SF	1897c		1904	Pantaleon	52	ESP	867		1901
EYBS						**FA**					
William	1852	GER	318c		1904	Chung Tuck	23	CHN	437		1866
EYELORF						**FAA**					
Frederick	30	SWE	9271		1868	Coy	23	CHN	3413b		1870
EYMANN						**FAAS**					
George	29	GER	E32		1886	Wm. E.	54	GER	F67		1886
EYMAT						**FABELA**					
George	3	SF	5370		1902	George	<1	SF	2969		1895
EYRANER						**FABENS**					
Edward (soldier)			5181		1901	Francis A.	58	MA	3421a		1872
						G. C./O. G., c/o	<1	SF	1739b		1872
EYRAUD						Grace Ellingwood	55	MA	6989		1904
Marcelene	1852	CAN	272c		1904	Sarah Field					Nov 1898
EYRE											
Edward Engle					Jan 1899	**FABER**					
Frank J.	16	SF	2417		1873	Charles J.	34	SF	6843		1904
H. A.	35	PA	E23		1885	Elise Mary					Aug 1899
Manuel	53	PA	5693a		1895	Henry C.	44	IL	6724		1900
W. L.	47		2499		1902	Jacob	1	SF	2897		1866
						Nicolaus	26	IL	5694a		1895
EYSELER						Peter	41	GER	1454		1869
James					Nov 1898	Wm. A.	55	NY	5893a		1895
EYTEL						**FABIAN**					
Rudolph	55	GER	447		1903	Delia	45	IRE	2863		1903
EZAVERY						Ellis	2	CAN	1140		1869
George	33	JAM	1071		1869	Henry	43	NY	3370		1894
EZEKEIL						James	40	NY	2367b		1895
Rebecca					Jul 1898	**FABISAK**					
EZEKIAL						Joseph C.					Oct 1899
Isabella	1	NY	7961		1868	**FABLER**					
						Theodore	30	IL	4225		1900

Key: a = 1st part of year; b = 2nd part of year; c = death certificate copy; c/o = child of

NAME	AGE OR YOB.	BIRTH PLACE	CERT. NO	ID	DEATH YEAR	NAME	AGE OR YOB.	BIRTH PLACE	CERT. NO	ID	DEATH YEAR
FABRE						**FAGEN**					
Augusta					Apr 1899	Emily A.	54	OH	7894		1900
FABRIS						Hazel Gertrude	<1	SF	5987		1896
——		SF	3742a		1895	Louis	60	CAN	2599		1900
Frank	33	AUS	8969		1903	Lucy Agnes	1	SF	306		1870
Pulcheria	4	SF	4333		1903	Rose	61	IRE	659		1902
FABUN						Terrence	41	CA	7749		1904
Dan H	6	CA	4899		1902	**FAGER**					
FACCINI						Carolina					Feb 1899
Nicclola					Jan 1899	**FAGET**					
FACCO						Glady	80	FRA	8755		1903
Catherine	74	IRE	6595		1903	**FAGGAINO**					
FACIE						Anna					Nov 1898
August	25	CA	7409		1902	**FAGIANI**					
FADDEN						Leopold	46	ITA	2601		1894
Clare	3	MN	8301		1903	**FAGLIAFERO**					
Edward	86	IRL	4078a		1895	Louis	1	SF	4099b		1870
Florence Edna	2	SF	2616		1903	**FAGNANI**					
George H.	52	CAN	7799		1904	Silvestro	1858	ITA	1134c		1904
FAGAN						**FAGUHAISEN**					
Catharine	62	IRE	3118		1902	Jessie Jane	<1	SF	1321		1869
Catharine	78	IRL	8288		1900	**FAGUNDES**					
Florence R.	10	CA	4096		1903	Mary R.	35	CA	4946		1903
James	65		3963		1900	**FAH**					
James (soldier)	42	SD	4447		1901	Ah	30	CHN	3407a		1872
John J.	37	LA	F78		1887	Lan	52	CHN	2984a		1872
Margaret	41	IRL	1883b		1872	Noe	<1	SF	6768		1896
Maria	58	IRL	7884		1901	**FAHER**					
Mary	1	SF	1319		1869	Charles H. (soldier)				1878	1900
Mary A.	69	IRL	1348		1894	**FAHERTY**					
Michael	40	IRL	1187		1870	——		SF	1438		1869
Thomas	35	IRE	6692		1868	**FAHEY**					
Thomas F.	1	SF	8658		1868	Ada	24	IL	5285		1904

Key: a = 1st part of year; b = 2nd part of year; c = death certificate copy; c/o = child of

NAME	AGE OR YOB.	BIRTH PLACE	CERT. NO	ID	DEATH YEAR	NAME	AGE OR YOB.	BIRTH PLACE	CERT. NO	ID	DEATH YEAR
Annie	77	IRE	4438		1904	**FAHRIG**					
Annie	31	CA	2826		1900	Frances	26	IL	2129		1902
Bridget	55	IRE	4677		1904	**FAHS**					
Catherine	69	IRL	151		1901	Herrmann	63	GER	5186		1904
Catherine Geneve	1	SF	9030		1903						
E./M., c/o		SF	5215		1895	**FAI**					
Michael	35	IRE	4627		1867	Joy		SF	6468a		1895
Stephen	32	IRL	3265		1870	**FAIGLE**					
Thomas	7	OR	8433		1868	Charles	1824	FRA	2332c		1904
Thomas	39	IRE	6271		1903	**FAIK**					
Thomas F.	1	SF	4159b		1870	Annia Helena	4	CA	4897a		1895
Thos.	45	IRL	F103		1889	**FAILEY**					
William	54	IRE	1268		1903	Charles	43	PA	6484a		1895
FAHLBUSCH						**FAILS**					
Florence Ethel	1901	SF	966c		1904	Jessie Lee	17	AZ	3115	Oct	1901
FAHLBUSH						**FAIR**					
William				Oct	1899	Bessie	<1	CA	6756		1903
						Caroline D.	35	NJ	1744		1902
FAHLHABER						Charles L.	35	NV	1745		1902
Jacob	25	NY	5571		1867	Frank	<1	SF	2205		1901
FAHLSTEN						James G.	63	IRL	3501a		1895
C. J. E.	48	SWE	384a		1871	**FAIRBANK**					
FAHRBACH						Charles	<1	CA	9203		1868
Christian Fred				Feb	1900	**FAIRBANKS**					
FAHRBACK						Anna	51	CT	3795		1903
George	61	GER	6833a		1895	Bertha	26	NY	1909		1901
FAHRENBACH						Peter	69	GER	1066		1869
Sophie					1899	**FAIRCHILD**					
FAHRENHOLZ						Augusta	4	PA	1031		1868
Henry	48	GER	1082b		1895	Benjamin R.				Mar	1900
FAHRENKRUG						G. E./Lucy, c/o	<1	SF	3749		1901
F. Christian	4	SF	562b		1872	Henrietta				Nov	1898
Sophie	1836	GER	790c		1904	Louisa	34	ENG	5291		1867
FAHRENWALD						Richard Hubbell	71	OH	5069		1903
William				Feb	1900	Sara K.	71	NH	1337		1900

Key: *a = 1st part of year; b = 2nd part of year;*
c = death certificate copy; c/o = child of

NAME	AGE OR YOB.	BIRTH PLACE	CERT. NO	ID	DEATH YEAR	NAME	AGE OR YOB.	BIRTH PLACE	CERT. NO	ID	DEATH YEAR
Troy E.					Feb 1900	FALCONE					
William W./Sophie E., c/o		SF	1269		1900	Emelia	11	SF	5777		1904
FAIRCLOUGH						FALCONER					
Jno. Edward	<1	CA	2095		1894	Robert S.	71	NS	2106		1903
FAIRE						FALDON					
Albert					Mar 1899	Peter	63	IRL	8496		1900
FAIRFAX						FALEN					
A. D.					Jan 1900	Albert					Jan 1900
FAIRFIELD						FALES					
Benjamin L.	55	MA	1106		1870	Mary K.	62	MA	989b		1872
Edward D.	<1	SF	1689a		1871	FALK					
John H. Bliffin	53	LA	5730		1902	Adolph	38	PRU	774a		1871
Joseph	25	CA	1927		1894	Albert					Feb 1899
William	47	NY	726		1901	Elsie Irene	4	SF	2115		1901
FAIRFOWL						Ernstine	38	PRU	7393		1902
Charles		SF	1763		1870	Isiah	<1	SF	729		1866
FAIRGRIEVE						Philip	68	PRU	6898		1902
Julia E.					1898	Samuel	64	GER	5436		1902
FAIRLEY						FALKENBERG					
Alexander	24	SCT	4039a		1895	Agnes Helena	1	SF	3039		1895
FAIRMAN						Caroline					Jan 1900
William B.	33	NY	3577		1867	FALKENBURG					
FAIRR						Henry C. (soldier)			5325		1901
Maria Inocenee	<1	SF	1746		1866	FALKENHAHN					
FAIRWARTH						Katherine	36	NY	F93		1889
Albert	<1	SF	1180		1869	FALKENSTEIN					
FAIRWEATHER						Henry					Jan 1899
FlorenceL.	1	SF	1050b		1871	FALKER					
FAKER						Albert	58	GER	5675		1904
Francis H.	20	IRE	805		1866	FALKIN					
FAKUI						C.	24	GER	F48		1885
Teie W.	<1	SF	635		1894	FALKINGHAM					
						Mary Jane	36	IRL	1971a		1872

Key: a = 1st part of year; b = 2nd part of year; c = death certificate copy; c/o = child of

NAME	AGE OR YOB.	BIRTH PLACE	CERT. NO	ID	DEATH YEAR
FALKNER					
William	58	CAN	1055		1868
FALL					
Jno. C.	84	VA	3099		1894
FALLAHELY					
Patrick	40	NY	2585		1894
FALLAN					
William J.	1	SF	8454		1868
FALLE					
Elias	50	ENG	F98		1889
FALLEN					
Christopher	35	IRE	1209		1869
Joseph J. (soldier)			258		1901
Oscar				Feb	1900
FALLENI					
Petro	39	ITA	1220		1869
FALLETI					
Joseph	26	ITA	4370		1903
FALLEUR					
Wm. Joseph	6	SF	109b		1895
FALLINAN					
John P.				Mar	1899
FALLMER					
——		SF	4353b		1870
FALLON					
Agnes	34	SF	6827		1904
Alice				Feb	1899
Annie	35	IRE	1515		1902
Annie				Apr	1899
Bridget Teresa	5	SF	1168		1869
Catharine	<1	SF	9836		1868
Catherine	1	SF	2799a		1872
Edward	1	SF	477		1870
Edward Francis	55	IRE	4959		1902

NAME	AGE OR YOB.	BIRTH PLACE	CERT. NO	ID	DEATH YEAR
Genevieve	<1	SF	3483a		1895
George Francis	<1	SF	1387		1869
Hugh					1899
J. C.	45	MN	1605		1902
James J.	46	MA	5970Jan		1901
James L.	68	IRL	3950a		1895
Katie	1	SF	4243b		1870
M. G., c/o		SF	2252		1873
Maggie	1	SF	1627		1866
Margaret	55	IRL	2232		1894
Margaret	62	IRL	1056b		1895
Mary	63	IRE	4097		1903
Mary Ann	6	SF	4112b		1870
Mary Anne	8	SF	981b		1871
Matthew	67	NY	4847		1901
Michael				Feb	1899
Michael	1850	MA	219c		1904
Michael (soldier)			2052		1901
Owen Gorge	<1	SF	1659		1866
Patrick	29	IRE	9481		1868
Patrick (soldier)			7139		1901
Peter M. (soldier)			859		1901
Thomas	4	SF	4058b		1870
William John	34	SF	8659		1904
FALLONSBY					
William	19	ME	1400		1869
FALLS					
Edith D.				Jan	1899
Stephen D.	80	ME	7903		1901
William Geo.	22	SF	134		1900
FALTINGS					
Arnold Christian	<1	SF	1549		1894
FALVEY					
Edw.	35	IRL	F31		1884
Edward A.	64	MA	2865		1902

NAME	AGE OR YOB.	BIRTH PLACE	CERT. NO	ID	DEATH YEAR	NAME	AGE OR YOB.	BIRTH PLACE	CERT. NO	ID	DEATH YEAR
FAMARISS						**FANNIE**					
Fanny	50	ENG	4339		1901	——	<1	SF	586		1894
FAMBRINI						**FANNING**					
Lina	2	CA	5880		1904	——			2421		1866
Ulisse	3`	ITA	8096		1903	Ellen M.	<1	SF	5184		1867
FAN						Gladys E.	37	NH	63		1903
Ah	44	CHN	6739		1868	James	60	IRL	3629		1900
Ah	17	CHN	1452		1869	John	73	IRE	6065		1904
Chin Song	35	CHN	281b		1871	John (marine)			8425		1901
Ung Wing	57	CHN	187		1865	Margaret	85	IRL	4040a		1895
Wing	51	CHN	5904		1867	Margaret	58	IRE	4334		1903
Wong Quong	66	CHN	1199a		1871	Mary	76	IRL	4130Dec		1901
Young	38	CHN	1315a		1871	Thomas/Maggie, c/o	1904	SF	56		1904
FANBEL						**FANNON**					
Philip	<1	SF	9636		1868	Matthew	<1	SF	513b		1872
FANCHI						Thomas	35	IRL	2998		1873
Silvio	47	ITA	30b		1895	**FANTERY**					
FANCU						Mary	<1	SF	1051		1868
Andrew J.	1	SF	1079		1869	**FANTINO**					
FANEN						——	70	CHI	F97		1889
J. Lucas	36	WV	1189		1869	**FANTPHAN**					
FANG						Gustave	2	SF	3580		1867
Sing	36	CHN	2102a		1872	**FANTRY**					
FANGOHR						George	<1	SF	6016		1867
Otto				Feb	1900	**FANUCCHI**					
FANJOY						Daniel	26	ITA	7492		1903
William H.	42	NB	6082		1867	Jabio/Cesera, c/o	<1	SF	3400		1901
FANNAR						**FAR**					
Richard J.					1898	Ah	40	CHN	1735b		1871
						Chew	25	CHN	1525c		1904
FANNAY						Coon	30	CHN	368		1870
John	11	NY	2748a		1872	Foy	<1	SF	634		1894
FANNIAN						**FARACO**					
John	29	IRL	179		1870	Eugene	1866	CA	345c		1904

Key: a = 1st part of year; b = 2nd part of year; c = death certificate copy; c/o = child of

NAME	AGE OR YOB.	BIRTH PLACE	CERT. NO	ID	DEATH YEAR	NAME	AGE OR YOB.	BIRTH PLACE	CERT. NO	ID	DEATH YEAR
FARACY						**FARIETO**					
Redmond	60	IRL	1095		1894	Felicite G. G.	29	MS	8405		1868
FARADAY						**FARIN**					
Jeanie B.	17	CA	4621		1901	Hende	63	PRU	9032		1868
FARBO						**FARINA**					
Angelo	<1	SF	448b		1895	Joseph	21	ITA	8023		1904
FARCY						**FARISH**					
John J				Feb	1900	Mary W.	60	NC	4318b		1870
FARENKAM						**FARKLAND**					
Olof Ferdinandt Larsen	79	DEN	5028		1902	Daniel	42	IRE	8359		1868
FARENTE						**FARLESS**					
Angelina	2	LA	4104a		1895	Thomas Ashley	1864	NY	1485c		1904
FARESS						**FARLEY**					
Carle	1	SF	3993		1870	Alice	<1	SF	1212		1870
						Alice	80	IRL	3790		1896
FARETTO						Chang	25	IRL	5288a		1895
Nicola	37	ITA	3879		1870	Daniel Edgar	71	NY	6690		1904
FARFAN						Edw.	45	IRL	F51		1885
Jose Marie	20	MEX	1884		1894	Elizabeth	78	IRE	1805		1902
FARGISE						Ellen	5	SF	1196		1870
Elizabeth	36	NY	1971		1866	Ellen	33	IA	5994		1904
FARGO						Elmer A.	6	SF	6371		1902
Calnn				Feb	1900	Henry Joseph	31	SF	8620		1903
Geo. B.				Feb	1900	Hugh	88	IRL	1680b		1871
Jerome B.	72	NY	3448		1896	James	7	CA	F4		1882
FARGUE						James	71	IRL	4578		1896
John P.				Mar	1899	James C.				Feb	1900
FARGUHARSON						James I.	35	CA	152b		1895
Jessie H.	1833	SCT	1356c		1904	Jas.	65	IRL	F52		1885
FARIA						Jeremiah	1	SF	333		1903
Frank D.	1884	CA	162c		1904	John	27	IRE	1314		1869
						Margaret	1	SF	8765		1904
FARIDELLA						Margaret	31	CA	5933		1896
Vincenzo	1	IL	1438		1900	Mary	55	IRL	659b		1895

NAME	AGE OR YOB.	BIRTH PLACE	CERT. NO	ID	DEATH YEAR	NAME	AGE OR YOB.	BIRTH PLACE	CERT. NO	ID	DEATH YEAR
Mary					Apr 1899	Epaphroditis S.	60	VT	2350		1900
Mary Ann	<1	SF	1625a		1871	Fannie P.	1850	NH	873c		1904
Mat/Annie , c/o	1	SF	2821		1903	Frederick E.	23	CA	7265		1901
Melvia	<1	SF	1627		1870	George L.	<1	SF	7795		1868
Patrick					1899	Louis Amesley	<1	SF	74b		1895
Peter	45	IRE	7801		1868	Louise	1829	LA	2814c		1904
Phillip	19	CA	F86		1887	**FARNUM**					
Richard	1	SF	378		1903	Eugene S. (soldier)			5692	Jan	1901
FARMAN						**FARO**					
Florence Eliza	1	SF	3093		1873	Frank	66	ITA	8357		1868
Mary Josephine	1866	CA	1454c		1904	**FAROW**					
FARMER						Walter/Etta, c/o	<1	SF	6063		1903
Albert Nathan	<1	SF	2525		1902	Walter/Etta, c/o	<1	SF	6064		1903
Amelia	54	JAM	3807		1902	**FARPEILHA**					
George E.					Mar 1900	George					Oct 1899
Henry A.	60	WAL	5237a		1895	**FARQUHAR**					
Huapella	7	CA	7609		1901	——	<1	CA	7821		1868
John	51	IRE	1204		1869						
Mary	<1	SF	3780		1900	**FARQUHARSON**					
Mary Florence	29	CA	598		1903	Charles Deas	66	SCT	2695		1895
Moses	63	JAM	5721		1903	John	54	MA	4116		1900
Thomas	69	ENG	3b		1895	**FARR**					
FARNAM						Albert St. Lawrence	<1	SF	2030		1900
Oliver G.	60	NY	170		1902	Alonzo	68	OH	F64		1886
FARNAN						Annie M.					Apr 1899
Patrick J.	56	IRE	4596		1904	Edwin	31	CA	4305		1903
FARNHAM						Katherine	1	SF	4758		1904
——			3908		1867	Lincoln T.	63	NY	5091		1904
Anna Rachel	63	ME	3614		1902	**FARRAEY**					
Eben	67	ME	3233		1894	Cornelius	55	IRL	2096		1894
John H.	1832	ME	2481c		1904	**FARRAH**					
Lillie	37	CA	1261		1902	Rachel Catherine					Feb 1899
William Hatfield	72	NY	609		1901	**FARRAN**					
FARNSWORTH						John	33	IRE	5384		1867
David L.	61	NH	1223		1900						

Key: a = 1st part of year; b = 2nd part of year;
c = death certificate copy; c/o = child of

NAME	AGE OR YOB.	BIRTH PLACE	CERT. NO	ID	DEATH YEAR
FARRAR					
Edward	62	ENG	323		1870
Fanny	2	SF	597		1870
Serafina	15	CAN	1660b		1872
FARRE					
Fred				Feb	1900
Fred A.	28	OH	770		1900
FARREL					
Marguerite				Jan	1899
Marie	35	IRL	F14		1883
Thos.	<1	SF	5806		1867
FARRELL					
——			9619		1868
Alonza	78	PA	2754		1902
Ann	<1	SF	485		1870
Ann	81	IRL	2581		1895
Ann	67	IRE	3876		1903
Annie	<1	SF	6866		1868
Annie Elizabeth	24	LA	2334a		1872
Anthony					1898
Bridget.	<1	SF	3134		1866
Cahterine				Aug	1899
Catharine	62	IRL	1212b		1871
Catherine	40	NY	4417		1902
Clarence Bernard	1	SF	9031		1903
D.	60		2661		1902
Eddy	2	SF	1365		1869
Edward	6	SF	3a		1871
Edward	6	SF	16a		1871
Edward (soldier)			2051		1901
Edward G.	49	NJ	4681		1896
Elizabeth				Apr	1899
Ella A.	30	SF	6701		1896
Frances	1	SF	925b		1871
Frank/Mamie, c/o	<1	SF	7053		1903

NAME	AGE OR YOB.	BIRTH PLACE	CERT. NO	ID	DEATH YEAR
Frank/Mamie, c/o	<1	SF	3945		1901
George	53	IRL	6749		1896
George Paul (soldier)			5043		1901
Gwenoline				Nov	1898
Harry Edward	39	CA	3585		1902
Herbert Vaughan	4	SF	1142		1869
James	27	IRL	3459b		1870
James	<1	SF	2012a		1872
Jeremiah	29	IRL	3136		1870
Jno. P.	11	CA	4860a		1895
John	50	IRL	912a		1871
John	37	IRL	F5		1882
John	34	NY	1093		1866
John	24	IRE	1224		1869
John				Jan	1899
John	1	SF	3877		1903
John	13	SF	1402		1903
John B.	66	IRL	2144		1900
John E. (soldier)			2050		1901
John J.	52	NY	1766		1903
John Joseph	35	CA	234		1900
John P.				Jan	1899
Joseph	72	IRE	7831		1903
Joseph	28	AUS	404		1901
Joseph				Jan	1899
Joseph (soldier)			1178		1901
Joseph L.	48	PA	6612	Feb	1901
Joseph M.	20	SF	2525		1901
Julia	1	SF	1039b		1871
Kate Agnes	23	SF	1922b		1895
Katherine	59	IRL	1760b		1895
Mamie	26	SF	3796		1903
Margaret	26	MA	2704		1866
Margaret Ellen	30	CA	6032	Jan	1901
Mark	34	IRL	7484		1901
Mary	30	NS	5498		1867

NAME	AGE OR YOB.	BIRTH PLACE	CERT. NO	ID	DEATH YEAR
Mary	51	IRL	3432	Nov	1901
Mary J.	84	IRL	2290		1900
Mary J.	60	ENG	1766		1900
Matilda Emily	1824	CAN	225c		1904
Matthew Wm.	65	IRE	2406		1902
Michael	51	IRL	6876		1895
Michael	70	IRL	2629		1895
Michael G.				May	1899
Michael J. (soldier)			7747		1901
Michael/Ellen, c/o		CA	9613		1901
Michl	20	IRL	F99		1889
Nick					1899
Patrick	61	IRL	642b		1871
Patrick	67	IRL	F45		1885
Patrick	40	IRE	1163		1902
Peter	35	CA	2766		1900
Phillip	30	IRE	652		1866
Rebecca	40	NY	4222		1896
Rebecca	1847	IRE	822c		1904
Robert	26	IRL	2519		1873
Samuel B.	50	IRL	2818		1894
Thomas	<1	SF	1646		1870
Thomas	75	IRE	6289		1902
Thomas	50	IRE	7242		1903
Thomas	50	IRL	4512		1896
Thomas	75	IRL	2095b		1895
Thomas	48	IRL	6531		1896
Thomas	48	IRL	6561		1896
Thomas F.	46	NY	1232		1901
Thomas, Sgt./Mrs., c/o	<1	SF	5839		1901
Thomas/Beatrice, c/o		SF	9718		1901
Timothy Ambrose	29	SF	725		1901
William	64	IRL	685b		1895
William				Mar	1899
William A,	69	KY	783		1901
William J.				Jan	1899

NAME	AGE OR YOB.	BIRTH PLACE	CERT. NO	ID	DEATH YEAR
William Werley	<1	SF	1303		1869
Willie G.				Jan	1900
Wm.	42	CT	4573a		1895
FARREN					
Andrew J.	30	CA	4070	Dec	1901
Bernard	40	IRL	2560		1895
Charles	33	IRL	8192		1900
Henry	35	IRL	105b		1872
John	35		931b		1872
John	4	SF	31b		1895
John W.	67	IRL	4900		1896
Loretta				Jan	1900
Margaret	<1	SF	883b		1872
Mary					1899
May	7	SF	6658a		1895
Nellie, c/o	<1	CA	5239		1895
Samuel Henry	5	SF	1285		1869
Thomas	1861	NY	1535c		1904
William P.	<1	SF	7173		1868
FARRES					
Mabel C.		CA	1753		1870
FARRIER					
James	58	SCT	3280		1866
Joseph	37	POR	8528		1901
FARRINGTON					
Ann	1841	IRE	2549c		1904
B. M. (soldier)			5182		1901
Charles L.	45	NY	3263		1870
E. P.	23	USA	4153	Dec	1901
James C.				Nov	1899
Joseph William	72	ME	6284		1896
Sarah B.				Oct	1899
FARRIS					
William Henry				Aug	1898

Key: a = 1st part of year; b = 2nd part of year;
c = death certificate copy; c/o = child of

NAME	AGE OR YOB.	BIRTH PLACE	CERT. NO	ID	DEATH YEAR	NAME	AGE OR YOB.	BIRTH PLACE	CERT. NO	ID	DEATH YEAR
FARRISEY						**FASA**					
Michael				Mar	1900	Carolina				Jan	1900
FARRO						**FASCIA**					
Joseph				Aug	1899	G.	43	ITA	F41		1885
Pasquale	43	ITA	6065		1903	**FASCIO**					
FARRON						Giacomo					1898
——		SF	1079		1870	**FASH**					
——		SF	370		1870	John H. A.	62	GER	4014	Dec	1901
Annie		SF	4472b		1870	**FASS**					
Ellen	2	SF	619		1870	Pauline	1857	GER	2795c		1904
Henry				May	1899	**FASSLER**					
FARROW						Sophie	39	SF	2299		1903
George (soldier)			7300		1901	**FAT**					
Susanah	69	NY	6135		1903	Ah	32	CHN	4a		1871
FARRY						Ah	32	CHN	17a		1871
John	63	IRE	7518		1904	Ah	36	CHN	3623		1867
FARSELL						Ah	28	CHN	3894		1867
Lottie	23	SF	7164		1900	Le Ah	32	CHN	2580a		1872
FARTHING						Lee	35	CHN	1299b		1872
Abner (soldier)			9561		1901	Mar	45	CHN	50b		1871
FARUNE						Won	37	CHN	2577		1866
Giovanna	<1	SF	1496		1870	Wong Sue	20	CHN	440a		1871
FARVEN						Yun	38	CHN	1096b		1872
Roy Leslie					1899	**FATH**					
FARWAE						Ah	55	CHN	440b		1872
——			9755		1868	**FAU**					
FARWELL						Ah	25	CHN	4937		1867
Agusta	2	SF	1962		1866	Lim	42	CHN	2514		1866
Charles	53	DEN	223		1865	**FAUBEL**					
Joseph	33	SF	7210		1902	Phillip	65	GER	9294		1901
Laura Ewing	30	SF	5845		1903	**FAUCI**					
W. C.	29	WI	F28		1884	Antonio	1	SF	4569		1904
Willard B.	74	MA	5622		1903	**FAUL**					
						George A. (soldier)			5690	Jan	1901

Key: a = 1st part of year; b = 2nd part of year; c = death certificate copy; c/o = child of

NAME	AGE OR YOB.	BIRTH PLACE	CERT. NO	ID	DEATH YEAR	NAME	AGE OR YOB.	BIRTH PLACE	CERT. NO	ID	DEATH YEAR
FAULDS						FAUSS					
John	1	SF	5995		1904	Amelia	5	SF	1264b		1871
						Louis A.	25	SF	638		1902
FAULHABER						Otto	2	SF	671		1870
Permin	70	GER	5641		1904	Otto	32	SF	7644		1904
						Otto	59	GER	1480b		1895
FAULK						William	<1	SF	1020		1902
William B.	25		3493		1903						
						FAVA					
FAULKENER						Amedeo	51	ITA	3045		1900
Henry	47	OH	957a		1871	Carolina				Jan	1899
						Etta	42	CA	5573		1904
FAULKNER						Maria Luisa	75	NE	3827	Nov	1901
Charles Edw.				Aug	1898						
Elizabeth Whitcomb	53	NY	1327		1901	FAVERIO					
Ellen	44	IRL	2453a		1872	John	41	ITA	6862		1895
Horace L.				Jan	1900						
James	50	IRL	1229a		1871	FAVERIS					
James	74	IRE	8097		1903	Edmund	41	FRA	3955		1903
John	40	IRL	1605		1870						
John	<1	SF	9353		1868	FAVOR					
Mary E.	<1	SF	112		1870	Mary Mabel	43	IL	4577		1901
William E.	26	MA	7754		1868						
						FAW					
FAULL						Ah	38	CHN	3315		1870
John	63	ENG	6480	Feb	1901						
Susan Helen				Feb	1899	FAWCETT					
						Carrie M.	35	IN	6636		1900
FAURE						Robert Edwin	<1	SF	6956	Feb	1901
Ambrose	34	FRA	3385		1900						
Emile				Jun	1899	FAWLER					
Frank	55	SWE	2043		1902	Alex	59	OH	2799		1895
Virginia				Jan	1899						
						FAWN					
FAUREEBER						Angela	40	CA	1959c		1904
Amelia	42	PRU	24a		1871						
						FAY					
FAURES						Alice Howard	10	MT	3857		1900
August Eugene				Apr	1899	Annie E. W.				Jan	1899
						Annie M.	46	IRL	4342b		1870
FAURRE						Bridget	65	IRL	1757b		1872
Baptiste/Emilie, c/o		SF	4145		1896	Bridget	75	IRL	4164a		1895
						Bridget M.	65	IRE	2952		1903

NAME	AGE OR YOB.	BIRTH PLACE	CERT. NO	ID	DEATH YEAR	NAME	AGE OR YOB.	BIRTH PLACE	CERT. NO	ID	DEATH YEAR
Catharine	28	IRE	1402		1869	William	40	OH	1290a		1871
Catherine	59	IN	5567		1902	William	82	IRL	F55		1886
Catherine				Jan	1899	William J.	35	NY	106a		1871
David	79	NY	6272		1903	Yit	28	CHN	776b		1871
Edward James Lee	27	SF	5211		1902	**FAYARD**					
Edward P.	44	IRL	1786a		1872	I. B., Jr.	76	FRA	864		1870
Elizabeth	<1	SF	1234		1869	**FAYET**					
Ellen	1	SF	1288		1869	Raoul (soldier)			1314		1902
Ellen	60	IRL	1396		1901						
Emelie	50	GER	4154Dec		1901	**FAYHEN**					
Frank	41	IL	5690		1902	Peter	28	GER	6575a		1895
Frank/Mary, c/o	<1	SF	3662		1901	**FAYLOR**					
Gussie	36	NY	6866		1900	Orpha Jane	54	VA	4589		1896
Harvey				Jul	1899	**FAYNA**					
Hoon	45	CHN	1845		1870	Thomas/Annie, c/o	1	SF	5842		1904
James	22	IRE	1025		1868	**FAYNAIS**					
James/Katie, c/o		SF	3651		1896	Honore	50	FRA	2857a		1872
John	3	MA	1309		1869						
John				Jan	1899	**FAZACKERLEY**					
John F.	37	NY	1282		1869	Sarah B.	48	MO	323		1901
Joseph K.	29	SF	5809		1903	**FAZIA**					
Mamie	37	SF	6520		1900	F. F./M., c/o				Oct	1899
Margaret	29	IRE	7119		1902	**FAZZIA**					
Margaret Irene				Nov	1898	Rosina					1899
Mary	36	IRL	166a		1871	**FAZZIO**					
Mary	52	IRL	4289		1901	Francesco M.	1	SF	3470		1903
Mary A.	68	IRL	913		1900	Giov./Angela, c/o		SF	6973		1900
Mary Ann	1	VA	1215		1869	**FEAGANS**					
Michael	30	IRL	1212b		1872	Alva (soldier)			431		1902
Michael Edward	5	CA	1377b		1871	**FEAKES**					
Peter	75	IRL	8558		1901	Vyone	4	OR	6253a		1895
Philip Stephen	59	NY	9095		1901	**FEALEY**					
Sarah	62	IRL	1719b		1895	Catherine	<1	SF	4574a		1895
Sophia				Feb	1900	Margaret	28	IRL	4626a		1895
Thomas	66	NY	6714		1903						
Walter	<1	SF	1642		1902						

Key: a = 1st part of year; b = 2nd part of year;
c = death certificate copy; c/o = child of

NAME	AGE OR YOB.	BIRTH PLACE	CERT. NO	ID	DEATH YEAR	NAME	AGE OR YOB.	BIRTH PLACE	CERT. NO	ID	DEATH YEAR
FEALY						**FEDELA**					
Dennis	30	IRE	7275		1868	Arne					Jun 1899
Mary Alice	6	SF	168		1870	**FEDER**					
FEAN						Rpbert					Nov 1898
Edith J.	36	SF	1736		1903	Samuel	63	PRU	4605		1901
Otis/Kate, c/o	1	SF	1739		1903	Sophie	1842	GER	1272c		1904
FEAREY						**FEDERIC**					
Sadie H.					1898	Juan	30	PHI	5b		1895
FEATHERSON						**FEDERLEIN**					
Daniel	41	ENG	6827		1868	Babette					Feb 1899
FEATHERSTON						Jay	41	NY	8484		1904
Mary	72	IRL	2685		1901	**FEDERSPEIL**					
FEATHERSTONE						Ludwig	38	DEN	F6		1882
Cecil Osmond	1	CA	1834		1903	**FEDLER**					
Peter Joseph	<1	SF	809a		1872	Franz	33	GER	3267a		1872
Thomas	29	IRL	1318		1870	**FEE**					
Thomas	<1	SF	2947		1873	Alfred Whitney	38	OH	9615		1901
FEBOREL						James	49	IRL	1500b		1895
Aunesto	58	FRA	1844a		1872	Nellie May					Feb 1899
FEBRUARY						**FEEHAN**					
Samuel J. (soldier)			2157		1901	Rose	<1	SF	8078		1903
FECHAN						Ursula E.	23	CA	6882		1904
William					1899	**FEELDS**					
FECK						Robert	42	ENG	4577		1896
Nichole	36	OH	1481a		1871	**FEELEY**					
FECKEN						Daniel	42	IRE	7456		1904
Cathrine	28	GER	3610		1870	Emelia	3	SF	9826		1868
FECKLIN						John	60	IRE	7864		1903
Frank					Oct 1899	**FEELING**					
FEDDEN						Eugene T. (soldier)			2210		1903
Thos.	55	GER	5121		1904	**FEELY**					
FEDDIGAN						Catharine	1	CA	589a		1870
Howard (soldier)			2209		1903	Ellen V.	30	ENG	8638		1903
						John C. (soldier)			8425		1900

Key: a = 1st part of year; b = 2nd part of year;
c = death certificate copy; c/o = child of

NAME	AGE OR YOB.	BIRTH PLACE	CERT. NO	ID	DEATH YEAR	NAME	AGE OR YOB.	BIRTH PLACE	CERT. NO	ID	DEATH YEAR
John McDonell	76	SCT	1607		1900	Timothy	55	IRL	1125		1894
Lucy	25	SF	8112		1901	William Henry	<1	SF	2831		1873
Mary Agnestam	17	SF	3498	Nov	1901	**FEENY**					
						John	30	IRL	1381b		1872
FEENEY						John	35	IRE	1350		1869
Andrew	45	IRL	2232		1901	John Patrick	<1	SF	1804b		1872
Anita Mabel	1	SF	8847		1903	Lawrence				Aug	1898
Annie	43	IRL	2478		1894	Matthew	1	SF	4155		1903
Bernard	28	IRE	1862		1866	Michael	23	IRE	9251		1868
Bessie				Jun	1899	Patrick	<1	SF	5952		1867
Bridget	53	IRL	1386		1894	William	76	IRE	7787		1902
Catherine				Jan	1900	**FEGAN**					
Edward					1898	Christopher	5	SF	3751		1900
Edward A.	30	IRL	4186		1900	John H.	67	IRE	932		1903
Frank J.	25	SF	8549		1900	Jos. F.	18	CA	5457		1896
James B.	33	SF	8372		1904	Mary E.	28	SF	4942		1896
Jas./Nellie, c/o				Nov	1898	Sarah Ann	5	SF	3102		1866
John	7	SF	1614		1870	**FEHERTY**					
John	37	IRL	357a		1871	Phillip				Feb	1900
John				Feb	1900	**FEHL**					
Joseph		SF	4219b		1870	Samuel				Oct	1899
Julia	78	IRE	8547		1868	**FEHLER**					
Lizzie	28	SF	1309		1894	Louise	<1	SF	1150		1900
Margaret	1	SF	2074a		1872	**FEHNEMANN**					
Martin	58	IRL	3491		1900	Bernhard	41	GER	5869		1867
Mary C.	27	CA	3689	Nov	1901	**FEHR**					
Michael P.	<1	SF	1284		1866	Mary				Apr	1899
Milton J.				Mar	1899	**FEHRENBACHER**					
Nicholas	<1	SF	1205		1869	Wilelm				Mar	1899
P./D., c/o	<1	SF	2934		1894	**FEHRENBUCHER**					
Patrick	60	IRE	8723		1904	Winnie				Nov	1899
Peter	2	PA	1062		1869	**FEIGE**					
Sister Eunice	32	CA	7244		1901	Albert	28	CA	600		1902
Stephen	56	IRE	3548		1902						
Stephen				Oct	1898						
Thomas	26	IRE	505		1866						
Thomas	57	NY	4692		1867						

Key: a = 1st part of year; b = 2nd part of year;
c = death certificate copy; c/o = child of

NAME	AGE OR YOB.	BIRTH PLACE	CERT. NO	ID	DEATH YEAR	NAME	AGE OR YOB.	BIRTH PLACE	CERT. NO	ID	DEATH YEAR
FEIGENBAUM						**FELD**					
Benedict	63	GER	3650		1896	George	<1	SF	1293		1869
Jullius/Rosa, c/o		SF	4649		1903	George	27	PRU	1354		1869
Louis	30	CA	2733		1894	John	57	GER	4187		1903
FEIL						**FELDHEIM**					
Lewis (soldier)			3033	Oct	1901	Nathan	63	BAV	6017a		1895
FEILIAN						**FELDMAN**					
William	34	IRL	1041		1870	Henry	51	GER	1529		1902
FEINEY						Paul	34	GER	1050		1868
John Thomas	<1	SF	1076		1869	**FELDMANN**					
FEINOLD						Burt	45	AUT	2196b		1895
J. S., c/o		SF	3067		1873	Louis	68	GER	2670		1900
FEINTUCH						Marget C.	<1	SF	2820		1873
Markus	75	AUT	3752		1900	**FELHEIN**					
FEIRLING						Caroline	3	SF	1011		1868
Liza	40	NOR	1353b		1895	**FELICE**					
FEISEL						Augustine	23	MEX	3055a		1872
James	28	SF	2503		1900	**FELIX**					
FEITEL						Edmund	36	MEX	F80		1887
——	<1	CA	8243		1868	Frederick	67	GER	1759b		1895
						G./V., c/o	<1	SF	715		1894
FEITELSOHN						Incarnation	4		2853		1866
Adolf	56	ROM	6033	Jan	1901	John George				Oct	1898
FEITSCH						Jose	<1	SF	2270		1901
George	38	GER	1800b		1872	**FELKER**					
Lucy	<1	SF	5236		1867	Louis B.				May	1899
FEIX						Oscar D.				Feb	1900
Charles	<1	SF	7807		1868	William	66	WI	5980		1904
John	18	PA	1349		1869	**FELKSHONE**					
FELBRETH						John	48	SWE	1199		1869
Mary E.	<1	SF	1022		1868	**FELL**					
FELCH						Conrad Peter	<1	SF	8629		1868
Noah	92	ME	6435		1900	Lillian	1	SF	5538		1904
						Orson	60	NY	9380		1868

Key: *a = 1st part of year; b = 2nd part of year;*
c = death certificate copy; c/o = child of

NAME	AGE OR YOB.	BIRTH PLACE	CERT. NO	ID	DEATH YEAR	NAME	AGE OR YOB.	BIRTH PLACE	CERT. NO	ID	DEATH YEAR
Solomon (soldier)			1234		1902	**FELT**					
Sylvester	39	MA	1447		1869	Cornelia E.	36	NY	360		1870
FELLA						Henry Jacob	3	SF	1083		1869
Frank/Lena, c/o	<1	SF	6757		1903	Louisa R.	<1	SF	1271		1869
Mary E.	50	GER	2251		1866	**FELTCH**					
Placidus	60	GER	6870		1868	Lillain C.				Aug	1898
FELLAND						**FELTMAN**					
Olavus T. (soldier)			5484	Jan	1901	Clemens	68	PRU	1087		1869
FELLDEN						**FELTON**					
Lars N.	40	SWE	2456		1894	Erastus W.	43	AR	4222		1902
FELLER						John	69	GER	956		1902
Augusta	27	GER	8055		1901	Kate Disbrow	22	NY	3293		1902
Otto	4	SF	2207		1901	**FELTZ**					
FELLERS						William	71	GER	5663		1902
Lavinia A.	79	OH	375		1900	**FELVEY**					
FELLET						Louisa	22	CA	6817		1902
George				Jul	1898	**FENBECK**					
FELLMER						John W.	<1	SF	1149		1900
Antone/Esther, c/o		SF	7182		1903	**FENBON**					
FELLOWS						Daniel	64	IRL	6467a		1895
Allen	<1	SF	5035a		1895	**FENDSEN**					
Benjamin D.	1	SF	1279		1869	Frederick	1861	GER	2128c		1904
Charles	26	OR	5020		1904	**FENECH**					
Hattie	41	MO	F16		1883	Louis Edward	<1	SF	535		1902
Kate J.	31	MA	441a		1871	**FENELIUS**					
Ruth H.	1	SF	942		1894	Frank B.	13	SF	6779	Feb	1901
Thomas	39	NY	1412b		1872	Lottie May	1877	CA	2890c		1904
FELLWORTH						**FENELON**					
Edmund				Feb	1900	H. S.	43		5747		1867
FELNET						**FENEU**					
Joseph	35	FRA	480		1870	——	<1	SF	1313		1869
FELSCHI						**FENG**					
John	27	SCT	1248		1869	Leu Heng	55	CHN	2090b		1895

Key: a = 1st part of year; b = 2nd part of year;
c = death certificate copy; c/o = child of

NAME	AGE OR YOB.	BIRTH PLACE	CERT. NO	ID	DEATH YEAR
FENN					
Alonzo	41	NY	1126		1869
Charles Francis				Mar	1899
Hattie M.	34	MO	7054		1903
James Henri	<1	SF	4898a		1895
John	32	IRE	7046		1868
Lawrence J.	1	SF	1173		1903
Lyman John	70	NY	8853		1900
FENNEL					
Cardine	63	GER	5803		1896
FENNELL					
James	42	MA	97b		1872
John	13	IRL	1134a		1871
Leslie F.	4	SF	3503		1902
Martin				Nov	1899
Mary E.	38	SF	2098		1901
Morine	3	SF	3778		1902
Peter	25	IRE	1066		1869
Robert P.	6	SF	228		1865
Thomas Francis	30	IL	8295		1901
Winifred				Nov	1899
FENNER					
Obedier B.	69	RI	2457		1894
FENNESSEY					
Edward J.	28	SF	6305		1904
Johanna	54	IRE	1140		1902
FENNESSY					
James	50	NY	7479		1904
Mary	1	SF	3656		1870
Mary	10	NY	1211		1869
Thomas	35	IRE	7395		1904
FENNETT					
Alfred Hugh	27	ENG	5274a		1895

NAME	AGE OR YOB.	BIRTH PLACE	CERT. NO	ID	DEATH YEAR
FENNEY					
Joseph				Jul	1899
FENNISTY					
John J.	4	SF	1676		1870
FENNON					
Emma M.	27	CA	3887a		1895
FENTHORCY					
Charles	<1	SF	3916		1870
FENTON					
Alace F.	3	NY	7690		1868
Cathrine	4	SF	1260		1866
Charles	1824	NY	511c		1904
Daniel Patrick	47	SF	6192		1896
Dolly	33	SF	923		1901
Francis	<1	SF	1058		1866
Francis (soldier)			5080		1901
Frederick M.	74	CT	211b		1895
James	<1	MA	1272		1869
James	76	IRL	8380		1901
John				Feb	1900
Joseph R	72	IL	4743		1902
Julia	3	SF	1466b		1872
Margaret	26	IRL	5530a		1895
Mary	1	SF	3311		1870
Mary E.	<1	SF	3119		1870
Mary Ellen	3	SF	2803		1866
Patrick	66	IRL	2978		1900
Rhoda Reynolds	83	PA	3364		1902
Samuel	37	IRE	1226		1866
Thomas (soldier)			137		1901
FENWICK					
Chas./M., c/o				Nov	1898
May				Oct	1898

Key: a = 1st part of year; b = 2nd part of year;
c = death certificate copy; c/o = child of

NAME	AGE OR YOB.	BIRTH PLACE	CERT. NO	ID	DEATH YEAR	NAME	AGE OR YOB.	BIRTH PLACE	CERT. NO	ID	DEATH YEAR
FEOUR						**FERGUSON**					
John James	56	ME	1378		1903	A./D., c/o				Apr	1899
FERAGGI						Alexander				Oct	1898
Teressa	2	SF	2551		1901	Alexander S.	68	NS	4606		1901
FERANTI						Alfred Graham	59	ENG	8387		1903
Angela	43	ITA	8529		1901	Alice	60	IRL	2973		1894
FERARI						Aloysino				Jul	1899
Guilio					1898	Ann	85	IRE	4426		1903
						Catherine				Oct	1899
FERBACK						Charles A.	62	LA	7100		1903
Harry/Kate, c/o	1	SF	170		1903	Daniel	32	PE	6321		1902
FERBUT						E./Mary, c/o		SF	7918		1900
Eugene	42	FRA	293		1865	Ellanor W.				May	1899
FERCHEN						Ellen L.	70	IRL	3861		1870
Cynthia	44	CA	8296		1901	Emma	35	MD	4840a		1895
FERCHIN						F. J.	25	IN	3438b		1870
Tressa H	19	OR	4841		1902	Frances A.	1859	IL	539c		1904
						G. H., c/o		SF	1683b		1872
FERCHLAND						George	92	ME	4784		1902
Ida	31	GER	6252	Feb	1901	George H.	49	MD	473		1903
Ida Cathe	<1	SF	6613	Feb	1901	Gladys	1	TX	1941b		1895
FERDERSPIEL						Harry	30	IL	5986		1896
Andrew	63	DEN	2853		1900	Harry Emile	46	WV	3722		1903
FERDINANDEZ						Henry	1	SF	3408		1903
Manuel	1	CA	3148a		1872	I.		SF	799		1866
FERDINANDSEN						J. Dwight	19	TN	6277	Feb	1901
George	19	SF	8119		1900	James	1837	ME	724c		1904
FEREIRA						James	1	SF	6066		1904
Jesus	3	MEX	890		1866	James P.	75	IRE	1521		1903
Manuel	30	POR	9076		1868	John	62	OH	9166		1868
						John (soldier)			219		1902
FERENADA						John Leland	71	IN	8227		1901
Frank/Teresa, c/o	1	SF	8722		1904	Joseph				Oct	1898
FERGUS						Kenneth M.				Jan	1900
Patrick	25	IRL	3630		1900	Lewis				Jan	1900
						Louisa Fauning	55	MA	1346		1869

Key: a = 1st part of year; b = 2nd part of year; c = death certificate copy; c/o = child of

NAME	AGE OR YOB.	BIRTH PLACE	CERT. NO	ID	DEATH YEAR
Malcolm				Oct	1899
Mary	46	IRE	1724		1902
Mary	77	IRE	7756		1903
Mary B.		OH	2005		1870
Nancy				Aug	1899
Norman	60	CAN	5511		1903
Patrick	38	IRL	990		1870
Robert	28	MD	1077a		1871
Robert	<1	SF	502		1866
Stewart Stephen	52	SCT	2044		1902
Susan C.	40	IL	24		1900
Thomas H.					1899
Thomas James	<1	SF	2934a		1872
W. T.				Aug	1898
William	44	FIN	533b		1872
William	65	IRL	4605		1896
William				Jul	1898
William H.	29	VA	2249		1903
William P.				Nov	1899
FERIA					
George , Jr.	32	MA	1166a		1871
FERIN					
Mary	6	NY	1096		1869
FERIOT					
Xavier	51	FRA	3738		1867
FERMAN					
Howard L.	3	SF	3150		1866
FERMER					
Aldrich	64	RI	1467		1900
FERNALD					
Charles H	26	ME	741b		1871
Clara D.	19	ME	6555		1868
Julia A.	1846	NY	642c		1904
William K.				Apr	1899

NAME	AGE OR YOB.	BIRTH PLACE	CERT. NO	ID	DEATH YEAR
FERNANDEZ					
A.(aka Chris Anderson)	33	DEN	1070		1870
Antonio	22	POR	4917		1867
Charles F.	1904	SF	273c		1904
Christina M.				Feb	1900
Fernando	40	POR	2152		1866
Francisco	41	MEX	2682a		1872
Joaquin	82	MEX	3242a		1872
Joseph M.	1868	CA	3173c		1904
Joseph N	46	NY	4842		1902
Manuel	20	CVE	1060		1866
Manuel J.	24	MA	2337		1903
Ramona	24	MEX	5163		1867
Richard/Susan, c/o	<1	CA	4900		1902
FERNE					
Esther					1899
FERNET					
Jean Baptist	60	FRA	8977		1868
FERNON					
Wesley				Jun	1899
FERO					
Catherine	71	IRE	5437		1902
FERRALL					
Joseph	40	MA	F39		1885
FERRAN					
Jean	56	FRA	5840	Jan	1901
FERRAND					
Eugene	42	FRA	1047		1870
Mathiew	51	FRA	6064		1867
FERRANTE					
Arthur	<1	SF	5927	Jan	1901
FERRARI					
Andrea	1832	ITA	1960c		1904
Andrew	2	CA	3974a		1895

NAME	AGE OR YOB.	BIRTH PLACE	CERT. NO	ID	DEATH YEAR
Antonio	1877	ITA	2700c		1904
Antonio	1	SF	546b		1895
Antonio	26	ITA	3225		1900
Colombo	65	ITA	6453		1903
Domenico	55	ITA	1267b		1872
Lorenzo	35	ITA	5512		1903
Luigi	41	ITA	639		1902
Luigi	45	ITA	177		1900
Luigi				Mar	1900
Luigia				Jul	1898
Pietro				Oct	1899
FERRE					
Antonio	77	SPA	8873		1903
Horace Russell				Jan	1899
Lucinda M.					1898
FERREA					
Katie	19	SF	3336		1902
Louis/Lena, c/o	<1	SF	5269		1896
Peter	28	SF	178		1900
Rose	19	SF	3836		1902
FERREIRA					
Caroline B.				Nov	1899
FERRELL					
Florence	27	MA	6285		1896
James	<1	CA	4281		1900
John	1	SF	1251		1869
FERREN					
Bridget	35	IRE	1262		1869
Lawrence	68	IRE	5171		1902
FERRENBECKIN					
William	1	SF	2301		1873
FERRER					
Abby M. Laflin	45	NY	482		1870
Ferdnando F.				Feb	1899

NAME	AGE OR YOB.	BIRTH PLACE	CERT. NO	ID	DEATH YEAR
Jos. L.	50	SPA	F68		1886
Manuel Y.	72	MEX	8273		1904
Rafael F. Labrot	78	SPA	6067		1904
FERRERE					
Alyrio	40	ITA	8074		1868
FERRERI					
Maria	40	ITA	906b		1872
FERRERO					
Giovanni	35	ITA	1141		1902
FERRETI					
Maria	34	ITA	F3		1882
FERRETTI					
Salvador	19	SF	4830		1896
FERRIA					
Anton	5	SF	1804		1894
FERRIE					
Francois	55	FRA	3946	Dec	1901
FERRIER					
Louis	8	SF	747		1901
FERRIGIARI					
John Babtiste	<1	SF	2253		1873
FERRIN					
George	52	MA	2301		1902
John	43	IRE	4961		1867
FERRIS					
Augustine	60	SPA	F35		1885
Chas.	45	IRL	F15		1883
Davis	1847	IRE	1488c		1904
Elizabeth	34	SCT	904b		1895
James J.	36	CAN	7834		1901
John E.	1869	WI	3006c		1904
Josiah	45	ENG	3830		1900
Mabel Dorothy	17	SF	620		1900
Margaret	1	SF	3527		1870

Key: a = 1st part of year; b = 2nd part of year;
c = death certificate copy; c/o = child of

NAME	AGE OR YOB.	BIRTH PLACE	CERT. NO	ID	DEATH YEAR	NAME	AGE OR YOB.	BIRTH PLACE	CERT. NO	ID	DEATH YEAR
Margaret	64	IRL	1097		1901	Joseph					1899
Michael	27	IRE	4599		1867	Loretta	6	KY	5310		1903
Patrick	58	IRL	3359a		1872	Mary	<1	SF	8758		1900
Theresa	<1	SF	3249		1870	Rebecca	70	NH	5247		1904
William James	18	SF	5419		1896	Walter	<1	SF	506		1902
Winifred	87	IRL	1044		1900	Walter	3	SF	5524	Jan	1901
FERRIT						**FERSON**					
Francis	<1	SF	1056		1868	James A.	54	NB	782		1902
FERRITER						**FESENDEN**					
Patrick	47	IRE	2501		1903	Walter W. (soldier)			7303		1901
FERRO						**FESSEN**					
Angela Mazza	<1	SF	7433		1903	Paul	43	GER	5369		1867
Angelo	1881	ITA	512c		1904	**FESSLER**					
Antonio	27	ITA	816b		1895	Anna	76	SWT	1355		1901
Emma	<1	SF	1969		1902	**FETHERI**					
Gio. B./Rosie, c/o		SF	2695		1900	Ernest/Alice, c/o				Mar	1899
FERROGGIARO						**FETHERSON**					
Annie				Jan	1900	Charles	2	SF	2781a		1872
Francesco	<1	SF	479		1902	**FETHERSTONE**					
Louis P.	24	ITA	4088		1902	Mary A.	1	CA	6086		1867
FERROGIARO						**FETT**					
Maria	25	ITA	568b		1895	——		SF	1388		1869
FERRONI						Henry	45	GER	2094		1894
Gelsumino	18	ITA	5007		1901	Johann Mathaus	30	GER	364b		1872
FERROT						William E.	31	CA	4098		1903
Armand				Jan	1899	**FETTERS**					
FERRU						Frank J.				Feb	1900
Jules	50	FRA	7898		1868	**FETTES**					
FERRY						Andrew	38	SCT	F75		1887
Edward	1	SF	5238a		1895	Catherine	38	SCT	F76		1887
Emily P.				Oct	1898	**FETY**					
Frances	1873	CA	1987c		1904	Peter	1	SF	1544		1866
Hazel	4	SF	5769	Jan	1901	**FETZ**					
J./F., c/o				Apr	1899	Adolph	26	SF	6031	Jan	1901

Key: a = 1st part of year; b = 2nd part of year;
c = death certificate copy; c/o = child of

NAME	AGE OR YOB.	BIRTH PLACE	CERT. NO	ID	DEATH YEAR
FEUCHEL					
Gretchen	34	GER	868		1901
FEUGER					
Henry M.	31	CA	5875	Jan	1901
FEURER					
Louis	27	OR	7390		1901
FEUSIER					
Edward D.	66	NY	5213		1902
Henry	60	NY	1158		1900
Louis	60	OH	5808		1904
FEUTNER					
Mary Francis				Feb	1900
FEUTON					
John H.	31	MA	F40		1885
FEUTREN					
Thomas M.	28	CA	6273		1903
FEVRE					
Auguste Francois	61	FRA	3715	Nov	1901
FEY					
Elizabeth	26	GER	1438b		1871
George B.	49	OH	1397		1901
Mary	<1	CA	3076		1902
FEYGE					
John	44	PRU	1284		1869
FEYOCK					
Conrad				Aug	1899
Frederik Conrad	29	GER	1422		1903
FIAFFAY					
Maria	44	FRA	6453		1867
FIAVRA					
Marion	35	CHL	9856		1868
FIBARICCE					
C., c/o	<1	SF	42b		1872
FIBIGER					
Geo Lea			7442		1902
FICE					
George	23	SF	3270		1902
Richard				Nov	1898
FICH					
Joseph	44	NY	1288b		1872
FICHETTE					
James A.	21	CA	1795		1894
FICHTNER					
Otto W.D.	8	SF	3504		1902
FICHTNES					
Emelie	27	GER	716		1866
FICK					
Hermann	62	GER	4445a		1895
Sing	70	CHN	1021		1902
FICKE					
Minna	33	GER	5056a		1896
FICKEN					
Amanda E. C. D.	<1	SF	3839		1870
Marlin				Jan	1900
FICKETT					
Alvus R.	75	ME	2527		1900
Stillman H.	78	ME	1805b		1895
FICKLIN					
——	<1	SF	1189		1869
FIDANZA					
Luigi	73	ITA	4126		1896
FIDDES					
Robert	50	CAN	4514		1903
FIDEL					
——			1865		1866

Key: a = 1st part of year; b = 2nd part of year;
c = death certificate copy; c/o = child of

NAME	AGE OR YOB.	BIRTH PLACE	CERT. NO	ID	DEATH YEAR	NAME	AGE OR YOB.	BIRTH PLACE	CERT. NO	ID	DEATH YEAR
FIDER						**FIELDS**					
Morris	4	SF	318		1870	Daniel L. (soldier)	24	PA	3561	Nov	1901
FIDLENGER						Edward (soldier)			8780		1901
Henry F.	24	ME	9543		1868	Elizabeth Jane				Oct	1898
FIE						Fredericka	33	IL	6279		1904
Ah	1	SF	612b		1872	John	46	MD	2701		1866
Che At	51	CHN	172b		1872	John				Jan	1900
Sing	30	CHN	894b		1871	Leroy	22	NC	6692		1902
FIEDLER						Thomas	45	MA	3299a		1872
Antone A.J.	<1	SF	4206		1896	William				May	1899
James R.	31	CA	8309		1903	**FIELITZ**					
Sophron	60	GER	8990		1903	Anna Katherine	93	GER	2648		1895
William H. (soldier)			1874		1900	Claus Carl Wm.					1899
FIEGL						**FIELIZ**					
Joseph	62	AUS	5905		1904	H.	60	GER	5367a		1895
FIEK						**FIENE**					
Ah	34	CHN	4238		1870	Emma	<1	SF	2452a		1872
FIELD						**FIENY**					
Ann	88	ENG	4233		1896	Catherine	3	SF	810		1866
Ann K.	60	ME	5611		1896	**FIERSAN**					
Ernst	<1	SF	2953		1866	Mary	1	SF	877b		1871
Eugene	<1		6536		1900	**FIESCHER**					
Frank	33	KS	7676		1900	Charles	40	GER	1914		1866
Frederick	67	MA	1143		1869	**FIEZISE**					
Frederick H./Hilda T., c/o		SF	2457		1901	Henry	54	ENG	6987		1900
George J.				Feb	1899	**FIFER**					
Gertrude	<1	SF	3159	Nov	1901	Joseph	38	OH	6715		1903
Hannah S.	84	ME	2978		1902	Mike	26	OH	3477		1896
Mary				Oct	1899	**FIFIELD**					
Nels Thorald	55	NOR	8310		1903	Mary J.	31	PA	1500a		1871
Sue Virginia	60	KY	1422		1901	Winthrop J.	<1	SF	4006		1867
FIELDING						**FIGEL**					
Samuel M.	64	OH	4184	Dec	1901	Isabel E.	61	NY	5768	Jan	1901
Thos.	48	ENG	2195		1894						

Key: *a = 1st part of year; b = 2nd part of year;*
c = death certificate copy; c/o = child of

NAME	AGE OR YOB.	BIRTH PLACE	CERT. NO	ID	DEATH YEAR	NAME	AGE OR YOB.	BIRTH PLACE	CERT. NO	ID	DEATH YEAR
FIGER						**FIGUERA**					
Benedict	76	GER	8756		1903	Maria	76	LA	3965		1900
Henry J.	37	OH	902		1902	**FIGUEROA**					
FIGERVA						Jesus	3	SF	5522	Jan	1901
Concepsion M	38	MEX	4785		1902	**FIGUIREDO**					
FIGIERO						Lenoria	<1	SF	1970		1902
Maria T. K.	84	MEX	1806		1894	**FIHE**					
FIGNERA						Geo. W.	24	OH	567b		1871
Louis	25	LA	2406a		1872	**FIHSILBRAND**					
FIGONE						R. Z.					1899
Allma				Feb	1900	**FILBEN**					
Angela	60	ITA	2291		1894	Dewey A.				Aug	1898
Angelo	31	ITA	4142a		1895	**FILFEASHER**					
Annie	33	SF	3597		1903	Dennis F.	40	CA	5999a		1895
Antonio	<1	CA	3119		1902	**FILGATE**					
Assunta	26	SF	3797		1903	Catherine				Aug	1899
David	50	ITA	3411		1902	**FILIABRALT**					
Domenico	63	ITA	524b		1895	P. D.	24	CAN	1773		1866
Edward	1901	SF	1848c		1904	**FILIPELLI**					
Emilia				Aug	1898	Angelo	41	ITA	3324		1895
Erin				Jan	1900	**FILIPICH**					
Francesco	77	ITA	5442		1904	Nichola				Aug	1899
G./M., c/o				Dec	1898	**FILIPPELLI**					
George				Jan	1900	Maria	20	SF	4938		1904
Giovanni	<1	SF	7430		1902	**FILKIN**					
Giuseppe					1898	Maggie	46	KY	5368a		1895
Guiseppe	1	SF	3042		1903	**FILKINS**					
Luigia Maria				Feb	1899	George E.	42	MA	F77		1887
Maria	74	ITA	8660		1904	**FILLEBROWN**					
Maria	16	SF	6623		1902	Henry H.	23	NH	3622		1867
Maria	<1	SF	2952		1902	James	55	MA	3420a		1872
Rosie	<1	SF	1279b		1895	**FILLGATE**					
FIGONI						Esther	3	SF	7927		1900
Antonio/Lizzie, c/o	<1	SF	6596		1903						
Giovanni	2	SF	1069b		1895						

NAME	AGE OR YOB.	BIRTH PLACE	CERT. NO	ID	DEATH YEAR
FILLGRAFF					
R.	62	GER	F70		1886
FILLION					
Albert	51	CAN	8079		1903
FILLIPPELLI					
Mary	31	ITA	7577		1904
FILLIPPI					
Andrea	1873	ITA	2452c		1904
FILLMORE					
Charles W.	1828	ME	3144c		1904
Esther R.	49	SCT	3710a		1895
George H.	41	MA	1105		1869
Jerome Adolphus	56	NY	6247		1902
Mary E.	38	CAN	8345		1900
FILMER					
Eliza M. A.	52	MA	1908		1894
William	74	ENG	6155		1900
FILMORE					
Clarence J.				May	1899
Marie	<1	SF	4899		1896
FILOGRASSO					
Jennie	2	SF	935		1900
FILOS					
Pietor A.	42	SWT	3169		1870
FILOSOFA					
Valentine				Oct	1899
FILPIN					
Richard	57	IRE	3655		1902
FILSENTHAL					
Caroline				Oct	1898
Philip	72	BAV	6148a		1895
FIMBREATH					
Arthur F.	1857	LA	138c		1904

NAME	AGE OR YOB.	BIRTH PLACE	CERT. NO	ID	DEATH YEAR
FIN					
Chun	21	CHN	2472a		1872
Tun Tin	23	CHN	720b		1872
FINALE					
Julia	4	SF	7410		1902
FINALY					
Arthur				Mar	1900
FINASCKSTED					
Emil	<1	SF	6968		1868
FINBURG					
Abraham	52	POL	2314a		1872
FINCH					
Emilia	4	NY	1110		1866
Frederick D.	24	NY	1678b		1872
Josephine	23	GER	2156		1866
Leona	25	IL	7586		1904
Thomas H.	57	OH	F13		1883
FINCK					
Antin/Alvis, c/o		SF	1295		1900
August	1852	FRA	1423c		1904
Edw.	48	GER	F25		1883
Henry	69	GER	2002		1902
John W.	45	GER	7019		1900
Machtelena	44	GER	7585		1902
FINDEA					
Edward				Feb	1900
FINDLEY					
Dorothy				Jun	1899
Richard	<1	CA	5765		1902
FINE					
Earnest	<1	SF	1048		1901
Edward Julian	3	CA	6408	Feb	1901
John J.				Aug	1898
W./D., c/o	<1	SF	2974		1894

Key: a = 1st part of year; b = 2nd part of year;
c = death certificate copy; c/o = child of

NAME	AGE OR YOB.	BIRTH PLACE	CERT. NO	ID	DEATH YEAR
FINEGAN					
Daniel				Oct	1899
William	36	SF	7055		1903
FINERTY					
Maggie	23	SF	3071		1894
William	1	SF	9709		1868
FINEY					
Arthur	6	SF	8694		1901
FING					
Ah	28	CHN	5057		1867
H.	25	CHN	2849		1866
Mar					1899
FINGER					
Catherine	1	SF	1662		1903
Eleanor	1	SF	1663		1903
Herman T.	34	LA	F1		1882
FINGLAND					
Robert	33	CAN	223b		1871
FINGLER					
Oscar J.	42	GER	5214		1902
FINK					
Freddie	4	SF	7645		1904
Jacob	49	GER	5852		1867
Jennie	23	AL	F58		1886
Minnie	10	SF	806		1902
Sophie				Jul	1899
FINKELSTEIN					
Gussie	<1	SF	1169b		1895
FINKENSTEDT					
——		SF	816		1870
FINKLE					
Michael	30	GER	F32		1884
FINKLER					
Antoinia De. A.				Mar	1899

NAME	AGE OR YOB.	BIRTH PLACE	CERT. NO	ID	DEATH YEAR
FINKNER					
Henry	41	MD	5677		1867
FINLAY					
Isabel A.				Aug	1898
Robert Alexander	25	AZ	8204		1903
William Henry	45	IRE	811		1903
FINLAYSON					
Mary Ada	34	VA	761b		1871
Robert	29	CAN	5974		1903
FINLEY					
Elizabeth H.	6	SF	3845		1867
Ellen	9	SF	1190		1866
James R. (seaman)			5822	Jan	1901
Johanna	62	IRL	2116b		1895
John W.				Nov	1899
Julia Harrington	17	IRL	230		1870
Louis G. (soldier)	30	TN	1852		1902
Margaret A.	52	DEN	4188		1903
Margaret J.				Jan	1900
Susan	<1	SF	1308b		1871
Thomas F.	<1	SF	1992a		1872
William H.	8	SF	9426		1868
FINN					
——		SF	1178		1869
Alfred	30	IRE	1429		1869
Anne	37	IRL	759b		1872
Berel	70	POL	6379		1904
Daniel	2	SF	3350		1873
Edward	30	IRE	6619		1868
Ellen	1	SF	1107		1869
Ellen	30	CA	1478		1894
Ellen					1899
Ellen Maria	70	IRL	2737		1895
Hannah	<1	SF	6293		1867
Harriette				May	1899

NAME	AGE OR YOB.	BIRTH PLACE	CERT. NO	ID	DEATH YEAR	NAME	AGE OR YOB.	BIRTH PLACE	CERT. NO	ID	DEATH YEAR
James W.	44	SF	7720		1903	Mary Jane	6	SF	1334b		1872
Jeremiah	83	IRL	216		1901	Michael	41	IRL	3342	Nov	1901
John	52	IRE	7396		1904	Patrick	24	IRL	3484a		1895
John Henry	5	CA	F88		1887	Patrick	83	IRL	122		1900
Kate	36	AUS	F37		1885	Patrick	57	NY	996		1901
Margaret	83	IRE	3549		1902	Peter	60	IRE	1701		1902
Mary	5	SF	93		1870	Simon	27	IRL	793b		1872
Mary	52	IRL	1657b		1872	Susan	76	IRL	1017		1900
Mary	77	IRL	6111	Jan	1901	Thomas	6	SF	1254		1869
Mary	64	IRL	6824	Feb	1901	**FINNERAN**					
Mary	74	IRL	4185	Dec	1901	Ann	35	IRE	4943		1902
Mary Ann	35	IRE	3467		1867	Lawrence P.	45	NY	1741		1901
Mary Ellen	2	SF	3153		1894	Martin	<1	SF	4097a		1895
Mathew	50	IRE	2670		1903	**FINNERTY**					
Michael	<1	SF	2334		1866	Ann or Curly Margret ??	55	IRL	6579		1900
Patrick	46	IRL	1590b		1871	Catherine	<1	SF	673a		1871
Susan	<1	SF	342		1865	Christopher P.				Mar	1899
Susan F.	27	MA	539		1870	Ellen, Mrs.	50	IRL	8894		1901
Timothy				Jul	1899	James	48	IRL	4873		1896
William	4	CA	946b		1872	James				Mar	1899
FINNAN						Julia Frances Loretta	1887	OR	725c		1904
Patrick	35	IRE	7254		1904	Martin	22	IRE	1035		1868
FINNARN						Samuel E.	1	SF	341		1865
Patrick	35	IRE	6943		1868	Thomas	49	PA	7471		1902
FINNCAN						**FINNEY**					
John (soldier)			7301		1901	Jane				Nov	1899
FINNEGAN						Mary J.	25	IRL	1265		1901
Catherine	50	IRL	4526		1901	Rusus N. (soldier)			66		1901
Edwin J.			5093		1903	William Webb	52	RI	3920		1902
Henry	32	USA	5282		1867	Willie S.	19	OH	3318		1873
Henry J.	16	SF	6562		1896	**FINNIE**					
John	<1	SF	2911		1902	Mary Ellen	30	CA	5523		1896
John	67	NY	4041		1896	William				Nov	1899
Josephine	1	SF	1260		1869	William Walter	28	NJ	8321		1901
Margaret	78	IRL	2671		1900						

NAME	AGE OR YOB.	BIRTH PLACE	CERT. NO	ID	DEATH YEAR	NAME	AGE OR YOB.	BIRTH PLACE	CERT. NO	ID	DEATH YEAR
FINNIER						**FIRCK**					
Joseph				Nov	1898	Wah	61	CHN	953		1894
						FIRDERER					
FINNIGAN						Frank H.	9	CA	1128		1869
Elizabeth Caroline	32	SF	8284		1903						
Eugenio Francis P.	1	SF	2479		1873	**FIREBAUGH**					
Henry J.	45	NY	5627		1896	Blanche L.	18	SF	937b		1895
John					1898						
John E.	46	NY	7578		1904	**FIRENZI**					
Josie C.				Mar	1899	Maria	<1	SF	6290		1902
Susan				Jan	1900	Rosa/D., c/o	1904	CA	888		1904
						FIRESTONE					
FINNING						Henry Thomas				Oct	1898
Catherine	69	IRL	1132b		1895						
James				Nov	1899	**FIRGGATT**					
						Antun				Mar	1900
FINNINGER											
Oscar A.				Mar	1900	**FIRMIN**					
						Francis C.					1899
FINSTERBUSCH											
Charles	76	GER	7037		1904	**FIRPO**					
Edwin J. C.				Oct	1898	Alfredo	<1	SF	7731		1904
						Francesco	1	SF	5021		1904
FINTON						Maria	<1	SF	825		1902
Patrick, c/o		SF	407b		1872	Melba	1901	SF	1374c		1904
FIORA						**FIRTH**					
Thomas	<1	SF	7895		1903	Joseph	<1	SF	4249		1896
						Joseph B.	74	ENG	4108	Dec	1901
FIORE											
Tomaso/Angelina, c/o	<1	SF	5438		1902	**FISCADE**					
						Joseph	48	CUB	1739		1900
FIORENTINI											
Domenico	30	ITA	3190		1895	**FISCHBACHER**					
						Ernst	37	SWT	2458		1902
FIORIO											
Eugenie/Silvio, c/o		SF	6278		1900	**FISCHBECK**					
						Albert Stanley	2	SF	450		1870
FIPPENGER						Annie	24	GER	1606		1902
——			4977		1867	Hermann R.	3	SF	9796		1868
FIPPINGER						**FISCHER**					
——			4978		1867	——	<1	SF	3824		1870
Eliso	34	GER	4967		1867						

Key: a = 1st part of year; b = 2nd part of year;
c = death certificate copy; c/o = child of

NAME	AGE OR YOB.	BIRTH PLACE	CERT. NO	ID	DEATH YEAR
Albert	39	GER	6239a		1895
Albert E.	2	CA	F73		1887
Charles N.	47	FRA	F7		1882
Charloth	57	GER	7038		1904
Charlotte	58	GER	4185		1900
Conradine	59	GER	4045		1903
Emma	30	NY	6291		1902
Emma	48	GER	831		1901
Ermina	60	GER	F2		1882
Frank/Clara, c/o	<1	SF	2220		1902
Franz	65	GER	4570		1904
George	56	PA	980b		1895
George	54	GER	4265		1901
Gottlobe	68	GER	4369		1901
Irene	3	SF	3401	Nov	1901
Johann				Aug	1898
John	<1	SF	428		1901
John C.	41	BAV	9761		1868
Joseph	<1	SF	490a		1871
Michel	66	FRA	4679		1902
Paul	44	SWT	987		1902
Susan E.				Feb	1900
Virginia Hayden	71	KY	3091	Oct	1901
Wilhelm (soldier)			2289c		1904
William/Louisa, c/o		SF	7072		1902
William/Selma, c/o	1	SF	5248		1904
FISCUS					
Ida Inez	44	NY	4269		1896
Mary	32	MA	6384		1867
FISH					
Alice	33	IRL	5654a		1895
Barbara A.	26	NY	2768a		1872
Charles	35	PA	3113		1870
Eliza	74	NY	748		1901
Esther N.	86	PA	6780		1903
Gauss Halsey	72	NY	5022		1904
Harriet A.	82	NY	2854		1900
Henry Papehin	65	NS	1682		1902
Julius	41	OR	2779		1902
Katherine					1898
Lena	93	GER	3532		1896
M. H./H. F., c/o	<1	SF	1735		1895
Mary Emma	<1	SF	5133		1867
Philip B. (soldier)			7526		1900
FISHBECK					
Rebecca	87	GER	8339		1900
FISHBONE					
Mendel/Jennie, c/o	<1	SF	2526		1902
FISHBOURNE					
Viola F.	19	SF	1563		1900
FISHEL					
Benjamin	67	BOH	5200		1901
Harry	1886	CA	3198c		1904
Morris	73	AUS	6691		1904
FISHER					
——	36	GER	1361		1869
Abram	54	MA	F21		1883
Alfred C.	25	KS	898		1903
Amelia	26	PRU	6319		1867
Antone	58	POR	4313		1902
Benj. Frank	31	MA	2514		1873
Carliss	1	CA	6614	Feb	1901
Catherine				Feb	1900
Catherine B.	67	NY	1211b		1895
Charles D.	6	CA	1076		1869
Charles H.	<1	SF	1185		1869
Charles J. (soldier)	34	TX	5377		1901
Daisy	26	CA	8757		1903
Daniel F.				May	1899
E. Addie	18	MA	254		1865

Key: a = 1st part of year; b = 2nd part of year;
c = death certificate copy; c/o = child of

NAME	AGE OR YOB.	BIRTH PLACE	CERT. NO	ID	DEATH YEAR	NAME	AGE OR YOB.	BIRTH PLACE	CERT. NO	ID	DEATH YEAR
Ebenezer	1	SF	986		1903	Martha	42	IL	4873		1902
Elizabeth Evelyn				Jul	1899	Martha J.				Apr	1899
Elizabeth, c/o	1	SF	6778		1904	Mary	71	IRL	9096		1901
Ella	4	CA	7301		1903	Mary				Aug	1898
Fannie	1839	AUS	1929c		1904	Mary	45	KY	4996		1904
Ford				Feb	1900	Mary A.	1	SF	4458		1867
Frederick	23	MI	3465		1900	Mary C.	61	IRE	6169		1904
George	33	GER	3554		1870	Mary Ellen				Apr	1899
George D.				Feb	1900	Mary Tatterson Ryer	65	NY	5085a		1896
Goerge W.	62	PA	3126		1895	Mrs.	65	GER	5624		1903
H./K., c/o	<1	SF	3603		1895	Nancie Amelia	62	ME	1172		1902
Hans	46	GER	6159	Jan	1901	Nancy Jane	49	IL	5598		1904
Harry (marine)			9242		1901	Nicholas				Oct	1898
Henry George	<1	AUS	930a		1871	Oliva Belle	43	CAN	7499		1904
Henry Q.	43	NY	7493		1903	Peter	30	SCT	2044a		1872
Hugh	71	IRL	3015		1900	Philander	67	MA	3227		1873
Ida M.	26	CA	1549		1901	Robert				May	1899
Jake				Aug	1898	Ruth	<1	SF	7725		1902
James McDaniel	18	SF	254b		1895	Sophie	35	SF	4099		1903
Johanna	38	BAV	1930		1900	Stephen (marine)			5952	Jan	1901
John	40	GER	6283		1896	Theador V. Q.	4	SF	1303		1869
John M.	44	GER	1545		1866	Thomas W.	42	DC	2268		1903
John S.	59	TN	4914		1904	W./B., c/o	<1	SF	4767		1895
Joseph	25	GER	1312		1901	Watson T.				Nov	1898
Kate	<1	SF	568		1894	William	54	GER	8025		1903
Lawrence William	<1	SF	2403		1873	William F./Lueya, c/o	<1	SF	6343		1904
Lizzie	48	NJ	6580		1896	William G.	<1	SF	2912		1901
Louis	28	GER	F61		1886	William J.	34	VT	7341		1902
Louis				Jan	1900	William Thomas	1	SF	1691a		1871
Lulu				Oct	1898	**FISK**					
Mabel Alice				Feb	1900	Andrew P.	26	MA	1859a		1872
Mabel Cloudman	<1	CA	7196		1900	E. A., Mrs.	35	CA	4487a		1895
Madie E.	38	CA	322		1901	Edward S.	38	MA	6097		1867
Margaret Frances	34	MA	1746		1902	Evelyn	<1	SF	7467		1903
Margarethe	48	GER	2559		1895	Fred Harland	32	CA	1066		1902
Maria	abt	IRE	8414		1904	Fredrick Andrew	<1	SF	695		1902

Key: a = 1st part of year; b = 2nd part of year;
c = death certificate copy; c/o = child of

NAME	AGE OR YOB.	BIRTH PLACE	CERT. NO	ID	DEATH YEAR
George Herbert				May	1899
Harry C. (soldier)			3698		1900
John Blanchard	75	MA	7613		1904
Merivah	81	CAN	2477		1903
FISKE					
Barbara	1		6803		1904
Edward J.				Oct	1898
Elizabeth A.	68	NY	625		1903
Estella	34	SF	7678		1903
Henry Gustavus	75	MA	756		1902
Henry Mortimer	72	MA	5120a		1896
William H.	41	CA	2290		1901
FISTELINI					
Pietro	31	SWT	80b		1872
FISTER					
Fred			7565		1902
FITCH					
——		SF	894		1870
Carrie	49	IA	8180		1904
Cornelia E.	39	NY	516b		1871
Ellen		SF	531		1866
Henry	37	GER	F8		1882
Julia	70	IRE	1971		1902
Julia C.				Oct	1898
Louise	27	NY	933b		1872
May	<1	SF	1257		1869
Miss E. May	32	NY	3908a		1895
Phipps			9478		1868
S. L.	42		3226		1900
FITGERALD					
May	32	MA	7806		1903
FITSCHEN					
Henry	58	GER	1548b		1895

NAME	AGE OR YOB.	BIRTH PLACE	CERT. NO	ID	DEATH YEAR
FITSIMMONS					
Catharine Elizabeth	<1	SF	1117b		1871
FITTER					
Louisa	33	GER	1682		1866
FITTS					
Hazel D.	5	SF	6767		1896
Milton D.	<1	SF	1479		1894
FITZ					
Henry	1	SF	3043		1903
Mary Frances	23	CAN	1642		1894
Patrick Simon	76	IRE	4997		1904
FITZ SIMMONS					
Margaret	69	IRL	3750	Nov	1901
FITZALAW					
Charlotte	<1	SF	6911		1903
FITZELL					
Mary E.	1	SF	3517		1903
FITZERALD					
James	55	IRL	3426		1896
FITZGERALD					
——			7547		1868
——		SF	1266		1869
——		SF	1417		1869
Alexander	20	NY	9473		1868
Alice Bridget	<1	SF	3240a		1872
Andrew	4	SF	1501		1866
Ann	34	IRL	4185b		1870
Ann	78	IRE	4571		1904
Ann	83	IRL	2791		1894
Annie	1	SF	1423		1903
Annie	22	SF	1009		1903
Annie	27	CA	5231		1903
Annie M.	26	FL	2693		1866
Archie E.	45	NV	7224		1904

NAME	AGE OR YOB.	BIRTH PLACE	CERT. NO	ID	DEATH YEAR	NAME	AGE OR YOB.	BIRTH PLACE	CERT. NO	ID	DEATH YEAR
Austin	80	IRL	3962		1900	James C.				Jan	1900
Bridget	80	IRE	5175		1903	James Elmo	3	SF	6207		1903
Caroline M.	<1	SF	2290		1866	Jane	24	NB	6021		1867
Catharine	5	SF	2184a		1872	Jas./Mary, c/o				Aug	1898
Catharine	76	IRE	1374		1869	Johanna	80	IRE	5574		1904
Catherine Agnes	1	SF	1232		1869	John	46	IRE	1968		1866
Catherine/Dennis, c/o		SF	3		1901	John	52	IRE	7617		1903
Chas.	25	WI	F54		1886	John	72	IRL	8967		1901
Daniel	34	CA	6344		1904	John					1898
David	<1	SF	3778		1867	John	50	IRL	3870	Nov	1901
David	27	CA	9295		1901	John S.	<1	SF	1208		1869
Edw.				Mar	1900	John T.	38	NY	2414		1900
Edward	1832	NY	2944c		1904	Joseph	24	IRL	1662		1870
Edward				Apr	1899	Julia	1	SF	3388a		1872
Edward				Apr	1899	Julia	<1	SF	1367		1869
Edward (soldier)			6932		1900	Kate	<1	SF	8031		1868
Edward (soldier)			4898		1901	Kate	35	IRL	1787		1900
Edward D.	6	CA	3261	Nov	1901	L./M., c/o				Oct	1899
Eli (Soldier)			2211		1903	Lily	<1	SF	263		1865
Eliza	80	IRL	2943		1895	Lizzie	38	CA	8177		1903
Eliza	8	CA	699a		1871	Lizzie	<1	SF	2803		1901
Ellie	43	NY	4922		1896	Lizzie Fitzgerald/Harry Magner, c/o	<1	CA	7055		1901
Emily Maud	<1	SF	2340a		1872						
Emma C.	48	NY	6384		1903	Loretta	1895	SF	967c		1904
Frances Marie	1893	SF	1988c		1904	Margaret	54	IN	5369a		1895
Frank C. (soldier)			874		1902	Margaret	67	IRL	2455		1901
George	54	MA	3537		1867	Margaret A.	5	NB	1048		1868
George W.	3	CA	7914		1904	Margarett	7	SF	1078		1869
Grace	1903	SF	2239c		1904	Margarett F.	55	IRE	1286		1869
Hannah	70	IRL	1966a		1872	Margret	<1	SF	8142		1868
Hannorah	70	IRE	4991		1903	Marion	<1	SF	1736b		1895
J.	52	NY	7262		1868	Mary	5	SF	1217		1869
James	29	IRE	1309		1869	Mary	36	IRE	5164		1904
James	<1	SF	1373		1869	Mary	57	IRL	5836a		1895
James	19	MA	1398		1869	Mary					1898
James	77	IRE	3114		1903	Mary	<1	SF	4749		1867

Key: a = 1st part of year; b = 2nd part of year;
c = death certificate copy; c/o = child of

NAME	AGE OR YOB.	BIRTH PLACE	CERT. NO	ID	DEATH YEAR	NAME	AGE OR YOB.	BIRTH PLACE	CERT. NO	ID	DEATH YEAR
Mary	35	IRE	1310		1869	William Francis	2	SF	3037		1873
Mary	40	IRE	4947		1903	William J.	41	WI	1399		1902
Mary Alice	<1	SF	1234		1869	William J.	30	MA	4846		1901
Mary Ann	60	IRL	176		1900	William Patrick	7	CA	4992		1903
Mary F.	<1	SF	3862		1870	William T.	45	CAN	2864		1903
Mary Jane	72	PE	3985		1903	William T.					1899
Maurice (soldier)			4539		1901	William W.	75	WI	2171		1900
Michael	4	SF	4665		1867	Wm.	45	IRL	884b		1871
Michael					Nov 1899	**FITZGERALDRGE**					
Morris	40	IRL	3731		1870	Andrew	27	IRL	663		1870
Morris	41	IRL	1262b		1871	**FITZGIBBON**					
Nelly	3	SF	3903		1896	David	75	IRE	3166		1903
Nicholas	59	IRE	5635		1902	Geroge T.					Aug 1899
Nicholas	67	IRL	4228		1900	Margaret	22	SF	931		1902
Patrick	80	IRL	1215a		1871	Maurice M.	76	IRE	6953		1902
Patrick	78	IRE	171		1902	Michael B.	41	IRE	1367		1869
Patrick	29	IRE	1323		1869	Thomas	70	IRE	3685		1903
Patrick R.	75	IRL	241		1901	**FITZGIBBONS**					
Richard	<1	SF	1181		1866	Harry J.	50	NY	3992a		1895
Richard	48	NY	5582		1903	J.	47		4676		1903
Richard A.	63	ENG	6392	Feb	1901	Mary	58	IRL	3604a		1895
Richard D.	64	ENG	3197		1903	Regina Josephine	<1	SF	4068		1896
Rose Ann	23	CA	515		1900	**FITZGIBON**					
Thomas	55	NY	F11		1883	Mary Ann	35	IRL	3858		1870
Thomas	34	ENG	635		1866	**FITZH**					
Thomas	32	PA	1417		1869	Margaret	37	IRE	556		1866
Thomas	1842	IRE	2333c		1904	**FITZHARRIS**					
Thomas	72	IRE	6750		1902	John	38	SF	3168		1900
Thomas	43	IRE	6851		1902	**FITZHENRY**					
Thomas	60	IRL	5595		1896	James	64	IRE	2248		1902
Thomas T.					Jan 1900	**FITZHUGH**					
Walter M.	1	SF	3854		1903	E. C.	62	VA	F26		1883
William	71	IRL	251b		1871	Peregrine					Jan 1899
William					Feb 1899	Sarah Margaret	84	MD	8678		1900
William (soldier)			138		1901						
William (soldier)			5688	Jan	1901						

Key: a = 1st part of year; b = 2nd part of year;
c = death certificate copy; c/o = child of

NAME	AGE OR YOB.	BIRTH PLACE	CERT. NO	ID	DEATH YEAR	NAME	AGE OR YOB.	BIRTH PLACE	CERT. NO	ID	DEATH YEAR
FITZJAMES						Frank	<1	SF	2467		1902
William					1899	Geo. Wm.	<1	SF	2714		1866
						George	2	SF	1364		1869
FITZLER						Gertrude	<1	CA	4677		1903
Fred E.	32	CA	8381		1900	Guy M.	28	NV	5731		1902
						Hugh				Jul	1899
FITZMADDEN						J./Ch., c/o	<1	SF	2776		1894
Fulton	<1		5028		1867	James	32	IRL	3503		1872
Maud	<1	SF	5027		1867	James	30	ENG	3532		1867
						James	72	IRE	757		1902
FITZMAURICE						James	7	SF	5975		1903
Allick	74	IRL	1281		1870	James	<1	SF	3907a		1895
Nellie	47	IRE	5128		1902	James	1904	SF	3145c		1904
Wm. M.				Jul	1898	James	69	IRL	8183		1901
						Jno.	44	IRL	5705a		1895
FITZMEYER						Jno. Edward	<1	SF	3342		1894
Christian	42	PRU	1199		1869	Jno. P., c/o		SF	181b		1872
						John	<1	SF	4755		1867
FITZPATRICK						John	<1	SF	8748		1868
——	29	SF	1705		1894	John	20	WI	5007a		1895
Annie	36	IRL	F66		1886	John				Feb	1899
Bernard	25	IRE	924		1866	John				Jul	1899
Bridget T.	55	NY	8329		1901	John Henry	27	SF	6402		1904
Carrie	<1	SF	3236		1895	Joseph	<1	SF	3253		1870
Catharine F.	3	SF	3013		1872	Julia Teresa	31	SF	1347		1894
Catherine	<1	CA	1598		1866	Margaret	21	SF	5291		1901
Catherine	56	IRL	6251		1896	Margaret				Jan	1900
Daniel	31	IRL	7005	Feb	1901	Margaret	47	IRL	6606a		1895
Dominick	<1	SF	1255		1894	Margaret A.				Feb	1900
Dora	28	IRL	4171b		1870	Martha	78	IRL	4156		1896
Edward	1841	IRE	1178c		1904	Mary				Jul	1899
Edward				Mar	1899	Mary	72	AL	5342		1904
Edward				May	1899	Mary Ann	60	IRL	35b		1871
Edward A.	<1	SF	1368		1869	Mary Clair	4	CA	9271		1901
Edward Joseph				Feb	1899	Mary E. G.	1872	SF	248c		1904
Elizabeth	1846	IRE	1849c		1904	Matthew				Feb	1899
F., c/o	<1	SF	3437a		1872						
Florence J.	<1	CA	1356		1901						
Francis					1899						
Frank	3	CA	7110		1904						

Key: a = 1st part of year; b = 2nd part of year;
c = death certificate copy; c/o = child of

NAME	AGE OR YOB.	BIRTH PLACE	CERT. NO	ID	DEATH YEAR
Michael	68	NY	F9		1882
Micheal	48	IRE	1353		1869
Patrick	28	IRE	9883		1868
Peter				Jun	1899
Reverend Timothy	53	IRL	5335a		1895
Sarah E.	<1	SF	5379		1867
Sarah E.	31	SF	1479		1902
Simon	76	IRE	4997		1904
Theresa	<1	SF	6171		1903
Thomas		SF	1084b		1871
Thomas				Apr	1899
Thomas	64	IRL	1456a		1871
Thomas J.	5	SF	6365	Feb	1901
William	61	IRE	57		1902
William E.	35	NV	3927		1900
Wm. H.	2	SF	273b		1871
FITZSCHE					
Rudolph	42	GER	953		1866
FITZSIMMONS					
Betsy	59	SCT	201		1901
Catherine Teresa	44	SF	2003		1902
Ellen	75	IRE	8620		1904
James	71	IRL	8592		1901
James E.	<1	SF	3341		1870
John	35	IRL	1324b		1871
Joseph	30	IRL	4015		1896
Margarey	1846	IRE	2482c		1904
Mary	50	IRL	F18		1883
Michael	68	IRL	3227		1900
Thomas	74	IRL	6362a		1895
FITZSIMONDS					
John F. (soldier)			6813		1900
FITZSIMONS					
Bridget E.	<1	SF	5961		1867
Cornelius				Oct	1899

NAME	AGE OR YOB.	BIRTH PLACE	CERT. NO	ID	DEATH YEAR
FIUD					
Marie	29	FRA	1835		1894
FIVAZ					
Louis Pierre	1838	SWT	2613c		1904
FIVEY					
Margaret	77	IRE	2166		1903
William J.				Apr	1899
FIX					
Charlotte				Feb	1899
FIXSEN					
Henry	27	GER	7550		1900
FLACH					
Josepha	67	GER	2129		1903
FLACK					
Catherine	68	NY	8661		1904
George D.	62	ENG	6254	Feb	1901
FLAGEOLLET					
Charles H.	63	FRA	3951a		1895
Hypolite	16	FRA	F43		1885
FLAGG					
Fannie	52	LA	8156		1904
FLAGHERTY					
——			7265		1868
John	68	IRE	2695		1866
FLAGLAN					
Sarah	78	NB	5676		1867
FLAGLER					
Lucy Ann	83	NS	6990		1904
FLAGLOR					
Frank A. J.	<1	SF	1657		1900
FLAHANAN					
Edgar	11	CA	3386		1900

Key: a = 1st part of year; b = 2nd part of year;
c = death certificate copy; c/o = child of

NAME	AGE OR YOB.	BIRTH PLACE	CERT. NO	ID	DEATH YEAR	NAME	AGE OR YOB.	BIRTH PLACE	CERT. NO	ID	DEATH YEAR
FLAHARTY						**FLANAGAN**					
Catherine	45	IRL	1373a		1871	Ann Isabel	<1	SF	5528a		1895
						Bernard	<1	CA	3780	Nov	1901
FLAHERTY						Catherine	49	IRL	4237	Dec	1901
——			7313		1868	Chas./Lucy, c/o				Feb	1900
Agnes	29	SF	4829		1903	Daniel	54	IRL	F27		1884
Ann	43	IRL	F22		1883	Edward	52	IRL	1999		1873
Annie	65	IRE	4893		1903	Edward	40	NH	6345		1900
Bridget	74	IRL	4019		1870	George	<1	SF	82		1865
Bridget	<1	SF	6727		1868	George Elmer	<1	SF	2468		1902
Cathrini	<1	SF	5183		1867	Hattie	8	SF	6045		1896
Eddie G.	26	CA	5336a		1895	Henry O'Connell	37	IRL	325		1870
George E.	1	CA	3763		1903	James/Kate, c/o	<1	CA	3869		1901
I.			1039		1866	John	50	IRE	2407		1902
James	35	QU	3607	Nov	1901	John	24	CA	6751		1900
John	<1	SF	1172		1869	John	36	IRL	3947	Dec	1901
Joseph D.					1899	John J.	33	NY	4476		1904
Katie	6	SF	2953		1903	Lawrence					1898
Madge	8	SF	6015		1896	Margaret	29	IRE	8758		1868
Margaret	1830	IRE	57c		1904	Margaret	48	IRE	2045		1902
Margaret Teresa	2	SF	1750b		1872	Margaret A.	<1	SF	1494		1900
Martin	30	CA	7150		1903	Margaret Elizabeth	<1	SF	1201		1894
Mary	67	IRL	6530		1896	Mary	18	SF	32b		1895
Mary				Nov	1899	Mary E.	30	CA	8693		1901
Patrick/Henrietta, c/o		SF	1083		1900	Michael	50	IRL	3877		1896
Peter E.					1898	Michael	50	IRL	7757		1900
Stephen	43	IRL	3169		1873	Patrick	71	IRL	3449		1896
Thomas	46	IRE	1445		1869	Patrick	64	IRL	3220	Nov	1901
William Henry	42	NY	1132		1903	Patrick	60	IRE	5353		1903
FLAIG						Patrick J.	42	IRE	3098		1902
Martin	28	GER	954b		1872	Thomas	33	IRL	280b		1872
FLAKE						Willie	1	CA	1367a		1871
Campbell W. (soldier)			1765c		1904	**FLANAGHAN**					
FLAKER						Kate	25	IRL	329a		1871
Kate	37	IA	2267		1903						

Key: *a = 1st part of year; b = 2nd part of year;*
c = death certificate copy; c/o = child of

NAME	AGE OR YOB.	BIRTH PLACE	CERT. NO	ID	DEATH YEAR
FLANDERS					
Bert G. (soldier)			6969		1900
Bert T. (soldier)			6812		1900
Lena	24	CA	610b		1895
FLANICH					
Eva	<1	SF	955		1894
FLANIG					
Elsie M.	<1	SF	2013		1894
FLANIGAN					
Frank J.	27	CAN	5784a		1895
James	<1	SF	6561		1868
Patrick	55	IRL	6885		1900
Wm.	45	IRL	F33		1884
FLANIHAN					
Patrick	36	IRE	6767		1868
FLANNAGAN					
Alice C.				Jul	1898
Edwin Samuel	4	SF	2116		1894
Ellen	1885	PA	1240c		1904
Patrick				Jul	1898
FLANNELLY					
Ann	62	IRE	1324		1903
Anne	1	SF	1639a		1871
James	37	SF	3661		1900
Margaret	Abt	IRE	1325		1903
Thomas	33	SF	8913		1900
FLANNELY					
John	51	IRL	2008b		1895
FLANNER					
Chas.	46	NC	F92		1889
FLANNERY					
Catherine	60	IRL	2137		1894
Chas.	43	IRL	1310		1894
James	40	IRL	F60		1886

NAME	AGE OR YOB.	BIRTH PLACE	CERT. NO	ID	DEATH YEAR
Mary	24	IRL	1656b		1871
Patrick	28	IRE	8589		1868
Thomas	30	IRL	694a		1871
FLANNEY					
Michael				Mar	1899
FLANNIGAN					
Laurcinca				Jun	1899
Mary	<1	SF	1194		1869
Mary				Mar	1899
T. J.	42	IRL	545		1894
FLATELY					
William E.	2	SF	9612		1901
FLATHERTY					
——	<1	SF	1222		1869
FLATHMANN					
Henry	1	SF	2213a		1872
FLATLAND					
Theodore	4	CA	8438		1904
FLATLEY					
Hannah	1	SF	486a		1871
Louis Francis	4	SF	5767		1902
Madeline Thersa				Jan	1899
William D.				May	1899
FLATLY					
J./M., c/o		SF	2105		1873
FLATTERY					
Kate E.	22	CA	2259		1894
FLAVEN					
J. E.	35	IA	2579		1895
FLAVILLE					
Louisa	36	NY	8478		1901
FLAVIN					
Mary	60	CAN	3812		1896

Key: a = 1st part of year; b = 2nd part of year;
c = death certificate copy; c/o = child of

NAME	AGE OR YOB.	BIRTH PLACE	CERT. NO	ID	DEATH YEAR
FLAXMAN					
Thomas	74	NS	787		1903
FLECK					
Francis Melvin	1	SF	9473		1901
Gustave	39	GER	5249		1904
FLEET					
George H.				Oct	1899
FLEETWOOD					
W./T., c/o				Mar	1899
FLEGER					
Catherine	<1	SF	21		1865
FLEISCHHAUER					
Beatrix W.	1	SF	1016a		1871
W. H.	1	NY	6673		1868
FLEISCHMAN					
Annabelle Louise	20	SF	5215		1902
C. V., c/o	<1	SF	243b		1872
Mathias/Martha, c/o				Jul	1899
William G.	3	SF	8939		1868
FLEISCHMANN					
Caroline	1	SF	1297		1866
John	72	GER	474		1903
Louisa	36	GER	278b		1872
FLEISHACKER					
Alfred	1	SF	1283		1866
FLEISHER					
Bertha				Nov	1898
Eva	74	AUS	8699		1904
Myrtle J.				Jan	1900
Wolf	67	AUS	7340		1904
FLEISHMAN					
——	<1	SF	8605		1868
Adelheia	1815	GER	2979c		1904
Charles L.				Mar	1899
Fredrick J.	35	SF	4306		1903
Isaac	4	SF	1137		1869
Moses	56	AUS	3196		1902
Raphael	<1	SF	2872a		1872
FLEISSNER					
Frances W.	64	GER	1548		1901
FLEISZIG					
Ahe	<1	SF	5337a		1895
FLEMER					
Louisa	45	SF	1631		1900
FLEMING					
——			8815		1868
Agnes L.	44	CA	736		1902
Alice			2239		1866
Ann	40	IRE	1444		1903
Arthur	62	PA	550		1901
Augusta	<1	SF	2611		1894
Bridget	53	IRE	3275		1866
Catharine				Nov	1898
Catherine	70	IRE	2130		1903
Catherine	73	IRE	4540		1904
Catherine Stella	<1	SF	1172		1869
Chas. B. (soldier)			7767		1902
Chas. B. (soldier)			7768		1902
Clarence T. (soldier)			248		1902
D./M., c/o	<1	SF	804		1894
David J.	21	MA	5217a		1896
Edna May	6	MO	5898		1903
Edward	26	CA	210b		1895
Edward G.				Feb	1899
Ellen	35	MA	2045		1900
Eugene	3	SF	1295		1869
Fanny Elizabeth	25	MO	141		1902
Florence	<1	SF	4620		1901
Frank	46	IA	7644		1903

Key: a = 1st part of year; b = 2nd part of year; c = death certificate copy; c/o = child of

NAME	AGE OR YOB.	BIRTH PLACE	CERT. NO	ID	DEATH YEAR
George H.	1	SF	740a		1871
Giles	23	PA	4226		1900
Harriet	1	SF	1174		1903
James	68	IRL	5522		1896
James B.	55	IN	2828		1902
James Howard	11	SF	1918		1900
James Stella					Feb 1900
John	2	SF	461		1870
John	25	AUS	F56		1886
John	50	IRE	1133		1903
John Knox					1898
John M.	70	GA	1972		1902
Joseph P.					1899
Julia					Feb 1899
Lillian M.	22	NY	2004		1902
Maggie	45	IRE	4650		1903
Marguerite	3	SF	1834		1894
Maria	85	SCT	2647		1895
Marie	40	IRL	1442		1870
Michael D.					Apr 1899
Nora E.					May 1899
Peter	69	SCT	6734a		1895
Thomas	58	FRA	8126		1901
Thomas F.					Feb 1899
Vara E.	49	IN	3237		1903
William	10	SF	1258		1869
William	84	IRE	737		1902
William B.	52	MA	4751		1901
FLEMMING					
Cathrine	3	NY	7861		1868
Frank B.	35	IL	6557a		1895
Jennie	2	SF	921b		1895
John	15	PA	1699		1866
Otto		SF	1350b		1872
Philip	62	IRE	6136		1903
William (soldier)			2049		1901
FLEMMINGS					
Eliza	85	IRL	4365	Dec	1901
FLENNCKEN					
R./C., c/o		SF	2039		1873
FLERES					
Mariannino	72	ITA	5093		1901
FLESCHMANN					
William	1	CA	1616b		1872
FLESMAN					
Mary Louise	51	OR	2578		1901
FLESSER					
Friedrick					Mar 1899
FLETCHER					
Agnes	1	SF	1186		1869
Annie	42	GER	8851		1904
Bernard	2	SF	1422		1869
Charles	<1	SF	7708		1868
Charles	76	RUS	1142		1902
Charlotte	60	ENG	5843		1904
David Waller					Mar 1900
E. P.	69	MI	8991		1903
Edith Christina	45	MA	3238		1903
Edward (soldier)			139		1901
Edward/Cecily, c/o					Jul 1898
Elizabeth	84	VA	6698		1900
Gordon	24	NE	6731		1904
Hannah	65	ENG	1412b		1895
Hattie Layell					Jan 1899
Henry	63	ENG	6694a		1895
J. A.	59	VT	2485		1873
James					Feb 1899
James	27	ENG	3598		1903
James P.	<1	SF	6096		1904
Jas.	69	PA	F20		1883

Key: a = 1st part of year; b = 2nd part of year; c = death certificate copy; c/o = child of

NAME	AGE OR YOB.	BIRTH PLACE	CERT. NO	ID	DEATH YEAR
John H.	52	ENG	1620		1870
Leroy D.	60	ME	7426		1904
Lydia	3	SF	9364		1868
Martha P.	15	SF	2579		1901
Mary	38	NB	1162		1870
Mary Alice	53	NY	6453		1904
Mary Ann	82	ME	1767		1900
Mary C.	53	NJ	6181		1902
Ormand (soldier)			3540		1900
Robert	59	IRE	6921		1868
Royal E.				Jan	1900
Sarah	21	CA	767b		1895
Selena Minna	1	SF	1000		1866
St. Clair	55	DC	2300		1903
Walter K./Mary E., c/o		SF	9248		1901
William					1899
William E.		CA	1261		1869
FLETT					
William	51	SCT	3831		1900
FLEUR					
Olga				Aug	1899
FLEURY					
Adolphe	1827	FRA	249c		1904
Ann	65	IRE	3683		1902
Ita	59	FRA	575		1866
John E. (soldier)			6745	Feb	1901
Sophie				Feb	1900
FLEUTIAIX					
Philippe Auguste	77	FRA	5443		1904
FLICK					
Bertha	<1	SF	1389		1870
Carl (soldier)	34	GER	1930		1901
Clara	<1	SF	1642		1870
Gustav	48	GER	4633		1896
Marguerite	53	BEL	6074		1902

NAME	AGE OR YOB.	BIRTH PLACE	CERT. NO	ID	DEATH YEAR
Philip/Mary		SF	5268		1896
William F.				Nov	1899
FLIEGELMAN					
Hannah				Mar	1899
FLINN					
Catherine M.	64	IRL	7733		1900
Dennis	28	VT	2998		1866
Elizabeth Anna	51	OR	2598		1900
Elizabeth M.	<1	SF	758		1902
Ellen E.	1	SF	661		1866
Mary	1830	SCT	1335c		1904
FLINT					
Almira Theresa	48	MA	4248		1896
Dres Jane E.	52	NY	F46		1885
Electa W.	<1	SF	2159a		1872
Frank R.	19	WI	6147	Jan	1901
Hanah B.	84	NS	485b		1895
Harry P.				Aug	1898
Horace P.	52	MA	2075b		1895
John	65	ENG	5965		1867
Samuel					1898
Thomas P.	45	MA	1131		1869
Wilson	46	OH	3435		1867
FLINTOFF					
Thomas	48	ENG	2041		1873
FLISCHMANN					
Johann	21	GER	5044		1867
FLISHMAN					
Jos.	<1	SF	4714a		1895
FLITNER					
Frank William	1847	ME	3062c		1904
FLOCKTON					
Charles Procton	1828	ENG	5c		1904

NAME	AGE OR YOB.	BIRTH PLACE	CERT. NO	ID	DEATH YEAR
FLOETER					
Herman Henry	1	SF	6611		1900
Minnie	3	SF	8248		1904
FLOHR					
G. F. M.		SF	6149a		1895
Kate	24	CA	4750		1901
FLOOD					
——		SF	199		1870
——			7527		1868
Ann	75	IRL	4655a		1895
Annie Elizabeth	2	SF	1659a		1871
Bernard , c/o		SF	2629a		1872
Bernard, c/o		SF	2466		1873
Bridget	72	IRE	5545		1902
Bridget	80	IRL	6721		1896
Charles B.	60	ME	5111		1901
Cora	42	CA	6673		1902
Edward Gavin	<1	SF	2269		1901
Edward N. (soldier)			96		1900
Emma	37	NY	7794		1900
Fred B.	37	IN	5599		1904
Grace	1	SF	9746		1868
Hugh	45	IRL	256b		1872
James	53	NY	F29		1884
James	35	CA	6379		1896
James				Jun	1899
James				Oct	1899
John Henry	<1	SF	693		1866
John Joseph	38	IRE	8325		1903
John Joseph				Aug	1898
Mary Ann	5	SF	2693a		1872
Mary Catherine	30	SF	949		1900
Mary Ellen	1	CA	3193		1873
Mary Emma	13	SF	1476		1866
Mary J.				Jul	1899

NAME	AGE OR YOB.	BIRTH PLACE	CERT. NO	ID	DEATH YEAR
Minnie E.	46	SF	7889		1904
Minnie S.	30	PA	696		1902
Patrick Joseph	52	NY	5928	Jan	1901
Rose A.	47	IRL	1690		1901
Theresa	60	IRL	748b		1895
FLORA					
——		SF	1152		1869
FLORENCE					
Andrew C.	28	CA	F84		1887
George		SF	589b		1871
FLORENTECK					
Maria Angelique	46	FRA	1652a		1871
FLORENTINE					
Alexander	67	NY	7564		1900
Edward (soldier)			6931		1900
FLORENTINO					
Josepha				Oct	1898
FLORES					
Adlia	1904	SF	2157c		1904
Alice	30	CA	3997		1900
Anastasia L.	<1	SF	1041		1868
Angela	25	CA	9855		1868
Antonio				Feb	1900
Candelario	33	MEX	1447		1869
Carlos	12	SF	3362	Nov	1901
Cayetano	25	CA	F69		1886
Francisco	35	MEX	3661		1903
Herbert A.	<1	SF	7721		1903
Jesus	22	MEX	8980		1868
John				Oct	1899
Joseph	5	CA	6495		1902
Joseph	49	CA	5844		1904
L./A., c/o		SF	976		1894
Manuel				Apr	1899
Marcus	<1	SF	5835a		1895

NAME	AGE OR YOB.	BIRTH PLACE	CERT. NO	ID	DEATH YEAR
Nicholas F.	45	WIS	8669		1868
Pilar	23	MEX	9694		1901
Policarpo	23	MEX	3000a		1872
Ramon B. (marine)			4388		1903
Refugio	23	CA	9974		1868
FLORETTA					
Vincenza	67	ITA	8391		1904
FLORINE					
John A.	6	SF	3998		1870
Juliana	8	MN	2285		1866
FLORIS					
Carlotta	<1	SF	5112		1901
FLOSI					
Adolfo	45	ITA	6433		1904
FLOTT					
William	41	DEN	1133		1869
FLOUTADE					
Eugenie P.	2	SF	4839		1867
FLOWER					
Susanna Tygeorge	49	GER	6191		1896
William	<1	SF	1693a		1871
FLOWERS					
Cecil				Aug	1898
Edward	52	CAN	1215		1866
Electa G.	46	VT	1374		1869
Mary P.	39	NY	5170		1867
FLOYD					
Ann	1813	NY	3220c		1904
Elizabeth				Aug	1899
George (soldier)			5691	Jan	1901
Henry	44	IRL	541a		1871
James	50		3940		1896
Miles Baird	3	SF	4606		1896
Robert W. (soldier)			4540		1901

NAME	AGE OR YOB.	BIRTH PLACE	CERT. NO	ID	DEATH YEAR
Thomas	75	ENG	3714		1896
William Wolf				Jul	1898
FLUBACHEN					
Henry	<1	SF	2095		1873
FLUBACHER					
Emily	1	SF	759a		1871
FLUEBACHER					
Cathrine	31	FRA	2200		1866
FLUES					
Emil				Nov	1898
FLUHAR					
Wayland Edward	32	OH	1315		1900
FLUHART					
F. M.				Oct	1898
Nancy	85	PA	3125		1895
FLUKE					
Charles Westley	68	IL	4968		1904
FLURM					
Julius	48	GER	5176		1867
FLUSHMAN					
Adelheia	1815	GER	2979c		1904
FLUSSNER					
Doris Augusta	3	SF	1058b		1895
FLUTH					
George	26	MO	3147		1902
Samuel A.	19	MO	2569		1900
FLUTSCH					
Bertha				Oct	1898
FLYNN					
Alice Margaret	<1	SF	1232b		1895
Anthony	<1	SF	815		1866
Anthony				Jan	1899
Catherine	<1	SF	1187		1869

NAME	AGE OR YOB.	BIRTH PLACE	CERT. NO	ID	DEATH YEAR	NAME	AGE OR YOB.	BIRTH PLACE	CERT. NO	ID	DEATH YEAR
Catherine	63	IRL	358b		1895	James	26	SF	7858		1901
Catherine	64	IRL	5417		1896	James A.	32	OR	2794		1903
Catherine	47	IRL	6903		1900	James A.	29	NY	4433		1901
Catherine				Oct	1899	James J.					1899
Cathrine I.	2	SF	981		1866	James W.				Mar	1899
D./C. H., c/o		SF	6483		1895	Jennie	39	BC	917		1903
Daniel Joseph	1	SF	212b		1871	Jno. Philip	20	SF	2321		1894
Denis	<1	SF	5587		1867	John	10	MA	2196a		1872
Denis	33	IRL	3258		1895	John	30	IRL	3224		1873
Dennis L.	51	IRE	6104		1903	John	32	IRE	3141		1866
Dominick	38	SF	6222		1900	John	26	IRE	5402		1867
Edith C.	<1	SF	7120		1902	John	47	IRL	3904		1896
Edw. F./Annie, c/o		SF	731		1900	John	40	CA	7345		1900
Edward	54	IRL	1973		1894	John	32	NY	3751	Nov	1901
Edward	60	IRL	6192		1900	John Henry	44	MO	4371		1903
Edward P.	31	LA	7271		1902	John J.	38	SF	4224		1902
Elizabeth	42	IRL	229		1870	John W.	38	SF	3023		1902
Elizabeth				Mar	1900	Joseph				Jul	1898
Ellen	29	IRL	1325a		1871	Joseph Bernard	1	SF	4077		1903
Ellen				Apr	1899	Juliette M.				Jul	1898
Ellizabeth	<1	SF	1448		1869	Lizzie				Apr	1899
Eveline Mary	<1	SF	7056		1903	Madeline G.	<1	CA	1332		1902
Evelyn M.	1	SF	791		1866	Maggie	<1	SF	8684		1868
Frances Victoria	2	SF	8464		1904	Margaret A.	25	SF	1431		1900
Francis	69	IRE	5213		1904	Margaret M.	24	SF	6525		1902
Frederick V.	28	SF	6513a		1895	Mary	<1	SF	4680		1867
George C.	<1	CA	1880		1902	Mary	<1	SF	761		1894
Hazel G.	6	SF	7563		1901	Mary	82	IRL	3824a		1895
Honora	54	IRL	94b		1871	Mary				Aug	1899
Hughie (soldier)			299		1902	Mary E.	<1	SF	1807b		1895
J. alias J. Gordon	28	ENG	4768a		1895	Mary E.	35	MA	3576	Nov	1901
J./M., c/o	<1	SF	2907		1873	Mary F.	44	CA	3511		1900
James	73	IRE	783		1902	May	25	SF	6624		1902
James	37	NV	1457		1902	May J.	27	SF	4482		1902
James	36	CA	7778		1903	Michael	67	IRL	3781	Nov	1901
James	48	IRL	1744		1894	Michael				Nov	1899

Key: a = 1st part of year; b = 2nd part of year;
c = death certificate copy; c/o = child of

NAME	AGE OR YOB.	BIRTH PLACE	CERT. NO	ID	DEATH YEAR
Michael	29	PA	1033		1903
Michael Terence	1	SF	1139		1869
Morris	56	IRL	2767		1901
Morris/Wilhelmina, c/o	1	SF	8415		1904
Nellie	9	SF	3197		1870
Owen	47	IRL	F79		1887
Patrick	40	IRE	1576c		1904
Patrick	75	IRL	3088		1900
Patrick B.	32	IRE	5173		1867
Patrick Henry	<1	SF	839		1894
Patrick J. (soldier)	25	IRL	3699		1900
Peter	30	PA	1404		1894
R. L.	38	NS	1488b		1871
Rose	<1	SF	2217a		1872
Sellie	32	CA	6610		1900
Thomas	30	IRL	2555a		1872
Thomas	45	IRL	1592b		1872
Thomas	19	NY	8418		1868
Thomas	87	IRE	6306		1904
Thomas	<1	SF	108b		1895
Thomas	74	IRL	6434		1900
Thomas					Mar 1900
Thomas C.	75	IRL	9014		1901
Thomas J.	<1	SF	8335		1868
Thomas J.					Jul 1899
Thomas J.					May 1899
Timothy		SF	1021b		1871
Timothy	55	IRL	F47		1885
Timothy	35	IRE	9910		1868
Timothy	68	IRL	7183		1900
Timothy I.	<1	SF	8779		1868
William	28	IRE	1057		1869
William	60		3725		1902
William	46	IRE	6808		1903
William	55	IRL	3235		1895
William					Aug 1899

NAME	AGE OR YOB.	BIRTH PLACE	CERT. NO	ID	DEATH YEAR
Winifred	1840	IRE	848c		1904
Wm.	56	IRE	5664		1902
Wm. J.					Mar 1900
FLYNT					
John W.					May 1899
FO					
Hi		CHN	6272		1896
FOARD					
Thomas	66	MD	1882b		1895
FOCACCI					
Maria	62	ITA	6992		1900
FOCCOCIA					
Giovannia	38	ITA	129b		1872
FOCHETTI					
Emilio	2	SF	1143		1902
FOCKE					
Julius	33	GER	F59		1886
Julius E.	26	GER	2772a		1872
FODERA					
Anthony/Rosa, c/o		SF	854		1900
Drew					Apr 1899
FOEADNEAU					
Willie	<1	SF	8749		1868
FOEDRICKS					
——		CA	1739		1870
FOEHNER					
Joseph	40	GER	8623		1901
FOERTSCH					
Emilie Louise					Aug 1898
Juanita	2	SF	7399		1903
FOFF					
Bertha	<1	SF	1257b		1895

*Key: a = 1st part of year; b = 2nd part of year;
c = death certificate copy; c/o = child of*

NAME	AGE OR YOB.	BIRTH PLACE	CERT. NO	ID	DEATH YEAR
FOGARTY					
——	<1	SF	3604		1870
Alicia				Jul	1898
Anna	2	SF	1602b		1871
Bridget	59	IRL	2705		1894
David	68	IRE	5607		1902
Edward	<1	SF	1702a		1871
Edward	1	SF	3285		1866
Elizabeth S.	3	SF	2861		1901
Ellizabeth	63	IRE	5155		1902
James	<1	SF	3353a		1872
James	1	SF	3217		1903
John C.	35	IRE	5280		1903
John J.				Jan	1900
Mary Adelaide	1	SF	469b		1872
Mattie A.				Apr	1899
Michael	1829	IRE	2435c		1904
Susan	33	SF	3409		1903
Thomas	68	IRE	5354		1903
Thomas Francis				Jan	1899
Walter T.	24	NY	5292		1902
William				Feb	1900
FOGE					
Christian	20	GER	4592		1901
Cord. Albert Claus	34	GER	3188Nov		1901
John Mathias	62	GER	2233		1901
FOGEL					
George	52	GER	541b		1871
Morris	29	CA	762		1901
Tillie	22	CA	1134		1903
Tina	63	GER	6912		1904
FOGERTY					
Ann Maria	8	SF	2136		1866
Catherine	33	IRL	1144b		1872
Elizabeth	55	IRL	2456		1873
James	<1	SF	1174a		1871
John	7	SF	833a		1871
Margaret	70	IRL	85		1900
FOGG					
Clara Belle	20	CA	F83		1887
George	46	ME	6760a		1895
Joseph S.	81	NH	4014a		1895
Leslie F.	42	ME	3964		1900
R. T.	64	NH	F101		1889
Walter B.	3	SF	1230		1869
FOGHEL					
Francisco	1827	AUS	1722c		1904
FOGLIA					
Frank	1903	SF	111c		1904
FOGT					
N.	67	FRA	5235a		1896
FOH					
Chun	22	CHN	225a		1871
FOICH					
James	27	SWT	3576		1870
FOIE					
Mark L.	1	SF	3373		1870
FOIN					
Frederick A.	66	GER	3344		1903
Harry F. (soldier)			4541		1901
FOIZEY					
Anne	67	CAN	4761		1904
FOK					
Le Tung	40	CHN	817b		1895
FOLDS					
H. S. (soldier)			9562		1901
FOLEY					
——	<1	SF	3548		1870
——	<1	SF	3853		1870

Key: *a = 1st part of year; b = 2nd part of year; c = death certificate copy; c/o = child of*

NAME	AGE OR YOB.	BIRTH PLACE	CERT. NO	ID	DEATH YEAR
——		SF	1366		1869
Alfred E.	1	CA	8225		1901
Alfred I.	<1	SF	4954		1867
Ann	6	SF	3772		1870
Anne	64	IRL	7562		1901
Annie J.				Aug	1898
Bridget	67	IRL	1098		1901
Catherine	7	SF	6735		1868
Catherine	78	IRL	4921		1896
Catherine	65	IRL	4309a		1895
Catherine	65	IRL	7525		1901
Catherine	56	IRL	2957		1900
Catherine	62	IRL	6723	Feb	1901
Charles Aloyuis	<1	SF	4909		1901
Charles P.	18	ENG	5272		1867
Colman	<1	SF	1001		1868
Cornelius J.	47	CT	6923		1902
Daniel				Feb	1899
Daniel	55	IRE	5602		1903
Dennis J.	24	CA	4945		1901
E.	27	SF	4607		1901
Edmond	45	IRL	728b		1872
Edward	75	IRL	571a		1871
Elizabeth	1	SF	673		1903
Elvira	56	MA	4366	Dec	1901
Frances	<1	SF	7910		1868
Francis Joseph	<1	SF	142		1902
Francis L.	3	CA	4187		1900
Frank	9	SF	7142		1902
Frank	55	IRL	1231b		1895
George	<1	SF	1508		1866
Hannah	85	IRE	784		1902
Hannah				Mar	1900
Hannah	66	IRE	114		1903
J./E., c/o	<1	SF	3501		1895
James	63	IRL	7902		1901

NAME	AGE OR YOB.	BIRTH PLACE	CERT. NO	ID	DEATH YEAR
James	50	IRE	6033		1902
James (soldier)			1944		1903
Jean Joseph	45	MA	8521		1900
Johanna	52	IRE	6403		1902
Johanna N.	58	GER	8663		1900
John	35	IRL	1634a		1871
John	<1	SF	838		1866
John	35	IRE	8189		1904
John			7228		1902
John	58	IRL	4207	Dec	1901
John	48	CT	2375		1901
John	1	SF	2231		1903
Joseph	<1	SF	1779b		1872
Joseph	<1	SF	3070		1894
Joseph D.	28	IRE	3855		1903
Joseph J.	33	MA	3764		1903
Julia	35	IRL	805		1894
Julia	45	IRL	4755		1896
Julia Agnes	2	SF	7614		1904
Lizzie	1	SF	1513b		1872
Loretta	<1	SF	8706		1903
Mamie	9	SF	4679		1903
Margaret	35	IRE	7376		1868
Margaret	65	IRE	1726		1902
Margaret Mary	<1	SF	7434		1903
Margarett	12	CA	1071		1869
Maria A.	51	ENG	1550		1901
Martin	27	PA	5063		1904
Mary	<1	CA	3092		1873
Mary	72	IRE	4592		1867
Mary	60	IRE	3450		1903
Mary	65	IRE	3723		1903
Mary	45	IRL	2461b		1895
Mary				Jul	1899
Mary				Mar	1899
Mary	6	SF	6115		1867

Key: a = 1st part of year; b = 2nd part of year; c = death certificate copy; c/o = child of

NAME	AGE OR YOB.	BIRTH PLACE	CERT. NO	ID	DEATH YEAR	NAME	AGE OR YOB.	BIRTH PLACE	CERT. NO	ID	DEATH YEAR
Mary A.	13	NY	1120		1870	William Aloysuis	1898	SF	1850c		1904
Mary A.	50	IRL	F17		1883	**FOLGER**					
Mary A.	95	IRL	1055		1894	Catherine	46	IRL	1548		1894
Mary Anna	37	ENG	586		1900	Charles M.	84	NY	2189		1902
Mary E.	<1	SF	2084		1866	Jane McArthur	39	SF	957		1902
Mathew	<1	SF	1643b		1871	Maria	48	CT	5582		1867
Michael	71	IRE	7415		1903	Mary Hallen	8	SF	1142		1869
Michael	42	MA	4244a		1895	Rachel C.	34	MA	2016a		1872
Michael				Jan	1899	Sarah Jane	67	NY	4147		1900
Michael	46	IRE	6065		1867	Seth	75	MA	1045		1900
Michael Joseph	39	CAN	7795		1900	**FOLK**					
Michael Richard	<1	SF	9015		1901	Lin	30	CHN	5798		1867
Michael/Mary, c/o		SF	8836		1903	Phillip	1	SF	939		1870
Morris	19	SF	6212		1900	**FOLKINBURG**					
N./E., c/o	<1	SF	3975		1895	Nelson H.	75	NJ	4404		1903
Patrick	43	IRL	464		1870	**FOLKMANN**					
Patrick	38	IRE	3896		1867	Peter F.	53	DEN	691		1870
Patrick	27	IRE	4397		1867	**FOLKS**					
Patrick	43	IRE	1373		1869	Bella	<1	SF	3125		1866
Patrick	83	IRE	8766		1904	**FOLLAINE**					
Patrick	61	IRE	6385		1903	William T	38	VA	4814		1902
Patrick	39	IRL	5041a		1896	**FOLLEFSEN**					
Patrick James	26	SF	6657a		1895	Benj. A. (soldier)			6814		1900
Q.	1	SF	3912		1870	**FOLLET**					
Risella	21	SF	5034a		1895	Russell	<1	SF	4786		1902
Robt. J.	<1	SF	1091		1869	**FOLLINOBY**					
Stella	27	LA	1719		1901	Elizabeth	<1	SF	3280		1894
Thomas	30	ENG	1124b		1872	**FOLLIS**					
Thomas	57	IRE	7480		1904	Annie Flood	57	NY	2540b		1895
Thomas	63	IRE	5466		1902	Margaret	66	IRL	3935		1900
Thomas				Apr	1899	Richard Holden	73	IRL	8270		1900
Thomas	42	MA	7618		1903	**FOLLNER**					
Thomas J.	5	NY	6019		1867	Albert	32	GER	7451		1868
Timothy	57	IRE	4597		1904						
William		CA	3204		1873						
William	60	IRL	4946		1901						

NAME	AGE OR YOB.	BIRTH PLACE	CERT. NO	ID	DEATH YEAR	NAME	AGE OR YOB.	BIRTH PLACE	CERT. NO	ID	DEATH YEAR
FOLSOM						Ait	38	CHN	6316		1903
Geo. D. F.	73	ME	2388b		1895	Buck Suey	34	CHN	172		1902
George Thorndyke	69	NY	5910		1902	Chang	30	CHN	1088		1869
George W.	18	NV	357b		1895	Che	42	CHN	2502b		1895
Rachel Ann	71	ME	4456		1896	Chee				Jan	1900
Walter H.	6	SF	132		1870	Cheong	40	CHN	3182		1894
FOLTZ						Ching Nea	46	CHN	4270		1896
Charles G.	33	GER	2856		1873	Chon Foo	43	CHN	698		1866
Michael	51	FRA	667b		1872	Chong	51	CHN	2533		1866
FON						Chow				Oct	1898
Lip				Nov	1898	Chun Yip	32	CHN	2884		1894
Mun	24	CHN	7245		1901	Chung	46	CHN	1516		1894
FONCERRADA						Chung					1898
Carlos Henrique	<1	SF	2673		1873	Chung Ham					1898
FONCILLASSARD						Chy Toon	40	CHN	5560a		1895
Joseph				Apr	1899	Ding Yuen				Nov	1898
FONCLERC						Dock Ben				Jan	1900
J.	50	FRA	4439		1896	Dung	42	CHN	575		1901
FOND						Fien or Fung Fon	62	CHN	7466		1903
William M.	44	CA	3716	Nov	1901	Fong	46	CHN	863		1870
FONDA						Foon	49	CHN	2232		1903
Helen K.				May	1899	Foy	42	CHN	5859		1896
Walter M.	<1	CA	3701a		1895	Gee				Nov	1898
FONER						Ging Ying	44	CHN	92		1903
Mary	36	IRE	1107		1869	Git	64	CHN	1896		1901
FONG						Hee	53	CHN	3662		1903
Ah	<1	SF	3459b		1870	Hing	36	CHN	7057		1903
Ah	29	CHN	2579a		1872	Hing				Mar	1900
Ah	30	CHN	7624		1868	Hip	41	CHN	1390		1869
Ah Gun	44	CHN	3274		1900	Hoy Chee	40	CHN	6378		1896
Ah Kit	26	CHN	F62		1886	Huey	1869	CHN	750c		1904
Ah Noe				Feb	1899	Ivy Gin	24	CHN	3902		1896
Ah On	42	CHN	6385		1900	Jet	36	CHN	837		1900
Ah See				Feb	1900	Jim King	25	CHN	3089		1900
						Jung	35	CHN	5086a		1896
						Jung Duck	38	CHN	8388		1903

NAME	AGE OR YOB.	BIRTH PLACE	CERT. NO	ID	DEATH YEAR
Kan	22	CHN	3238		1870
Kee	36	CHN	4640		1902
Kee	50	CHN	8117		1903
Kim	55	CHN	1832		1902
King Fang	37	CHN	8648		1900
King Gong				Oct	1899
Lim	34	CHN	1206		1870
Ling	39	CHN	5443		1896
Ling				Jan	1900
Loong luong	52	CHN	8621		1903
Lung Fook	41	CHN	7211		1902
Lung Hew	25	CHN	773b		1871
Lung Why	33	CHN	6253	Feb	1901
Man	42	CHN	1413b		1895
Mau				Oct	1898
Ming	31	CHN	855b		1895
Mon Jom	31	CHN	8392		1904
Mun	28	CHN	F23		1883
On	53	CHN	3629		1902
Pong	38	CHN	8968		1901
Quai	60	CHN	1199		1901
Sen Oi	52	CHN	6572		1904
Sha Song	56	CHN	5660	Jan	1901
Shew Lui				Jun	1899
Shing	35	CHN	3140	Oct	1901
Shun	27	CA	4109	Dec	1901
Sing	35	CHN	5785		1903
Sit Dow					1899
Slick Num	55	CHN	2280		1894
Son King	51	CHN	209b		1895
Sun				Jan	1899
Ten	55	CHN	29		1902
Tung	52	CHN	661		1902
Un Sue	44	CHN	6971		1904
Wade H. (soldier)	22	VA	8880		1900
Wing Ning	32	CHN	1144		1902

NAME	AGE OR YOB.	BIRTH PLACE	CERT. NO	ID	DEATH YEAR
Yet	40	CHN	8743		1901
Yino	50	CHN	924		1901
You	1863	CHN	2290c		1904
Yow	32	CHN	7044		1902
Yu "Wen	52	CHN	4180		1896
Yuck Goon	51	CHN	8835		1901
Yun On				Jan	1900
FONIET					
Charles	64	AUS	1702		1902
FONN					
Chow	44	CHN	1471		1866
FONSECA					
John, Jr.	24	ESP	1057b		1895
FONTAINE					
Alfred (soldier)			3034	Oct	1901
Mary Ann	40	MN	2172		1900
FONTANA					
Domenico	44	ITA	3518		1903
Frank				Mar	1899
Luisa					1898
FONTANINI					
Guiseppe	25	ITA	5333		1903
FONTENEAN					
Victor Michael				Oct	1899
FONTENEAU					
Isaline Marie	83	SWT	1111		1900
FONTES					
Alexandrine	45	FRA	4815		1902
Carulindo	6	CA	2912		1903
Manuel	21	CA	7993		1904
FONTZ					
Joseph	<1	SF	8709		1868
FONZER					
Andrew	50		3782	Nov	1901

NAME	AGE OR YOB.	BIRTH PLACE	CERT. NO	ID	DEATH YEAR
FOO					
Ah	35	CHN	2511a		1872
Ah	28	CHN	2887a		1872
Ah	33	CHN	427		1865
Chin Fay	53	CHN	1371		1870
Chong	24	CHN	1706		1870
Gee	40	CHN	1772		1870
Jew Bing	1846	CHN	2618c		1904
John	30	CHN	3175		1870
Jung Mun	1859	CHN	1991c		1904
Lee Hun	17	CHN	7811		1868
Lee Kung	1848	CHN	1993c		1904
Leony Ah	21	CHN	1454		1869
Quong				Jan	1900
Sam Lak	27	CHN	1357		1870
Tom	1868	CHN	2094c		1904
Tong	28	CHN	4237b		1870
Toy	13	SF	2311b		1895
Wee Chin	43	CHN	81		1870
FOOHN					
John, c/o		SF	1566b		1872
FOOK					
Ah	30	CHN	1707		1870
Ah	28	CHN	738a		1871
Ah	26	CHN	401b		1872
Ah	35	CHN	5337		1867
Ah	2	SF	5344		1867
Ah	23	CHN	6849		1868
Ah	29	CHN	1049		1868
Chang	40	CHN	776a		1871
Ching C.	38	CHN	1409		1870
Chung	27	CHN	3424b		1870
Hee	42	CHN	1472		1870
Kan	22	CHN	186b		1872
Kong	45	CHN	7619		1868
Lee Joe	1854	CHN	2899c		1904
Leon Ah	24	CHN	1155		1869
Lin	29	CHN	1524		1870
William Winter	58	MS	5642		1904
Yee Wing	22	CHN	1639b		1871
FOOLEY					
Mary	38	IRL	2877		1901
FOOM					
Mo Nue	45	CHN	2043		1903
FOON					
Ah	38	CHN	1158		1869
Chan	1851	CHN	1663c		1904
FOONG					
Ah Fong	10	SF	5841	Jan	1901
Ng	52	CHN	2190		1902
FOORMAN					
Simon	82	GER	3996		1900
FOOSE					
Adele	1877	SF	2614c		1904
FOOT					
Minerva	33	CA	1088		1869
FOOTE					
Bertha Isabel				Feb	1900
Blanche	23	CA	2958		1900
Ernest Emery	1	SF	2131		1903
Henry Stewart	<1	SF	8080		1903
Hugh	70	IRL	4086	Dec	1901
John	38	NY	4759		1904
Joseph H.					1898
FOOTIN					
———			2045		1870
FOPIANO					
Louisov	2	NY	3572		1867
Maria	5	SF	1653b		1872

Key: a = 1st part of year; b = 2nd part of year; c = death certificate copy; c/o = child of

NAME	AGE OR YOB.	BIRTH PLACE	CERT. NO	ID	DEATH YEAR
Rosa	19	ITA	1397b		1871
FOPPIANI					
Teresa	<1	SF	3125a		1872
FOPPIANO					
Alvina	2	SF	8422		1903
Andrea	26	ITA	1121		1869
Angelo					1899
Enrico	1	SF	33		1903
Flora	1	SF	3624		1896
Francisco	76	ITA	6066		1903
Giovanni	50	ITA	3139	Oct	1901
James	32	CA	7026	Feb	1901
Joseph	4	ITA	3138	Oct	1901
Pietro	72	ITA	2167		1903
Pietro	2	SF	6496		1902
FORAN					
Bernardin Frances	24	SF	8393		1904
Edward F.	53	PA	5032		1903
James	63	IRE	8232		1903
Mary	37	IRL	3478		1896
Patrick				Apr	1899
FORANSEN					
Ollof	40	NOR	2832		1866
FORBES					
Agnes	42	GER	6236a		1895
Andrew	73	NY	3961		1900
Andrew Bell	78	NJ	3808		1902
Cecil	1904	CA	2483c		1904
Eileen	53	SCT	6703	Feb	1901
Eliza Ann				Feb	1899
Ellen				May	1899
Fannie	34	SF	360		1900
Frank	50		405		1901
George W.	<1	SF	3776		1867
Henrietta A.	48	CA	4894		1903

NAME	AGE OR YOB.	BIRTH PLACE	CERT. NO	ID	DEATH YEAR
James	78	SCT	5388		1903
James Sty	22	NY	3670		1867
John	46	SCT	2205		1873
Robert Christie	33	SCT	3437		1900
Samuel	10	SF	465a		1871
Thomas	50	MA	3245		1866
Victoria Jane				Nov	1898
William H.	48	NY	5504		1904
FORBIS					
John L. (soldier)			3679		1900
FORCADA					
Joseph	62	SPA	4758		1902
Mariana					1899
Vincent	18	CA	1550		1894
FORCHE					
Elisha (soldier)			806c		1904
FORD					
Almeron	72	NY	4388	Dec	1901
Ann	52	IRL	6061	Jan	1901
Ann	62	NY	3116	Oct	1901
Annette	<1	CA	2432		1902
Augustus	1882	SF	2671c		1904
Bartholomew	10	MA	339b		1871
Benjamin	40	ENG	5911		1902
Bridget	54	IRL	3379		1870
Bridget	<1	SF	1275		1869
Bridget	70	IRL	523b		1895
Catherine	45	IRE	1605		1903
Charles	34	SF	6528		1903
Daniel	22	IRL	520b		1871
Daniel	70	IRL	6299		1900
Daniel J.	5	NY	7379		1868
Daniel William	<1	SF	1395		1901
Dickie	1904	SF	464c		1904
Edward	42	CA	4901		1902

NAME	AGE OR YOB.	BIRTH PLACE	CERT. NO	ID	DEATH YEAR	NAME	AGE OR YOB.	BIRTH PLACE	CERT. NO	ID	DEATH YEAR
Edward	9	SF	1351		1869	Mary	72	TN	3148		1902
Elizabeth	3	SF	1274		1869	Mary				Oct	1899
Elizabeth Bridget	<1	SF	1207		1869	Mary A., Mrs.	72	NY	2803		1894
Ella	<1	CA	3384		1902	Mary E.	<1	SF	8732		1903
Ellen	31	IRL	1506b		1871	Mary H.	17	CA	5783	Jan	1901
Ellen	<1	SF	298a		1871	Matthew W.	53	NY	4619		1901
Ellen				Jan	1900	Michael	36	IRL	967		1870
Ellen A.				Jul	1899	Michael	65	IRL	1886		1894
Emily W.	71	MA	3892		1896	Michael C.				Jan	1900
Eva/John W., c/o	<1	CA	9127		1901	Patrick	39	IRL	2838		1873
Frank	50	USA	1243		1869	Phineas	36	NY	8774		1868
Fred F.	<1	SF	6579		1896	Robert	44	MD	3599		1870
Frederick					1899	Steven	52	IRL	6832a		1895
George C.	<1	SF	2863		1894	Susan	61	IRE	5521		1902
Henry				Mar	1899	Timothy	40	IRL	4339b		1870
Henry C.	52	VT	806		1894	Timothy	76	IRL	484b		1895
Henry Geo.	<1	SF	1398		1869	William	64	IRE	988		1902
Henry I.	39	ENG	1382		1870	William	47	ENG	5529a		1895
Henry/Mary, c/o	1832	ITA	1961		1904	William	85	ENG	1223		1869
James	37	CAN	2027		1903	William M. (soldier)			3035	Oct	1901
James B.	41	MA	3560		1896	William T.	27	SF	4111		1902
Jeremiah J.	2	SF	1194		1866	Willie E.	35	WV	6983	Feb	1901
John	80	IRL	1451		1900	Wm.	63	MD	1885		1894
John				Mar	1899	**FORDE**					
John	80	IRL	1451		1900	Agnes	21	CA	501b		1895
John E.	1	SF	925		1870	Mary J.				Feb	1900
Joseph	70	IRL	5682		1896	R. H./A., c/o		SF	447		1895
Joseph A.	30	SF	3341		1894						
Joseph A.	52	MD	1188b		1895	**FORDEN**					
Josephine	32	IRL	3218		1870	James V. (soldier)			2570		1900
Julia				Jan	1899	**FORDERN**					
Lillian May	24	SF	8970		1903	A./R., c/o	<1	SF	3154		1894
Mack				Nov	1898	**FORDHAM**					
Margaret	23	IRE	3446		1902	Robert B., Jr.	<1	SF	1444b		1871
Martin	70	IRE	2132		1903	William	72	ENG	2954		1903
Mary	3	SF	4097b		1870						

Key: *a = 1st part of year; b = 2nd part of year;*
c = death certificate copy; c/o = child of

NAME	AGE OR YOB.	BIRTH PLACE	CERT. NO	ID	DEATH YEAR	NAME	AGE OR YOB.	BIRTH PLACE	CERT. NO	ID	DEATH YEAR
FORDI						FORMAN					
Edward	39	IRE	2072		1902	Annie	<1	SF	7748		1900
						Edward A. (soldier)			142		1901
FORE						Lillie	1	NV	3146		1866
Ah	30	CHN	7509		1868	Philip	32	NJ	5308a		1895
Dare	33	CHN	1218		1869	Sands W.	52	IL	4221	Dec	1901
						William Bishop	50	NY	7777		1904
FOREMAN						Wm./Annie, c/o		SF	2841		1895
Bernard	<1	SF	1537		1870						
Eugene	18	MN	46b		1872	FORMET					
Henry Louis				Aug	1898	Francois	86	FRA	4367		1902
J. B.	41	OH	4932a		1895						
John	83	ENG	1572b		1895	FORMHALE					
Mabell H.	3	SF	4016		1870	Caroline	56	GER	3524a		1895
FORESTER						FORNA					
Henry	<1	SF	489a		1871	Marta	48	ITA	8546		1904
Henry B.	33	NY	1650a		1871						
						FORNER					
FOREY						Jacob B.	74	GER	3856		1900
Bridget	52	IRL	7096		1900						
						FORNERIS					
FORG						Alberto/Melvina, c/o		SF	8624		1901
Ah Chew				Oct	1898						
						FORNEY					
FORGE						Gertrude				Mar	1899
Clara M.	31	MA	3663	Nov	1901	Sam /, c/o				Jan	1900
FORGENSEN						FORNI					
Christian				Mar	1899	Frederico					1898
Peder or Peter	18	NOR	7494		1903						
						FORNIER					
FORGERT						Justine				Oct	1898
Emile/Bertha, c/o	1904	SF	874		1904						
						FORNOFF					
FORIA						Charles				Feb	1900
Francis	<1	SF	1322		1869						
						FORREST					
FORIGIANI						Agnes	73	SCT	4184		1900
Francesco	3	SF	3169		1900	Alexander	69	SCT	7815		1901
						Emma	53	ENG	1479b		1895
FORK						Fanny	14	CA	8310		1868
Tree Sea				Apr	1899	James					1899
						Margaret A.	<1	SF	4986		1867

*Key: a = 1st part of year; b = 2nd part of year;
c = death certificate copy; c/o = child of*

NAME	AGE OR YOB.	BIRTH PLACE	CERT. NO	ID	DEATH YEAR	NAME	AGE OR YOB.	BIRTH PLACE	CERT. NO	ID	DEATH YEAR
Mervin	1	SF	4541		1904	**FORSTON**					
Nellie				Aug	1898	Geo H.				Jan	1900
Robert A.	29	PA	4449		1902						
William	50	IRE	5832		1902	**FORSYTH**					
William Drummond				Jul	1898	Alice A	<1	SF	856		1894
						Annie M.				Jul	1899
FORRESTER						Doris	4	ENG	7832		1903
John D.	1	CA	7532		1868	Ernest E.	27	BAH	5080a		1895
Marian	25	CA	7564		1901	George Cephus				Jul	1898
						Helena				Nov	1898
FORREY						Maggie	50	IRL	569b		1895
Lucy Helen	4	SF	2141a		1872	Walter B.				Feb	1899
FORRISTER						**FORSYTHE**					
James H.	41	NC	1371		1869	Chas. Leslie				Mar	1900
FORS						Elijah				Nov	1899
Henry	52	PRU	18		1870	Frederick Jacob		SF	1098b		1871
Peter	33	SWE	1058		1903	Fredrick I.	1	SF	6537		1868
						Jack McCarthy				Jun	1899
FORSATZ						**FORTADO**					
Matilda	28	MA	2358		1901	Anibal J.	56	POR	1522		1903
FORSEE						**FORTE**					
Cordelia Catherine	22	MO	3090		1866	Maria	<1	SF	1881		1902
FORSELL						**FORTES**					
August	33	SWE	7143		1902	Joseph	1	AUS	8228		1868
Elfrida M.	<1	SF	4622		1901	**FORTIER**					
FORSELT						Elizabeth				Aug	1899
Annie M.				Jun	1899	Pierre Auguste	86	FRA	7348		1900
FORSMAN						**FORTIN**					
Nancy J.	73	ME	6361a		1895	Adolph	37	FRA	9269		1868
FORSTER						Sarah	<1	SF	9253		1868
Bertina C.	22	SF	2219b		1895	**FORTMAN**					
Fredrick	59	SWE	7842		1900	Frederick H.	2	SF	1364		1869
Jennie	48	NY	1000b		1895	Fredrick	<1	SF	550		1866
Louis	49	GER	7582		1900	Henry	64	GER	7583		1900
Pewter B.	40	SAX	1417		1869						
Wm.	57	ENG	1803		1894						

Key: a = 1st part of year; b = 2nd part of year;
c = death certificate copy; c/o = child of

NAME	AGE OR YOB.	BIRTH PLACE	CERT. NO	ID	DEATH YEAR
FORTMANN					
George					Jan 1900
FORTOUL					
Honori	61	FRA	259b		1871
FORTRIEDE					
Henry	66	GER	812		1903
FORTRO					
Joseph I.	69	NY	8856		1901
FORTSON					
Harry H.	33	CA	3608		1896
FORTUNAS					
Leonidas	52	GRE	4641		1902
FORTUNE					
——			1043		1868
James A.	50	IRL	396b		1872
Josephine M.	<1	SF	2252a		1872
Mary	66	IRL	92b		1871
Susan May	30	SF	2730		1900
Thomas	62	IRL	761b		1872
Thomas	2	SF	2729		1866
FORTURICE					
Annie	<1	SF	2923		1895
FOS					
Isidore	54	FRA	7646		1904
FOSE					
Patrick	30	IRL	2573a		1872
FOSGATE					
Edmund					Feb 1899
FOSGETT					
Caroline	69	NY	1693		1901
FOSGRAVE					
G.					Aug 1899

NAME	AGE OR YOB.	BIRTH PLACE	CERT. NO	ID	DEATH YEAR
FOSHAY					
Frank W.	13	SF	4059b		1870
FOSLER					
Fay					Mar 1900
FOSS					
Caroline	58	GER	1542		1870
Charles	42	NOR	8362		1903
Edward	44	NOR	8747		1904
Hazel	1	SF	705		1903
Julian	41	NY	4510b		1870
Katie E.	1	IA	1072		1869
Mary	75	IRE	5846		1903
Ouscar	73	NH	1054		1902
Sarah					Aug 1898
William					Oct 1898
FOSSET					
Leon	53	FRA	1564b		1871
Leonie Henriette	1	SF	122b		1871
FOSSEY					
Charles A.	1856	CAN	2372c		1904
FOSSUM					
Olena	65	NOR	3294		1902
Sivert	72	NOR	3295		1902
FOSTARDO					
Geario	1	SF	1161		1870
FOSTER					
——	<1	SF	1139		1869
A. S.	61	RI	1182a		1871
Albert	9	CA	7435		1903
Alden T.	73	NY	2931	Oct	1901
Alice	13	BC	3026a		1872
Annie E.	3	NY	1088		1870
Annie Gertrude	26	NB	4302		1896
Antonio	30	AZO	5939		1867

Key: *a = 1st part of year; b = 2nd part of year; c = death certificate copy; c/o = child of*

NAME	AGE OR YOB.	BIRTH PLACE	CERT. NO	ID	DEATH YEAR	NAME	AGE OR YOB.	BIRTH PLACE	CERT. NO	ID	DEATH YEAR
Caroline	47	OH	7521		1868	Martha J.	75	NH	5786		1896
Charles	<1	SF	2541b		1895	Mary	1	CA	1197		1903
Charles C.	39	VT	380		1865	Mary E.	51	PA	5940		1902
Charles O.	26	CA	2206		1901	Mary Jane	<1	SF	3530a		1872
Chas. W,	68	SWE	232b		1895	Mary L.	<1	SF	3138		1870
Daniel	71	ENG	7441		1901	Mary Winter	41	IL	2293b		1895
Edward	52	MO	4227		1900	May Morton	32	CA	4998		1904
Elizabeth	48	CA	232		1903	Pauline Lee	30	CA	7364		1904
Emily E.	57	CAN	4137		1902	Pierce C.				Jul	1899
Emily G.	78	GER	7482		1901	Samuel	62	MA	8677		1903
Emma	<1	SF	5884		1902	Sophia	63	ENG	7452		1901
Ernest M.				Jan	1900	Theresa				Aug	1898
Francis	6	SF	3181		1870	Thomas	84	PA	6939		1903
Frank W. (soldier)			140		1901	William				Nov	1898
Frederick W.	32	ENG	8375		1900	William (soldier)			4785		1901
George	58	ENG	5665		1902	William H.	51	ME	1010		1868
George I.	50	MA	1168b		1872	Zephaniah (soldier)			5795		1904
George Mathew	75	ENG	2790a		1872	**FOSTMANN**					
George W.	75	RI	1205		1870	Henry	<1	SF	918		1866
George W.	1	CA	6207		1896						
Georgiana	29	ENG	1307		1869	**FOTBRIDGES**					
Harry	<1	SF	83a		1871	Benjamin/Martha, c/o	<1	SF	6013		1902
Harry Wylie	40	SF	5787		1902	**FOTHERINGHAM**					
Hugh	70	GER	1561		1902	Mary	37	SF	2160b		1895
Isaac	77	NY	8076		1868	**FOTSCH**					
Jane				Jan	1899	Charles (soldier)			3283	Nov	1901
John	56	ENG	58		1902	**FOUGERE**					
John	37	DEN	390		1865	Elysee	80	FRA	3652		1896
John A.				Jan	1900	**FOULHERS**					
John P.	69	VT	1136		1901	Male	<1	SF	4469a		1895
Joseph Austin	23	SF	5309		1896	**FOULK**					
Julia	71	IRL	4455		1901	Harry Edward				Jan	1899
Julia	45	IRL	3649		1896	**FOULKE**					
Kenneth	<1	CA	8402		1900	Edwin J.	43	DC	1888b		1872
Maj. Sam A.	30	ME	391a		1871						
Marion	40	MN	4368		1902						

Key: *a = 1st part of year; b = 2nd part of year;*
c = death certificate copy; c/o = child of

NAME	AGE OR YOB.	BIRTH PLACE	CERT. NO	ID	DEATH YEAR	NAME	AGE OR YOB.	BIRTH PLACE	CERT. NO	ID	DEATH YEAR
FOULKERS						**FOUX**					
Helene Sophie				Nov	1899	Alfred (soldier)			561		1902
FOULLES						**FOWKE**					
John	27	TAH	4760		1867	William	3	AUT	7037		1868
FOUNKE						**FOWKES**					
Louisa	2	SF	3422b		1870	Elizabeth	65	IRL	3234		1894
FOUNTAIN						**FOWLER**					
Anthony	48	NY	5583		1903	Albert G. Jr.	20	NY	5759		1867
Chester	25	CA	4115		1900	Catherine	45	IRL	F82		1887
Minerva E.	43	IL	F95		1889	Charles Edgar	23	NY	5232		1903
Richard	3	SF	709		1866	Charlotte J.				Jan	1900
Victor	1833	CAN	2409c		1904	Daniel F.	40	MI	1089		1869
Washington A.	24	NY	3307		1873	Darius D.				Mar	1899
William H. (landsman)			5689	Jan	1901	E. B.	49	MA	6532		1896
FOUQUEZ						Edgar Coursen	50	PA	4248		1903
Eugene	51	FRA	1250		1869	Edith	<1	SF	2804		1901
FOURCAD						Edward	<1	CA	1368		1869
Maria T.	40	FRA	2085		1866	James F.	48	ENG	672a		1871
						Jennie E.	1	CA	1075		1869
FOURGOUS						John	61	CAN	5344		1902
Bertrande	48	FRA	2443b		1895	John A.	50	MA	619		1902
Theophile	25	FRA	8767		1904	John Henry	<1	SF	1121		1869
FOURNESS						Julia				Feb	1900
——		SF	1431		1869	Margaret A.	66	NY	4291		1896
William	62	ENG	826		1902	Mary	57	IRE	3471		1903
FOURNEY						Nellie B.	28	SF	4405		1903
Augiente Philip	70	FRA	1092		1869	Roy A.	20	CA	8579		1904
FOURNIER						Thomas L.	43	ENG	5296		1867
Claudino	56	FRA	5822		1867	Warren				Feb	1900
Pierre	62	FRA	4b		1895	William	44	ENG	501		1900
FOUTE						Wm. Henry				Aug	1898
Robert Chester	63	TN	541		1903	**FOWLES**					
FOUTS						Stephen				Jan	1900
Maria	65	GER	3498		1896	**FOWLIE**					
						William/Edna, c/o				Jul	1899

Key: a = 1st part of year; b = 2nd part of year;
c = death certificate copy; c/o = child of

NAME	AGE OR YOB.	BIRTH PLACE	CERT. NO	ID	DEATH YEAR
FOWN					
Chin Moon	40	CHN	5304		1867
FOX					
Anna	29	CAN	9803		1868
Annie	51	IRL	466a		1871
Annie	45	IRL	8667		1901
Artie A.	56	PA	3999a		1895
Barbara	57	SWT	4444a		1895
Benjamin	<1	SF	3995		1870
Bridget	38	IRL	6867		1900
Camille G.	1881	SF	3385c		1904
Daniel	40	IRL	F65		1886
Ellen	5	SF	163		1865
Florence Annie	<1	SF	8303		1900
Frank T.	<1	CA	2662		1902
George O.	33	WI	6494	Feb	1901
Hannah Mary	23	IN	2456		1901
Harry	<1	SF	698b		1872
Humphrey B.	22	MA	669b		1872
I. I.	34	IRE	923		1866
J. G.				Mar	1899
James	22	GER	212		1865
James P.	<1	AUS	1632		1870
Jessie				Nov	1898
John	60	IRE	1043		1866
John	5	SF	4144a		1895
John				Jul	1898
John Arnold	1	IL	2913		1903
John E.	1	NY	1025		1868
Joseph			1040		1866
Joseph (soldier)			8779		1901
Joseph B.	1	SF	8701		1868
Joseph S. (soldier)	27		7925		1901
Katie	36	IRL	2159b		1895
Louisa R.	24	PA	302		1865

NAME	AGE OR YOB.	BIRTH PLACE	CERT. NO	ID	DEATH YEAR
Margaret	1	SF	4072b		1870
Margaret Angeline	9	SF	2005		1902
Mary	54	IRE	7397		1904
Mary	70	GER	6236		1903
Mary E.	74	KY	4675a		1895
Otto				Nov	1898
Paul (soldier)			7302		1901
Richard	51	ENG	6260		1867
Robert L. (soldier)			6255		1900
Sarah	24	OH	4488a		1895
Susan	30	IRL	2558		1895
Teresa	66	BOH	56b		1895
Theodore	45	NY	7607		1900
Theresa				Feb	1900
Thomas	62	IRL	5008		1901
Thomas	67	TN	5355		1901
Thomas	70	NY	1495		1900
Thomas William	29	SF	1170b		1895
William L.	1903	CA	528c		1904
FOXBRIDGES					
Martha	37	MA	3934		1903
FOY					
Charles	19	CHN	1880a		1872
Elizabeth	1	AUT	1012		1868
Jno. B.	4	SF	4486a		1895
John J.				Feb	1900
John/Julia, c/o	<1	SF	8394		1904
Martin	65	IRL	5245a		1896
Michael	43	IRE	1185		1869
Ming	47	CHN	1528		1866
On	37	CHN	2335b		1895
Sarah				May	1899
William	57	ME	894b		1872
Young Sing	29	CHN	8720		1903

Key: a = 1st part of year; b = 2nd part of year; c = death certificate copy; c/o = child of

NAME	AGE OR YOB.	BIRTH PLACE	CERT. NO	ID	DEATH YEAR	NAME	AGE OR YOB.	BIRTH PLACE	CERT. NO	ID	DEATH YEAR
FOYE						**FRAHER**					
Francis	1	SF	2546		1894	Aloysius	<1	SF	7228		1903
Franklin E.	25	SF	4705		1904	**FRAHM**					
George W.	60	ME	7841		1900	Ernest Henry	<1	CA	1692		1901
M.	28	CHN	2204		1866	Ernest P.	47	GER	7372		1903
Margaret				Aug	1898	George	51	GER	7101		1903
Mary Alice	<1	SF	1704		1894	Margarethe W.	82	GER	6883		1904
Warren	42	ME	1398		1870	Peter	31	DEN	278		1870
William		SF	982		1866	**FRAINE**					
FOYLE						Robert (soldier)			65		1901
Robert A.	76	NY	26		1901	**FRAIR**					
FOYS						Rachel				Jan	1900
(twins)		SF	1447		1869	**FRAISS**					
FPRD						Jean/Marie, c/o		SF	2106		1895
Margaret				Oct	1899	**FRAISSON**					
FRABRIZIO						Ann	<1	SF	8666		1868
Miclelie	40		995		1901	**FRAIZET**					
FRAEHAUF						W.	70		5027		1902
Minnie				Jun	1899	**FRAMDLING**					
FRAETES						Charles (soldier)	47	GER	6076	Jan	1901
Manuel	50	POR	2617		1903	**FRANCE**					
FRAGER						——			8348		1868
A. M.	56	POR	4290		1901	Arthur H.	1	SF	8494		1904
Stanislas	57	FRA	643b		1872	Clyde Ol			6274		1903
FRAGLEY						George W.				Jan	1899
Albert H.				Aug	1898	Henrietta	18	CAN	8282		1868
Charles Francis	1	SF	2235		1873	**FRANCES**					
Ellen	54	IRE	7371		1903	Alice				Nov	1898
John M.	28	MO	2076b		1895	Fanny	50	VA	585		1903
Joseph Henry	34	SF	4939		1904	James	24	GA	2058		1900
Mary Ellen	19	SF	334b		1895	John F.	49	ENG	3137		1903
FRAGOZO						Miriam	<1	CA	4969		1896
Rafaela	51	MEX	1090		1900	**FRANCESCHI**					
						Antonio	29	ITA	3294	Nov	1901

Key: a = 1st part of year; b = 2nd part of year;
c = death certificate copy; c/o = child of

NAME	AGE OR YOB.	BIRTH PLACE	CERT. NO	ID	DEATH YEAR	NAME	AGE OR YOB.	BIRTH PLACE	CERT. NO	ID	DEATH YEAR
Emelio/Marianna, c/o	<1	SF	6899		1902	Frank H.	28	ENG	1117		1869
Henry	8	SF	8557		1901	Frederick	1904	SF	1357c		1904
John B.				Mar	1899	Frederick W.	1	SF	2529		1894
						Gerald	<1	SF	51		1900
FRANCESCHINI						Grosvenor	1824	ENG	620c		1904
Charles				Mar	1899	Harold Bertram	1	SF	4698		1896
Ilia	<1	SF	6154		1900	Henry	57	IRE	706		1903
Mary Estella				Jan	1899	Herbert	18	CA	2671		1901
						James	1	SF	1373		1869
FRANCESSCHI						Jno. A.	43	IL	5672a		1895
Agnes Birdie	<1	SF	2052		1894	John	44	EIN	746a		1871
						John	m	SF	3253		1866
FRANCH						John				Jan	1899
Claire				Aug	1898	Joseph/A., c/o				Jan	1899
						M./C., c/o		SF	1706		1894
FRANCHI						Mary	20	MA	3013		1870
Arcangelo	41	ITA	7077	Feb	1901	Mary			3838		1867
Chas.	57	ITA	6365		1900	Mary				Feb	1899
Franco	40	ITA	1445		1903	Mary Lecount	76	PA	7008		1902
Pietro	<1	SF	4664		1901	Nestlyn	28	SCT	1928		1900
						Nina	<1	SF	3040		1895
FRANCHIM						Phylis	1	CA	4598		1904
Geovanni				Oct	1898	Robert C.	80	PA	5954		1904
						Samuel P.	1	SF	1253a		1871
FRANCHINI						Thos.	40	ENG	F19		1883
Joseph	52	FRA	5418		1896	William	56	MA	3600		1867
FRANCIAS						**FRANCISCA**					
Charles G.	42	FRA	1923		1870	Manuel	27	POR	6750		1904
FRANCIN						**FRANCISCO**					
Hans	50	GER	4514a		1895	——	<1	SF	3107		1895
						Amaro Jose	32	AZO	1244b		1871
FRANCIS						Antonio	33	GRE	1214		1869
——	<1	CA	6456		1896	Antonio	45	WIS	1304		1869
Albert				Jan	1899	Joseph	50		1703		1902
Albion Lacartes	60	VT	1861		1902	Manuel	23	CPV	1040		1901
Andrew	23		3318		1866						
Anna	45	IRE	3123		1866						
Clarence	30	KS	5847		1903						
David	<1	SF	576		1901						
Emily S.	35	NY	4340		1901						
Frank	67	CA	F102		1889						

Key: a = 1st part of year; b = 2nd part of year;
c = death certificate copy; c/o = child of

NAME	AGE OR YOB.	BIRTH PLACE	CERT. NO	ID	DEATH YEAR	NAME	AGE OR YOB.	BIRTH PLACE	CERT. NO	ID	DEATH YEAR
Marrif Phebe					Feb 1900	**FRANEY**					
						Patrick C. (marine)			7746		1901
FRANCK											
Elizabeth	2	SF	1068		1869	**FRANIE**					
Matilda	68	GER	3021		1902	Jane	30	IRL	1003b		1872
FRANCKLIN						**FRANK**					
Mina	41	PRU	309		1870	____	24	FRA	8641		1868
FRANCO						____	1	CA	3327		1903
Antonio	73	ITA	1125b		1895		<1	CA	2348		1894
Elizabeth	1	SF	5206a		1896	____	<1	SF	3108		1895
Mariano					1899	Andrew	32	CHI	4470a		1895
Refugio					Apr 1899	Anna	45	GER	882a		1871
Simone	40	ITA	889		1901	Anna	1	SF	8213		1868
FRANCOEUR						Augustus Fred	<1	SF	3170		1900
David T.	42	NY	5623		1903	Camelia	4	SF	7290		1868
FRANCOFISA						Carolina	88	GER	3741a		1895
Casario	45	MEX	1165		1869	Caroline	5	SF	2170a		1872
FRANCOIS						Emanuel	62	GER	429		1901
____			1832		1866	Emil	23	GER	1092		1869
Ceroule	<1	SF	3525a		1895	Emma	40	GER	2827		1900
M.	30	FRA	F42		1885	Ephraim	72	AUS	5396		1904
FRANCONI						Frederick	45	GER	910		1870
John	38	SWT	6532		1868	Frederick S.	45	NY	4540		1896
FRANCOONE						George R.	1	SF	1289		1870
____			6320		1867	Haucheon	<1	SF	1475b		1871
FRANCOUIS						Henry	1	SF	2817		1873
Nora	2	SF	4661		1867	Henry	67	GER	502		1900
FRANCOVICH						Herbert					Apr 1899
Antonio Nick	1904	SF	997c		1904	Herman	<1	SF	5420		1867
Antonis F.	<1	SF	875		1902	Isaac (soldier)			2212		1903
FRANE						Isaac M.	1861	PA	58c		1904
Alexander	55	FRA	5881		1867	James	43	GER	4034		1896
Charles	30	PRU	253a		1871	Jennie	<1	SF	5409a		1895
						Johannes	1835	GER	1784c		1904
FRANERY						Jos./Minia, c/o		SF	2292		1895
James					Aug 1899	Kassel					Oct 1899

Key: a = 1st part of year; b = 2nd part of year; c = death certificate copy; c/o = child of

NAME	AGE OR YOB.	BIRTH PLACE	CERT. NO	ID	DEATH YEAR
Linda				Nov	1898
Louis	26	WIN	8323		1868
Louis	56	BAV	621b		1895
Louis (soldier)			2213		1903
Louis A.	4	SF	1053		1868
Louis J.	45	CA	2953		1902
M., c/o		SF	588b		1872
Mary Ellen	<1	SF	3605		1867
Mathilda	20	SF	1867b		1895
Minnie	1864	CAN	1536c		1904
Minon	54	NY	2303		1873
Moses J.	59	NY	6003	Jan	1901
Paul	42	GER	7938		1904
Philip	83	GER	1184		1894
Richard T. (soldier)			7125		1900
Salome	59	GER	1200		1901
Samuel	53	PA	3061		1895
Sophie				Oct	1899
William C.	39	MA	4223		1902
William E.	22	KY	8133		1904
FRANKA					
Anthony	34	NY	7750		1904
FRANKAL					
Joseph	1	SF	165b		1872
FRANKE					
Christine				Jan	1900
Florence J.	23	SF	4067a		1895
Livia	55	GER	6441		1896
Mary E.	35	IRL	6748		1896
Paul/Anna, c/o		SF	1671		1900
Rudolph				Feb	1900
William/Anita, c/o		SF	536		1902
FRANKEL					
Bertha	64	PRU	3740a		1895
Kanchen				Jul	1898

NAME	AGE OR YOB.	BIRTH PLACE	CERT. NO	ID	DEATH YEAR
L. B., c/o		SF	1296		1869
FRANKENBACH					
Walburga	83	GER	6597		1903
FRANKENBURG					
Charlotte	74	AUT	7703		1901
FRANKENSTEIN					
Harmond	38	GER	9742		1868
FRANKENTHAL					
Jacob	65	GER	5199		1901
FRANKI					
Antonio	25	ITA	1342b		1871
FRANKL					
Leopold	78	AUT	6791		1896
FRANKLIN					
Amelia A.	52	POL	5910		1896
Anna Augusta	<1	SF	3077		1866
Blake/Amelia, c/o	<1	SF	3810		1901
Bridget	63	IRL	5759		1896
Caroline	57	POL	8463		1904
Hy	32	OR	530		1901
James	56	ENG	1269		1903
Jane, c/o		SF	1245		1869
John	35	IRE	1043		1868
Louisa				Jul	1899
Margaret Nelson				Feb	1899
Martha	19	SF	6647		1903
Moses	9	SF	579a		1870
Sarah	66	GER	2914		1903
Thomas	73	IRE	9007		1903
William	<1	SF	2736		1895
William H. (soldier)			7745		1901
FRANKS					
——			8988		1868
George Mortimer	39	NY	5766		1902

Key: a = 1st part of year; b = 2nd part of year;
c = death certificate copy; c/o = child of

NAME	AGE OR YOB.	BIRTH PLACE	CERT. NO	ID	DEATH YEAR	NAME	AGE OR YOB.	BIRTH PLACE	CERT. NO	ID	DEATH YEAR
James	77	GER	3022		1902	Alexander	60	ENG	683a		1871
						Alexander	56	SCT	4845		1901
FRANLY						Alexander E.	76	CAN	3169		1895
Elisabeth	1	SF	812b		1871	Amelia M.	52	NY	1362		1869
FRANNSICH						Daniel	32	NS	30		1900
Mary				Jan	1900	Daniel				Mar	1899
FRANO						Ellen	80	CAN	2433		1902
Eilen	<1	SF	644		1894	Francis L.	6	SF	148		1870
FRANS						Harriett Emma	59	OH	3862		1896
Isaac	28	RUS	4559a		1895	Irwin W.				Aug	1898
FRANTRETTER						Isabella R.	67	NS	6482		1903
Amelia E.	<1	SF	3664		1870	J. P./A., c/o	<1	SF	3279		1894
FRANZ						James Gray				Jul	1898
Felix (soldier)			8778		1901	James K.	15	SF	7457		1904
Frederick W. (soldier)			7140		1901	James R.				Jan	1900
FRANZEN						James Robert	32	CA	4138		1903
Ida	1	SF	2050a		1872	Jane A.	<1	SF	2346		1902
Wm./Louise, c/o	<1	SF	5938		1903	Janet	50	AFR	233		1903
FRANZINA						Jean Isabella	31	NY	7246		1901
Martin				May	1899	John	1828	SCT	3146c		1904
FRANZINELLI						John P./Agnes, c/o		SF	3941		1896
Antonio				Oct	1899	Margaret A.				Jan	1900
FRAOEST						Robina Gordon				Jan	1899
——		SF	4268b		1870	Simon J.	1867	PE	599c		1904
FRAPOLLI						William P.	57	CAN	6607		1904
Silvia	32	SF	6226		1904	Wm. O.	45	NS	6074a		1895
FRARY						**FRASH**					
Elizabeth	68	NY	9614		1901	Charles H.	15	SF	4766a		1895
FRASCH						**FRASIER**					
Frederick				Jun	1899	Hobert	18	CA	1763		1901
						Julia A.	33	ME	8206		1900
FRASEN						**FRATCHER**					
John	21	ENG	2015		1873	Robert H.	1	SF	5501		1867
FRASER						**FRATES**					
——	<1	SF	3585		1870	Emmanuel	30	WIS	3597		1867

Key: a = 1st part of year; b = 2nd part of year;
c = death certificate copy; c/o = child of

NAME	AGE OR YOB.	BIRTH PLACE	CERT. NO	ID	DEATH YEAR	NAME	AGE OR YOB.	BIRTH PLACE	CERT. NO	ID	DEATH YEAR
Mary	39	CA	1932		1902	D.	63	NB	1806b		1895
FRATILLAIRE						Edna J.	3		F91		1889
William J.	42	CA	6702		1896	Evelyn B.	38	NY	4313		1901
FRATILLI						Henry C.	53	PA	475		1903
Fornanda	<1	SF	2291		1901	Ida May	<1	SF	3254		1870
FRATINGER						J. J.	54	IRL	1581a		1871
Anthony M.	53	OH	5984a		1895	James	11	CA	F81		1887
FRATOS						Mary Jane	1	SF	7032		1868
William J.	8	SF	4208		1896	Ulysse H.	1	SF	6102		1867
FRAUENHOLZ						**FRAZIER**					
Hugo	52	GER	3060		1895	Arteg	4	CA	F71		1886
FRAVEGA						Edith May	22	CA	1418		1902
Giovanni/Catherina, c/o		SF	5523		1901	John					1898
Maria					1899	Louis				Feb	1900
Nicola	37	ITA	4143a		1895	Mary	1904	SF	3353c		1904
FRAVOR						Nettie L.	34	IA	1479		1901
James H.	80	NY	8495		1904	**FREABIE**					
FRAWLEY						Henrietta	47	ENG	3369		1894
Bertha	73	IRL	7080		1900	**FREAOD**					
Elizabeth	24	IRL	4075b		1870	——			3654		1867
Johanna	70	IRE	186		1903	**FRECHETTI**					
John	62	IRE	2222		1902	Louis E.	45	CAN	5585a		1895
Katie	1849	AUT	918c		1904	**FRECRICKS**					
Mary	<1	SF	1470b		1871	William	34	GER	9043		1868
Patrick	44	IRL	3205a		1872	**FRED**					
FRAY						Leon/Florence, c/o		SF	7982		1900
Frederick/Mary, c/o		SF	4207		1896	**FREDELL**					
FRAZEE						Fredericka Georgina	1900	CA	1307c		1904
Charles (soldier)			3092c		1904	Fredrica Georgina	42	SWE	8202		1900
Mary Eliza	66	IRE	6625		1903	**FREDERICK**					
FRAZER						——	1	SF	6608		1904
Alfred	55	AR	2922		1873	Charles	77	GER	179		1901
Annie Matilda	<1	SF	1148		1869	Christian	57	PRU	1373		1869
Catherine	69	OH	6970		1903	Chs. Patrick	<1	SF	2669		1873

Key: a = 1st part of year; b = 2nd part of year;
c = death certificate copy; c/o = child of

NAME	AGE OR YOB	BIRTH PLACE	CERT. NO	ID	DEATH YEAR
George A.				Nov	1899
George H.	48	GER	2513a		1872
Harry (soldier)			3078		1903
FREDERICKE					
Chs. Maurice	1	SF	497a		1871
FREDERICKS					
——	45	GER	F38		1885
Allura E.	48	NY	2528		1900
Amelia	53	GER	7111		1904
Anna Pearl	26	NV	2578		1895
Elizabeth	2	AUS	1755		1870
Emily	60	GER	119b		1872
Fritz J.	18	SF	3700a		1895
J./A., c/o		SF	5695		1895
Jacob C.	53	GER	5345		1902
Joseph	70	GER	4947		1901
Sophie	33	GER	247		1870
William H.	1	SF	373		1870
FREDERICKSEN					
Christian	67	DEN	5996		1904
FREDERICKSON					
Ann R.	55	IRL	5681a		1895
Bridget	37	IRE	5070		1903
Charles	55	DEN	8379		1901
Gesna Adolphus	57	GER	5859a		1895
Jennie Patrina	24	DEN	2516		1903
Johann Gotthief	32	GER	5739a		1895
FREDERICKSRD					
Henry	37	GER	796		1870
FREDIANI					
Francisco	32	ITA	7102		1903
Fredriano	26	ITA	1768		1894
FREDIN					
Axel (soldier)			9117		1901
FREDLEND					
Adey	1904	CA	1898c		1904
FREDMA					
Pasquele	27	ITA	2736a		1872
FREDRICK					
Chas. W.				Feb	1900
Herman/Katie, c/o	<1	SF	7826		1904
Roy	<1		7256		1904
FREDRICKS					
——	<1	CA	8244		1868
Ann E	29	PA	3697		1870
Joseph Theodore	12	CA	1192		1869
Lana	1	SF	483		1866
FREDRICKSON					
Anthony S.	<1	SF	3183		1870
Gertrude	54	GER	4485a		1895
John	60	DEN	9094		1901
FREDRIKSON					
Frank	45	FIN	5467		1902
Thekla	45	SWE	8562		1900
FREE					
Elizabeth	70	KY	8724		1904
FREECHTLE					
Charles Anton	<1	SF	9059		1901
FREED					
Seamon/Mathilda, c/o		SF	2003		1900
FREEL					
William H.	23	NY	8901		1868
FREELAND					
Agnes S.	28	CAN	5838	Jan	1901
Mercy	67	USA	1200b		1872
Sarah F.				Jun	1899
FREELING					
——			1009		1868

Key: a = 1st part of year; b = 2nd part of year;
c = death certificate copy; c/o = child of

NAME	AGE OR YOB.	BIRTH PLACE	CERT. NO	ID	DEATH YEAR
FREELUND					
Andrew	45	SWE	1212		1902
FREEMAN					
Allen M.	54	IL	8224		1901
Annie	1826	IRE	889c		1904
Capt. C. N.	43	MA	1997a		1872
Carline A.	<1	SF	5786		1867
Caroline	75	GER	2466		1900
Catherine, c/o	<1	CA	379		1900
Charles (soldier)			2048		1901
Charles/Mary, c/o	<1	SF	1410		1895
Clarence	<1	SF	270b		1872
Clyde	17	IN	3205	Nov	1901
Edward Allen	47	MA	4369		1902
Edward D.				Nov	1899
Edward D.				Nov	1899
Edward Ely	50	IA	6068		1904
Edward W.	1864	ME	3034c		1904
Emma	45	CA	2571		1900
George	50	ENG	7564		1868
Henry	51	GER	F10		1882
James	58	MA	7588		1868
James (soldier)			9563		1901
James E.	79	NY	6831a		1895
Jane Elizabeth Whiting	73	WV	6016a		1895
John (soldier)			3036	Oct	1901
Josephine E.	47	MS	F90		1889
Laura E.					1898
Mary M.	56	IA	8378		1901
Matilda	1819	IRE	2891c		1904
Matthew				Jun	1899
Ora K.			4010	Dec	1901
Per Enoch	71	SWE	2875		1900
Robert				Jan	1900
Simeon B.	70	MA	6009		1867

NAME	AGE OR YOB.	BIRTH PLACE	CERT. NO	ID	DEATH YEAR
T. E.	52	ME	F24		1883
T. K. S.				Oct	1898
Thomas D. (soldier)	27	TX	932		1902
William	33	PA	730a		1871
William	37	MA	1155		1869
William H. (soldier)	26	CA	4760		1904
FREER					
Grace				Apr	1899
FREES					
John B./Lucy H., c/o	<1	SF	835		1895
Lucy H.	36	CA	836b		1895
FREESE					
Fred	<1	SF	1605		1901
John H.	53	GER	1078		1901
O. S.	54	ME	7780		1900
Samuel W.	47	ME	6040		1903
W. Henry	67	ME	5060a		1895
FREESIS					
George	5	SF	1185b		1871
FREETHY					
Mary E.	<1	SF	5738		1896
FREI					
E./E., c/o	<1	SF	4674		1895
FREIBERG					
Emma	35	SWE	4539		1896
FREIDLANDER					
Julius	17	ENG	1186		1869
FREIDLER					
Oscar Karl Gebhart	55	GER	9319		1901
FREIDMAN					
William	55	RUS	6202	Jan	1901
FREIE					
Henry, c/o	<1	SF	3160		1866
Herman		SF	687		1870

Key: a = 1st part of year; b = 2nd part of year; c = death certificate copy; c/o = child of

NAME	AGE OR YOB.	BIRTH PLACE	CERT. NO	ID	DEATH YEAR
FREIL					
Hannah	43	IRE	2247		1866
FREILING					
Catherine	33	IRL	1260b		1872
Catherine	<1	CA	5847		1867
Peter		SF	4417b		1870
FREIRMUTH					
Annie	68	IRE	6195		1904
FREISMUTH					
Hervey I.	1	SF	8288		1868
FREITAS					
Charlotte F.	28	ENG	7188		1868
Jons	24	AZO	3450		1896
Thomas	1	SF	180		1901
William Walter	3	SF	4422		1901
FREMON					
William N.	49	MO	3514		1896
FREMY					
Annie					Mar 1900
FRENCH					
Adah Frederick	<1	SF	889b		1895
Alise	1	SF	7442		1901
Alphens P.			7141		1901
Arthur	<1	SF	8530		1901
Augusta L.	84	ME	1295		1903
Catherine Spottswood	42	IRL	6528a		1895
Charles					1899
Chas. Edward	24	SF	547b		1895
Edward					Aug 1899
Ernst					Jan 1900
Eva Mildred	31	CA	2618		1903
Frank J.					Jan 1899
Franz	65	AUT	7483		1901
Gladys A.	1	SF	8639		1903

NAME	AGE OR YOB.	BIRTH PLACE	CERT. NO	ID	DEATH YEAR
Hayes Clifton	61	ENG	5732		1902
John (soldier)	25		6280		1904
John Gessner	1890	MN	1241c		1904
John Henry					Jan 1899
Lillie Francis	1	SF	1371		1869
Malvern L.	26	PA	226c		1904
Mary	52	VA	2704		1894
Mary					1899
May B.					1898
Moses B.					Aug 1899
Nellie	1	SF	139a		1871
Sarah E.	76	IN	3220		1902
Virginia Ann	37	NC	1437b		1871
Wheeler L.	4	SF	1615		1870
FRENCHTWANGER					
Sigmund	1853	BAV	3470c		1904
FRENDENTHAL					
John					1899
FRENGER					
Maria	44	GER	3799a		1895
FRENGILLE					
Hippole	38	FRA	1390		1869
FRENGS					
Annie Jane	71	IRL	1338		1900
FRENNA					
Sarah E.	42	MA	1419		1902
FRENSCHEL					
Albert	53	IA	1170		1902
FRENZEL					
Erdmann August	48	GER	6924		1902
FRERICHS					
Meta Christine	81	GER	4089		1902
FRERNIER					
Julius B..					Jun 1899

Key: a = 1st part of year; b = 2nd part of year;
c = death certificate copy; c/o = child of

NAME	AGE OR YOB.	BIRTH PLACE	CERT. NO	ID	DEATH YEAR
FRESE					
Rudolf Gading	2	SF	4145a		1895
William	48	GER	7151		1903
FRESEUS					
Martha	30	MEX	1285		1869
FRESIUS					
John E.				Jan	1899
FRESSLIES					
John S. F.	<1	SF	97		1865
FRET					
Carl Victor	35	FIN	2183		1894
FRETICH					
Robert	56	GER	2413		1900
FRETUS					
Manuel F.	<1	MA	1000		1868
FRETZ					
B. P.	56	PA	4832		1867
FREUD					
J. Richard	44	NY	4787		1902
FREUDENTHAL					
Cecelia M.	53	ENG	6559		1902
FREUND					
F. A.	71	GER	2775		1894
Philip	69	GER	7648		1900
FREUNDSHUH					
Charles P.				Jan	1900
FREUSDORF					
Otto	45	GER	8563		1900
FREY					
Alfred	<1	GER	3072		1894
David	71	GER	6542	Feb	1901
Edward Walter	23	SF	3269		1903
Frederick	42	NY	1691		1901

NAME	AGE OR YOB.	BIRTH PLACE	CERT. NO	ID	DEATH YEAR
George W. (soldier)			300		1902
Gustave				Jun	1899
Hattie				Jun	1899
Jacob	44	GER	F63		1886
James	20	SF	6904		1900
John	45	GER	1076b		1871
Leonard (soldier)			3037	Oct	1901
Marguerite Helen	<1	SF	3578a		1895
Nellie				Jan	1899
Sophie	<1	SF	966b		1895
William	38	GER	7345		1903
FREYERMUTH					
Mary Emma	37	IN	7552		1904
FRIADLANDER					
Areine	<1	SF	5278		1902
FRIBERG					
John	30	SWE	881		1900
FRICAUDE					
Eugene Bertin				Feb	1899
FRICERO					
Frank	5	SF	9126		1901
FRICHETTE					
Marie Rosa D.	45	CAN	2988		1895
FRICHIS					
Joseph				Oct	1899
FRICK					
Adelaide Constonia	65	IOM	8802		1900
Dominique	78	FRA	757		1866
Samuel	45	NS	5175		1867
Thomas	64	PA	1629		1903
Willie	2	SF	2865a		1872
FRICKE					
Eva	39	USA	4208	Dec	1901
Gustave, Jr.	1	SF	202		1901

NAME	AGE OR YOB.	BIRTH PLACE	CERT. NO	ID	DEATH YEAR	NAME	AGE OR YOB.	BIRTH PLACE	CERT. NO	ID	DEATH YEAR
FRICKER						FRIEDMAN					
Louisa	1	SF	3306		1895	Chas.	58	PRU	3027		1873
						Edna	10	SF	3447		1896
FRICKS						Elba	1839	RUS	2291c		1904
Henry (soldier)			3450	Nov	1901	Elizabeth	38	CAN	2986a		1872
						Hannah	1	NY	1031		1868
FRIDECK						Hannah	53	GER	2107		1903
Charles (soldier)			5550	Jan	1901	Harry	24	RUS	3876		1896
FRIDEGER						Henry/Deborah, c/o		SF	7141		1902
Jacob	73	SWT	7257		1904	Inga Marie	25	NOR	6529		1896
FRIDERICK						Isaac	66	POL	4868		1904
Augusta	64	GER	F12		1883	Isiah	<1	SF	8017		1900
FRIED						Jacob	44	POL	2701		1873
Leopold	4	SF	1600a		1871	Julius, Capt.				Jan	1900
FRIEDBERG						Lawrence H.	10	SF	1585		1902
Frank				Aug	1898	M., c/o				Dec	1899
						Madeline B.				Feb	1899
FRIEDEL						Max M.	44	RUS	6576a		1895
Alexander	<1	SF	1199		1869	Mendel L.	1	SF	3609		1867
Charlotte Bertha	2	SF	1297b		1872	S.	54	GER	1350		1870
Frederick T.	68	GER	406		1900	Sam/Gertrude, c/o	1	SF	5997		1904
Hermiena F.	2	SF	7753		1868	Samuel	41	HUN	3236		1903
FRIEDERICH						FRIEDMANN					
Gustav	54	GER	5251		1902	Frank	6	SF	5214		1904
Henry/Flora, c/o	1904	SF	139		1904	I./F., c/o				Oct	1899
FRIEDHOFER						Marcus	67	GER	922		1901
Augustus	38	GER	2955a		1872	FRIEDRICH					
FRIEDLANDER						Charles Gottfried	66	GER	6725		1900
Ernest	56	GER	5324		1902	Henry	74	GER	6692		1904
Hulda	60	GER	7779		1900	John Wm.	17	CA	243		1900
Israel				Jan	1900	Marie	76	GER	2649		1895
Joseph				Nov	1898	Robert A.	57	KY	4948		1903
Pauline	73	GER	1077		1901	FRIEDRICHS					
Ruth J.	<1	CA	2864		1894	Wm. D.	1879	SF	2946c		1904
FRIEDLENDER											
Wille	<1	SF	3275		1873						

Key: a = 1st part of year; b = 2nd part of year;
c = death certificate copy; c/o = child of

NAME	AGE OR YOB.	BIRTH PLACE	CERT. NO	ID	DEATH YEAR	NAME	AGE OR YOB.	BIRTH PLACE	CERT. NO	ID	DEATH YEAR
FRIEDRICK						**FRIESENHAUSEN**					
Ann E.	72	GER	3469b		1870	John	78	GER	4418		1902
FRIEL						Mary				Jul	1899
Abraham	22	NY	923		1870	Wilhelm	1	SF	1380		1869
Edward Patrick	3	SF	1860		1903	**FRIESKE**					
James A. (soldier)			9629		1901	Julius E.	50	GER	6281		1904
Philip	50	FRA	F34		1885	**FRIETAG**					
William				Apr	1899	Kaskel	72	GER	2701		1903
FRIEMAN						**FRIETAS**					
W.	40		8894		1868	Frank	21	MA	5539		1904
FRIEND						Manuel	30	POR	1000		1868
Abbie C.	1	NV	610b		1871	Mary Joseph	1875	CA	2334c		1904
Elizabeth	30	SWT	116		1902	**FRIEZE**					
Fredrick L.	24	MA	1007		1868	Henrietta	41	PRU	1944b		1872
FRIERMUTH						John, c/o		SF	1938b		1872
Geo. A.	42	MA	F57		1886	**FRIGANOVICH**					
Sarah				Jan	1900	Antonia	6	SF	3844	Nov	1901
FRIERY						Elena					1899
Mary	92	IRE	2829		1902	**FRIGGERIO**					
FRIES						Pietro	32	GER	1551b		1872
Albert Steinalt	<1	SF	1601b		1895	**FRILEY**					
Amalia	34	GER	8311		1903	Claude	73	FRA	2368		1894
Andreas Jacob	1	SF	3221	Nov	1901	Daniel M.	53	MI	989		1902
Annie	33	NY	5009		1901	Florence A.				Mar	1899
Edward L. (soldier)			367		1900	Oscar M.	<1	SF	4228a		1895
Henry E.		SF	1248b		1895	**FRILL**					
Joseph/Amelia, c/o	<1	SF	8233		1903	——	<1	SF	3675		1870
L./A., c/o	<1	SF	1569		1894	**FRINCKE**					
Leopold/Annie, c/o		SF	1590		1895	Henry	27	CA	F94		1889
FRIESE						**FRINK**					
Mary Mathilda	27	OH	2822		1903	Elisabeth				Feb	1899
FRIESENHANSEN						George Washington	75	NY	2930		1902
John A.				Jul	1899	Wallace	<1	SF	7973		1868

Key: a = 1st part of year; b = 2nd part of year; c = death certificate copy; c/o = child of

NAME	AGE OR YOB.	BIRTH PLACE	CERT. NO	ID	DEATH YEAR
FRINTERA					
Anna	<1	SF	1368		1900
FRIPP					
John	54	SWT	1185		1902
FRISBIE					
James	78	ME	3213		1895
Leni Cornell				Aug	1899
Wm. D.	34	NY	2207		1873
FRISBY					
Albert W. (soldier)			7304		1901
FRISCH					
Albert T.	<1	SF	3454		1867
Herman H.			5412	Jan	1901
John G.	33	GER	378		1865
Willie	3	SF	8428		1868
FRISCO					
Maggie	13	SF	7314		1900
FRISE					
Hannah	1887	IL	2108c		1904
FRISH					
Khristian A.	54	FIN	4991		1902
FRISK					
Malcom S.				Mar	1900
FRIST					
Nicholas	46	FRA	1045		1866
FRITCHI					
Rudolph	29	SWT	1099a		1871
FRITSCH					
Joseph L. (soldier)			7142		1901
Lorenz	55	GER	6336	Feb	1901
Wm.	43	GER	F36		1885
FRITZ					
Anton /, c/o				Jan	1900

NAME	AGE OR YOB.	BIRTH PLACE	CERT. NO	ID	DEATH YEAR
Carl	50	GER	7290		1902
Frida				Jul	1898
George Lewis	<1	CA	1314b		1871
Henry	11	CA	5215		1867
Herbert	3	SF	5033		1903
Herman	<1	SF	2080		1866
Jacob	1867	GER	2292c		1904
John	2	SF	2052		1866
John	79	GER	8226		1901
Joseph R.	32	GER	6105		1903
Kittie	<1	SF	4970		1896
William C.	26	CA	6583		1902
Wm. Harold	1	SF	330		1900
FRITZE					
Gustav	55	GER	F50		1885
FRITZON					
Fred C.				Mar	1900
FRITZSCHE					
Minnie	28	NY	2970		1895
FROCHLICH					
Augusta	55	GER	4036		1900
FRODSHAM					
——	<1	SF	94a		1871
John	59	ENG	1945b		1872
FROESE					
F. W.	1844	PRU	3147c		1904
FROGILLO					
N./Catherina, c/o	<1	SF	2130		1902
FROHMAN					
Barbara	61	GER	4439		1904
Julia	2	SF	7407		1868
Max				Aug	1898
FROHMANN					
Alfred	1	SF	3		1865

Key: a = 1st part of year; b = 2nd part of year;
c = death certificate copy; c/o = child of

NAME	AGE OR YOB.	BIRTH PLACE	CERT. NO	ID	DEATH YEAR	NAME	AGE OR YOB.	BIRTH PLACE	CERT. NO	ID	DEATH YEAR
FROHN						**FROUD**					
Emma	1	GER	1391		1869	Jane	73	ENG	8020		1901
John M.	62	GER	4209		1896	**FROYAN**					
FROID						Patrick	35	IRE	1871		1866
Ebba Helwig				Jul	1898	**FRREDERICKS**					
FROLICH						Anne	54	IRL	1681		1894
Robert					1898	**FRUBOSO**					
FROMAGE						Louis	<1	SF	2654a		1872
Thoesphilis	44	FRA	F72		1887	**FRUDENBERG**					
FROMBERG						J. M.	14	CA	F49		1885
Auna	<1	SF	1323		1869	**FRUEGLE**					
Gustave (soldier)			136		1901	Mathew	50	IRL	650		1870
Isaac	66	RUS	4040		1896	**FRUGOLIN**					
Wm.	7	CA	6877		1895	Angela T.	<1	SF	316a		1871
FROMENT						**FRUHE**					
Benjimin C.					1899	Millicent				Aug	1899
FROND						**FRULAND**					
John				Nov	1899	Endui J.	1868	NOR	2357c		1904
FRONLEIA						**FRUMAN**					
Salvatore				Feb	1900	John E.					1899
FROSCH						**FRÜS**					
C. J. H.	18	GER	F53		1885	Chas. Stenalt	73	DEN	5061a		1895
FROST						**FRUSH**					
Benjamin	24	NOR	6513		1900	Carl V.	50	MD	6237a		1895
Ellen, Mrs.	74	IRL	2670		1901	**FRY**					
Floyd Finus	1	MN	5575		1904	Albie	1829	IRE	2588c		1904
John Henry	46	ME	1863		1900	Cary H.	59	KY	2708		1873
Joyce M.	3	SF	8733		1903	Charles T.	<1	SF	5385		1901
Julia A.	63	NY	2684		1901	Elizabeth	<1	SF	1250		1869
Laura				Jul	1899	Ernest O.	1880	IL	1487c		1904
Mary A.	66	GER	2220b		1895	Frank (soldier)			2214		1903
Wm. H.	37	NB	797		1870	Freddie	4	SF	598		1894
FROSTER						John	66	GER	434		1866
——		SF	1126		1869						

NAME	AGE OR YOB.	BIRTH PLACE	CERT. NO	ID	DEATH YEAR
John D., Col.	81	KY	5599	Jan	1901
Margaret Teresa				Jun	1899
Stanley	<1	SF	2783		1873
T. J., c/o		SF	2843a		1872
Thomas Jefferson	69	MO	5444		1904
FRYAR					
Maggie	23	ID	8395		1904
FRYDENDELLKOL					
Mary	75	IRL	3522	Nov	1901
FRYE					
Alfred	63	ME	6363		1902
Mary/Jesse, c/o	<1	SF	2099		1901
Nellie May	12	CA	4575a		1895
Wm. R.	47	IRL	2444b		1895
FU					
Hoo	36	CHN	245		1865
FUCHIKAWA					
Masaku	31	JPN	7364		1902
FUCHS					
——			4996		1867
——		CA	4997		1867
——		SF	1245		1869
Chattarina	43	GER	1273		1869
Elizabeth	82	SWT	1591b		1895
George/Emma, c/o	1904	SF	1930		1904
Geroge				Oct	1899
Henry	56	GER	7647		1904
Johann	1841	GER	849c		1904
Joseph	44	BOH	785		1902
Martin	50	FRA	2876		1900
FUCICH					
Steve	22	AUS	7077		1904
FUCIK					
Paul	57	AUS	8181		1904

NAME	AGE OR YOB.	BIRTH PLACE	CERT. NO	ID	DEATH YEAR
FUCK					
Sam	40	CHN	1427		1869
FUE					
Hung	25	CHN	892b		1871
Wye	46	CHN	2126		1873
FUEHRIG					
Dora C.	1855	GER	1375c		1904
FUENTIS					
Joseph	39	CHI	4120b		1870
FUERETIS					
Maria	40	MEX	1248a		1871
FUESGUSS					
Jacob (soldier)			7143		1901
FUGALI					
John W. (soldier)			6930		1900
FUGE					
Robert	67	GER	8888		1903
FUGEL					
Mary	30	CA	2310b		1895
FUGSCHIBERG					
Martha				Feb	1900
FUHE					
Ah	32	CHN	1017		1870
FUHRER					
John	45	SWT	499		1901
FUHRMAN					
Henry N.	66	GER	304b		1871
FUHRMANN					
Maria				Oct	1899
FUI					
Ah	46	CHN	6904		1868
FUILL					
James H.	21	NS	964		1870

Key: a = 1st part of year; b = 2nd part of year; c = death certificate copy; c/o = child of

NAME	AGE OR YOB.	BIRTH PLACE	CERT. NO	ID	DEATH YEAR	NAME	AGE OR YOB.	BIRTH PLACE	CERT. NO	ID	DEATH YEAR
FUITH						Elmer Lelon	9	IA	987		1903
Simon				Jan	1899	Francis Pearl				Apr	1899
						George E.	38	ENG	6956		1900
FUJIMOTO						George Selvista	<1	SF	1214		1901
Tomakicki	42	JPN	7358		1900	Harriet M.	85	MA	8787		1903
FUJIWARA						Henry				Mar	1899
Jinzo	41	JPN	1973		1902	Joseph G.	49	SF	2913		1894
FUJIYAMA						Martha H.	54	AUS	445		1900
Yone	2	SF	3837		1902	Mary A.	64	NB	5704a		1895
FUKUMOTO						Mary E.	1	SF	3247		1870
Mohu	23	JPN	3412		1902	Mary Rose	19	WIS	1311		1869
FUKUSIMA						Matilda	60	ENG	4806a		1895
Iwakishi				Jul	1898	Patrick	35	IRL	F89		1887
						Philip Oscar	46	GER	5165		1904
FULBERG						Sophia	40	CHN	1034		1868
Carl O.				Feb	1900	Thomas	74	ME	7453		1901
FULDA						William	28	ENG	5655		1867
Minnie, Mrs.	73	GER	5842	Jan	1901	**FULLERS**					
FULFOY						Thomas				Jul	1899
Mary Alice	16	SF	5275a		1895	**FULLERTON**					
FULKERTH						Annie				Jan	1899
Asa Shiew				Oct	1898	John H.				Jan	1900
FULLARD						Thomas E.	31	IRE	697		1902
Emma R.	<1	SF	3682		1867	**FULLIP**					
Hannah I.	66	NY	357		1901	Teresa	65	HUN	2904		1900
Mary C.	36	SF	1133b		1895	**FULLMAN**					
FULLEN						Anne	50	DE	539b		1871
George	81	IRE	7896		1903	**FULLMER**					
Maud	52	NV	8046		1900	John A.	42	USA	1349		1869
FULLER						**FULLUM**					
Annie	1868	CA	3426c		1904	Kate	25	CA	7883		1901
Charles H.	32	ME	3297a		1872	Thomas	34	CA	5500	Jan	1901
David	74	NY	6485		1904	**FULMORE**					
Edward Lincoln	48	PA	5557		1903	John	60	MA	4456		1901
Ellis A.	70	NY	1902		1870						

Key: a = 1st part of year; b = 2nd part of year; c = death certificate copy; c/o = child of

NAME	AGE OR YOB.	BIRTH PLACE	CERT. NO	ID	DEATH YEAR	NAME	AGE OR YOB.	BIRTH PLACE	CERT. NO	ID	DEATH YEAR
FULTON						Bee	45	CHN	5676		1904
Adelaide	53	NS	7915		1904	Chee	30	CHN	64		1903
Charles	1	SF	1142		1869	Chin	26	CHN	1100		1902
Charles Alexander	2	SF	6238a		1895	Chong				Nov	1899
Edwin	<1	NY	3224		1870	Chow	27	CHN	3220		1866
Emily J.				Nov	1899	Chum	37	CHN	3577a		1895
Florence E.	15	SF	6252		1896	Chung				Jan	1900
Hannah	82	PA	1974		1894	Fong	35	CHN	6881		1868
John	54	CT	3427		1896	Gwy	42	CHN	6275a		1895
Louisa	<1	CA	F74		1887	Hi	20	CHN	1250		1869
Lydia	22	MA	1758b		1871	Hing Wo	51	CHN	6818		1902
Oliver	<1	SF	344b		1871	Hoy	36	CHN	F104		1889
Ray F.			5094		1903	Jen Gong	36	CHN	434a		1871
Samuel	59	NS	1443b		1895	Law	54	CHN	3558		1903
William	70		6249		1904	Linn	15	SF	4056a		1895
William Edward	<1	SF	1274		1869	Loon	50	CHN	3684		1902
William H.	32	CA	3472		1902	Lun	27	CHN	1410		1870
Willie A.	<1	SF	2007		1866	Nung	41	CHN	1368b		1872
Willis C. (soldier)			7305		1901	Quan Com	21	CA	7056	Feb	1901
						San Gee	67	CHN	900		1870
FUME						Sea Ku				Oct	1898
E. C., Mrs.	26	NB	F96		1889	Thoy Yeo				Jan	1899
						Toy	48	CHN	790a		1871
FUN						Toy Mon	27	CHN	2738		1895
Ah	25	CHN	2836		1866	Yee		CHN	569b		1872
Ah Wong	32	CHN	6843a		1895	Yip Quong	40	CA	7883		1904
Lum	1870	CHN	325c		1904	Yung				Oct	1898
Sun Let	1879	CHN	2913c		1904						
						FUNK					
FUNCKE						Arthur K.	27	OH	1720		1901
Robert C.	31	AUT	4821		1904	Eliza	53	IN	9493		1901
						Fred	1885	CA	2373c		1904
FUNE						Geo. E.	26	IL	1262		1869
Ah	15	CHN	7687		1868	Gustave	32	GER	5810		1903
Ah	22	CHN	8490		1868	J. A.	1869		465c		1904
						Nicolaus	61	GER	439a		1871
FUNG						William	36	GER	6616a		1895
Ah	46	CHN	1838		1870						
Ah	28	CHN	3859		1870						
Ah	32	CHN	271		1870						

NAME	AGE OR YOB.	BIRTH PLACE	CERT. NO	ID	DEATH YEAR	NAME	AGE OR YOB.	BIRTH PLACE	CERT. NO	ID	DEATH YEAR
FUNKE						FURLEY					
Florence May	1874	MO	346c		1904	Edward	40	IRL	F44		1885
FUNKENSTEIN						John F.	<1	SF	2772		1866
Abraham	<1	SF	3697		1867	John F., c/o	<1	SF	1119b		1872
FUNNELL						Margaret	60	IRE	7073		1902
Jos. Richard	3	LA	2587		1873	FURLONG					
FUNO						Bella	5	SF	1623b		1872
Kum You	26	CHN	3019		1873	Delia Sullivan	33	IRE	4189		1903
FUOG						Mary	1	SF	9902		1868
Katherine	72	SWT	4960		1902	Mary	65	IRE	5722		1903
FUR						Mary					1898
Long	30	CHN	6220		1867	Mary Anne		SF	8531		1901
Long	30	CHN	6232		1867	Mattew Wm.	66	RI	1270		1894
FURBUSH						Nicholas	<1	SF	1411b		1895
Alice	<1	SF	1103b		1871	Thomas	60	IRE	7160		1902
Ellis Wells	28	CA	2133		1903	Thomas				Oct	1898
Jose	35	MA	F87		1887	Thomas J. (soldier)	36	ENG	4356		1901
Moses	83	ME	6044		1896	FURMAN					
FURCELLO						John A.	1	SF	4933		1867
Giovanni	<1	SF	5603		1903	FURNER					
FUREY						Lulu G.				Jul	1898
William	72	IRL	5094		1901	FURNESS					
FURGER						Charles F.	41	MA	6543	Feb	1901
Joseph	8	SF	5176		1903	Sarah A.	1	SF	5752		1867
FURGERSON						FURNEY					
Roger J.	3	SF	9128		1901	John	40	IRE	1214		1866
FURGESON						FURNISS					
——			4913		1867	Annie				Jul	1898
David A. (soldier)			7577		1900	FURR					
Virgil J. (soldier)			7663		1900	Guy A. (soldier)			141		1901
FURGUSON						FURRAR					
——	38	IRE	8975		1868	Louise	<1	CA	5355		1903
						FURRER					
						Albin	42	SWT	4594		1903

Key: a = 1st part of year; b = 2nd part of year;
c = death certificate copy; c/o = child of

NAME	AGE OR YOB.	BIRTH PLACE	CERT. NO	ID	DEATH YEAR	NAME	AGE OR YOB.	BIRTH PLACE	CERT. NO	ID	DEATH YEAR
Charles	62	GER	8287		1900	**FUSTHS**					
Marie	32	SWT	404b		1895	Bertha	<1	CA	4903		1902
FURRIO						**FUSZ**					
Bastiano	26	ITA	6600Feb		1901	Peter				Nov	1898
FURRY						**FUSZY**					
Le Roy K.	14	CA	4902		1902	John F.				Jan	1899
FURSH						**FUTA**					
John	38	PA	F85		1887	Masato	24	JPN	2465		1900
FURSTENTHAL						**FUTTER**					
Raphael	<1	SF	2432a		1872	Jennie	78	GER	2580		1895
FURTADO						John				Jan	1899
Emilia Rosa	3	SF	369b		1871	Rebecca	1852	GER	1805c		1904
FURUYA						**FUZIKI**					
Risuke	24	JPN	3998		1900	Tomizo	29	JPN	5286		1904
Yoshiteru	22	JPN	876		1902	**FUZIOKA**					
FURY						Yosisaburo	27	JPN	1215		1901
Ellen	53	IRL	3840		1896	**FY**					
FUSCO						Ah	35	CHN	F30		1884
Margherita	1	SF	1204		1903	Wong Com	47	CHN	2490		1866
FUSELLI						**FYANO**					
Maria	45	ITA	5090		1902	Leonard	1875	ENG	319c		1904
FUSILEER						**FYARCE**					
John	42	GER	3034		1873	——		SF	3078		1870
FUSILIER						**FYARD**					
Sarah Ann	32	IRE	1710		1866	Maria	<1	SF	3293		1870
FUSILLET						**FYFE**					
Louise F. A.	<1	CA	1398		1894	Andrew A.	1829	SCT	890c		1904
FUSLECO						William/Jane, c/o	<1	SF	5601		1903
Antone	7	MEX	1212b		1895	**GABB**					
FUSON						Clarence	<1	SF	4155Dec		1901
Mary E.	66	NY	1137		1901	Minnie	28	SF	4822		1904
FUSSENEGGER						**GABBS**					
Carl	40	AUS	3726		1902	Albert L.	1843	OH	140c		1904

Key: a = 1st part of year; b = 2nd part of year;
c = death certificate copy; c/o = child of

NAME	AGE OR YOB.	BIRTH PLACE	CERT. NO	ID	DEATH YEAR
GABEL					
Mary	34	GER	1107a		1871
GABERT					
Julia	58	FRA	4769a		1895
GABIN					
Mary Marcella	<1	CA	6565		1900
GABLE					
Claude			1226		1903
GABRICK					
Thomas	35	GER	5122		1904
GABRIEL					
Annie M.	52	GER	G40		1885
Arthur	1	SF	2671		1903
Fred		SF	1882		1902
Louis	40	MD	7836		1901
Mary		SF	1883		1902
Mary				Jan	1900
William E.	1	SF	4678		1904
GABRIELLEA					
N. L. N.				Mar	1899
GABRIELLI					
G./M., c/o		SF	4043		1896
GABRIELSEN					
Flora	39	ENG	5135a		1896
GACCARD					
Louis/Maria, c/o				Jan	1900
GAD					
Flora				Oct	1899
GADBURG					
J. K./Fannie, c/o		CA	2431		1900
GADBURY					
Pearl	3	SF	3235		1894

NAME	AGE OR YOB.	BIRTH PLACE	CERT. NO	ID	DEATH YEAR
GADDEN					
——	20	SAN	8111		1868
GADDI					
Alfredo	5	SF	1112		1900
GADDINI					
Angelo	<1	SF	4271		1896
John	52	ITA	5123		1904
GADDY					
Charles (soldier)			7145		1901
GADING					
Adelia				Aug	1899
GADNER					
Ellen	34	MA	2053		1894
GADSCH					
Ernest	69	GER	1683		1902
GAENZ					
Carl, c/o		SF	2821		1873
GAERBER					
Jos.	57	AUT	G53		1885
GAERIE					
Henry Edwin	1	OH	1155		1869
GAETCKE					
Augusta	31	GER	6388a		1895
GAETGEN					
Emma	36	LA	1280b		1895
GAETING					
Mary	29	SF	5586a		1895
GAETJEN					
Hermann F.	2	SF	5427		1904
GAEVERT					
Fred W.	28	PA	180b		1895
GAFFENEY					
Stephen	44	PA	6303	Feb	1901

NAME	AGE OR YOB.	BIRTH PLACE	CERT. NO	ID	DEATH YEAR
GAFFEY					
Ann E.	85	IRE	1833		1902
Mabel	20	SF	1034		1903
GAFFIGAN					
John James	<1	SF	1280		1869
Mary				Mar	1899
GAFFNEY					
Annie	28	CA	4342		1896
Annie	58	IRL	9146		1901
Bernard	62	IRL	4635		1896
Charles H.	35	NY	1147		1869
Ed.	18	CA	554		1900
Henry T.	44	AUS	6326		1900
James				Nov	1898
James				Nov	1899
James P.	1874	SF	3354c		1904
John	<1	SF	1132b		1872
John				Jan	1900
M.				Mar	1900
Marie	30	CA	7664		1903
Mary	1842	IRE	1455c		1904
Mary	68	IRE	6994		1903
Michael	72	IRE	2073		1903
Michael				Jan	1900
Michael H.	70	IRE	7615		1904
Patrick M.				Jan	1900
Rose	31	ENG	2296		1866
Thomas				Feb	1900
GAFFORI					
Chas. F. E.	74	GER	6577a		1895
GAFNEY					
Jennie B.	39	SCT	4288b		1870
Jeremiah	63	IRL	1349		1894
GAFVO					
Joseph	<1	SF	513a		1871

NAME	AGE OR YOB.	BIRTH PLACE	CERT. NO	ID	DEATH YEAR
GAGAN					
Edward M.	24	CA	3715		1896
Ellen	64	NY	7895		1900
Grant Watson	1868	CA	3427c		1904
John	34	CA	1330		1901
Mary Elizabeth	56	MA	2800		1895
Mary J.	65	RI	6643	Feb	1901
Thomas	73	IRE	5343		1904
Thomas	78	IRL	4899a		1895
Thos.	50	IRL	G24		1883
Walker W.	4	SF	2751		1894
GAGE					
Harriet M.	56	CT	1083a		1871
James Crosby	1829	IRE	2923c		1904
Maria Fisher	54	ME	4816		1902
Wm. L.	36	MA	2750		1873
GAGEN					
Mary H.	<1	SF	7395		1868
Philip	40	IRL	1648b		1872
Thomas R.	41	SF	6248		1902
GAGGINI					
G.	72	ITA	3725		1900
GAGLALIDO					
Coforiani B.	1	SF	387		1865
GAGLIARDINI					
Josephine	19	SF	4802		1903
GAGLIARDO					
Mary	<1	CA	2338		1873
Pasquale	63	ITA	4229		1900
GAGNE					
Sophie	58	FRA	332b		1872
GAGUEUR					
Frank	43	FRA	G95		1889

NAME	AGE OR YOB.	BIRTH PLACE	CERT. NO	ID	DEATH YEAR	NAME	AGE OR YOB.	BIRTH PLACE	CERT. NO	ID	DEATH YEAR
GAGUS						William Richard	76	MD	8215		1904
Delia	75	MA	7704		1904	**GAINEY**					
						Cathrine	75	IRL	4563		1901
GAHAGAN						Jane	40	NB	689		1901
John	38	MA	4796		1904	John Raymond				Mar	1899
Richard	80	IRE	2865		1903						
						GAINKE					
GAHAGEN						Herman	40	GER	8507		1900
Hannah				Mar	1899						
						GAINOR					
GAHAN						Thomas				Oct	1898
Michael	59	VA	3319		1900						
						GAIONE					
GAHILL/BRYAN						Jenny M.	40	CA	997		1901
A.				Mar	1900						
						GAJIOLA					
GAHL						Anita	58	MEX	3828		1903
Anna	1	CA	34		1903						
						GAKEL					
GAHNSTROM						Lewis	43	GER	449b		1895
John	62	SWE	4080		1900						
						GAKEN					
GAIGAN						Joseph	<1	SF	1191		1869
William				Jan	1900						
						GALA					
GAIL						Louisa	<1	SF	8016		1868
Bernard				Aug	1899						
						GALAGHER					
GAILLARD						Peter	<1	SF	1356		1869
——	<1	SF	10		1870						
Joseph	65	BEL	1404		1903	**GALAGIN**					
Marie				Nov	1898	John James	1	SF	2586a		1872
Zoelina M.	1835	LA	3048c		1904						
						GALAPSIN					
GAIMALIS						Francis	45	FRA	1271		1869
Gort	40	GRE	310		1902						
						GALARDO					
GAIN						Josephine G.				Apr	1899
Herbert J.				Oct	1899	Leonardo	73	MEX	2897		1901
Wong Gok	1854	CHN	2842c		1904						
						GALATOIRE					
GAINES						George	<1	SF	1740		1900
Henry Alonzo				Oct	1898	Josephine	5	FRA	5929	Jan	1901
Paul				Mar	1900						
						GALBANO					
T. O./Pieser, c/o	1	SF	1010		1903	Vincenzo	25	ITA	G97		1889

Key: a = 1st part of year; b = 2nd part of year;
c = death certificate copy; c/o = child of

NAME	AGE OR YOB.	BIRTH PLACE	CERT. NO	ID	DEATH YEAR	NAME	AGE OR YOB.	BIRTH PLACE	CERT. NO	ID	DEATH YEAR
GALBERG						**GALESPY**					
Peter C. H.	65	DEN	3120		1902	Cecilia	30	PRU	231		1870
GALBRAITH						**GALEWSKY**					
Hazel Josephine	<1	SF	3528a		1895	Simon	38	PRU	1361		1869
William	68	IRL	2059		1900	**GALEY**					
GALBREATH						Paul	26	FRA	4989a		1895
Samuel				Nov	1899	**GALIGHER**					
GALBREITH						Laura Annette	49	OH	3138		1900
Margarat Ann	7	NB	769b		1871	**GALIMBERTI**					
GALE						Charles				Feb	1899
——	<1	CA	1365		1869	**GALINDO**					
Benjamin A.	46	ENG	3058		1873	Francisca	20	CA	2345		1866
Benjamin Franklin	57	OH	1267		1901	Guadalupe	33	CA	4609a		1895
Edward N.	30	MO	999		1900	**GALINGER**					
Grace	6	SF	4679		1904	Theresa	1	SF	721b		1871
Jeremiah Wilson				Oct	1898	**GALIRU**					
Leonard O.	33	NY	5392		1867	John Joseph				Jan	1899
Lewis E. (soldier)			7144		1901	**GALL**					
Lucinda H.	66	IN	6282		1904	Morris H.	33	PRU	9230		1868
Lucy A. E.				Oct	1898	Sylvester			2515c		1904
Mary A.	61	IRE	8233		1904	**GALLACHER**					
Raymond John	1	SF	1887		1894	John				Aug	1899
Roxana	71	VA	5805		1896	**GALLAFENT**					
S./Anna, c/o				Jul	1899	Barnard	47	ENG	3856		1903
Thomas M.			3467a		1872	**GALLAGHER**					
GALEA						——			2086		1870
Andrea	48	MAL	5250		1904	——		IRL	1897a		1872
GALEHOUSE						——		SF	2955		1866
Frederick	72	OH	7189		1904	——			5388		1867
GALENSKY						——			8973		1868
Louis	6	CA	8885		1868	Agnes	19	CA	3783	Nov	1901
GALES						Alexander	82	FIN	1401		1869
Margaret	52	BEL	1851		1900	Alice	<1	CA	3727		1902
Mildred				Jan	1900	Ann	70	IRL	7485		1901

Key: a = 1st part of year; b = 2nd part of year; c = death certificate copy; c/o = child of

NAME	AGE OR YOB.	BIRTH PLACE	CERT. NO	ID	DEATH YEAR	NAME	AGE OR YOB.	BIRTH PLACE	CERT. NO	ID	DEATH YEAR
Anne	78	IRE	1303		1866	Francis			7100		1902
Annie	5	CAN	3562		1870	George	33	SF	2823		1903
Annie	18	PA	1034		1868	George (soldier)	34	CA	6946		1904
Annie	65	IRE	3370		1903	George A.	5	SF	5435		1867
Annie	65	IRE	7567		1903	Harvey	41	PA	6322		1902
Annie J.	21	SF	6151a		1895	Henry	63	NY	8870		1901
Anthony Owen	28	SF	8804		1904	Henry	32	CA	1414b		1895
Arthur	2	SF	5740a		1895	Hugh	72	IRE	1190		1869
Bernard	73	IRL	166		1900	Hugh	<1	SF	754		1900
Bridget				Jun	1899	Hugh W.	29	CA	1500		1900
Catherine	27	IRL	1183a		1871	James	67	IRE	2979		1902
Catherine				Jun	1899	James	67	IRL	8854		1900
Catherine Jane	65	IRE	1967		1903	James				Jan	1899
Catherine M.	55	IRL	5338a		1895	James				Feb	1900
Cathrine	1	ME	9416		1868	James A.	34	IA	5172		1902
Charles, Mrs.	56	NY	6695a		1895	James G.	15	SF	7797		1900
Chas. F.	<1	SF	1220		1869	James L.	77	MI	4078		1903
Dan D. (soldier)			3270		1903	Jennie J.	33	CA	6326a		1895
Daniel	69	IRE	3221		1902	Joanna	69	NY	8234		1903
Daniel Joseph	48	MA	283		1900	John	34	IRL	1606		1870
Dennis	36	SCT	3779		1902	John	9	SF	1766		1870
Edward	75	IRE	494		1866	John	37	IRE	3337		1866
Edward	37	IRE	8522		1904	John	63	IRE	6680		1903
Edward Charles	1904	SF	1489c		1904	John				Jun	1899
Edward H.	1	SF	8145		1868	John (soldier)			7126		1900
Edward Jos.			1227		1903	John J.	1	SF	5122		1867
Edward P.	<1	SF	6612		1900	John P.	42	IRE	1440		1869
Edward/Margaret, c/o		CA	5666		1902	John T.	5	SF	8043		1868
Eliza J.	2	SF	3631		1867	John Vernon				Feb	1899
Elizabeth	23	SF	6237		1900	John/Madge, c/o	1	SF	8465		1904
Elizabeth	76	IRE	4599		1904	Joseph	34	IRE	1436		1869
Elizabeth Jane	3	SF	1146		1869	Joseph	47	IRL	4201a		1895
Ellen	1848	IRE	1154c		1904	Joseph				Oct	1898
Ellen	78	IRE	235		1902	Julia A.	63	MO	6984	Feb	1901
Ellen	67	IRL	5500a		1895	Kate	31	SF	5554	Jan	1901
Farrell	69	IRE	3761		1902	Katharine	40	IRE	1737		1903

NAME	AGE OR YOB.	BIRTH PLACE	CERT. NO	ID	DEATH YEAR
Letitia/M. J., c/o	<1	SF	981		1895
Lillian M.	1871	SF	3174c		1904
Lily E.	46	MO	5786a		1895
M. J./M., c/o		SF	6331		1895
Maggie	25	PA	5971	Jan	1901
Marcella E.	<1	SF	2835		1894
Margaret					1899
Mary	82	IRL	919b		1871
Mary	<1	SF	8340		1868
Mary	57	IRE	759		1903
Mary	71	IRL	2315		1900
Mary	80	IRL	4454		1901
Mary				Jul	1899
Mary				Jan	1900
Mary A.	<1	SF	928b		1872
Mary Allena	60	IRL	6358		1900
Mary Amalia	1	SF	1184		1869
Mary Anne	3	SF	816b		1871
Mary E.	4	SF	1361		1869
Mary Ellen	<1	SF	9257		1868
Mary F.		SF	3011		1870
Mary F.				Jun	1899
May	32	MN	2866		1902
Michael	<1	SF	1963		1866
Michael	72	IRE	2029		1903
Michael	1852		791c		1904
Michael J.					1899
Michael R.	49	MA	5804		1896
Mollie	28	SF	4314		1902
Nancy	65	IRE	1630		1903
Neil	30	IRE	1167		1869
Neil, Rev.	38	IRE	5581		1867
Nellie	27	IRE	5156		1902
Patrick	1	SF	4158b		1870
Patrick	45	IRL	1266		1901
Patrick					1898

NAME	AGE OR YOB.	BIRTH PLACE	CERT. NO	ID	DEATH YEAR
Patrick C.	25	IRL	6337	Feb	1901
Patrick H.	51	IRE	6470		1902
Philip (soldier)			8426		1900
Sarah E.	1	SF	820		1870
Sarah J.	67	ME	4440		1904
Susana	6	CAN	3306		1870
Theresa	59	IRL	7006	Feb	1901
Thomas	37	SF	4501		1901
Thomas	1828	IRE	2240c		1904
Wallace J.				Aug	1898
William	<1	SF	5562		1867
William	20	SF	1498		1900
William A.		SF	1086b		1871
William P.	3	ME	8202		1868
Winifred	78	IRL	8330		1901
Wm.	50	IRL	G30		1883
Wm. R.				Mar	1900
GALLAGHER					
——			1608		1866
GALLAINT					
Charles A.	32	NY	1840		1866
GALLAN					
Elizabeth	65	PA	2128		1894
John	38	VT	1156		1869
GALLAND					
Fredericke	67	GER	3044		1903
Samuel A.	20	PRU	6483		1868
GALLANT					
Joseph H.	31	RI	4112		1902
Mary	<1	SF	1357		1901
GALLARCA					
Macario	<1	SF	4642		1902
GALLARD					
Selina	<1	CA	4441		1867

Key: a = 1st part of year; b = 2nd part of year;
c = death certificate copy; c/o = child of

NAME	AGE OR YOB.	BIRTH PLACE	CERT. NO	ID	DEATH YEAR
GALLARDO					
Durelio Louis	38	MEX	1420		1869
Pedro	<1	SF	3141		1873
Rosa Lopez de	25	MEX	2985		1873
GALLAVAN					
Jeremiah					Apr 1899
GALLAWAY					
Nicholas	65	ENG	4680		1903
GALLEAND					
Elizabeth	74	MA	G67		1886
GALLEANO					
Ben	33	ITA	1745		1894
Benedetto	22		1967b		1872
GALLEGER					
Francis B.	36	CA	4202a		1895
GALLEGOS					
Emily Louise	23	SF	4600		1904
Ignacia	75	COR	2511		1873
Manuela	74	COR	6403		1904
Teresa	64	COR	5346		1902
GALLEIGHER					
John	32	IRE	1228		1866
GALLEN					
Ella	6	SF	2316		1900
Eloysius					Aug 1898
James W.	1879	IRE	1023c		1904
Mary A.	32	IRE	6283		1904
Rosie					Aug 1898
GALLETTA					
A./Mary, c/o		SF	4082		1900
GALLI					
Americo	<1	SF	7442		1900
Angelo	24	ITA	2445b		1895
Cecilia	<1	SF	1782b		1895

NAME	AGE OR YOB.	BIRTH PLACE	CERT. NO	ID	DEATH YEAR
Emilio	57	ITA	4940		1904
Emma	11	SF	1670b		1895
Ida	<1	SF	8081		1903
Vincenzo					Mar 1899
GALLIANO					
Antonio	<1	SF	4181		1896
Celestine					Apr 1899
Emma	65	ME	1806		1902
GALLIARD					
Mary E.	44	KY	6934	Feb	1901
GALLIARO					
Maria	31	ITA	4292		1896
GALLICK					
Irene	1	SF	2154		1894
Lilie	<1	SF	2111		1894
Nicolaus/Mary, c/o	<1	SF	6234		1900
GALLIENT					
Joseph M.	36	MD	1913		1866
GALLIER					
Teresa	<1	SF	5458		1896
GALLIGAN					
James	72	IRL	9616		1901
Julia					Nov 1899
Margaret	64	IRL	140b		1895
Michael	50	IRL	8364		1900
Thomas James	11	SF	249b		1872
GALLIGHAN					
Patrick	38	IRL	1523b		1872
GALLIGHER					
Humphrey	13	MA	584a		1870
GALLIGOS					
Philomina	29	MEX	1149		1869
GALLINELLAHIN					
Delfine	15	CA	1118		1870

Key: a = 1st part of year; b = 2nd part of year;
c = death certificate copy; c/o = child of

NAME	AGE OR YOB.	BIRTH PLACE	CERT. NO	ID	DEATH YEAR
GALLIPENE					
Adelaide	18	CA	1485a		1871
GALLMISCH					
Jean	64	SWT	5081a		1895
GALLON					
Ann	49	IRE	2866		1903
John	2	SF	3871	Nov	1901
Melville E.	<1	SF	4556		1903
GALLOWAY					
James D.	75	NY	5071		1903
Kattie K.	11	SF	3975		1870
GALLWAY					
Philip	44		1213		1870
GALLWEY					
David				Jul	1898
GALLY					
John	80	ALS	2602		1894
GALPIN					
Elizabeth E.	26	VT	6438		1867
GALT					
B.	40	GER	1388		1869
GALTIER					
Jean Marie	69	FRA	8600		1904
GALUSHA					
Chas. H.				Jul	1898
GALVAN					
Johanna	2	NY	1405		1869
GALVIN					
Agnes	<1	CA	2191		1902
Catherine	26	SF	3829		1903
Claire R.	<1	SF	6292		1902
Daniel				Aug	1899
Edward C.	1	CA	3239		1903

NAME	AGE OR YOB.	BIRTH PLACE	CERT. NO	ID	DEATH YEAR
Ellen	<1	SF	6425		1867
Ellen					1899
Helena	20	IRL	1268		1901
James	62	IRL	6358		1896
Jeremiah	35	IRL	3710		1870
Jeremiah	52	IRL	2906a		1872
Jeremiah	48	IRE	5954		1902
Jeremiah	30	IRL	7904		1901
John	31	PA	5023		1904
Joseph				Aug	1898
Margaret	38	IRE	4015		1902
Maria	20	IRE	1371		1869
Mary				Oct	1899
Mary Ely	58	MA	7009		1902
Michael	61	IRE	698		1902
Michael	70	IRE	4315		1902
Michael	<1	SF	75b		1895
Patrick	35	IRE	4759		1902
Peter F.	<1	CA	9426		1901
Thos.	20	SF	1315		1901
Timothy				Feb	1899
William	35	IRL	1783b		1872
William	35	NY	1950b		1872
William I.				Mar	1899
GALVISH					
James Mervin					1898
GAMA					
Miguel	<1	SF	5526	Jan	1901
GAMACH					
Florence	1861	MA	968c		1904
GAMAGE					
Anstis	55	MA	3106a		1872
GAMBA					
Felici	56	ITA	5661	Jan	1901
Guiseppe	1	SF	7183		1903

Key: a = 1st part of year; b = 2nd part of year;
c = death certificate copy; c/o = child of

NAME	AGE OR YOB.	BIRTH PLACE	CERT. NO	ID	DEATH YEAR
GAMBARASE					
Eddie	1	SF	5024		1904
GAMBARINO					
Guiseppe	21	ITA	873a		1871
GAMBEL					
Hamilton B.	34	PA	5018		1867
GAMBER					
Henry	40	GER	G29		1883
GAMBILL					
Charles D.				Jul	1898
Julia C.	38	KY	3002		1870
GAMBITZ					
Kady	73	GER	4063		1902
Regenie	54	AL	4307		1903
GAMBLE					
Alexander				Feb	1900
Annie	21	SF	403		1903
Bridget				Feb	1900
Chas. J. (soldier)			7115		1900
Frederick C.	15	SF	2185		1894
James	76	IRL	5955		1896
John M.				Mar	1900
John W.				Mar	1900
Laura					1899
Leland Thompson	11	SF	5105a		1895
Willa	<1	SF	6307		1904
William P.	43	CA	1835		1903
GAMBO					
Helma, c/o	<1	CA	3754		1900
GAMBOA					
Jesus Pablo	26	MEX	1074		1866
GAMBOLD					
Anthony	33	GER	3337		1902

NAME	AGE OR YOB.	BIRTH PLACE	CERT. NO	ID	DEATH YEAR
GAMBS					
Ernest F.	43	MD	5733		1902
GAMERSTON					
Margaret				Oct	1899
GAMIS					
Jesus	32	MEX	G56		1885
GAMMA					
Albert	<1	SF	1987		1901
Caspari	18	SWT	3009		1894
Gallus	52	SWT	4706		1904
Moritz	<1	SF	2503b		1895
GAMMELL					
C. F.	31	CA	6507		1896
GAMMON					
John C./Nellie, c/o	<1	SF	8045		1904
GAMPERS					
George W.				Jan	1900
GAN					
Duck	33	CHN	384		1900
Gin	65	CHN	7597		1900
Herbert J.				Oct	1899
P./A., c/o				May	1899
Sing	40	CHN	3110		1895
Sing	44	CHN	1846		1900
Soon Yuen					1898
Yun	49	CHN	559		1900
GANAKA					
——	45	SAN	1032		1868
GANARD					
Thomas	1	SF	731b		1871
GANBALDI					
Attilra	2	SF	838a		1871
GANCO					
Bernard	35	FRA	2349		1894

NAME	AGE OR YOB.	BIRTH PLACE	CERT. NO	ID	DEATH YEAR
GANDE					
Edward A.	26	IL	4628a		1895
GANDENZIO					
James D./Virginia, c/o	1	SF	93		1903
GANDER					
Andres	30	FRA	2842		1895
Charles T.	<1	SF	1850b		1895
Fred	1859	SWT	2057c		1904
GANDERSON					
George Thomas	<1	SF	1899b		1872
GANDLEY					
John J.	47	NY	1421		1900
GANDSINDT					
Lepold	29	PRU	8390		1868
GANDY					
General (soldier)			1853		1901
William E. (soldier)			6529	Feb	1901
GANEARD					
Thomas Hall	1846	NY	2980c		1904
GANEY					
John Francis	20	SF	5325		1902
Julia	55	IRL	6409	Feb	1901
Patrick	55	IRL	2619		1895
GANG					
Gee Ah	50	CHN	G45		1885
Young	48	CHN	1164		1869
GANGHREN					
Peter	40	IRE	9419		1868
GANGLOFF					
Emil (soldier)			2215		1903
Henry A.	5	SF	3811		1867
GANGNON					
Philomaine M.	1887	CA	27c		1904

NAME	AGE OR YOB.	BIRTH PLACE	CERT. NO	ID	DEATH YEAR
GANIGI					
Sadakichi	31	JPN	998b		1895
GANN					
George W.	40	NY	5538		1867
William	38	CA	123		1900
GANNEY					
Daniel	17	CA	1369		1900
GANNICH					
Frank	50	AUT	534		1900
GANNON					
Bridget	39	IRL	2196		1894
Cecelia	3	SF	1807a		1872
James Peter	<1	SF	348b		1872
John	20	IRE	1662		1866
John				Jun	1899
Joseph	34	IRL	1570		1894
Joseph H.	38	SF	5029		1902
"Major"	57	IRL	G66		1886
Mary	<1	SF	2886		1894
Mary Ellen	1	SF	1920		1866
Patrick	18	IRE	1189		1869
Peter William	6	SF	2467		1900
Thomas	32	IRE	392		1865
Thos.	60	IRL	2097		1894
William I.	<1	SF	798		1866
GANONG					
James (soldier)			5487	Jan	1901
GANS					
Charles W.				May	1899
GANSEVOORTANC					
James	78	NY	1501		1902
GANSO					
William H.	19	SF	5784	Jan	1901

NAME	AGE OR YOB.	BIRTH PLACE	CERT. NO	ID	DEATH YEAR
GANSTVINDT					
Anna L.	2	CA	8134		1868
GANTER					
Charles A.					1899
Julia A.	39	SF	6679	Feb	1901
GANTERT					
Hermann	50	GER	4069		1896
GANTINE					
Paul	70	FRA	8971		1868
GANTNER					
Mathias Joseph	60	NOR	2855		1900
Richard	69	GER	6454		1903
GANTZ					
Henry	40	GER	3181		1873
GANZERT					
Dorothea	44	GER	2761a		1872
GANZHOM					
George	4	SF	1033		1868
GAP					
Chin Sot	55	CHN	3120		1895
GARAHAM					
H. C.			1200c		1904
GARARD					
Mary Louisa	6	SF	1099		1869
GARASCHT					
Harry				Nov	1898
GARASSINO					
Joseph	<1	SF	4526		1867
GARAVENTA					
Angelo	66	ITA	3198		1903
GARBANNO					
Lawrence					1899

NAME	AGE OR YOB.	BIRTH PLACE	CERT. NO	ID	DEATH YEAR
GARBARINO					
Andrea	32	ITA	330b		1871
Antone				May	1899
Beatrice	1897	SF	1273c		1904
John	<1	SF	3816		1867
Lawrence					1899
Michael Louis	44	CA	5173		1902
Rose				Feb	1900
Salvatore	1850	ITA	1682c		1904
GARBER					
Ashley K.	25	CA	807		1894
Eugene R.				Jul	1898
Guilford S.	1875	IN	1041c		1904
GARBINA					
Ersiglia	1	SF	9984		1868
GARBINI					
Amedeo	60	ITA	8039		1901
Emilia	9	SF	1857b		1872
Eugene	<1	SF	2169		1866
Joseph	37	CA	4440		1896
Louigi	5	CA	9675		1868
Luigi	<1	SF	1381		1869
Luigi				Nov	1898
GARBORINO					
Joe	28	ITA	8328		1900
GARBUTT					
Augusta	49	NY	5246a		1896
John				Mar	1899
GARCELON					
C. C.	54	ME	5121a		1896
GARCIA					
Albert	3	CA	59		1902
Anastasia	26	MEX	8008		1900
Angelina				Jul	1898

Key: a = 1st part of year; b = 2nd part of year;
c = death certificate copy; c/o = child of

NAME	AGE OR YOB.	BIRTH PLACE	CERT. NO	ID	DEATH YEAR
Ascencion	85	MEX	968b		1895
Benita				Jul	1898
Callie	25	NC	4578		1901
Carman	82	MEX	2168		1903
Carnation	23	CHI	3304		1870
Dolores	20	MEX	4303b		1870
Evaresta	61	CHL	1458		1903
Evelyn C.	1	SF	5356		1903
G./D., c/o		SF	8138		1900
George	<1	SF	6046		1896
Gertrude	25	MEX	4460		1867
Jenaro	14	CA	634a		1871
Jennie	<1	SF	951b		1895
John	70	POR	7010		1902
John	6	SF	7651		1901
Joseph				Oct	1899
Joseph S.	78	POR	4527		1901
Lella	<1	CA	9425		1901
Louis	<1	SF	9847		1868
Louis					1899
Louisa E.	70	ME	382		1902
Loupi				Jul	1898
M.	33	CHI	5311		1896
Manuel	25	MEX	1574b		1895
Margaret, Mrs.	50	MEX	4823.a		1895
Maria				Nov	1898
Marsalina Cardoza	23	AZO	5643		1904
Mary	<1	SF	8183		1868
Medardo/Hortence, c/o				Jul	1898
Miquel	1876	CHL	2374c		1904
Ramona M.	<1	SF	8373		1904
Rosie	1	SF	4249		1903
Simond	24	CA	6481	Feb	1901
Tiburcia	40	MEX	8942		1901

GARCIE

NAME	AGE OR YOB.	BIRTH PLACE	CERT. NO	ID	DEATH YEAR
Nichola S.	<1	SF	8287		1868

NAME	AGE OR YOB.	BIRTH PLACE	CERT. NO	ID	DEATH YEAR
GARCILON					
Annie	23	NY	3137		1870
GARDE					
Catherine				Aug	1898
GARDELLA					
C. J./Mable , c/o	1904	SF	1851		1904
Giovanna	63	ITA	4455		1901
Guiseppi	60	ITA	565		1903
Serafina	25	ITA	7677		1900
GARDEMAN					
Louis	33	FRA	589a		1871
GARDEN					
James	39	SCT	356		1870
Johnathan Harry				Aug	1898
GARDENER					
Arthur W.	12	CA	4601		1904
Charles	53	JAM	3512		1900
Clarence	18	RI	9649		1901
Francis B.	39	ME	304b		1872
Geo.	57	NJ	G51		1885
Lila	<1	SF	1598		1894
Louis	26	FRA	768		1866
Walter S.	<1	SF	2131		1902
GARDENIER					
Walter	<1	SF	3610		1867
GARDENMEYER					
M. Dorathea	79	GER	3784	Nov	1901
GARDES					
Henry	38	GER	1233b		1895
GARDILLA					
Felipe	67	ITA	7398		1868
GARDINA					
Peter F. (USN)			4061		1903

NAME	AGE OR YOB.	BIRTH PLACE	CERT. NO	ID	DEATH YEAR	NAME	AGE OR YOB.	BIRTH PLACE	CERT. NO	ID	DEATH YEAR
GARDINEN						Marie (aka Anna Mary)	76	ALS	2995	Oct	1901
William T.	40		1738b		1872	Matthew	56	CAN	7416		1903
						Noah E. (soldier)			220		1902
GARDINER						Rebecca	1829	IRE	28c		1904
Aurelia B.	59	NY	3116		1900	Samuel	75	PA	4182		1896
Caroline	72	VA	1862		1902	Selena	3	SF	9159		1868
Elizabeth Ann	35	IRL	95b		1871	Thomas E. (soldier)			7127		1900
Francisco S.	35	NJ	6758	Feb	1901	W./R., c/o	<1	SF	4471		1895
James L.	35	VT	7921		1868	William	<1	SF	231		1900
Russell				Mar	1899	William H./Annie, c/o	1	SF	5287		1904
William C.	27	CA	6889	Feb	1901	William J. (soldier)			2055		1901
GARDNER						**GARDNIR**					
Ada Emily	29	NY	2672		1903	William					1899
Algernon Avery (soldier)			5485	Jan	1901	**GARDON**					
Annie	<1	SF	1642		1901	Alfred	67	FRA	1505		1894
Arthur M.	49	MA	4316		1902	**GAREGHLY**					
Benjamin				Mar	1900	Joseph B.	19	CA	1047		1900
Daniel				Apr	1899	**GARELL**					
Ellen	54	IRE	1374		1869	Hannah	35	NY	1367		1869
Eugene	38	ALS	2598		1901	**GARERY**					
Eugene/Mary, c/o		SF	5310		1896	Charles	52	FRA	921		1866
Francis J.		SF	4562b		1870	**GARESCHE**					
Francis Jos.				Jul	1899	Francis	3	NV	2417		1866
Frank	6	SF	4528		1901	John	1	NV	2422		1866
Frederic A.				Nov	1899	**GARETT**					
George	38	IRL	1864		1900	Edwin L. (soldier)			6818		1900
George F.	5	SF	8355		1868	Edwin L. (soldier)			6996		1900
James			3957		1902	**GARETY**					
James C.					1899	James F.				Feb	1899
James H.	<1	SF	8083		1868	Minnie A.	26	DC	3296		1902
James P. (soldier)			3320		1900	**GAREY**					
Jennie/Lewis, c/o	<1	CA	2223		1902	Kate E.	1	SF	285		1865
John	57	IRL	2925		1873	**GARFIELD**					
John	40	GER	2765		1903	Emma J.				Jun	1899
John Nicolaus	90	GER	6716		1903						
John W. (soldier)			2450		1900						

NAME	AGE OR YOB.	BIRTH PLACE	CERT. NO	ID	DEATH YEAR
GARGAN					
Catherine	69	IRL	3700		1900
Edward	68	IRL	705		1901
John J.	65	AME	7212		1902
Theresa V.	33	SF	7628		1902
GARGARO					
Domenico				Jan	1899
GARGONVICH					
Antonio	21	DAL	2932		1866
GARHART					
William	1829	PA	701c		1904
GARIBALDA					
Emelia	3	SF	125		1870
GARIBALDI					
A. T., c/o				Aug	1898
Eugenia	<1	SF	6240a		1895
Frederico	1	SF	6052		1902
Lorenzo	20	ITA	9097		1901
Lucca	35		6346		1900
Maria	52	ITA	2223		1873
Maria	<1	SF	5271		1896
Maria Rosa	2	SF	380		1901
Norma	6	CA	1909		1894
S./S., c/o				Nov	1899
Sarah	32	SF	1692		1903
GARIBAY					
Catalina	1	SF	2764a		1872
GARIN					
John	80	IRL	3237		1894
Nellie Matilda	28	SF	670		1894
GARISON					
Elizabeth				Aug	1898
GARITY					
Catherine	77	IRL	1037a		1871

NAME	AGE OR YOB.	BIRTH PLACE	CERT. NO	ID	DEATH YEAR
Phillip	82	IRE	3969		1867
GARLAND					
Abbie A.	46	NH	1336b		1895
F. A.	44	ME	9957		1868
Fred Curtis	<1	CA	585		1900
Patrick	64	IRL	2233		1894
GARLAND (OR GRIVES)					
William C.	21	CA	4389	Dec	1901
GARLICK					
Fannie	69	GER	5998		1904
GARLINDI					
Carmen	32	MEX	835		1870
GARLISCH					
Fredrick A.	22	GER	2106		1866
GARME					
Gamans/Kitty, c/o	<1	SF	8190		1904
GARMELAND					
Frances	56	FRA	4786a		1895
GARMON					
Elbert	30	MO	3986		1903
GARNBACK					
A.	65	GER	4383a		1895
GARNEAU					
Ella Theresa	14	SF	4591a		1895
Gaspar	3	SF	2337		1873
Gaspard	73	CAN	8610		1900
GARNER					
Frederick				Oct	1899
William F.				Nov	1898
GARNETT					
John	70	NY	3240		1903
Lewis A.	79	VA	9647		1901
Marion Lee	3	SF	254		1870

Key: a = 1st part of year; b = 2nd part of year; c = death certificate copy; c/o = child of

NAME	AGE OR YOB.	BIRTH PLACE	CERT. NO	ID	DEATH YEAR	NAME	AGE OR YOB.	BIRTH PLACE	CERT. NO	ID	DEATH YEAR
GARNETTE						**GARRETT**					
Lydia G.				Nov	1898	Annie	57	ENG	813		1903
						Celestia H.	43	IA	6159		1904
GARNIER						Evaline Mabel				Nov	1899
Alphonse	58	FRA	7213		1902	Francis G.	68	ENG	9147		1901
Emily				Jul	1899	Frederick	60	ENG	4450		1902
Frederick	64	FRA	978		1901	James	1846	ENG	2947c		1904
GARNIL						James H.			2322		1866
Alma	<1	SF	2945		1895	Julia				Aug	1899
GARNION						Lionel William	5	SF	5030		1902
Andrew	30	NGR	1156		1869	Martha Jane	71	MO	1769		1903
GARNISS						May	34	CA	1836		1903
James Rodgers	73	NY	620		1902	Minnie	35	CA	6317		1903
GARONE						Peter G. (soldier)			7589		1901
John	70	ENG	8381		1901	Robert S.				Aug	1898
GARRAND						Samuel	1849	IRE	748c		1904
Gabriel D.	39	SF	7468		1903	Samuel R.	<1	CA	503b		1872
GARRARD						Sidney T.				Feb	1900
Hatsell	43	CAN	6131		1902	Thomas	45	SF	6529		1903
Jean	36	FRA	1096		1866	W. M./S. L., c/o	<1	SF	2778		1894
GARRATT						**GARRETTY**					
Catherine	62	ENG	1046a		1871	John				Oct	1899
Harry B.	40	SF	5833		1902	**GARRIAS**					
Mary B.	2	KY	1691		1870	Martha	20	CHI	1024		1870
GARRAUD						**GARRIBLE**					
Alexander J. V.	41	SF	1011		1903	Amanda	44	CA	6566		1900
Alexander L.	1	SF	359b		1895	**GARRIC**					
Zelia	29	NV	1516b		1895	E.	40	FRA	754b		1871
GARRELSON						**GARRICK**					
Jane H.	85	CT	3519		1903	James H.	1859	ENG	1592c		1904
GARREN						**GARRIDO**					
Louis	73	AUS	2108		1903	Albert	16	CA	6759	Feb	1901
GARRETSON						**GARRIGAN**					
John De Witt	60	NY	4341		1901	Edward	24	CA	143		1902

Key: a = 1st part of year; b = 2nd part of year;
c = death certificate copy; c/o = child of

NAME	AGE OR YOB.	BIRTH PLACE	CERT. NO	ID	DEATH YEAR
Margaret	13	SF	2363		1873
Mary	1	SF	1349b		1872
GARRIGUES					
Anton/Blanche, c/o		SF	8640		1903
Melanie	33	FRA	2271		1901
GARRIOCK					
Earnest	20	ENG	7897		1903
GARRISON					
A. G.	38	UT	1339		1900
Frank L.				Mar	1900
Mary Ann	50	NJ	1237		1869
GARRITSEN					
Henry	65	HOL	1836		1894
GARRITY					
Ann	50	IRL	2696		1895
Anne	52	IRL	6032a		1895
Edward Peter	1	SF	7010		1904
Hannah M.	1847	MA	320c		1904
Henry T.	11	SF	1420		1902
Katherine R.	30	IRE	115		1903
Martin	45	USA	5445		1904
Owen	46	IRL	2348a		1872
Patrick	49	IRE	1123		1869
Patrick	67	IRL	2731		1900
Peter	57	MA	1624		1902
Thomas	34	CA	5988		1896
GARRONE					
Felix	53	FRA	279b		1872
GARRY					
Catherine				Jan	1900
Margarett	4	SF	1073		1869
Mary				Mar	1900
Michael				Nov	1898
Thomas		SF	1097		1869

NAME	AGE OR YOB.	BIRTH PLACE	CERT. NO	ID	DEATH YEAR
GARSIDE					
Catherine Mary	50	IRE	5734		1902
GARSON					
Andrew, Mrs.	58	BAV	6566a		1895
Henry	59	GER	5844	Jan	1901
Jane	1849	IRE	2109c		1904
GARTELMANN					
Catharina	29	GER	1019b		1871
GARTHORNE					
George Henry, Jr.	15	CA	2843		1895
GARTHWAITE					
Richard	41	ENG	5359		1867
GARTLAND					
Bernard	77	IRE	5608		1902
Patrick	1848	IRE	2892c		1904
GARTLEMANN					
Henry				Jun	1899
GARTLEY					
Sarah J.	55	IA	933		1903
GARTMAN					
Robert (soldier)	35	SWT	4336		1901
GARTNER					
Banni	30	GER	1664b		1871
Charles	62	GER	3017	Oct	1901
John C.	21		7866		1900
GARTNETT					
Morris	65		1913		1900
GARTZ					
William	4	WIN	9958		1868
GARUCON					
Edw./Birdie, c/o				Jul	1898
GARVAN					
John	2	MT	6380		1904

Key: a = 1st part of year; b = 2nd part of year; c = death certificate copy; c/o = child of

NAME	AGE OR YOB.	BIRTH PLACE	CERT. NO	ID	DEATH YEAR
Rosa	1882	CHL	1199c		1904
GARVEY					
——		SF	883		1870
Catherine	30	IRL	598		1871
Catherine	57	IRL	3035a		1872
David S.	33	IRL	2033		1894
Francis				Feb	1900
James (soldier)			5486	Jan	1901
James Monroe	72	NY	262		1900
John (soldier)			7116		1900
Julia	65	IRE	4317		1902
Mary				Mar	1900
Steven	2	SF	1046		1868
William	40	CA	7918		1903
William	72	IRE	3635		1903
William B.	38	NY	1658		1900
GARVIE					
George	26	SCT	686b		1895
GARVILLE					
Francois	45	FRA	4414b		1870
GARVIN					
——			1899		1870
Annie Mary	<1	SF	8205		1903
Cathrine	<1	SF	6059		1867
Theo. G. (soldier)			1179		1901
Thomas C.	35	NY	1257		1869
William	57	NY	8290		1904
GARVISH					
Carlos	78	NH	4719		1903
GARWIN					
Timothy	40	IRE	5643		1867
GARWOOD					
William F.	1	SF	9763		1868
Wm. Thomson	65	PA	3413		1902
GARY					
Peter E.	1	SF	4097		1896
GARZOLI					
Peter				Mar	1900
GASCHLIN					
Francis	79	SWT	3550		1902
GASHIN					
George J.	<1	SF	5103		1867
GASKER					
Joseph	19	FRA	1355b		1871
GASKILL					
Chas. C.				Jul	1898
Ellen	74	NY	4803		1903
Hattie	41	ME	3743a		1895
GASKIN					
Annie	<1	SF	7969		1868
J. P.				Nov	1898
GASPAR					
Frank Cardoza	1881	POR	540c		1904
GASPARI					
Carmella	<1	SF	650		1900
Louis	56	FRA	35		1870
GASPER					
George Frank	45	SF	1237		1903
Lucy Ellenede	40	CA	1458		1902
GASQUET					
Horace	68	FRA	3735		1896
GASS					
James			6410	Feb	1901
Joseph M.	59	FRA	9299		1868
Julius A.	43	GER	6601	Feb	1901
Pauline	1857	GER	2795c		1904

NAME	AGE OR YOB.	BIRTH PLACE	CERT. NO	ID	DEATH YEAR
GASSERT					
Elizabeth	10	SF	2161		1866
W.	40		6123		1904
GASSMAN					
Theodore	45	GER	8091		1900
GASSMANN					
Anna Amelia	<1	SF	191b		1872
Emelie	60	FRA	8161		1901
John Baptiste				Mar	1899
GASSNER					
Alfred Joseph				Nov	1899
GASTIGER					
Emile	1876	GER	3262c		1904
GASTOLDI					
Ed	1860	ITA	3125c		1904
GASTON					
Harry F.	1	SF	3692		1870
Hugh A.	52	NJ	6752		1868
John W.	1859	CA	1042c		1904
GASTRO					
Joseph	18	POR	9625		1868
GATELEY					
Delia	68	IRL	9148		1901
GATELY					
Alice				Oct	1899
Anna	<1	SF	1020		1868
Catherine	63	IRL	990		1894
Charles C.	9	SF	9143		1868
Frank (soldier)			2054		1901
James	29	NY	1432		1869
James J.	28	CA	G61		1885
John	70	IRE	3138		1903
Joseph	5	SF	1222		1869
Mamie	36	SF	6491		1900

NAME	AGE OR YOB.	BIRTH PLACE	CERT. NO	ID	DEATH YEAR
Martin	62	IRL	2538		1873
Mary	34	IRE	6263		1867
Patrick J.	50	IRL	2765		1895
T. I.	36	IRE	534		1866
Thomas B.	68	IRE	7619		1903
William	80	IRL	2281		1873
William	28	NY	2415		1866
GATES					
A. L.				Apr	1899
Augusta Elmira	54	NY	3703		1903
Charles Raymond	1904		193c		1904
Doratha	<1	SF	3679		1867
Edwin/Mabel, c/o	1	SF	1924		1903
Emery P.	37	CA	7705		1904
Emmarilia M.	51	IA	3430		1902
George K.	31	AL	2954		1902
Hanna K.	55	NY	199a		1871
Hannah M.	24	MA	1382		1869
John	29	PA	1702		1870
Orpha	33	NY	3321a		1872
GATEWOOD					
George (soldier)			7214		1900
GATH					
John	34	HAN	3447a		1872
GATIER					
Francis E.	51	FRA	732		1900
GATIN					
Maurice	7	CAN	8084		1901
GATLEY					
Maggie	28	CA	2273		1894
Richard/Mary, c/o	<1	SF	8915		1901
GATLIN					
Cyril	<1	SF	8357		1900

Key: a = 1st part of year; b = 2nd part of year;
c = death certificate copy; c/o = child of

NAME	AGE OR YOB.	BIRTH PLACE	CERT. NO	ID	DEATH YEAR	NAME	AGE OR YOB.	BIRTH PLACE	CERT. NO	ID	DEATH YEAR
GATLKAU						**GAUCKLE**					
Max	8	IL	546		1894	Lena	32	GER	4457		1896
GATMAN						**GAUDENZIA**					
Rachael				Oct	1898	James/Virginia, c/o	1	SF	5881		1904
GATTANINI						**GAUGHAN**					
Guiseppe	<1	CA	9272		1901	James (soldier)			2216		1903
GATTE						**GAUGHOM**					
John	<1	SF	461 b		1872	Catherine		SF	4114b		1870
GATTER						**GAUGHRAN**					
Frederick	34	GER	7045		1902	James	1835	IRE	513 c		1904
GATTO						John					1898
Ernesto	2	SF	4318		1902	**GAUL**					
Giambattisti				Oct	1899	David	4	SF	1815b		1872
Guiseppe	62	ITA	3311		1873	James	65	IRL	6396		1896
John				Nov	1899	John	38	IRE	6853		1868
Mamie				Nov	1899	Thomas Francis	1904	SF	3395c		1904
Maria	46	ITA	7843		1900	**GAULD**					
Risa	38	ITA	3976a		1895	Annie	27	SCT	5957a		1895
Tinna	18	SF	6019a		1895	James A.	49	SCT	8304		1900
GATTOL						**GAULENSAK**					
Aurelu L.	19	PAN	6503		1904	Johann Martin	67	GER	1798		1900
GATZE						**GAULEY**					
Otto	38	GER	1093		1900	James A.	50	NY	1358		1869
GAUBATZ						James A.	49	NY	1359		1869
Freida	23	GER	5934		1896	Margarette M.	1	OH	1247		1869
William	26	GER	5912		1896	**GAULINA**					
William George	<1	SF	977		1894	Babtish	42	ITA	G36		1884
GAUBERT						**GAULT**					
Joseph	1831	FRA	2436c		1904	Thomas E. (soldier)	60	NC	4797		1904
GAUCH						**GAUNON**					
Katie	31	CA	3893		1896	Elizabeth				Aug	1898
Welhelmina	59	GER	2805		1901	Tony				Feb	1899
GAUCHET											
Thiebauld	23	FRA	1373		1869						

NAME	AGE OR YOB.	BIRTH PLACE	CERT. NO	ID	DEATH YEAR
GAUSMAN					
Juan Antonio	2	CA	1105b		1872
GAUTER					
Charles A.					1899
Frank				Jan	1899
GAUTIER					
Conrad (soldier)			1457		1901
Marie Louise	<1	SF	5857		1867
GAVALN					
Bridget	85	IRL	3486b		1870
GAVAN					
Dominick	44	IRE	4399		1867
GAVEEN					
——		SF	2909		1866
GAVELY					
Frank R.				Mar	1900
GAVEN					
Bernard				Jun	1899
Irene					1899
John	46	NY	5894		1896
GAVER					
John	78	MD	2338		1903
Rebecca	1822	MD	2796c		1904
GAVETE					
Alfred	54	FRA	G85		1887
GAVIGAN					
Marlin	53	IRL	1671b		1895
Thomas (soldier)			2053		1901
GAVIN					
——			7277		1868
Ellen	29	IRE	7341		1868
Ellen	41	NY	7652		1901
James J.	38	IRL	G1		1882
Lizzy	<1	SF	5201		1867

NAME	AGE OR YOB.	BIRTH PLACE	CERT. NO	ID	DEATH YEAR
Mary	76	IRE	4595		1903
Mary Ann	1	SF	6145		1867
Mary Ellen	22	SF	5334		1903
Mary J.	25	SF	8707		1903
Michael B.				Nov	1899
Patrick	69	IRE	3910		1903
Rose	50	IRL	4117		1900
Thomas	<1	CA	1281		1869
Wm. Henry	38	CA	2801		1902
GAVITT					
Capt. George H.	49	RI	1946a		1872
Elvy H.	42	ENG	G6		1882
GAVRAN					
John	5	SF	3439a		1872
GAY					
Charles	76	MA	3077		1902
Elizabeth	48	ENG	3100		1894
Elmira L.	73	MA	2618		1895
Frederick	<1	SF	4910		1901
Houn	32	CHN	1877		1870
James L.	<1	SF	4394		1867
Jenette Mary				Jan	1899
John G.	70	SCT	1619b		1895
Lincoln G. (soldier)			7306		1901
Lucy	16	CA	G19		1883
Margaret T.				Aug	1899
Peter	43	FRA	2505		1900
Sophia M.	27	ENG	323b		1871
Theobald				Feb	1900
GAYA					
Wm.	37	SF	1340		1900
GAYER					
Henry H.				Mar	1900
GAYLER					
Newton A.	78	VT	2337b		1895

Key: a = 1st part of year; b = 2nd part of year;
c = death certificate copy; c/o = child of

NAME	AGE OR YOB.	BIRTH PLACE	CERT. NO	ID	DEATH YEAR
GAYLOR					
Edward	<1		1185		1901
GAYLORD					
Charles Manford	11	NE	9697		1901
Christopher	59	ENG	5576		1904
Edward P.	61	NY	1640b		1895
Wm. H.	46	NY	G13		1882
GAYMOT					
Jean	6	SF	2293		1894
GAYNE					
Robert	35	MA	8135		1868
GAYNOR					
Annie	50	IRL	3350		1896
Catherine	68	IRL	4282		1900
Martin	75	IRE	4370		1902
Mary				Oct	1899
Mathew	38	IRE	5539		1867
Patrick W.	67	IRL	2647		1900
William Henry	4	SF	84b		1872
GAYNORD					
Edward	45	IRL	2859a		1872
GAZARI					
Antone	24	AUT	G38		1884
GAZELL					
John				Aug	1899
GAZELLE					
Mittie Smith	28	TX	8601		1904
GAZIN					
Marie Godal					1898
GAZZARA					
Giosue	51	ITA	784		1901
GE					
Chung	38	CHN	2600		1895
En Lui				Nov	1899
Hue Loy	25	CHN	1883b		1895
Ka Wah				Nov	1899
Pok	30	CHN	3452		1896
Sing Chung	61	CHN	2197b		1895
You	35	CHN	4325		1896
GEAN					
Edward	<1	SF	2234		1901
GEANEY					
Ellen	83	IRE	7568		1903
GEANNETTE					
Katherine	2	SF	8532		1901
GEARE					
Ira	1	SF	1621		1900
GEARHARDT					
William	60	GER	8685		1904
GEARHART					
Roy F. (soldier)			2060		1901
GEARING					
——		SF	481		1870
GEARTY					
James	64	IRE	4869		1904
GEARY					
——			1359		1870
Bridget E.					1898
Catharine A.	2	OR	3364		1873
Cathrine	<1	SF	4893		1867
Daniel	22	ME	1271		1869
Edward D.	15	IL	1205		1903
Edward P.	<1	SF	505		1870
Ellen	32	IRL	424a		1871
Francis L.	4	CA	299		1870
Henry Joseph	42	MA	509		1903
Henry T.	70	IRL	2888		1900
James				Mar	1900

Key: *a = 1st part of year; b = 2nd part of year;*
c = death certificate copy; c/o = child of

NAME	AGE OR YOB.	BIRTH PLACE	CERT. NO	ID	DEATH YEAR
Jas. M.				Jan	1900
Jennie				Jan	1900
Jeremiah J.	78	IRL	8363		1900
John A.	<1	SF	1108b		1895
John Daniel				Oct	1898
John Doe				Jul	1898
John Henry	14	NY	2028		1866
Kate	<1	SF	1973		1866
Kate F.	43	MA	1942b		1895
Mary S.					1898
Michael	46	NY	1185		1869
Mollie Frances					1898
Woodbridge				Mar	1900
GEBBELS					
Bertha	60	GER	3371		1894
GEBEL					
Grace Dorothy	1	SF	8285		1903
GEBHARD					
Frederick G.	69	GER	6295		1900
GEBHARDT					
A.	22	MO	1441b		1872
Anna Marie	72	GER	2024		1901
Fred	34	SF	5830		1896
John	74	GER	825		1903
Mathilda Julia	36	CA	7956		1900
Michael	23	CA	882		1900
Theresia	65	GER	4611		1896
GEBHART					
Henrietta	2	SF	833		1866
GEBREY					
James	58	LA	2629		1894
GECKLER					
John				Jul	1899

NAME	AGE OR YOB.	BIRTH PLACE	CERT. NO	ID	DEATH YEAR
GEDDER					
Albert	44	GER	4841a		1895
GEDDES					
Alexander	37	IA	2064		1870
Alexander M.	27	NY	1848		1870
Charles	83	NS	3724		1903
Elizabeth	<1	SF	999a		1871
George	1837	NS	112c		1904
George G.	30	NS	1112		1870
Margaret La Rose	31	CA	6160		1904
Samuel				Feb	1900
William M.	5	SF	4372b		1870
GEE					
Ah	35	CHN	30b		1871
Ah	25	CHN	1904		1866
Ah	35	CHN	4969		1867
Ah	30	CHN	1256		1869
Ah	27	CHN	1414		1869
Ah	27	CHN	5495		1867
Ah Way				Jan	1900
Ah Wing	51	CHN	5371		1902
Aug Yit				Aug	1898
Bing Lang				Oct	1899
Cang Chung	50	CHN	2870		1894
Charley	58	CHN	7616		1904
Chong				D	1898
Chong Kwong	56	CHN	3551		1902
Chow				D	1899
Chow Kam	<1	SF	6530		1903
Chung	19	SF	891		1901
Chung				Jan	1900
Chung Chow				Nov	1898
Coy	75	CHN	4283		1901
Di	26	CHN	6184a		1895
Epp				Oct	1898

NAME	AGE OR YOB.	BIRTH PLACE	CERT. NO	ID	DEATH YEAR	NAME	AGE OR YOB.	BIRTH PLACE	CERT. NO	ID	DEATH YEAR
Fong	51	CHN	7291		1902	P./C., c/o	<1	SF	3405		1894
Foo	32	CHN	6878		1895	Poan	51	CHN	7740		1902
Foo				Jan	1899	Poch	24	CHN	3197		1902
Frank	1	CA	465b		1895	Pong	35	CHN	G71		1886
Ge How				Oct	1899	Ring	58	CHN	1910		1894
Gee Slue	54	CHN	4969		1904	Shew	46	CHN	3222		1902
Gong	39	CHN	30		1902	Tin Chung	32	CHN	3241		1894
Goy				Nov	1898	Tin Yee	50	CHN	7761		1900
Guey	44	CHN	5723		1903	Tong Chung	60	CHN	6514a		1895
Gun (or Yuen) Jue	50	CHN	1235		1902	Tung				Jul	1898
Hee Shen	61	CHN	4874		1904	Un	40	CHN	3508a		1872
Ho	33	CHN	357		1870	Ung	28	CHN	152		1865
Hoo Chu	50	CHN	5416		1902	Wah				Dec	1899
How				Dec	1899	Wah On	46	CHN	6372		1902
How Hong				Jan	1900	Wm./Nellie, c/o	<1	SF	1315		1895
Hung	49	CHN	2442		1903	Wm./Nellie, c/o	<1	SF	1316		1895
Hung	59	CHN	4314		1901	Yon Gee				Oct	1899
Jan	41	CHN	1663		1866	Young	61	CHN	2160		1866
Jang				Feb	1899	**GEER**					
Jay Young	48	CHN	3343	Nov	1901	Richard	72	ENG	5483a		1895
Jin	53	CHN	1443		1900	**GEFFE**					
Ka Yen	25	CHN	1236		1902	Charles	44	GER	3677		1896
Kay Yuen	47	CHN	5357		1903	**GEFFKE**					
Kee Gi	42	CHN	3987		1903	Margarethe	75	GER	6226		1902
Kee Quork	41	CHN	1641		1901	**GEFFS**					
Ki Wah				Jul	1899	Henry D.			3820		1902
Kim Wook	1	CA	7526		1901	**GEFKEN**					
Lew Wah	54	CHN	6804		1904	Helen				Nov	1898
Lim				Oct	1899	**GEFOROS**					
Long Eue	38	CHN	3881		1870	George	27	GRE	5505		1904
Lunn				May	1899	**GEGEN**					
Millicent	77	ENG	4624		1901	Margaret	<1	SF	1743		1866
Ming	37	CHN	8483		1900	**GEGGUS**					
Mon On Shee	60	CHN	4515		1903	Nanny	40	GER	699		1894
Mon Yee				Oct	1899						
Mun	40	CHN	9668		1868						

NAME	AGE OR YOB.	BIRTH PLACE	CERT. NO	ID	DEATH YEAR	NAME	AGE OR YOB.	BIRTH PLACE	CERT. NO	ID	DEATH YEAR
GEGHEN						David	<1	SF	4717		1896
Edward	1865	IRE	2184c		1904	William C.					Nov 1899
GEGNAT						**GEIKE**					
Marie Victorine	30	FRA	132b		1872	Richard					Oct 1899
GEGOETROUSIEE						**GEIL**					
Gustave	<1	SF	1311		1894	Christine					Mar 1900
GEGOX						**GEILER**					
Conrad F.					Jan 1900	Andrew	42	GER	2641		1873
GEHAGAN						**GEILS**					
Christina	<1	SF	589b		1872	Carrie	51	AL	3843a		1895
GEHERTY						Catherine	54	GER	1496		1900
Julia					Jan 1899	Clara H.	1	SF	1418		1869
GEHL						Elenora Helena	<1	SF	3492a		1872
Louis	72	GER	2293		1900	**GEIMANN**					
GEHRELS						William F.					Jan 1899
Wilhelm A.	33	GER	5472		1867	**GEINDLACK**					
GEHRET						Fritz					Jul 1898
Sophie	61	SWT	7417		1903	**GEININI**					
GEHRICKE						John	14	SF	1087		1869
Frances Cunningham	66	PA	4441		1903	**GEIS**					
GEHRIG						Henry	60	GER	7515		1902
Ferdinand					May 1899	**GEISE**					
GEHRING						Henry A.	61	GER	1986a		1872
Theodore (soldier)			4542		1901	**GEISEENDORFER**					
GEHRKE						Frederick	1	SF	955b		1871
Charles	24	GER	4788		1902	**GEISEL**					
GEIB						John	38	GER	6592		1868
Christine					Mar 1900	**GEISHACKER**					
Edward	<1	SF	5656a		1895	Mary	65	IRL	1696		1901
GEICK						Matthias					Mar 1899
Johann Frederick	79	GER	4090		1902	**GEISINGER**					
GEIGER						Lydia M.	46	OH	2527		1902
Andrew	49	GER	861b		1871						

Key: a = 1st part of year; b = 2nd part of year;
c = death certificate copy; c/o = child of

NAME	AGE OR YOB.	BIRTH PLACE	CERT. NO	ID	DEATH YEAR
GEISSLER					
Joseph				Jan	1899
GEIT					
Christine				Mar	1900
GEITE					
Ah	25	CHN	3494b		1870
GEITNER					
R./K., c/o		SF	6354		1895
GEIU					
Un	33	CHN	8487		1868
GEIZEL					
Balzar W.	30	GER	G73		1886
GEL					
Jno.	37	SCT	G37		1884
GELBAR					
Isaack	1902	SF	321c		1904
GELBART					
Margaretha	51	ENG	5785a		1895
GELES					
George P.				Jan	1900
GELINANCE					
John	41	FRA	1173		1869
GELINAS					
Mary J. L.	<1	CA	3450b		1870
GELINI					
Maria	3	NY	6284		1904
GELLEN					
Dominick				Jan	1900
GELLERT					
Louis	74	GER	5388		1901
Mary	42	GER	1571		1894
Yetta	70	GER	6102		1896

NAME	AGE OR YOB.	BIRTH PLACE	CERT. NO	ID	DEATH YEAR
GELLISS					
Ada T.	<1	SF	2532a		1872
GELOWSKY					
Louisa, c/o	<1	SF	1361		1869
GEMIGNIANI					
Deonisiso/Clementina, c/o	1	SF	65		1903
GEMINANI					
Louis	<1	SF	1870b		1872
GEN					
Ah	25	CHN	1590		1870
Ah	34	CHN	3054		1870
Li	50	CHN	8519		1900
Tong Gin				Nov	1899
Young				Nov	1899
GENDAR					
Edward F.	90	NY	3472		1903
John A.	<1	SF	2912		1902
John W.	58	NY	7860		1904
Josephine E.	<1	SF	9218		1868
GENDOTTI					
Marguerite A.	12	FRA	5904		1896
Theresa	19	CA	7817		1901
GENE					
Mary D.	51	CT	2752		1894
GENERTICK					
Julius	68	GER	5386		1901
GENESER					
Mon Chung	27	CHN	1515b		1895
Waller	<1	SF	1458b		1895
GENEVE					
Louis	75	FRA	2009b		1895
GENEVIEVE					
	1	SF	4845		1904
Vincentia	1904	SF	1376c		1904

Key: a = 1st part of year; b = 2nd part of year;
c = death certificate copy; c/o = child of

NAME	AGE OR YOB.	BIRTH PLACE	CERT. NO	ID	DEATH YEAR
GENGETTE					
Joseph	66	CAN	8365		1900
GENGNAGEL					
Jacob	61	MD	5843	Jan	1901
GENICH					
Anton	37	SWT	853b		1872
GENILLER					
Gabriel	35	FRA	771a		1871
GENKEBBERGER					
Maggie	1	SF	1352		1869
GENOLA					
Teresa				Nov	1898
GENOS					
Joseph	68	POR	7373		1903
GENOVESSA					
Gesfino	7	ITA	645		1901
GENRICH					
Gertrude T.				May	1899
GENSLER					
Michael	71	GER	2267		1902
GENSOSEL					
Edward Leon	3	SF	1240		1869
GENSTA					
——			5327		1867
GENSWINDT					
Margaret	68	IRL	6253		1896
GENTH					
Charles	51	PA	3271		1903
Joseph	32	OH	462		1870
GENTHNER					
Gustave	27	ME	8639		1868
Sarah	3	SF	8910		1868

NAME	AGE OR YOB.	BIRTH PLACE	CERT. NO	ID	DEATH YEAR
GENTILI					
Evristo	30	ITA	1693		1903
GENTRY					
Cornelius F. (soldier)			4543		1901
Kate	73	GER	1380		1903
GENTY					
Amelia	59	FRA	3228		1900
John	72	IRL	5008a		1895
GENZEL					
Martha	61	GER	5166		1904
GENZEN					
A. Mary	35	GER	3965		1896
GEO					
Mun Lee Chee	20	CA	3171		1900
Wan Woo	49	CHN	8198		1900
GEOFFROY					
Leon	1852	FRA	2375c		1904
Margaret	47	PA	3363	Nov	1901
GEOGER					
William C. (soldier)			1087		1900
GEOHAGAN					
Michael	71	IRL	2898		1901
GEON					
Lenong				Dec	1899
Liuong				Dec	1899
GEONEY					
Jeremiah, Jr.	1888	SF	2981c		1904
Jeremiah, Jr.	1888	sf	2981c		1904
GEONG					
leo	51	CHN	7611		1900
GEORGE					
——	<1	SF	7108		1868
——	<1	SF	3344		1894

Key: a = 1st part of year; b = 2nd part of year;
c = death certificate copy; c/o = child of

NAME	AGE OR YOB.	BIRTH PLACE	CERT. NO	ID	DEATH YEAR
Ameboi	2	GRE	5465a		1895
Antone				Feb	1900
Augustus	1	CA	1113		1903
Charles	<1	SF	5086		1867
Christ	56	GRE	222		1900
Eliza	42	NY	1483		1870
Ermina	60	GER	G5		1882
Francis S.	37	CAN	1697		1894
Harvey	76	NY	7816		1901
Henry Cowell	67	ME	1609		1901
<Japanese>	17	JPN	5992	Jan	1901
John A.	5	CA	3316		1866
Joseph	<1	SF	366b		1871
L.		SF	558a		1870
Martha	<1	CA	5787		1896
Mary Annetta	55	PA	6318		1903
Max	6	SF	1859		1866
Ming	42	CHN	6558a		1895
Peter	40	GER	867		1866
Peter	46	GRE	1925		1903
Pierre	68	FRA	792b		1895
Rosa	64	POR	6381		1904
Russell M.	<1	SF	3515		1896
Thomas W.	16	MA	7507		1868
Wesley	65	SC	2078b		1895
GEORGESON					
Louis C.				Feb	1899
GEORGI					
Masoero	40	ITA	4564		1901
GEORGIANA					
——	1	CA	6732		1904
Antonia	<1	SF	6194		1867
GEORGIANNA					
Isadora	<1	SF	1065		1869
GEOSTH					
M./S., c/o	<1	SF	3075		1894
GEOU					
Tin On	60	CHN	23		1900
GEOVELT					
——			7674		1868
GEOVRNI					
Porfiarate	7	ITA	1400		1870
GEPHARDT					
Louis	31	NY	7039		1904
GEPHRENSON					
Charles L.	26	LA	8005		1868
GEPPERT					
George W.	1878	OH	998c		1904
GERABERK					
Frank	71	HUN	7335		1900
GERAGHTY					
Annie	40	IRL	360b		1895
Annie Kristine	71	IRE	8249		1904
John	7	SF	885		1870
John J.				Dec	1898
Patrick	1856	IRE	772c		1904
GERAHTY					
James P.	1	SF	9437		1868
GERALD					
David V.	31	RI	585a		1871
GERANAND					
Wm.	38	GER	4627a		1895
GERARD					
Ausgustine	6	SF	8035		1868
Frank R.	59	SWT	2025		1901
Julian				Feb	1899
Marcel	47	FRA	7649		1900

Key: a = 1st part of year; b = 2nd part of year; c = death certificate copy; c/o = child of

NAME	AGE OR YOB.	BIRTH PLACE	CERT. NO	ID	DEATH YEAR	NAME	AGE OR YOB.	BIRTH PLACE	CERT. NO	ID	DEATH YEAR
GERARDI						GERDINE					
Accursco	15	ITA	8312		1903	Michael O.	30	SWE	8472		1868
Josephine	19	SF	1714		1900	GERDING					
Maria Rosa	78	ITA	8946		1903	Henry	1869	GER	2158c		1904
Martha	37	SF	5501a		1895	Lizetta	64	GER	1793		1901
Vita	2	NY	8473		1903						
						GERDIS					
GERARDIN						Carsten	59	GER	255b		1895
Marie	37	FRA	1169a		1871	GERE					
						Mary Ann	6	SF	1861		1903
GERASCH											
Fredrich	32	GER	6620		1868	GEREKEN					
						Elizabethe Margarethe H.	6	SF	1475b		1872
GERASKOWSKY											
alias Eskey Charles	45	RUS	793b		1895	GERET					
						Robert J. L.	2	SF	5033		1867
GERATY											
Patrick W.	34	IRL	230b		1871	GEREY					
						John	47	ENG	8067		1868
GERBER											
Catherine	66	GER	8297		1901	GERGOSTATHIS					
Jerre B.	79	ALS	5561a		1895	Dimitrius	19	GRE	1974		1902
Mathew	22	GER	1200		1900						
						GERGUS					
GERBERDING						August	43	GER	3206Nov		1901
Albert	50	SF	6954		1902						
Mary J.	77	VA	1405		1903	GERHARD					
						August /Nellie, c/o	1904	SF	113		1904
GERCKE						F.	38	PRU	6680		1868
Amelia	68	GER	9591		1901						
Charles William	70	GER	9513		1901	GERHARDT					
Minna	1845	GER	2376c		1904	Caroline				Jul	1898
						Charles	68	GER	8641		1903
GERCKEN						Katharine	85	GER	1366		1902
Ernest H.	65	GER	3473		1902						
William F.	59	GER	7229		1903	GERHARDY					
						Charles	34	GER	1530b		1871
GERDES						Henry P.	34	SF	8622		1900
John	37	GER	2314		1901						
Lena A.	19	SF	861		1903	GERHOW					
Maria	45	GER	G57		1885	Gertrude E.	<1	SF	4003		1896
Sarah Maude	1	SF	1012		1903	GERICHTEN					
						Anna P.	27	GER	7862		1868

Key: a = 1st part of year; b = 2nd part of year;
c = death certificate copy; c/o = child of

NAME	AGE OR YOB.	BIRTH PLACE	CERT. NO	ID	DEATH YEAR	NAME	AGE OR YOB.	BIRTH PLACE	CERT. NO	ID	DEATH YEAR
GERIN						**GERLECIDE**					
Jacob	4	SF	1255		1869	Leonora	<1	SF	6699		1900
GERING						**GERLOFF**					
Wm.	52	GER	G88		1887	Franze A.	1904	SF	3007c		1904
Wm., c/o	<1	SF	1247b		1872	Fritz Heinrich J.				Jan	1899
GERION						**GERMAIN**					
Domingo	36	SPA	759		1866	Henry	74	MA	G41		1885
GERISHTEN						**GERMAN**					
Anna C. P.	<1	SF	6105		1867	Reyes Silvas de	50	MEX	4000		1900
GERITTE						**GERMANSEN**					
——			9933		1868	Kroslet	<1	SF	1725		1900
GERITY						**GERMINI**					
Joseph P.	<1	SF	1020		1868	Denis	40	SWT	2214		1873
GERKASSKY						**GERNANDT**					
Max/Glate, c/o	1904	SF	2672		1904	George	5	SF	5667		1902
GERKEL						Henry	2	CA	4477		1904
——			1019		1868	**GERNER**					
GERKEN						Frances, c/o	<1	CA	536		1900
Henry				Nov	1898	**GERNET**					
Metta	78	GER	5677		1904	Otto	19	PA	7827		1900
Peter	42	GER	2450		1866	**GERNIGNANI**					
GERKIN						Dionisio/Clementina, c/o		SF	2767		1900
Henry				Mar	1899	**GEROGHTY**					
GERLACH						Bernard	47	IRL	180b		1872
Anna Margaretha	58	GER	4915		1904	**GEROLAN**					
Conrad	??	GER	5162a		1895	Jule	35	FRA	1377		1869
Edward	32	DC	9698		1901	**GEROLANI**					
Elizabeth	47	GER	5482		1896	Giovanni	23	ITA	4949		1903
Friedrich	80	GER	1294		1900	**GEROLD**					
G./C., c/o		SF	2282		1873	Philip	46	GER	G92		1889
Geo. E.	36	GER	G12		1882	**GERONE**					
George	49	GER	2816		1895	Alexandrina	47	FRA	2041		1870
John	26	MD	7436		1903						
John	60	GER	3199		1903						

NAME	AGE OR YOB.	BIRTH PLACE	CERT. NO	ID	DEATH YEAR	NAME	AGE OR YOB.	BIRTH PLACE	CERT. NO	ID	DEATH YEAR
GERRA						**GERSTERBENG**					
Encarnacion	51	MEX	1028		1868	——	<1	SF	3207		1870
GERRAN						**GERSTLE**					
Lizzie	1849		1766c		1904	Lewis	77	GER	3365		1902
Marcieu	38	FRA	4608a		1895	**GERSTMAYER**					
GERRARD						Bertha	1827	GER	1219c		1904
John Blaisdell	87	VT	6615Feb		1901	**GERSTNER**					
Lawrence	63	FRA	5344		1904	William	44	NY	5568		1896
GERRE						**GERTEL**					
Susie	30	SF	5938a		1895	Bertha	23	PRU	691		1866
GERRERA						**GERTRUDE**					
Raphael		SF	1713		1870	———	<1	SF	5252		1902
GERRIC						**GERTZ**					
M.	5	CA	G55		1885	Anna M.	63	IRL	1695		1901
GERRICK						Edward					Apr 1899
Frank (soldier)			347		1900	John (soldier)			3680		1900
GERRISH						**GERTZEN**					
Martha Ann	1829	MA	702c		1904	Johanna Dorathea	31	GER	3552		1902
GERRY						**GERVASI**					
Erna	1904	CA	1931c		1904	Vito					May 1899
John Henry	64	MA	4529		1901	**GERZ**					
GERSAN						Joseph	<1	SF	6726		1900
Esther	<1	SF	8529		1868	**GES**					
GERSHNER						William	50	Eng	2342		1894
John B.					Mar 1900	**GESCAS**					
GERSON						Manuel/Dolores, c/o		SF	4817		1902
Clara	1881	GER	347c		1904	**GESCH**					
GERST						Alice					Nov 1898
Garrison	65	GER	4464		1903	**GESSAD**					
GERSTENBERG						Harry	<1	SF	5216a		1895
Henrietta	<1	SF	1274		1869	**GESSAN**					
GERSTENBERGER						Amilda					Feb 1899
Paul					Feb 1900						

Key: a = 1st part of year; b = 2nd part of year;
c = death certificate copy; c/o = child of

NAME	AGE OR YOB.	BIRTH PLACE	CERT. NO	ID	DEATH YEAR	NAME	AGE OR YOB.	BIRTH PLACE	CERT. NO	ID	DEATH YEAR
GESSEN						GETTS					
——			2049		1866	Maria	<1	SF	3478b		1870
GESSIEN						GETTY					
Ot./W., c/o		SF	5225		1895	Annie	8	GER	462a		1871
GESSLER						Ellen	<1	SF	1120		1869
Charles	15	SF	7994		1904	Esther A.	85	NJ	4516		1903
GET						GETZ					
Fong	50	CHN	891b		1871	Joseph	60	PRU	6722		1896
GETCHEL						Mary A.	82	GER	138		1900
Mary	62	NY	8708		1903	GETZEL					
GETCHELL						Alfred Wilhelm Heinrich	<1	SF	1367		1902
Estella Catherine	22	CA	6699		1902	GEURARA					
James J.	69	ME	379		1901	Alphonse E. C.	66	CAN	2630		1894
Mary F.				May	1899	GEURIN					
McKinley	6		8678		1903	John	29	IRL	1979		1870
GETHERS						GEUTHNER					
William	1	CA	6693		1904	Margaret				Aug	1898
GETHINGS						GEVARA					
Catherine	76	IRE	7074		1902	Antonia	44	MEX	1959a		1872
GETLAON						GEVERSON					
Laura	<1	SF	360b		1871	Peter H.		SF	748		1870
GETOMADO						GEW					
——			1738		1870	Ah	31	CHN	1080b		1872
GETTEN						Do Hong	15	CA	785		1901
William	2	MA	2481		1866	Shoo				Feb	1899
GETTENS						GEYER					
Daniel	74	IRL	358		1900	Mary Louise	2	MN	1424		1869
GETTIGAN						Rena	21	CA	7964		1904
Winnay	24	NY	1016		1868	GHEEN					
GETTINGS						Matilda V.	<1	SF	1515		1866
Samuel A.	65	KY	3139		1903	GHEZZI					
GETTLESON						Guiseppe/Guiseppina,	c/o	SF	6285		1904
Louis	6	SF	1091		1869						

NAME	AGE OR YOB.	BIRTH PLACE	CERT. NO	ID	DEATH YEAR	NAME	AGE OR YOB.	BIRTH PLACE	CERT. NO	ID	DEATH YEAR
GHIBANDI						**GHISELIN**					
Raffaella	<1	SF	192b		1895	James T.	63	MD	4513		1896
GHIBARDUCCI						**GHISELLI**					
D. A., c/o				Nov	1898	Amadeo				Nov	1899
GHICK						Frank P.	<1	SF	4948		1901
Elizabeth	73	GER	7844		1900	Lloyd Jos	<1	SF	1213		1902
GHIGLIAZZA						Lorenzo	2	SF	632		1900
Antonio	43	ITA	8889		1903	Luigi	3	SF	4017a		1895
GHIGLIOTTI						**GHISI**					
Eugene	4	SF	669		1894	O./A., c/o	<1	SF	3929		1895
GHILARDI						**GHISLO**					
Evelina	1	CA	1965		1901	Giocomo	30	SWT	1407		1869
GHIO						**GHISSOLTO**					
Agostina	1	SF	5882		1904	Giov.	33	ITA	1746		1894
Felice	82	ITA	2195		1903	**GHOW**					
Giuseppe	32	ITA	7516		1902	Hing	29	CHN	1113		1869
Ida	1900	SF	77c		1904	**GI**					
Joseph/Catterina, c/o		SF	9200		1901	Gum	21	CHN	875		1866
Maria	39	ITA	4213		1903	**GIACOMAZZI**					
Mary	2	SF	6308		1904	John B.	50	SWT	5417		1902
Vittorio	3	SF	2996Oct		1901	**GIACOMINI**					
GHIOLDI						James B.	49	SWT	1499		1900
Colastina	27	SWT	913		1901	**GIACOMO**					
GHIORRZO						L.	45	ITA	G44		1885
Luigi	32	ITA	5848		1903	**GIAMBRA**					
GHIORSO						Guiseppe	1904	SF	2982c		1904
Giuseppe	35	ITA	9249		1901	Guiseppe	1904	SF	2982c		1904
Guiseppe				Jul	1898	**GIAMBRUNO**					
GHIORZO						Luigi	<1	SF	1955		1902
Paulo	25	ITA	2432		1900	**GIAMMATEC**					
GHIOTTO						Otavio	36	ITA	1620b		1872
Eddie	1	SF	3921		1902	**GIAMMUGNANI**					
Emilio				Nov	1899	Antonio	53	ITA	5420		1896

NAME	AGE OR YOB.	BIRTH PLACE	CERT. NO	ID	DEATH YEAR
GIAMPOLINI					
Maria	1	SF	6126		1896
GIAN					
Franceschi				May	1899
GIANETTI					
Guiseppi	43	ITA	2824		1903
GIANETTONI					
Hattie	40	CA	3499		1896
GIANFRANCESCHI					
Adelina				Jan	1899
Ugo				May	1899
GIANINI					
Caterina	24	ITA	6509		1903
Geacomo	50	SWT	3372		1894
Guiseppe	<1	SF	4683		1896
GIANNELLI					
Giorgina	22	SF	7500		1904
GIANNETTI					
Giuseppe	47	ITA	5876	Jan	1901
GIANNI					
Alberto	20	ITA	1664		1903
Giovanni	32	ITA	2469		1902
Isola	44	ITA	94		1903
GIANNINI					
Amadeo				Nov	1898
Ancha	25	CA	1362		1900
Francesco	1	SF	7027	Feb	1901
Henry G.				Nov	1899
Henry Joseph	16	SF	1420		1869
John	46	SWT	8668		1901
Joseph				Oct	1899
Mary				Feb	1899
Natale	52	ITA	7258		1904
Rosa				Feb	1899

NAME	AGE OR YOB.	BIRTH PLACE	CERT. NO	ID	DEATH YEAR
Rudolph	1904	SF	792c		1904
Russell Silom	1	SF	2744		1901
Virginia	<1	SF	3887		1867
GIANOLA					
Louis	<1	SF	6526		1902
GIANOTTI					
Gilarda	36	SWT	5446		1904
Nicolo	52	ITA	4367	Dec	1901
GIB					
Who	65	CHN	1423b		1871
GIBB					
Beatrice Hays	27	CA	6349		1903
James	<1	SF	2184		1894
Leonard Daniel	1	SF	2302		1902
Lovina	24	IL	6685		1868
Lucy	1	SF	3478		1867
GIBBENS					
W./N., c/o				Aug	1899
GIBBIE					
William	80	IRE	760		1903
GIBBIN					
Mary A.	33	IRE	1051		1868
GIBBON					
Hannah	53	IRL	3351		1896
John A.				Nov	1899
Viola C.	3	SF	6823		1868
GIBBONS					
Catherine	44	NY	5428		1904
Isabella	46	IRL	2455a		1872
James	25	IRL	280a		1871
James	52	NY	5031		1902
James	48	MA	4315		1901
Jane	<1	SF	3189	Nov	1901
John	40	IRL	808b		1872

Key: a = 1st part of year; b = 2nd part of year; c = death certificate copy; c/o = child of

NAME	AGE OR YOB.	BIRTH PLACE	CERT. NO	ID	DEATH YEAR
John	5	WA	4532		1867
Josephus	<1	SF	2926		1900
Julia	66	IRL	8379		1900
Katie	1	SF	2697		1895
Margaret E.	17	OH	6631		1868
Margaret L.	1	SF	5728		1904
Marie Raymond				Jul	1899
Mary	40	OH	5140		1901
Mary A.	<1	SF	4266		1901
Mary Ann	3	ID	6114		1867
Miles	1	SF	8230		1868
Patrick D.	3	CA	1297		1869
Sarah	70	IRE	9032		1903
Sarah	28	SF	1351		1894
Thomas	69	IRL	5106a		1895
Virginia Pearl	28	CA	1721		1901
William	<1	CA	1604b		1872
William	56	NY	5870		1902
GIBBS					
Alexander	<1	SF	2014		1894
C. V. S.	75	RI	6119		1900
Charles F.	35	ME	2192		1902
Francis P.	<1	SF	9943		1868
George P.				Jan	1900
George W.	72	RI	2504b		1895
Harriet E.	75	NC	1948		1901
J. H.	54	MA	G49		1885
James	45	CAN	4904		1902
John S.	62	MA	1389a		1871
Josephine	3	SF	1013		1868
Julia Ziegler	54	ME	5292		1901
Martha S. G.	34	RI	7993		1868
Reuben F.	61	VT	3813		1896
Sarah	72	PA	1421		1894

NAME	AGE OR YOB.	BIRTH PLACE	CERT. NO	ID	DEATH YEAR
GIBEAN					
Albert J.				Feb	1900
Isac/Jeanne, c/o		SF	2430		1901
GIBEAU					
Gerald	1	NV	3410		1903
GIBELIN					
du Py Ernest	71	FRA	1912b		1895
GIBLEN					
James F.	10	SF	3961		1870
GIBLIN					
Gertrude Margaret	20	SF	4665		1901
James Henry	35	CA	2913		1902
Jas.	40	IRL	G26		1883
Josephine	3	CA	6075		1902
Michael	48	IRL	3172		1873
Thomas/Eunice, c/o		SF	603		1900
Timothy J.	73	IRL	4490a		1895
William				Oct	1899
GIBLON					
Patrick				Feb	1899
GIBNEY					
Andrew D.	52	SCT	18b		1895
Catharine		SF	2203a		1872
Ellen	29	IRE	6479		1868
Ellen	37	SF	8580		1904
James	48	IRE	310		1865
James	1876	CA	1179c		1904
James Clyde	<1	SF	537		1902
Jennie	19	IRL	2202		1900
Margaret	29	SF	1502		1902
Maria	43	IRE	8495		1903
GIBON					
Mary	56	FRA	152b		1872
Thomas				Aug	1899

Key: a = 1st part of year; b = 2nd part of year; c = death certificate copy; c/o = child of

NAME	AGE OR YOB.	BIRTH PLACE	CERT. NO	ID	DEATH YEAR
GIBOT					
Anthony				Feb	1899
GIBOURET					
Alphonse				Nov	1898
GIBSON					
Abbey B.	77	ME	4502		1901
Alexander	4	SF	1181		1869
Alice	45	IRL	G47		1885
Anna	37	IRL	94		1870
Anne				Jan	1899
Charles Frederick	34	NB	5072a		1896
Charles W.	49	ENG	1256		1869
Daniel	37	MA	1451		1869
Delia	30	SF	212		1903
Dorothy Bonnard	1	CA	820		1894
Eddie A.	12	CHN	1444		1869
Frederick (soldier)			2530		1900
George	22	CA	3520		1903
George Edwin	72	DEN	6825	Feb	1901
Hannah	33	IL	3857		1903
Henry B.	<1	SF	1523		1870
Herbert	<1	SF	7418		1903
J. H.	41	MI	1520a		1871
James E.	54	MA	6849		1903
John				Jan	1899
Joseph	41	MA	4484		1867
Josephine, c/o	<1	SF	2877		1900
Julia	51	IRL	4238	Dec	1901
Margaret J.				Jun	1899
Mary	35	MA	G11		1882
Mary	66	ME	2768		1900
Mary	62	IRE	1135		1903
Mary J.	38	IRL	2751a		1872
Mary M.				Oct	1899
Matthew M.				Jul	1898

NAME	AGE OR YOB.	BIRTH PLACE	CERT. NO	ID	DEATH YEAR
Olemy	45	PA	5371a		1895
Oren Bennett	80	ME	95		1903
Phibe	74	ENG	6325a		1895
Richard	42	IRE	1747		1902
Rose	1	SF	1940		1866
Sarah	<1	SF	2108b		1895
T. Abel	<1	SF	1669b		1872
Thomas	46	ENG	2828		1900
Thomas				Aug	1899
W. H.	26	CA	3222	Nov	1901
William	25	NY	6975		1900
William Franklin	46	SEA	6881		1902
Wm. B.	2	CA	6277a		1895
GIDDINGS					
Anna	26	CA	3513		1900
Calvin	31	OH	3366		1866
GIDNEY					
William E.	38	NY	5294		1867
GIDOW					
Leon	66	FRA	6436		1900
GIE					
Ton Chong	1873	CHN	2531c		1904
GIEBEL					
Bertha	20	CA	7346		1903
GIEHRLEIN					
August	1	SF	4768		1867
GIEHRS					
Jacob				Jan	1900
GIELON					
Albert	<1	SF	716		1894
GIELOW					
Charles G.	59	GER	233b		1895
GIERMAN					
H. C.	66	GER	2020		1873

Key: a = 1st part of year; b = 2nd part of year;
c = death certificate copy; c/o = child of

NAME	AGE OR YOB.	BIRTH PLACE	CERT. NO	ID	DEATH YEAR
GIERY					
George					Dec 1899
GIES					
Anna Daisy Witham	32	SF	8870		1904
August	34	SF	6217		1900
Kilian					Dec 1899
Lilian F.	<1	SF	1710		1894
Rosa	2	SF	1150		1870
GIESE					
Carl Adolph	50	GER	6382		1904
Frederick					Feb 1899
Jurgen					Aug 1898
GIESEA					
Jennie					Oct 1898
GIESECKE					
William	43	GER	1530		1902
GIESIN					
Martha E.	23	PA	4682		1896
GIESLAR					
Matilda	42	CA	8111		1904
GIESLER					
Albert	79	SWT	4843		1902
GIFFEN					
Mary A.	34	OH	429a		1871
GIFFIN					
——			7734		1868
Christianarth	60	NY	1621		1894
Ira A.					Jan 1900
GIFFORD					
Charles Edward					Dec 1898
Elizabeth	71	ENG	27		1901
Georgiana	<1	SF	8297		1868
Hazel R.	24	CA	6497		1900
John R.	1851	ENG	3355c		1904

NAME	AGE OR YOB.	BIRTH PLACE	CERT. NO	ID	DEATH YEAR
Paul J.	33	MA	7286		1868
Willard G. (soldier)			1165		1901
GIFT					
Fannie	24	IL	1389		1866
GIFTER					
Charles	75	NY	3579a		1895
GIGGUS					
Charles	38	GER	8868		1868
GIGLIA					
Joseph	26	CA	788		1903
GIGNA					
Aristides Pierre	<1	SF	1575a		1871
GIGNAT					
Jean Baptiste	<1	SF	4553		1867
Pierre	62	FRA	5371		1904
GIGON					
E./P., c/o		SF	5192		1895
E./P., c/o		SF	5193		1895
Eliza	37	SF	31		1902
Polycarpe	40		274c		1904
GIHON					
Thomas					Aug 1899
GILARDI					
Salvatore	19	ITA	4290		1903
Salvatore	1	SF	1296		1903
GILBART					
John Edmund	1	SF	2893		1902
Wm.	60	ENG	3073		1894
GILBERT					
——			7214		1868
Auguste	79	FRA	6076		1902
Caroline					Mar 1899
Chandler L.	33	ME	9379		1868
Charles	28	FRA	2216		1873

NAME	AGE OR YOB.	BIRTH PLACE	CERT. NO	ID	DEATH YEAR
Charles	<1	SF	1443		1866
Charlie A.	<1	SF	1121		1869
Christ	25	CA	5655a		1895
Christopher J.	58	LA	5141		1901
Curtis C.	5	MA	6640		1868
D. W.	30	OH	1485b		1872
Edward Ernest	<1	SF	878		1894
Elizabeth				Oct	1899
Elizabeth Sprague	52	MA	7527		1901
Ellen, c/o	<1	SF	715b		1872
Emil	50	FRA	7936		1900
Fannie M.	1	SF	672b		1871
G. A.	51	NY	1361		1869
George M.	<1	SF	4850		1867
George S. N.	44	PA	2732		1873
Henry	40	TN	2547		1901
James A.	1904	CA	1593c		1904
James A.	60	FRA	1365		1900
Jane (Pam) E.	45	USA	G7		1882
John L.			5823	Jan	1901
John/Ida, c/o	<1	SF	1765		1901
Joseph E.	30	TN	6957	Feb	1901
L./F., c/o	<1	SF	3745		1895
Margaret				Oct	1898
Mary	43	NY	2339		1903
Max	5		1323		1869
Mortimer Thomas	58	IL	1022		1902
Robert A.	69	ENG	4720		1903
Rosalie M.				Jan	1900
Thomas R.	34	NB	2927		1866
Walter	35		3223	Nov	1901

GILBERTSON

NAME	AGE OR YOB.	BIRTH PLACE	CERT. NO	ID	DEATH YEAR
Annie	18	AUT	3789		1867

GILBO

NAME	AGE OR YOB.	BIRTH PLACE	CERT. NO	ID	DEATH YEAR
Evelina	11	MI	2582		1895

GILBRIDE

NAME	AGE OR YOB.	BIRTH PLACE	CERT. NO	ID	DEATH YEAR
Elizabeth	3	SF	309b		1895

GILBURN

NAME	AGE OR YOB.	BIRTH PLACE	CERT. NO	ID	DEATH YEAR
Mary	37	KY	1951		1894

GILCHRIST

NAME	AGE OR YOB.	BIRTH PLACE	CERT. NO	ID	DEATH YEAR
James/Agnes, c/o	<1	SF	508		1902
John G.	73	SCT	2046		1902
Kate	34	IRE	1296		1869
Mary	40	IRL	2499a		1872
Mary McGregor				Mar	1899

GILDEMEESTER

NAME	AGE OR YOB.	BIRTH PLACE	CERT. NO	ID	DEATH YEAR
Adrain H.	39	HOL	7094		1868

GILDEMUSTER

NAME	AGE OR YOB.	BIRTH PLACE	CERT. NO	ID	DEATH YEAR
William	1	SF	3425		1867

GILDENMEISTER

NAME	AGE OR YOB.	BIRTH PLACE	CERT. NO	ID	DEATH YEAR
Frank				Jun	1899

GILDERSLEVE

NAME	AGE OR YOB.	BIRTH PLACE	CERT. NO	ID	DEATH YEAR
Emmet W.				Jan	1900

GILED

NAME	AGE OR YOB.	BIRTH PLACE	CERT. NO	ID	DEATH YEAR
Muriel, c/o		SF	8986		1901

GILES

NAME	AGE OR YOB.	BIRTH PLACE	CERT. NO	ID	DEATH YEAR
Edd./Susan, c/o	<1	SF	1506b		1872
Kate	62	IRL	3240		1894
Mary E.	80	IRE	7152		1903
Robert	53	IRL	130b		1871
Robert	60	NS	2109		1903
Rollin	1	SF	4788		1867
William	25	IRE	3576		1867
William	55	MA	4809		1896
William Henry	<1	SF	2816		1873

GILESPEY

NAME	AGE OR YOB.	BIRTH PLACE	CERT. NO	ID	DEATH YEAR
John	1	SF	951a		1871

GILFEATHER

NAME	AGE OR YOB.	BIRTH PLACE	CERT. NO	ID	DEATH YEAR
James	60	IRL	2017		1870

Key: a = 1st part of year; b = 2nd part of year;
c = death certificate copy; c/o = child of

NAME	AGE OR YOB.	BIRTH PLACE	CERT. NO	ID	DEATH YEAR
James	1	CA	2648		1873
James	51	LA	5977		1903
James				Jan	1900
GILFETHER					
Owen	1839	MA	3063c		1904
GILFILLAN					
Archibald F	47	PA	4718		1902
GILFOIL					
Catherine		SF	4096b		1870
GILHOOLY					
John	60	IRL	2415		1900
John				Feb	1900
Thomas	1	SF	7341		1904
GILHULY					
Helen Josephine	8	SF	5691		1902
Hugh	67	IRL	4015	Dec	1901
Katie				Jul	1899
GILKEY					
A. M. (soldier)			4544		1901
Stanley G.	1879	IL	3292c		1904
GILKYSON					
Albert R.	45	CA	7184		1903
GILL					
Annie	40	IRL	3566		1896
Bridget	<1	SF	3235		1866
Catharine	50	IRE	6968		1903
Catherine	71	IRL	2015		1894
Ellen	37	IRE	7471		1868
Emma	<1	CA	690a		1871
Herbert	10	CA	5132		1903
Horatio B.	44	NY	987		1870
Howard	<1	SF	6147		1902
James	27	MA	9479		1868
John				Feb	1899

NAME	AGE OR YOB.	BIRTH PLACE	CERT. NO	ID	DEATH YEAR
John T.	35	CA	8595		1903
Joseph	37	CA	7679		1903
Kate	55	IRE	3798		1903
Mabel E.	21	ENG	4757		1896
Martha	1	SF	9768		1868
Mary	<1	SF	5860		1867
Mary	101	IRE	5834		1902
Mary	84	IRL	1480		1894
Matthew	40	ENG	G87		1887
Michael	23	IRE	9565		1868
Robert	44	IRL	1629		1870
Robert S.	45	ENG	G79		1887
Stephen Andrew	1	SF	640		1902
Thomas	32	CA	7919		1900
Thomas	68	IRL	6213		1900
Wm./Margaret, c/o				Aug	1898
GILLADUCCI					
Philimena				Feb	1899
GILLAM					
Howard				Feb	1900
John	71	PA	3295	Nov	1901
GILLE					
Henry Robert	<1	SF	5682a		1895
GILLEECE					
James	59	IRE	8257		1903
GILLELEAND					
A. L. (soldier)			7118		1900
GILLEN					
Charles	1	SF	8127		1868
Charles J.	54	IRE	6995		1903
Delia	42	MA	3663		1903
Edward	24	IRL	132a		1871
James	42	NY	G21		1883
John	60	IRL	2463b		1895
Mary	65	IRL	3970		1900

Key: a = 1st part of year; b = 2nd part of year; c = death certificate copy; c/o = child of

NAME	AGE OR YOB.	BIRTH PLACE	CERT. NO	ID	DEATH YEAR	NAME	AGE OR YOB.	BIRTH PLACE	CERT. NO	ID	DEATH YEAR
Michael	36	IRE	4882		1867	W. D.				Jan	1900
William	54	IRE	1607		1902	William	33	IRL	1312a		1871
						William H. (soldier)			5044		1901
GILLERAN						Wm.				Jun	1899
Ernest	45	TX	808		1900						
Patrick	1834	IRE	1537c		1904	**GILLESPY**					
William	55	IRL	1996b		1895	——			6606		1868
William H.	<1	SF	1074		1869						
						GILLET					
GILLEREN						Annie	41	FRA	1101		1869
——			6970		1868	Aristide				Nov	1899
Mary Ann	3	SF	2622		1866						
						GILLETT					
GILLERLAIN						Isaac Copley	57	NY	4456		1901
Dennis J.	24		7454		1901	Lucetta R.	74	NY	7565		1901
						Mable F.				Mar	1900
GILLERMO											
Avila	50	MEX	1521b		1871	**GILLEY**					
						Elizabeth	61	IRE	6148		1902
GILLESPIE											
——			7035		1868	**GILLIAN**					
Alex G.	1825	SCT	2484c		1904	David	32	CAN	1833b		1895
Andrew				Mar	1900						
Ann	47	ENG	8144		1868	**GILLICE**					
E. A.	2	SF	2147		1866	Charles Edward	7	SF	690		1901
George A.	54	IRE	6227		1904	Mary Ellenndo	6	SF	1067		1902
George Arthur	14	SF	2817		1895						
James	<1	SF	1390		1866	**GILLICK**					
James	42	IRE	6645		1868	Mathew		SF	4459b		1870
James				Jul	1899						
Kate	22	NY	2078a		1872	**GILLIECE**					
Lawrence	48	IRL	4581b		1870	John K. , c/o				Jan	1899
Mary J.	1843	IRE	3396c		1904	**GILLIES**					
Patrick				Dec	1899	S.F./Natina, c/o	1904	SF	695		1904
Richard W.	73	NB	838		1900						
Sarah Beutner	84	WIN	1632		1900	**GILLIG**					
Thomas	<1	SF	409		1870	John	74	OH	3224	Nov	1901
Thomas (soldier)			3038	Oct	1901	John A.	5	SF	3523	Nov	1901
Thomas Jefferson				Feb	1900	**GILLIGAN**					
Thos.	56	IRL	4515a		1895	Agnes	1	CA	2893		1903
						Arthur	25	NH	1381		1903
						Christopher				Jan	1900
						James	6	SF	887		1894

Key: a = 1st part of year; b = 2nd part of year;
c = death certificate copy; c/o = child of

NAME	AGE OR YOB.	BIRTH PLACE	CERT. NO	ID	DEATH YEAR
Jno. Jos.	10	MA	3960a		1895
John/Bridget, c/o	<1	SF	577		1901
Margarette	1904	CA	2241c		1904
Mary				Aug	1899
Matthew A.	65	IRL	8479		1901
Michael	55	IRL	3717	Nov	1901
Paul C.				Jan	1899
Peter	34	IRE	4672		1867
GILLIHAN					
Allen Warburton				Oct	1898
GILLILAN					
Lizzie E.	26	OH	2132		1902
GILLILAND					
Wm. M./L. G., c/o	<1	SF	6364		1895
GILLIN					
Bernard	27	IRE	5493		1867
GILLINGHAM					
Charles	62	ENG	8009		1868
Katie A.	26	MA	2114		1873
GILLINGS					
Honora	73	IRL	6554		1900
GILLIO					
B. Gillio Bernardo		NM	1135c		1904
Joseph	1903	SF	1242c		1904
GILLIONS					
Frank	42	ITA	4214		1903
GILLIRAN					
Margaret	58	IRL	6313a		1895
GILLIS					
Angus	21	NS	7230		1868
Wm. C.	4	SF	6150a		1895
GILLISPIE					
John	74	SCT	1444b		1895
John Francis	26	SF	4149		1900

NAME	AGE OR YOB.	BIRTH PLACE	CERT. NO	ID	DEATH YEAR
Kate/Christhian Frank, c/o	1	CA	3045		1903
Thomas J./Katherine, c/o	<1	SF	8191		1904
GILLIT					
Martin M.	84	VT	7068		1900
GILLIWAY					
John George	60	IRL	6760	Feb	1901
GILLMAN					
Albert A.	43	NH	9225		1868
Harriet				Dec	1898
Joseph Nicholson Fred	22	WI	2340		1903
GILLMANN					
Victoria				Oct	1898
GILLMOR					
Anna A.	33	NY	3336		1870
Jno. B.	57	IRL	3744a		1895
GILLMORE					
Aggie	7	SF	3118		1866
GILLON					
Ann E.	10	SF	1483		1866
Mary Ann	5	CA	1503		1866
Thomas	<1	SF	3456b		1870
Thomas	<1	SF	3788		1870
GILLS					
Kate	28	IRE	8959		1868
GILLSON					
James	43	IRL	2076a		1872
GILLULY					
Eliza Ann	28	SF	4831		1896
GILLYGAN					
James M.	<1	SF	8339		1868
GILMAKER					
Levi	74	GER	958		1902

NAME	AGE OR YOB.	BIRTH PLACE	CERT. NO	ID	DEATH YEAR	NAME	AGE OR YOB.	BIRTH PLACE	CERT. NO	ID	DEATH YEAR
GILMAN						John				Feb	1899
Blanche I.	29	CA	7706		1903	John	9	SF	977		1901
Charles Alfred	<1	SF	7833		1903	John J.	50	IRL	5270		1896
Charles E.				Mar	1900	John W. A.	38	NY	7903		1868
Edward	<1	SF	3922		1902	Leeman	30	CA	2979		1900
Eliza D.	75	NY	3653		1896	Mary	54	IRE	5233		1903
Emely P.	15	CA	9604		1868	Michael				Feb	1900
George W.	54	NH	1114		1869	Nora	2	SF	3599		1903
Henry	74	ME	3156		1894	Patrick	38	IRL	7028	Feb	1901
John				May	1899	Richard George	1	SF	5540		1904
Mary A.				Nov	1899	Robert E.				Dec	1898
Sarah Louise	85	NH	7859		1901	Samuel	77	NB	6758		1903
W. A.	60	ME	350a		1871	Stephen D.	77	NH	1682		1894
Washington	15	MA	266		1865	Thomas	56	IRL	1870		1900
GILMARTIN						Walter A. (soldier)			7959		1901
William H.	3	NY	1029		1868	**GILMOUR**					
GILMORE						George D.	70	SCT	4905		1902
——	<1	SF	8607		1868	Michael	104	IRE	7292		1902
Albert L.	7	CA	1852		1866	**GILPIN**					
Catherine	1858	IRE	823c		1904	Charles W. (soldier)			7307		1901
Cecil Hazel	1	SF	4992		1902	Hiram (soldier)			272		1901
Charles Cutting	55	NH	4420		1902	William P.				Mar	1900
Charles Lester	1	SF	5174		1902	**GILROY**					
Elaine I.	1	CA	1656b		1895	Hattie May	23	SF	4371		1901
Eugene G.	<1	SF	3137		1873	James	36	IRL	1700		1870
Eva F.	<1	SF	8133		1868	Mary Ella	53	NY	1316		1900
Frederick	47	MA	5794		1867	T.	65		2333		1901
George				Nov	1899	Thomas	63	IRL	5718a		1895
Harry A.	<1	SF	2168		1866	**GILSON**					
Harry C.				Jan	1899	Charles	36	SF	1748		1900
James	48	IRE	933		1902	Henry	39	MA	6098		1867
James	47	IRL	862b		1895	Sarah R.	<1	WA	1737b		1895
James A.	<1	SF	1932		1866	**GILSTEAD**					
James B.	38	NY	3577	Nov	1901	Amanda	45	SWE	8364		1903
Jas.	54	IRL	G22		1883						

NAME	AGE OR YOB.	BIRTH PLACE	CERT. NO	ID	DEATH YEAR	NAME	AGE OR YOB.	BIRTH PLACE	CERT. NO	ID	DEATH YEAR
GILSTRAP						**GINDROZ**					
Sarah A.	52	IL	5718		1896	Emile	45	FRA	G43		1885
GILTMEN						**GINE**					
Daniel Francis	<1	SF	7190		1904	Wong Sung	22	CHN	3265a		1872
GIM						**GINGERICH**					
How	1854	CHN	32c		1904	William	49	PA	6846Feb		1901
Jang	1864	CHN	1402c		1904	**GINGG**					
GIMBEL						Conrad	37	SWT	G2		1882
Annie	1	SF	1176		1869	Johanna	46	GER	6062Jan		1901
William					Mar 1899	**GINGRAS**					
GIMMEL						Alcade (soldier)			2158		1901
Peter	51	BAV	1320		1869	**GINLEA**					
GIMMELL						Elena	<1	SF	3298a		1872
Louisa M.					Jan 1900	**GINN**					
GIMPEL						George A.	38	CA	8298		1901
Paul	38	FRA	1549b		1895	**GINNAAN**					
GIN						James	55	IRL	765b		1871
Ah	1	SF	1818a		1872	**GINNOCHIO**					
Ah	18	CHN	3907		1867	Attilio	35	ITA	40c		1904
Ah	25	CHN	7829		1868	**GINNS**					
Ah	34	CHN	9132		1868	Albert A.	1	SF	1549		1866
Ah Sham	44	CHN	548b		1895	**GINOCCHIO**					
An	32	CHN	1420		1869	Dominico	48	ITA	6363a		1895
How Guen					Nov 1899	Giovanna	38	ITA	1270		1903
Lin Cuy	38	CHN	1140		1894	Guisseppie	53	ITA	3709		1870
Mon		CHN	1077		1869	Mary G.					Dec 1898
Sue Fook					Mar 1899	Pietro	40	ITA	1800		1900
Wa Mon					Aug 1899	**GINOICHIO**					
Yet Zow					Nov 1899	John	<1	SF	1026		1868
GINACA						**GINSBERG**					
Charles	1	SF	7338		1868	A.		SF	2128		1873
GINARDINI						Mary					Aug 1898
Prospero	20	SWT	2656a		1872						

NAME	AGE OR YOB.	BIRTH PLACE	CERT. NO	ID	DEATH YEAR
GINTER					
Joseph	28	GER	478		1866
GINTY					
Alila Lillian	18	CA	3988		1903
John	35	IRL	1924a		1872
GIOMETTI					
Alfredo	1904	SF	2016c		1904
Alfredo	<1	SF	8326		1903
GIONG					
Ang Mig	45	CHN	7413		1900
GIORDANO					
Nicholas J.	1889	LA	2850c		1904
GIORDONA					
Josephine				Dec	1898
GIORETTI					
Louis	54	ITA	3664	Nov	1901
GIORNO					
Luigi	6	SF	1669b		1895
GIOVACCHINI					
Guiseppe	64	ITA	5600		1904
GIOVACHINI					
Emilio	48	ITA	1956		1902
GIOVANARI					
Gaetano	64	SWT	3915		1867
GIOVANETTI					
Catherine	<1	SF	5939		1903
GIOVANIS					
Montiverdi	45	ITA	1874		1866
GIOVANNACCI					
Frank	43	SWT	5908a		1895
GIOVANNETH					
Annibale/Ercolina, c/o	<1	SF	7669		1904

NAME	AGE OR YOB.	BIRTH PLACE	CERT. NO	ID	DEATH YEAR
GIOVANNETTI					
Pietro	57	ITA	4629		1904
Salvatore				Jan	1899
GIOVANNI					
Cedro	23	ITA	5839a		1895
Colson	43	ITA	239		1870
Paierotti	25	AUS	3560		1867
Spenhiani	34	GRE	655b		1871
Valassini	35	ITA	G91		1889
GIOVANNINI					
Alouisious A.	4	SF	304		1900
Angelo/Domenica, c/o		SF	4424		1901
Daniele	60	ITA	6506		1896
Francesco	61	ITA	6571	Feb	1901
Luigi	8	SF	7186		1902
GIOVANNONI					
Emilia	1	SF	2301		1903
Giorge	25	SF	7732		1904
Guido	<1	SF	1246		1901
Kristide				Mar	1899
P./E., c/o		SF	4609		1896
GIPPERT					
Anna Maria	1	SF	8523		1904
GIRARD					
Achille	53	FRA	1198b		1871
Aimée Thérese	55	FRA	4004		1896
Francois Pierre	84	SWT	6004	Jan	1901
George	33	FRA	304		1865
Henriette		SF	1885		1870
Ida Alice	1	CA	1926		1903
Justine	33	FRA	2641		1903
Leon	17	CA	3349		1900
Pete	<1	SF	1007		1868

Key: a = 1st part of year; b = 2nd part of year;
c = death certificate copy; c/o = child of

NAME	AGE OR YOB.	BIRTH PLACE	CERT. NO	ID	DEATH YEAR	NAME	AGE OR YOB.	BIRTH PLACE	CERT. NO	ID	DEATH YEAR
GIRARDI						GIRWOOD					
Guiseppe	22	ITA	4630		1903	Robert B.	<1	SF	5357		1901
Ianazia	50	ITA	7		1902	GIRY					
GIRARDOH						Aime	71	FRA	5335		1903
Susanne M.	79	SWT	7846		1904	Camille	Abt	NY	1665		1903
GIRAU						Victoria	72	FRA	1586		1902
Henriette	<1	SF	4091		1902	GISCARD					
Marie	35	FRA	7955		1900	Pierre Emile	<1	SF	5036a		1895
GIRAUD						GISENE					
Benjamin	60	FRA	3878		1903	Therise	24	FRA	1768		1900
Eugene	55	FRA	967b		1895	GISI					
GIRAUDAN						Emil	40	SWT	5625		1903
Rosalie	62	FRA	8550		1900	GISIN					
GIRETI						John F.	9	SF	7443		1900
Adolfo	33	ITA	1742b		1872	GISLER					
GIRGI						Charles	7	CA	3830		1903
Niccoli	40	ITA	406		1901	Maria	47	SWT	1216		1901
GIRIMELLI						GISSON					
Genoveffa	1	NY	5032		1902	Pierre	67	FRA	4100		1903
GIROCCHIO						GIT					
Luigi	35	ITA	3101		1894	Ah	32	CHN	1215b		1872
GIROIN						Yee Chong	1848	CHN	2771c		1904
Harriet J.	30	CA	2450		1894	GITCHILL					
GIROT						Elizabeth	77	VA	1140		1869
Anna	1	SF	8120		1868	GITIGAN					
Emily	7	SF	754a		1871	——			2047		1866
Mary I.	<1	SF	922b		1895	GITTENS					
Peter Geo.	4	SF	8549		1868	John	53	IRE	1229		1869
GIRRARD						GITZEL					
Hugh	36	IRE	3801		1867	Ernst				Oct	1898
GIRSCH						GIUFFRE					
Daniel Joseph	<1	SF	2459		1902	Bartolom./Caterina, c/o	<1	SF	1975		1902
Hedwig	<1	SF	922		1900						

Key: a = 1st part of year; b = 2nd part of year;
c = death certificate copy; c/o = child of

NAME	AGE OR YOB.	BIRTH PLACE	CERT. NO	ID	DEATH YEAR	NAME	AGE OR YOB.	BIRTH PLACE	CERT. NO	ID	DEATH YEAR
GIULLIANA						**GLADSON**					
Sarvera	55	MEX	2593		1866	Florence	19	SF	7400		1903
GIUS						**GLADSTONE**					
Ottilia	1	SF	4250		1896	William	68	ENG	3942		1896
GIUSTI						**GLADWIN**					
——			4313		1867	Bertha Louise	9	SF	2059		1873
Adele	70	ITA	5885		1902	Emily A.	73	NY	86		1900
Antonia		SF	554b		1871	George Samuel	73	NY	1835		1900
Ida	1	SF	5447		1904	W. H., c/o		SF	2858a		1872
Johanna E.	27	IRL	3265		1873	**GLADYS**					
Lina		SF	6963		1900	Mary					Oct 1899
GIUSTO						**GLAHN**					
Antonio	46	AUT	448		1870	Cathrina	<1	SF	2530		1873
GIVEN						**GLAIN**					
George	50	IRE	7343		1868	Thomas H.			3791		1902
Gillispy	6	MD	2064		1866	**GLAIZE**					
John H.			2599		1902	Edward	78	FRA	8535		1903
GIVENCHY						**GLANCEY**					
Charlotte C.	<1	SF	1120		1869	Stephen	27	IRE	7541		1868
GIVENS						**GLANN**					
Arthur	1	UT	1708		1894	Frederick	53	DEN	3656		1902
George	35	VA	1213b		1872	**GLANVILLE**					
Jacob (soldier)			1031		1900	Mary Ellen	35	CA	4427		1903
GIVLIN						Viola B.	<1	SF	938b		1895
Michael	53	IRE	6249		1902	**GLAS**					
GLACKIN						Fred W.	2	SF	7579		1868
John/Kate, c/o	<1	SF	8274		1904	**GLASAR**					
GLACKSEN						George	50	MA	3825a		1895
John (soldier)			7622		1900	**GLASBY**					
GLADDEN						Albert (soldier)			3543		1900
Morgan J. (soldier)			807c		1904	**GLASER**					
GLADOWISKI						August J.C.	48	GER	5169a		1895
August					Dec 1898	Edwin	<1	SF	4042		1896

NAME	AGE OR YOB.	BIRTH PLACE	CERT. NO	ID	DEATH YEAR	NAME	AGE OR YOB.	BIRTH PLACE	CERT. NO	ID	DEATH YEAR
Henry	42	GER	2077b		1895	**GLASSMAN**					
Sarah	25	PER	5072		1903	Simon	1	SF	5059		1867
GLASFORD						**GLASSON**					
——	<1	SF	290a		1871	C.W./Jane, c/o	<1	CA	6209		1902
GLASGON						**GLASSPOOLE**					
Samuel	2	SF	8373		1868	Robert	27	WI	1217		1901
GLASGOW						**GLAUCH**					
Martha A.	63	IRL	6533		1896	Olga B.	46	NY	3965	Dec	1901
GLASHEEN						**GLAVENICH**					
William				Jun	1899	Gaspar	67	AUS	5326		1902
GLASO						**GLAVIN**					
Rudolph	49	GER	418		1902	Joseph	1904	SF	3093c		1904
GLASON						**GLEASON**					
Mary	72	IRE	429		1865	Ann	68	ENG	3966		1900
GLASS						Arthur E. (soldier)			6531	Feb	1901
Bertie				Jan	1899	Bertha Elizabeth	2	SF	1324		1869
Catherine	76	ME	1594c		1904	Bridget	35	IRE	1295		1869
Dora	27	GER	1003		1868	Bridget M.	47	IRL	3428		1896
Elizabeth	70	ENG	206		1865	Catherine	24	MA	8572		1868
Frederick	39	SF	4658		1904	Catherine E.	42	MA	950b		1895
Hamilton W.	11	CA	2739		1895	Clara				Oct	1898
Harry H.				Jul	1899	Clorinda Rose	1877	CA	2293c		1904
J. R.	35	ENG	3612		1870	Edward G.	54	NY	1349		1902
John	42	OH	1002		1868	Fanny	65	IRE	877		1902
John	54	NY	1015		1868	Fred C. (soldier)			2056		1901
Julius, c/o	<1	SF	1318		1869	Fred I. (soldier)			7147		1901
Nellie E.	29	SF	4934a		1895	Geo.	<1	SF	2480		1894
Simon	38	SF	2152		1873	Harry E. (soldier)			6933		1900
GLASSEN						Henry			1228		1903
Charles	1861	GER	395c		1904	James (John)	60	NY	5525	Jan	1901
GLASSFORD						John	55	IRE	7040		1904
Elizabeth	55	IRL	1230a		1871	John	75	IRE	8182		1904
Nancy	54	IL	674		1903	John Joseph	<1	SF	1366		1869
						Joseph O'N.				Jan	1900

NAME	AGE OR YOB.	BIRTH PLACE	CERT. NO	ID	DEATH YEAR
Kate	1859	IRE	1180c		1904
Martin	35	IRE	8004		1868
Mary	40	IRL	1432		1870
Mary	1	SF	3534		1867
Mary	<1	SF	1562		1902
Mary	80	IRL	5289a		1895
Mary A.	55	MA	3746a		1895
Mary A.	62	NY	3395		1896
Mary E.	3	SF	199		1865
Mary E.	<1	SF	4337		1867
Mary F.	8	NY	334		1865
Michael	70	IRL	5771	Jan	1901
Patrick	14	NY	7704		1868
Peter J.				Oct	1899
Thomas	<1	SF	50		1865
Thomas	65	IRL	6152a		1895
Thomas Allen	68	NY	4419		1902
Thos. L.	23	CA	8228		1901
Timothy	62	IRE	5345		1904
Timothy James	2	SF	1396		1869
William	41		5372		1904
William	84	IRE	7751		1904
GLEAVES					
James Malcolm	49	OH	3872	Nov	1901
GLEDDEN					
Johanna	72	IRL	2272		1894
GLEERSUP					
Chas. (soldier)			7215		1900
GLEESEN					
Michael Aloysious	15	SF	9098		1901
GLEESON					
Edward C.				Nov	1898
Ella Margaritte	26	SF	4335		1903
Francis W.	25	CA	330		1902
Hannah	32	SF	6826	Feb	1901
James H.	<1	SF	1111b		1872
John	63	IRL	2493		1901
Margaret	1	SF	8632		1868
Martin	24	IRL	1497		1900
Mary Allice	<1	SF	4909		1867
Patrick				Apr	1899
William John	1	SF	1282		1869
GLEETHMAN					
Jacob/I., c/o				Feb	1900
GLEHER					
Henri	56	FRA	1021		1868
GLEIN					
Margarethe	74	GER	2899		1901
GLEINOW					
Tho. Aloyious	<1	SF	1602a		1871
GLEISON					
Timothy	88	IRE	5234		1903
GLENDER					
Henry L.	2	SF	3521		1902
GLENDINNING					
Harry Alden Wallace	2	CA	3364	Nov	1901
GLENDON					
James/Louise, c/o	<1	SF	3752		1901
GLENN					
Charles A.	23	NJ	3762		1902
Clara	1	SF	800b		1871
David	49	SF	3183		1894
James Edward	<1	SF	252		1870
John H.	45	MN	6395		1896
Thomas	75	IRL	254		1900
Walter Miles	<1	SF	5788		1902
William	11	CA	5372		1902
GLENNAN					
Margaret J.	59	NY	8581		1904

Key: a = 1st part of year; b = 2nd part of year; c = death certificate copy; c/o = child of

NAME	AGE OR YOB.	BIRTH PLACE	CERT. NO	ID	DEATH YEAR	NAME	AGE OR YOB.	BIRTH PLACE	CERT. NO	ID	DEATH YEAR
GLENNIE						**GLINDEN**					
George M. S.	31	SCT	5527	Jan	1901	Bridget	29	IRL	1430b		1871
John Burke	1	SF	826		1903	James	43	IRL	1047b		1871
						Martin H.	40	SF	8098		1903
GLENNON						Mary Margaret	1	SF	7779		1903
Florence, c/o	<1	SF	2172a		1872						
						GLINDERMANN					
GLESON						Geo. W.	2	SF	110b		1895
Bridget Francis	<1	SF	1391		1869						
Ellen	34	IRL	1427b		1871	**GLISMANN**					
						Johan	37	GER	1439		1869
GLESSMAN											
A. J.	abt	GER	9695		1901	**GLITZKE**					
						Theodor	39	GER	2312b		1895
GLESTON											
Noland	67	MA	8494		1868	**GLOCK**					
						Helene	36	GER	4823		1904
GLICK											
Allen				Mar	1900	**GLODE**					
Mary	55	GER	4147a		1895	Dennis				Feb	1900
Ray	23	SF	3728		1902						
						GLOOTZ					
GLIDDEN						Adolph	55	GER	5062a		1895
Ada W.				Dec	1898	John P. M.	57	GER	8695		1901
Auvilla	1834	IN	2198c		1904						
Charles E.	36	MA	1270		1869	**GLOR**					
Emile	65	MA	3704a		1895	Hermann	28	SWT	G10		1882
Mary P.	34	CHI	2831a		1872						
						GLOSSER					
GLIDDON						Geo./C., c/o		SF	1769		1894
Edward	6	SF	1012		1866						
Frank	27	ME	1427b		1872	**GLOVER**					
Grace	18	ENG	1722		1900	Alice	<1	CA	3385		1902
Neva	15	CA	7995		1904	Annie/John, c/o		SF	3176		1902
						Frank S.				Jan	1900
GLIDEN						George F.	1	SF	1338b		1895
George W.	35	NH	2985		1866	Hannah				Mar	1899
						James				Feb	1899
GLIGO						James E.	33	CA	4602		1904
Guiro	58	AUS	5288		1904	Johanna	4	SF	1061b		1872
						John	33	IL	1121		1866
GLINDEMAN						John	63	MA	7314		1868
Maria	67	GER	551		1901	John (soldier)			3039	Oct	1901

Key: a = 1st part of year; b = 2nd part of year;
c = death certificate copy; c/o = child of

NAME	AGE OR YOB.	BIRTH PLACE	CERT. NO	ID	DEATH YEAR	NAME	AGE OR YOB.	BIRTH PLACE	CERT. NO	ID	DEATH YEAR
John P.				Jan	1900	Margaret				Feb	1899
Mary Agnes	2	SF	2356a		1872	Margaret Mary				Apr	1899
Robert	40	ENG	3284		1870	Martin (soldier)			861		1901
Samuel	40	NY	5443		1903	Mary Elizabeth	1	SF	1162		1869
GLUCK						Mary Ellen	16	SF	430		1901
Jacob	23	GER	1183		1870	P./L., c/o				May	1899
Regina W.				Aug	1898	Patrick/Elizabeth, c/o		SF	5105		1903
GLUCKSMAN						Thomas/Margaret, c/o		SF	3275		1900
Fanny	1	SF	1736		1870	Timothy	65	IRL	5226		1901
GLUECK						Veronica	<1	SF	4864		1903
George	29	GER	6404		1904	Virginia	<1	SF	1640		1901
GLUHAN						Virginia Mary	<1	SF	1694		1901
Nellie	<1	SF	8890		1903	**GMEHLICH**					
GLUMM						Herrman	53	GER	5886		1902
Frank E. (soldier)			5811	Jan	1901	**GNIP**					
GLUSING						Chong	24		1954b		1872
Tim	34	GER	1460b		1872	**GNOBEL**					
GLUYAS						Abraham	10	GER	1513b		1871
Geo. E. C.	27	VA	2226		1866	**GNOCCHIS**					
Henry Jane	<1	SF	162		1870	Albert	1	CA	G83		1887
Jane Everett	53	NY	7029	Feb	1901	**GNOS**					
May Duncan	<1	SF	2874a		1872	Carl	3	SF	2888		1894
GLYIM						**GO**					
Mary A.	47	IRL	G82		1887	Ah	55	CHN	4825		1867
GLYN						Bing Lin	34	CHN	4370		1901
Gertrude	<1	SF	4842a		1895	Buck Ming	28	CHN	8002		1900
GLYNN						Chew Chung				Feb	1899
Catherine	1	SF	1161		1869	Chung Han	47	CHN	1964b		1895
Daniel S.	48	IRL	1598		1900	Get Chang	40	CHN	1029b		1895
Fredrick	<1	SF	1282		1866	Ging Guey	71	CHN	3799		1903
James	69	IRL	6411	Feb	1901	Gum Di	49	CHN	5883		1904
John	29	ME	7926		1901	Kin Bon				Jun	1899
Kate	70	IRE	4603		1904	Mon Chin Shee	52	CHN	6228		1904
Margaret	64	IRE	3093		1903	Moon Leong Sea	79	CHN	8512		1901
						See				Jan	1900

Key: *a = 1st part of year; b = 2nd part of year; c = death certificate copy; c/o = child of*

NAME	AGE OR YOB.	BIRTH PLACE	CERT. NO	ID	DEATH YEAR
Tim San				Jan	1900
Wong Shee				Dec	1899
Yoong	42	CHN	4442		1904
GOAD					
Wm.	37	ENG	G50		1885
GOATZ					
Charles	36	FRA	375b		1872
GOBENER					
Henry N.	<1	SF	3355		1866
GOBEY					
Frank	56	CAN	2818		1895
GOBIT					
Marie Therese	<1	SF	1572b		1871
GOBLAI					
Gustave	7	CA	1772		1866
GOBLE					
James E.	70	NY	7757		1903
John E.	63	ENG	8709		1903
Nellie	33	SF	8984		1901
GOBRILLE					
Jane	62	NY	5358		1903
GOBY					
Jane				Dec	1899
GOC					
Dora	32	KS	5019a		1895
GOCHET					
Ludwig Wilhelm	5	SF	1266		1869
GOCHEY					
Thos./Thelma, c/o				Jan	1899
GOCK					
Johann	1	SF	5397		1904
GODAHL					
Edwin J. (soldier)			5693	Jan	1901

NAME	AGE OR YOB.	BIRTH PLACE	CERT. NO	ID	DEATH YEAR
GODAIR					
Henrietta Francesca	20	CA	500		1901
GODAN					
Francis	65	FRA	G84		1887
GODART					
Juliette	<1	SF	744b		1872
GODCHANCE					
G.		SF	889		1866
GODCHANT					
Nathan	2	FRA	418		1865
GODCHAUX					
Alfred L.		SF	1549b		1871
Egennie	<1	CA	3886		1870
Elisa				May	1899
Frank	<1	SF	3306a		1872
Lazard	76	FRA	3553		1902
Lucien				Aug	1899
Sophie				Oct	1899
Sylvain				Aug	1898
GODCHEAUX					
N.	39	FRA	2695a		1872
GODDARD					
Anthony M.	1837	IA	1398c		1904
Charles/Mary, c/o	<1	SF	8805		1904
Riley	38	ENG	273		1865
Theresa S.	35	CA	4044		1902
GODDEN					
James Henry				Jan	1899
GODE					
——			1064		1869
GODEAU					
Adrain	1	SF	7181		1868
Parfait Eugene	42	SF	4209	Dec	1901

Key: a = 1st part of year; b = 2nd part of year;
c = death certificate copy; c/o = child of

NAME	AGE OR YOB.	BIRTH PLACE	CERT. NO	ID	DEATH YEAR	NAME	AGE OR YOB.	BIRTH PLACE	CERT. NO	ID	DEATH YEAR
GODENOR						GODHUE					
William	55	ENG	1158		1866	Wm.	57	MA	2777		1894
GODENS						GODI					
Jno. D.	62	HOL	5063a		1895	Iris	1903	SF	1024c		1904
GODESKI						GODICKA					
Pauline	1875	SF	428c		1904	William Francis	<1	SF	1365		1869
GODET						GODINEZ					
Jeanne	1837	FRA	1308c		1904	Panfilo	38	MEX	903		1902
Louis	79	FRA	6504		1904	GODIT					
GODFREY						Louis	<1	SF	1422		1869
Albert Edward	1	SF	7650		1901	GODKIN					
Aliene	1	SF	934		1902	Nellie	25	SF	3406		1894
Annie	3	SF	2802		1866	Susan Agnes	1	SF	5417		1867
Augustus	48	MA	2280a		1872	GODLEY					
Christoher	49	RI	1924		1870	Montgomery				Jan	1900
Dennis				Mar	1899	Montgomery				Jan	1900
Florilla S.	26	CT	8380		1868	GODOY					
George B.	1838	ENG	2410c		1904	Jose A.	55	NGR	1376		1869
George J. (soldier)			4545		1901	Juana	21	MEX	6309		1904
George T.	33	SF	4604		1904	Louis Alberto	2	MEX	1174b		1871
Helen	49	OH	6210		1902	GODREY					
Irabella D.	67	IRL	2531		1900	John	60	NY	3704		1903
James Michael	<1	SF	9199		1901	GODSCHAND					
Jeremiah J.	62	IRL	1115b		1872	——	<1	SF	3487b		1870
John T.				Jun	1899	GODSIE					
Lidia S.	27	MA	319		1865	——		SF	1144		1869
M. A.	<1	SF	5483		1867	GODSIL					
Mary	<1	SF	2459		1894	James	58	IRE	3561		1903
Mary Florence	13	NV	8089		1904	John Henry				Jun	1899
Michael	77	IRE	1400		1902	Timothy	57	IRL	8490		1900
Mildred, c/o		CA	6572		1901	GODSMARK					
Nathaniel A.	68	MA	644b		1895	Thomas G.			3958		1902
Rebecca B.				Feb	1900						
William				Jan	1900						

Key: a = 1st part of year; b = 2nd part of year;
c = death certificate copy; c/o = child of

NAME	AGE OR YOB.	BIRTH PLACE	CERT. NO	ID	DEATH YEAR	NAME	AGE OR YOB.	BIRTH PLACE	CERT. NO	ID	DEATH YEAR
GODT						**GOETHALS**					
Hans Peter					May 1899	Harry					Aug 1898
GODWIN						**GOETJEN**					
Harold M.			1229		1903	Charles/Mollie, c/o	1	SF	6947		1904
GOE						Hattie					Jan 1899
Annie Ann					Jun 1899	Hermann					Mar 1899
Ong	20	CHN	1487a		1871	Richard	5	CA	G48		1885
William	67	OH	431		1901	**GOETTE**					
GOEBBELS						George	22	SF	5978		1903
Alina	4	IL	2234		1894	**GOETZ**					
GOEBEL						Anna	46	FRA	8985		1901
Chas.	67	GER	9650		1901	Anna P.	1	SF	8752		1868
Frederick N.	45	GER	1287		1869	Balthasar	64	GER	1684		1902
Jacob (soldier)			6819		1900	Bartholomew	53	GER	4239Dec		1901
GOEBENER						Harry	48	GER	1125		1870
Henry	64	GER	6915Feb		1901	Henry	34	NY	398b		1895
Johanna L.	1	SF	1932		1870	Joseph	1	SF	766b		1871
GOEBNER						Joseph, Jr.	17	NY	874b		1872
Elizabeth	37	GER	2242a		1872	Joseph/Bertha, c/o	1	SF	2795		1903
John	1	SF	2241a		1872	Leopoldine	58	AUT	6700		1900
GOECKE						Peter	14	NY	3923		1870
Albert (soldier)			821		1900	Peter	34	NOR	G9		1882
GOEHR						Rudolph	45	GER	6681		1903
Edna Elizabeth	5	SF	7629		1902	**GOETZE**					
GOEPP						Edith	<1	SF	1172b		1895
Amelia	27	GER	2597a		1872	Henry	57	GER	4282a		1895
GOEPPERT						Joseph Eroll	1	SF	4680		1904
Annie Caroline	30	GER	571		1902	**GOEZ**					
GOERSS						Elizabeth	67	GER	5064		1904
Gertie S.	49	CAN	2792		1894	**GOFF**					
GOESSEL						Almon B.	1832	NY	2948c		1904
Paul	40	GER	1884		1902	Chas. P.	70	VT	G74		1886
						Lucius M.	55	IN	6867Feb		1901
						Sarah	45	CA	6250		1904

Key: a = 1st part of year; b = 2nd part of year; c = death certificate copy; c/o = child of

NAME	AGE OR YOB.	BIRTH PLACE	CERT. NO	ID	DEATH YEAR
GOGAN					
Ann	38	IRE	5612		1867
Elizabeth	65	IRL	6905		1900
John	45	IRE	7427		1904
William	40	LA	4183		1896
GOGER					
Kunigunda	82	GER	789		1903
Phoebe	26	KY	1460b		1871
GOGGIN					
Charles Francis	1904	CA	3035c		1904
Daniel J.	20	SF	1524		1900
John	43	IRL	6723		1896
Kate	25	CA	2530		1894
Mary Ann	4	SF	2075		1873
Norah	57	IRL	4608		1901
Richard	67	KY	3791		1896
Richard D.	<1	SF	1125		1901
GOGNE					
C.	1877	ITA	3428c		1904
GOH					
Ah	40	CHN	3008a		1872
GOHLICH					
Margaret	47	GER	4482		1896
GOHLINGHORST					
Geo. J.	40	GER	G17		1882
GOICOVICH					
Spiro	20	AUS	271		1903
GOIGAN					
Bridget	65	IRL	3702a		1895
GOININI					
Annie	1	SF	4310a		1895
GOK					
Soy Hing	35	CHN	2911		1873

NAME	AGE OR YOB.	BIRTH PLACE	CERT. NO	ID	DEATH YEAR
GOLCHER					
Samuel Lingard	24	MN	978		1894
GOLD					
Ab	56	PRU	2093		1866
GOLDARACENA					
Polonia	67	ESP	3864a		1895
GOLDBAUM					
Louis					Apr 1899
Rosa Gertrude	1	SF	1265		1869
GOLDBECK					
Chas.	71	GER	5251		1904
GOLDBERG					
Alexander	8	TX	1654		1903
Annie	62	GER	7293		1904
Charles	66	DEN	5327		1902
Daniel	75	RUS	8481		1901
Frank J. (soldier)			6817		1900
Harrold J.	1	SF	5537		1903
Hilda	25	SF	5480		1904
Isaac	68	RUS	9449		1901
J./ L., c/o					Dec 1899
Louis	72	GER	212b		1895
Malka	9	CA	7020		1900
Phillip					Jun 1899
Rebeccah	21	PRU	3952a		1895
Solomon	81	GER	3272		1903
Walter W.	18	ND	9540		1901
William					Aug 1899
GOLDBERT					
George R.	18	GA	501		1866
GOLDBLATH					
Isador					Oct 1899
GOLDBURG					
Edna R.	1886	MN	2263c		1904

Key: a = 1st part of year; b = 2nd part of year;
c = death certificate copy; c/o = child of

NAME	AGE OR YOB.	BIRTH PLACE	CERT. NO	ID	DEATH YEAR	NAME	AGE OR YOB.	BIRTH PLACE	CERT. NO	ID	DEATH YEAR
GOLDCHMIDT						GOLDING					
Katie	27	SF	191b		1895	James	70	SCT	7247		1901
						John	40	UT	9696		1901
GOLDEN						Thos.	53	CA	3124		1894
——		SF	703		1870						
Anna	57	IRL	1529b		1895	GOLDKUHL					
Annie	64	IRL	1896		1900	Mary E.	36	CT	5919a		1895
Bernard	27	CA	G15		1882						
Claude	<1	CA	670		1900	GOLDMAN					
Edward	48	NY	3101		1873	Alfred J.	40	SF	3046		1900
Edward	40	IRE	5038		1867	Benjamin	71	RUS	7704		1901
Edwin (soldier)			4038		1900	Cyril M.				Feb	1900
George A.	37	MA	139b		1895	Evelyn Mae	32	SF	572		1902
Hugh M.	29	IRL	4240	Dec	1901	Hannah	56	GER	5934a		1895
James	58	IRL	234b		1895	Hugh	1	SF	3347		1870
James F.	5	CA	8916		1900	Irving	1887	SF	2017c		1904
Jo's. L., c/o	<1	SF	2601a		1872	J. W. , c/o		SF	1990		1873
John	62	IRE	8406		1903	J., c/o	<1	SF	2284a		1872
John Wm.	53	NY	5601	Jan	1901	Jacob	62	BAV	2489		1900
Margaret	69	IRL	4862a		1895	Joseph	76	PRU	6137	Jan	1901
Matthew James	1864	NY	529c		1904	Joseph/Evelyn, c/o		SF	509		1902
Patrick	60	IRE	3521		1903	Leopold	44	HUN	3871		1902
Patrick	37	IRE	379		1903	Louis	53	PRU	2796		1903
Robert B. (soldier)			5326		1901	Mansfield	3	SF	5626		1903
Simon	29	IRE	1250		1869	Rosia	3	SF	1979b		1895
Thomas	37	ME	1368		1869						
Thomas	34	MI	2292		1901	GOLDMEYER					
Thomas				Mar	1900	Louis	77	GER	7359		1900
Thomas E.	31	SF	6788		1900						
Thomas J. (soldier)			2217		1903	GOLDNER					
Winifred	1	SF	1088		1869	Julie	1827	GER	194c		1904
						Julius	73	PRU	6172		1903
GOLDENSON											
Martha Rebecca	44	POL	3628a		1895	GOLDRICK					
						James				Mar	1900
GOLDER						John	40	NY	1445		1869
Theresa	2	CA	3136		1866	GOLDRING					
						Hanna	1	SF	3127		1895

Key: *a = 1st part of year; b = 2nd part of year;*
c = death certificate copy; c/o = child of

NAME	AGE OR YOB.	BIRTH PLACE	CERT. NO	ID	DEATH YEAR	NAME	AGE OR YOB.	BIRTH PLACE	CERT. NO	ID	DEATH YEAR
GOLDSBERRY						Julius P.	44	NY	6985	Feb	1901
Wm. D.	53	IN	5276a		1895	Lea	<1	CA	1382b		1895
						Lena	<1	SF	1608		1902
GOLDSCHMIDT						Leon	53	POL	6831		1903
Adolph				Jul	1899	Louis	1903	SF	1538c		1904
Gretchen	6	SF	4950		1903	Louis	53	NY	6149		1902
Samuel	6	AZ	1705		1900	Louis/Dora, c/o		SF	1622		1900
GOLDSHEIN						M., c/o				Nov	1899
Jacob		SF	2054		1894	Margaret	45	MA	3003		1903
GOLDSMITH						Margaret	32	NY	3609		1896
Alfred	3	SF	3086a		1872	Marks	1	SF	9336		1901
Alice	33	NV	1238		1903	Maurice	1854	NJ	1962c		1904
Berdie				Aug	1898	Moris, c/o	<1	SF	1655		1895
David S.				Mar	1900	P./T., c/o	<1	SF	4382		1895
Edward	56	GER	2556		1900	Samuel	1835	POL	3263c		1904
Elkin	37	GER	1069		1869	Simon	<1	SF	5934		1867
George				Aug	1899	Sophie			5910		1903
Jeanette S.				Dec	1898	William	46	SF	3402	Nov	1901
Julius	39	GER	G14		1882	**GOLDSTEM**					
Lewis	50	GER	G42		1885	Moses	48	RUS	5356		1901
Moses	1	SF	2364		1866	**GOLDSTINE**					
Sam/Carrie, c/o	<1	SF	6868		1901	Louis	2	SF	296a		1871
Sylvian	1903	CA	1595c		1904	**GOLDSTOHN**					
William (soldier)			7443		1904	Morris	50	PRU	1938a		1872
GOLDSON						**GOLDSTON**					
Alexander	33	WIN	3173		1873	Dave	1	SF	2570		1866
GOLDSTEIN						Israel	44	PRU	6434		1867
Bertha L.				Oct	1898	**GOLDSTONE**					
Charles H.	<1	CA	6170		1904	Bertha				Jan	1899
Dora	34	RUS	1984		1900	Dorian	<1	SF	1817		1894
Helena	75	GER	1269		1901	Edwin H.	<1	SF	1038		1868
Henry	59	RUS	6303		1896	Eliza	49	ENG	1517		1894
Henry	62	POL	2224		1902	H.	75	RUS	2397		1894
Hiram P.	57	NY	3600		1903	Maria	1	SF	7042		1868
Jacob/Sarah, c/o	<1	SF	5034		1903	Mildred Phyllis	<1	SF	3841		1896
Joseph/Sarah, c/o	<1	SF	1643		1901						

Key: a = 1st part of year; b = 2nd part of year;
c = death certificate copy; c/o = child of

NAME	AGE OR YOB.	BIRTH PLACE	CERT. NO	ID	DEATH YEAR
Percy	33	SF	4478		1904
Rae	23	SF	8524		1904
GOLDSTROUGH					
Margaret					Oct 1898
GOLDTHWAITE					
W.B.					Nov 1899
William					Oct 1899
GOLDWATER					
Amelia	65	ENG	599		1903
Jacob	39	NY	7191		1904
Michael	82	GER	7437		1903
GOLERIE					
Roland	58	FRA	751b		1872
GOLEY					
George	5	SF	6061		1867
GOLL					
John H.	1841	GER	1899c		1904
GOLLER					
Emma M.					Oct 1899
H. J./E., c/o	<1	SF	3238		1894
H. J./E., c/o	<1	SF	3239		1894
Jno.	53	GER	G65		1886
GOLLNICK					
Rudolph	36	GER	8596		1903
GOLLY					
Anita	<1	SF	4342		1901
Lena	55	WI	6386		1903
Leon	50		4993		1902
GOLZIO					
Batista	2	ITA	934		1903
GOMAR					
Sarah	8	SF	1063		1870
GOMES					
John F.	87	POR	7957		1903
Joseph	50	POR	2047		1902
Mariano					Mar 1899
GOMEZ					
Dolores					Feb 1899
Edward	1	CA	1666		1903
Ella Carmelita	<1	CA	3474		1902
Esignia	26	CA	6694		1904
Geronimo	36	COL	215b		1871
Jennie	1	RI	4291		1903
John Henry	21	CA	4016		1902
John Henry	43	POR	7419		1901
Jose	25	WIS	4279b		1870
Joseph	28	CO	1796		1903
Louisa	39	SF	6770		1896
Manuel	31	POR	8696		1901
Manuel Silva	29	POR	1084a		1871
Mary Isabella	25	WIS	5946		1867
Migele	2	SF	8269		1868
Petra	52	MEX	3520		1867
Prudencia	<1	SF	1582a		1871
Rafaele	62	SPA	7214		1902
Rosa	<1	SF	8160		1901
GOMOND					
Nelce	44	CAN	4824		1904
GON					
Ding Gui	38	CHN	6506		Feb 1901
GONAILHARDON					
Mary L.					Jul 1899
GONCALVES					
Anita May	<1	SF	6958		Feb 1901
GONDOLFO					
Charles	10	SF	6724		Feb 1901
GONEIZ					
Encarmacion	7	CA	1318		1866

Key: a = 1st part of year; b = 2nd part of year;
c = death certificate copy; c/o = child of

NAME	AGE OR YOB.	BIRTH PLACE	CERT. NO	ID	DEATH YEAR	NAME	AGE OR YOB.	BIRTH PLACE	CERT. NO	ID	DEATH YEAR
GONELLA						Concepcion	38	MEX	7122		1903
Giuseppe	55	ITA	6700		1902	Ernesto	50	ITA	6160	Jan	1901
						Esmelinda	11	SF	5992		1867
GONG						Felice	22	MEX	9424		1868
Chan Long	45	CHN	2129		1866	Irene Victoria	<1	SF	4651		1903
Gee Wood	46	CHN	1713		1900	John	<1	SF	960		1866
Ging	30	CHN	8577		1900	John	40	AZO	4784		1896
Gung	1862	CHN	3126c		1904	Jose Maria	56	MEX	8597		1868
Guy Sen	27	CHN	1809b		1895	Mary	25	MEX	142		1903
Lep	32	CHN	2166a		1872	Modesta	30	MEX	3307		1894
Ong	17	CHN	256a		1871	Peter	20	MEX	443a		1871
Ong	34	CHN	1450a		1871	William	<1	SF	4299		1867
Ong	34	CHN	2487a		1872						
Sue Hing	29	CHN	1808b		1895	**GONZALEZ**					
						Elena	<1	SF	6337		1867
GONGUE						Frank P.	18	MEX	7818		1900
Wisalia	40	GRE	1431		1869	Margaret	39	IRL	3533		1870
						Margaret	26	SF	2601		1900
GONNELLA						Mariano E.	55	CA	3831		1903
Annie	48	ITA	2745		1901						
						GONZALS					
GONSALEZ						Ralph	1904	SF	447c		1904
Juan	49	MEX	717a		1871						
Margaret				Nov	1898	**GOO**					
						Emma Wasley	30	CA	7805		1900
GONSALVES						Gee Yuck	28	CHN	863b		1895
Julian	49	POR	575		1900	Moon			2949c		1904
Manuel	<1	SF	1612		1870	Moon				Jan	1899
						Yum Nom	47	CHN	3838		1902
GONSOLIN											
Eugene/Marie, c/o	1	SF	8466		1904	**GOOCH**					
						Alice B.	21	CA	91		1902
GONUAIE											
John M.	<1	SF	184b		1872	**GOOD**					
						Fred (soldier)			6394		1900
GONYEAU						George	49	SCT	7349		1900
John B.	63	CAN	925		1901	Helene M.	76	OH	943		1894
						Henry	63	IRE	7342		1904
GONYEN						John	54	NY	5750		1903
Burney (soldier)			7148		1901	Joseph Christian	66	SWT	419		1902
GONZALES											
Brazil	23	MEX	5387		1901						
Catarina	3	SF	9344		1868						

Key: *a = 1st part of year; b = 2nd part of year;*
c = death certificate copy; c/o = child of

NAME	AGE OR YOB.	BIRTH PLACE	CERT. NO	ID	DEATH YEAR
Michael (soldier)			1540		1900
W. F.					Aug 1898
William P.	20	NJ	4937		1902
GOODALE					
Grace Marie	<1	CA	6455		1903
GOODALL					
Charles					Aug 1899
George A.	1	SF	9634		1868
George H.	<1	SF	2034		1894
Junnialla	32	OH	775		1900
GOODCHILD					
Edward	56	ENG	1412		1866
Mary	83	NY	3904		1900
GOODELL					
Charles	29	MA	5427		1867
Mary Florilla	1	CA	5607		1867
Sarah	85	MA	5955		1902
GOODENOUGH					
Alice	5	SF	4262		1900
GOODENOW					
George V.	21	CA	1928		1894
GOODERHAM					
Sadie	33	SF	5577		1904
GOODFELLOW					
Edw./Margaurite., c/o		SF	1791		1901
Felix	abt	ENG	8593		1901
Summerfield Stephen	72	PA	7192		1904
GOODFRIEND					
Ferris	18	CA	8560		1901
Tessie					Dec 1898
GOODHUE					
Daniel	69	ME	6701		1902
Eddie	<1	SF	2887		1894
Frank B.	29	PA	6630		1904
Lizzy			2412		1866
Margaret	23	CA	1445b		1895
Margaret	3	SF	1574a		1871
GOODKIND					
Caroline					Feb 1899
Meyer	71	GER	7336		1900
GOODLING					
John W. (soldier)			7749		1901
GOODMAN					
A.	51	PRU	G54		1885
Adele	64	GER	4823a		1895
Albert	30	SF	8159		1901
Cathrine	58	MA	9184		1868
Charles David	1904	SF	891c		1904
Chas. F.					Feb 1900
Eli					Mar 1900
Elias		POL	5590		1867
Ella					Aug 1898
Ephraim	30	CA	2117		1894
G. S.	52	HOL	1002		1868
George	75	AUS	7706		1904
George W.					Jan 1899
H.	19	MI	6484		1896
Helen	70	GER	7334		1900
Henry	1867	SF	999c		1904
James S. (soldier)			2218		1903
Laura	39	MI	1030b		1895
Lewis K.	63	NY	7835		1901
Louise Jane	71	MO	862		1903
Lyman B.	27	NY	9459		1868
Mary	50	IRL	G77		1887
Selma	28	SF	3499		Nov 1901
Simon	51	RUS	4127		1896
W.I.					Feb 1900

NAME	AGE OR YOB.	BIRTH PLACE	CERT. NO	ID	DEATH YEAR
GOODMANN					
Dorah	8	SF	747b		1871
GOODMURPHY					
Edith Eminson	1	SF	1933		1902
GOODMURPHYIA.					
Annie	30	SF	1929		1894
GOODNIGHT					
Rufus	51	NC	8594		1901
GOODRICH					
Devane					Mar 1900
Elizabeth	60	VA	982b		1895
Elliott D.	49	NY	5541		1904
Eugenia M.	24	CA	899		1900
Harriet Elizabeth					Mar 1899
John F.	18	MO	2916		1866
Lucinda Clark	50	NY	759		1902
Robert L. (soldier)	35	TN	1880		1900
Sidney Everett	51	NY	6786		1902
William					Nov 1898
GOODSELL					
De Courcy M.	82	NY	3989		1903
GOODSPEED					
Lucy C.	51	WI	4608		1896
Rilano					Jan 1899
GOODSTEIN					
Hannah	1823	POL	2516c		1904
GOODWIN					
Benjamin F.	64	NH	4406		1903
Frederick S.	<1	SF	1423		1869
H.	77	VA	2505b		1895
Harry Blair	33	OH	7517		1902
Howard C.	<1	SF	2829		1900
Jas. Porter					Feb 1900
John F.	39	MA	1768		1902
Joseph	<1	SF	1412		1869
Laura	57	VA	1738		1903
Lillian					Apr 1899
Lydia W.	79	RI	6534		1896
M. D., Mrs.	27	CA	1148		1869
Maria Dolores Laura	1	SF	1352		1869
Mary Ann	<1	SF	1362		1869
Mary W.	1848	NY	1577c		1904
Michael	62	IRL	1028b		1895
Myron H.	68	NY	4758		1896
Peter/Ellen, c/o					Mar 1899
Solomon	37	NH	3620		1867
William	24	NB	2024		1902
GOODYEAR					
Everett F.	33	IA	4017		1902
GOOGINS					
Lawrence M. (soldier)			5045		1901
GOOK					
Lee Gas	48	CHN	341b		1872
Sue Hoo Hoy	39	CHN	G76		1886
GOOLD					
——	<1	SF	3984		1870
P./E., c/o	<1	SF	3529		1895
P./E., c/o	<1	SF	3530		1895
GOOMER					
Francis					Nov 1898
GOON					
Ah	68	CHN	2059a		1872
Jue	66	CHN	6732		1902
Lai Gong	27	CHN	5644		1904
Lee		CHN	G18		1883
Quon Lee	41	CHN	2260		1900
Weg	13	CHN	716b		1872

Key: a = 1st part of year; b = 2nd part of year;
c = death certificate copy; c/o = child of

NAME	AGE OR YOB.	BIRTH PLACE	CERT. NO	ID	DEATH YEAR
GOONG					
Gee Lock	25	CHN	848		1870
GOORSKEY					
Peter (soldier)			6615		1900
GOOSSANS					
J. J.	42	BEL	18a		1871
GOOT					
Ah	<1	SF	2069		1866
Gnook	24	CHN	6453	Feb	1901
Waldemar Duvey				Dec	1898
GOOTEGUT					
Caroline	1	SF	3479b		1870
GOOTHMANN					
Henry	<1	SF	2000		1894
GOOU					
Ann	36	CHN	712b		1871
GOPCEVIC					
Harry A. L. F.	31	SF	5542		1904
Harry A. L. F./M. M., c/o	1	SF	5601		1904
GOR					
Knoin Joe	25	PUR	2644		1901
GORADT					
Frank	<1	SF	1635		1900
GORAMLY					
Patrick	56	IRE	2499		1866
GORBET					
Louisa F.	2	SF	1377		1870
GORDAN					
Henry	66	IRL	5569		1896
John Aloyisius	4	SF	1101a		1871
GORDEN					
Amelia L.	47	AFR	3038		1870
Charles W.	<1	SF	8208		1868

NAME	AGE OR YOB.	BIRTH PLACE	CERT. NO	ID	DEATH YEAR
George A.	<1	SF	209a		1871
Mary C.	<1	SF	9307		1868
Mattie	37	ID	3554		1902
William	40	NY	9284		1868
GORDON					
——	22		1332b		1871
Ada Myrtle	12	CA	3907		1896
Alexander	59	NS	8327		1903
Alexander C.	72	NH	5095		1901
Alicia Moore				May	1899
Amherst	75	NY	2325		1902
Andrew Leslie				Oct	1898
Carlotta F.	43	ENG	488		1870
Charles				Jan	1899
Charles H.	70	ENG	1271		1903
Cuthbert Powell	50	VA	3190	Nov	1901
Edward Payson	35	CAN	6985		1902
Elizabeth	<1	SF	1124		1869
Elizabeth				Mar	1900
Elnor	42	MA	3429a		1872
Fred (soldier)			466		1902
George	48	MA	3544		1870
George	49	ENG	1216		1869
George	9	SF	7519		1904
George	69	IRL	6769		1896
George Gorum				Mar	1899
George P.	51	NS	459		1901
George W.	51	MI	2122		1900
George/Mary, c/o		SF	8261		1901
Gracie				Jun	1899
J.	35		4923		1896
James C.	34	NY	3807		1870
John	45	NY	1265		1869
Joseph	26	SF	2885		1894
Lem (soldier)			2710		1901
Lillian Kate	1	SF	1459		1903

Key: a = 1st part of year; b = 2nd part of year;
c = death certificate copy; c/o = child of

NAME	AGE OR YOB.	BIRTH PLACE	CERT. NO	ID	DEATH YEAR
Louisa	52	ENG	217		1901
Maggie				Feb	1900
Mary	1844	IRE	1101c		1904
Mary A.	73	SCT	4372		1903
Mary J.				Feb	1899
Mary Jane	<1	SF	537		1870
Max				Feb	1899
Michael				Jan	1899
Mollie	22	SF	8467		1904
Morris (soldier)			822		1900
Nellie	55	MA	2830		1902
Noah Henry	72	NH	9250		1901
Patrick				Dec	1898
Patrick Joseph	1869	IRE	2411c		1904
Samuel A.	57	ENG	7472		1902
Sheldon S.	64	NY	6863		1895
Thomas	61	IRE	2766		1903
Thomas	81	IRL	5290a		1895
W.	60		2867		1902
W./M., c/o	<1	SF	2865		1894
William (soldier)		NY	3541		1900
Wm./M., c/o	<1	SF	3526		1895
GORE					
Deborah Parsons				Jan	1899
John H.	<1	SF	1017		1868
William Robert				Jun	1899
GOREE					
Charles F.			2600		1902
GOREN					
A./M., c/o		SF	4971		1895
GORESUCH					
Charles			7149		1901
GOREVAN					
James	83	IRE	2094		1902
Mary Ann	70	IRE	1035		1903

NAME	AGE OR YOB.	BIRTH PLACE	CERT. NO	ID	DEATH YEAR
Thomas Joseph	37	CA	5175		1902
William P. J.	34	CA	7315		1900
GORF					
J./A., c/o		SF	4489		1895
GORFINKEL					
Aaron	76	POL	3260		1895
Rebecca	10	SF	1558b		1872
GORHAM					
Anna Elizabeth	75	MA	7827		1904
Charles M.	9	SF	4890		1867
Eliza F.	67	ME	3394		1896
Emily A.	82	NY	4188a		1895
J.	55	IRE	9794		1868
James				Jan	1899
John	60	IRL	525b		1895
John Anderson	1	CA	578		1901
Sarah L.	37	CT	4002		1867
Thomas Melton	1	SF	8806		1904
GORHEY					
John	46	MA	4652		1903
GORINGA					
Crus	38	MEX	965a		1871
GORMAN					
Adaline, c/o	1	CA	4846		1904
Andrew James	50	LA	1667		1903
Anna	1	SF	8791		1868
Annie	55	IRL	2687		1901
Annie G.	2	SF	2632a		1872
Bernice Irene	<1	CA	4596		1903
Catherine	2	SF	8792		1868
Charles L.				Oct	1898
Clara C.	28	SF	8817		1903
David O.	34	IRE	295		1865
Edward	28	IRL	3016		1900
Ellen	2	SF	1271		1869

Key: a = 1st part of year; b = 2nd part of year;
c = death certificate copy; c/o = child of

NAME	AGE OR YOB.	BIRTH PLACE	CERT. NO	ID	DEATH YEAR	NAME	AGE OR YOB.	BIRTH PLACE	CERT. NO	ID	DEATH YEAR
Ellen	81	IRE	7865		1903	**GORMLEY**					
Frances				Mar	1899	John	70	IRL	1383b		1895
George	55	IRE	2541		1866	Margaret	28	IRE	4678		1867
George	1	SF	579		1901	Mary Ann	35	IRE	1126		1869
James	40	NY	1707		1894	Mary E.	<1	SF	859		1866
James	39	IRL	5505		1896	Michael	29	IRE	959		1902
James	70	IRL	4316		1901	Nellie	<1	SF	2177		1873
James Emmett	30	SF	3678		1896						
John	65	IRE	4215		1903	**GORMLY**					
John	44	IRL	8092		1900	Annie	12	SF	3157a		1872
John	46	IRL	2123		1900	Elizabeth A.	<1	SF	9646		1868
John F.	64	IRL	6256	Feb	1901						
Jos. F.	<1	SF	2990		1894	**GORNAN**					
Lucy	13	CA	8127		1901	Margaret	1	CA	487b		1872
Margaret	35	SF	2894		1903	**GORRICK**					
Margaret	67	IRE	7193		1904	Leonard L.				Jan	1900
Margaret Louise				Oct	1898	**GORRIE**					
Mary	3	SF	4589b		1870	James Osborne	30	MN	2894		1902
Mary	54	IRE	4825		1904	**GORRINGER**					
Mary	73	IRE	7828		1904	Henry	36		7041		1904
Mary Elizabeth	3	SF	1249		1869	**GORS**					
Mary Ellen	<1	SF	1472b		1871	Michael	64	IRL	6761a		1895
Michael	22	IRL	3881		1870	**GORSIN**					
Michael	64	MO	3923		1902	John	48	AUS	7521		1903
Michael	78	IRL	6278	Feb	1901	**GORSSON**					
Michael	66	IRE	5927		1904	Charles				Jun	1899
Mollie	<1	SF	190b		1895	**GORSUCH**					
Page Bennett	1	SF	4996		1896	Henry W.				Jun	1899
Pat	30	IRE	1126		1869	**GORTE**					
Peter Francis	<1	SF	96b		1871	Maria	46	GER	4607		1896
Richard Francis	43	MA	8700		1904	**GORTON**					
Simon	67	IRL	8041		1901	Hilda Doris	<1	SF	5895	Jan	1901
Timothy	45	IRE	7058		1903	**GORYL**					
William	19	CA	G3		1882	Lloyd A.	<1	SF	3753		1900
William Henry	29	CA	4734		1904						

Key: a = 1st part of year; b = 2nd part of year;
c = death certificate copy; c/o = child of

NAME	AGE OR YOB.	BIRTH PLACE	CERT. NO	ID	DEATH YEAR	NAME	AGE OR YOB.	BIRTH PLACE	CERT. NO	ID	DEATH YEAR
GOSCH						**GOSTMER**					
Henry	26		8585		1868	Simon	29	PRU	1833a		1872
GOSDORF						**GOT**					
Leopold B.	82	GER	2975		1894	Hung	61	CHN	7868		1900
GOSLAND						**GOTANDA**					
William T.				Feb	1900	Ayai	1904	SF	2437c		1904
GOSLER						**GOTCHAUX**					
John	41	GER	1596a		1871	Leon	5	FRA	1268b		1871
GOSLINE						**GOTELLI**					
John A. (soldier)			1315		1902	George	26	SF	7225		1904
GOSLINER						Giovanni				Jan	1899
Aaron S.	45	GER	4016	Dec	1901	Joseph	16	SF	2685		1903
Bella	23	CA	2182b		1895	L./A., c/o		SF	6081		1896
Joseph	47	GER	3259		1895	Margherita				Mar	1899
Julius	53	GER	5739		1896	**GOTH**					
Minnie	84	GER	3736		1896	Emma Louise				May	1899
Simon	69	GER	1198		1903	Johann	41	GER	2625		1900
Theresa	45	ENG	1221		1894	**GOTHER**					
GOSLINSKY						Anne	38	IRE	2442		1866
Elias	60	GER	4514		1896	**GOTSCHALK**					
GOSMAN						Jos.	60	AUT	2999a		1872
Maria Rosalia	6	SF	2630		1873	**GOTTE**					
GOSNEZ						George	<1	SF	1684b		1871
Jose	22	NIC	1270		1869	**GOTTEI**					
GOSS						Lillie	<1	SF	7364		1868
Elizabeth	56	IRE	5418		1902	**GOTTIG**					
G.A.				Oct	1899	L.	1	SF	841		1870
John	3	MA	390a		1871	**GOTTLIEB**					
Mary	<1	SF	1022		1870	Louis J.	75	GER	8734		1903
Mary E.	78	OH	8916		1901	William	24	CO	6650		1896
Mathilda P. S.	39	ENG	2718		1866	**GOTTSCHALK**					
GOSSAGE						Alice	7	IA	1227		1869
W. S.	27	CA	6644	Feb	1901	Elise	1	SF	8531		1868

Key: a = 1st part of year; b = 2nd part of year;
c = death certificate copy; c/o = child of

NAME	AGE OR YOB.	BIRTH PLACE	CERT. NO	ID	DEATH YEAR	NAME	AGE OR YOB.	BIRTH PLACE	CERT. NO	ID	DEATH YEAR
Fred K.	30	CA	G33		1884	Wm.	68	IRL	2322		1894
John T. H.				Feb	1900	**GOUL**					
Marcus	62	GER	1317b		1895	Frank	35	BAV	6850		1868
Nora	<1	SF	2229		1866	**GOULD**					
GOUAILHARDOU						Albert Robertson	50	ME	4131	Dec	1901
Mary L.				Jul	1899	Ashley Cooper	<1	SF	9164		1868
GOUCH						Azaph	48	VT	1713b		1872
Chan	37	CHN	1397		1866	Earle E.				May	1899
GOUDET						Edward	49	CT	1201		1869
Adrien	29	FRA	8470		1900	Eliza Jane	9	SF	2949		1873
GOUDY						Francis L. (soldier)			2059		1901
Jullien/Angelae, c/o	<1	SF	6925		1902	Frank (soldier)			7150		1901
Justin	1903	SF	892c		1904	Franklin	51	NH	2415		1873
Justine Margueritte	1	SF	2272		1901	George O.	32	ME	2260		1866
GOUEL						James	53	ME	6387		1903
Mary	44	GER	2731		1873	James G.	49	MA	666a		1871
GOUGE						James R.	31	NY	365b		1872
J. H.	36	SF	2686		1901	John C.	1849	IRE	396c		1904
GOUGEL						Juanita				Mar	1899
Simon	29	FRA	837a		1871	Lucy A.	31	ME	1026		1868
GOUGH						M.	30	IRL	4212b		1870
Al, Jr.	1	SF	699		1870	Maria	81	MA	8562		1903
Bridget	31	IRL	3225a		1872	Mary Ann		SF	4259b		1870
Catherine	34	IRL	828b		1872	Mary Ann	35	ENG	2906		1873
Chas. H.	67	MD	502b		1895	Peter	21	MI	567		1866
E. F.	29	NY	6847		1868	Seriah H.	1836	ME	2615c		1904
Harry O.	40	MD	1488		1870	Thomas				Oct	1899
John L.	47	IRL	134		1870	Walter E.	39	SF	7518		1902
John Patrick	<1	SF	1489a		1871	William B.	40	VT	3338		1866
Lottie	16	SF	4146a		1895	William O	73	NH	4643		1902
Michael Joseph	<1	SF	1440a		1871	**GOULDIN**					
Patrick, c/o	<1	SF	2011a		1872	Thomas	75	Eng	182		1901
Son	20	CHN	2057		1870	**GOULET**					
Thomas	34	MD	4803		1867	Isidore	75	CAN	7800		1904

NAME	AGE OR YOB.	BIRTH PLACE	CERT. NO	ID	DEATH YEAR
GOUMEZ					
———	70	ITA	6872		1903
GOUMONT					
Edward	40		2868		1902
GOUNAT					
Pierre	27	FRA	4719		1902
GOUNSKY					
Joseph B.	60	POL	3726		1900
GOURLEY					
Mary	1867	CA	1102c		1904
GOURSAN					
Joseph	38	FRA	749b		1895
GOURSOLLE					
Clementina	1901	CA	2701c		1904
GOUSTIAUX					
Albertine Celestine Adelina	63	FRA	5940		1903
GOUSY					
Ling	45	CHN	317b		1871
GOUT					
Leontine	<1	SF	3485a		1895
GOUTIE					
Jean Oscar	44	FRA	1772b		1871
GOVE					
Catherine L.	60	IRE	8138		1903
David Merritt	46	SF	2044		1903
Henry M.	37	WA	4955		1896
Mary	56	IRL	3858		1900
GOW					
Aung	38	CHN	1063		1866
Chin Shar	1850	CHN	989c		1904
Get	33	CHN	1927		1900
Leong Sung	55	CHN	1696		1894
R. T.	40		3631		1900

NAME	AGE OR YOB.	BIRTH PLACE	CERT. NO	ID	DEATH YEAR
Sen Si				Jan	1900
Yow				Dec	1898
GOWAN					
George	37	SCT	842b		1871
John M.	<1	SF	3924		1867
William	50	PA	8940		1901
GOWEN					
Theresa Adelaide				Nov	1898
GOWENLOCK					
Robert	67	SCT	1770b		1872
GOWEY					
Wm. A./Rosetta, c/o		SF	1770		1900
GOWING					
Louie W. (soldier)			7151		1901
GOY					
Yua	26	CHN	478b		1872
GOYEN					
Alice				Aug	1899
GOYER					
Clara	48	OR	6674		1902
GOYHENEIX					
Marie	45	CA	7226		1904
GOZZOLO					
Joseph G.	1	SF	1033		1868
GRABAU					
Hermanda				Aug	1899
GRABB					
George	42	PRU	1047		1868
GRABE					
Herman	24	GER	3221		1866
GRABILL					
Auguste	74	PA	6077		1902

Key: a = 1st part of year; b = 2nd part of year;
c = death certificate copy; c/o = child of

NAME	AGE OR YOB.	BIRTH PLACE	CERT. NO	ID	DEATH YEAR
GRABOUSKY					
Joseph				Feb	1900
GRACCHI					
G./R., c/o		SF	5037		1895
Giovanni	17	ITA	3910	Dec	1901
Maria	12	SF	3685		1902
GRACE					
Calvin Willing	8	CA	2730		1903
George	<1	SF	3343		1894
James	47	IRE	2233		1903
John B.	7	SF	3172		1900
John P.	45	SCT	966		1870
John R.	24	SF	5628	Jan	1901
Joseph H.	1867	SF	1181c		1904
Margaret Ursula	<1	SF	322		1900
Patrick	41	SF	5448		1904
Sarah Ellen	28	MA	1789		1902
Timothy C.	52	IN	6005	Jan	1901
Walter D.	15	CA	G63		1885
William	30	MA	5620a		1895
GRACEY					
Anna	60	IRL	4527a		1895
GRACIA					
Florence E.	<1	SF	2055b		1895
GRACIER					
Alice	2	SF	1540		1866
Charles R./M., c/o		SF	2271		1895
GRADEROHL					
Benj[n]	<1	SF	8270		1868
GRADVIEU					
Mary E.	20	MD	447		1870
GRADWOHL					
Bertha	<1	SF	1695b		1871
Isaac	1	NV	9525		1868

NAME	AGE OR YOB.	BIRTH PLACE	CERT. NO	ID	DEATH YEAR
Mathilda	<1	SF	3421b		1870
Meyer	72	GER	8340		1900
GRADY					
Andrew	70	IRL	6827	Feb	1901
Anne O.				Dec	1899
Annie	1877	SF	3429c		1904
Augustus	24	SF	4752		1901
Bridget	73	IRL	2784a		1872
Catharine	20	NY	621		1870
Catherine	24	SF	7259		1904
Ellen	60	IRL	4409		1896
Ellen	50	IRL	3307		1895
Frank	35		4308		1903
James O.	1	SF	5257		1867
Johanna	84	IRE	5811		1903
John	50	NJ	2882		1895
John	70	GER	4457		1901
John				Dec	1898
Joseph	<1	SF	1615		1900
Margaret	64	IRE	4762		1904
May Aloysia	1882	SF	1025c		1904
Michael				Oct	1898
Nellie	36	MA	5877	Jan	1901
Richard J. (soldier)			2709		1901
Thomas	35	CA	2341		1903
Thomas Henry	38	SF	6275		1903
Thomas P.	21	SF	2603		1894
W. M./Kitty, c/o	1	SF	116		1903
William	47	ENG	6078		1902
GRAEBER					
Ralph	2	MA	6926		1902
GRAEF					
Hilton	16	CA	2755		1902
GRAEFENACKER					
Leo	45	GER	3308		1895

Key: a = 1st part of year; b = 2nd part of year;
c = death certificate copy; c/o = child of

NAME	AGE OR YOB.	BIRTH PLACE	CERT. NO	ID	DEATH YEAR
GRAEME					
David	1	SF	5809		1904
GRAF					
Albert	36	BAV	1318		1869
Amalia	56	GER	758		1870
Erika	1	GER	8686		1904
H.	<1	SF	1239		1866
Haver	44	GER	237		1900
Herman	21	GER	1480		1902
Mina	2	SF	3693		1896
Oscar	20	SF	3560		1903
William Otto	<1	SF	6771		1896
GRAFE					
Joseph					Apr 1899
GRAFF					
Eugenie A.	3	NY	130		1870
Justian J.	74	SWT	3559		1903
Mary A.	66	SWT	8245		1900
GRAFIL					
William	<1	SF	5600		1867
GRAFT					
George W. (soldier)			4546		1901
GRAFTON					
Mary/Edward, c/o	<1	CA	1907		1902
GRAGERT					
John (soldier)			3578		1900
GRAGG					
John S.			6722		1902
GRAGLIA					
Michael					Aug 1898
GRAHAM					
Alfred	<1	SF	4760		1902
Alice	<1	SF	7293		1902
Alice	<1	SF	847b		1895

NAME	AGE OR YOB.	BIRTH PLACE	CERT. NO	ID	DEATH YEAR
Alice J.					Nov 1898
Amelia	23	NE	1350		1902
Andrew	62	IRE	761		1903
Ann	80	ENG	4720		1902
Arthur/Emma, c/o	1904	SF	3175		1904
Bridget	58	IRL	3908		1896
Bridget	50	IRL	2389b		1895
Caroline					Dec 1898
Catharine M.	40	IRL	1518b		1871
Cathrine I.	1	CA	6772		1868
Clara Augusta	53		1340		1894
Clinton W. (soldier)			5038		1901
Daniel	74	NY	4707		1904
Edward B.	70	ENG	2617		1895
Edward F.	<1	SF	5035		1903
Elenor L.	22	MA	6890		1868
Elizabeth	26	SF	1110		1894
Elizabeth A.	46	PA	8256		1903
Emma L.	4	SF	4011		1867
Frank J.					Nov 1899
George	49	IRE	4348		1867
George					Jul 1898
Gracie	<1	SF	2198		1894
H. A./E. C, c/o					Oct 1898
Hannah	32	SF	2581		1901
James	2	NY	3761		1867
James	67	SCT	3928		1900
James	47	CAN	5896	Jan	1901
James E.	42	IRL	1978a		1872
James Edward	<1	SF	319b		1872
Jennie Chest	27	CA	6581		1896
John	29	PA	1292		1869
John	50	IL	6828	Feb	1901
John	62	MO	1036		1903
John A.	24	MA	3062		1895
John S.	60	IRE	2740		1866

NAME	AGE OR YOB.	BIRTH PLACE	CERT. NO	ID	DEATH YEAR
John T.				Jan	1899
Joseph	49	IRL	5528	Jan	1901
Julia	66	ENG	5768		1902
Julia				Oct	1899
Lena	<1	SF	1712		1894
Lilly	24	CA	2696		1900
Louise	46	GER	6424		1903
Mabel	3	CA	G23		1883
Martha Switser				Jul	1898
Mary	33	ENG	1375		1870
Mary	49	IRL	1350		1894
Mary				Nov	1898
Mary Jane	61	IRE	6436		1902
Nancey	60	IRL	89		1870
Nelson	50	ENG	692b		1872
Peter	37	VA	1315		1870
Remato	1	CA	52		1900
Rose	74	IRL	8652		1901
Sally S.				Mar	1899
Sarah	30	CA	357		1903
Sarah	1821	KY	2309c		1904
T. Mitchell	<1	SF	2200		1873
Therese	6	SF	1139		1869
Thomas	48	IRL	952b		1871
Thomas	64	IRE	5373		1902
Thomas	37	CA	9646		1901
Viola				Feb	1900
Walter A.				Jul	1899
William	<1	SF	1790		1902
William	64	IRL	7030	Feb	1901
William				Oct	1899
William A.	9	NY	239b		1871
William F. (soldier)			3781		1900
William G.	19	MT	8546		1900
Wm./Margaret, c/o		SF	1564		1900
Zack Montgomery	3	SF	1139		1869

NAME	AGE OR YOB.	BIRTH PLACE	CERT. NO	ID	DEATH YEAR
GRAHAN					
Robert Wesley	22	CA	80		1901
GRAHMAN					
Josephine				Jan	1900
GRAHN					
Jno C,	57	GER	G69		1886
GRAIF					
Carl T.	44	NJ	4516a		1895
GRALL					
Andrew	47	GER	G4		1882
GRALOUSKY					
Joseph				Feb	1900
GRAM					
Neils T.	52	DEN	1666		1901
GRAMER					
Fidelia	73	GER	G31		1884
GRAMLICH					
Jeannetta	46	GER	5157		1902
GRAMLING					
Robert (Peter)	60	OH	G90		1889
GRAMLY					
Patrick	56	IRE	2499		1866
GRAN					
John	36	AUT	G78		1887
GRAN?					
Sarah	<1	MA	1197		1869
GRAND					
Albert	39	AUS	6196		1904
Sarah	1	SF	8604		1868
GRANDAIS					
Auguste	65	FRA	1037		1868
GRANDEAU					
Francis	51	FRA	4900		1867

NAME	AGE OR YOB.	BIRTH PLACE	CERT. NO	ID	DEATH YEAR	NAME	AGE OR YOB.	BIRTH PLACE	CERT. NO	ID	DEATH YEAR
GRANDFIELD						GRANGER					
Lizzie M.				Dec	1899	Annie	50	NY	1272		1903
GRANDI						GRANICE					
Josephe				Aug	1899	Catherine Keogh	1861	SF	1043c		1904
GRANDIDIER						GRANLE					
Pierre	40	FRA	571		1866	Nicholas C.	1	SF	54		1865
GRANDINETTI						GRANNAN					
John	31	ITA	6483		1903	Michael	62	IRL	3527a		1895
GRANDMOUGIN						GRANNIS					
Anna	72	FRA	7243		1903	George W.	75	CT	5293		1901
GRANDON						James G.	5	SF	8157		1904
Patrick	70	IRL	611b		1895	GRANNUCCI					
GRANDONA						S./M., c/o		SF	6276		1895
Joseph	57	ITA	1189b		1895	GRANQUIST					
Maria I.	<1	SF	4327		1867	Mary	23	FIN	905b		1895
GRANE						GRANSAND					
Kate Rich	54	MO	3703a		1895	Fred H./Mary E., c/o	<1	SF	7829		1904
Michael (soldier)			8065		1900	GRANT					
GRANER						——	<1	SF	3646		1870
Fredericka	77	GER	2227		1900	Adam	75	SCT	6515		1904
GRANETTONI						Agnes Frances				Aug	1899
Stephen E.				Feb	1900	Angus	<1	SF	6193		1900
GRANEY						Anna C.	29	CA	5928		1904
Ellen	65	IRE	8053		1903	Benjamin	49	ME	690		1870
GRANFIELD						Charles	44	ME	2037		1866
Della	22	CA	3990		1903	Charles	43	MA	2710		1895
Earl J.				Jan	1899	Charles Watson	58	MA	3579		1900
Margaret	72	IRE	1101		1902	David				Jun	1899
Mary J.	52	IRE	6648		1903	E./Clare M., c/o				Jan	1899
Thos.	55	IRL	G35		1884	Edward	66	IRL	7959		1900
W. M., c/o				Apr	1899	Emily	61	NY	4644		1902
GRANGE						Frank W.	<1	SF	131a		1871
Nellie E.	22	CA	2804		1894	Frederick I.	1	SF	793		1870
						George	<1	SF	9008		1903

Key: a = 1st part of year; b = 2nd part of year;
c = death certificate copy; c/o = child of

NAME	AGE OR YOB.	BIRTH PLACE	CERT. NO	ID	DEATH YEAR
Henry E.	44	ENG	8057		1901
Henry F.				Jan	1900
James A.	54	CAN	2012		1903
James C.	1	SF	1078		1869
James D.	54	IL	5956		1902
Jas. D.				Dec	1899
Jno. T.	49	CAN	3155		1894
John C.	1	SF	852		1870
John Frederick	1	SF	3044		1866
John R.	<1	SF	305b		1872
Joseph	53	MA	5827		1867
Joseph	65	MA	96		1903
Joseph	<1	SF	3041		1895
Joseph (soldier)			273		1901
Josephine L.				Aug	1899
Laurence	45	IRL	3901		1870
Lewis T.	2	SF	1090		1869
Marion	1		6717		1903
Mary	67	IRL	890		1901
Mary	63	IRL	4340	Dec	1901
Mary E.	<1	SF	8152		1868
Mary R.	6	SF	3182		1895
Nellie	46	MA	1988		1901
Pauline I.				Jan	1900
Peter				Nov	1899
Raymond	20	NV	4916		1904
Richard A.	34	SCT	7996		1904
Thomas	2	SF	359		1900
Wm. Edward	<1	SF	1028b		1872
Wm. H.	37	NY	812		1870
GRANUCCI					
Eugenio	1	SF	7707		1904
Joseph	3	CA	4875		1896
Margherita	2	SF	5600	Jan	1901
Salvator	<1	SF	976		1901
Tomaso				Jan	1900

NAME	AGE OR YOB.	BIRTH PLACE	CERT. NO	ID	DEATH YEAR
GRANVEST					
Fredericke M. L.				Feb	1900
GRANVILLE					
Margaret	1	SF	688b		1871
Mary A.	28	SF	4457		1901
Maurice W.				Jul	1899
Thomas	59	IRL	5800a		1895
GRANWELL					
Leonard	32	SWE	7722		1903
GRANZ					
Louis	53	GER	7343		1904
GRAPEL					
Joan Heinrich	50	GER	3947		1902
GRAPENGATER					
Carl/Emilie, c/o	<1	CA	5845		1901
GRAPER					
Louise	61	GER	4138		1902
GRAS					
Joseph	67	FRA	4341	Dec	1901
GRASER					
Anna	34	SF	6645	Feb	1901
GRASIN					
Philip H.	64	BAV	G94		1889
GRASS					
Annie E.	<1	SF	8944		1903
Elisabeth				Aug	1898
GRASSELL					
Ollie	1	CA	6404		1902
Ollie E.				Jan	1900
GRASSER					
Babetta	50	CA	4044	Dec	1901
GRASSHOFF					
Albert	1	SF	5674		1867

Key: a = 1st part of year; b = 2nd part of year;
c = death certificate copy; c/o = child of

NAME	AGE OR YOB.	BIRTH PLACE	CERT. NO	ID	DEATH YEAR	NAME	AGE OR YOB.	BIRTH PLACE	CERT. NO	ID	DEATH YEAR
GRASSIL						GRAVE					
Paulina	3	SF	1970		1866	Bernard	57	GER	5873		1903
GRASSMANN						Henry				Feb	1899
Emily	2	SF	1609		1870	Henry				Jan	1899
GRASSO						Herman	52	GER	2500		1902
Costantino	84	ITA	3297		1902	GRAVEN					
Felice	<1	SF	4623		1901	Howard	2	CA	870		1901
GRATE						GRAVES					
Eva E.	24	OH	488b		1895	Ann S.	1824	ENG	850c		1904
GRATER						Charles (soldier)			3542		1900
John	13	PA	5796		1867	Clarence	<1	CA	5740		1896
GRATH						E. A.	48	LA	1375		1869
George				Oct	1899	Edward	1856	IRE	2018c		1904
GRATHEIS						Emma	48	VA	1869b		1895
Adolphe L.	3	SF	4202b		1870	Gertie	<1	SF	5570		1896
GRATHMANN						Gertrude				Mar	1899
Richard	35	GER	4057a		1895	Hazel W.				Feb	1899
GRATTAN						Hiram Throop	77	NY	2095		1902
William S.	14	SF	2052a		1872	James	77	CT	2107b		1895
GRATTEN						Jessie, c/o	<1	SF	7566		1901
Lucy	49	IRE	7641		1868	Johanna	6	SF	3122		1866
GRATTO						John M.	70	CT	2997	Oct	1901
Margaret M.				Aug	1899	Joshua	36	ENG	2550		1866
GRATTON						Mary B.				Nov	1899
Augusta Kate	31	MI	4064		1902	Maynard G. (soldier)	23	MO	3047		1900
Joseph Edward	4	CAN	1348		1869	Paul	55	FRA	7681		1868
GRAUERHOLZ						Rector Chiles	15	SF	4789		1902
Adele	31	SF	2732		1900	Thos./Daisy, c/o		SF	4037		1900
GRAUFIELD						William	<1	SF	3755		1896
Matthew L.	1903	SF	3049c		1904	GRAWNEY					
GRAUSTWAIN						Thomas J.	9	SF	183a		1871
Rosa	37	SWT	8216		1904	GRAY					
						——		SF	1105		1869
						Ada Turner	64	OH	4785		1896
						Agnes (alias Mahoney)				Feb	1900

Key: a = 1st part of year; b = 2nd part of year;
c = death certificate copy; c/o = child of

NAME	AGE OR YOB.	BIRTH PLACE	CERT. NO	ID	DEATH YEAR	NAME	AGE OR YOB.	BIRTH PLACE	CERT. NO	ID	DEATH YEAR
Agnes alias Mahoney				Feb	1900	Henry A.	47	MA	515b		1871
Agnes Mahoney (alias)				Feb	1900	Henry W.				Nov	1898
Anna A.				Jul	1899	Herbert	29	KY	2700		1902
Bernard	<1	SF	7168		1904	Iam	1	SF	4340b		1870
Beulah				Jan	1899	J. F./M., c/o		SF	2861		1873
Burton E.	28	IA	4993		1903	James	67	VA	3735	Nov	1901
Bustie	5	SF	1908		1900	James				Mar	1900
Carrie M.	7	SF	2312		1866	James (soldier)			7152		1901
Catherine	2	SF	1260		1869	James W.	<1	SF	8374		1904
Catherine				Jan	1899	Jane	88	PA	5379		1896
Charles	35	ENG	2018		1870	John	43	MA	2168		1873
Cynthia I.	<1	SF	5705		1867	John	40	IRL	G62		1885
Delia E.	55	ME	8085		1901	John	70	ENG	3654a		1895
Dorothea H.	68	IRL	4609		1901	John J.	1847	SCT	3397c		1904
Earl Watson	11	CA	8363		1903	John L.	27	MA	7420		1901
Edw. A.	26	NY	6080		1896	John M.	67	KY	4971		1896
Edward S.				Mar	1899	John Richard				Mar	1899
Elizabeth				Aug	1899	Lawrence F.			7653		1902
Elizabeth C.	71	ME	3924		1902	Lewellyn	54	MO	3634	Nov	1901
Ellen	59	IRL	1344b		1872	Lillie Louisa	1	SF	1061		1869
Ellen	84	IRL	8700		1900	Lina Ruby	<1	CA	766b		1895
Ellen				Aug	1899	Margaret Spencer	55	MO	4020		1903
Emitt				Oct	1898	Maria				Mar	1900
Etta W.	42	CA	4895		1903	Maria	19	CA	6c		1904
Fannie H.				Oct	1899	Martha	70	ENG	6247		1867
Frank (soldier)			721		1902	Mary	27	IRE	26		1865
Frank John	38	SF	5419		1902	Mary	<1	CA	5414		1867
George A. (USN)			4062		1903	Mary E.	43	KY	741		1900
George E.	44	ENG	G59		1885	Mary Jane	41	OH	2580		1901
George T.	<1	SF	9494		1901	Matilda	78	GER	8525		1904
Geraldine	<1	CA	520		1900	Melinda M. Am	62	NY	3811	Nov	1901
Harold	<1	CA	323		1900	Rebecca K.	35	GER	5887		1902
Harry F.	34		904		1902	Robert (soldier)			6471		1900
Hazel	<1	SF	1109		1894	Robert A.	52	ME	3411		1903
Helen Elizabeth	1	SF	4708		1904	Robert Burns	23	SF	5636		1902
Henrietta	67	ENG	408		1870	Robt Frederick				Aug	1899

NAME	AGE OR YOB.	BIRTH PLACE	CERT. NO	ID	DEATH YEAR
Sadie	30	ENG	7584		1900
Samuel	40	ENG	3128		1895
Samuel (soldier)			271		1901
Sarah	77	IRL	1569b		1872
Susan H.	62	NJ	3968		1900
Sybil	<1	SF	4148		1900
Theodore/May K., c/o	<1	SF	2378		1902
Theodore/May K., c/o	<1	CA	6286		1904
Thomas (soldier)			7750		1901
Thomas M. (soldier)			7153		1901
Walter E.	<1	SF	8310		1904
Walter John	<1	SF	1394		1900
William	42	MA	6251		1904
William (soldier)			432		1902
William J.	2	SF	85a		1871
Wilmer Lewis	<1	SF	1427		1869
Wm.				Jan	1900
Wm. B. (soldier)			6815		1900
GRAYBILL					
George A./Charlotte, c/o		SF	2504		1900
GRAYDON					
Mary	49	NY	5941		1903
GRAYMION					
Emanuel	58	FRA	3291a		1872
GRAYSON					
Robert R.	35	CA	610		1901
Sanford W.	58	IN	3969		1900
GRAZER					
Edwin	1904	SF	2589c		1904
GRDT					
Elmer E.	<1	SF	8710		1900
GREAME					
Mary	47	CA	5522		1902

NAME	AGE OR YOB.	BIRTH PLACE	CERT. NO	ID	DEATH YEAR
GREAN					
George E.	66	MA	3063		1895
GREANCY					
———			6240		1867
GREANEY					
Bridget				Jun	1899
Thomas	50	IRE	7587		1904
GREANY					
Elise	58	GER	6204	Jan	1901
Henry J	21	CA	4906		1902
John T.	43	CA	8916		1903
Mary	31	IRE	6249		1867
Michael	71	IRE	960		1902
GREB					
Conrad J.	73	GER	4245a		1895
GRECCA					
Anna	<1	SF	6780	Feb	1901
GRECO					
Arcangelo	45	ITA	1868b		1895
Pasquale				Mar	1899
Vincenzo				Mar	1899
GREEHY					
Mary Feleta	<1	CA	4044		1896
GREELEY					
Ann	20	IRL	4933a		1895
George	60	IRL	53		1900
Mary	32	NV	8871		1904
Mary P.				Jul	1899
Nora	70	IRE	4101		1903
Sarah B. C.	81	NH	1792		1901
GREELY					
Ann	77	IRE	790		1903
Bridget	74	IRL	3533		1896
Cyral	5	SF	1207		1903

Key: a = 1st part of year; b = 2nd part of year;
c = death certificate copy; c/o = child of

NAME	AGE OR YOB.	BIRTH PLACE	CERT. NO	ID	DEATH YEAR	NAME	AGE OR YOB.	BIRTH PLACE	CERT. NO	ID	DEATH YEAR
Edward E.	21	ME	3180		1866	Ellen	24	NY	3220		1870
T./D., c/o	<1	SF	4068		1895	Ellen	38	IRE	7733		1904
T./M., c/o	<1	SF	3408		1894	Ellen, c/o		CA	417		1895
						Emma L.	37	SF	8669		1901
GREEN						Erashois H.	73	ENG	8311		1904
——	<1	SF	46a		1871	Eric				Oct	1899
Abe/Etta, c/o		SF	1672		1895	Eva	<1	SF	1296		1870
Abraham	54	GER	6991		1904	Frances Moulton	1883	CA	1989c		1904
Albert	23	GER	G89		1889	Fred E.				Jan	1900
Albert	27	FRA	9175		1901	Furlow W. H.				Jul	1898
Albert L.				Jan	1899	George	34	IRL	942		1870
Alfred Augustus				Mar	1899	George	45		5290		1904
Alice C.	30	CA	4844a		1895	George	1	CA	899		1903
Alonzo	90	OH	4186	Dec	1901	George	68	ENG	4994		1902
Anna	21	VA	2418a		1872	George				Feb	1899
Anna	68	IRE	8026		1903	George G.				Jul	1898
Annie May				Feb	1900	Georgie	17	CA	3004		1903
Arabella	40	CA	3325		1895	Hannah	34	CA	4458		1896
Areneth	43	ENG	4925		1867	Harold	6	CA	4995		1902
Avarilla	20	CA	5955		1904	Harold John	<1	SF	3555		1902
Catherine	1	SF	5289		1904	Harriett	24	CA	3911		1903
Cathrine	32	IRE	4632		1867	Harry	1	SF	1175		1903
Charles	37	DEN	5846	Jan	1901	Hattie C.	35	NY	1048		1868
Charlotte	1	SF	9065		1868	Helen	58	GER	4187	Dec	1901
Chas. A.	34	CA	7522		1903	Helena	1842	FL	1358c		1904
Chas. G./Georgia, c/o	1	SF	2673		1903	Helena	1904	CA	2073c		1904
Clara Agnes				Nov	1898	Henry O. (soldier)			8428		1900
Clinton	4	SF	857		1894	Herbert/Jennie, c/o	1	CA	2558		1903
Daniel	23	CA	1620		1900	Idaho	<1	SEA	1309		1870
David	40	NY	G39		1884	Isabel	68	NY	3556		1902
David	1	SF	1288		1869	Isabella	1	SF	7483		1868
Dora	45	SF	3412		1903	J. Harry	40	CA	2779		1894
Edmund				Aug	1899	Jacob	74	POL	8725		1904
Edward				Feb	1899	James	44	NY	3270		1873
Elbert			5095		1903	James E.	64	PA	1297b		1895
Eliza J.	56	NY	5444		1896	Johana				Dec	1898
Elizabeth	23	IRE	4251		1867						

NAME	AGE OR YOB.	BIRTH PLACE	CERT. NO	ID	DEATH YEAR
Johannius Percy A.	<1	SF	2213b		1895
John	90	IRL	6521		1900
John	65	IRL	1125		1900
John B. A.				Oct	1898
John D.	1904	SF	2950c		1904
John H.	74	ENG	4629		1903
John/V.John, c/o				Dec	1899
Jose B.	<1	SF	95a		1871
Joseph J.	25	SF	4081		1900
Julia Bayliss	41	IN	4096		1896
Kate	21	IRE	4709		1867
Lavinia	37	ENG	263b		1871
Leah Bead	1	SF	9638		1868
Lewis	16	NY	1388		1869
Lilly A. Fatesque	3	SF	1151		1869
Linna	1	CA	43b		1871
Lizzie	27	CA	6412	Feb	1901
Lloyd	4	CA	7486		1901
Louisa	48	GER	G86		1887
Mamie C.	24	CA	1720b		1895
Margaret	39	IRL	1782b		1872
Margret	<1	SF	4428		1867
Marguerite	1904	SF	541c		1904
Marion				Aug	1898
Marvin Wheeler	62	NY	900		1903
Mary				Jul	1899
Mary E.				Jul	1899
Mary F. S. S.	1	BC	3531		1870
Michael	70	IRE	538		1902
Michael	25	IRL	3711a		1895
Nellie	2	SF	559		1866
Nellie	54	MA	2079b		1895
Nicholas	45	GRE	2028		1903
Oliver	45	NY	2586		1866
Olivia	43	JAM	1422		1900
Patrick	59	CAN	510		1903
Paul Theodore	<1	SF	2557		1902
Peter	53	HOL	3816		1896
R. H.	70	ENG	5341		1896
Raymond Robert	<1	SF	6211		1902
Rebecca	83	IRL	5360		1896
Richard James	25	NB	1548b		1871
Robert A.	41	CA	3900	Dec	1901
Sadie				Oct	1898
Sarah	69	NY	3109		1895
Sarah	70	IRL	5421		1896
Seth	62	NY	G80		1887
T. Felix	<1	SF	3011		1873
Thomas	67	IRL	8649		1900
Thomas	70	IRL	4232		1900
Walter	<1	SF	6355		1867
Walter D. (soldier)			4547		1901
Watson				Jun	1899
Wiliam H. (soldier)			606		1901
William	64	IRE	7275		1903
William	80	IRL	6974		1900
William	60		1046		1900
William	61	FIN	3966	Dec	1901
William				Feb	1899
William	1826	GER	1703c		1904
William A.	4	SF	695		1870
William B.	3	SF	3800		1903
William F.	60	RI	3229		1900
William Granville	1	SF	5346		1904
William Thomas	49	NM	2045		1903

GREENAN

NAME	AGE OR YOB.	BIRTH PLACE	CERT. NO	ID	DEATH YEAR
Fanny				Mar	1900

GREENBAUM

NAME	AGE OR YOB.	BIRTH PLACE	CERT. NO	ID	DEATH YEAR
Beckie	32	LA	4579		1901
M., c/o				Dec	1899
S.	40	POL	G70		1886

Key: a = 1st part of year; b = 2nd part of year;
c = death certificate copy; c/o = child of

NAME	AGE OR YOB.	BIRTH PLACE	CERT. NO	ID	DEATH YEAR
GREENBERG					
Caroline	76	SAX	2458		1901
Charles	44	DEN	662		1902
Marie	69	CA	2734		1894
Minnie	18	GER	G34		1884
Rebecca	1880	CA	3221c		1904
GREENBERRY					
Grant			7654		1902
GREENBURG					
Sam				Feb	1900
GREENE					
Anne	<1	SF	1181b		1872
Annie E.	70	NH	6205	Jan	1901
Bessie M.				Oct	1899
Charles	65	NY	152		1901
Daniel	73	IRE	6310		1904
Francis H.	<1	SF	6646	Feb	1901
Frederick Wiebe	<1	SF	2458		1894
Henry E.	68	SF	153b		1895
Irene C.	24	MI	3662		1900
Isabella	<1	SF	1203a		1871
James A. (soldier)			1879		1900
Jessa Vail	33	AL	1436		1869
John	<1	SF	1704		1902
Joseph Raymond	3	SF	6750		1896
Marshall S. (soldier)			1970		1900
Mathias	42	GER	1592		1870
Oliver Duff	71	NY	6516		1904
Oliver E. (soldier)			7751		1901
Ransom	75	NY	4861		1896
Robert (soldier)			270		1901
Robert S.	<1	SF	5177		1903
Rose	<1	SF	1584		1870
William	59	IRL	301b		1871

NAME	AGE OR YOB.	BIRTH PLACE	CERT. NO	ID	DEATH YEAR
GREENER					
Paolo C.	<1	SF	4656		1867
GREENFIELD					
Alexander Clarke	1861	NS	2739c		1904
Beverly Carsar				May	1899
GREENHALGH					
Richard B.	38	ENG	3960		1867
GREENHAM					
Frederick	70	IRL	4229a		1895
GREENHOOD					
Bertha G.	35	AUS	3199c		1904
Eddie	1	CA	5731		1867
Herman	45	AUS	5423		1867
GREENHOW					
Margaret B.	1864	SCT	1456c		1904
GREENIER					
Christiana				Jan	1900
GREENLAW					
Florence Jenett				Jul	1898
George W.	1865	MA	1061c		1904
John				Nov	1898
Lillie Ann	55	IRL	1943b		1895
M. E.	53	MA	4861a		1895
Mervynn B.	1	SF	5543		1904
GREENLEA					
Edward			7566		1902
GREENLEAF					
——			2078		1866
——		SF	1097		1869
James	27	CA	7989		1901
GREENLIEF					
——			6972		1868
GREENLIN					
Herbert	3	CA	6515		1900

Key: a = 1st part of year; b = 2nd part of year; c = death certificate copy; c/o = child of

NAME	AGE OR YOB.	BIRTH PLACE	CERT. NO	ID	DEATH YEAR
GREENSLIT					
Fred D.				Feb	1900
GREENWALD					
Clarence R.				Dec	1898
Gustav	5	SF	5920		1867
Jacob	74	GER	3635	Nov	1901
Joseph	45	KY	516		1900
William	32	GER	807		1902
GREENWAY					
Ellen	60	IRL	2932	Oct	1901
GREENWELL					
Harry S.	1881	CA	1262c		1904
James P.				Jul	1899
GREENWOOD					
Annette	<1	SF	1697b		1872
Annita				Oct	1899
Catherine A.	30	BC	1087		1903
Charles W.	2	SF	1422b		1872
Edna H.	1882	CA	3320c		1904
Elizabeth	1841	MA	1291c		1904
H.	23	POL	1418		1869
Hannah				Mar	1899
John	64	ENG	G72		1886
William	34	SF	4230		1900
GREER					
Alexander G.	75	PA	660b		1895
E., c/o		SF	423b		1872
Eliza	30	IRE	169		1865
Emma S.	9	SF	1490b		1871
Frances				Jul	1899
John S.				Aug	1898
Laura	<1	SF	1173		1869
Mary M.				Feb	1900
Mary W.	38	IRL	926a		1871
Sarah	1839	IRE	3127c		1904

NAME	AGE OR YOB.	BIRTH PLACE	CERT. NO	ID	DEATH YEAR
William	62		7648		1904
GREETHAUSEN					
Henry	34	GER	2767a		1872
GREFFE					
Josephine	66	FRA	6959	Feb	1901
GREGA					
George	57	AUT	4731a		1895
GREGAN					
Mary Ann	<1	SF	1077b		1871
GREGANS					
Mary Jane	7	SF	973		1870
Phillip	<1	SF	8000		1868
GREGG					
Charles G.	18	CA	352b		1872
Chas.	26	LA	5924		1867
Ellen	42	IRE	8444		1903
Jane Lowe				Nov	1899
John C.				May	1899
Joseph M.	31	VT	1000		1868
Sarah A.	78	PA	2767		1903
GREGGY					
Julia	40	IRL	2853		1873
GREGO					
Stefano	4	SF	1748		1902
GREGOIRE					
Joseph Herire	57	FRA	925a		1871
Pauline				Mar	1899
GREGOR					
Selma	16	GER	4426		1896
GREGORI					
Rudolph	8	SF	1176		1903
GREGORY					
———	<1	SF	4843a		1895
Amelia	1822	GER	1377c		1904

Key: a = 1st part of year; b = 2nd part of year;
c = death certificate copy; c/o = child of

NAME	AGE OR YOB.	BIRTH PLACE	CERT. NO	ID	DEATH YEAR
Annie M.	46	IRL	5628		1896
Catherine E.				Aug	1898
Catherine P.	<1	SF	1229b		1872
Charles C.			6480		1902
Cornelia	65	NS	173		1902
Elizabeth W.	91	ENG	358		1901
Fred L.			6338	Feb	1901
George D.				Apr	1899
George Henry				Feb	1899
Henry	44	GA	2747a		1872
Hugh Mcullough	68	NY	8642		1903
James N.	41	NJ	4481		1896
Richard	62	ENG	1282		1869
S.	32	GA	2214a		1872
Samuel C.				Apr	1899
Victor J.	52	LA	7885		1903
W./H., c/o		SF	1271		1894
William	48		779b		1895
William D. (soldier)			6530	Feb	1901
William W. (soldier)	28	NY	3771	Nov	1901
GREIF					
Amalie B. M.	35	SF	1708		1900
Catherine	1866	SF	1275c		1904
John	81	GER	1919		1900
John Milton, Jr.	1	SF	4605		1904
GREIG					
Guiroz				Nov	1899
L.B.	45	SCT	2364a		1872
Regugio				Nov	1899
William				Oct	1899
GREINER					
Amelia				Jul	1898
GREIST					
Stella	5	SF	8235		1903

NAME	AGE OR YOB.	BIRTH PLACE	CERT. NO	ID	DEATH YEAR
GREIVE					
Gertrude Katherine	1903	SF	2412c		1904
GRELARTO					
Manuel Francisco	20	WI	1065a		1871
GRELLA					
Alesandro	40	ITA	2867		1903
GRELLEN					
George				Mar	1900
GREMMAN					
Cintha Inez	9	MO	6196a		1895
GREMMER					
Joseph				Oct	1899
GREMMINGER					
Walter V.	<1	SF	4924		1896
GREMMLER					
Jakob	79	GER	3350		1900
GRENADE					
Euchere	55	BEL	2098a		1872
GRENAN					
James ?? (soldier)			6816		1900
GRENELL					
Hart I.	69	NY	4231		1900
GRENET					
Adele P.	<1	SF	3993		1867
GRENEY					
John	30	IRE	1310		1869
GRENHAM					
Deane T.	60	IRL	4446a		1895
GRENIER					
Julia	67	CAN	5114		1901
GRENLICH					
John	33	AUS	6460		1900

Key: a = 1st part of year; b = 2nd part of year;
c = death certificate copy; c/o = child of

NAME	AGE OR YOB.	BIRTH PLACE	CERT. NO	ID	DEATH YEAR
GRENMAN					
Guy	<1	SF	4423		1901
GRENNAN					
Ellen D.	25	CA	7248		1901
James F.	12	SF	2369a		1872
Joseph F.	29	SF	5073		1903
Peter				Jan	1899
Wm. M.	27	SF	1816		1894
GRENNELL					
Henry S.	2	SF	2759		1866
GRENNEN					
Edward I. (soldier)			301		1902
GRENNIENSTEIN					
Anne E.				Feb	1900
GRENNIGER					
Daniel	73	GER	1834		1902
GRENOIULLEAU					
Marie	39	FRA	1697a		1871
GRENONILLIAN					
Jules L.	6	SF	732		1870
GRENTHER					
Sarah Evaline Thompson	33	SF	8246		1900
GRENZEBACH					
Frances Nelson	67	NY	1949		1903
GRESHAM					
Amos	42	GA	4572		1904
GRESHEN					
George	39	GER	9740		1868
GRESLEY					
Thomas T.	76	ENG	5930	Jan	1901
GRESS					
Charles				Jun	1899
Charlotte				Nov	1898

NAME	AGE OR YOB.	BIRTH PLACE	CERT. NO	ID	DEATH YEAR
George E.	53	GER	3657		1902
GRESSLER					
Earnest/Anna, c/o	<1	SF	5835		1902
GRESTEL					
J./E., c/o	<1	SF	2431		1894
GRETE					
Augusta Frederika	4	SF	1137		1869
Charles	<1	SF	1994		1866
(child)		SF	5689		1867
Henry	14	NY	7465		1868
GREUET					
Margrita Euguie	1	SF	351b		1871
GREUL					
Charles J.	41	NY	6150		1902
GREUNER					
——	47	NB	1361		1869
GREVE					
Frank	31	CA	8559		1901
Wm.				Jan	1900
GREVES					
Annie Bernice	1	SF	5602		1904
Mannie				Jul	1898
Margaret B. W.	24	NY	3312a		1872
GREWER					
Galen Lamar	1	SF	3127		1866
GREY					
Arthur S.	11	CA	7244		1903
Edwin G.	<1	SF	914		1870
Ellen	26	IRL	1152		1870
Gladys	<1	SF	539		1902
John	24	IRL	G64		1886
Louis				Apr	1899
Mary	<1	SF	1260		1869
Maud	1904	SF	2110c		1904

Key: a = 1st part of year; b = 2nd part of year;
c = death certificate copy; c/o = child of

NAME	AGE OR YOB.	BIRTH PLACE	CERT. NO	ID	DEATH YEAR
Moses	55	MA	1608b		1871
Thomas	58	IRL	410b		1872
Victoria				Feb	1900
GREYBECK					
C.	45	GER	8022		1868
GREYE					
Irene/Egbert, c/o		CA	6890		1901
GRIBBEN					
Wm.	22	CA	G68		1886
GRIBBIN					
Alexander Francis				Dec	1898
GRIBBLE					
Albert (soldier)			5796		1904
Edith	53	WI	2868		1903
John B.	60	ENG	5374		1902
GRIDER					
Luther E.			7567		1902
GRIDLEY					
C. V.				Jul	1898
Inez	6	CA	5836		1902
GRIEBEL					
August	35	GER	2490a		1872
GRIEDER					
Annie	1	SF	5398		1904
GRIEG					
Ignatz	39	GER	1061		1866
GRIENBERG					
Clara	76	GER	2572		1900
GRIENER					
L. G./J., c/o	<1	SF	2836		1894
GRIENLY					
Charles P.	46	NY	445		1866

NAME	AGE OR YOB.	BIRTH PLACE	CERT. NO	ID	DEATH YEAR
GRIER					
___			4828		1867
Esther	61	IRL	3906		1896
Geo. A.			G25		1883
Isaac	82	PA	2837		1894
Sarah Caroline	58	OH	706		1901
GRIERSON					
Francisca	2	CA	2581		1873
GRIESE					
Elizabeth	85	GER	3503		1903
GRIESSEN					
Louise	95	GER	1358		1901
GRIESWALD					
George W.	64	NY	5956		1904
GRIEVE					
Robert				Jul	1899
GRIEWATZ					
Peter T. (soldier)			8781		1901
GRIFALBA					
Asumsion	1	SF	468a		1871
GRIFF					
William				Mar	1900
GRIFFEN					
Alice				Oct	1899
Janies			1125b		1871
John	<1	NY	6361		1867
GRIFFIN					
___			5430		1867
Abrena Jane	1876	CAN	2983c		1904
Abrena Jane	1876	CAN	2983c		1904
Addie	<1	SF	965		1894
Alice	19	MT	5678		1904
Alice	abt	ENG	8836		1901
Alice				Oct	1899

Key: a = 1st part of year; b = 2nd part of year;
c = death certificate copy; c/o = child of

NAME	AGE OR YOB.	BIRTH PLACE	CERT. NO	ID	DEATH YEAR	NAME	AGE OR YOB.	BIRTH PLACE	CERT. NO	ID	DEATH YEAR
Andrew				Oct	1898	Jeremiah	67	IRL	3230		1900
Annie	60	IRL	3845	Nov	1901	Jessie Edna	31	ME	272		1903
Bridget	1829	ENG	2851c		1904	Johanna	59	CA	1640		1900
Bridget	58	IRL	7896		1900	John	<1	SF	1706		1866
Catherine	19	LA	1153		1869	John	68	IRL	3846	Nov	1901
Catherine	1	SF	6018a		1895	John				Oct	1899
Catherine	51	IRL	244		1900	John Henry	1904	SF	563c		1904
Catherine Virginia	4	SF	794a		1871	John W.				Nov	1898
Coleman Joseph	62	NY	9228		1901	John Warren	20	CA	3782		1900
Cora May	<1	CA	3586		1902	John, Mrs.	40	IRL	G52		1885
Daniel F. (soldier)			862		1901	Joseph H. (soldier)			3040	Oct	1901
Dennis	29	IRL	6703		1896	Josephine	1876	IRE	41c		1904
Edwin C.	1	SF	5845		1904	Lydia S.	62	MA	532a		1871
Edwin W.	<1	CA	1859		1894	Lynch	77	MD	8728		1868
Elizabeth	72	IRE	6041		1903	Magaret S.	78	PA	591a		1871
Ellen	<1	SF	1420b		1872	Margaret	49	OH	6304	Feb	1901
Ellen	46	IRL	1711		1894	Margarett Jane	4	CA	1225		1869
Ellen	56	IRL	6695a		1895	Maria Marciell	16	SF	1288b		1871
Ellen E.	8	MA	5476		1867	Mary	35	IRL	2583		1873
Frances	2	SF	1133		1869	Mary	6	SF	1178		1869
Frances Helen	3	MA	4421		1902	Mary	69	IRE	5347		1902
Frank D.	39	SF	4573		1904	Mary	75	IRL	2524b		1895
George	2	SF	8038		1868	Mary A.	50	CA	8139		1903
H. W.	21	ME	9447		1868	Mary Alice	11	SF	3372		1896
Helen				Jul	1898	Mary L.	36	SF	476		1903
Henry	35	ENG	5201		1901	Maurice	62	IRL	8318		1900
Hugh				Oct	1899	Michael	24	IRE	8547		1904
J. W.	30		919c		1904	Michael	66	IRE	7059		1903
James	2	SF	3032		1870	Michael	64	IRL	4384a		1895
James	68	ENG	511		1903	Michael A.				Nov	1898
James				Dec	1898	Nettie	22	SF	1504		1894
James (soldier)			4548		1901	Patrick	37	IRL	3334		1873
James J.	1829	IRE	1636c		1904	Patrick	47	IRL	G81		1887
James/Carmen, c/o	1	SF	5744		1904	Patrick				Jul	1898
Jane	61	IRE	5060		1902	Pauline Elizabeth	16	NV	3559a		1895
Jeremiah	24	IRE	2025		1902	R. S.	21	ME	1354b		1895

Key: *a = 1st part of year; b = 2nd part of year;*
c = death certificate copy; c/o = child of

NAME	AGE OR YOB.	BIRTH PLACE	CERT. NO	ID	DEATH YEAR
S. A.	55	NY	1074		1869
Sarah	1	SF	584b		1871
Thomas (soldier)			7308		1901
Thomas B.				Jul	1898
Thomas F.	1869	SF	2333c		1904
Thomas Francis	<1	SF	2439		1873
Thomas J.				Apr	1899
Wallie (soldier)			9118		1901
Walter (soldier)			543		1901
Walter E.			6484		1903
William	<1	SF	1299		1869
William D.	41	SF	3911	Dec	1901
William F.	25	SF	1329		1901
William F.	1	SF	621		1901
William H.	7	SF	7024		1868
William J.	22	SF	3718	Nov	1901
William P.				Jun	1899

GRIFFING

NAME	AGE OR YOB.	BIRTH PLACE	CERT. NO	ID	DEATH YEAR
Isaac	38	PA	959b		1871

GRIFFINS

NAME	AGE OR YOB.	BIRTH PLACE	CERT. NO	ID	DEATH YEAR
——			6918		1868

GRIFFIS

NAME	AGE OR YOB.	BIRTH PLACE	CERT. NO	ID	DEATH YEAR
Jeremiah W.	41	NY	661b		1895

GRIFFITH

NAME	AGE OR YOB.	BIRTH PLACE	CERT. NO	ID	DEATH YEAR
——			3674		1867
Adam	abt	KS	1989		1901
Alexander			1541		1866
Anellie Agnes	<1	SF	2673		1894
Anna Maria	31	NY	7248		1868
Anthony J.				Feb	1899
Edwin L.	46	CA	6527		1902
Elizabeth	50	DC	6327		1896
Esther Sophia, Mrs.	61	NY	6437		1902
F. J.	19	CA	1531b		1895
Frances Gertrude	1904	SF	2673c		1904

NAME	AGE OR YOB.	BIRTH PLACE	CERT. NO	ID	DEATH YEAR
George	<1	SF	7365		1901
Hannah G.				Dec	1899
Hannah M.	72	NJ	6761	Feb	1901
Harold (soldier)			7528		1900
James	27	IRE	1758		1866
James J.	45	CA	2431		1901
John	25	WAL	G46		1885
Louisa				Aug	1899
Maggie	1	SF	7558		1868
Margarett	45	IRE	1312		1869
Mary A.	1	SF	1462		1870
Robert	35	WAL	1249		1869
Thomas Hamlin	70	WAL	3054		1902
Vivian Susan	1	CA	7078		1904

GRIFFITHS

NAME	AGE OR YOB.	BIRTH PLACE	CERT. NO	ID	DEATH YEAR
Amanda	37	CA	7095		1901
Charles	73	ENG	5375		1903
Elizabeth	38	IRE	3770		1867
James				Jul	1899
Mabelle F.	26	SF	3999		1900
Mary	69	IRL	5161a		1895
Robert	34	WAL	6254a		1895
T. Alfred				Feb	1899

GRIFFO

NAME	AGE OR YOB.	BIRTH PLACE	CERT. NO	ID	DEATH YEAR
Joseph	<1	SF	503		1900

GRIGGS

NAME	AGE OR YOB.	BIRTH PLACE	CERT. NO	ID	DEATH YEAR
Austin (soldier)			7748		1901
Hollis S.	1890	CA	3398c		1904
Mark	<1	SF	5216		1902

GRIGOR

NAME	AGE OR YOB.	BIRTH PLACE	CERT. NO	ID	DEATH YEAR
Eliza Janet				Jul	1899

GRIGSBY

NAME	AGE OR YOB.	BIRTH PLACE	CERT. NO	ID	DEATH YEAR
Harvey/Grace, c/o	<1	SF	7847		1904
Ileane Catherine	1	SF	6913		1904
Margaret/James C., c/o		SF	2334		1901

NAME	AGE OR YOB.	BIRTH PLACE	CERT. NO	ID	DEATH YEAR
William H.	45	SF	6203	Jan	1901
GRILL					
Catherine				Dec	1899
GRILLIO					
Vincent	14	CA	G93		1889
GRILLONE					
Francesco	48	ITA	4205		1900
GRIM					
Allen M.	6	SF	9120		1868
GRIMANI					
Antonio James	1837	ITA	3264c		1904
GRIMAUD					
Rosalie Anastasie Lucie	1886	FRA	1243c		1904
GRIMED					
JF/E	<1	SF	3236		1894
GRIMES					
Ann	95	IRL	9031		1901
Annie				Aug	1898
Annie				Dec	1899
Clarissa	72	CT	1437		1869
Edward	34	SF	5328		1902
Emma	2	SF	1640		1870
Fred Chandler	52	MA	7302		1903
James	1	SF	7463		1868
James	38	IRE	1267		1869
James	38	IRE	1267		1869
James Lowry	76	IL	2915		1903
James P.	<1	SF	9097		1868
John	35	IRE	6302		1867
Michael	82	IRE	357		1902
Patrick	44	IRE	9340		1868
Samuel (soldier)			863		1901
GRIMLEY					
Mary	42	SF	5911		1896

NAME	AGE OR YOB.	BIRTH PLACE	CERT. NO	ID	DEATH YEAR
GRIMM					
——	<1	SF	3464b		1870
A.A.	2	SF	897		1870
Adam	64	GER	7075		1902
Albert H.	4	CA	763		1901
Bertha A.	3	SF	474		1870
Blanche/Robt. Smith, c/o	<1	CA	2214		1901
Charles	<1	SF	3294		1872
Charles H.	42	GER	6790		1868
Emil Francis	63	GER	4211		1896
Emily	5	SF	891		1870
Frederick	42	GER	6425		1903
Henry A.	1	SF	672		1870
J. Charles (soldier)			2058		1901
Margarette	<1	SF	1251		1869
Mary	34	OR	7752		1904
Matthias	68	GER	1049		1901
Teresa	<1	CA	1446		1901
GRIMSELL					
Thomas H. (soldier)			923		1902
GRIMWOOD					
Edward Dewey				Feb	1899
GRINBERG					
Herman				Dec	1898
GRINDLEY					
Joseph M.				Jun	1899
Thomas R.				May	1899
GRINNELL					
H. W.	25	MA	3057		1866
John Jay				Jul	1899
GRISCHOTT					
George Leland	4	CA	493		1903
GRISEKE					
——	<1	SF	1278		1869

Key: a = 1st part of year; b = 2nd part of year;
c = death certificate copy; c/o = child of

NAME	AGE OR YOB.	BIRTH PLACE	CERT. NO	ID	DEATH YEAR
GRISON					
Marie B.	47	FRA	26		1871
GRISSIM					
Montgomery E., c/o				Feb	1899
GRIST					
Lilian W.				Jul	1898
GRISWOLD					
Augustus Henry				Jan	1900
Carrie L.	68	NY	6366	Feb	1901
Ed/Rose, c/o	<1	SF	2944		1895
Edward Jno.	19	SF	658		1894
James A.	42	CT	7223		1868
Nellie Gertrude	1876	CA	1704c		1904
GRITTS					
Katherin Dora	24	CA	5281		1903
GRIVES (OR GARLAND)					
William C.	21	CA	4389	Dec	1901
GROAH					
Geo.	41	GER	G32		1884
GROASSER					
Joe/Rosie, c/o				Feb	1899
GROBEFEND					
Elsie C.	7	CA	762		1894
GROCE					
Joseph L.	<1	SF	9122		1868
GROENEVELT					
Carl Gustave	78	GER	3991		1903
GROEPEN					
Marie	32	GER	2011		1873
GROEZINGER					
Elizabeth	68	GER	1001b		1895
Emile A./Emma, c/o	1	SF	5705		1904
Gottlob	79	GER	3241		1903

NAME	AGE OR YOB.	BIRTH PLACE	CERT. NO	ID	DEATH YEAR
Robert				Jan	1899
GROGAN					
Jno. Joseph				Mar	1900
Morton				Nov	1898
Tho. Francis M.	15	NY	475		1871
William	25	IRL	4557b		1870
GROH					
Joseph (soldier)			4549		1901
GROIZARD					
Francis				Jul	1899
GROLL					
Raymond (soldier)			8066		1900
GROLLMAN					
Julius	40	GER	1152		1871
GROLLMANN					
——			8757		1868
GRONDONA					
Azelia Leonita	9	SF	6847	Feb	1901
GRONI					
Antonio Loriano	42	SPA	2220		1873
GRONLT					
Marie E.	22	FRA	2396		1894
GROOCH					
Ken				May	1899
GROOM					
Henry	69	ENG	3374		1873
James	<1	SF	1214		1902
Juanita	1	CA	7215		1902
Lydia	70	ENG	2376		1873
Roger	70	IRE	5603		1904
GROOMS					
James	40	MS	2647		1873

NAME	AGE OR YOB.	BIRTH PLACE	CERT. NO	ID	DEATH YEAR
GROOTEWAL					
Nicholas (soldier)			8778		1904
GROPPER					
Karl Emil	3	SF	310		1903
GROSBAUM					
Sophie	79	GER	4156		1903
GROSCETTA					
Marietta					Nov 1899
GROSGEBAUER					
Annie F. E.		SF	1858		1870
Emma A. S.	<1	SF	362b		1871
John F.	<1	SF	988		1872
GROSH					
JennieFlorence	12	SF	1369		1871
GROSHON					
Wm. Alexander	<1	SF	6912		1903
GROSMAN					
Wilhelmina	1860	GER	1026c		1904
GROSO					
Mary	13	SF	1266		1869
GROSS					
——			4448		1867
Alexander	<1	IL	2743		1866
Alfred G.	32	CA	1102		1902
Annie Elizabeth	20	NY	8056		1901
Caroline					Mar 1899
Caroline					Nov 1899
E.S.	64	MA	2662		1872
Elizabeth	43	GER	1187		1869
Frank M.	33	GER	3569		1870
Fred Otto	41	GER	2410		1903
G. R./Lena, c/o	<1	SF	4110		1901
Hannah	32	PRU	1394		1869
John	58	GER	1572		1870
John					Nov 1899
Joseph	<1	SF	2315		1866
Joseph	<1	SF	2866		1866
Joseph P.					Dec 1898
Lilly	15	NV	G16		1882
Louis	70	AUT	2711		1895
Marie	3	SF	5273		1896
Martha E.	31	GER	5158		1902
Mary Amelia	1	CA	945		1872
Minnie	26	NY	8538		1900
Philip	57	POL	5751		1903
William (soldier)			5183		1901
GROSSE					
Charles Paul	45	GER	8662		1904
Enrico	38	ITA	1945		1866
GROSSKREUTZ					
Amanda	29	GER	3223		1902
GROSSMAN					
Abraham					Oct 1898
Annie	1	SF	2054b		1895
Daniel					Mar 1900
George					Oct 1899
Henry	20	MI	2175		1900
Marks	72	POL	5523		1902
Morris L./Annie, c/o		SF	1910		1901
Morris M.	49	NY	1103		1902
Nancy					Feb 1899
GROSSMANN					
Minnie	9	SF	3403		Nov 1901
GROSWIND					
Edward	1	SF	6631		1904
GROSZ					
George	49	FRA	6706		1868

Key: a = 1st part of year; b = 2nd part of year; c = death certificate copy; c/o = child of

NAME	AGE OR YOB.	BIRTH PLACE	CERT. NO	ID	DEATH YEAR
GROTE					
Frank C.	27	CA	6311		1904
GROTEFEND					
Elsie C.	7	CA	762		1894
GROTH					
Frederick/Martha, c/o	<1	SF	4405		1901
Karsten Henry	69	GER	5217		1902
GROTHAM					
Peter	41		1106		1869
GROTHAUS					
Ferdinand				Dec	1899
GROTHEER					
Louis	27	SC	1337b		1895
GROTHWOHL					
Charles Kaufman	76	FRA	3317		1902
GROTYEN					
George	39	PA	3986		1867
GROUGEN					
Joseph	1857	IRE	2924c		1904
GROUGUET					
Henri	45	FRA	7249		1901
GROULT					
Adele	42	FRA	1304		1866
GROUNDS					
Mary A.	27	SF	8480		1901
GROUSSIN					
Francois	49	FRA	1457		1866
GROUT					
Ernest C. (soldier)			860		1901
GROVE					
Jonathan	32	IRE	4446		1867
Mary	62	KY	5726	Jan	1901
Samuel	60	OH	6326		1896

NAME	AGE OR YOB.	BIRTH PLACE	CERT. NO	ID	DEATH YEAR
GROVER					
Benjamin Percy	66	ME	4045		1902
Elise C.	20	TN	2876		1866
Hannah Folsom				Mar	1900
Thomas	70	MD	2558		1902
GROVERS					
Mat/Sarah, c/o				Feb	1899
GROVES					
Catherine	<1	SF	1258		1869
Catherine	66	CAN	6497		1902
Dana				Feb	1900
James	50	ENG	4610		1896
GROVON					
Joseph S.	<1	SF	2294		1894
GROWMEL					
Louisa	1	SF	2402		1872
GROWNEY					
Elizabeth	<1	SF	3719		1870
Terence	65	IRE	2478		1903
Theodore	68	MA	2359		1901
GRUAN					
Andrew	60	PA	5468		1902
GRUBB					
Bernice A. G.	<1	SF	1104		1902
Dilla Lorgine	42	OR	3765		1903
Samuel Nicholas	67	MD	1668		1903
GRUBBS					
Hayden Y. (soldier)			8427		1900
GRUBE					
Henry	26	GER	659		1894
GRUBER					
Alexander James	60	MA	8815		1900
Charlotte	53	DEN	5460		1896
Martha Antonia	<1	SF	5031		1867

Key: a = 1st part of year; b = 2nd part of year;
c = death certificate copy; c/o = child of

NAME	AGE OR YOB.	BIRTH PLACE	CERT. NO	ID	DEATH YEAR	NAME	AGE OR YOB.	BIRTH PLACE	CERT. NO	ID	DEATH YEAR
						Frank	47	PA	6869		1900
GRUBERT											
Martha	18	GER	3636		1903	**GRUNIG**					
						Emma Laura	23	CA	6737		1900
GRUCHENSKY						Fred W.	29	CA	99		1900
Marks	54	NY	3074		1894	Henry	48	GER	G28		1883
GRUENBERG						**GRUNIGEN**					
Arthur	32	CA	5506		1904	Louisa Margrethe V.	<1	CA	2501		1902
GRUENING						**GRUNIH**					
August C.				Jul	1899	Herman	33	GER	835		1872
GRUM						**GRUNISSA**					
Francis Edna	1	CA	2292		1894	Marie		SF	5064a		1895
GRUMBO						**GRUNNAGLE**					
Joseph G.	<1	SF	1609		1902	George	76	FRA	6659		1904
GRUN						Mary Lucille	46	IRL	9296		1901
——	<1	SF	3473b		1870	**GRUNSHAW**					
GRUNAUER						Wm.	62	ENG	6786a		1895
Moses				Dec	1898	**GRUNWALD**					
GRUNBERG						Alexander	54	PRU	1265		1872
Charles	52	NOR	4351a		1895	Gustav	5	SF	5920		1867
GRUNBOUYN						**GRUSH**					
H.		SF	1443		1869	David	1831	OH	3008c		1904
GRUND						**GRUSZKIEWICZ**					
Rudolph	41	GER	1550		1870	Joseph	19	GER	6132		1902
GRUNDELL						**GRUTZMACHER**					
Thomas Oswald	33	CAN	3522		1903	Elizabeth	42	ENG	5057a		1896
GRUNDMANN						**GRUWELL**					
Caroline	71	PRU	4082b		1870	Henry	19	CA	2672		1900
John	34	GER	5162		1867	**GSCHWANDNER**					
GRUNEBERG						Joseph				Nov	1898
Carl	47	PRU	3455		1867	**GSCHWIND**					
GRUNER						Albert	3	SF	1181		1869
Ferdinand				Mar	1899	Remo	75	SWT	2234		1903
Frances				Feb	1900						
Francis				Feb	1900						

Key: a = 1st part of year; b = 2nd part of year;
c = death certificate copy; c/o = child of

NAME	AGE OR YOB.	BIRTH PLACE	CERT. NO	ID	DEATH YEAR
Gu					
Chung				Feb	1899
Guadagne					
Enela	<1	SF	6584		1902
Gualt					
Maria	83	FRA	8137		1903
Guamas					
Joseph	25	ISI	2973		1866
Guan					
Chan Chow				Apr	1899
Fon Ewe				Dec	1899
Gun Oh				Aug	1899
Kay				Dec	1898
Lung				Dec	1899
Guandlack					
William H.	6	SF	1440		1869
Guanziroli					
L./M., c/o		SF	6505		1895
Guaraglia					
Attilio A.	6	SF	1372b		1895
Luigi	58	ITA	3967		1900
Guaragna					
Accurso/Vianzina, c/o		SF	4634		1896
Guaraldi					
Seconda	1	NY	7670		1904
Guardini					
V/M., c/o	<1	SF	76		1895
Guardino					
G./M., c/o		SF	5459		1896
Guastafson					
Edith	4	SF	791b		1895
Guatelli					
Cesare	<1	SF	1709		1894

NAME	AGE OR YOB.	BIRTH PLACE	CERT. NO	ID	DEATH YEAR
Giovanni				Mar	1899
Gubleman					
Ernest C.			1114		1903
Gucchi					
Concessa	2	SF	1126		1894
Gucero					
Louis	1	MEX	6647	Feb	1901
Guckenheimer					
Marx	61	GER	1349		1900
Gudely					
John	1	SF	4826		1904
Gudhaus					
Fred, c/o	<1	SF	3044		1873
Gudmundson					
Carrie				Feb	1900
Gudxinsky					
Charles	1	SF	839b		1871
Gue					
Fow	24	CHN	1663a		1871
Geon Chan	37	CHN	1019		1870
Loo	40	CHN	839		1866
Ti				Feb	1899
Guegand					
Jean Marie	42	FRA	4210	Dec	1901
Guelfi					
Orlando	37	ITA	2074		1903
Guellemin					
Juliett	6	SF	1100		1866
Guen					
Ene				Oct	1899
Leang Ah	28	CHN	1363		1869
Ung	30	CHN	476b		1871

      Key: a = 1st part of year; b = 2nd part of year;
c = death certificate copy; c/o = child of

NAME	AGE OR YOB.	BIRTH PLACE	CERT. NO	ID	DEATH YEAR	NAME	AGE OR YOB.	BIRTH PLACE	CERT. NO	ID	DEATH YEAR
GUENIN						**GUERRERO**					
Eleanore				Oct	1899	Dorothy H.	1904	SF	3036c		1904
						Tuzal	2	CA	6549		1904
GUENLEY											
Charles	<1	SF	2338b		1895	**GUERROLLO**					
Edward	41	CA	2674		1903	Prudencio	<1	SF	1040		1868
GUENTHER						**GUERRSAN**					
Charles (soldier)			7117		1900	Christina	<1	SF	6135		1867
Charles Francis	2	GER	5637		1902	**GUERSBUHLER**					
GUEP						Aeine	50	SWT	1007		1868
Gottlieb F.	70	PRU	713b		1871	**GUESME**					
GUERCIA						Melaine	81	FRA	1256		1894
Savalatorine	34	ITA	7617		1904	**GUESS**					
GUERELLO						Geo.				Mar	1900
Amelia	4	CA	1008		1868	James H., c/o	<1	SF	2225a		1872
GUERIMAN						**GUESSER**					
——		SF	1241		1869	Frank				Feb	1900
GUERIN						**GUEST**					
——			6214		1867	Mary A.	28	NY	3625		1896
Fitz W.	57	IRE	258		1903	T./M., c/o		SF	3451		1896
Frederic	75	FRA	7079		1904	**GUEY**					
G. C.	32	OH	5342		1896	Fai	49	CHN	6182		1902
James M.	24	CAN	2391a		1872	**GUFFETT**					
John				Jul	1899	Robt.	59	PA	G96		1889
Margaret	58	IRL	3150		1895	**GUGANOVICH**					
Steve	29	CA	7325		1903	Francesca	<1	SF	5191a		1895
Theophile B.	49	FRA	3995	Dec	1901	**GUGELSBERGER**					
GUERKINK						Annie				Oct	1898
Charlotte	51	USA	1050		1901	William	38	SF	8663		1904
GUERRA						**GUGGER**					
Dewey	5	SF	5359		1903	Samuel	25	SWT	7445		1868
Juanna F de	68	MEX	691a		1871	**GUGLIEMINA**					
Rafael	<1	SF	9991		1868	Giacomina	32	SWT	4541		1896
GUERRAZRO											
Maddalena	<1	SF	993a		1871						

Key: a = 1st part of year; b = 2nd part of year;
c = death certificate copy; c/o = child of

NAME	AGE OR YOB.	BIRTH PLACE	CERT. NO	ID	DEATH YEAR	NAME	AGE OR YOB.	BIRTH PLACE	CERT. NO	ID	DEATH YEAR
GUGLIERI						**GUILFOY**					
Francisca	38	MEX	5912		1902	James	50	ENG	2169		1903
GUGNY						**GUILFOYL**					
William (soldier)			7217		1900	Teresa	<1	SF	5365		1867
GUHNE						**GUILFOYLE**					
Fritz				Mar	1899	Catherine				Jan	1899
GUHRING						Frances	50	IRL	2331		1901
Geo.	35	GER	G58		1885	Mary E.	1	SF	3663		1870
GUIBBINI						**GUILIANELLI**					
Shalby	1904	SF	114c		1904	Miliano	1	SF	1706b		1895
GUICHET						**GUILIANI**					
Francis	62	FRA	2947		1894	Antonio	54	ITA	8082		1903
						Giovanni	1	SF	8496		1903
GUICHOSHI						Guelfo	37	ITA	5604		1904
Mariano	28	GUA	3524	Nov	1901	**GUILLAS**					
GUICK						J. M.	77	FRA	2856		1900
——			6428		1867	**GUILLAUME**					
GUIDER						Baldi Bartel	82	FRA	1225a		1871
Mary Motelda	45	IN	9427		1901	**GUILLEMARD**A.E					
GUIDI						Alfred Jos.	33	SF	1405		1894
Arcangelo	55	ITA	2244		1900	**GUILLEN**					
Armando	1904	SF	2702c		1904	Ada	24	TN	4444		1867
GUIDICE						Ada	<1	SF	5675		1867
C. J. (soldier)			7529		1900	Jesus C.	4	MEX	1728		1866
GUIGNARD						**GUILLERMET**					
John	80	SWT	2432		1901	F. P.	35		5568		1902
GUILBERT						**GUILLIUM**					
Emma	57	ENG	11		1900	Angelique	<1	SF	2065		1894
William J.	25	SF	7309		1904	Cecile	8	SF	8250		1904
GUILD						**GUIMIER**					
A.M.				Jul	1899	Angele, Mme.	35	FRA	8941		1901
GUILFORD						**GUIN**					
Maria Barbara	<1	SF	1764		1901	John Walter	<1	SF	1362		1869

Key: a = 1st part of year; b = 2nd part of year;
c = death certificate copy; c/o = child of

NAME	AGE OR YOB.	BIRTH PLACE	CERT. NO	ID	DEATH YEAR	NAME	AGE OR YOB.	BIRTH PLACE	CERT. NO	ID	DEATH YEAR
On	46	CHN	4542		1904	**GUINOCCHIO**					
						Pietro					Dec 1898
GUINAN											
Andrew	52	CAN	2686		1903	**GUINOLA**					
						Frank	1	SF	1104		1869
GUINASSO											
Amelia E.	<1	SF	7620		1903	**GUION**					
Angelo	1866	ITA	29 c		1904	Annie	25	SF	5065		1904
Angelo	<1	SF	3905		1896	Clara D.M.	76	CUB	4210		1896
Francesco T.	56	ITA	8040		1901	Elijah	69	NY	4234		1896
Frederick L.					Apr 1899						
Marie					Nov 1898	**GUIOTT**					
Stella Ida					Nov 1898	Christina	62	GER	2269		1903
Theresa, c/o					Dec 1898	**GUIRACH**					
						Rosa	<1	CA	1171b		1895
GUINCE											
Michael H.					May 1899	**GUIRARD**					
						Augusta	56	LA	2600		1900
GUINCH											
Marie K.	25	DEN	G60		1885	**GUIRE**					
						Michael	58	IRE	6531		1903
GUINCIO											
Pietro	69	ITA	6286		1896	**GUIREY**					
						W. C.	<1	SF	172a		1871
GUINDON											
Eugene F.	22	WT	G75		1886	**GUIROLO**					
						Luigi		ITA	8469		1868
GUINER											
Joseph	29	MO	3493		1867	**GUIROZ**					
						Refugio					Nov 1899
GUINESSO											
Annie					Feb 1900	**GUIRTI**					
						Sidney S.	6	SF	8732		1900
GUINICH											
Alexander	49	SCT	1077		1869	**GUISPERT**					
						Julius	<1	SF	6138		1867
GUINN											
Ida May	35	CAN	5394		1896	**GUISTE**					
John	<1	SF	1189		1869	Francesca/Bianca, c/o		SF	1904		1900
Mary Ellen	2	CA	9603		1868	**GUISTI**					
						Caroline	61	FRA	1206		1903
GUINNANE						Lina	<1	SF	6850		1903
Lulu	11	SF	5899		1903						
Mary	54	PA	7260		1904	**GUISTO**					
Mary Frances	20	SF	5252		1904	Domenic	65	ITA	7569		1903

Key: a = 1st part of year; b = 2nd part of year;
c = death certificate copy; c/o = child of

NAME	AGE OR YOB.	BIRTH PLACE	CERT. NO	ID	DEATH YEAR
Frank	63	ITA	4542a		1895
GUITTARD					
Etienne A.				Jul	1899
Eva	<1	SF	1300b		1872
GUIVARA					
Eutimia	60	MEX	2336b		1895
GULARDO					
Anne	32	AUS	G27		1883
GULDEMANN					
Agusta	36	GER	7153		1903
Dora	5	SF	7398		1904
Henry	35	GER	2351		1900
GULENE					
Martin	50	FRA	417b		1871
GULIEROR					
Frank	1	CA	1074		1869
GULLE					
Louis	4	ITA	2824		1873
GULLIKSEN					
James	50	NOR	616		1894
GULLINAN					
Michael	61	IRE	1160		1869
GULLIVER					
Harriett	76	ENG	5569		1902
GULLIXSON					
Ellen J.	<1	SF	4897		1867
Henry A.	<1	SF	4896		1867
GULLMAN					
Charles	33	GER	1062		1869
GULLOPENA					
F. Maudalena	18	SF	1327a		1871
GULLSSAZ					
E. L.			G20		1883

NAME	AGE OR YOB.	BIRTH PLACE	CERT. NO	ID	DEATH YEAR
GUM					
Ah	35	CHN	3133		1870
Ah	40	CHN	5710		1867
Ah Won				Jun	1899
Chan	<1	SF	2479		1894
Choie	24	CHN	892		1870
GUMBINNER					
J. L.	58	GER	3914		1867
Sven	59	SWE	2905		1900
GUMELIN					
Edwin	3	CA	1603b		1895
GUMM					
Willie	4	SF	6137		1903
GUMMER					
Chas J.	37	HI	G8		1882
Frederick Channing	60	AUT	5176		1902
GUMMUS					
Martin	1849	RUS	644c		1904
GUMP					
Gustav				Dec	1898
GUN					
Ah	23	CHN	144		1865
Ah	42	CHN	3292		1866
Ah	28	CHN	1320		1869
Die	56	CHN	6351		1902
Lep Gum				Feb	1899
Luin	<1	CHN	1172		1869
You	<1	SF	1125		1866
GUNALACH					
Jacob	76	GER	2989		1894
GUNAR					
Thos. P.				Mar	1900
GUNARAS					
George	63	GRE	1105		1902

Key: a = 1st part of year; b = 2nd part of year;
c = death certificate copy; c/o = child of

NAME	AGE OR YOB.	BIRTH PLACE	CERT. NO	ID	DEATH YEAR
GUNDELACH					
John	60	GER	3948	Dec	1901
GUNDERSEN					
Ellen Francis	7	SF	2292		1900
GUNDERSON					
Alfred	30	SF	6573		1904
Christian	42	NOR	2879a		1872
H. C.	39	NOR	7111		1868
John	40		6787		1902
Ole (soldier)			7527		1900
GUNDLACH					
Henry	65	GER	2080		1873
Martha				Feb	1899
GUNDRY					
Ida				Mar	1899
GUNETTI					
Eugenia	1	SF	512		1903
GUNG					
Duck	45	CHN	5627		1903
Ngin Bina	54	CHN	4870		1904
Si Kay				May	1899
GUNI					
Shey				Feb	1900
GUNN					
――			1887		1866
Annie	40	MA	2093		1900
Belinda Frances	2	SF	3203		1873
Frances	5	SF	1946		1900
Frank L.			3821		1902
Gertrude Christina	1873	CA	141c		1904
Helen	45	NY	8083		1903
Hugh	85	SCT	8482		1901
Jennie	58	IRE	3809		1902
John	8	SF	7783		1868
John Michael	37	ENG	1131		1869
Mary Agnes	<1	SF	2294		1866
Propero C.	2	SF	258		1865
Robert T.	51	AUS	2197		1894
Robert W.	46	CAN	2098		1894
Walter J.	26	SF	6759		1903
William	65	SCT	3496a		1872
GUNNAR					
Patrick	69	IRL	1001		1894
GUNNARSON					
Augusta				Jan	1899
GUNNING					
Clara F.	26	SF	6960	Feb	1901
Edward	<1	SF	1366		1869
Frank				Nov	1899
Thomas	10	SF	1969		1870
William (soldier)	27	PA	2788		1900
GUNNISON					
Albert	72	NH	7103		1903
Andrew Joseph	79	NH	7701		1902
C. Robert	68	NOR	8892		1900
GUNNOUD					
Roderick	54	IRE	641		1902
GUNST					
Abraham	83	GER	4943		1896
GUNTER					
Charles	1	SF	1128		1869
GUNTHER					
Isabella S.	59	NY	8182		1900
Joseph D.	54	FRA	6912		1868
William	<1	SF	5467		1903
GUNTLI					
Peter	31	SWT	8382		1901

Key: a = 1st part of year; b = 2nd part of year;
c = death certificate copy; c/o = child of

NAME	AGE OR YOB.	BIRTH PLACE	CERT. NO	ID	DEATH YEAR	NAME	AGE OR YOB.	BIRTH PLACE	CERT. NO	ID	DEATH YEAR
GUNTREN						**GURMA**					
Mathilda	34	SWT	5735		1902	Margaret	<1	SF	4884		1901
Willie	<1	SF	2674		1894	**GURMONDEY**					
GUNTRUM						B.	36	FRA	3720		1867
John B.	49	GER	1208		1869	**GURNER**					
GUNTZ						Clinton				Oct	1898
Agnes	10	SF	1530b		1895	**GURNEY**					
Martin	43	GER	1312		1894	Fred	1	SF	358		1903
GUNY						**GUROVITZ**					
Chuve (alias)	40	CHN	1438b		1895	Odon			1230		1903
GUNZBURGER						**GURRCOSTA**					
Johanna	73	GER	3930a		1895	A.	85	MLT	2624		1900
Nathan E.	1	SF	2053b		1895	**GURRDUIN**					
GUOLIOS						M./V., c/o	<1	SF	763		1894
James	18	GRE	7866		1903	**GURROLA**					
GUONG						Josephine	30	MEX	3012		1870
Bing				Aug	1898	**GURRY**					
Lee	25	CHN	3676		1870	Edward J.	1	SF	3716		1870
GUOS						**GURULE**					
John				Jan	1899	Petronile (soldier)			8782		1901
GUOY						**GUS**					
Am	30	CHN	2924a		1872	Edward I.	<1	SF	5370a		1895
GUPTILL						William	<1	SF	3183		1895
Mary	50		1177		1903	**GUSCETTI**					
Willard W.	69	NY	7253		1902	Viola Sophie	<1	SF	6016		1896
GURGANAS						**GUSCONI**					
William Frances	1	SF	1249a		1871	Ridgway (soldier)			7216		1900
GURLEY						**GUSINA**					
Goldie	14	IA	6302	Feb	1901	Anna	<1	SF	1432a		1871
Mary	60	IRL	1769		1900	Marco	43	AUT	2137a		1872
GURLONG						**GUSINO**					
John M.	3	SF	1082		1869	Elizabeth	23	DAL	929a		1871

Key: a = 1st part of year; b = 2nd part of year; c = death certificate copy; c/o = child of

NAME	AGE OR YOB.	BIRTH PLACE	CERT. NO	ID	DEATH YEAR
GUSMA					
Marco	43	AUT	2137a		1872
GUSMAN					
Felicita	5	SF	2472		1873
Lewis	7	SF	3671		1867
GUSMANI					
Giovanno	<1	SF	1237b		1871
Mary	56	IRE	918		1903
GUSS					
Ellis L. (soldier)			269		1901
GUSSINO					
Angelo	55	ITA	6255	Feb	1901
GUSSLER					
Broadwell Kruse				Jan	1899
GUSTAFSEN					
Lillie L.	24	SF	2648		1900
GUSTAFSON					
Daniel	21	IL	7778		1904
Edgar	<1	SF	7401		1903
George H.	<1	SF	5696a		1895
Hedvig F.				Jul	1898
Oscar William				Feb	1899
S./W., c/o				Feb	1899
GUSTAN					
Morris N.	42	VT	8697		1868
GUSTAVSON					
Gustav	42	FIN	2291		1900
Oscar Edwin	<1	SF	1584		1900
GUSTEFSON					
Peter August	1846	SWE	1201c		1904
GUSTIN					
James William				May	1899
Mattie E.	29	ME	310		1900
GUSTY					
Albert				Jun	1899
GUT					
Ah	25	CHN	9449		1868
Elice				Mar	1899
Fong	36	CHN	7965		1904
Geam Lan	48	CHN	3040a		1872
Saisey	27	CHN	3039a		1872
GUTAFSON					
Axel	26	SWE	5979		1903
GUTBERLET					
Helena	<1	SF	9841		1868
GUTFELD					
Martha				Jan	1900
Morris				Nov	1898
GUTGELUCH					
Louis	30	GER	1373		1869
GUTH					
George	59	GER	8251		1904
GUTHEARTZ					
George	70	IL	8161		1903
GUTHRIE					
Claud	85	SCT	1035		1868
Frances M. Ashley	68	KY	5786		1903
Jane				Mar	1899
Martha	26	ENG	9532		1868
Mary	88	IRL	3943		1896
Minerva Holitha	1856	OH	1425c		1904
Walter H.				Dec	1899
GUTIERREX					
Candido	78	CHN	4597		1903
GUTIERREZ					
Euphemia E.	1	SF	1244		1869
Pedro F.	<1	SF	397		1870

Key: a = 1st part of year; b = 2nd part of year;
c = death certificate copy; c/o = child of

NAME	AGE OR YOB.	BIRTH PLACE	CERT. NO	ID	DEATH YEAR	NAME	AGE OR YOB.	BIRTH PLACE	CERT. NO	ID	DEATH YEAR
GUTIERRZ						**GUTTRIDGE**					
Maria E.	6	SF	7194		1868	W./E., c/o		SF	2339		1873
						William I.	3	SF	337		1865
GUTMAN											
Fan Adams	55	RUS	9531		1868	**GUTTZEIT**					
						Lena				Feb	1899
GUTMANN											
David	45	BAV	1328		1901	**GUY**					
						Eugene				Oct	1898
GUTSCH						Kearns				Jul	1899
Gustav Friedrich Alexander	73	GER	4241	Dec	1901	Michael H.	60	CA	5770	Jan	1901
GUTSCHOW											
E./A., c/o		SF	991		1894	**GUYATT**					
						Lennie	16	SF	2332		1901
GUTTE											
Julius	72	GER	1945		1900	**GUYEN**					
						Eliza	35	GER	2094		1873
GUTTEMAN											
Barbara	45	GER	2529		1900	**GUYER**					
						Charles E. (soldier)			2057		1901
GUTTENRY											
Wutter	<1	SF	1020		1868	**GUYOT**					
						Hortense	31	FRA	1657b		1871
GUTTER											
Alfred Siegfrid				Aug	1898	**GUYTON**					
Ida Emma	17	GER	4666		1901	Earl E.			7655		1902
GUTTERMANN						**GUZMAN**					
Lena	46	GER	1989		1903	Richard A.	48	MEX	1807		1902
GUTTERSON						**GWIN**					
Ina Maria	44	VT	5957		1902	Mary Elizabeth Hampton	86	KY	9648		1901
						Ralph				Jul	1899
GUTTERY											
Robert	27	GER	5188		1867	**GWINN**					
						Arthur (soldier)			7146		1901
GUTTMAN											
David	32	PRU	1821a		1872	**GWYNETTE**					
						John M. W.	51	MA	1741b		1872
GUTTNER											
John				Mar	1900	**GWYNN**					
						Solon	38	CA	685		1902
GUTTO											
Henry	55	GER	5372a		1895	**GWYTHER**					
						Eliza	80	ENG	9033		1903
GUTTREDGE											
Ellen Louisa	3	SF	1316		1869						

Key: a = 1st part of year; b = 2nd part of year; c = death certificate copy; c/o = child of

NAME	AGE OR YOB.	BIRTH PLACE	CERT. NO	ID	DEATH YEAR	NAME	AGE OR YOB.	BIRTH PLACE	CERT. NO	ID	DEATH YEAR
GYBSON						**HAAN**					
G. W.	40	ME	7008		1868	John	41	GER	1585b		1872
GYGAX						**HAAS**					
Ernest/Sophie, c/o	<1	SF	8807		1901	Adelheid	66	GER	7553		1904
GYLE						Charles					Dec 1898
Hauchen					Dec 1898	Charles N.	2	CA	6913		1903
Pauline	1	CA	828b		1871	Elizabeth	33	GER	1582		1866
GYLORD						Esther					Jan 1900
Wilber H.	1843	IL	893c		1904	Franklin	<1	SF	1324		1869
H						George	39	GER	606a		1870
Catherine					Jan 1899	Henry	10	NJ	602a		1870
HA						Henry					Mar 1899
Lung Chou	43	CHN	762b		1871	Jesus Ricardo	1	MEX	1066		1900
Mong Chung She					Feb 1900	Johann	46	GER	2819		1866
Wah Lock	56	CHN	6914		1904	John	43	IA	2619		1903
HAACK						Joseph	1904	SF	2951c		1904
Gustave	42	GER	5282		1903	Lottie Elizabeth	27	DC	4721		1903
Jacob	42	GER	1150		1869	Margaret	15	SF	1634		1900
Matilda	23	NY	6418		1900	Salomon	78	GER	4935a		1895
HAAF						Sam'l., c/o		SF	388b		1872
Jacob	59	GER	966		1894	Samuel	71	GER	5410a		1895
HAAG						Susanna	49	GER	2736		1894
Chas.	42	GER	3140		1903	Tessie	37	NY	8285		1900
Francesca, Mrs.	66	GER	6b		1895	**HAASE**					
George A.	24	IN	5744		1896	Auguste					Jul 1899
Julius/Fannie, c/o	1	CA	4512		1904	Christian	<1	SF	3347a		1872
Katherine					May 1899	Doris S.	3	SF	3392		1870
HAAKE						Fritz	31	GER	6070		1867
Bertha	22	CA	1532b		1895	Herman A.	27	CA	H173		1887
Della	26	SF	2675		1903	Richard H.	35	NY	7666		1900
Henry	38	SF	6955		1902	**HABELIN**					
J. C.	50	GER	H57		1884	Mary L.	1	SF	9430		1868
Oliver	22	SF	7867		1900	**HABELZS**					
						Abraham	41	AUT	8184		1901

Key: a = 1st part of year; b = 2nd part of year;
c = death certificate copy; c/o = child of

NAME	AGE OR YOB.	BIRTH PLACE	CERT. NO	ID	DEATH YEAR	NAME	AGE OR YOB.	BIRTH PLACE	CERT. NO	ID	DEATH YEAR
HABENICHT						HACHMAN					
Geo./A., c/o					Nov 1898	Henry	31	GER	1720b		1871
HABERLAN						HACHMANN					
Thomas	34	CA	4849		1901	Laura V.	37	CA	7326		1903
HABERLEN						HACHOR					
Jos. Patrick	<1	SF	1334a		1871	Wm.	65	GER	5621a		1895
HABERLI						HACHOWAY					
Fredrick	68	SWT	4505		1901	Rebecca W.	82	ME	1613		1900
HABERLIER						HACK					
Mary Ann	29	IRL	628a		1871	Lena	39	GER	1136		1903
HABERLIS						Mary M.	21	OR	143		1903
Isaac	3	AUT	H18		1882	Susana Rosena	81	GER	5895		1896
HABERLY						HACKE					
Fredric Valentine	24	CA	2980		1900	Christoph	73	GER	7665		1903
HABERMACHER						HACKELE					
Ferdinand	64	SWT	7841		1901	Charlie	1	SF	6637		1868
HABERMAN						HACKENBERG					
Antonette					Feb 1899	Ewald	54	GER	1691		1900
HABICH						HACKER					
Charles M.	49	FRA	1447		1901	Gertrude	14	CA	6327		1900
Esperance	66	FRA	1273		1903	Loring Joseph	<1	SF	2991		1894
Mary					Aug 1899	HACKETT					
HABULAND						A. Cornell	1904	SF	2242c		1904
Minna	22	CA	858		1894	Catherine, c/o	<1	SF	7227		1904
HACE						David A.	1	SF	2768		1903
——	<1	SF	1104		1869	Edward Henry	29	SF	6405a		1895
HACH						Emily					Jan 1899
——	<1	SF	1058		1869	James	64	IRL	7853		1900
HACHETTE						Jno. J., Dr.	60	IRL	4866a		1895
Roy M.	8	SF	6897		1900	John			7101		1902
HACHKOFLER						John C.	32	NY	8861		1868
Caroline A.	39	NY	1280		1869	Lewis B.	28	CA	H183		1889
						Maggie A.	1	SF	3089		1870
						Mannie	75	IRL	1973		1870

NAME	AGE OR YOB.	BIRTH PLACE	CERT. NO	ID	DEATH YEAR
Mary Clara	79	MD	4092		1902
Michael	47	IRL	550b		1895
Owen	47	IRL	H31		1883
P.	65	IRL	H102		1886
Patrick	60	IRL	54		1900
Powhattan T. (soldier)			5488	Jan	1901
Sarah	<1	CA	1152a		1871
Thomas	27	ENG	8831		1868
Thomas				Apr	1899
HACKH					
John	59	GER	1270b		1872
HACKLEY					
Robert J.				May	1899
HACKMAIER					
P.K., c/o				Jul	1898
HACKMAN					
Charles				Feb	1900
John				May	1899
HACKMANN					
Fred				Nov	1898
HACKMEIER					
Lottie , c/o	1904	CA	2550		1904
HACKSTON					
Charles Edward	<1	SF	1114		1900
Elizabeth Grace				May	1899
John	33	ENG	8758		1903
HACKWARD					
William	50	ENG	3664		1900
HACTOIF					
Charles	61	NY	4872		1904
HADANO					
Kakuyemon	30		7021		1900
HADDIN					
Lucretia A.	15	MA	1062		1869
HADDOX					
Enoch, Jr. (soldier)			7458		1904
HADELER					
Claudina E. I.	1	SF	8233		1901
Louis	19	OH	1380b		1871
HADEN					
———			8534		1868
HADENFELDT					
Charles	59	GER	8497		1903
J. A. M.	1	SF	1055b		1872
HADERLE					
John				Jun	1899
HADLEN					
Henry	69	GER	245		1901
HADLER					
———			3143		1866
Anna Auguste	31	GER	5185a		1896
Elizabeth	36	MA	2435		1901
Frida M.				Jul	1898
HADLEY					
Albert B.	5	MA	3036		1866
Annabelle				Nov	1898
Helen	1860	WAL	1396c		1904
Moses F.	76	MA	4503		1901
Nellie J.	41	MA	6171		1904
HADLIGH					
Lewis	30	CA	2295		1894
HADLY					
Emma Gertrude	2	SF	3117		1866
HADNETT					
Jeremiah W.	64	IRL	1722		1901
HADSELL					
Charles				Jun	1899

Key: a = 1st part of year; b = 2nd part of year;
c = death certificate copy; c/o = child of

NAME	AGE OR YOB.	BIRTH PLACE	CERT. NO	ID	DEATH YEAR	NAME	AGE OR YOB.	BIRTH PLACE	CERT. NO	ID	DEATH YEAR
HADVER						HAFHEIM					
Henry	<1	SF	7827		1868	Louis	55	GER	1683		1894
HAE						HAFNER					
Ah	22	CHN	1374		1869	Francis Charles	<1	SF	1841b		1872
HAECKL						Johanna Maria	<1	SF	425a		1871
Charles	34	CA	5187		1904	HAFT					
HAELY						Ebenezer E.	71	PA	6660		1904
John	<1	SF	3913		1867	HAGAN					
HAERA						——			1568		1866
Frank	68	GER	1399		1901	Catharine	38	IRL	H101		1886
HAERFET						Celia				Mar	1900
Henry	<1	SF	1360		1869	Charles	37	AUS	725b		1895
HAERSFERING						Ciscelay	36	IRL	2306a		1872
Meyer		SF	2013		1870	James E. (soldier)			3041	Oct	1901
						John	1	SF	847b		1872
HAESLOOP						Joseph	<1	SF	1443		1869
Frederick	70	GER	4448a		1895	Joseph D.			7383		1902
HAETSCHE						M. B.	34	IRL	1866a		1872
——		SF	1215		1869	Mary	60	IRL	6870		1900
						Mary Ann	6	SF	637		1866
HAETTEL						Mave E.	18	RI	8121		1900
C. J.				Jan	1900	Patrick	38	IRE	1173		1869
HAFERHOM						Patrick M.	31	IRL	944b		1871
Mary	27	GER	820b		1872	Sarah Jane	<1	SF	2187		1866
HAFERKORN						Thomas	50	IRL	3829		1870
Anton Frederick	<1	SF	1424b		1872	Y. Carlos	<1	MEX	1376		1869
Frederick A.	68	SWT	6718		1903	HAGARTY					
HAFFEY						Jeremiah	<1	SF	3869		1870
Ann	75	IRE	7588		1904	John	55	IRL	H35		1883
Catherine				Feb	1900	Mary	4	CA	9063		1868
Frank Z.	36	MO	1934		1902	HAGATA					
Thomas	26	SF	4021		1903		28	JPN	888		1903
HAFFORD						HAGE					
Elizabeth	55	GER	4972a		1895	August/Cleora, c/o	1	SF	2825		1903

NAME	AGE OR YOB.	BIRTH PLACE	CERT. NO	ID	DEATH YEAR
Octavia M.	47	IL	1127		1869
Robert	<1	SF	3763		1902
HAGEDON					
Anna H. B.	75	GER	5133		1903
HAGEDOON					
Henry	<1	SF	3978a		1895
HAGEDORN					
Edna F.	21	SF	5570		1902
Fred				Feb	1899
John			7384		1902
Mildred	<1	CA	8865		1900
Peter	33	HOL	1759		1866
Willie	10	SF	1172		1894
HAGEMAN					
Sarah A.	28	ENG	5787a		1895
W. S.	47	PA	222		1901
HAGEMANN					
C./M., c/o		SF	4542		1896
Emily M.	29	MD	70b		1872
Katie C.	18	SF	4319		1902
Peter	59	NOR	1378		1869
Philip	50	GER	4227		1903
HAGEMEISTER					
Bertha				Aug	1899
HAGEMMON					
Louisa	23	GER	4260		1867
HAGEN					
Elizabeth	1863	ENG	824c		1904
Frederick	24	GER	2417		1900
Fritz O. (soldier)			7154		1901
Henry	58	GER	4864a		1895
Mary				Apr	1899
Max	53	PRU	3665	Nov	1901
Samuel J.	21	SF	8408		1900

NAME	AGE OR YOB.	BIRTH PLACE	CERT. NO	ID	DEATH YEAR
HAGENAUER					
Florence				May	1899
George V.				May	1899
HAGENMEYER					
Gebhard	69	GER	8533		1901
HAGENON					
Richd.	45	GER	H52		1884
HAGENVIAMP					
H. F. George	<1	SF	4517		1867
HAGERMAN					
Bernard	72	GER	83		1901
HAGERTY					
Alice	36	IRL	2906		1895
Anna M.				Nov	1899
Catharine	34	IRL	3663		1900
Daniel	32	IRL	1069b		1872
Daniel Stevens	3	SF	395b		1872
Elizabeth	27	NY	1197		1869
James Henry	<1	SF	2005		1900
Kate	1	SF	1029		1870
Margaret	65	IRL	460		1901
Margaret L.				Jan	1899
Mary	60	IRE	5546		1902
Mary Frances	35	IRE	6034		1902
Susan	36	IRL	6573	Feb	1901
William K.	3	MA	1681		1870
HAGG					
John A. (soldier)			221		1902
HAGGAN					
Fanny	<1	SF	1353		1869
HAGGART					
James	43	SCT	1317		1901
HAGGARTY					
Judson B.	<1	SF	9145		1868

NAME	AGE OR YOB.	BIRTH PLACE	CERT. NO	ID	DEATH YEAR
Timothy	15	NY	3966		1870
HAGGERTY					
——	<1	SF	1175		1869
George	78	IRL	5296		1901
Jno.	40	NY	1890		1894
Julia	28	IRL	3126a		1872
Margaret	39	IRL	3758		1896
Mary	26	SF	4680		1902
Michael/Delia, c/o	<1	SF	3024		1902
Peter	60	IRL	H53		1884
Richard	60	IRL	2272b		1895
Timothy	42	IRE	1277		1869
HAGGETT					
A. O.	45	ME	H152		1887
Myrtle H.	13	SF	3196		1900
HAGGIN					
Dr. J. B.	62	KY	3374		1894
Henry	64	NY	6365a		1895
HAGGLUND					
Charlotte	75	SWE	7154		1903
Helen Marian				Apr	1899
HAGGWALL					
John H.	1849	SWE	2140c		1904
HAGIN					
Saidee Louise	24	IL	6956		1902
HAGLER					
Erhardt	83	SWT	4293		1896
Pierre Oswald	5	SF	5293		1896
HAGMAN					
Carl Wilhelm	<1	CA	6383		1904
Nicholas August	<1	CA	6384		1904
HAGNER					
Oliver	23	USA	5218a		1896

NAME	AGE OR YOB.	BIRTH PLACE	CERT. NO	ID	DEATH YEAR
HAGSTROM					
Anna Constance	<1	SF	3262	Nov	1901
Della	7	SF	979		1901
Luisa, Mrs.	38	NOR	1138		1901
HAGUE					
Arthur V.				Dec	1899
Stephen	68	GER	9496		1901
HAHN					
——	<1	SF	1154		1869
Adelaide	60	NY	3250		1902
Alfred	26	GER	H129		1886
Arther	<1	SF	8462		1868
Arthur	1	SF	1239		1903
August	59	GER	551b		1895
Augusta	29	GER	1215		1869
Bella	<1	SF	1172		1869
C. C.	27	GER	742a		1871
Elizabeth Barbara	74	GER	663		1902
Esther	8	AUS	3630		1902
Ferdinand	47	GER	1180a		1871
Franz Joseph	43	AUT	2576		1894
George	49	GER	H198		1889
George H.	29	GER	1974		1870
Henry	63	GER	4990		1901
Ida	1	SF	8535		1868
J./Carrie, c/o		SF	6455		1900
John	<1	SF	7501		1904
John	50	GER	324		1901
John William	76	GER	2196		1903
Lea	40	SF	4786		1896
Lena Marie	2	SF	1083b		1895
Lisette	1	SF	3208		1870
Louis Henry				Jan	1900
Margaret A.	52	MD	1020		1900
Martha	36	GER	1993		1873

NAME	AGE OR YOB.	BIRTH PLACE	CERT. NO	ID	DEATH YEAR
Philippina	27	OH	4374b		1870
Rudolph J.	<1	SF	749		1901
Theresa	67	GER	1794		1901
HAHNE					
August	49	GER	392		1870
Babette	75	GER	5010		1901
HAHR					
Emma	<1	SF	39b		1872
HAI					
Tai Chew				Jul	1898
HAIBLE					
Constant	45	GER	2046		1903
HAIDER					
Marie	<1	SF	5311		1903
HAIFFLE					
Robert (soldier)			6830		1900
HAIGHT					
Anna H.	27	NY	9029		1868
Cameron	6	SF	2464		1866
Clarence	11	SF	2043		1870
Diana	93	NY	4093		1902
Ella F.	4	SF	8576		1868
F. M.	66	NY	857		1866
Fred Billings	1861	SF	1739c		1904
George A. (soldier)			3684		1900
H. H., c/o	<1	CA	1878b		1872
Harrison	1827	NY	621c		1904
Henry	48	NY	1155		1869
HAILE					
Anton	65	GER	5558		1903
Catherine	1	SF	748b		1871
Susan Duncan	1821	KY	2129c		1904
HAILER					
Albert	34	SF	4443		1904

NAME	AGE OR YOB.	BIRTH PLACE	CERT. NO	ID	DEATH YEAR
HAIN					
Abigal K.	70	NH	1251		1869
Alonzo	40	CA	H23		1883
HAINES					
Clara F.	36	SF	1908		1902
Clifford				Mar	1899
Elena P.				Feb	1900
Elizabeth A.	26	OH	218		1901
Ervin D.	31	IN	4085		1900
James	21	ME	1196		1869
James M. (soldier)			3546		1900
Roy/Gwen, c/o	1904	CA	142		1904
Samuel A.	48	IL	1976		1902
HAINEY					
Maria	1	SF	2613		1873
HAINGUE					
Martial	27	SF	927		1901
Merovee	64	FRA	3842		1896
HAINQUE					
Maggie	19	MA	1011		1866
Rosalie	76	FRA	32		1902
HAIO					
John	38	CHN	2243a		1872
HAIR					
Elizabeth	63	ENG	1364b		1872
Frank	1	SF	6852		1902
Maria M.	67	SWT	4517		1903
HAIRSTON					
Peter			7568		1902
HAIS					
Sarah Ann	47	MO	430b		1895
HAISING					
Henry	35	GER	279b		1871

Key: a = 1st part of year; b = 2nd part of year;
c = death certificate copy; c/o = child of

NAME	AGE OR YOB.	BIRTH PLACE	CERT. NO	ID	DEATH YEAR	NAME	AGE OR YOB.	BIRTH PLACE	CERT. NO	ID	DEATH YEAR
HAISLEY						HALDER					
Clifford (soldier)			5047		1901	Richard	40	GER	5578		1904
HAIST						HALDINAN					
John	42	GER	3149		1902	John				Jul	1898
HAIT						HALDORN					
——		SF	1190		1869	Howard	<1	CA	7080		1904
HAKANSON						HALDORSEN					
Solomon	<1	SF	3375		1896	Haldor	63	NOR	5909a		1895
HAKE						HALE					
Charles W. (soldier)			2848		1901	Arthur Charles	<1	SF	4261		1902
Fred	37	GER	3310		1895	Caroline F.	61	CT	1373		1870
						Delia	47	IRL	4879		1896
HAKER						E. T.	50	OH	3092	Oct	1901
George F.	39	SF	1890		1903	Edward P.	53	ENG	1761		1870
William Carl Ludwig	1830	GER	1276c		1904	Ezekiel (soldier)			5053		1901
HAKES						Grace				Jul	1899
Arlington O.	22	NY	7007	Feb	1901	Hannah H.	1834	DC	2212c		1904
HALAHAN						Herbert	37	CA	3256		1894
Patrick	26	IRE	5879		1867	Irving W. (soldier)			1881		1900
HALAKER						James P.	27	CA	5420		1903
Charles I.	<1	CA	1108		1901	Jesse C.				Feb	1900
HALBERG						John Thomas				Mar	1899
Peter R.	36	LA	2236		1866	Kathleen	27	SF	4534a		1895
HALBERSTADT						Leonard				Feb	1899
Carl	50	GER	H128		1886	Lucy L.				Oct	1899
HALCK						Lydia Maria				Feb	1899
Clifford Elmore	18	SF	4865		1903	Mahala	19	CA	7610		1901
						Stephen B. (soldier)			8789		1901
HALD						Thomas Harold	1	SF	3719	Nov	1901
Willie Henry	1	CA	6306		1896	William	63	NY	2377		1873
HALDAN						Wm.	45	MD	H55		1884
Eda Rebecca	24	SF	1643		1894	Wm. F.	45	ME	H27		1883
HALDEN						Zeltner S.	89	ME	4681		1903
Ada	20	ME	3165		1866	HALEMKAMP					
Edith Van Bergen	<1	SF	1714		1894	Peter	26	KY	1367		1869

Key: a = 1st part of year; b = 2nd part of year;
c = death certificate copy; c/o = child of

NAME	AGE OR YOB.	BIRTH PLACE	CERT. NO	ID	DEATH YEAR	NAME	AGE OR YOB.	BIRTH PLACE	CERT. NO	ID	DEATH YEAR
HALERON						Mary	40	IRL	3484b		1870
M. T.	76	IRL	5488a		1895	Mary	45	IRL	1612b		1871
						Mary	1839	IRE	1826c		1904
HALEY						Mary				Feb	1900
——			2781		1866	Mary A.	34	MA	1823b		1872
Adeline S.	85	CT	1165		1900	Mary A.	<1	SF	8762		1868
Alfred J.	3	SF	4248b		1870	Mary Kate	40	SF	2980		1902
Anny	21	IRE	6178		1867	Michael	60	IRL	2202a		1872
Bridget	72	IRL	342b		1872	Michael	1	CA	3170		1866
Bridget	59	IRE	7194		1904	Morris	62	IRL	5256		1901
Charles C.	43	CA	1316		1901	Patrick				Jan	1900
Charles Stanwood	67	ME	8230		1900	Raymond				Oct	1898
Claire Edna	4	SF	4342	Dec	1901	Rebecca	1	SF	8530		1868
Cyril	<1	SF	4831		1903	Rose	55	IRL	3909		1896
Delia				Jan	1900	Rose				Feb	1900
Edward	60	IRL	H141		1887	Ruth	2	SF	926		1901
Edward	1873	NY	3148c		1904	Sarah	32	IRE	6522		1868
Esther	67	IRL	4947a		1895	Thomas	<1	SF	1410		1869
Esther Ann	<1	SF	1068		1869	Thomas	31	IRL	3880		1870
Frank			7569		1902	Thomas A.	31	MA	7666		1903
Hannah	70	IRE	2370		1903	Thomas/Kate, c/o	1	CA	1556		1903
Hannah	68	IRE	5348		1902	Willard G.	37	CA	1563		1902
Honora	78	IRL	2709a		1872	William	67	NF	2115		1902
James H.	Abt		2443		1903	William H.	38	WI	7500		1902
James L.	19	SF	4410		1896	William Henry	36	CA	843		1903
John	85	IRE	6675		1902	William J. (soldier)	23		8258		1903
John	62	CAN	7310		1902	William K.	<1	SF	2434		1873
John	69	IRL	3605a		1895	William T.	6	SF	6944		1868
John	65	IRE	1059		1903	**HALFERTY**					
John Justin				Mar	1899	Frank				Nov	1899
Josephine				Jul	1898	**HALFNER**					
Julia	4	IRE	1099		1869	Chas. (soldier)			7623		1900
Julia	25	IRE	1153		1869	**HALFORD**					
Julia	30	SF	1237		1902	Margaret	30	IRL	4003		1870
Margaret	47	IRE	1236		1869						
Maria L.	1	SF	230a		1871						

Key: a = 1st part of year; b = 2nd part of year; c = death certificate copy; c/o = child of

NAME	AGE OR YOB.	BIRTH PLACE	CERT. NO	ID	DEATH YEAR
HALFREY					
Frank J.				Mar	1900
HALISY					
Hannah	40	NS	5566		1867
HALK					
Agnes Hazel	1	SF	117		1903
HALKINS					
Christine	26	GER	3410		1894
HALL					
——	<1	SF	1248		1869
Abraham				Nov	1899
Albert Smith	79	ME	7144		1902
Alexander	28	VT	636		1866
Alexander H.	25	CAN	17		1870
Alice	23	CA	646		1901
Annie Kristine	42	MA	8291		1904
Arthur (soldier)			1282		1902
Bell S.	1829	NH	2703c		1904
Cathrine	27	IRL	207a		1871
Charles	74	MO	8346		1900
Charles				Nov	1899
Charles Galbraith	1866	MD	793c		1904
Charles Henry	55	MD	4287		1901
Charles O. (soldier)	25		5050		1901
Charlotta	81	ENG	1610		1901
Clara	13	OR	7607		1868
Earl V.	32	IA	97		1903
Edmund	1837	NY	2551c		1904
Edward	24	VT	188		1865
Edward	74	IRL	8917		1901
Edward B.	50	MA	H107		1886
Edwin	48	ME	5649		1867
Elden W.	23	ME	1399		1869
Eliza Jefferson	68	ENG	1700a		1871
Elizabeth F.				Jan	1900

NAME	AGE OR YOB.	BIRTH PLACE	CERT. NO	ID	DEATH YEAR
Emma, Mrs.	47	WI	5339a		1895
Eveline	63	WI	5392		1901
Frances B.	48	MA	2244b		1895
Frank	32	SF	3729		1902
Frank M.	53	MI	6042		1903
Franklin	<1	NV	2521a		1872
Fred C.	47	OH	5374a		1895
Frederic				Dec	1898
Frederick S.				Feb	1900
G.	50		H125		1886
G./A., c/o				Aug	1899
George	28	IRE	1439		1869
George	<1	SF	1819		1894
George				Jun	1899
George	1875	CA	773c		1904
George J.				Oct	1898
George W.	2	SF	459		1870
George W.				Feb	1900
Harry				Apr	1899
Henry	38	SWE	534b		1872
Henry N. (soldier)			4696		1901
Herbert E.	50	NY	1722b		1895
Hulda Irene				Oct	1898
Irwin W.	1	CA	2013		1903
Isaac Reynolds	60	NY	2264		1900
Isabelle R.	1873	SF	2740c		1904
Isora	22	IA	6710		1868
Iva	<1	SF	1610		1902
J. E.	62	MA	1534		1901
James	50		3525	Nov	1901
James A.	29	CA	1529		1900
James N.				Oct	1899
James O. (soldier)			8581		1901
James T (soldier)			473		1901
James Vincent	61	ENG	1186		1894
Jennie E.				Nov	1898

Key: a = 1st part of year; b = 2nd part of year;
c = death certificate copy; c/o = child of

NAME	AGE OR YOB.	BIRTH PLACE	CERT. NO	ID	DEATH YEAR	NAME	AGE OR YOB.	BIRTH PLACE	CERT. NO	ID	DEATH YEAR
Jessie May	27	GA	6250		1902	Richard	55		1611		1901
John	39	NY	5874		1903	Richard				Dec	1898
John	42	IL	3502		1896	Richard B.				Jan	1899
John	68	NY	6194		1900	Robert Wm.	21	NY	362a		1871
John	69	ENG	6426		1903	Ruth	85	CT	3850		1870
John F.	48	ME	887		1870	Samuel A. (soldier)			67		1901
John M.	<1	SF	3967	Dec	1901	Samuel J.	30	TN	675		1903
John P.	60	AUS	762		1903	Sarah A.				Jul	1898
John S. (soldier)			4698		1901	Sarah G.	86	CT	2342b		1895
John W.	22	PA	3829		1900	Stephen (soldier)			8787		1901
Joseph S.		SF	1762		1870	Teresa I.	4	NB	9433		1868
Lary J. (soldier)			3235	Nov	1901	Theodor L.	57	NY	8444		1901
Laura May	7	CA	648		1903	Thomas	50	ENG	420b		1872
Lizie	1	CA	6632		1904	Thomas (soldier)			8		1902
Lucy Estelle	35	TN	5		1901	Thomas Fred	44	VT	948a		1871
Maggie E.				Feb	1900	Thomas J.	32	ENG	844a		1871
Margaret C.	45	IL	1693		1900	Thomas J.	47	ENG	H153		1887
Margaret Elizabeth	35	NY	7669		1902	Thomas L.	56	ENG	4599b		1870
Margaret L.	49	CT	2294b		1895	Waldo B.	24	CA	3610		1896
Maria E.	41	SF	7806		1900	Walter Paul	4	CA	909		1870
Martha Peabody	37	RI	725		1900	William	53	IRL	2639		1873
Martha V.	50	NY	6120a		1895	William	35	OH	1844		1866
Mary	28	NY	847a		1871	William	7	NB	9864		1868
Mary	28	IRE	6609		1904	William	63	NY	4336		1903
Mary	40		4019		1900	William	67	OH	6229		1904
Mary Ann	67	ENG	7971		1900	William	64	SC	3152		1895
Mary L.	7	NB	9854		1868	William	75	IRL	2981		1900
May				May	1899	William				Aug	1898
Mildred A.	42	CA	6528		1902	William (soldier)			7155		1901
Milton, Jr.	58	MA	1159		1869	William C.			1257		1903
Myrtle	1	SF	2533		1903	William J. (soldier)			2077		1901
Myrtle C.	1869	OH	1000c		1904	William Joseph	<1	SF	1566a		1871
Netherton H.	38	IL	6206	Jan	1901	William R. (soldier)			8784		1901
Nicholas	39	MD	4040		1900	Winnie	9	IL	1208		1903
Olivia	77	NY	84		1902						
Peter Herbert Arnold	<1	SF	1057		1894						

HALLADAY

NAME	AGE OR YOB.	BIRTH PLACE	CERT. NO	ID	DEATH YEAR
Guy Whitney				Aug	1898

Key: a = 1st part of year; b = 2nd part of year;
c = death certificate copy; c/o = child of

NAME	AGE OR YOB.	BIRTH PLACE	CERT. NO	ID	DEATH YEAR
Mary Jane	28	IRL	5170a		1895
HALLAHAN					
Eugene	70	IRL	5422		1896
Jas./D., c/o					Jun 1899
May	18	CA	1761b		1895
HALLARON					
J. L.	29	IL	H178		1889
HALLASEY					
John	29	MO	7927		1901
HALLEDEN					
——		SF	764		1870
HALLEN					
John	7	CA	446		1900
Peter	62	FRA	2419		1873
twins/o Edw.	<1	SF	1862b		1872
HALLER					
Augusta	31	SF	7898		1903
Carolina	<1	SF	2186		1866
Catherine	43	FRA	3695		1896
Harriet	30	IL	311		1903
Howard P.					Feb 1900
Joseph B. (soldier)			7309		1901
Margeret	76	FRA	3429		1896
Marie C.	65	GER	3783		1900
William, Mrs.	21	CAN	2918		1866
HALLET					
Laura A.	56	ME	2674		1900
Mary L.	<1	SF	2927		1900
Thomas A.					Nov 1898
HALLETT					
Bessie Lavaun	24	WI	2252b		1895
Catherine	76	CAN	7712		1900
George Henry	1823	MA	2536c		1904
Jane Mirialla					Oct 1898

NAME	AGE OR YOB.	BIRTH PLACE	CERT. NO	ID	DEATH YEAR
Lillian	38	OH	3173		1900
Margaret	35	MD	4451		1902
Oliver Gray					Aug 1899
Sarah E.	38	MA	2992		1866
HALLEY					
Albert M.	1	SF	4252		1867
Frank M.	19	ME	5815		1867
Mary Ellen	2	SF	455		1866
HALLGRIFFETHE					
James					Feb 1899
HALLICKSON					
Peter					Jan 1899
HALLIDAY					
Frank M.			7570		1902
James	1864	ENG	2243c		1904
Thomas	47	IRL	4492a		1895
William					Jul 1899
HALLIDEN					
Fernando L.	3	SF	4148a		1895
HALLIDIE					
Andrew Smith	64	ENG	7430		1900
Curt E. (soldier)			7662		1900
HALLIGAN					
Alexander	1860	IRE	78c		1904
Mary	1836	IRE	1001c		1904
Thomas					May 1899
HALLIGER					
John	42	ENG	1036		1866
HALLIHAN					
James/Delia, c/o		SF	8808		1901
Kate	40	IRL	1660		1894
Mary		SF	1068		1902
HALLINAN					
——		SF	2921		1866

Key: a = 1st part of year; b = 2nd part of year;
c = death certificate copy; c/o = child of

NAME	AGE OR YOB.	BIRTH PLACE	CERT. NO	ID	DEATH YEAR
Cyril Nathanial	1889	SF	466c		1904
John J.	42	IRE	6388		1903
John J.	41	NY	2631		1895
Kate	35	IRE	3053		1866
Loyd Daniel					Nov 1898
Mary	<1	SF	3104		1870
Mary Ellen					Nov 1899
Sarah Augusta	26	SF	5188		1904
Thomas H.	40	IRL	1954a		1872
W./C., c/o		SF	111		1895
HALLIWIN					
Agness					Nov 1898
HALLMAN					
Fannie					Oct 1899
James J. (soldier)			8430		1900
HALLMEYER					
Charles G.	35	GER	3117	Oct	1901
HALLOCK					
James Fanning	70	NY	1669		1903
HALLONQUIST					
——	58	SWE	6706a		1895
HALLORAN					
Annie	35	SF	3005		1903
Bridget				Mar	1900
D. N. S.					Nov 1899
James	61	IRL	7937		1900
John	55	IRE	4407		1903
Michael	34	IRL	1838		1894
HALLOWAY					
Bert	58	NY	2313b		1895
Bertram E.				Feb	1899
Robert	41	ENG	7411		1902
HALLOWELL					
Ellen	50	SF	2587		1894
Saml. E.	51	ENG	H158		1887
HALLQUIST					
Mary	35	IRL	2863		1901
HALLSWORTH					
Herbert Leslie	49	ENG	6616	Feb	1901
HALLYWOOD					
Ann	31	IRL	1202a		1871
HALMEN					
Alex	47	FIN	6499		1900
HALOORSEN					
Marlin	41	NOR	4187		1896
HALPIN					
Ann	37	IRE	8571		1868
Hannah	61	GER	1467a		1871
Hannah	73	IRL	2469		1900
John S.				Jun	1899
Thomas	40	IRE	1776		1866
HALSEY					
Anna Louisa	3	SF	1141		1869
Annie	44	SF	4084		1900
Earl/Josephine, c/o		CA	3025		1902
James/Nellie, c/o	1	SF	1564		1903
Jennie E.	1	SF	1421		1869
Nellie	36	SF	4002a		1895
Ruth	<1	SF	1238		1902
Sarah M.	63	NY	6211a		1895
William Clark	19	NY	5785	Jan	1901
Willie	3	SF	1993		1866
HALSING					
Iver M.	1859	NOR	2213c		1904
HALSTEAD					
Joel	38	NY	2234		1866
HALSTED					
Edson	43	NY	4735		1867

NAME	AGE OR YOB.	BIRTH PLACE	CERT. NO	ID	DEATH YEAR
HALSTROM					
K. H.	32	SWE	1573		1870
HALTY					
Gottfried					Aug 1898
HALVARSON					
Fannie	<1	SF	4555		1896
HALVERSON					
Christian	42	NOR	H180		1889
Eliza	62	IRL	1100		1901
Halver	40	NOR	8263		1901
John S.	1903	SF	1457c		1904
HALVORSEN					
Charlott Maria	37	SF	2900		1901
Oscar	1	SF	7394		1902
Samuel					Dec 1898
HALY					
Dolly	6	SF	972b		1871
Elizabeth	29	IRE	1856		1866
Jeremiah	31	IRE	6996		1868
HAM					
Abigal K.	70	NH	6109		1867
Ah	27	CHN	1159		1869
Ah Fong					Dec 1898
Charles	75	NY	1891b		1895
Chuck	33	CHN	2200		1900
Eng Ling					Jul 1899
Et Gae	52	CHN	3580		1900
Fan King					Dec 1899
Fang Bun	67	CHN	5701		1896
G.	50	MA	4992a		1895
Gang Shung					Apr 1899
Gook Hang	44	CHN	6631		1896
Gue Sing	50	CHN	3777		1896
He Guen					Jun 1899

NAME	AGE OR YOB.	BIRTH PLACE	CERT. NO	ID	DEATH YEAR
Jow					Aug 1898
Kew Fat					Jul 1898
Koon Ka					Feb 1900
Lin					Nov 1898
Lung	44	CHN	5729		Jan 1901
Muu Bov					May 1899
Pun Chun					Oct 1898
Say	40	CHN	8349		1904
Sen Toy					Oct 1898
Stephen (soldier)			3494		1903
Tan	29	CHN	967		1900
Tin Pin	45	CHN	3243		1894
William	40	ENG	8178		1903
William	34	IRL	1393a		1871
Won Chung Chu					Jun 1899
Wy	57	CHN	865b		1895
Yet	44	CHN	7917		1904
Yue Quen					Dec 1898
HAMA					
Hikojiro	27	JPN	7187		1902
HAMADA					
Unosuke	1880	JPN	1511c		1904
HAMAGUCHI					
Masataro					Aug 1899
HAMAKER					
Morse R.	67	PA	3872		1902
HAMAN					
Ella V.	49	ME	7909		1900
George					Mar 1900
HAMANO					
Tomajiro	39	JPN	2335		1900
HAMBER					
Gustav	30	FIN	H106		1886

NAME	AGE OR YOB.	BIRTH PLACE	CERT. NO	ID	DEATH YEAR	NAME	AGE OR YOB.	BIRTH PLACE	CERT. NO	ID	DEATH YEAR
HAMBERG						HAMILAN					
Amy Louise	7	SF	4374		1901	Johanna McDonald	42	CA	3587		1902
Elba Viola	<1	SF	3909		1900						
John	33	FIN	H20		1882	HAMILL					
						Anitha C. H.				Feb	1900
HAMBERRY						Charles P.	45	IRL	2959		1900
Chow Sun	21	CHN	1309a		1871	Gwendoline M.	<1	SF	5652		1896
James	<1	SF	1246a		1871	Jno.	38	MA	1389		1894
						Louisa				May	1899
HAMBLIN						Miriam Douglas	17	NE	8134		1904
Admiral	1	SF	1257		1869	Rose	59	IRL	6049a		1895
						Sarah A.	1	SF	4446b		1870
HAMBRECHT						William	47	IRE	1574		1866
Bertha	30	GER	992		1900						
						HAMILTON					
HAMBU						——	26	MI	5196		1867
Ketota Virginia	<1	SF	2706		1894	Alfred	52	DC	4763		1867
						Alva	19		2602		1895
HAMBURG						Andrew	65	IRL	4636		1896
Louise F.	35	NY	6319		1903	Andrew	28	MA	2990		1895
						Annie	38	CA	4763		1904
HAMBURGER						Annie	79	IRL	1911		1901
Gustav	63	GER	3224		1902	Annie C.	39	CA	3010		1895
John B.	30	SWT	8769		1868	C., c/o				Dec	1899
Margaret	63	GER	1947		1900	Cathrine	25	SCT	3219		1870
Morris	60	GER	117		1902	Charles	27	CA	2099		1894
Samuel	32	PA	1315		1894	Charles Frederick	47	IRL	1423b		1872
						Charles N.	32	NY	1092		1866
HAMELSON						Christopher	74	PA	H96		1885
Claus	30	SWE	4543		1896	David	60	NV	1525		1900
						David H.	56	CAN	5450Jan		1901
HAMENWAY						Edward	32	MD	1571		1900
Geo. W.	42	MO	H98		1885	Edwin E. (soldier)			2063		1901
						Elizabeth	80	IRL	203		1901
HAMER						Ernest	<1	SF	6223		1900
George G.	73	MD	8247		1900	Ethel Mary	3	CA	8513		1901
Oliver	57	OH	7978		1903	F.F.				Dec	1899
HAMERLY											
William	50	PA	118		1902						
HAMERTON											
John William	53	ENG	1159		1903						
William	73	ENG	3776		1896						

Key: *a = 1st part of year; b = 2nd part of year;*
c = death certificate copy; c/o = child of

NAME	AGE OR YOB.	BIRTH PLACE	CERT. NO	ID	DEATH YEAR	NAME	AGE OR YOB.	BIRTH PLACE	CERT. NO	ID	DEATH YEAR
Florence Edna	18	MN	2913		1901	Peter	65	IRL	H147		1887
Frank	62	AUT	3544	Nov	1901	Phebe T.	44	WI	5461		1896
Frank H.	29	NY	1400		1869	Robert	28	CAN	3283		1870
George E.	29	MS	4499b		1870	Robert	35	IRE	8948		1868
George/Anne, c/o	<1	SF	432		1901	Robert	83	IRE	7867		1903
George/Annie, c/o	<1	SF	3475		1902	Robert	1904	SF	2590c		1904
Harry	45	CAN	6809		1903	Robert B.	38	IRE	5129		1902
Harry	28	CA	2335		1901	Sarah	64	PA	284		1870
Harry C.	<1	SF	4018		1902	Sarah	60	ENG	554a		1871
Helen	<1		1421		1902	Susan	37	JAM	H60		1884
Henry	40	MD	138b		1872	Thomas	72	ENG	8206		1903
Henry B. (soldier)			2135		1901	Thomas	67	KY	3832		1903
Henry Harold	1898	CA	1263c		1904	Thomas V. (soldier)			2649		1900
Howard	24	MO	7621		1903	Thos., c/o	<1	SF	10b		1872
Ida	<1	SF	3542		1870	Troy (soldier)			8786		1901
Isabella Zoe	20	JAM	1858b		1872	William	56	IRL	4536b		1870
J. T./H. W., c/o		SF	2620		1895	William	46	PA	197b		1872
James	68	ME	914		1900	William	37	CA	7081		1904
James (soldier)			7218		1900	William				Jun	1899
James A.	58	IN	3879		1903	Wm.	83	MA	5292a		1895
James Francis	1	SF	877b		1872	Wm. Henry	20	CAN	4667		1901
James L.	33	SF	5788		1896	Wm. J.	59	CAN	3115		1903
James Thomas	71	SCT	7854		1900	**HAMLIN**					
Jas. S./Annie, c/o	<1	SF	6312		1900	Ethel W.				Jun	1899
John	2	CA	1672		1870	Henry Gerke	<1	SF	483a		1871
John H.				Jul	1898	Henry H.				Jan	1900
John J.			7156		1901	**HAMLOW**					
John Wesley	66	PA	3992		1903	Thomas Wm.	<1	SF	974a		1871
Joseph	84	IRL	2746		1901						
Manifred				Jan	1900	**HAMM**					
Margaret A.	51	IL	3263	Nov	1901	Sarah E.	1824	ME	1359c		1904
Mary	40	IRE	5049		1904	**HAMMAND**					
Mary E.	28	NY	5095		1867	John Francis	4	SF	1272		1869
Matilda M.	73	IRL	8595		1901	**HAMMAR**					
Matthew	51	NY	666		1900	Ellen	42	NY	2857		1900
Noble	81	IN	1968		1903	Lars F.	73	SWE	383		1902

Key: a = 1st part of year; b = 2nd part of year;
c = death certificate copy; c/o = child of

NAME	AGE OR YOB.	BIRTH PLACE	CERT. NO	ID	DEATH YEAR
Oliver	37	SWE	H166		1887
HAMMEL					
Anna	2	NJ	1268		1869
Jessie	35	MD	4901		1896
HAMMELL					
Mary Edward	68	KY	8582		1904
Thomas	65	IRL	6127		1896
HAMMER					
Ann	1837		1492c		1904
Carrie A.	27	SF	7741		1902
Chas. P.	30	SWE	2253b		1895
Christopher J.	19	PA	1438		1894
Francis J.				Feb	1900
Frederick	62	GER	6111		1902
Hattie	27	CA	236		1902
Ida	<1	SF	3949	Dec	1901
John G. (soldier)			5812	Jan	1901
HAMMERBERG					
Carl	76	GER	4070		1896
HAMMERGREN					
Carl O.	32	SWE	9009		1903
HAMMERQUIST					
August Bertel	3	CA	6891	Feb	1901
HAMMERS					
Henrietta Elizabeth	1850	LA	2159c		1904
HAMMERSCHLAG					
Annie	48	NY	1692		1900
Francis J.	1	SF	3523		1903
HAMMERSCHMIDT					
Carl Henry Ferdinan	25	SF	1297		1903
Charles	47		2875c		1904
Pauline	2	SF	1117		1869
HAMMERSMITH					
Charles				Feb	1900

NAME	AGE OR YOB.	BIRTH PLACE	CERT. NO	ID	DEATH YEAR
Charles/May, c/o		SF	501		1901
Elizabeth	1853	GER	825c		1904
James R.	1	SF	1137		1903
HAMMERSTEIN					
Anton	28	BAV	6462		1868
HAMMES					
Frank	26		8629		1904
Nellie H.	<1	SF	4754		1867
HAMMET					
Mary				Feb	1900
HAMMILL					
Henry	34	IRL	1912b		1872
HAMMIT					
Margaret	1	TN	3260		1873
William	1866	VA	1490c		1904
HAMMITT					
Edwd.	17	TN	H74		1885
HAMMOND					
Albert O'Connor	17	SF	2715a		1872
Amy	<1	SF	1634b		1871
Arthur	70	IRL	3878		1896
Benjamine	2	SF	5081		1867
Cathrine	41	IRE	7683		1868
E. L./ M., c/o				Jul	1898
Edna Belle				Jan	1899
Edna May	24	CA	7753		1904
Emily L.				Jul	1899
Frederick				Mar	1900
George	31	GER	9060		1868
George				Dec	1899
Harold Oliver	<1	SF	4083		1900
Harrold Earl	9	SF	3338		1902
Hattie	73	MA	3386		1902
James	47	NS	1253		1870

Key: a = 1st part of year; b = 2nd part of year; c = death certificate copy; c/o = child of

NAME	AGE OR YOB.	BIRTH PLACE	CERT. NO	ID	DEATH YEAR
Jane A.	61	IRE	2110		1903
Jennie E.				Mar	1900
John	68	RI	4230b		1870
John	46	IRL	957b		1872
John	38	OR	901		1903
John	69	MA	2628		1900
Joseph H.	62	ME	2689		1901
Lee J.		SF	1648		1870
Mary	6	SF	1268		1869
Maude E.	15	SF	3288		1894
Pleasant H. (soldier)			7310		1901
R. W.	36	MA	H100		1886
Richard Pindell	42	SF	1720		1900
Rosana	<1	SF	4750		1867
Sallie E.	36	LA	5839		1867
Sallie Thornton	7	SF	1124		1869
Stephen M.	25	SF	3090		1900
Tho.	44	IRL	1527a		1871
William H.	53	MA	7081		1900
HAMMONDS					
Lillian G. E.	1	SF	2928		1900
HAMMONN					
Mary J.	40	IRE	2788		1866
HAMMONS					
James	1819	IL	429c		1904
HAMON					
Delia	33	SF	2866		1894
HAMPSHAW					
Mary Ann	43	ENG	7475		1868
William	47	ENG	938		1870
HAMPSHIRE					
Ella	43	NJ	1397		1900
HAMPSON					
Joseph	38	OH	1945b		1895

NAME	AGE OR YOB.	BIRTH PLACE	CERT. NO	ID	DEATH YEAR
Olive	54	OH	8824		1904
Percy C. (soldier)			3042	Oct	1901
HAMPTON					
Ada Virginia	19	OH	1051		1901
Charles C.	1844	ENG	774c		1904
Edna Millicent				May	1899
Edward W.				Jan	1900
Gertrude				Jul	1899
John				Oct	1898
Mary A.				Jan	1899
Mary Charlotte	<1	SF	8749		1900
Robert L.			1258		1903
HAMUT					
Mary	4	SF	1102		1869
HAN					
Ah	30	CHN	562b		1871
Ah	26	CHN	2018a		1872
Chin Eta S.	26	CHN	5277a		1895
Get Hing	40	CHN	H108		1886
Hun	26	CHN	1073		1866
Ming	50	CHN	5806		1896
Wee	30	CHN	2300		1866
HANAGAN					
John J.	1	SF	3890		1870
HANAH					
Margaret	75	BAV	1705		1902
HANAK					
Albert	73	AUT	773		1900
HANARATTY					
Ruth Anna	4	SF	8622		1903
HANAVAN					
Alice	25	IRE	2738		1866
Bridget	55	IRE	1655		1903
William	15	SF	3047a		1872

Key: a = 1st part of year; b = 2nd part of year;
c = death certificate copy; c/o = child of

NAME	AGE OR YOB.	BIRTH PLACE	CERT. NO	ID	DEATH YEAR	NAME	AGE OR YOB.	BIRTH PLACE	CERT. NO	ID	DEATH YEAR
HANCE						HANDERS					
George	30	SCT	4721		1902	Ephram	52	NY	1277		1870
HANCK						HANDLAR					
Christian	51	FRA	3236		1870	Ella	24	GER	8400		1901
Jacob	15	LA	1403		1869	HANDLEY					
HANCOCK						Bertram				Jul	1899
Anne	56	IRE	2479		1903	Catherine	48	IRL	H176		1889
David C.				Nov	1899	Eliza A.	61	ME	2933	Oct	1901
John	70	MA	2362		1873	Frank R.	1874	OR	1596c		1904
John	30	SF	2673		1895	Frank Raymond, Jr.	4	CA	7837		1901
Josephine Agnes	43	IRL	4156	Dec	1901	Henry Harrison	40	CA	1483b		1895
Mary Ann	53	FRA	5632	Jan	1901	Patrick				Jan	1900
Mary F.	61	PA	2235		1894	HANDLON					
Philima Mary	1	IA	1252		1869	Richard	76	IRE	6805		1904
Rubertie M.	1	CA	380b		1872	HANDLOS					
Samuel	66	IRL	2296		1894	J. W.				Dec	1898
Vic/Marie, c/o		SF	1570		1900	HANDLY					
William	1	SF	1096		1869	Ellen	55	IRE	1333		1902
HANCSHETT						Margaret	81	IRE	6639		1902
Jose J.	59	IN	6602		1902	HANDMAN					
HAND						Ervin	6	SF	7400		1868
Addie C.	20	CT	412a		1871	HANDMANN					
Albert	52	OH	6276		1902	Clementina J.	68	GER	8816		1900
Emma	1	SF	1366		1866	Clementina Josephine	68	GER	8723		1900
Frances Amelia	1866	AUT	59c		1904	Erevin	1838	GER	1852c		1904
Hattie W.	36	ME	H50		1884	HANDRICKS					
John	36	IRE	2366		1866	Frank				Jan	1900
N. T.	52	NY	5058a		1896	HANDRIGHT					
Norman Edward (soldier)			5327		1901	Patrick J.	65	NY	4373		1901
HANDEL						HANDSCHUMACHER					
Albert C.	42	PA	4518		1903	John	<1	SF	1069		1902
HANDERKIN						HANDY					
Emma B.	<1	SF	3521		1867	Edward	<1	SF	6885		1868
						Harry P. (soldier)			2160		1901

Key: a = 1st part of year; b = 2nd part of year; c = death certificate copy; c/o = child of

NAME	AGE OR YOB.	BIRTH PLACE	CERT. NO	ID	DEATH YEAR
Lizzie	49	CA	3531a		1895
Thos.	49	SEA	3142		1894
HANDYSIDE					
Wm. London Beard	42	SCT	4519		1903
HANEALAN					
Mary E.	2	SF	9940		1868
HANEGRESS					
Adele	31	GER	5811		1902
HANEKE					
Sophie	76	GER	1087b		1871
HANEN					
Richard	48	KY	6271		1902
HANES					
Charles P.					May 1899
HANEY					
Ellen	4	SF	1097		1869
Emily Frances	72	WV	6986Feb		1901
Henry Haight	<1	SF	1123		1869
Hugh	54	IRL	3298		1895
James C.	86	MA	1151		1900
John G.	<1	SF	1310		1869
Mary		SF	360b		1872
Michael Joseph	<1	SF	367b		1872
HANFORD					
Mary	80	IRE	8664		1904
William H.	64		1921		1870
HANG					
Fa Doy					Jul 1899
Ga					Jan 1899
Kay					Oct 1898
Lee Yung	48	CHN	1349b		1871
Sun	46	CHN	1360		1869
Wee	51	CHN	1392b		1871
Yee	56	CHN	2853a		1872

NAME	AGE OR YOB.	BIRTH PLACE	CERT. NO	ID	DEATH YEAR
HANGE					
L./B., c/o	<1	SF	3345		1894
HANGLING					
James B.	29	MA	158a		1871
HANICH					
Frank	44	AUT	549b		1895
HANIFEN					
Dennis	68	IRL	6736a		1895
HANIFIN					
Josiah P.	<1	SF	1225		1866
Morris	24	IRL	1221a		1871
HANIFY					
Albert/Clara, c/o		SF	5178		1903
Annie Jane	1860	NY	3200c		1904
Clara	33	CA	5179		1903
John Meiler	2	SF	4184		1896
Mary, Mrs.	63	IRL	2004		1900
HANIGAN					
Lizzie	38	CA	9673		1901
HANIPLE					
Franz	41	SWT	507		1866
HANISCH					
Anna	63	GER	7702		1902
HANIVAN					
Patrick	40	IRE	207		1865
HANK					
Melvin M. (soldier)			5186		1901
HANKE					
Charles J.			5018		1903
HANKEL					
Charles	22	GER	1503a		1871
HANKINS					
Chas. E. (soldier)			1460		1901

Key: a = 1st part of year; b = 2nd part of year; c = death certificate copy; c/o = child of

NAME	AGE OR YOB.	BIRTH PLACE	CERT. NO	ID	DEATH YEAR	NAME	AGE OR YOB.	BIRTH PLACE	CERT. NO	ID	DEATH YEAR
HANKLEY						Peter	75	IRL	3127		1894
Frank (soldier)			2075		1901	Peter/Anna, c/o		SF	1966		1895
						Vickey, c/o				Dec	1899
HANKS						William C.	43	CA	5449		1904
Edith	1877	CA	1002c		1904	William F.	29	AUS	2652		1895
Ellen J.	51	ME	3010		1894	William H.	1	SF	586		1903
Kate	49	IRL	H113		1886						
Mary				Feb	1900	HANLIN					
Walter Stanley	56	OH	2295		1900	Koenig	35	IRE	3460		1867
HANLAN						HANLON					
John Archibald	1901	SF	1309c		1904	Anastasia Maud	<1	SF	6278a		1895
						Ann	75	IRE	6112		1902
HANLANX						Daniel	52	IRL	2914		1901
——			1836		1870	Daniel J./Josephine, c/o	<1	SF	3198		1902
						Dolores	1904	SF	1081c		1904
HANLAS						Edward O.	50	IRE	477		1903
Peter Hanlon	<1	CA	3709		1867	Elizabeth	23	IRL	3120a		1872
						Emilie D. F.				Dec	1898
HANLEY						Erasmus	38	DEN	1251		1869
——			7561		1868	John	40	IRL	1129		1870
Albert T.	<1	SF	7040		1868	John				Jul	1898
Daniel	58	IRL	429a		1871	John	85	IRE	513		1903
Ellen Adelaide	23	CA	6454		1904	John J.	42	CA	171		1903
Frances Gamba				Dec	1898	Joseph A	32	SF	4744		1902
George W.				May	1899	Katie	1844	IRE	320c		1904
Howard F.	5	SF	5494		1902	Katie			3201	Nov	1904
J. H.	40		275c		1904	Margaret	54	IRE	7791		1868
Jeannie	16	CA	1409b		1872	Mary Agnes	<1	SF	1315b		1872
Johana	39	IRL	916		1870	Peter	26	ENG	1143		1894
Johanna	20	IRL	4143b		1870	Richard	58	IRL	2588		1894
John	40	IRL	6320		1900	Richard/Mary, c/o		SF	4516		1896
John J.	47	NY	1421		1900	Rosie	2	SF	4178		1902
John Joseph	7	SF	2858		1900	Welsh	60	IRL	3759		1896
Margaret	32	ENG	3492		1900						
Mary Ann	<1	CA	83		1865	HANLRINSON					
Michael	45	MA	1330b		1872	Alfred	36	PA	7692		1868
Michael	56	IRE	6914		1903						
Patrick	80	IRL	1206a		1871						
Patrick/Nancy, c/o				Aug	1898						

Key: a = 1st part of year; b = 2nd part of year;
c = death certificate copy; c/o = child of

NAME	AGE OR YOB.	BIRTH PLACE	CERT. NO	ID	DEATH YEAR	NAME	AGE OR YOB.	BIRTH PLACE	CERT. NO	ID	DEATH YEAR
HANLY						HANNAN					
Anne	76	IRL	2963a		1872	Alfred T.	35	ENG	7295		1900
Annie	51	NY	2769		1903	Ann	35	IRE	1057		1868
James	3	NY	1074		1869	Dennis J.				Jan	1900
Mary	83	IRL	3578	Nov	1901	Edward	1	SF	7794		1868
Thomas J.	34	CA	6252		1904	Edward				Apr	1899
Wm.				Nov	1899	Johanna	66	IRE	7141		1904
						John F.	50	NY	5942		1903
HANN						John/Jean, c/o		SF	1385		1895
Julius	42	GER	H58		1884	Margaret	82	IRE	7245		1903
						Martin	27	MA	H94		1885
HANNA						Mary	60	IRE	6083		1867
Anna C.				Aug	1899	Mary A.	24	SF	8496		1904
Catherine	38	NY	4504		1867	Michael J.				Feb	1900
Daniel N.	34	SF	4371		1902	Patrick E.	67	IRL	4045	Dec	1901
Francis A.	1	SF	1138		1903	Robert	72	IRL	5502a		1895
Jane	1883	CA	485c		1904	William D.	24	SF	7905		1901
Jas.	34	IRL	H133		1886						
John, Jr.	334	PA	677a		1871	HANNAY					
Joseph T.	51	IRE	7723		1903	Allen W.	1902	CA	3430c		1904
Kate	1866	CA	3064c		1904						
Nellie	12	CA	1395		1869	HANNEFORD					
Robert	1823		486c		1904	William	31	ENG	115a		1871
Robert W.	30	PA	4309		1903						
Sarah				Jun	1899	HANNEKE					
Thomas	18	IL	4458		1901	Herman	42	GER	1331		1901
HANNACKE						HANNELLY					
William	<1	GER	1028		1868	Joseph J.	<1	SF	5100		1867
HANNAFORD						HANNEY					
Catherine	68	IRE	2663		1902	——	<1	CA	3500		1867
HANNAH						HANNIFIN					
George	27	NY	710		1866	Bridget	26	MA	3971		1900
John Clarence	51	MO	2073		1902						
Levi	64	ME	3501		1896	HANNIGAN					
Robert B.	25	CAN	7807		1903	John C.				Oct	1899
						Mary	50	IRE	2916		1903
						Patrick	58	IRE	6053		1902

Key: a = 1st part of year; b = 2nd part of year;
c = death certificate copy; c/o = child of

NAME	AGE OR YOB.	BIRTH PLACE	CERT. NO	ID	DEATH YEAR	NAME	AGE OR YOB.	BIRTH PLACE	CERT. NO	ID	DEATH YEAR
HANNING						HANOVN					
John	57	IRL	1124b		1871	Patrick	25	CAN	3871		1870
HANNIVER						HANOWER					
Mary	5	SF	4046		1903	James	50	SCT	1188		1900
Nora W.				Jun	1899	HANRAHAN					
HANNON						John	<1	CA	7		1870
——			1054		1868	John (soldier)			2697		1900
——		SF	1429		1869	Margaret	50	IRL	5719		1896
Abbie	50	IRE	6505		1904	Michael	70	IRE	5745		1904
Catherine (foundling)	1	SF	1421		1869	HANRAHEN					
Eugene	40	CA	3225		1902	Honora	5	SF	9939		1868
Hannah T.	2	SF	8282		1901	HANRATTA					
Hugh				Oct	1898	George	1	SF	7819		1900
James Joseph	6	SF	6695		1904	HANRATTY					
Joseph	47	IRL	2482		1894	Walter John	1	SF	1797		1903
Mary	70	IRE	3867		1867	HANRETTY					
Mary	50	IRL	6773		1896	Elizabeth H.	3	SF	7098		1900
Thomas	40		826c		1904	HANS					
Thomas				Jul	1899	Edward W.				Jan	1900
Thomas (soldier)			5185		1901	Jacob	35	BAV	1291		1869
Thos. C.	35	IRL	H184		1889						
HANNUM						HANSACO					
Ralph	22	OH	3352		1900	John Peter	28	NOR	5840		1867
HANON						HANSALEIT					
Ralph	35	CA	8112		1904	Albert	39	GER	H13		1882
HANORA						HANSAN					
Mathias/Anna, c/o	<1	CA	6601		1902	Emma				Dec	1898
HANORIH						HANSBROUG					
Benjamin				Feb	1900	Stockton	<1	SF	935		1902
HANOVAN						HANSBROUGH					
Bridget	74	IA	4722		1902	Elmar C.	1	SF	5495		1902
HANOVER						George				Dec	1898
——	<1	SF	1101		1869	HANSCHILDT					
						Dean	12	OR	6782		1903

Key: a = 1st part of year; b = 2nd part of year;
c = death certificate copy; c/o = child of

NAME	AGE OR YOB.	BIRTH PLACE	CERT. NO	ID	DEATH YEAR
HANSCOM					
Clarabell	53	MA	1107		1901
HANSECKE					
Robert				Apr	1899
HANSEL					
Elanore				Oct	1899
John Carl	1	SF	5700		1896
HANSELL					
——			2157		1866
Caroline S.	63	PA	3534		1896
Emma ?	52	NY	5742a		1895
Minnie J.	2	SF	2733		1866
Sarah M.	12	NY	6698a		1895
William S.	51	CA	7940		1904
Wm. E.	65	PA	H163		1887
HANSELLE					
Carry M.	7	SF	1334		1870
HANSEN					
Alfred	<1	SF	2092		1866
Alfred	<1	SF	7899		1903
Alice P.	1	CA	3912		1903
Almo	7	SF	4087	Dec	1901
Andreas	45	GER	1482b		1895
Andrew	58	DEN	1946b		1895
Andrew	34	NOR	2138		1894
Andrew Peter	50	SWE	8403		1901
Andy L. L.	16	SF	4272		1896
Anita	<1	SF	4580		1903
Anna	33	DEN	6485		1903
Anna				Feb	1899
Anna Helena				Dec	1898
Annie Bertha	53	NOR	8462		1901
Bertha	27	NOR	6961	Feb	1901
Bertha M.				Jul	1898
Carrie	32	DEN	5913		1902

NAME	AGE OR YOB.	BIRTH PLACE	CERT. NO	ID	DEATH YEAR
Cathrine	1	SF	4131b		1870
Celma Nikoline	<1	SF	4251		1896
Charles	64	NOR	1808		1902
Charles	33	NOR	2977		1894
Charles				Apr	1899
Charles A.	40	DEN	1258b		1895
Charles L.	28	NV	4157	Dec	1901
Chas. W.			6984		1900
Chas./Emma, c/o		SF	1937		1900
Chris	38	NOR	5571		1896
Chris L.	45		3557		1902
Chrisitian M.				Jan	1900
Christian	28	PRU	6655		1868
Christina				Aug	1898
Christine D.				Oct	1899
Clara Ann				Nov	1898
Daniel	74	SWE	6884		1904
Eddie C.	<1	SF	1649		1866
Edward	59	DEN	8783		1900
Elizabeth	63	IRL	6607		1896
Ella	1864	CA	2777c		1904
Ellen Christian	<1	CA	1935		1902
Emil	31	DEN	5012		1901
Eveline	1	SF	3451		1903
F.				Oct	1898
Fannie	70	GER	552		1901
Ferdinand	49	DEN	3264	Nov	1901
Francis E.				Feb	1900
Frederick	76	GER	4994		1903
Geo. T.				Mar	1900
Geo./Annie M., c/o	<1	SF	848		1895
George	<1	SF	2434		1900
George				Nov	1898
George H.	45	MI	2592		1903
George R. N.	22	SF	8497		1904
Gustav	20	NOR	3833		1903

Key: a = 1st part of year; b = 2nd part of year; c = death certificate copy; c/o = child of

NAME	AGE OR YOB.	BIRTH PLACE	CERT. NO	ID	DEATH YEAR	NAME	AGE OR YOB.	BIRTH PLACE	CERT. NO	ID	DEATH YEAR
Gustave	30	SWE	5134		1903	Maggie	44	NY	3055		1894
H.	55	DEN	5343		1896	Margaret	1841	IRE	2893c		1904
H./A., c/o				Jan	1899	Marie Bodil	62	DEN	6719		1903
Hans	31	GER	1990		1903	Marie E.	38	GER	92		1902
Hans	64	DEN	3414		1902	Marie E., Mrs.	38	CA	4273a		1895
Hans A.				Aug	1899	Marie Emilie	22	CA	2225		1902
Hans Albert	27	DEN	6195		1900	Martha E.	5	SF	7406		1868
Hans Andrew	35	DEN	5727		1867	Martin	74	NOR	6970		1903
Hans C.	1841	DEN	794c		1904	Martin C.	3	SF	3237		1895
Hans Nelson	52	GER	2411		1903	Mary	30	IRL	1112b		1871
Harold	1	SF	8989		1901	Mary	<1	SF	2914		1902
Harry	28	GER	1013		1903	Mary	28	DEN	5444		1903
Harry Edward	1859	NOR	2825c		1904	Mary		SF	2147		1900
Helen E.	1885	NOR	2160c		1904	Mary	37	SWE	3265	Nov	1901
Henning				Jul	1898	Mary				Nov	1898
Henry	62	DEN	8629		1900	Mary				Mar	1899
Henry E. (soldier)			7311		1901	Mary E.	28	CA	6323		1902
Herold	35	GER	9077		1868	Mary E.				Feb	1899
Hilga Maria	1	SF	1468		1900	Matthais				Dec	1899
Isadore (soldier)			3682		1900	Mona Browne	3	SF	2604		1900
James	56	DEN	3046		1903	Neals	25	DEN	561a		1871
Jens C.	36	NOR	7997		1904	Nels (soldier)			4788		1901
Johan P.	77	NOR	7935		1903	Nels J.	48	DEN	461		1901
Johanna	25		2236		1901	Olaf	1864	NOR	2359c		1904
John	1860	DEN	42c		1904	Olaf	54	NOR	5180		1903
John	33	DEN	4098		1896	Ossian F. W. (soldier)	29		5414	Jan	1901
John A. G.	64	GER	6485		1896	Otto	7	SF	1223		1894
Julia	64	GER	6034	Jan	1901	P. H./Selma, c/o		SF	2883		1895
Katherine				Jul	1898	Paul A., c/o				Dec	1898
Kirsten				Mar	1899	Paul A., c/o				Dec	1898
L. T./Marie, c/o		SF	2273		1895	Peter	28	DEN	1195b		1872
Lars				Dec	1898	Peter	34	GER	8329		1904
Lili Henricka	<1	DEN	8474		1903	Peter	67	NOR	7246		1903
Lizzie	25	SF	3438		1900	Peter	50	NOR	4661		1896
Louis				Jun	1899	Peter, Jr.	<1	SF	538b		1872
Lucinda				Nov	1898	Rise Andrea	4	SF	6405		1902

NAME	AGE OR YOB.	BIRTH PLACE	CERT. NO	ID	DEATH YEAR
Rosie	20	SF	3736	Nov	1901
Samuel E. (soldier)			3043	Oct	1901
Serviene	50	NOR	5143		1901
Sophie				Aug	1899
Sophie				Jan	1900
Susan/Christopher, c/o	<1	CA	7374		1903
Thomas	35	NOR	9		1902
Thomas				Nov	1899
Thora Lillian	1	SF	2917		1903
Tillie	7	SF	4017	Dec	1901
Turo	32	NOR	3671a		1895
Walter Frances	3	CA	4326		1896
William	1826	DEN	348c		1904
Z.C./Christina, c/o	<1	SF	6969		1903
HANSER					
Abraham				Aug	1898
Louisa				Jan	1899
HANSING					
Karl/Catherine, c/o	<1	SF	2237		1901
HANSLER					
Anna	4	SF	4490b		1870
HANSLLE					
Clara	14	SF	1274		1870
Nelly D.	2	SF	1273		1870
HANSOM					
Edwin Cutta	1	SF	1063		1869
HANSON					
——		SF	4198b		1870
——		SF	4462b		1870
——			7698		1868
Abel Harrison	71	VT	7366		1901
Ada	<1	SF	2667		1873
Albert A.	<1	SF	2740		1895
Andrew	28	DEN	1075		1866
Andrew	60	DEN	8701		1904

NAME	AGE OR YOB.	BIRTH PLACE	CERT. NO	ID	DEATH YEAR
Andrew G.	78	PA	7724		1903
Andrew K.	42	DEN	1213		1866
August	25	NOR	153a		1871
Baby	<1	SF	2868		1894
Bearnard	1	SF	2731		1903
Belle F.	30	IL	1839		1894
Benjamin W.				Oct	1899
Caroline A.	60	DEN	4190		1903
Caroline Mead				Jul	1899
Charles	1825	GER	2894c		1904
Charles			2894	Nov	1904
Charles (soldier)			2072		1901
Charles M.	49	DEN	2113		1873
Charlotte				Jul	1898
Chas. A.	38	NOR	5240a		1895
Chris	4	SF	1585		1900
Christian P.	<1	SF	1569		1866
Clara	<1	SF	1086		1869
Clara	<1	CA	1611		1902
D.	28	GER	1037		1868
Elisha	16		1012		1870
Ellen	36	MA	3018	Oct	1901
Erasmus	38	DEN	6073		1867
Eveline	<1	SF	7481		1904
F. C. M.	<1	SF	1443		1869
Francis C.	64	NY	5199		1867
Frank	34	NY	H19		1882
G. B./J., c/o				Jun	1899
George C.	<1	SF	1638b		1871
Habs				Oct	1898
Harry				Jan	1900
Harry/Louisa, c/o	1	CA	4513		1904
Hays R.			1259		1903
Hazel	<1	CA	3048		1900
Henry	82	NOR	3558		1902
Ida	24	NY	1146b		1872

Key: a = 1st part of year; b = 2nd part of year;
c = death certificate copy; c/o = child of

NAME	AGE OR YOB.	BIRTH PLACE	CERT. NO	ID	DEATH YEAR	NAME	AGE OR YOB.	BIRTH PLACE	CERT. NO	ID	DEATH YEAR
James J.	1	SF	1164		1869	**HANSSMANN**					
Jas. B.	45	NOR	H79		1885	Helena				Jul	1899
Jno. A.	29	SWE	5486a		1895						
Johanna M.	25	SWE	402b		1872	**HANTINE**					
John	28	SWE	2423a		1872	James	57	NY	3511		1867
John C.	67	SWE	1504b		1872	**HANTON**					
John Henry	<1	SF	476b		1872	John E.				Dec	1898
Julius	27	DEN	2370		1866	Wm.	54	CAN	3348		1894
Lirris	1848	DEN	487c		1904	**HANTRIGSEN**					
Louis				Nov	1899	Alfred				Jan	1900
Louis	36	NY	7990		1901	**HANTZIO**					
Mary Ann	90	ENG	7694		1900	Steve	1877	GRE	1378c		1904
Mary Josephine	45	NY	5399		1904	**HANVENSACK**					
Michael O'Brien	<1	SF	3162		1873	twins		SF	287		1870
Milof				Jan	1899	**HAOWE**					
Neil	25	DEN	3471		1867	Montgomery	1823	NH	894c		1904
Nicholas	1904	SF	645c		1904	**HAPERMAN**					
Oscar B.				Jun	1899	William	<1	SF	3156		1866
Peter	41	GER	2670		1873	**HAPFUER**					
Peter	26	GER	9330		1868	Ferdinand				Feb	1899
Peter	57	SWE	5769		1902	**HAPGOOD**					
Robert	36	SWE	1257		1900	Charles				Mar	1900
Theodore	35	NOR	5932		1867	**HAPPENSBERGER**					
Theodore H.	24	SF	2620		1902	Julius	<1	SF	994		1866
Thomas	1877	WI	1932c		1904	**HAPPERSBERGER**					
Thomas G.	41	GER	6617	Feb	1901	Frank	40	GER	358		1870
Walter	38	IL	1119		1869	**HAPPERSETT**					
Walter (soldier)			6473		1900	Reese	55		2579		1866
Wilhelmine	47	GER	6563		1896	**HAPPY**					
William Joseph	<1	SF	1313		1869	Lillian E.	1	CA	5787	Jan	1901
William/Gunda, c/o	1904	SF	1666		1904	**HAQUETTE**					
Wm.				Mar	1900	August	51	FRA	2915		1901
Wm. Henry	1	IA	1223		1869	**HAR**					
HANSSEN						Ah	44	CHN	1370		1869
Asmus	6	GER	5066a		1895						

NAME	AGE OR YOB.	BIRTH PLACE	CERT. NO	ID	DEATH YEAR
Chou/Sun On, c/o	<1	SF	7872		1900
Loy He	46	CHN	5506		1896
HARA					
Mary Louisa	31	CA	4827		1904
Sen				Aug	1898
HARAKER					
Mary	45	IRL	4514b		1870
HARAMURA					
Tokimoski				Mar	1899
HARANT					
Annie	27	SF	970		1900
HARASZTHY					
Arpad	60	HUN	3049		1900
HARBACH					
Arthur	<1	CA	4790		1902
Daniel L.	68	MI	5108a		1895
HARBENGARTEN					
Joseph	62	GER	3913		1903
HARBER					
Richard B. (soldier)			7157		1901
Sam/Sady, c/o	1	SF	4337		1903
HARBIES					
Henry	2	CA	1716		1903
HARBOE					
Christian	51	DEN	1459b		1895
HARBOSH					
Joseph				Oct	1899
HARBOUR					
Theodora				Oct	1898
HARBURN					
James F.	72	IRL	705		1900
HARBUT					
Marie	48	FRA	2191		1894

NAME	AGE OR YOB.	BIRTH PLACE	CERT. NO	ID	DEATH YEAR
HARBY					
Josepha S.	32	MEX	7062		1868
HARC					
Daniel	59	IRL	868a		1871
HARCOURT					
Elizabeth	44	CAN	5255		1901
HARDCASTLE					
George F.	23	ENG	4745		1867
HARDE					
William L.	41	SF	4343		1901
HARDEE					
Margaret F.	1879	SF	7c		1904
HARDEMAN					
Burton N.				Feb	1900
Gabriel	1904	SF	2244c		1904
HARDEN					
Frank M.				Feb	1900
Rutledge (soldier)			7312		1901
HARDER					
Albert	52	GER	3958a		1895
Charles	46	GER	1189		1869
Elenore A.	39	GER	3588		1902
Elsmore Ruth	1	SF	1110		1901
Johan H.	77	GER	2819		1895
Nicholaus	49	GER	2607		1900
Pauline	72	GER	8457		1900
HARDERBERGH					
Maria	80	NY	4961		1902
HARDERICK					
Chas. M.	8	SF	806b		1872
HARDERS					
Edward S.	36	SF	8839		1901
Fred T.	78	GER	8070		1904
John J.	11	SF	7378		1868

NAME	AGE OR YOB.	BIRTH PLACE	CERT. NO	ID	DEATH YEAR	NAME	AGE OR YOB.	BIRTH PLACE	CERT. NO	ID	DEATH YEAR
Margaret				Nov	1898	W. A.	39	NY	H167		1887
						William B.	38	NY	7868		1903
HARDEY											
Marie	48	FRA	1395		1869	**HARDINK**					
						Henrietta A.	2	SF	779		1870
HARDGRAVE											
Elizabeth F.	<1	SF	454		1866	**HARDMYER**					
						Marie	25	SWT	1057		1868
HARDGROVE											
Elizabeth	34	IRE	6919		1868	**HARDT**					
						Ernest	57	GER	8407		1903
HARDIE											
Claus	60	GER	4150a		1895	**HARDWICK**					
Philip				Aug	1898	Annie Jean				May	1899
						Arthur (soldier)			7769		1902
HARDIGAN						Charles L.	1	SF	979b		1871
Michael F.	48	IRL	H61		1884	Richmond	22	MA	698a		1871
HARDIMAN											
Anne	71	IRL	3266	Nov	1901	**HARDWIG**					
Edward	1	SF	1261a		1871	Fredrick	34	GER	9312		1868
Francis	<1	SF	2254		1873	**HARDY**					
May	<1	SF	2739a		1872	——		SF	1083		1869
Patrick	74	IRL	3365	Nov	1901	Bernice	18	CA	8497		1900
						Bernice				Apr	1899
HARDIMANS						Cathrine	35	OH	5328		1867
——		SF	1109		1869	Frances				Feb	1900
						Francis J.	39	VA	7201		1868
HARDIN						Frank	64	IRL	19b		1895
Amy	<1	SF	1239		1902	Franklin D.	22	MA	9654		1868
John	45	ENG	2389		1873	George	36	ENG	5703		1867
William K.			7571		1902	Grace Anna	3	CA	6324		1902
						John Thomas		SF	961		1902
HARDING						Michael	82	IRL	6823a		1895
——			2733		1900	Rebecca C.	20	IL	6294		1867
Charles				Feb	1900	Reginald	<1	SF	8463		1900
Charles M. (fireman)			6230	Feb	1901	Samuel (soldier)			1316		1902
Charles S.				Jan	1900	Sarah S.	55	MA	1388b		1872
Edward				Apr	1899	Walter R.		SF	4193b		1870
George				Jan	1900	William	<1	SF	2905		1895
James Ignatius	48	SF	3409		1894	William (soldier)			6826		1900
Jas. R.	44	MA	H137		1886						
Nellie	25	ME	H59		1884						

NAME	AGE OR YOB.	BIRTH PLACE	CERT. NO	ID	DEATH YEAR	NAME	AGE OR YOB.	BIRTH PLACE	CERT. NO	ID	DEATH YEAR
HARE						**HARGRO**					
Ada E.	<1	SF	3151		1870	James	72	VA	21b		1895
Albert	<1	SF	7993		1903	Mary E.	54	PA	4520		1903
Dennis O.	40	IRE	1265		1869	**HARINGTON**					
Ellen	72	IRE	9010		1903	Timothy	34	IRE	5558		1867
Fannie L.	33	SF	4179		1902						
Fanny	1	SF	796b		1871	**HARIS**					
						Sarah G.	21	NY	5352a		1895
Fredrich	1	SF	512		1866						
Hugh	24	IRE	4722		1903	**HARISON**					
James	35	CA	78		1900	Jas./A., c/o		SF	5837		1895
Joseph T.	72	OH	4405		1901	**HARKANSON**					
Mary	86	IRE	5389		1903	Olaf	51	SWE	1602		1894
Stanislaus D.	23	SF	7885		1901	**HARKER**					
						Asa	67	NJ	548		1894
HAREEN											
David	53	IRE	6138		1903	**HARKIN**					
						Michael	<1	SF	4551		1867
HARES											
Reginald C.	24	WV	2770		1903	**HARKINS**					
						Anna, Mrs.	68	MD	5656		1867
HARFORD						Charles B.	74	IRE	7998		1904
Evangeline	8	SF	1293		1869	Daniel H.	66	MA	3839		1902
						Dennis	55	IRE	6517		1904
HARGADEN						Edward Allen	1	CA	2360		1901
John	21	IRE	4380		1867	Eilen Mary	<1	SF	4543a		1895
Michael	68	IRE	4735		1904	Elizabeth	6	CA	1067b		1871
HARGAN						Elizabeth	66	IRE	3704		1902
Martha	5	MA	1378		1869	James	55	IRL	2688		1901
HARGER						Joseph	35	IRL	1272		1894
John	67	OH	803		1900	Katherine	1855	OH	3065c		1904
HARGES						Margaret	94	IRE	6227		1902
Frederick	38	GER	1391		1869	Mary A.	50	IRL	3245		1894
HARGRAVE						Mary Ellen	1	CA	7303		1903
Henry				Dec	1899	Michael	37	IRL	1683a		1871
James W. (soldier)			2533		1900	Patrick	65	IRE	7734		1904
John F. (soldier)			2849		1901	Patrick	38	IRL	3847	Nov	1901
Walter J.	26	SF	310b		1895	Robert H.	20	SF	540		1902

Key: a = 1st part of year; b = 2nd part of year;
c = death certificate copy; c/o = child of

NAME	AGE OR YOB.	BIRTH PLACE	CERT. NO	ID	DEATH YEAR	NAME	AGE OR YOB.	BIRTH PLACE	CERT. NO	ID	DEATH YEAR
Robert L.	70	MD	2100a		1872	**HARLIGAN**					
Rosana				Apr	1899	David J.	35	IRL	1929		1900
Sadie Ellen				Jan	1900						
William L.	34	CT	2929		1900	**HARLIN**					
						O. W.	49	SWE	3543		1867
HARKINSON											
Francis R.	30		5725		1903	**HARLINSTURN**					
						Chas./Christina, c/o	<1	SF	647		1901
HARKIUS											
Ellen	60	IRL	3441		1900	**HARLOCK**					
						Hanna L.	1	SF	4018		1867
HARKNESS						Margaret C.	30	OR	9719		1901
Agnes	69	NY	8262		1901	Robert E.	59	ENG	9130		1868
Harry Wilson	80	MA	383		1901						
John J.	59	CT	1201a		1871	**HARLOE**					
						John D.	30	IRL	528a		1871
HARLACHER						Mary				Oct	1898
Julia A.	25	CA	573		1902						
						HARLOW					
HARLAN						Aaron	65	OH	6540		1868
Josiah	73	PA	1102b		1871	Alnura				Feb	1900
Marcus	4	SF	1358		1869	Annie Elizabeth	36	CA	9592		1901
Margaret M.	32	NY	6215		1867	Claude				Mar	1899
						Elizabeth M.	30	SCT	2673		1900
HARLAND						Eva	<1	SF	3931		1867
Christina	70	CAN	2517		1903	Sarah	22	IRE	3112		1866
Mary				Jun	1899						
						HARM					
HARLEGI						Moses	5	SF	4533a		1895
George	<1	SF	3469		1867						
						HARMAH					
HARLEIN						Eliza Jane				Jan	1899
Amanda	47	OH	6891		1868						
						HARMAN					
HARLEM						Albert	16	SF	2601		1895
Henry J.	42	ENG	2625		1901	Ellen	31	ENG	668		1901
						Francis James	2	SF	764		1900
HARLEY						Fred E./Emily, c/o	<1	SF	5958		1902
Anna	61	NY	5752		1903	Hubert	<1	CA	8192		1904
Catherine	1	CT	2308		1866	Ida L.	16	CA	312		1903
George J.				Oct	1898	John	45	IRL	H171		1887
James M.	66	ENG	6305		1896						
Jno. A.	67	KY	5446a		1895						
Milton F.	62	IRL	7782		1900						

Key: a = 1st part of year; b = 2nd part of year;
c = death certificate copy; c/o = child of

NAME	AGE OR YOB.	BIRTH PLACE	CERT. NO	ID	DEATH YEAR	NAME	AGE OR YOB.	BIRTH PLACE	CERT. NO	ID	DEATH YEAR
HARMED						HARNEDY					
Susan	40	NY	1062		1869	Mary	38	IRL	6848	Feb	1901
HARMES						HARNER					
Dorothea	78	GER	5504a		1895	Mary, c/o	<1	SF	1659		1894
Frederick W.	46	IL	3589		1902	HARNESS					
HARMN						Wm. J.				Feb	1900
Mathias	63	RUS	1771		1894	HARNETT					
HARMON						Edwd., c/o	<1	SF	1180b		1872
——		SF	2935		1866	Michael	<1	SF	3316a		1872
Andrew	59	NY	2844		1895	William F.				Feb	1899
Catherine	<1	SF	1222		1894	HARNEY					
Effie W.	32	ME	2765		1873	Benjio C.	32	OH	1634b		1872
Elizabeth	60	ENG	5896a		1895	Daniel				Feb	1899
Frederick	30	NY	H14		1882	Elizabeth A.	<1	SF	3349		1894
Geo. H.	<1	SF	4419		1867	James C.	31	IRE	4703		1867
James A.	39	ME	3002a		1872	John	<1	NY	1027		1866
Joe E.	38	SCT	3451		1894	Leslie	9	SF	6760		1903
John	45	MD	5124		1904	Mary	45	IRE	118		1903
Joseph	40	GER	5356		1867	William E. (soldier)			2067		1901
Nancy M.	65	IN	4944		1896	HARNISCH					
Orris Vance	28	ME	2302		1903	John C.	55	DEN	4605		1867
Philip	62	ENG	1186		1902	HARNISEN					
HARMS						Nellie	35	WAL	5375		1902
Hans	50	GER	2426b		1895	HARNISH					
Henry W.	<1	SF	3875		1870	Franklin B.	58	PA	1835		1902
Jergen	32	GER	8260		1868	HARNOTT					
Louise	33	CA	3996	Dec	1901	Jos.	29	CA	H112		1886
Meta C. M.				Oct	1898	HARNS					
HARNAH						Zeth/Mary, c/o				Jan	1899
Ellen	40	IRL	H1		1882	HARNWELL					
HARNATTA						Robert John	18	SF	2079		1902
John Joseph				Feb	1900	HARNY					
HARNED						Hannah	37	IRE	3215		1866
Edith M.	<1	SF	3889		1870						

Key: a = 1st part of year; b = 2nd part of year;
c = death certificate copy; c/o = child of

NAME	AGE OR YOB.	BIRTH PLACE	CERT. NO	ID	DEATH YEAR	NAME	AGE OR YOB.	BIRTH PLACE	CERT. NO	ID	DEATH YEAR
HARO						**HARPHAM**					
Shintaro	16	JPN	6941		1903	Clara G.	39	SF	8917		1903
HAROLD						**HARRAHEL**					
Charles	1821	IRE	3431c		1904	Jeremiah	29	IRL	1641b		1871
James	78	IRE	3391		1903	**HARRELL**					
John W.	64	IRL	796		1900	Eugene G.			6173		1903
Rose Mary				Dec	1899	Francis J.	<1	SF	9034		1903
HAROWITZ						Friedreka	42	CA	4645		1902
Simon	33	GER	6664		1900	Katherine	<1	CA	4099		1896
HARPENDING						Mary E.	1847	IN	2336c		1904
Benj. W.	47	KY	2195a		1872	**HARRIES**					
Lillian	21	KS	9542		1901	Horatio B.	38	ENG	4139		1902
HARPER						**HARRIGAN**					
A. E.	30	MA	H130		1886	Arthur Joseph				Oct	1898
Benjamin C.	41	ENG	258		1900	Cornelius	76	IRE	3730		1902
Charles J.	36	ENG	2490		1900	Cornelius	72	IRL	5390		1901
Charles T.	56	ENG	9428		1901	Daniel	92	IRE	1440		1869
Fred	55	MD	6463		1868	Dennis Cornelius	35	CA	5144		1901
Glyds	<1	SF	2747		1901	Florence E.	<1	SF	1420		1900
James L.	<1	SF	9112		1868	J. Timothy				Oct	1899
John M.	21	IRL	764		1894	James Joseph	42	CA	6853		1902
Josette	<1	SF	5171a		1896	John	54	IRE	7237		1902
Leslie J.				Feb	1899	John (soldier)	48	CA	3905		1900
Lucy Hoppe	78	VA	3091		1900	John James	<1	SF	5931	Jan	1901
Mary	60	ENG	6389		1903	John Matthew	4	SF	6763	Feb	1901
Mary C.				Oct	1898	Mary	50	IRL	1300b		1895
Mary J.	43	IRE	1326		1903	Michael	45	IRL	2072		1873
Moon Wang Shee	30	CHN	348		1900	Timothy	1838	IRE	1900c		1904
Richard	4	AUT	3690		1867	**HARRIGER**					
Robt. C.	30		H195		1889	Elizabeth Jane	1871	CA	3265c		1904
Sarah Jane	42	SF	1888		1894	**HARRIMAN**					
Thomas	43	IRE	4483		1902	George C.	34	ME	1158		1869
William	54	ME	1313a		1871	Milton B.				Apr	1899
Wm. D. (soldier)			1461		1901	Minerva C.	29	CA	5040a		1895

Key: a = 1st part of year; b = 2nd part of year;
c = death certificate copy; c/o = child of

NAME	AGE OR YOB.	BIRTH PLACE	CERT. NO	ID	DEATH YEAR
William G.	22	VT	5079		1902
HARRINGREN					
Ellen	45	IL	6444a		1895
HARRINGTON					
——		CA	5619		1867
Adeline				Apr	1899
Ann	55	IRL	3860		1900
Annie	59	IRL	8944		1901
B.	72	ME	7586		1902
C. J.	54	IRE	5254		1904
Caroline	2	CA	1191		1869
Catherine	59	IRL	793b		1871
Catherine	<1	SF	3238		1866
Charles	20	MA	647		1870
Charles J.	37	CA	5253		1904
Clare	1	SF	3006		1903
Cornelius	60	IRL	H131		1886
Corrnelius	27	IRE	6312		1867
Dan'l./Mary, c/o		SF	8921		1900
Daniel	35	IRL	1289b		1871
Daniel	<1	SF	191		1865
Daniel	29	MA	2095		1900
Daniel D.	35	IRE	2307		1866
Daniel Joseph	30	SF	6106		1903
Dennis	<1	SF	107b		1871
E. F. A., c/o				Jul	1898
Edgar D. (soldier)	20		6051		1904
Frances				Oct	1899
George	74	VT	6458		1896
George/Georgina	1	SF	8602		1904
Georgiana /Geo H., c/o		SF	7780		1903
Hannorah	45	IRE	4745		1902
Hazel	<1	SF	3214		1895
Henry	35	IRE	788		1866
Irene M.	<1	SF	6508		1896

NAME	AGE OR YOB.	BIRTH PLACE	CERT. NO	ID	DEATH YEAR
James	<1	SF	647b		1872
James (soldier)			6256		1900
James (soldier)			7128		1900
James (soldier)			7220		1900
James C.				Dec	1899
James E.	22	CA	5123a		1896
Jane	22	IRL	1117b		1872
Jas.	16	CA	H2		1882
Jas.	30	PA	H177		1889
Johanna	88	IRL	1907		1870
Johanna				Dec	1898
John	1	SF	1403		1870
John	28	DE	H189		1889
John	26	IRE	5070		1867
John	1820	IRE	1806c		1904
John	33	CA	7703		1902
John		SF	713		1870
John	1842	NY	795c		1904
John B.	ABT	IRE	8c		1904
John C.	35	MA	1157		1869
John C.	62	MA	3007		1903
John D.	37	SF	6438		1902
John J.	24	IRL	1730		1870
John Mark	22	NV	2955		1903
John P.	53	IRL	4263		1900
John W.	66	ME	6869	Feb	1901
Joseph	59	IRL	2416		1900
Joseph				May	1899
Julia	1867	IRE	1292c		1904
Julia	22	CA	2119		1894
Katherine E.	24	CA	4311		1901
Lee	<1	SF	6849	Feb	1901
Lizzie B.	21	LA	8246		1868
Margaret	55	IRL	4877		1896
Margaret	<1	SF	1645		1901
Margaret T.	3	SF	1196		1869

Key: a = 1st part of year; b = 2nd part of year; c = death certificate copy; c/o = child of

NAME	AGE OR YOB.	BIRTH PLACE	CERT. NO	ID	DEATH YEAR
Martha	12	SF	3351		1894
Mary	42	IRL	2782		1873
Mary	65	IRL	6775		1900
Mary A.	77	IRL	4343	Dec	1901
Mary C.	26	NJ	60		1902
Mary E.	1	SF	1640		1866
Mary E.	<1	SF	8778		1900
Matthew J.	27	CA	4557		1903
Moses H.	45	ME	1037		1903
N. P.				Aug	1899
Nancy	63	IRL	592		1900
Nellie A.	22	SF	8837		1901
Owen	60	IRL	H87		1885
Patrick	63	IRL	3064		1895
Patrick H. (soldier)			4697		1901
Richard J.				Oct	1898
Ruby Agnes				Aug	1898
Thomas	50	IRL	2352		1894
Thomas	1838	IRE	2984c		1904
Timothy	67	IRE	8798		1868
Timothy	38	IRL	5935		1896
Timothy, c/o	<1	SF	2145a		1872
(twins)	<1	SF	713a		1871
William F.	32	CA	514		1903
William H.	61	NY	7399		1904
William Pierce	77	ME	3601		1903
William R.	1	CA	7958		1903
HARRIS					
——			5136		1867
——			8919		1868
——			9962		1868
A. L.				Oct	1899
Abraham				Dec	1898
Agnes	56	IRL	1109b		1895
Albert (soldier)			5052		1901
Alex	32	MI	5212		1903

NAME	AGE OR YOB.	BIRTH PLACE	CERT. NO	ID	DEATH YEAR
Allen Maclain	38	ENG	1951b		1872
Andrew C.	1	CA	1551		1866
Angeline	53	MA	1756		1870
Anna	<1	SF	501		1872
Bell, Mrs.	28	SF	6257	Feb	1901
Ben	17	SF	5957		1896
Benj. H.	2	SF	2463		1866
Benjamin Eliza	75	KY	871		1901
Benjamin W.	68	RI	2895		1903
Bernhard	1	SF	1145		1870
Carelein	37	PRU	3276		1873
Cecilia	3	SF	1314		1894
Cecilia	64	PRU	3347		1894
Charity	21	VA	3263a		1872
Charles M.	41	ENG	1446		1903
Charles North	62	NY	6751		1902
Charles Parsons				May	1899
Charles W.	43	CA	4736		1904
Chas. A. (soldier)			7770		1902
Claude H. (soldier)		VT	3619	Nov	1901
Collin B.	37	WI	2459		1901
Daniel/Sarah, c/o				Aug	1898
David	57	MD	547		1894
David	<1	SF	8483		1901
David	60	RUS	6822a		1895
Dora	31	PRU	1003		1868
Dora	82	PRU	448		1903
E. E. (soldier)			6434	Feb	1901
Edward	65	NJ	6651		1896
Edward				Mar	1900
Eldridge (soldier)			7313		1901
Elias B.	75	NY	776		1900
Elisha	42	RI	1140		1869
Eliza	60	IRL	2947		1895
Eliza Wheeler	56	NH	6789		1868
Elizabeth	58	VA	1944b		1895

Key: a = 1st part of year; b = 2nd part of year; c = death certificate copy; c/o = child of

NAME	AGE OR YOB.	BIRTH PLACE	CERT. NO	ID	DEATH YEAR	NAME	AGE OR YOB.	BIRTH PLACE	CERT. NO	ID	DEATH YEAR
Emily V.	53	VA	6854		1902	John	34	SCT	2303		1903
Ernestine	63	POL	3522		1902	John N.	32	NY	3817		1867
Etta				Mar	1900	Joseph	23	ENG	H164		1887
Eva	1	CA	5683		1867	Joseph	1	SF	6454		1867
Fanny	42	GER	1115		1903	Joseph				Aug	1899
Florence				Oct	1898	Juanita Adeline	1901	SF	969c		1904
Florence/Oscar, c/o		CA	1218		1901	Julia E.	53	NY	199		1902
G., Mrs.	70	GER	1150		1869	Kanchen				Jul	1898
Geo. A.	56	MA	4306		1896	Kate	32	CA	6036a		1895
George	32	PRU	3227		1866	Kate	33	CAN	4592a		1895
George	1822	NY	2641c		1904	Laurence V. (soldier)			6396		1900
George D.	31	NS	6752		1896	Lillie	41	CA	3200		1903
George W.	68	MA	2332		1900	Lillie	1	SF	3413		1903
Hardy	33	CAN	1603		1900	Louis B.	15	SF	2399		1900
Harman	50	PRU	546b		1871	Louis/Fanny, c/o	<1	SF	8396		1904
Harry	1875	SF	1155c		1904	Louisa		SF	5959		1902
Harry	<1	SF	1213b		1895	Mabry L., Jr. (soldier)			2219		1903
Henrietta	8	SF	7960		1900	Marie	<1	SF	7906		1901
Henry Albert				May	1899	Marshall/Susie, c/o	1904	SF	1963		1904
Hulda	56	PRU	8099		1903	Mary	45	IRL	2375		1873
Irene	<1	SF	637		1894	Mary	12	SF	1126		1869
Irving Bernard				Mar	1900	Mary	37	SF	8759		1903
J.	30	MO	2619		1866	Mary	59	IRL	2916		1901
Jacob	45	RUS	7212		1868	Mary/William, c/o	1904	SF	1539		1904
Jacob				Jan	1899	Mathias	23	GER	1091b		1871
Jake/Rosa, c/o	1904	SF	3399		1904	Mathias L. (soldier)			6395		1900
James	35	ENG	6122		1867	Meta				Apr	1899
James	23	IL	1278		1869	Mitchell G.	72	GER	7310		1904
James	43	ENG	4344		1896	Mollie	96	POL	1670		1903
Jane	<1	SF	2085a		1872	Moses	<1	SF	3139		1870
Jane	68	ENG	5181		1903	Moses	54	POL	2382a		1872
Jane W.	34	IRE	6684		1868	Moses	14	SF	7165		1900
Joe	76	NY	H70		1885	Nellie				Feb	1899
John	25	WIN	2093		1870	Pauline	72	PRU	5720a		1895
John	21	AL	6829		1868	Perry (soldier)			2062		1901
John	60	IRL	6279	Feb	1901	Peter	71	CAN	3019	Oct	1901

Key: a = 1st part of year; b = 2nd part of year;
c = death certificate copy; c/o = child of

NAME	AGE OR YOB.	BIRTH PLACE	CERT. NO	ID	DEATH YEAR	NAME	AGE OR YOB.	BIRTH PLACE	CERT. NO	ID	DEATH YEAR
R.C.	80		447		1902	Cora	2	SF	8098		1868
Rebecca	<1	SF	1045		1868	E.F.K.	29	MA	4568b		1870
Reinhard	<1	SF	5085		1867	Elizabeth				Dec	1898
Robert W.	<1	SF	2846		1866	Emily S.	69	MA	4211	Dec	1901
Ruth Harris	1	SF	3533a		1895	Fannie H.	27	MA	2036		1873
Sarah				Aug	1898	Florence Nightingale	38	SF	3092		1900
Sarah				Feb	1899	Frederick	41	NJ	35		1903
Sherman	45		2876c		1904	Fredericka	67	GER	4406	Dec	1901
Simon	28	PRU	8b		1871	George	47	NS	683		1870
Simon	64	PRU	447		1900	George	35	ME	1018b		1872
Solomon	66	GER	3469		1900	George				Mar	1900
Stephen L.	29	SF	6035		1902	George (soldier)			2294c		1904
Theresa	67	AUT	1920		1900	George F.	60		7999		1904
Thomas				Jan	1899	George W.	67	KY	4289		1901
Thomas	55	ENG	3476		1902	Grace Jane	<1	SF	3004		1873
Thomas W.	35	CAN	1145		1902	Gussy W.	5	SF	521		1870
Tillie				Jan	1900	H.	27	NY	677		1866
Toby	<1	SF	354b		1872	Harold	1	SF	3705		1903
W.				Nov	1899	Harry	27	CA	5724		1903
Walter T.	22	TX	6948		1904	Horace	44	NH	1444		1869
Walter W. (soldier)			7375		1900	Ida Ethel				Mar	1899
William	2	SF	1098		1869	James	10	CA	2111		1903
William A.	52	MI	4158	Dec	1901	James H./Maud, c/o		SF	4630		1903
William H.	8	SF	3581		1870	John	38	NY	8970		1868
William H.	60	VA	4754		1901	John	45	NOR	2735		1894
Wm.	63	MD	2390b		1895	Joseph Charles	46	ENG	5235		1903
						Joseph J.	57	ENG	155		1901
Harrison						Joseph S.	10	SF	4544b		1870
A./F., c/o		SF	278		1895	Lehna	65	GER	2738		1894
Abbie A.	68	MA	8234		1901	Lola Frances				Jun	1899
Abraham				Feb	1899	Luke H.	58	NY	8563		1903
Albert Franklin	12	SF	1747b		1871	Lydia G.	58	RI	219		1901
Annie Louise	27	SF	3141		1903	Margaret	65	ENG	7538		1868
Beha	<1	SF	105		1900	Margaret	72	WV	2014		1903
Benjamin	53	USA	105		1901	Martha	39	CA	2621		1902
Caroline A.	28	SF	6733		1902	Mary	4	MO	915b		1872
Chas. (soldier)			8431		1900						

Key: a = 1st part of year; b = 2nd part of year;
c = death certificate copy; c/o = child of

NAME	AGE OR YOB.	BIRTH PLACE	CERT. NO	ID	DEATH YEAR
Mary	71	ENG	3630a		1895
Mary	45	BC	5389		1901
Mary	34	SF	5957		1904
Mary Eilen	21	SCT	6389a		1895
Massellon Matthew	<1	CA	5721a		1895
Nathaniel	<1	CA	752		1866
Otis W. (soldier)			7314		1901
P.	55	ENG	4216		1903
Patrick H.	44	AUS	4504		1901
Philip Julian	27	SF	5573		1896
Randolph				Mar	1899
Richard				Nov	1899
Robert T.	15	KS	3387		1900
Sarah Marie Mrs.	41	UT	4681		1902
Sidney	<1	SF	7469		1903
Thomas D.				Aug	1898
Walter Henry	<1	SF	5503a		1895
Weber				Mar	1900
William	42	LA	549a		1871
William	42	NB	1237		1869
William Joseph	26	SF	119		1902
William S.	45	PA	7391		1868
William Walter	4	CA	6406		1904
HARRISS					
Charles S.	1866	CA	542c		1904
HARRISTAD					
Kornelius	60	NOR	H179		1889
HARROLD					
Charles W.	35	MA	718		1894
George	52	MA	4941		1904
Laura	<1	SF	6277		1902
Mary Ann	92	NY	8848		1903
Nellie A.	32	MA	3505b		1870
Richard	67	NY	36		1903
Thos. C.	1	SF	1714		1866

NAME	AGE OR YOB.	BIRTH PLACE	CERT. NO	ID	DEATH YEAR
HARRUB					
Ernest/Alma, c/o	1	SF	2676		1903
HARRY					
——	<1	SF	827		1902
Christine	39	DEN	5934	Jan	1901
George	26	RUS	2588		1866
Gerald	<1	SF	5837		1902
Hannah	70	IRE	7395		1902
John	30	ENG	1999		1870
Lilie May	17	CA	6521a		1895
HARRYHAUSEN					
Annie	42	CA?	3366	Nov	1901
HARSCH					
August (soldier)			7158		1901
HARSTROMBERG					
Bernard H. W.				Mar	1899
HART					
Ada	1	SF	3980a		1895
Alice Isabella				Nov	1898
Anna				Dec	1899
Anne Miss	43	CA	6900		1902
Arch Coombs	32	ME	8943		1901
Augustus L.	53	IN	82		1901
Babette				Apr	1899
Barbette	83	GER	621		1900
Barney				Oct	1898
Bartholomew	22	MA	8988		1901
Bernard	53	IRL	2282a		1872
Bridget	58	IRE	8381		1868
Catherine	75	IRE	6406		1902
Catherine L.	1882	CA	227c		1904
Charles	45	GER	2552		1901
Charles B.	58	OH	6406		1896
Conrad				Feb	1900
Darcas	63	IRL	5831		1896

Key: a = 1st part of year; b = 2nd part of year;
c = death certificate copy; c/o = child of

NAME	AGE OR YOB.	BIRTH PLACE	CERT. NO	ID	DEATH YEAR	NAME	AGE OR YOB.	BIRTH PLACE	CERT. NO	ID	DEATH YEAR
Dominick	31	IRE	7009		1868	John A.	43	ENG	2601		1901
Earl Reber	4	CA	6454	Feb	1901	John B.	27	CVE	4759		1867
Elizabeth	25	IRL	590b		1870	John L.	35	IRL	3033		1873
Elizabeth	54	NY	7337		1900	Joseph	79	IRL	7528		1901
Florence	26	SF	1631		1903	Leah				Feb	1900
Frances				Dec	1899	Lillie				Oct	1898
Frank W.	65	PA	8208		1900	Loyd Phillipp	<1	SF	5956		1896
Fredrick J.	64	GER	1215		1902	Margaret	52	ENG	918b		1871
George	30	ENG	H103		1886	Margaret	3	SF	397a		1871
George	37	ENG	2100		1894	Margaret Mary	<1	SF	2398		1894
George				Jul	1898	Marion	1888	CA	1062c		1904
George D./Wanda, c/o		SF	8720		1901	Mary	36	IRE	6167		1867
Harry H. alias: Jos.	33	NJ	2780		1894	Mary Ann	<1	SF	7968		1868
Henry	48	ENG	4791		1902	Merle (soldier)			294		1903
Henry F. (soldier)			5697	Jan	1901	Michael	67	IRE	3664		1903
Hyman	73	POL	8539		1900	Naomi R.	75	OH	3801		1903
James		CA	625		1866	Nellie	33	RI	7311		1902
James	<1	SF	5706		1867	P. A./Lizzie, c/o		SF	376		1900
James	37	NY	550		1894	Patrick	35	CAN	H72		1885
James	82	IRE	1502		1903	Peter	55	IRE	1358		1869
James (soldier)			3044	Oct	1901	Richard B.	30	CA	3366		1902
James B.	19	CA	764		1901	Robert	40	ENG	H30		1883
James Jos.	66	NY	2976		1894	Robert	20	CA	1049		1900
James M. (soldier)			6825		1900	Rose				Feb	1900
Jeannette	6	SF	8000		1904	Sallie C.	51	IRL	4246a		1895
Jennette Hopps				Feb	1900	Samuel				Jun	1899
Jessica N.	36	TN	6471		1902	Terrance	<1	SF	458		1866
John	<1	SF	43b		1872	Thomas	40	IRE	8360		1868
John	45	IRE	6665		1868	Thomas	<1	SF	1269		1869
John	28	SF	4746		1902	Thomas	51	NY	7428		1904
John	33	NY	4447a		1895	Thomas	29	IRE	1011		1868
John	69	IRL	5029a		1896	William	25	SF	4581		1903
John	91	IRL	900		1900	William	70	IRL	7567		1901
John	34	IRL	4434		1901	William (soldier)			6398		1900
John	76	IRL	3207	Nov	1901	William (soldier)	33	IL	5046		1901
John				Oct	1899	William H., Jr. (soldier)			4699		1901

Key: a = 1st part of year; b = 2nd part of year; c = death certificate copy; c/o = child of

NAME	AGE OR YOB.	BIRTH PLACE	CERT. NO	ID	DEATH YEAR
William N.	35	CA	2295b		1895
Wm. (soldier)			8785		1901
Wm. P.	35	IRL	1837		1894
HARTE					
Gregory P.	60	OH	5452	Jan	1901
Harry J.	7	SF	4944		1902
John Patrck	4	CA	645		1894
Julie L., Mrs.	30	PA	H85		1885
Michael				Nov	1899
Patrick (soldier)			6821		1900
Robert M.	<1	SF	5983		1867
HARTER					
Alexander	83	NY	4372		1902
Oliver L. (soldier)			944		1901
HARTERIUS					
Clarence E.	1884	NE	2642c		1904
HARTERY					
Edward	25		1926		1870
HARTFORD					
Ann	44	IRL	1947		1870
Benjamin	47	NH	7165		1868
Jenny	1	SF	1749		1866
Joseph	<1	SF	3509		1870
Sarah E.	36	MO	3886		1870
Thomas	37	SF	7502		1904
HARTIGAN					
John	42	IRE	1215		1869
Mary Jane	<1	PA	1301		1869
William I.	<1	SF	4686		1867
HARTING					
Caroline	25	SWT	5017		1867
Charles	<1	SF	6113		1867
William (soldier)			6763		1900

NAME	AGE OR YOB.	BIRTH PLACE	CERT. NO	ID	DEATH YEAR
HARTJE					
Florence Louise	1	SF	1327		1903
Hilda L. A.				Aug	1898
HARTLEY					
Albert	1903	SF	673c		1904
Frank E.	18	NY	905		1870
J. M./Dora, c/o	1	SF	234		1903
Richard	45	IRL	621a		1871
HARTLING					
Gussie	1860	CA	3386c		1904
HARTMAN					
Anthony	<1	SF	2236		1894
Artie/Lena Faver, c/o	<1	SF	7859		1904
Charles	<1	CA	1193a		1871
Charles				Feb	1899
Charles/Minnie, c/o	1	SF	3880		1903
Cilly	29	BAV	370b		1872
Emil Adolph	<1	SF	1272		1869
Ernest	35	CA	8305		1900
Gertrude	53	ENG	642		1902
J. William, c/o		SF	2707		1873
Jahan	26	GER	2332		1866
Jno. D.	82	SWE	2564		1894
John	<1	CA	1191a		1871
John W.	38	GER	220a		1871
Joseph				May	1899
Philemena	<1	CA	1192a		1871
Theresa M.	26	OR	6212		1902
Tillie				May	1899
William	60		5507		1904
HARTMANN					
Addy	22	SF	794b		1895
Adolph	44	GER	2914a		1872
Adolph	40	GER	H34		1883
C. F.				Nov	1899

Key: a = 1st part of year; b = 2nd part of year;
c = death certificate copy; c/o = child of

NAME	AGE OR YOB.	BIRTH PLACE	CERT. NO	ID	DEATH YEAR
Charles	1875	CA	276c		1904
Christoph	1	SF	807b		1871
Emile C.	32	SF	5699		1896
Emily	<1	SF	1275b		1871
Frank			4490	Dec	1901
George	1879	CA	448c		1904
Henry	66	GER	5065a		1895
Henry	70	GER	4286		1901
J.	67		2934	Oct	1901
John F.				Nov	1899
Louisa A.	<1	SF	7785		1868
Mary Ann	<1	SF	7243		1868
Nicholas	42	GER	3184		1873
Nicholaus	29	SF	1111		1894
Ruth	<1	SF	8788		1903
Vitris Grayland	8	CA	224		1901
HARTMANSHENN					
John	49	GER	1523		1903
HARTMENSHENN					
Jno./M., c/o	<1	SF	3957		1895
HARTMEYER					
——	1	SF	7998		1868
HARTNELL					
Ellen	31	MA	6733		1868
Maria	22	SF	4314a		1895
HARTNESS					
——			7556		1868
HARTNETT					
Henrietta L.	82	NY	3690	Nov	1901
Hjohn J.	18	IRL	7928		1900
Jeremiah	49	SF	2494		1901
John P. (soldier)			6832		1903
L./L., c/o		SF	1675		1895
Margaret	40	IRL	719		1894
Michael	50	IRL	890a		1871
Michael	80	IRL	6236		1900
Morris				Dec	1898
Nellie	<1	SF	1734b		1872
Thomas	35	IRE	2270		1903
William	57	IRL	5380		1896
HARTNETTE					
James David	1	SF	6566		1903
HARTNEY					
Stephen	44	NY	4277b		1870
HARTON					
Leanora	22	LA	6208		1867
HARTSHINE					
——	<1	SF	5185		1867
HARTSHORN					
Elldridge G.	81	MA	7842		1901
Elum D. (soldier)			474		1901
HARTSHORNE					
Julian Norton	30	NY	1102		1869
Wm. R.	63	NJ	101		1870
HARTSOUGH					
Frank W.	<1	SF	6067		1867
Mary Louise	57	NY	7188		1902
Mary Susan	1840	MO	163c		1904
HARTTER					
Cecelia	1	SF	1798		1903
Walter A.	22	SF	1667		1901
HARTUNG					
Conrad	<1	SF	615a		1871
Maria	3	SF	9822		1868
Rosa	8	SF	2021a		1872
HARTWELL					
George F.	45	CAN	6580		1900
Jerry	78	LA	7861		1904
Margaret	11	SF	220		1901

Key: a = 1st part of year; b = 2nd part of year; c = death certificate copy; c/o = child of

NAME	AGE OR YOB.	BIRTH PLACE	CERT. NO	ID	DEATH YEAR
Samuel H.				Dec	1898
HARTWIG					
Charles				Aug	1899
HARTY					
John	64	IRL	2427b		1895
Maggie	27	SF	4871		1904
Roger	62	IRE	2193		1902
Thomas	<1	SF	270b		1871
HARTZ					
Maria	34	FRA	624b		1872
Meta	62	GER	2535		1900
HARTZBERG					
Annie	21	POL	3977a		1895
HARTZE					
Nineita P.	58	CAN	1930		1894
HARVEY					
Albert Joseph	58	ME	8721		1901
Alice	<1	SF	503b		1895
Andrew	61	NS	2826		1903
Annie M.	10	CA	H77		1885
Arthur	1	SF	7097		1900
Ch. A.	65	NY	2155		1894
Charles				Oct	1899
Charles C.	68	ENG	3747a		1895
Chas. C.	68	ENG	4165a		1895
Dennis	42	IRE	5645		1904
Dorothea				Jun	1899
Edward	39	ENG	7488		1901
Elizabeth	1845	NY	349c		1904
Elizabeth Aurelia	35	LA	548b		1872
Florence	36	SF	6983		1900
Frederick W.	73	ENG	2626		1901
George F.	24	SF	5629		1896
Harry W.	25	ENG	1924b		1895
Hebbert				Nov	1898

NAME	AGE OR YOB.	BIRTH PLACE	CERT. NO	ID	DEATH YEAR
J.	29	ENG	134a		1871
James J.	41	NY	7083		1900
Jas. Ernest				Jun	1899
Johanna	38	IRL	7152		1900
John	35	IRL	498b		1871
John	53	IRL	H121		1886
John Oliver				Nov	1898
Lizzie	32	IRL	872		1901
Louisa	38	GER	4128		1896
Lucy	75	ENG	4907		1902
Margaret	50	SCT	2111		1873
Margaret				Feb	1899
Mary	5	CA	3725		1867
Mary	60	IRE	8292		1904
Mary L.	42	CA	5770		1902
Nellie R.	21	RI	H168		1887
Peter/Catherine, c/o	<1	SF	8217		1904
Phoebe	65	NS	1173b		1895
Robert	24	IRE	1371		1869
Rose	52	DC	416b		1871
Sarah E.	49	OH	7463		1900
Thaddeus	40	MA	H143		1887
Thomas	49	IRL	1913		1901
William	38	NY	1381		1870
William (soldier)			9564		1901
HARVY					
Lilian B.	1	SF	3774		1867
HARWOOD					
Edward	4	TX	1209		1903
Frank L.	22	MI	6781	Feb	1901
Jane	81	NY	6885		1904
Jane Elizabeth	64	NY	6651		1902
Margaret	52	ENG	4413		1867
Rufes	53	ME	5560		1867

Key: a = 1st part of year; b = 2nd part of year; c = death certificate copy; c/o = child of

NAME	AGE OR YOB.	BIRTH PLACE	CERT. NO	ID	DEATH YEAR	NAME	AGE OR YOB.	BIRTH PLACE	CERT. NO	ID	DEATH YEAR
HARY						**HASKEL**					
Maria	36	GER	962		1902	Wm.	40	ENG	3137		1894
HASBACH						**HASKELL**					
Otto	42	PRU	9547		1868	Charles	50	MA	1192		1869
HASBRONCK						Charles					Dec 1899
Maud Florence	1	SF	1069a		1871	Chauncy Orlando	77	VT	3118	Oct	1901
HASBROUCK						Clara					Dec 1899
Joseph	62	NY	3526	Nov	1901	Daniel H.					May 1899
						Edward C.	22	ME	7899		1868
HASBUCH						Frank H.	<1	SF	2377a		1872
Albert	5	SF	9944		1868	George S.					Oct 1899
HASE						Harry H.					Jul 1898
Charles	<1	CA	3352		1896	Helen Frances	3	SF	1633b		1871
Fred	<1	SF	2603		1900	Jessie A.	2	SF	5716		1867
HASELTINE						John					Oct 1899
Charles Ebenezer	80	ME	4479		1904	John M.	31	ME	1152		1869
Hagen	58	MA	1381		1869	Katherine F.	48	MA	2296b		1895
Mariette Woodward	54	MA	8971		1903	Mary A.	61	IRL	4120		1900
Robert E.	54	IL	8021		1901	Mary Eliza		SF	1787a		1872
						Mary Lord	69	ME	3848	Nov	1901
HASENBERG						Nikles G.	42	SCT	1437		1869
Mary Ellen	33	IRL	1391b		1872	Sarah A.	52	NJ	4317b		1870
HASERLY						Sarah Alice					May 1899
John				Nov	1899	Willis Gilbert	45	ME	863		1903
HASHAGEN						**HASKETT**					
Ellen	23	IRL	2042a		1872	George K.					Feb 1900
Herman	62	GER	5848	Jan	1901						
Sarah	53	IRL	4530		1901	**HASKILL**					
						Geo. H. H.	51	MA	4656a		1895
HASHIGAMI						Herbert/Dorothy, c/o	1904	SF	1491		1904
Hunizo	33	JPN	3439		1900						
HASHIMOTO						**HASKINS**					
B.	42	JPN	2480		1903	Bridget M.					Jul 1899
Henzo	27	JPN	7869		1900	Daniel					Mar 1899
						James	74	ENG	909		1894
HASHINS						John	42	NY	6280		1867
Mary	2	SF	764a		1871	Lily					Apr 1899

NAME	AGE OR YOB.	BIRTH PLACE	CERT. NO	ID	DEATH YEAR	NAME	AGE OR YOB.	BIRTH PLACE	CERT. NO	ID	DEATH YEAR
Mary	63	IRE	4682		1903	**HASSELWANDER**					
Mary Blanche	38	CA	6089		1902	Rudolph	<1	SF	5039a		1895
Samuel	24	IN	2470		1902	**HASSENPFLUG**					
HASLEHURST						Frederick	74	GER	7082		1900
Helen Eva	2	SF	2982		1900	**HASSETT**					
HASLER						John	16	CA	2174		1900
Willie F. Paul	<1	SF	3056		1894	Julia	53	IRE	6079		1902
HASLETT						William	33	CA	8726		1904
Arthur	16	CA	6486		1896	**HASSETTE**					
David	1	SF	181b		1895	Patrick	48	IRE	1208		1869
Leah	1	SF	935		1903	**HASSEY**					
HASLEY						Dollie Frances	22	CA	6735		1900
Margaret Alice	<1	SF	5084a		1895	Frank	65	NJ	3373		1896
William	35	SCT	289b		1871	**HASSMANN**					
HASRAUCH						Franz	50	GER	488b		1872
Frank					Jan 1900	**HASSMEYER**					
HASS						Oscar	33	GER	3242		Nov 1901
Abraham	58	GER	3834		1903	**HASSON**					
Henry	29	GER	1153		1869	James C.	55	MD	8400		1868
HASSARD						**HASSTED**					
Morley E.					Jun 1899	Maggie					Aug 1899
HASSE						**HAST**					
Carl H. W.	<1	SF	6407		1896	Prince S.	50	MA	2280		1866
HASSELBUSCH						**HASTINGS**					
John					Mar 1900	Appolos	67	VT	2862		1901
HASSELGREN						Ashley	50	MA	2436		1873
A./M., c/o					Nov 1899	Carrie L.	24	OH	6426		1867
HASSELL						Charles	<1	SF	815a		1871
Montgomery Prescott	2	SF	1693b		1872	E. O. F.	61	OH	H192		1889
HASSELMANDER						Frank	78	NY	6649		1903
John					Jan 1900	Frederic Hamilton	42	NY	2197		1903
HASSELMEIER						G. A., c/o		SF	2863		1873
John C.	35	GER	3075		1900	George	40	MA	2848		1866
						George A.	1872	CA	726c		1904

Key: a = 1st part of year; b = 2nd part of year;
c = death certificate copy; c/o = child of

NAME	AGE OR YOB.	BIRTH PLACE	CERT. NO	ID	DEATH YEAR	NAME	AGE OR YOB.	BIRTH PLACE	CERT. NO	ID	DEATH YEAR
George Alexander	87	NH	3665		1903	Theodore Henry Jr.	31	SF	6957		1902
Isabel I.	17	CA	1242		1870	Thomas		SF	636b		1871
Josephine	<1	SF	5894a		1895	Wiliam			8135		1904
Julia M.	31	MO	3001		1866	Wm. H.	19	NY	750		1870
Stephen	31	IRL	5083a		1895	**HATCHER**					
HASTLER						Martha J.	3	SF	7880		1868
Charles G.	<1	SF	7916		1904	**HATFIELD**					
HASTTICK						Adnan				Feb	1900
Joseph	31	GER	6227		1867	Clarence N.	31	MA	5929		1904
HASWELL						George A.				Apr	1899
Lorena D.	1875	CA	322c		1904	Kate	28	CA	6992		1904
Mary W.	24	NY	2275		1894	Wm.	49	ENG	H63		1884
Viloa Wyman	56	NY	7121		1902	**HATHAWAY**					
HATA						Andrew H.	68	MA	3009		1902
Yone	1	SF	5450		1904	Anna	28	MN	2489b		1895
HATAYE						Anna Chand	70	NY	3450		1894
Mautaro	48	JPN	6927		1902	Barnaby W.	54	RI	4567		1867
HATCH						Braddock R.				Jan	1900
——		SF	1205		1869	Charles W.	1	CA	3428b		1870
Albert J.				Jan	1900	Chas. W.				May	1899
Annie Wilson	1876	TX	250c		1904	Clifford	10	MA	5521		1867
Burton C., Jr.				Aug	1899	E. V., Dr.				Dec	1899
Charles				Jan	1900	Emma	35	ME	3486a		1872
Clara E.	56	ME	7375		1903	Frederick C.	16	CA	8129		1901
Ella Augusta	53	WI	440		1900	Haron Davis				Jan	1899
Festus	<1	SF	1475a		1871	Jennie	25	ME	8041		1868
Harriet	63	NY	5312		1896	Martha A.	50	MD	2336		1900
Jane	28	PA	1205		1869	Prudence	<1	SF	940		1900
Junius Loring	77	NH	5360		1903	**HATHERTON**					
Kate	37	IRL	4601b		1870	Edward A.	60	ENG	5000		1896
Marvin D.	60	VT	3367	Nov	1901	**HATHORNE**					
Nellie Louise	39	CT	H142		1887	Georgia Adelaide	31	ME	5579		1904
Richard	<1	SF	1135		1869	**HATHWELL**					
Ruth	<1	CA	448		1902	Jackson	47	IL	4681		1904
Sanford	29	NY	1164		1869						

Key: a = 1st part of year; b = 2nd part of year;
c = death certificate copy; c/o = child of

NAME	AGE OR YOB.	BIRTH PLACE	CERT. NO	ID	DEATH YEAR
HATJE					
Marie J.	79	GER	4212	Dec	1901
HATL					
Ceddie	2	SF	1913		1870
HATMAN					
Adeline	29	SF	5466a		1895
HATMARO					
Charles Henry	6	SF	1173		1869
HATSFIELD					
Frederick (soldier)			6940		1900
HATTA					
Taichiro	23	JPN	325		1901
HATTENFIELD					
Thomas			7572		1902
HATTER					
Manhias	55	GER	2612		1894
HATTON					
Annie	49	PA	5914		1902
Francis J.	52	FRA	8281		1901
John	<1	SF	142b		1895
Mary	65	IL	7520		1904
R./F., c/o				Mar	1899
HAUB					
Catherine	4	SF	1748		1870
Conrad C. W.	4	SF	3087		1873
Katie	25	GER	1152b		1895
Margaretha	12	GER	5893		1867
HAUBERT					
Helen A.	91	ENG	7653		1900
HAUBRICH					
Eugenia	<1	SF	1775b		1872
HAUCK					
Lucey W.	10	PA	851		1870
S./F., c/o		SF	944		1894
Steven	38	SF	8443		1901
Susie				Jun	1899
William	17	IN	8597		1901
HAUD					
George W.	66	NJ	8042		1901
HAUER					
Augusta				Nov	1898
HAUF					
Adam	65	GER	7203		1900
HAUFRAU					
Patrick		SF	674b		1871
HAUGH					
Mary	35	IRL	H42		1883
HAUGHEY					
Francis	8	SF	657b		1871
HAUGHN					
Margaret Teresa	1	SF	2176a		1872
HAUGHT					
Joseph C. (soldier)			143		1901
HAUGHTON					
Annie	2	SF	3141	Oct	1901
Ellen Barbaris	6	SF	2581		1902
Jane	1844	ENG	2438c		1904
Joseph P.	5	SF	5445		1903
Mary Catherine	1	SF	5658		1903
HAUGHY					
Helen C.	60	ENG	3150		1902
James	74	IRE	313		1903
HAULL					
James	60	IRL	5444a		1895
HAUNAN					
Sarah Ann	3	WI	1214		1869

Key: *a = 1st part of year; b = 2nd part of year;*
c = death certificate copy; c/o = child of

NAME	AGE OR YOB.	BIRTH PLACE	CERT. NO	ID	DEATH YEAR
HAUPHEY					
James	1	SF	8827		1868
HAUPT					
Fredrick	36	PRU	5492		1867
HAUSBROUGH					
Elmer				Nov	1898
HAUSCHEN					
P./K., c/o		SF	4491		1895
HAUSCHILDT					
Edward	16	GER	4570b		1870
Theis	40	GER	H6		1882
HAUSE					
Max				Dec	1899
HAUSEN					
Annie M.	28	SF	833		1901
C., c/o		SF	2458		1873
Conrad Louis	<1	SF	1564b		1872
Emma E.	38	SWE	6986		1902
HAUSENMEYER					
Mary	<1	SF	1016		1868
HAUSER					
Charles	1861	NOR	1767c		1904
Clara	<1	SF	662b		1895
Elizabeth	56	GER	8564		1903
George	58	GER	8710		1903
George/Hallie (twin), c/o	<1	SF	6405		1904
Hattie	1	SF	6844		1904
Henry	37	SF	3273		1903
Joseph Leonard	40	FRA	1296b		1872
Julia	53	GER	6605		1896
Leo	2	SF	4375		1901
Louisa	25	GER	316b		1895
Margaret B.	1867	ME	488c		1904
Rosine, Mrs.	57	SWT	5524		1902

NAME	AGE OR YOB.	BIRTH PLACE	CERT. NO	ID	DEATH YEAR
HAUSHIELD					
Harry	42	GER	5253		1902
HAUSILL					
George Frank	35	CA	7261		1904
HAUSMAN					
H.	52	GER	626b		1872
Lizzie	<1	SF	415b		1871
Wenzel	50		4996		1902
HAUSMANN					
Albert	34	GER	5194a		1895
Carrie A.	32	NY	8987		1901
Frank				Jan	1900
Henry	35	GER	1124		1869
Hetty	1	SF	4953		1867
Joseph	55	BOH	6113		1902
Raymond H.	2	SF	3388		1900
HAUSSLER					
Mary	59	IRL	5169a		1896
HAUSTEIN					
Alfred	42	AUT	1892b		1895
HAUSTON					
Frank T.	2	SF	1431		1869
HAUTE					
Emilie	5	CA	9273		1901
HAUTMAN					
Samuel	19	PA	761		1866
HAUTON					
Henry Edward	1	SF	16		1901
HAUTWEIN					
Jacob C.	40	GER	4233		1900
HAUX					
Saug F				Jan	1899

NAME	AGE OR YOB.	BIRTH PLACE	CERT. NO	ID	DEATH YEAR	NAME	AGE OR YOB.	BIRTH PLACE	CERT. NO	ID	DEATH YEAR
HAUXHURST						HAVILAND					
Caroline	93	CT	6347		1900	Albert (soldier)			5328		1901
HAUZERLING						Augustus E.	<1	SF	1565		1870
Jos.	50	GER	H90		1885	Jno. T.	63	NY	489b		1895
HAVARD						Michael	74	IRE	4832		1903
Edith	47	ENG	7495		1903	HAVISIDE					
HAVEBREUCK						Charlotte B.	54	ENG	8536		1903
Leonard	41	BEL	H190		1889	HAW					
HAVEN						Fou	52	CHN	630b		1871
Lucy Cushing	2	CA	1413		1869	Gay Wing				Mar	1899
Ramond	<1	SF	1316		1894	Lew	30	CHN	339b		1872
William L.	34	NY	1231		1866	Sam Gan				Dec	1898
HAVENS						See Wee	30	CHN	3433a		1872
Cathrine E.	49	NY	4005		1870	HAWES					
Gertrude Goewey	36	CA	8679		1903	Caroline	42	NY	1289		1869
Ida May	29	NV	6598		1903	Caroline	67	KY	1085b		1895
Richard F. (soldier)			7530		1900	Elizabeth	67	IRL	8838		1901
HAVER						George Hazelton	51	MA	2917		1901
Harold				Oct	1898	Harvey L.	77	PA	6083		1896
Katie	1866	SF	775c		1904	Horace	59	CT	721a		1871
HAVERLY						Lucy R.	<1	SF	1024		1868
Henry/Mary, c/o	<1	SF	3020		1901	Raymon S.	1	SF	320b		1895
HAVERMAN						HAWK					
Aron P. (soldier)			3683		1900	Harry	49	CA	5559		1903
HAVERTY						James S.	<1	SF	2156		1894
F., Mr./Mrs., c/o				Dec	1899	HAWKAMP					
Lewis Melville	<1	SF	4151		1900	A./H., c/o		SF	1807		1894
Thomas/Josie, c/o	<1	SF	6113		1901	HAWKE					
HAVESCHER						John Charles	46	ENG	671		1900
Fred W. (soldier)	22	GER	3093		1900	HAWKES					
HAVEY						Anna A. K.	45	ME	1852b		1872
Cornelius F.			6481		1902	John William				Jul	1899
John M.	11	CT	1417		1869	HAWKETT					
						William G.	44	CA	6662	Feb	1901

Key: a = 1st part of year; b = 2nd part of year;
c = death certificate copy; c/o = child of

NAME	AGE OR YOB.	BIRTH PLACE	CERT. NO	ID	DEATH YEAR	NAME	AGE OR YOB.	BIRTH PLACE	CERT. NO	ID	DEATH YEAR
HAWKINDS						**HAWLEY**					
Margaret	62	MO	8533		1900	A.	40		3925		1902
						Benjamin Franklin	38	MI	2395		1873
HAWKINS						Carmelita E. B.				Apr	1899
A. S., Col.				Aug	1899	Charles W.				Feb	1899
Alice D.	46	CA	4560		1901	David Nicholas	78	CT	5236		1903
Amasa J.			5413	Jan	1901	Dora				Nov	1899
Arthur L.	26	CA	3728		1900	E.A.	67	CT	H47		1883
Charles	28	NY	2759		1873	Edith Violet	<1	SF	1912		1901
Charles H. E.	1	SF	2545		1866	Ella Mann	29	NY	1418b		1871
Chauncey A.	25	NY	8578		1900	Ella Woart	46	NY	4119a		1895
Clarence B.			2601		1902	Grace Alice	2	SF	439b		1872
David	55	NY	560		1900	Grace Dunbar	59	MA	2766		1895
Dorothy G.	1	CA	3167		1903	Hope	63	ENG	5373		1904
Emma B.	28		6720		1903	J./A., c/o	<1	SF	2401		1894
Francis	<1	SF	194b		1895	James Holt	34	CAN	6017		1903
George	41	ENG	7549		1902	Mary J.				Mar	1900
Grace	1874	OR	350c		1904	Minnie Laura	39	ENG	144		1902
Howard Merrill	8	SF	2513		1901	Samuel	59	ENG	3069	Oct	1901
James	26	IRL	1139a		1871	Wm. Eben	<1	SF	5814		1867
John	41	SCT	48b		1872	**HAWN**					
John A.	32	NOR	1305b		1871	John	74	PA	7819		1901
Lewis C.			5560		1903						
Mary	34	SF	1448		1901	**HAWORTH**					
Philip M.	1	CA	5975		1867	James	78	ENG	2481		1903
Ruth May	<1	SF	8680		1903						
William J.	78	NY	4997		1902	**HAWS**					
						Albert S. J.	72	CAN	3447		1902
HAWKS											
J. D.	57	NY	1206		1869	**HAWTHORN**					
Minnie Fredericka	37	IRE	380		1903	Cooney J. (soldier)			5049		1901
HAWKSLEY						**HAWTHORNE**					
James Horace	18	IL	936		1903	Alexander	22	SF	5772	Jan	1901
						Dora	29	GA	7228		1904
HAWKSWORTH						Edward				Aug	1899
Charles/Katie, c/o	<1	SF	6958		1902	Harry J.				Oct	1898
Katie	25	CA	7011		1902	William A.	1823	PA	875c		1904
						William T.			3226		1902

Key: *a = 1st part of year; b = 2nd part of year; c = death certificate copy; c/o = child of*

NAME	AGE OR YOB.	BIRTH PLACE	CERT. NO	ID	DEATH YEAR
Wislar					Jan 1900
HAWTON					
Elizabeth Lait	56	ENG	3328		1903
HAXTHAUSEN					
Marcell	22	GER	4683		1903
HAY					
Allen	33		3712		1870
Andrew	36	IRL	H162		1887
Chum	10	CA	1975		1894
Duur	32	CHN	3177		1870
Helen Ellen Elizabeth	24	ME	3048		1873
Hong	44	CHN	1691b		1872
Janette Chase Davis					Jul 1898
John W.	28	LA	6509		1896
Lenora Agnes					Dec 1899
Mary Catherine	82	IRE	6959		1902
Mary I					Jul 1898
Peter					Dec 1898
Randolph R.	43	IL	1518		1894
Robert	36	SCT	3185a		1872
Sue	19	CHN	1881		1870
William Gilbert	33	SF	3321		1900
HAYBOURNE					
Charles	40	IRL	1645b		1872
HAYCROFT					
James Charles					Feb 1899
HAYDEN					
——			5074		1867
Bert W.			7656		1902
Bridget	54	IRL	1352		1894
Charles W.	<1	SF	9661		1868
Delia	50	AUT	4019		1902
E.	<1	SF	2661a		1872
Edward	3	SF	1233		1869
Edward					Aug 1899
Edward S.	1	IL	3337		1870
Edwin, c/o		SF	818b		1872
Elizabeth	54	IRL	4317		1901
Frank C.					Jan 1900
James	73	IRL	2655		1873
James	41	CT	7667		1900
James	67	IRL	894		1901
James Francis	1	SF	9016		1901
James/Kate, c/o		SF	4472		1901
John	29	IRE	1410		1866
John	21	CA	923		1900
John C./Mary, c/o		SF	950		1900
John/Maud, c/o		SF	6345		1904
Kate	58	MA	7425		1900
Katherine	53	IRL	923b		1895
Louis P. N.	<1	SF	2274a		1872
Margaret	42	IRL	3126		1894
Margaret Cleary	56	IRL	2801		1895
Mary	<1	SF	1305		1869
Mary	57	IRE	4598		1903
Michael	33	IRE	5050		1867
Patrick					Nov 1898
Peter	43	IRL	H29		1883
Thos.	35	IRL	2981		1873
Wilbur (soldier0			3544		1900
HAYDIN					
Lawrence	38	IRL	82b		1871
HAYDOCK					
Thomas M.	58	ENG	8162		1901
HAYDON					
Edward	36	IRL	1951		1870
HAYEN					
Heinrich B.	26	GER	964a		1871
HAYES					
——			7621		1868

NAME	AGE OR YOB.	BIRTH PLACE	CERT. NO	ID	DEATH YEAR	NAME	AGE OR YOB.	BIRTH PLACE	CERT. NO	ID	DEATH YEAR
Agnes M.	28	SF	6772		1896	Eugene	24	SF	2664		1894
Angie	34	SF	1721		1900	Fannie M.	52	NS	6813a		1895
Anna	<1	SF	3252		1873	Frank D.				Feb	1900
Anna	1836	IRE	514c		1904	Frank Joseph				May	1899
Annastatia A.	50	IRE	936		1902	Fred	70	ENG	3160	Nov	1901
Annie	1835	IRE	2778c		1904	Genevieve	<1	SF	4676a		1895
Annie	32	SF	8664		1900	George R. B.	49	IRL	5136a		1896
Annie	3	SF	1045a		1871	Geraldine	<1	SF	4385a		1895
Bartholomew I.	<1	SF	8037		1868	Hazel Ethel	9	CA	3505		1902
Bridget	40	IRE	1535		1866	Helen	28	CO	462		1901
Bridget	<1	SF	1380		1869	Henry	65	ME	8835		1900
Bridget	78	IRL	4273		1896	Henry W.	50	NH	1050		1868
Bridget	63	IRL	3493		1900	Ida M.				Jun	1899
Bridget	46	CAN	1360		1901	Isaac	64	MI	2435		1900
Catherine	4	PA	1030		1868	Isabelle	1834	IRE	2643c		1904
Catherine	65	IRE	2434		1902	J.M./Teresa, c/o	<1	SF	2831		1902
Catherine	75	IRL	5445		1896	James	76	IRE	6251		1902
Catherine	73	IRL	1596		1900	James	44	NY	2439		1894
Charles	<1	SF	1668b		1872	James A./Annie, c/o		SF	6047		1896
Charles	6	CA	384		1901	James E.				Dec	1898
Charles E.	41	CA	6810		1903	James W.	32	MO	3955a		1895
Charles Thomas	33	SF	4304		1896	Jas.	45	IRL	H32		1883
Cornelius	10	SF	7764		1868	Jeremiah	70	IRE	3706		1903
Cornelius	45	IRE	1359		1869	Johanna	74	IRE	3666		1903
Daniel	20	SF	6708a		1895	John	55	IRL	3408b		1870
Daniel				Dec	1899	John	36	IRL	1118b		1872
David	34	SF	2739		1894	John	33	IRE	9105		1868
Delia	33	IRL	2886a		1872	John	70	IRL	2398		1900
Delia	33	IRL	3931a		1895	John				Feb	1899
Denis L. (soldier)			1292		1901	John B.	63	ME	2167a		1872
Dennis A.	25	SF	2574		1900	John Bergin	21	SF	7367		1901
Dennis E.	69	IRE	5508		1904	John E. (soldier)			945		1901
Dennis T.				May	1899	John F.	70	IRL	786		1901
Ebenezel J.	1880	SF	1003c		1904	John F. (soldier)			8251		1901
Edward	55	IRE	5729		1904	John H.	37	SF	5274		1896
Ellen Cecilia	1	SF	3091		1866	John W.				Mar	1900

Key: a = 1st part of year; b = 2nd part of year;
c = death certificate copy; c/o = child of

NAME	AGE OR YOB.	BIRTH PLACE	CERT. NO	ID	DEATH YEAR	NAME	AGE OR YOB.	BIRTH PLACE	CERT. NO	ID	DEATH YEAR
Joseph B.				Feb	1900	William	1869	CA	1336c		1904
Joseph P.	56	IRL	907b		1895	William	30	IRL	6653		1896
Lusia	17	SF	466b		1895	William J.	52	OH	4653		1903
Margaret	40	IRL	H75		1885	William J.	53	NY	7705		1901
Maria Kisling	68	NY	8389		1900	Wm.		DEN	H49		1883
Mary	74	IRE	6544		1868	Wm.	52	IRL	H145		1887
Mary	<1	SF	1191		1869	Wm.	60	IRL	4234		1900
Mary	2	SF	1352		1869	**HAYFRON**					
Mary	50	SC	7344		1904	Ester	68	IRE	348		1865
Mary A.	60	MA	1115		1869	**HAYHOE**					
Mary Ann	36	NY	715b		1871	John	<1	SF	197b		1871
Mary Ann	2	SF	520		1866	**HAYLOCK**					
Mary Elizabeth	1	SF	6455	Feb	1901	Jane				Dec	1899
Mary P.	1	SF	1311		1869						
May, Mrs.	28	CA	5895a		1895	**HAYMAN**					
Michael	47	NY	3079		1894	George/Winifred, c/o	1	SF	5451		1904
Michael J.	65	IRL	225		1901	Rosalind C.				Dec	1898
Michael Joseph	10	SF	3011		1895	**HAYMANN**					
Minnie	32	SF	5256		1903	A.				Oct	1899
Patrick	49	IRE	9282		1868	**HAYMON**					
Patrick	1882	IRE	164c		1904	G.S./Winifred, c/o	<1	SF	3055		1902
Patrick	33	IRL	5423		1896						
Patrick	66	IRL	2600		1901	**HAYNE**					
Patrick (soldier)			1542		1900	George	1	SF	109a		1871
Peter	69	IRL	6757a		1895	James J.	42	NY	9230		1901
Susan				Jan	1900	Joseph	85	IRL	4657a		1895
Thomas	45	IRL	855		1870	Julia	60	IRL	1804a		1872
Thomas	35	IRL	583a		1870	Patrick	60	IRE	5953		1867
Thomas	53	IRE	2892		1866	Robert G.	7	NY	3372		1866
Thomas	<1	SF	3962		1867	**HAYNES**					
Thomas	59	IRL	1113		1900	Benjamin	30	CA	7266		1901
Tilden H.			7573		1902	G. E.	35	MA	5788a		1895
Timothy	84	IRL	138		1870	James P.	<1	SF	8889		1868
Timothy	48	IRL	238		1870	John	55	IRE	1368		1902
William	57	IRL	2859		1873	John	73	PA	4139		1903
William	<1	SF	1293		1869	John M.	34	MO	8011		1903

Key: a = 1st part of year; b = 2nd part of year;
c = death certificate copy; c/o = child of

NAME	AGE OR YOB.	BIRTH PLACE	CERT. NO	ID	DEATH YEAR	NAME	AGE OR YOB.	BIRTH PLACE	CERT. NO	ID	DEATH YEAR
Lee V. (soldier)			7315		1901	Franklin	66	ME	676		1903
Lucinda R.	32	VA	1518		1871	Mary	1	CA	3797		1870
Margaret	72	IRE	1382		1903	Salome	36	ME	8095		1868
Patrick	50	IRL	H83		1885	**HAYWORTH**					
Thomas J.	40	VA	413a		1871	Edgar O.			4113		1902
HAYS						**HAZARD**					
Bartholomew	36	IRE	6096		1867	Roxann R.	82	MA	1112		1894
Eugene	<1	SF	143a		1871	**HAZE**					
James	53	IRE	3168		1866	Thomas	46	IRE	1079		1869
John J.	<1	SF	6680a		1895	**HAZEL**					
Maranda G.	53	MO	2789		1900	John	60	IRE	1659		1902
Timothy	27	IRL	193b		1895	**HAZELTON**					
HAYSAHI						G. P.					Aug 1899
H.					Mar 1900	**HAZEN**					
HAYSE						Luella	38	CA	8401		1901
John					Jul 1899	Violet	27	CA	6725		Feb 1901
HAYWARD						**HAZLET**					
Allie	<1	SF	3176		1873	L. B./Bertha, c/o	<1	SF	3812		1901
Aloinza	81	VT	5706		1904	**HAZLETT**					
Carrie	72	NY	6139		1903	James	76	MD	5943		1903
Carrie May	1	SF	2013		1873	**HAZZARD**					
Darwin Leonard	71	NY	3056		1902	Andrew	65	IRL	1151b		1895
George	67	NY	3972		1900	Michael	36	IRE	4651		1867
Hannah Elizabeth	83	ENG	9672		1901	**HE**					
Lewis A.	53	VT	6582		1900	Chung He	43	CHN	2890		1873
Pedro C.	1	SF	8670		1868	He Qum	54	CHN	6896		1868
Samuel W.	<1	CA	1823		1866	Kin	20	CHN	304		1870
Verna	1876	MN	1827c		1904	Lee	22	CHN	135b		1872
Warren Francis	<1	SF	1186		1901	Lee Sing	42	CHN	1854a		1872
HAYWARDS						Lin	20	CHN	1593a		1871
Richard	45	IRL	1298b		1895	Lynn	18	CHN	1952		1870
W. B./Juanita, c/o		SF	6713		1900	One	54	CHN	1907b		1872
HAYWOOD						**HEACOCK**					
Albert	30	ME	8078		1868	Franklin Thomas	4	SF	150		1900
Carrie	55	MI	7808		1903						

NAME	AGE OR YOB.	BIRTH PLACE	CERT. NO	ID	DEATH YEAR
HEAD					
Addison Emmit	73	NY	3975		1902
Alexander	53	ENG	H25		1883
Eliza Clement	72		8561		1901
Fred./Catherine, c/o	<1	SF	3093		1901
George	47	GER	3405		1867
HEADLY					
Jas. T.	67	OH	878		1902
HEADRICK					
Birdie	1	SF	2163		1873
HEAL					
Leon	26	ME	2238		1866
HEALAN					
Eliza Agnes	4	SF	1219		1869
HEALD					
Alice M.	18	ME	3533a		1872
John	52	ME	259b		1872
Joseph	<1	SF	2398a		1872
Libby J.		CA	1919		1870
HEALER					
Paul				Jun	1899
HEALEY					
Annie				Nov	1898
Bernard J.	32	MO	3506		1902
Burchard	55	IRL	3800a		1895
Carrie H.	3	CA	6697		1868
Catherine	51	IRL	3567a		1895
Charles Stout	63	CAN	4102		1903
Daniel	51	IRL	5219a		1896
Daniel J.	31	NY	3785		1900
Delia				May	1899
Dennis	29	IRL	6485a		1895
Dennis E.	<1	SF	5921		1867
Elizabeth	39	MA	7808		1900

NAME	AGE OR YOB.	BIRTH PLACE	CERT. NO	ID	DEATH YEAR
George H.	62	CAN	781b		1895
Hannah				Jan	1900
Harriet C.	1	SF	1280		1869
Helina	20	SF	7294		1904
Herbert	<1	SF	4094		1902
Jas P.	54	IRL	H12		1882
John	<1	SF	3214		1873
John	62	IRL	983b		1895
John	71	IRE	6971		1903
Katy	2	MA	1212		1869
Margarett	39	IRE	1260		1869
Martha	26	CA	7834		1903
Mary Ann	<1	SF	1277		1869
Mary E.				Mar	1899
Peter	73	IRL	1935		1901
Rachel N.				Oct	1899
Theresa				Aug	1899
Thos. F.				Mar	1900
W.J./Annie, c/o	<1	SF	2402		1895
Willis G. (soldier)			924		1902
HEALING					
James	56	ENG	2048		1902
HEALY					
——			6132		1867
Alex	43	SCT	H97		1885
Anna	<1	CA	10		1900
Catherine	2	MA	806b		1871
Catherine				Oct	1899
Charlotte	6	SF	1240		1903
Daniel	75	IRE	6172		1904
Daniel	65	IRL	4863a		1895
Daniel	74	IRL	8484		1900
Donald Jos.	<1	SF	2691		1873
Edward				Oct	1898
Elbert P.	39	ME	724		1870

NAME	AGE OR YOB.	BIRTH PLACE	CERT. NO	ID	DEATH YEAR
Elizabeth				Feb	1900
Everett G.	<1	SF	1233b		1871
Freddy	7	SF	4962		1867
George S.	2	SF	317		1870
James				Jun	1899
James H.	2	SF	1855b		1872
James/Frances, c/o	1904	SF	2517		1904
Jeremiah				Dec	1899
John	26	IRL	H191		1889
John	<1	SF	5743		1896
John	47	IRL	9201		1901
John (soldier)			7376		1900
John H.	40	IN	3437b		1870
John L.		SF	3468b		1870
John M. (soldier)			6890		1900
Joseph	1	SF	986		1870
Joseph Mathew	<1	SF	9035		1903
Joseph W.				Feb	1899
Margaret	35	IRE	7472		1868
Margaret	<1	SF	7739		1868
Margaret	67	IRL	2768		1901
Mary E.	22	NY	1151b		1872
Michael	48	IRE	1156		1869
Michael A.	1839	GA	1310c		1904
Michael F.	52	IRL	604		1900
Myles A.				Dec	1899
Nora	16	SF	2199		1894
Peter	23	MA	H93		1885
Stanislaus	<1	SF	5631		1896
William				Jan	1900
Wm. T.	<1	CA	5903		1867
HEANEY					
Angela Beatrice				Jul	1898
Ann	80	IRL	5932	Jan	1901
Arthur George				Oct	1898
Jno. Jas.	<1	SF	6567a		1895
John	67	IRL	2334		1900
John				Nov	1898
Mary Jane	35	AUT	5915		1902
Michael	70	IRL	888		1894
Michael J.	36	SF	7189		1902
Patrick	60	IRL	1153b		1895
Rose				Jan	1899
Thomas F.	69	NY	2250		1903
HEANY					
Mary A.				Feb	1900
Mary E.	<1	SF	3289		1870
HEAP					
Tong	45	CHN	H68		1885
HEAPHY					
Mary	34	IA	3177		1902
Mary A.	<1	SF	4862		1896
Michael	65	IRE	8526		1904
HEAPS					
William W. (soldier)			7771		1902
HEARD					
Jos.	37	NY	H36		1883
Walter	49	ENG	8848		1868
HEARLE					
Rose	23	SF	6761		1903
HEARN					
Bartholomew	81	IRL	6574	Feb	1901
Beula A.				Mar	1900
Chas./Bertha, c/o				Mar	1900
Harry	24	CA	1851b		1895
James	45	IRE	3274		1903
Marion Louise	4	SF	2062		1900
Mary	2	OR	1227		1869
HEARNE					
Mary A.	1839	IRE	3432c		1904

NAME	AGE OR YOB.	BIRTH PLACE	CERT. NO	ID	DEATH YEAR
Moses Alexander	70	NC	5609		1902
William H. J.	27	CA	2046		1900
HEARNEY					
George	48	IRL	978b		1871
Margaret	54	IRE	1836		1902
Michael	56	IRL	8886		1900
HEARON					
Simon/Catherine, c/o	1	SF	1088		1903
William Leo				Jul	1898
HEARRMAN					
Andrew	52	GER	1911		1894
HEART					
John	40	IRE	906		1866
Offie	4	SF	1918		1866
HEARTY					
Alice	2	SF	1035		1868
HEATH					
Ada S.				Jun	1899
Annie	1846	ENG	1044c		1904
Edward L.	Abt	MA	3047		1903
F. P.				Jan	1900
Harriet M.	80	ENG	5203		1901
Jemima J.	58	ENG	2550		1873
Margaret Elizabeth	71	VA	244		1901
P. Laura Robene	6	SF	1224		1894
Richard Tilden	1859	SF	2741c		1904
Thomas P.	3	SF	6954		1868
Ulysses G.			7574		1902
Vera	<1	CA	2120		1901
William	40	ENG	4303		1896
William Ralston	34	CA	1551		1901
HEATHRINGTON					
Thomas	23	IRE	1396		1866

NAME	AGE OR YOB.	BIRTH PLACE	CERT. NO	ID	DEATH YEAR
HEATLIE					
Eliza	57	SCT	1460		1903
HEATON					
Catherine	68	ENG	3737		1896
Charles H.	44	OH	1270		1901
Geoffrey I.	8	SF	5218		1902
Warren	1823		1705c		1904
HEAVEY					
Christine A.	21	CA	1949		1901
HEAVISIDE					
Robert	57	ENG	4764		1904
HEBER					
Maria	63	GER	1834a		1872
HEBERLING					
Wm. A.				Feb	1900
HEBERT					
Josephine Marian	<1	SF	2192		1894
HECCLINK					
Matilda	1	SF	4993		1867
HECHT					
Amelia Kaufmann	47	VA	7890		1904
Babetta	69	AUT	3042		1895
Emanuel	48	GER	1668		1901
Isaac	62	GER	1134b		1895
HECIMOVITCH					
Joe	36	AUS	4873		1904
HECK					
Victor V.	61	LA	4095		1902
HECKEL					
Agnes	31	GER	487		1900
HECKER					
——		SF	1351		1869
Gottlieb	37	GER	3492b		1870

Key: a = 1st part of year; b = 2nd part of year;
c = death certificate copy; c/o = child of

NAME	AGE OR YOB.	BIRTH PLACE	CERT. NO	ID	DEATH YEAR
Heinrich	30	GER	4401b		1870
Theresa	45	GER	3299		1894
HECKERT					
Conrad	<1	NY	6106a		1895
HECKET					
William	5	CA	2890		1894
HECKMAN					
Edward	1827	GER	1244c		1904
Mary	41	NY	3008		1903
Thomas	67	GER	2651		1895
HECKMANN					
Herman	54	GER	6683		1900
HECOX					
Oscar Theodore	63	IL	3602		1903
HECTIN					
Thomas	75	ENG	8375		1904
HECTOR					
Abraham	70	SWE	8902		1900
Oswald/Winnie, c/o	1904	SF	2264		1904
HEDBERG					
Andrew	36	SWE	4203a		1895
Hilda Maria	12	MI	3863		1896
HEDDEN					
Mary					May 1899
HEDGES					
Daniel T.	65	IN	7680		1903
James	22	KY	5858		1902
Manuel					Jan 1899
William T. (soldier)			5698	Jan	1901
HEDGWEIN					
Frederick (soldier)			4550		1901
HEDINGER					
Richard	47	MA	5420		1902

NAME	AGE OR YOB.	BIRTH PLACE	CERT. NO	ID	DEATH YEAR
HEDLEY					
Thomas	42	ENG	3376		1896
HEDLIND					
Adolph					May 1899
HEDLUEND					
Mary	32	CA	174		1902
HEDQUIST					
Harry W.	4	SF	7550		1902
HEDRICK					
Albert	15	CA	3654		1896
Augusta L.	20	VA	1132a		1871
Don C. (soldier)			7159		1901
L.	40		3976		1902
Robert H. (soldier)			6477		1904
HEE					
Ah	32	CHN	3351		1870
Ah	22	CHN	103a		1871
Ah	32	CHN	1458a		1871
Ah	25	CHN	2257a		1872
Ah	15	CHN	3378a		1872
Ah	33	CHN	H10		1882
Ah	<1	SF	2465		1866
Ah	34	CHN	7466		1868
Ah	22	CHN	8257		1868
Ah	35	CHN	1143		1869
Ahe	50	CHN	1370		1869
Cho	23	CHN	4796		1867
Come	20	CHN	1305		1869
Kee	22	CA	7405		1900
Li	24	CHN	1205b		1872
Lin	32	CHN	789b		1871
Lon Jon	25	CHN	3954a		1895
Long	32	CHN	3239		1870
Lun	19	CHN	2325		1866
Mei	35	CHN	1077		1869

NAME	AGE OR YOB.	BIRTH PLACE	CERT. NO	ID	DEATH YEAR
Sang	46	CHN	1220b		1872
Sing	43	CHN	5034		1867
Tie	31	CHN	384b		1871
Toy	26	CHN	3014		1870
Woon Jock	53	CHN	7926		1900
Wy	30	CHN	450b		1871
HEEB					
Carolina	6	SF	2021		1873
George (soldier)			2066		1901
Philipp	71	GER	3329		1903
HEEG					
Laurence	1839	GER	2704c		1904
HEEGAARD					
Harriet					Jan 1899
HEEGLER					
Sophia A. B.	<1	SF	3419b		1870
HEELY					
Julia	<1	SF	1180		1869
HEEMAN					
Charles (soldier)		PA	7316		1901
HEENAN					
Agnes	9	SF	284		1900
Daniel	51	NY	1334		1902
HEENEY					
John					Oct 1898
Mary J.	72	IRE	7966		1904
HEENIZ					
Henry	<1	SF	2691a		1872
HEERDINK					
George F. J.	<1	SF	1281		1869
HEESEMAN					
Ethel G.	1	SF	4990a		1895
HEETH					
Elise					Nov 1898

NAME	AGE OR YOB.	BIRTH PLACE	CERT. NO	ID	DEATH YEAR
George Christian	39	GER	722		1902
Louise	1	SF	825b		1871
HEFFEMAN					
Mabel W.					Apr 1899
HEFFEMIN					
William	<1	SF	1360a		1871
HEFFERAN					
Joseph F. (soldier)			275		1901
Thomas	33	IRE	7164		1868
HEFFERMAN					
Helen M.	<1	CA	153		1901
James					Dec 1899
Mary	30	IRL	4151b		1870
Michael	62	IRL	1855b		1895
HEFFERNAN					
Catherine E.	12	SF	1740		1903
Francis Ignatius	18	SF	3151		1902
Henry T.	40	SF	2049		1902
Johanna Mary Josephine	55	IRE	4320		1902
Michael					Apr 1899
Nellie Hayes					Dec 1898
Peter	42	IRE	480		1903
William	55	IRL	185		1901
Wm.	48	IRE	2881		1866
HEFFIRN					
Margaret	28	IRL	2666		1873
HEFFNER					
John	44	GER	3186a		1872
HEFFREN					
Genevieve M.	<1	SF	5445a		1895
HEFFRON					
Mary B.	61	LA	4250		1903
Michael (soldier)			467		1902

NAME	AGE OR YOB.	BIRTH PLACE	CERT. NO	ID	DEATH YEAR	NAME	AGE OR YOB.	BIRTH PLACE	CERT. NO	ID	DEATH YEAR
HEFFUN						HEHIR					
Martin				Mar	1900	Dennis	35	IRL	48	b	1871
HEFTER						HEICHEMEYER					
Joseph	<1	SF	919		1866	John J. (soldier)			2161		1901
HEFTY						HEID					
Mathias	66	SWT	7434		1900	Christopher G.	56	GER	7818		1901
HEGARTY						HEIDE					
Jeremiah	45	IRE	4763		1903	D. Sanders	72	GER	1060b		1895
John	65	IRE	4251		1903	Thos. A. (soldier)			8429		1900
Maggie	29	IRL	3908		1900	HEIDENGER					
Patrick D.	33	IRE	6043		1903	Mary	35	IRE	8788		1868
Patrick/Norah, c/o		SF	8164		1900	HEIDINGER					
HEGE						Charles F.	1	SF	8723		1868
Mary Jane P.	22	IRE	1972		1866	HEIDOHM					
HEGELER						William A.				Jan	1900
Henry Frederick	82	GER	4896		1903	HEIDOHRM					
HEGEMAN						John/Annie, c/o		SF	3415		1902
Louise Harold	94	NY	6709a		1895	HEIDORN					
HEGER						Emma	22	CA	6538		1896
R./W., c/o				Apr	1899	HEIDSECK					
Vincent (soldier)			2162		1901	Adolph	59		5631	Jan	1901
HEGG						HEIER					
J. R.			6320		1903	John J.	48	GER	4284		1901
HEGLER						HEIFFNER					
John Henry	53	CA	8893		1900	Doroplea M. C.	37	GER	734		1866
HEGMANN						HEIGEL					
Gustav	42	GER	1141		1901	Sarah	60	IRL	6704	Feb	1901
HEGNER						HEILACKER					
Bert				Aug	1898	William G.	44	GER	828		1870
HEHAN						HEILBERGER					
Mary	<1	SF	3616		1867	Chas.	30	GER	4825a		1895
HEHER						HEILBRON					
Michael	48	IRL	H161		1887	Grace/Herrold, c/o	1	CA	494		1903

Key: a = 1st part of year; b = 2nd part of year;
c = death certificate copy; c/o = child of

NAME	AGE OR YOB.	BIRTH PLACE	CERT. NO	ID	DEATH YEAR	NAME	AGE OR YOB.	BIRTH PLACE	CERT. NO	ID	DEATH YEAR
Rosie	19	NY	6035a		1895	**HEINBURG**					
						Ernest W Sun	46	GER	6914		1868
HEILESEN											
Ole	37	DEN	2563		1894	**HEINCH**					
						Azes	31	OH	1312		1869
HEILIG											
William (soldier)			5695Jan		1901	**HEINCKEN**					
						Herman	75	GER	3592		1900
HEILMANN											
Francis Walker	27	SF	6107a		1895	**HEIND**					
						Emma	26	CA	H118		1886
HEILSCHER											
Welhemina H.	31	GER	8505		1868	**HEINE**					
						Bernhard	21	GER	H135		1886
HEIM						Chas.	28	GER	H45		1883
Arthur R.	2	SF	9030		1901	Harry	35	GER	5610		1902
Babette			Oct		1898	Martha			Dec		1899
Gottleb Fred		SF	1972		1870	Sarah			Feb		1899
Gottlieb	1837	GER	2552c		1904	Wilhelmini			Jun		1899
John Jacob		SF	1971		1870						
Joseph	26	SWT	3458a		1872	**HEINEBERG**					
Long	45	CHN	3272		1866	Levy	83	GER	2786a		1872
						Rika			Jan		1899
HEIMAN											
Clara	38	HI	6153a		1895	**HEINECK**					
						Carl Julius	56	GER	724b		1895
HEIMBURG											
H.	53	GER	1000a		1871	**HEINEKEN**					
						Albert Christian	73	GER	8803		1900
HEIN											
Ah	24	CHN	1448		1870	**HEINEMAN**					
Ah	25	CHN	1414		1869	Charles A.	35	NY	1576		1901
Ann Burke	65	IRL	1867		1901	Minna			Dec		1898
Hans	69	GER	5469		1902	Recha	77	PRU	8631		1904
John G.	48	GER	1183		1869						
Mollie	25	SF	4283a		1895	**HEINEMANN**					
						―――	<1	SF	1400		1869
HEINBERG											
Benjamin	73	GER	840		1894	**HEINEMEYER**					
						Elizabeth	1904	SF	1512c		1904
HEINBORN						Wm.	32	GER	384		1902
Harvey	<1	SF	1614		1894						
						HEINES					
HEINBRIGGE						Frida	1	SF	4022		1903
Louis	32	HAN	512		1870						

Key: a = 1st part of year; b = 2nd part of year; c = death certificate copy; c/o = child of

NAME	AGE OR YOB.	BIRTH PLACE	CERT. NO	ID	DEATH YEAR	NAME	AGE OR YOB.	BIRTH PLACE	CERT. NO	ID	DEATH YEAR
HEINICKE						**HEINZ**					
Magdelena	1844	GER	2337c		1904	George	<1	SF	3469a		1872
HEINIEKE						George	<1	SF	8052		1868
Jennie	30	NY	H82		1885	Henry	50	ENG	9060		1901
HEININGER						Jacob (soldier)			8790		1901
Charles John	7	SF	4761		1902	Katharine Eliesa	<1	NY	5620		1867
HEINNY						Kathrina	66	GER	2066		1894
Nachasia	35	NS	6898		1868	Lizzie/Carl, c/o		SF	6174		1896
HEINO						Lorenz	76	GER	6661		1904
Rose	28	CA	2507b		1895	Peter			Feb		1900
HEINOLD						**HEINZE**					
———	<1	SF	1161		1869	Annie	27	SF	7725		1903
						Carl F.	61	GER	3956		1903
HEINRICH						**HEIPNEN**					
Adale	64	FRA	8760		1903	Franz Deidrich	1	SF	2271		1873
Amelia	1	SF	5170a		1896	**HEISE**					
Gustave	27	NY	4158		1902	Anna	22	GER	2626		1900
Henry			Apr		1899	Hermann	68	GER	8358		1900
HEINRICHSEN						**HEISEL**					
Heinrich	42	GER	1004		1902	Kate	40	CA	6721		1903
HEINRICK						Peter	49	GER	5930		1904
P. H.	43	GER	1445		1869	**HEISER**					
HEINROTH						———		SF	4574b		1870
Walter			Oct		1898	Anna Maria	43	GER	2138		1866
HEINS						**HEISIG**					
Elizabeth	32	GER	2248		1873	Charles			Feb		1899
Henry H.	20	GER	H111		1886	**HEISLER**					
Peter D.	30	SF	7523		1903	Henry	1871	IL	1182c		1904
HEINSEN						**HEISTER**					
Henry	72	GER	3242		1903	Jacob	58	GER	6789a		1895
Maria	73		7551		1900	Mary E.	25	SF	1573		1894
HEINSOHN						**HEITH**					
Edwin L. F.	<1	SF	643		1902	Margaret	75	NF	2786		1901

NAME	AGE OR YOB.	BIRTH PLACE	CERT. NO	ID	DEATH YEAR	NAME	AGE OR YOB.	BIRTH PLACE	CERT. NO	ID	DEATH YEAR
HEITHAUS						HELANDER					
Robert	18	GER	1230b		1872	William	51	FIN	5182		1903
HEITMAN						HELBER					
Herman			7276		1903	John	45	GER	2742c		1904
HEITMANN						HELBING					
Nicholas				Apr	1899	Mary		SF	597b		1871
Nicolaus	57	GER	8264		1901	Otts	15	SF	2701		1902
HEITMEYER						HELBUSH					
Wm.	<1	SF	2308		1894	Henry H./Anna, c/o	<1	SF	2026		1902
HEITT						HELD					
Russell W.	22	OH	6034a		1895	Chas. A.	4	SF	5922		1867
HEITZ						Emma Georgina	26	SF	9320		1901
Minnie	1869	SF	2453c		1904	Ernest	<1	SF	1069		1869
HEITZEBERG						Evangeline	2	SF	1070		1869
Aristide Paul	71	FRA	5452		1904	John C.	42	MA	1927		1903
Catherine Theresa	82	IRE	8789		1903	Justus	62	GER	1853b		1895
						Justus	62	GER	1873b		1895
HEITZELMANN						Mary P.	<1	SF	6938		1868
Peter	54	GER	2602		1900	HELDER					
HEIVER						James K. (soldier)			277		1901
William	65	GER	717		1894	HELDON					
HEIZENBERGER						John	40	NY	9849		1868
Joseph	33	GER	1092a		1871	HELEN					
HEIZMAN						James Harvey				Dec	1898
George Henry	31	SF	2173		1900	HELEW					
L.	1	SF	822		1866	John Doe				Apr	1899
Lorenz	33	GER	293		1870	HELEY					
Magdalena C.	59	GER	4041		1900	Christopher				Apr	1899
HEIZMANN						Julia A.	70	IRE	481		1902
Christian	46	GER	4291		1901	HELGERSON					
George J. W.	<1	SF	5283		1867	John	60	NOR	5720		1896
HEKIS						V. Antonata	<1	SF	6459		1896
Ann	2	AUS	4186b		1870	HELGISON					
						Emil				Jul	1898

Key: a = 1st part of year; b = 2nd part of year;
c = death certificate copy; c/o = child of

NAME	AGE OR YOB.	BIRTH PLACE	CERT. NO	ID	DEATH YEAR
HELGOSH					
Lorenzo L.	1	SF	5587a		1895
HELGOTH					
Henry L.	29	SF	1923b		1895
Maria Tesesa	5	SF	9573		1868
HELIN					
Antone					Mar 1899
Emma L.	2	CA	H11		1882
HELJESON					
Helje	79	SWE	5468		1903
HELKE					
Charles	79	GER	7057	Feb	1901
HELL					
Benjamin	76	MA	1299b		1895
HELLAGE					
Elizabeth, c/o	<1	SF	1426		1869
HELLAR					
Mary E.	42	IL	2429b		1895
HELLBERG					
Lucy Warrick	36	NJ	81		1901
HELLEN					
Estella	<1	CA	H67		1885
HELLER					
Babette	56	BAV	H187		1889
Edward H.	36	NY	1398		1869
Emanuel Martin					Jan 1899
Martin	72	GER	1601		1894
HELLERA					
Doloros	36	PAN	5543		1867
HELLERS					
Henry	45	GER	7230		1903
HELLIER					
William	80	ENG	3202c		1904

NAME	AGE OR YOB.	BIRTH PLACE	CERT. NO	ID	DEATH YEAR
HELLING					
Alfred/Anna, c/o					Nov 1898
HELLINGER					
Adin Stanley	1	SF	1298		1894
HELLIS					
John	27	MI	1114		1869
HELLMAN					
Estella	2	CA	1136		1869
HELLMANN					
Richard	80	ENG	5219		1902
HELLMER					
Fred	33	CA	68		1900
HELLMUTH					
Theophine M.					Oct 1898
HELLQUIST					
Charles Adolph	10	SF	6303		1900
HELLREIGLE					
Lewis (soldier)			6937		1900
HELLSTEN					
Otto Wilhelm	20	FIN	5400		1904
HELLSTROMMER					
Charles H.	62	SWE	2981		1902
HELLWIG					
Frederick	64	GER	4998		1902
Otto Reinhardt	20	CA	2869		1902
HELM					
Christ	60	GER	5484		1896
James Harvey					Dec 1898
Oras			7670		1902
Sarah A.	1849	CAN	1706c		1904
HELMBERG					
August	41	FIN	7452		1900

Key: a = 1st part of year; b = 2nd part of year;
c = death certificate copy; c/o = child of

NAME	AGE OR YOB.	BIRTH PLACE	CERT. NO	ID	DEATH YEAR
HELMBREN					
Johain T.	3	SF	6884		1868
HELMER					
John	65	GER	3873		1902
Lucie				Dec	1898
William				Jan	1899
HELMERS					
Marie	45	GER	4222	Dec	1901
Niels Samuel	75	SWE	553		1901
Victor S.	32	SF	7869		1903
HELMHE					
William	29	GER	780a		1871
HELMHOLZ					
Catharine	48	GER	6788		1902
HELMKE					
Frederick	47	GER	3244		1894
Henry	27	GER	1064		1869
HELMKEN					
Frederika	1	SF	2528		1873
Margaretha	<1	SF	8498		1868
HELMONTE					
Fredricka		GER	1391		1869
HELMS					
Henry W.	65	GER	2047		1903
John E. A.	58	GER	545		1900
John J.	53	ENG	5135		1903
Theresa	60	SWT	5361		1896
HELSEN					
Palmer				Mar	1900
HELSING					
Agnes	45	SWE	8207		1903
HELSLEY					
Cornelius	58	OH	3502a		1895

NAME	AGE OR YOB.	BIRTH PLACE	CERT. NO	ID	DEATH YEAR
HELSON					
Salomon				Feb	1900
HELSTRUP					
Edward		SF	4173b		1870
HELTVATER					
E. Maria C.	<1	SF	163		1870
HELY					
E. S.				Aug	1899
Walker Raymond				Aug	1898
HEM					
Gee Fung	61	CHN	93		1902
Gook Yang	1	SF	381		1903
HEMANS					
Francis	75	ENG	3844a		1895
HEMBERGER					
Julia	57	GER	7568		1901
HEMEBOHL					
William L. (soldier)	29	NY	2134		1901
HEMEBRIGHT					
Harry/Agnes, c/o		SF	6426		1896
HEMELRIGHT					
Harry G.	31	OH	5789	Jan	1901
HEMEN					
Mary, Mrs.	28	SF	20b		1895
HEMME					
Louis	68	GER	2931		1902
HEMMEL					
Alice	42	GER	3392		1903
HEMMENWAY					
Albert L.	29	SF	1084b		1895
R. W. S.	16	NY	3507b		1870
Wm. P.	43	MA	2538a		1872

Key: a = 1st part of year; b = 2nd part of year;
c = death certificate copy; c/o = child of

NAME	AGE OR YOB.	BIRTH PLACE	CERT. NO	ID	DEATH YEAR	NAME	AGE OR YOB.	BIRTH PLACE	CERT. NO	ID	DEATH YEAR
HEMMING						**HENARIE**					
——			7135		1868	Mary Ann	74	MA	6306	Feb	1901
Margaret	20	NY	1411		1869	**HENAUGHAN**					
HEMMISON						Margaret	1	CA	1273		1894
John	32	DEN	1061		1869	**HENCHEN**					
HEMPEL						Julius				Nov	1899
Amalie	75	GER	6156		1900	**HENCHEW**					
Frederick	49	GER	6427		1903	Helena C.	2	SF	836a		1871
Herman	67	GER	8991		1901	**HENCKE**					
Hermann	29	PRU	3867		1870	Antone	28	DEN	6659a		1895
HEMPHILL						**HENCKEL**					
Albert G. (soldier)			2076		1901	Harry E. G.	<1	SF	1166		1900
Joseph	48	IRL	6957		1900	**HENCKEN**					
Thomas S.	28	PA	2320		1866	——			1654		1866
Walter S.			7575		1902	Annie Maria	<1	SF	6734		1868
HEMPSTEAD						Elizabeth Ann	32	MD	1341b		1872
Arthur (soldier)			4281		1901	Henry Thos.	<1	SF	3375		1894
HEMPT						**HENCKLEY**					
Joseph	64	AUS	7012		1902	Emma R.	<1	SF	673		1866
HEMROTH						**HENDEE**					
Oscar Herman	35	GER	1401		1902	E.B.	47	VT	722b		1871
HEMS						**HENDELL**					
George T.	29	ENG	1546		1870	Samuel	50		2076		1902
HEMSWORTH						**HENDERLING**					
James W.	10	SF	4787		1896	Herman	19	SWT	5391		1901
HEN						**HENDERSEN**					
Ah	31	CHN	9242		1868	Jacob	48	DEN	1842		1866
Ah			9244		1868	**HENDERSHOTT**					
Foo	24	CHN	1417		1869	Henny	23	CA	1427		1894
Jack	45	CHN	4525b		1870	**HENDERSON**					
Jack	45	CHN	4542b		1870	A. N.				Dec	1899
Kie	41	CHN	893b		1872	Anders J.				Jan	1899
Kung	<1	SF	706		1894	Andrew William	14	WA	3171		1866
Loo	27	CHN	3522		1870						

Key: a = 1st part of year; b = 2nd part of year; c = death certificate copy; c/o = child of

NAME	AGE OR YOB.	BIRTH PLACE	CERT. NO	ID	DEATH YEAR	NAME	AGE OR YOB.	BIRTH PLACE	CERT. NO	ID	DEATH YEAR
Ann Eliza	1823	IRE	2036c		1904	Louis	<1	SF	1259		1894
Arthur Irvington	3	SF	3603		1903	Louisa	24	CA	4368	Dec	1901
Arthur L.	50	MI	7365		1902	Margaret Pendergast				Aug	1898
Auther B.	2	NV	2105		1866	Mary A.	1851	MA	1379c		1904
Cath. Maria	1	SF	1151		1869	Nellie Jane	<1	SF	1129		1869
Catherine	70	NS	5011		1901	Phoebe H.	<1	CA	2323		1894
Chas. (soldier)			6934		1900	Robert	38	SCT	8113		1904
Chas. W.	30	CA	5042a		1896	Robert A.	71	NB	2528		1901
David	61	ENG	3199		1902	Roy D.			6052		1904
Duncan	75	PE	7554		1904	Sarah	70	PE	1587		1901
E. R.	38	NY	9198		1868	Thomas	54	SCT	1674b		1895
Edna	3	SF	6783		1903	Thomas (soldier)			544		1901
Edward Thomas	32	SF	449		1902	Waller H.	<1	SF	861b		1872
Egbert Ffrench (sic)	29	CA	273		1903	Walter	<1	SF	1697		1901
Ernest H.	34	NY	1398		1901	William	58	SCT	5638		1902
Esther	<1	SF	6067		1903	William	52	ENG	6855		1902
Ethel Olive	<1	SF	4998		1896	William	<1	SF	2599		1901
Eurancy	69	LA	1749		1900	William (soldier)	45	SCT	10		1902
Francis H.	40	IRE	5760		1867	William (soldier)	24	TN	702		1901
Fred L.	42	SF	2467b		1895	William Hall				Aug	1898
Fred L.	40	CA	9495		1901	William J.	29	SF	4186		1896
Garfield (soldier)			280		1901	William/Minna, c/o	1	SF	1671		1903
George				Dec	1898	Willie	5	CA	1164b		1871
Guy M. (soldier)			282		1901	Willie Stein	5	SF	566		1866
Hamsen				Jun	1899	Wm. P.	38	IRL	889b		1872
Harry (soldier)			2790		1900	**HENDLEY**					
Henrietta	3	OR	1055		1868	Frank Eastman	10	SF	2477a		1872
Isabella				Dec	1899	George W.	26	MA	1820a		1872
J H	34	OR	4874		1902	Samuel I.	49	KY	503		1866
James	82	ENG	4310		1903						
James				Oct	1898	**HENDRICK**					
James (soldier)			4789		1901	Daniel				Feb	1900
James Scott	67	SCT	2237		1894	**HENDRICKS**					
John	42	ME	4979		1903	Arthur Llewellyn	22	CO	5810		1904
Justus	38	SWE	1243b		1872	Baby	1	CA	8498		1904
Lena, c/o				Jul	1899	Emma	46	WIN	6140		1904

NAME	AGE OR YOB.	BIRTH PLACE	CERT. NO	ID	DEATH YEAR
Eolene	4	CA	1660		1902
Josephine	19	NY	1367		1869
Peter	51	GER	1207		1900
Raymond	19	CO	7758		1903
HENDRICKSON					
Amanda	27	FIN	6114		1902
C.	48	NOR	5411a		1895
Ed.	34	GER	H172		1887
Edward B.	<1	SF	1448		1869
George	46	SWE	2268		1902
Grace	3	SF	818		1870
Henry /Katri, c/o	1	SF	2534		1903
John	1870	FIN	1137c		1904
John (soldier)			4551		1901
Julia K.	44	GA	1048		1868
Victor	35	FIN	4792		1902
Walter	<1	SF	6735a		1895
Wm.	55	NY	2446b		1895
HENDRIE					
William A.	82	CT	6648Feb		1901
HENDRIES					
Frank W.	28	MO	H123		1886
HENDRY					
Hayes D. (soldier)			7772		1902
James	38	MA	1368		1869
John	43	SCT	9827		1868
Lucy	35	ENG	952		1900
Mary Isabella	35	SF	662		1900
Peter	<1	CA	7987		1868
Robert M. A.	<1	SF	7988		1868
Sarah	72	ENG	4122		1900
William	32	SF	8761		1903
HENDRYK					
Rebecca	63	MA	2186		1894

NAME	AGE OR YOB.	BIRTH PLACE	CERT. NO	ID	DEATH YEAR
HENEBERRY					
Andrew	56	IRL	6539		1896
HENEBERY					
Margaret T.	1	SF	3399		1870
Mary E.			1718		1870
HENEGAN					
Edward	35	IRE	5906		1867
HENEGHAN					
Timothy (soldier)			68		1901
HENER					
Fred	45	GER	H140		1886
HENERDIEZ					
Saids/Clayapas, c/o		SF	1568		1895
HENERITTA					
Henry		SF	1860		1870
HENERSY					
Jerem/Joseph, (twins)	<1	SF	364		1870
HENERY					
Adolphus G.	<1	SF	2730		1866
HENESSY					
Martin	1	SF	2672a		1872
HENEY					
Ann	72	IRL	3517		1900
Juliana				Jan	1900
Margaret	<1	SF	1956a		1872
Wm.	56	ME	H196		1889
Wm. J.	51	NY	2400		1894
HENG					
Ho Foo	27	CHN	158		1872
HENGELHAND					
Edward				Feb	1900
HENGOLANKER					
Ivan				Aug	1898

NAME	AGE OR YOB.	BIRTH PLACE	CERT. NO	ID	DEATH YEAR	NAME	AGE OR YOB.	BIRTH PLACE	CERT. NO	ID	DEATH YEAR
						Timothy	4	SF	721		1872
HENGUIE											
Victorine	<1	SF	1385		1866	**HENNE**					
						Addie	<1	SF	1005		1902
HENICKE						Francisca	49	WI	7845		1900
Walter Edward	33	CA	3298		1902						
						HENNEBERRY					
HENIER						Andrew	63	IRL	6210a		1895
Herman	<1	CA	H138		1886	Catherine	68	IRL	9674		1901
						Catherine A.	44	IRL	8398		1900
HENIG											
Albert (soldier)			4039		1900	**HENNECORT**					
						Jean H.	59	FRA	1403		1869
HENING											
John Frederic Wm.	<1	SF	221		1871	**HENNESEY**					
						Alice F.					Nov 1899
HENIPIN						Mary J.		SF	4095b		1870
Alice	65	IRL	1270		1870						
						HENNESSEY					
HENKEL						Alice					Feb 1900
Charles H.	40	IN	2263		1900	Alice Margaret	<1	SF	2983		1900
						Arthur (soldier)			8783		1901
HENKIN						Bessie	1	SF	3719a		1895
Annie	2	SF	7970		1868	Charles A.	39	NY	5202		1901
						Elizabeth	1839	IRE	2537c		1904
HENKS						Frank J.	<1	SF	784		1900
Alexander V.					May 1899	George Richard	3	SF	7767		1901
						Henry					Aug 1898
HENLAT						Humphrey	<1	SF	312b		1895
Jabez					Nov 1898	James	54	IRL	4001a		1895
						James	23	SF	6987Feb		1901
HENLEY						James (soldier)			6472		1900
Alonzo (soldier)			2064		1901	John					Feb 1899
Amanda E.	61	KY	7608		1900	John	29	SF	1741		1903
Estelle	15	NV	7749		1900	Margaret	48	NH	2698		1900
Hiram T.	29	IN	853		1870	Mary	55	ME	5931		1904
James Thomas	47	IN	1052		1901	Mary Berdina	<1	SF	581b		1895
Julia A.					Oct 1899	Patrick	33	IRE	1381		1869
Marion					Mar 1900	Peter	1822	IRE	1380c		1904
Patrick	45	IRL	415		1872						
HENN											
Dora	28	ENG	5483		1896						
HENNAN											
Jacob					Oct 1898						

NAME	AGE OR YOB.	BIRTH PLACE	CERT. NO	ID	DEATH YEAR
HENNESSY					
Charles	<1	SF	4851		1867
Charles	25	KS	6115	Jan	1901
Elizabeth C.	72	ENG	3504		1896
Ellen	60	IRE	7311		1904
James	42	IRE	7720		1868
James				Oct	1899
John	60	NY	113b		1895
John Pope				Jan	1900
Joseph	1	SF	3524		1903
Lawrence	33	IRE	6447		1867
Margaret	37	IRE	1040		1868
Marie	34	IRE	3604		1903
Mary	<1	SF	8118		1868
Mary	78	IRE	8389		1903
Murtha				Mar	1900
Richard	35	ENG	7202		1868
Richard	56	IRL	4865a		1895
Roy Thomas	<1	SF	8230		1901
Wesley J. (soldier)			6397		1900
William	40	IRE	5274		1867
William J.	21	SF	7207		1900
HENNESY					
Daniel	50	IRE	2341		1866
HENNEY					
James	34	NY	902		1903
Maggie K.	16	SF	2412		1903
HENNIG					
Katie	61	GER	5789		1902
Thelma Marie	1904	SF	1337c		1904
HENNIGAN					
Bridget				Dec	1898
HENNING					
Chas.				Feb	1900
F. M.	60	GER	898		1894

NAME	AGE OR YOB.	BIRTH PLACE	CERT. NO	ID	DEATH YEAR
Frank	22	GER	1169		1869
Hannah	36	IRE	1172		1869
John	74	GER	H16		1882
John S.	33	VA	2774		1866
Mary	1	CA	7082		1904
Mary Ella	17	SF	8218		1904
Samuel L.	49	SC	1383		1903
Sophia H.	34	PRU	717		1872
W.	40	GER	H81		1885
Walter J.	28	SF	6129		1896
William	36	GER	1334		1871
HENNINGER					
Burt (soldier)			8067		1900
Elise	28	GER	7653		1901
HENNINGS					
Fred	50	GER	5036		1903
Nancy				Nov	1899
HENNINGSEN					
John	35	GER	828		1902
HENNISKE					
Henry	55	GER	H185		1889
HENNISSY					
Mary T.	85	IRL	4458		1901
Mrs.	64	IRE	6401		1867
HENOCH					
Edmund	1	SF	3218		1903
HENON					
Charles	23	CA	6230		1904
Walter	30	CA	4753		1901
HENQUINET					
Louis I.	2	SF	8103		1868
HENQUIST					
Victoria	26	BEL	8395		1868

Key: a = 1st part of year; b = 2nd part of year;
c = death certificate copy; c/o = child of

NAME	AGE OR YOB.	BIRTH PLACE	CERT. NO	ID	DEATH YEAR	NAME	AGE OR YOB.	BIRTH PLACE	CERT. NO	ID	DEATH YEAR
HENRATTY						**HENROTTE**					
John				May	1899	Narcine	34	BEL	H148		1887
HENRI						**HENRY**					
Marchand	46		1323		1869	——			7361		1868
Monique	31	FRA	1747		1894	——	<1	SF	6498		1902
HENRICH						——	<1	SF	5832		1896
Helene	60	GER	3117		1900	Adelbert J.	40	CA	727		1903
Jacob	30	FRA	263b		1895	Alfred				Jun	1899
HENRICHS						Alfred				Oct	1899
Bernhardina	63	GER	1034		1894	Annie	<1	SF	1372		1869
HENRICI						Arthur				Jul	1899
Jeanette Ritter	42	IL	5888		1902	Benjamin J.	71	PA	2460		1894
Randolf	<1	SF	3900		1870	Bertha	<1	SF	1194		1869
William Julius Edward	60	GER	6253		1904	Bertha Elizabeth				Nov	1898
						Bridget Madeline	30	IRE	4252		1903
HENRICKSON						Charles	39	NOR	2542		1866
Herman	29	FIN	4828		1904	Charles	<1	SF	1146		1902
Peter	40	GER	7778		1868	Charles				Nov	1899
HENRICO						Chas. (soldier)			8794		1901
Emal, c/o	<1	SF	268b		1872	Cynthia	68	OH	5254		1902
						Edward A. (soldier)			2711		1901
HENRIKSEN						Ellen Maria	<1	SF	3262		1872
Bernhard Ed.	49	CA	7695		1900	Emil	62	FRA	2648		1894
HENRIOLLE						Emma	61	ME	6787a		1895
Argiat Katie	<1	SF	993		1894	F. T.				Nov	1899
HENRIOULLE						George	36	NB	7440		1868
Elizabeth Victoria	17	CA	707		1903	George				Feb	1900
Louis Joseph	13	SF	8563		1901	Guy Vernon	1	NY	1508		1871
HENRIQUES						Hannah	43	GER	4515		1896
Abraham L.	<1	SF	1703		1866	Henry	36	ENG	1773		1870
Adolph Francisco	1	SF	113		1871	Herbert	2	SF	1821b		1872
Annie L.	<1	SF	2018		1873	Isaac	74	RUS	1957a		1872
David	70	JAM	6618a		1895	James				Jul	1899
HENRIX						Jeanne Alice	28	ENG	2112		1903
Anna Margretha	54	GER	2027		1902	Johanna	65	IRL	6606		1896

NAME	AGE OR YOB.	BIRTH PLACE	CERT. NO	ID	DEATH YEAR
John	45	IRE	1487		1866
John	36	IRE	4793		1902
John	58		1216		1902
John	72	SWT	6707a		1895
John B.					Nov 1898
John P	37	SF	4908		1902
Joseph	<1	SF	5985a		1895
L. C.	58	NY	1087		1869
Lucien C. F.	1	SF	8514		1901
Mae	34	SF	221		1901
Margaret Landers	64	NY	4435		1901
Mari	22	SF	457		1870
Martha	24	IRE	5561		1903
Mary					Nov 1898
Mary A.	40	SF	4764		1903
Mary Beatrice	30	ME	8768		1904
Mary F.	26	SF	1698		1894
Mary Louisa	24	NY	4885		1867
Michael	35	IRL	4973a		1895
Nellie, c/o	<1	CA	1797		1894
Newlon					Feb 1900
Ray (soldier)	23	MI	5888		Jan 1901
Robert	25	PA	4794		1867
Rose M.	64	IRE	2797		1903
Samuel	64	GER	2056b		1895
Samuel T.	45	PA	3373a		1872
Sarah Grace					Nov 1898
Saunders	34	NY	160b		1871
SylvanusH.	61	NY	1007b		1871
Thomas	<1	SF	1042		1868
Watson Hoyt					Nov 1898
William	56	NY	2026b		1895
William	50	IRL	2699		1900
William J.	23	OH	507		1870
William J.	<1	SF	7826		1868
Wm.	64	MD	1457		1894

NAME	AGE OR YOB.	BIRTH PLACE	CERT. NO	ID	DEATH YEAR
Wm. Emil, Jr.	2	SF	787		1901
Wm. G. (soldier)			7222		1900
HENSCHEL					
H. L.	57	GER	9297		1868
HENSEL					
Heinrich	78	GER	9033		1901
HENSEN					
Hens/Ella, c/o	<1	SF	3050		1900
Jas.	73	HOL	1889		1894
HENSEY					
Margaret	54	NY	1706		1902
HENSHAW					
Edward Tyler	51	IL	2526		1901
Helen Emma	73	NY	9337		1901
HENSING					
Meta	73	GER	8919		1901
HENSLEY					
Francis	<1	SF	7745		1868
Robert (soldier)			2163		1901
S. J.	<1	SF	7744		1868
William D.	29	CA	7459		1904
HENTE					
Joseph					May 1899
HENTON					
Athol A.	15	NY	3454		1894
HENTSELL					
Ed/Nellie, c/o	<1	CA	184		1901
HENTZ					
Auigustus H.					Jan 1900
HENTZEL					
Emily T.	74	OH	3785		Nov 1901
John W.	1855	OH	749c		1904
Victor	<1	SF	1551		1894

Key: a = 1st part of year; b = 2nd part of year;
c = death certificate copy; c/o = child of

NAME	AGE OR YOB.	BIRTH PLACE	CERT. NO	ID	DEATH YEAR	NAME	AGE OR YOB.	BIRTH PLACE	CERT. NO	ID	DEATH YEAR
HENTZELL						HEPWORTH					
Augustus Joseph	48	OH	3231		1900	Susan				Mar	1900
Nellie	22	CA	998		1901						
Sarah E.				Oct	1899	HER					
						A. H.	3	SF	2274		1866
HENURY						Ling	31	CHN	2337		1866
Daniel V. B.				Nov	1899						
						HERALD					
HENWOOD						Edai	<1	SF	4808a		1895
Emily M.	72	ENG	4321		1902	Owen	1851	IRE	1103c		1904
HENZE						HERAN					
David	35	MA	1033		1894	Edna S.	5	SF	120		1902
Francis C.	25	MN	1625		1902						
						HERASONN					
HENZIE						Robert D.	<1	CA	8402		1901
Louis	abt.	GER	1140		1901						
						HERBENT					
HEOMANN						William	31	CA	7421		1901
Caroline	<1	SF	6697a		1895						
						HERBERGER					
HEONG						Emma	<1	SF	7051		1868
Ah	23	CHN	5		1870						
In	42	CHN	1095b		1872	HERBERT					
						Cathrine A.	<1	SF	9175		1868
HEOY						Charles F.			1260		1903
Young Wing	54	CHN	9338		1901	Charles/Annie, c/o	1	SF	5167		1904
						Chas.	19	IL	H99		1885
HEPBURN						Florence	<1	SF	5753		1903
Charles/Margaret, c/o	<1	CA	2756		1902	George	<1	SF	6788a		1895
William H.	1	SF	3411b		1870	Gladys M.	<1	SF	2935	Oct	1901
						James	45	NY	1909a		1872
HEPBURNE						John	47	IRE	7726		1903
Henry L.	47	CT	6006		1867	John	66	ENG	1014		1903
						John Edward				Jan	1899
HEPP						Joseph	10	SF	4322		1902
Caroline	20	SF	1386b		1895	Julia	18	NY	3584		1903
						Louis	60	FRA	9782		1868
HEPPERT						Mary	26	CAN	3346		1894
Clara	<1	SF	1661		1902	R. H.	52	IRL	H156		1887
						William	45	IRE	903		1903
HEPPLER											
Belle				Dec	1899						
HEPSWORTH											
John M.	42	NY	154		1865						

Key: a = 1st part of year; b = 2nd part of year;
c = death certificate copy; c/o = child of

NAME	AGE OR YOB.	BIRTH PLACE	CERT. NO	ID	DEATH YEAR
HERBET					
Louise	42	GER	2133		1873
HERBORG					
Cristian	51	DEN	5340a		1895
HERBST					
Catherine				Dec	1898
Catherine C.				Dec	1898
Elsa	6	SF	311b		1895
Francis	53	GER	4365a		1895
HERBSTRITT					
Jos.	36	GER	4338		1903
HERCZEL					
Rosalia	35	HUN	172		1903
HERD					
George	43	ENG	8404		1901
HERDCH					
Emil	22	GER	3943		1870
HERDINK					
John	54	HOL	H24		1883
HERDMAN					
Henry F. C.	21	IND	5910a		1895
HERDT					
Christian H.	<1	SF	82b		1872
HEREDIA					
Dolores	82	MEX	2915		1902
HEREFORD					
Flora J.	41	SF	6231		1904
William S.	52	MO	8527		1904
HERFORTH					
Susanna	1904	SF	30c		1904
HERGARTEN					
E. C.	47	GER	H132		1886

NAME	AGE OR YOB.	BIRTH PLACE	CERT. NO	ID	DEATH YEAR
HERGER					
Catherine	36	SWT	4191		1903
HERGET					
Elenore W.	28	AUT	1957		1902
HERGFELDER					
Herman	65	BAV	2307		1894
HERGOTT					
Justin	1874	PA	3293c		1904
Margaret Ellen	1904	SF	674c		1904
Peter				Apr	1899
HERING					
Caroline	3	SF	3238		1895
Caroline Augusta	69	GER	990		1902
Thomas	65	IRE	200		1902
Walter	<1	SF	2094		1900
HERINGHI					
Bernardo		SF	3302		1870
Bernardo	77	AUT	3267	Nov	1901
HERINGLAKE					
Augusta c.	1842	GER	1360c		1904
HERION					
Celestein				Jan	1899
HERIOT					
Edgar L.	78	SC	3725		1903
George P.	1	CA	5013		1901
HERITAGE					
John Wesley	76	NC	4599		1903
Mary	67	SCT	4096		1902
HERKENS					
Eildart	69	GER	612b		1895
HERKNER					
James Webb	53	NY	2433		1900

NAME	AGE OR YOB.	BIRTH PLACE	CERT. NO	ID	DEATH YEAR
HERLEHY					
Daniel				Jul	1898
Edward	1	NJ	8326		1868
Francis	2	NY	817b		1872
William/Eliz., c/o		SF	4521		1903
HERLETS					
Nellie	55	IRE	1958		1902
HERLICHY					
Dennis	2	CA	1603		1866
Mary	10	MA	8533		1868
HERLIEHY					
Catherine	73	IRE	2798		1903
HERLIHY					
——			7434		1868
Bartholemew	1	SF	1377		1869
Catherine	68	IRL	1317		1894
Cornelius				Dec	1898
Gregory	<1	SF	2802		1895
Margaret	6	CA	1587		1902
Margaret	67	IRE	5037		1903
Maurice	74	IRL	5875		1896
Patrick	73	IRE	1014		1868
Richard (USN)			4389		1903
Vincent Joseph				Oct	1899
HERLIKY					
Patrick H.	3	CA	2737		1894
HERLILNY					
Daniel	36	IRL	2061		1900
HERLING					
Louis	43	NJ	4999		1896
HERLITZ					
Emily Maud	37	CA	6782	Feb	1901
HERLON					
Ingrid Carrie	46	SWE	890b		1895

NAME	AGE OR YOB.	BIRTH PLACE	CERT. NO	ID	DEATH YEAR
HERMAL					
Jean Baptiste	72	FRA	7296		1900
HERMAN					
August	32	NY	8817		1900
Catherine	55	IRL	3102		1894
Clarence	1	SF	5509		1904
Ernest (soldier)			7122		1900
George	45	GER	5692		1902
George C.	<1	SF	9062		1901
Harry	29	GER	4444		1903
Jacob				Oct	1898
John	<1	SF	434b		1871
Joseph	<1	SF	8390		1903
Julius	37	GER	218b		1872
Louis	2	SF	718b		1871
Lucien	74	LA	H84		1885
Margaret	<1	SF	4579		1896
Marie A.	56	GER	6928		1902
Otto	31	GER	1480b		1871
William	18	NY	4284b		1870
William	1879	CA	1458c		1904
HERMANDEZ					
Milton (soldier)			4786		1901
HERMANN					
Alexander	40	GER	1433		1869
Angelica	1	SF	3775		1867
Christopher	44	GER	7382		1904
Fred				Mar	1899
Georg	1823	SWT	2377c		1904
Jno.	45	GER	H17		1882
Lena				Jun	1899
Mary	<1	SF	5742		1896
Mary A.				Jun	1899
Oscar	43	SF	857		1900
Peter	45	DEN	695a		1871

NAME	AGE OR YOB.	BIRTH PLACE	CERT. NO	ID	DEATH YEAR
Sussie	34	GER	7870		1900
W./E., c/o					Apr 1899
HERMELINE					
Justine Weill	92	GER	3977		1902
HERMES					
John	59	GER	6776		1900
HERMMELE					
Fredrick	38	GER	3856		1870
HERMON					
Frank (soldier)			1463		1901
HERN					
Byron/Amelia, c/o	<1	SF	6804		1901
Henry C.	44	RI	2428b		1895
Lizzie	19	MA	918		1894
HERNAN					
Michael					Dec 1899
HERNANDERZ					
Petra	26	CA	7979		1903
HERNANDEZ					
Adela					Nov 1898
Maria	12	MEX	1721b		1895
Santos	19	MEX	619		1894
HERNDON					
John (soldier)			4787		1901
HERNEN					
Patrick	26	IRE	8471		1868
HERNEY					
Austin		SF	2073		1870
HERNMANN					
Ferdinand	39	SWT	8347		1900
HERO					
Matilda	1	SF	1708		1866

NAME	AGE OR YOB.	BIRTH PLACE	CERT. NO	ID	DEATH YEAR
HEROLD					
Albert E.					Aug 1899
Eva	61	GER	4810		1896
George	36	GER	3590		1902
Jacob	19	SF	1386		1901
Marie L.	33	FRA	6681		1896
Phillip Roy	<1	SF	3907		1900
Roy	<1	SF	5849		1903
Ruth V.					Aug 1899
Violet Louise	<1	SF	6213		1902
Walter					Jan 1899
HERON					
William	45	SCT	2971		1895
William/Ada, c/o					Dec 1898
HERONIMO					
——		NGR	3271		1866
HEROT					
Antoine Chevalier	48	FRA	3463a		1872
HEROTY					
Kofiy					Aug 1899
HERPICH					
Ottilie	46	GER	4514		1904
HERRE					
Adolph Jules	34	SF	4770a		1895
HERRERA					
Amador	40	CHL	5469		1903
Mary H.	42	ENG	6836		1868
HERRGUTH					
Sam F.	60	GER	H33		1883
HERRICK					
Edward					Apr 1899
Fanny L.					Dec 1899
Fredrick B.	<1	SF	3242		1870
George E.	70	VT	8162		1903

NAME	AGE OR YOB.	BIRTH PLACE	CERT. NO	ID	DEATH YEAR
George Rees	<1	CA	7155		1903
Medora B.				Oct	1899
William A.	56	VT	1273b		1871
HERRIN					
Edward Nelson	63	ME	5628		1903
Michael	1852	ME	2553c		1904
HERRING					
Ethel May	1	SF	4373		1903
George D.	28	SF	2096		1900
Henry P.	60	NY	8231		1901
John M.				Feb	1900
Polly Nye	88	CT	580		1901
Rudolph	42	GER	1236		1869
HERRINGTON					
A. A. (soldier)			5184		1901
Sophia M.	31	SF	2491		1900
HERRIS					
Caroline	<1	SF	3179		1870
Francis	5	SF	1076		1869
HERRMANN					
Conrad	49	GER	5993Jan		1901
George	<1	SF	8179		1903
HERRON					
Azariah (soldier)			9565		1901
Hager	44	TN	1149		1869
Sarah Louisa	62	IRL	3784		1900
Thomas	41	CAN	1820		1870
William/Alice A., c/o	<1	CA	4114		1902
HERSAM					
Grace D.	32	NH	8484		1901
HERSCHBERG					
Therese	<1	SF	209b		1871
HERSCHFIELD					
——		SF	3127		1870

NAME	AGE OR YOB.	BIRTH PLACE	CERT. NO	ID	DEATH YEAR
HERSCHLER					
May Ann	29	CA	5294		1902
HERSEE					
George	47	ENG	110a		1871
HERSEY					
Arthur B. (soldier)			9119		1901
Elizabeth Peabody	1809	NH	2591c		1904
HERSFELD					
Clara Sophia	<1	SF	521b		1872
HERSH					
——			1938		1866
Dr. E. W.	35	GER	H11		1886
HERSHFIELD					
Roger Herbert	1	SF	3373		1894
HERT					
Dorathea	76	ALS	5136		1903
Katherine	62	GER	6108		1903
HERTAL					
Jacob	17	GER	1063		1869
HERTEL					
Edward August	44	GER	1187b		1871
Elyse	72	GER	1599		1894
HERTEMAN					
Eugene	42	FRA	1450b		1872
HERTENSTEIN					
William J. (soldier)			8630		1904
HERTH					
Charles	35	GER	34b		1871
HERTIG					
Michael	49	GER	358		1902
HERTING					
Henry	44	GER	6140		1903

Key: a = 1st part of year; b = 2nd part of year;
c = death certificate copy; c/o = child of

NAME	AGE OR YOB.	BIRTH PLACE	CERT. NO	ID	DEATH YEAR	NAME	AGE OR YOB.	BIRTH PLACE	CERT. NO	ID	DEATH YEAR
HERTY						Alfred Herbert	29	SF	9149		1901
Sarah Ann	3	SF	2971		1873	Gotleibe	55	GER	1409		1869
HERTZ						**HERZOY**					
Caroline	72	GER	3775		1896	Mary	44	GER	2347		1873
Charles	1	SF	1889		1870	**HESKETH**					
Peter	26	DEN	1947b		1895	Cathrine	<1	SF	3344		1870
HERTZEL						Hester B.	<1	SF	4909		1902
George W.				Nov	1898	Irene	16	SF	2001		1894
May Virginia	39	WI	664		1902	Joseph E.	33	SF	5639		1902
HERV?						Joseph Henry	59	NY	4367		1896
Elmer	2	SF	5196a		1895	Mary	33	ENG	4527b		1870
HERVAGAULT						Mary Theresa	28	SF	4235		1896
Clemence M.	49	FRA	6082		1896	**HESKETT**					
HERVE						Catherine				Jul	1899
Aurora	1859	SF	1245c		1904	James T. (soldier)			278		1901
Charles Francis	<1	SF	1358b		1872	**HESLEP**					
Mary E.	<1	SF	3679		1896	Judge A. M.	85	PA	H86		1885
HERWIG						**HESPE**					
Christine	<1	SF	6705a		1895	Susanna	36	SF	422		1900
HERY						**HESPICH**					
Joseph M.	65	GER	2340b		1895	Marie Isabelle Artemise	14	MN	2271		1903
HERZBERG						**HESS**					
——		SF	4312b		1870	Andrew J.	55	MD	H26		1883
——		SF	1441		1869	Benjamin Lintner				Aug	1898
Barbra Christina	21	CA	879		1902	Bernard W./Bertha, c/o		SF	864		1895
Christian	35	HAN	4042b		1870	Chas	39	CA	4765		1903
Christian				Oct	1898	Christian	1	SF	792a		1871
Julia	63	GER	4288		1901	Edward	9	SF	985		1870
Solomon	91	GER	8100		1903	Edward				Dec	1899
Zeppe Hinda	58	RUS	5395		1896	Elizabeth	38	GER	515		1870
HERZO						Emily	1	SF	877		1866
Anna				Mar	1900	Francisca	73	GER	15b		1871
HERZOG						George	1	SF	903b		1871
——		SF	1178		1869	George B.	72	MD	6018		1903

Key: *a = 1st part of year; b = 2nd part of year;*
c = death certificate copy; c/o = child of

NAME	AGE OR YOB.	BIRTH PLACE	CERT. NO	ID	DEATH YEAR
Helena				Feb	1900
Jacob	67	GER	5390		1903
James W.			1288		1903
Lewis	67	LA	937		1903
Luther P.	58	IN	5451	Jan	1901
Margareta	96	GER	3948		1902
Mary	15	GER	6441		1867
Mathilde	70	GER	2627		1901
Rebecca	24	HAN	331		1870
Robert	3	SF	5458		1867
Rosa Anna				Oct	1899
Sarah	44	CA	3414		1900
HESSE					
Anna	37	CA	3997	Dec	1901
Frank	41	GER	4590		1896
Julius	64		2360c		1904
HESSEL					
Amelia	83	BAV	829		1902
HESSELMEYER					
Theodore	85	GER	4346		1896
HESSEN					
A., c/o		CA	2000		1873
HESSIAN					
Patrick	<1	SF	1133		1869
Richard	45	CA	763		1903
HESSION					
John Martin Valentine	37	SF	7839		1901
Patrick/Mary, c/o		SF	5470		1902
Robert H.	42	SF	84		1901
HESSLER					
John				Oct	1899
Lilly	40	SF	6993		1904
Wm.	68	GER	1603		1894

NAME	AGE OR YOB.	BIRTH PLACE	CERT. NO	ID	DEATH YEAR
HESTER					
John Martin	<1	SF	2139a		1872
Luella Craven	27	CA	8498		1903
Mary	35	IRE	4995		1903
HESTHAL					
Bertha	40	GER	9034		1901
Mary M.	80	GER	7587		1902
HESTILOW					
Charles (soldier)			2068		1901
HETHE					
Francis	42	VA	542		1866
HETHERINGTON					
Elizabeth	82	IRL	5113		1901
Joseph	50	MI	4206		1900
HETHRINGTON					
John	56	ENG	2531		1894
HETNIAN					
Charles	29	GER	295b		1872
HETSCH					
Carl	30	GER	1159		1869
HETTICH					
Francis J.	3	SF	228a		1871
HETTINGER					
Charles	57	GER	6328		1896
Margaret	59	GER	5846		1904
HETTLE					
Annie	64	IRE	4373		1902
Celia Irene	20	SF	1949b		1895
HETTRICH					
Caroline L.	47	NY	2341b		1895
HETTY					
Louis B.	39	CA	179		1900

Key: a = 1st part of year; b = 2nd part of year;
c = death certificate copy; c/o = child of

NAME	AGE OR YOB.	BIRTH PLACE	CERT. NO	ID	DEATH YEAR	NAME	AGE OR YOB.	BIRTH PLACE	CERT. NO	ID	DEATH YEAR
HETZEL						HEUSSLER					
Edward Charles	44	PA	314		1903	Rosina	88	SWT	864		1903
Edward/Isabel, c/o		SF	7959		1903						
						HEUSSMANN					
HETZER						John C.	43	GER	2665		1902
Katherine	54	GER	8665		1904						
Marjorie Grace				Dec	1899	HEUSTEN					
						Jacob	34	SWT	2371		1873
HEUBACH											
Ellen	75	IRE	6107		1903	HEUTERKIS					
						John	69	GER	1286		1869
HEUCK											
Edward	42	GER	1975a		1872	HEVERIN					
Herman H.	52	GER	3271a		1872	Michael	70	ENG	214b		1895
						HEVRIN					
HEUER						Annie Aileen	1	SF	7870		1903
Philip	62	GER	6103		1896						
Philip	62	GER	5574		1896	HEW					
						Chock				Jul	1898
HEUERMANN						Fat Toy	<1	SF	3466		1900
George Adolph	1	SF	2361		1901	Fook	38	CHN	5168		1904
Veronica Adelaide	1903	SF	1246c		1904	Won	32	CHN	3262		1873
HEUFNER						HEWER					
Otto Charles	59	GER	7708		1904	George	1	SF	9796		1868
						W.	82	ENG	2775a		1872
HEUPEDEN						William	45	ENG	5525		1902
Franz	<1	SF	4149a		1895						
						HEWITT					
HEURCUX						Daniel W.	66	NY	4699		1896
Chas./Josephine, c/o	<1	CA	4170		1901	Isaac Lathrop	88	NY	9081		1901
						Jennie	28	NY	1046		1866
HEUREUX						John James	30	IRL	3017		1900
Edward	62	CAN	6724		1896	Joseph A.	44	ENG	6736		1900
						Mary Rebecca	60	ENG	6486		1904
HEURIKUN						Paul	1	SF	1422		1869
Sarah				Feb	1899	Sarah Ella	53	ME	2015		1903
HEURY											
John				Feb	1899	HEWLETT					
						Palma Baker	76	NY	3374		1896
HEUSCH											
Chas.	44	GER	H40		1883	HEWRY					
						Wm.	50	IRL	H91		1885
HEUSIER											
Henry	69	GER	1126		1901						

NAME	AGE OR YOB.	BIRTH PLACE	CERT. NO	ID	DEATH YEAR
HEWSON					
Bell	36	CA	4504		1903
Caroline S.	2	SF	780		1894
Conrad	51	IRE	94		1902
Lillie	1841	WV	1637c		1904
Martin	47	NS	1037		1870
Selby D., Jr.	5	SF	3200		1902
HEWSTON					
Emily	68	DE	1600		1894
Emmett Roland	35	SF	2983		1903
Jennie	48	PA	9530		1901
L. B.	58	VA	3871		1867
Robert James	<1	SF	1531		1902
HEXANDRINE					
Bernou F.	34	FRA	346		1865
HEXTER					
Fannie	68	GER	8047		1900
Kaufman	69	GER	3192		1895
HEXTROM					
Herman/Emma, c/o	1	SF	1565		1903
HEY					
——	1	SF	1399		1869
Amelia	43	OH	4312		1901
Fred	54	GER	3826a		1895
HEYBAND					
Patrick	39	IRE	1087		1869
HEYDENABER					
Adelia	1904	SF	2895c		1904
Henry G.	1	SF	1060		1903
HEYDENFELDT					
Ima Octreigh	28	CA	5439		1902
HEYDENINCH					
Emil	39	NY	8018		1900

NAME	AGE OR YOB.	BIRTH PLACE	CERT. NO	ID	DEATH YEAR
HEYDENREICH					
W.	60	GER	H186		1889
HEYDEURICH					
Caroline					Aug 1898
HEYEN					
Hannah	62	IRL	1211		1900
John	65	GER	5183		1903
HEYER					
John A.	1867	GER	489c		1904
HEYERMANN					
Charles/Bridget, c/o	<1	SF	3786		1900
Frederick	39	CA	8597		1903
HEYFRON					
Ellen	70	IRL	3018		1900
Margaret	78	IRE	2799		1903
HEYL					
George	72	GER	1424		1901
HEYMAN					
Jacob	66	GER	7848		1904
Leopold	24	PRU	8388		1868
Sluva	84	GER	5727		Jan 1901
HEYMANN					
Edmund	55	GER	8351		1901
HEYMANS					
Alexander					Oct 1899
HEYN					
Ernest					Jun 1899
HEYNEMANN					
Edward	54	GER	1059b		1895
Hermann	70	GER	843		1902
Louis	75	GER	4925		1896
HEYWOOD					
Annie A.	1	SF	4444b		1870

Key: a = 1st part of year; b = 2nd part of year;
c = death certificate copy; c/o = child of

NAME	AGE OR YOB.	BIRTH PLACE	CERT. NO	ID	DEATH YEAR
HI					
Ah	51	CHN	5478		1867
Gong	26	CHN	1574		1870
Kew Young	55	CHN	5564	Jan	1901
Lee	59	CHN	6751		1904
HIALTE					
Charles (soldier)			7377		1900
HIARTDAHL					
Sophie				Mar	1899
HIATT					
Ella	36	CA	3914		1903
HIBBARD					
Ellen	2	OR	2022		1870
Harry G.				Jan	1900
Minerva	59	KY	5749a		1895
HIBBERT					
Florence E.	30	CA	7503		1904
Irene J.	1	SF	2822		1873
HIBBETTS					
Jacob R.				Aug	1899
HIBBINS					
George Leslie	1904	CA	1933c		1904
HIBBS					
Frank T.				Feb	1900
HIBINO					
Masaji	28	JPN	3322		1900
HICK					
Philip S.				Jan	1900
HICKCI					
Lily Frances	<1	SF	650b		1872
HICKCOY					
Edward G.	62		2440		1866

NAME	AGE OR YOB.	BIRTH PLACE	CERT. NO	ID	DEATH YEAR
HICKEL					
O. H./L., c/o			1387		1894
HICKEN					
___		SF	730		1870
HICKERSON					
Mary/ Joseph, c/o		CA	183		1901
HICKEY					
Catherine	50	IRL	5630		1896
Catherine	1837	IRE	228c		1904
Catherine E.	76	MO	4404		1901
David	34	IRL	1547		1870
Elizabeth	<1	CA	1368		1869
Elizabeth	53	IRL	4832		1896
Emmet	29	CA	6228		1902
Emmett	38	NY	6410		1896
Helen	40	IRE	3009		1903
James	54	NB	6276		1903
James (soldier)			8791		1901
John	61	ENG	4185		1896
John J.	61	NY	8809		1901
John/Margaret, c/o		SF	5168		1896
Josephine	30	MA	7281		1900
Julia Mary	34	SF	1089		1903
Julia T.	26	IRL	5309a		1895
Kate	75	IRL	6962	Feb	1901
Leslie	<1	SF	7727		1903
Margaret	35	IRL	1744b		1872
Maria	68	MA	4723		1903
Mary	72	IRL	6408		1896
Mary Ann	52	IRE	6434		1904
Michael	38	IRL	5530	Jan	1901
Nellie M.	25	CA	2294		1900
Nora	48	IRE	7960		1903
Patrick				Aug	1899
Patrick	1864	CAN	675c		1904

Key: *a = 1st part of year; b = 2nd part of year; c = death certificate copy; c/o = child of*

NAME	AGE OR YOB.	BIRTH PLACE	CERT. NO	ID	DEATH YEAR	NAME	AGE OR YOB.	BIRTH PLACE	CERT. NO	ID	DEATH YEAR
Sarah	63	IRE	760		1902	Mary	21	CA	7565		1900
Thomas	2	CA	3014		1866	Thomas	36	ENG	3222a		1872
						Thomas J.	40	PA	1852b		1895
HICKLING						William	44	NY	396a		1871
Charles E.	28	ENG	3468		1900	Wyatt G. (soldier)			5048		1901
HICKMAN						**HICKSON**					
David C. (soldier)			6478		1904	Francis	1	SF	1740		1866
E. R.	31	FL	2874		1866	Henry	1	SF	6500		1868
George	<1	SF	2730a		1872	Julia Frances	67	MA	5489		1903
H.	42	DE	2021		1866	**HICKSTEDT**					
HICKMANN						Herman C.	56	GER	520		1902
Katherine	38	IN	8598		1903	**HIDALGO**					
HICKMON						Conception	35	MEX	4407b		1870
Alice	1	CA	5147		1867	**HIDALJO**					
HICKOK						Manuel	35	CHL	1424		1869
Sarah	50	SF	1058		1894	**HIDEYE**					
Virginia A.				Jul	1899	Hori	24	JPN	6680		1896
William B.	79	NY	1566		1903	**HIDNER**					
HICKOX						John				Jan	1899
Frank B.				May	1899	**HIE**					
Geo. C.	71	OH	121		1902	Ten	19	CHN	947		1870
John Henry	80	OH	1633		1900	**HIEBBS**					
Wesley	<1	SF	120b		1872	Ida M.	46	NY	7871		1903
HICKS						**HIEGEL**					
Charles W.	6	NV	5396		1896	Frank A.				Aug	1899
Daniel Dean	2	CA	5596		1867	**HIELDEBRAND**					
Edward	43	PA	4531		1901	Fabian	34	GER	6435		1867
Edwin S.	<1	SF	5585		1867	**HIENDS**					
Gertmide	<1	SF	454		1870	Margaret	38	IRL	2083		1873
Ivan			3711		1902	**HIENSEN**					
John Francis	<1	SF	1477a		1871	Charles/Emily, c/o	<1	SF	2664		1902
Josephine	<1	SF	8925		1868	**HIEP**					
Leslie L.			1289		1903	Fernand				Dec	1899
Lilly				Nov	1898						
Margaret	53	ENG	H71		1885						

Key: a = 1st part of year; b = 2nd part of year;
c = death certificate copy; c/o = child of

NAME	AGE OR YOB.	BIRTH PLACE	CERT. NO	ID	DEATH YEAR	NAME	AGE OR YOB.	BIRTH PLACE	CERT. NO	ID	DEATH YEAR
HIERNICHEL						**HIGGINBOTHAM**					
Valentine				Jan	1899	George B.	38	IRL	2794		1873
HIESTANT						**HIGGINS**					
Barbara	74	GER	7482		1904	——			3058		1866
HIESTER						——			5508		1867
Amos C.	59	OH	2391b		1895	——			5888		1867
Elwood Clinton	39	OH	4910		1902	——	<1	SF	1077		1869
Lily	29	SF	9593		1901	——	<1	SF	1422		1869
HIETLAND						Agnes	1	SF	4999		1904
Mary	69	SCT	8058		1901	Anita Augusta	2	SF	4042		1900
HIETSCHER						Anna E.	63	NY	5195a		1895
Christian	55	GER	H157		1887	Arthur	19	CA	6020a		1895
HIGAN						Benjamin F.				Oct	1898
James (soldier)			6820		1900	Bernard	38	IRE	8801		1868
HIGBEE						Bridget	51	IRL	3368	Nov	1901
Earl	1	SF	3414		1903	Bridget	75	IRL	8596		1901
James T.	55	NJ	5249		1867	Caroline	54	PE	2399		1894
Samuel	1900	CA	2439c		1904	Edward	<1	SF	58b		1871
Thornton	1972	MO	2674c		1904	Edward			H126		1886
Thornton/Lizzie, c/o		SF	1099		1901	Edward H.	10	CA	1038		1868
HIGBIE						Edward M.	30	SF	6007	Jan	1901
Alfred	86	NY	1723		1901	Edward Peter				Mar	1900
						Ellen	45	IRE	6589		1868
HIGBY						Ellen	70	IRL	1096		1894
Ephram B.	74	NY	765		1901	Esther	30	CA	4610		1901
Jeanette	<1	SF	276b		1895	Eugene D.	4	SF	2316		1866
HIGEL						Frank J.	32	CA	H175		1889
Alois				Oct	1898	Harry L. (soldier)			3045	Oct	1901
HIGGANS						Hellen	<1	SF	3418b		1870
James J. (soldier)			6828		1900	Isabelle	27	SF	4480		1904
HIGGENS						James	53	PE	2992		1894
Ellen	<1	SF	1045		1868	James H.				Aug	1899
Janes	47	IRL	423		1900	James J.				Mar	1900
						James W. (soldier)	32	CT	6779		1904
						Jas.	35	MA	H73		1885

Key: a = 1st part of year; b = 2nd part of year; c = death certificate copy; c/o = child of

NAME	AGE OR YOB.	BIRTH PLACE	CERT. NO	ID	DEATH YEAR	NAME	AGE OR YOB.	BIRTH PLACE	CERT. NO	ID	DEATH YEAR
Jennie A.				Feb	1900	Patrick	33	ENG	5371		1867
Jennie M.	1868	CA	2952c		1904	Patrick	<1	SF	5748		1867
John	50	CA	3686		1903	Patrick C.	57	IRL	7838		1901
John M.	9	SF	6277		1903	Richard	35	IL	879b		1895
John N.			28		1901	Richard	47	IRL	5373a		1895
John/Jennie, c/o	1904	SF	2852		1904	Robert	34	IL	3720	Nov	1901
Joseph	<1	SF	866b		1895	Rose	41	IRL	6935	Feb	1901
Joseph A.	13	CA	1033		1868	Sertins H.	1	SF	2703		1866
Joseph B.				Jan	1899	T./A., c/o	<1	SF	2440		1894
Joseph F.			2413		1866	Thomas				Jan	1899
Joseph H.	33	CA	4157		1903	William	1	SF	213b		1872
Kate	<1	SF	2867		1894	William	82	IRL	4494a		1895
Katie	29	IRL	3396		1896	William	65	IRL	951		1900
Kattie	52	IL	1202		1894	William				Dec	1898
Lewis	<1	SF	1837		1866	William J.	<1	SF	2354		1866
Lewis				Nov	1898	William J.	<1	SF	7793		1868
Lottie	30	SF	2161b		1895	William L. (soldier)			6400		1900
Margaret	7	SF	2932		1873	Winifred	62	IRL	3694		1896
Margaret	<1	CA	5531		1867	Winnifred				Feb	1899
Margaret	66	IRE	6151		1902	Wm.	48	IRL	H38		1883
Mark Joseph	<1	SF	424b		1872	Wm. J.	38	SF	2326		1903
Mary	<1	SF	3114		1873	**HIGGINSON**					
Mary	48	IRL	2506b		1895	Carrie A.				Jul	1898
Mary	52	IRL	1657b		1895	Margaret	24	IRE	7142		1904
Mary	80	IRL	112b		1895	Mary Elizabeth	40	NY	1258		1894
Mary	60	IRL	5425		1896	Richard H.	57	ENG	480		1902
Mary				Jan	1900	Sarah Ethel	11	SF	1257		1894
Mary Ann				Jul	1898	Thomas/Marg., c/o	<1	CA	7143		1904
Mary Christina				Nov	1898	**HIGGS**					
Mary E.	44	MD	1677b		1871	Alice	16	SF	4682		1902
Mary E.	36	SF	2353		1900	Benj. Frank	72	OH	6560?		1901
Mary Isabell				Aug	1899	Henry Geo.	13	SF	1204		1869
Maurice	1849	IRE	1876c		1904	**HIGH**					
Michael	40	IRL	1717b		1871	Henry	1834	GER	876c		1904
Michael	60	IRL	727		1901	Wm.	24	PA	H109		1886
Monica Justinia	42	AUS	4118		1900						

Key: *a = 1st part of year; b = 2nd part of year; c = death certificate copy; c/o = child of*

NAME	AGE OR YOB.	BIRTH PLACE	CERT. NO	ID	DEATH YEAR	NAME	AGE OR YOB.	BIRTH PLACE	CERT. NO	ID	DEATH YEAR
HIGHET						**HILDEBRAND**					
Charles				Mar	1899	Anna				Jul	1899
HIGHFIELD						Anna B.	35	CA	2444		1903
William (soldier)	31	IL	3515		1900	Annie G.	1	SF	5363		1867
HIGHLAND						Auguste	28	GER	1846		1866
Edward I. (soldier)			1462		1901	B. J.				Nov	1899
HIGHLEY						Christine	26	GER	8660		1868
Bernard G. (soldier)			4552		1901	Conrad	32	GER	5719a		1895
HIGHTOWER						Conrad	51	GER	243		1901
Helen M.	<1	SF	6367	Feb	1901	George	54	GER	8027		1903
HIGUERA						Gustav C.				Nov	1899
Emidio Samuel	35	CA	1406		1903	Hans	65	PRU	1694		1870
HIILLMANTEL						Henrietta	56	GER	H21		1882
Caroline	1836	GER	1426c		1904	Jennie	20	OR	4372		1901
HILAND						John				May	1899
John Harold	<1	SF	3191		1895	Lillian Annie	<1	SF	7835		1903
HILARITA						**HILDEBRANDEN**					
——	<1	CA	4600		1903	Mary F.	<1	SF	3568		1867
HILBERT						**HILDEBRANDT**					
Edward/Florence, c/o		SF	4001		1900	——		SF	876		1870
John C.				Jul	1899	Adolph R.				Aug	1899
John J.	<1	SF	7455		1868	Dora	76	GER	6652		1902
HILBERTSEIMER						Edward	62	GER	7939		1904
Peter	37	GER	1357b		1871	Fred	46	GER	2133		1902
HILBON						Henry	58	GER	4493a		1895
Franklin Charles	14	SF	5347		1904	J. Henry	2	SF	990b		1871
HILBOURN						Louisa	35	SF	6575	Feb	1901
James A.	33	IA	5080		1902	Margaretha	1839	GER	2896c		1904
HILCKER						Martin	28	PRU	1192		1869
Charles	32	GER	8163		1903	**HILDENBRAND**					
HILD						Dorodess		SF	1055		1866
Elizabeth	7	SF	5972	Jan	1901	Margaret E.				Jul	1899
Ellen				Mar	1899	Michael	52	FRA	1631b		1871
						HILDERBRANK					
						H.	22	GER	H46		1883

Key: a = 1st part of year; b = 2nd part of year; c = death certificate copy; c/o = child of

NAME	AGE OR YOB.	BIRTH PLACE	CERT. NO	ID	DEATH YEAR
HILDRETH					
Concheta	2	SF	5944		1903
Kate G.	27	NY	4492b		1870
HILE					
John J.	21	NY	8852		1868
HILES					
Bartholen	1872	CA	1264c		1904
HILEZ					
Charles F.				Feb	1900
HILGENBERG					
Julius	<1	SF	1517b		1895
HILKEN					
Johann F. A.	<1	SF	3432		1867
HILKEPEL					
J. T.	60	GER	H69		1885
HILL					
Agnes G.	52	IRE	5470		1903
Alice F.	37	CA	2832		1902
Andrew E.	28	NY	1101b		1871
Anna L.				Oct	1899
Annie	77	NJ	4794		1902
Augusta C.	70	NH	3583		1903
Benjamin S.	54	ME	5812		1902
Capt. John	52	NY	787		1870
Catharine	42	IRL	777		1870
Catherine	62	IRE	574		1902
Charles	72	IRE	1304		1869
Charles	<1	SF	2351		1894
Charles E.	40	ME	2138		1873
Charles S.				May	1899
Charles S./Florence T., c/o	<1	SF	1422		1902
Clarence (soldier)			274		1901
Dunaus	33	ME	281a		1871
Edith E.	3	CA	9155		1868

NAME	AGE OR YOB.	BIRTH PLACE	CERT. NO	ID	DEATH YEAR
Edward B./Florence, c/o	1	CA	865		1903
Elizabeth	30	PA	1436		1869
Ella	40	NY	706		1900
Ellen M.	35	LA	7321		1868
Elvira B.	64	NY	1854b		1895
Ethel	15	CA	7277		1903
Evelyn C.	37	MA	1362		1869
Frank A.			3547		1900
Frank E.	30	MA	6936	Feb	1901
Frank I.				Dec	1898
Fred H.	28	PA	1831b		1872
Fred R.	27	IRL	989		1870
George A.	78	MA	1187		1902
George F.	48	NY	1837		1903
George O. (soldier)			2159		1901
George W.	71	DE	5741a		1895
Godfrey S.	65	SCT	8603		1904
Harriet Lawrence				Jul	1898
Harry	30	ME	H48		1883
Harry S.	<1	SF	7421		1868
Helma	30	SWE	61		1902
Henry	27	NOR	2099		1873
Henry	69	IRE	7104		1903
Henry F. (soldier)			7773		1902
J.	55	IRL	H88		1885
James	40	IRE	9614		1868
James	70	SCT	145		1902
James				Nov	1899
James A.	48	ENG	4271		1867
James F. J.	3	SF	3823		1867
James S.	76	ENG	6232		1904
James T. (soldier)			8432		1900
James V.				Jul	1899
Jennie	76	OH	5453		1904
Jennie				Dec	1898
John				Dec	1899

NAME	AGE OR YOB.	BIRTH PLACE	CERT. NO	ID	DEATH YEAR	NAME	AGE OR YOB.	BIRTH PLACE	CERT. NO	ID	DEATH YEAR
John A.	37	ME	1422		1869	Sarah	48	IRL	1392a		1871
John H.	30	ENG	2421		1873	Sarah E.	1	SF	8425		1868
John J.	32		79c		1904	Sidney Stanton	<1	CA	3535		1896
John J.				May	1899	Stephen (soldier)			4204	Dec	1901
John P. (soldier)			4553		1901	Thomas	41	MA	7952		1868
Joseph (marine)			5009		1903	Thomas	58	IRL	8762		1900
Joseph C.	32	ME	6975		1868	Thomas F.	1	SF	6161		1867
Joseph H.	4	SF	1311		1866	Timothy W.	20	VT	4015a		1895
Joseph P.	1	SF	6854		1868	Wilhelm H.	32	GER	1523a		1871
Josie	32	SF	5091		1902	William C.	40	USA	1437		1869
Lawrence	1904	CA	3235c		1904	William G.	35	CA	5646		1904
Lee Mum		CHN	7326		1868	William H.	43	SF	3178		1902
Leonard	45	NY	9408		1868	Wm. J.				Mar	1900
Leslie				Feb	1899	**HILLABRAND**					
Louis B.	32		4323		1902	George				Aug	1898
Lucretia	19	CA	9918		1868	**HILLANDBRADT**					
Margaret Mary	48	TN	1532		1902	C./F., c/o		SF	2118		1894
Marian Mercer	68	NJ	5602	Jan	1901	**HILLARD**					
Mark			6226		1903	Benjamin	65	VA	1141		1894
Marlen				Mar	1900	Charles	75	SWT	3737	Nov	1901
Mary	67	IRE	5293		1902	Frank	20	MD	2002		1873
Mary	51	IRL	1636		1894	Kathyrine Hampton	21	VA	1707		1900
Mary A.	57	IRE	4631		1904	Ruth Mildred	2	CA	5790		1902
Mary A.	70	IRL	4166a		1895	Virginia Lee	6	SF	179b		1872
Mary Annie	27	OR	7519		1902	**HILLASHIP**					
Mary E.	75	ME	407		1901	Alfred	15	ENG	3430b		1870
Mary E.				Oct	1898	**HILLEAGUIRE**					
Maud	34	ENG	2251		1903	John	5	SF	1090		1869
Myra K.	29	ME	9486		1868	**HILLEBRAND**					
N. S./B., c/o				Oct	1899	Rosa				Oct	1898
Nellie	17	SF	3631		1896	**HILLEBRANDT**					
Norman Clark	<1	SF	8219		1904	Johan H. H. C.	<1	SF	1702b		1872
Ormonde David	<1	SF	8220		1904	**HILLEHANDT**					
Phebee B.	12	CAN	1644		1901	Heinrich				Mar	1900
Sadie P.				Nov	1898						
Samuel	28	PA	196		1870						

Key: a = 1st part of year; b = 2nd part of year;
c = death certificate copy; c/o = child of

NAME	AGE OR YOB.	BIRTH PLACE	CERT. NO	ID	DEATH YEAR
HILLELL					
John I.	1	SF	283		1865
HILLEN					
Florence E.	24	CA	H51		1884
HILLENBRAND					
Edward	62	GER	566		1903
HILLENBRANDT					
M./H., c/o					Dec 1898
HILLENS					
Minnie Elizabeth	9	SF	7250		1901
HILLER					
John H.	1	SF	1195		1869
Matthias	33	GER	8475		1903
Moses	48	NY	2972		1866
Nath	50	MA	H9		1882
HILLERY					
Maude Ethelda	<1	SF	1522b		1872
HILLIARD					
Eunice S.	76	PA	5707		1904
John	65	NH	1873		1870
Josie	<1	SF	2385a		1872
Millie	35	NY	33b		1895
HILLING					
Nathaniel B.	25	IL	2330		1866
HILLIS					
James	50	IRL	5082a		1895
Mark A. (soldier)			6323		1900
HILLMAN					
Abigail					Oct 1898
Henry	53	NOR	H146		1887
Henry	43	GER	1247		1866
Henry					May 1899
Henry C. (soldier)			8788		1901
Jane	31	ENG	1481b		1895

NAME	AGE OR YOB.	BIRTH PLACE	CERT. NO	ID	DEATH YEAR
Jennie	1	SF	4481		1867
John	30	NOR	8750		1900
John	59	GER	7861		1901
Regina Henrietta	39	PA	3426a		1872
HILLMINTH					
Nelly					Jul 1899
HILLS					
——		SF	1238		1869
Edward M.	46	NY	7083		1904
Frank M.	51	MA	6845		1904
Henry	35	ENG	789		1870
Isiah R.	49	ENG	4534b		1870
Jennie	16	CA	7807		1900
John Joseph	<1	SF	730b		1872
Mary /Edward, c/o	1904	CA	467		1904
HILLYARD					
John			6198		1903
HILLYER					
Carrie W.					Jun 1899
James	35	ENG	2146		1900
HILMER					
Charles Henry Ludwig	69	GER	5295		1901
HILNE					
Peter W. (soldier)			6259		1900
HILPERT					
John E.	48	NY	1969		1903
HILPISCH					
Carl Otto	1872	GER	2779c		1904
Jacob	52	GER	4911		1901
HILRATH					
George	<1	SF	1206		1869
HILS					
Frederick Albert	<1	SF	421b		1871
Herman H.					Dec 1898

NAME	AGE OR YOB.	BIRTH PLACE	CERT. NO	ID	DEATH YEAR
HILSKA					
Paul	27	FIN	3780		1902
HILSZ					
Fred	57	GER	3840		1902
HILTON					
Benjamin	26	NY	5117		1903
C. W.	30	NY	6187		1867
Charles B.				Nov	1899
Florence Louise	7	CA	6425		1896
Henry	29	ME	9744		1868
Henry/Kate, c/o				Mar	1899
Lydia A.	70	ME	6886		1903
Stanford	74	ME	37		1903
HILTS					
Nettie	11	CA	1011b		1871
HILTZINGER					
Gottlieb	52	SWT	3968	Dec	1901
HIM					
Ah	36	CHN	2087a		1872
Ah	16	CHN	9382		1868
HIMBERT					
Bertha	<1	SF	1287		1894
Bertha	<1	SF	1292		1894
Hans	10	SF	7346		1900
HIMEBAUGH					
Agnes E.	56	ME	8195		1904
HIMENBERG					
Georg	46	GER	3387		1902
HIMES					
Howard/Evochia, c/o	<1	SF	5030		1896
HIMMELBERGER					
Oliver (soldier)			2073		1901
HIMMELMANN					
H. W./M., c/o		SF	2946		1895

NAME	AGE OR YOB.	BIRTH PLACE	CERT. NO	ID	DEATH YEAR
Henry W./Nellie, c/o		SF	9162		1901
William D.	31	SF	6684		1900
HIMMELSTERN					
Gerald J.	1	SF	3142		1903
HIMND					
Graham				Dec	1899
HIN					
Ah	2	SF	4294b		1870
Ah	30	CHN	2689		1866
Ah	44	CHN	4242		1867
J.	50	CHN	3210		1873
Sevi	45	CHN	1132		1869
Tong Chung	35	CHN	1258b		1871
HINCH					
John	33	GER	170b		1872
Richard	45	CAN	2960		1900
HINCHIOSE					
Ellen	65	IRE	9435		1868
HINCHMAN					
C. H./Hettie, c/o	<1	SF	2050		1902
HINCK					
Henry J.	58	GER	8901		1900
Lorenz	1840	GER	2265c		1904
HINCKEN					
Elias J. (soldier)			946		1901
HINCKLEY					
Ezra				Apr	1899
Hannah Melzard	83	MA	7391		1901
Harry L.	<1	SF	1666a		1871
John	71	ME	1055		1902
L. E.	47	MA	1415		1869
Mildred	16	CA	2468		1900
HINCKLY					
Alvah C.	1	AUT	7087		1868

Key: a = 1st part of year; b = 2nd part of year;
c = death certificate copy; c/o = child of

NAME	AGE OR YOB.	BIRTH PLACE	CERT. NO	ID	DEATH YEAR
Samuel A.	39	ME	1004		1868
HIND					
William P. A.	39	IA	521		1900
HINDE					
Charles Wm.	2	SF	2226		1873
HINDERS					
Wilhelmina	<1	SF	3376		1866
HINDES					
Jay Gordon	50	MD	4683		1902
Mary Frances	39	CA	2532		1900
HINDLE					
Frank Aliene	7	SF	2201		1900
Hannah				Mar	1899
HINDS					
Ellen Gertrude	46	MA	644		1902
Joseph M.			4029	Dec	1901
Sumner B.	42	ME	4478b		1870
Violet/Loring, c/o	1	SF	8416		1904
William	66	IRE	5813		1902
HINE					
Nelson	<1	SF	2525b		1895
HINES					
——		SF	1198		1869
Bridget	38	IRE	8623		1903
Frederick (soldier)			1129		1900
George	40	CA	3525		1903
J. C.				May	1899
John		SF	1135b		1895
John	85	IRL	6430a		1895
John				Feb	1899
John (soldier)			2164		1901
Joseph (soldier)			6827		1900
Mary	<1	SF	1156		1869
Mary Edith	<1	CA	551		1894

NAME	AGE OR YOB.	BIRTH PLACE	CERT. NO	ID	DEATH YEAR
Michael	30	NY	H92		1885
Michael	40	IRE	3027		1866
Wm. F.	36	MD	H78		1885
HING					
Ah	24	CHN	234b		1871
Ah		CHN	298b		1871
Ah	31	CHN	643b		1871
Ah	45	CHN	2509		1872
Ah	39	CHN	7633		1868
Ah	23	CHN	1513		1870
Hong	43	CHN	6261		1867
King	40	CHN	1724		1866
Lang	32	CHN	912		1870
Lee	20	CHN	4402b		1870
Louis				Jul	1899
Luie	28	CHN	775b		1871
Mun	34	CHN	214a		1871
Quong	29	CHN	2116		1873
Tjer	1861	CHN	2124c		1904
Wong	45	CHN	842		1866
Yee	29	CHN	3042a		1872
Yue	51	CHN	231b		1871
Yum	32	CHN	782b		1872
Yung	26	CHN	1922a		1872
Yung	<1	SF	2464		1873
HINGALL					
Anna	1	SF	1075		1869
HINGREN					
Gustaf A. (sailor)	42	FIN	6346		1904
HINK					
Carstus	<1	SF	3350		1894
Henry M.	35	GER	6033a		1895
HINKEL					
Elenora	<1	SF	3529a		1872
Joseph	42	SF	5730		1904

Key: a = 1st part of year; b = 2nd part of year; c = death certificate copy; c/o = child of

NAME	AGE OR YOB.	BIRTH PLACE	CERT. NO	ID	DEATH YEAR
Mary	43	ENG	5949		1867
Selby William	2	SF	813		1901
HINKELBUN					
Rose Marie	<1	OR	2471		1902
HINKLE					
Caspar Edward	34	AUT	6229		1902
Walter S.				Feb	1899
William Timothy	1	SF	2119		1901
HINKLEY					
Florence R.				Dec	1899
Geo. G.	47	MA	3532a		1895
Oliver	71	ME	7058	Feb	1901
HINKS					
Gael W. August	23	GER	633b		1871
HINKSON					
Addison C.	28	CA	7470		1903
HINMAN					
Anna M.	45	PA	2460		1902
HINN					
Ah	32	CHN	440		1866
HINNEMAN					
Olive	<1	CA	8039		1900
HINNS					
J. C. C.	<1	SF	1417		1866
HINPRING					
Israel	<1	SF	2542		1873
HINRICH					
Rudolph	67	GER	2870		1902
HINRICHS					
Claus J. C.	<1	SF	1872b		1895
Emil	1	SF	2771		1903
John F.				Nov	1898
William F.	33	CA	6972		1904

NAME	AGE OR YOB.	BIRTH PLACE	CERT. NO	ID	DEATH YEAR
HINSBERG					
Charles				May	1899
Theodore F.				Dec	1899
HINSCHEIN					
Helen	<1	SF	2930		1900
HINSDALE					
George S.	77	CT	7678		1900
HINSHAW					
Barbara	<1	SF	5668		1902
HINSMELRICK					
Edward				Apr	1899
HINSTER					
Lewis T.				Jul	1899
HINTEMANN					
Katherine Sophia A.	<1	SF	5033		1902
HINTERMAN					
Marcelly				Jan	1899
HINTERMANN					
Hilda Annie	7	SF	6339	Feb	1901
HINTON					
Mary Ella	<1	SF	6709		1868
William C.	<1	SF	3636	Nov	1901
HINTZEMAN					
George	55	FRA	5151		1867
HINZ					
August C.	1841	GER	277c		1904
Julia E. A.	41	SF	6063	Jan	1901
Margarethe A.	53	GER	3342		1895
Mary Jane	65	MD	6626		1903
HINZE					
Alice	23	SF	2339b		1895
HIPKENS					
Mary Jane				Feb	1899

Key: a = 1st part of year; b = 2nd part of year;
c = death certificate copy; c/o = child of

NAME	AGE OR YOB.	BIRTH PLACE	CERT. NO	ID	DEATH YEAR	NAME	AGE OR YOB.	BIRTH PLACE	CERT. NO	ID	DEATH YEAR
HIPKINS						Emily	53	GER	H116		1886
Jese Carr	2	NZL	1429		1900	Fanny	42	GER	471a		1871
						Gilton	2	SF	9095		1868
HIPPELY						James	<1	SF	324		1900
Charles Alexander	51	PA	4543		1904	Joseph	37	FRA	2721a		1872
HIPPERT						Joseph	74	GER	2434		1901
Margarthe					Dec 1899	Regina	70	NY	404		1903
HIPPLER						Solomon E.	65	GER	H115		1886
Charles L. (soldier)			1972		1900	**HIRSCHFELD**					
HIPPO						Dora					May 1899
Julia					Jan 1899	Emile	1867	ENG	1156c		1904
HIPPS						George J.	36	NY	5025		1904
David C.					Jul 1898	Louis	59	GER	33		1902
J.	33	CA	5788		Jan 1901	Walter	36	ENG	3516		1900
HIRAMOTO						**HIRSCHFELDER**					
Kaitaro	1869	JPN	646c		1904	A.			79		1870
HIRANO						Aaron	47	GER	6459		1867
B.					Jan 1899	Antone	60	POL	4833		1903
HIRASHI						Rosa	12	SF	250a		1871
Yoshinatsu/Rio, c/o	<1	SF	7801		1904	Samuel/Ada, c/o	1	SF	5679		1904
HIRAYAMA						**HIRSCHFIELD**					
T.	35	JPN	8990		1901	Peter	63	GER	205		1901
HIRD						Wiliam	76	BAV	223		1901
Ellen J.					Dec 1898	**HIRSCHMAN**					
Jane	87	IRE	173		1903	Jerome					Mar 1900
HIREAL						**HIRSCHPRING**					
Mary	85	IRL	8726		1900	Meyer	35	POL	1371		1869
HIRON						**HIRSHENSON**					
Matilda	4	FRA	456a		1871	David	1844	RUS	1045c		1904
Victor					Nov 1898	**HIRSHFELD**					
HIRREL						Emma	<1	SF	1299		1869
Sarah					Dec 1899	Herman	59	GER	2780		1902
HIRSCH						**HIRSINGER**					
Bruno	80	GER	7438		1903	Anna Maria					Jun 1899

Key: a = 1st part of year; b = 2nd part of year; c = death certificate copy; c/o = child of

NAME	AGE OR YOB.	BIRTH PLACE	CERT. NO	ID	DEATH YEAR	NAME	AGE OR YOB.	BIRTH PLACE	CERT. NO	ID	DEATH YEAR
HIRST						Florida Virginia	29	IL	1389		1869
Harry Herbert				Dec	1899	Hollis	75	CAN	3418		1896
						James	52	PA	3691	Nov	1901
HIRSTEL						James L.	71	NY	5933	Jan	1901
——			6940		1868	Martha				Aug	1899
Carrie	1	SF	6205		1867	William F.	5	SF	424		1870
Edward H.	45	FRA	7578		1868						
						HITCHCOX					
HIRT						Harry	62	ENG	5291		1904
Albert	55	GER	3467		1900						
Bonifacious				Apr	1899	**HITCHENS**					
Robert George	31	SF	3701		1900	Elisabeth	70	IRE	235		1903
Theobold				Mar	1900	**HITCHINGS**					
						William	21	PA	6035		1867
HIRTH											
Elizabeth H.	61	OH	3930		1900	**HITCHINS**					
Henry	39	GER	7604		1868	James Henry				Feb	1899
HIRVET						**HITEMAN**					
Mrs.	14	FRA	1109		1869	Lottie M.	1872	OR	1138c		1904
HIS						**HITMAN**					
Yen Ben				Oct	1899	Stella M.	<1	HI	1359		1901
HISA						**HITT**					
Toyota				Oct	1899	Wm. A.				Mar	1900
HISCOX						**HITTE**					
Margurete	29	CAN	405		1903	Mariette	45	FRA	6892	Feb	1901
HISGEN						**HITTELL**					
E. C.	50	NY	8769		1900	Elsie C.	71	GER	3973		1900
						George W.	33	CA	5013		1867
HISLOP						John S.	75	PA	6576	Feb	1901
Robert C.	13	SF	8871		1901						
						HITTICK					
HISSEY						Whilhemina	1	SF	1679		1866
Thomas				Oct	1898						
						HIVANEY					
HISSION						Patrick	33	IRL	1949b		1872
Patrick/Mary, c/o	<1	SF	2194		1902						
						HIXON					
HITCHCOCK						Arthur C.				Jul	1899
Edward				Aug	1899	O.		CA	614		1866
Edward A.				May	1899	Omri	36	CAN	668a		1871

Key: a = 1st part of year; b = 2nd part of year;
c = death certificate copy; c/o = child of

NAME	AGE OR YOB.	BIRTH PLACE	CERT. NO	ID	DEATH YEAR
HIXSON					
Walter D.	40	CA	5814		1902
HJEHN					
Andrew O.				Jan	1899
HJORTH					
Louis	65	DEN	5662	Jan	1901
HLAWIN					
Frank	62	AUT	3440		1900
HO					
Ah	40	CHN	1240b		1871
Ah	19	CHN	7061		1868
Ah	24	CHN	8688		1868
Back Chow				Feb	1899
Bow	45	CHN	62		1902
Chang Kuong				Jul	1898
Chin	22	CHN	1085		1870
Chin	32	CHN	145		1865
Chin	30	CHN	1163		1869
Chow	32	CHN	70		1870
Chu Hom	44	CHN	6348		1900
Chune	26	CHN	3165		1870
Dai	41	CHN	2075		1902
Fang				Mar	1899
Gee	41	CHN	6696a		1895
Hing	39	CHN	2533		1873
Hing	23	CHN	1812		1866
Hing Bong	47	CHN	2702		1902
Hoy	27	CHN	1138b		1895
Hue Lee	83	CHN	598b		1871
Hung	60	CHN	1533		1902
Kai				Oct	1899
Kim	35	CHN	3670a		1895
Leong Lei	75	CHN	5820a		1895
Lin	25	CHN	1273		1869
Ling	26	CHN	5063		1867

NAME	AGE OR YOB.	BIRTH PLACE	CERT. NO	ID	DEATH YEAR
Lup Wing				Aug	1899
Man Ngue	24	CHN	1503		1903
Mon Chin She	26	CHN	4682		1904
Mu				Jun	1899
Mun				Nov	1899
Nai	42	CHN	2283		1873
Nim	49	CHN	4804		1903
Non				Aug	1899
Ping She				Dec	1899
Poi Mon	41	CHN	3345		1873
Poy Tin	54	CHN	1388		1894
Qui	25	CHN	1637		1870
San Yuen				Mar	1900
Shee	40	CHN	6537		1896
Shee Tyng Un	26	CHN	2573		1873
Sin	28	CHN	183		1865
Sun	26	CHN	6993		1868
Tung	24	CHN	1204b		1872
Wan	22	CHN	1254		1869
Woey	59	CHN	6293		1902
Yan				Dec	1898
HOADES					
Thedore L.	<1	SF	3809		1870
HOADLEY					
Charles H.	31	SF	4305		1896
Milo/Catherine, c/o	<1	SF	6618		1901
HOAG					
Katherine				May	1899
S. Cushing	45	NY	1246b		1872
Sarah Ann	80	NY	2906		1900
Wm. C.				Mar	1900
Wm. I.	1	SF	4824a		1895
HOAGLAND					
Jane Van	66	NY	2951a		1872

Key: a = 1st part of year; b = 2nd part of year; c = death certificate copy; c/o = child of

NAME	AGE OR YOB.	BIRTH PLACE	CERT. NO	ID	DEATH YEAR
HOAGS					
Chas. R.	6	CA	H134		1886
HOAR					
Annie E.					May 1899
Joseph A.	24	NY	1573		1901
Martin	21	SF	992		1894
Sidney Francis (soldier)			2061		1901
Thomas (soldier)			8874		1900
HOARE					
Henry	53	ENG	380		1900
Julia	30	IRL	2974a		1872
Nicholas	<1	SF	746		1866
William H.	29	ENG	6359		1867
HOBAN					
Patrick					Oct 1898
HOBBS					
Benjamin	73	MA	3505		1896
Detlief/Catherina, c/o		SF	7598		1900
Edward	35	IRL	H174		1887
George	14	HI	9000		1868
Hiram H.	68	ME	7490		1900
John K. C., Jr.	2	SF	6536		1896
Walter (soldier)			9351		1901
HOBBY					
Leander (soldier)			7753		1901
HOBE					
George J.	74	GER	448		1900
Harriett	19	SF	4312a		1895
William F.	28	SF	5693		1902
HOBEM					
George W.					Jan 1899
HOBEN					
Henry	57	GER	5596		1896
HOBLEN					
Ann	65	ENG	4503		1867
HOBLES					
——			5548		1867
HOBRON					
Minerva S.					Feb 1899
HOBSON					
——	<1	SF	1368		1869
Alice M.					Nov 1899
Anna Pagel	20	CA	9032		1901
Charles (soldier)			7317		1901
Harry	47	ENG	1469		1900
John	1	SF	9395		1868
Lydia A.	24		1962b		1872
Martha A.	48	ENG	3609		1870
Mary B.	59	IRL	547a		1871
Sarah					Nov 1899
Thomas R.	51	ENG	8445		1903
HOCE					
Bridget	33	IRE	3790		1867
HOCH					
F. Henry August	<1	SF	1593b		1871
HOCHGASTEL					
Frederika	34	GER	6030		1867
HOCHREITER					
Maria	87	GER	1423		1901
HOCHSTADLER					
Jacob	42	GER	4691		1867
HOCHSTADTEN					
Maggie	46	NY	8920		1901
HOCHSTADTER					
Flora	3	CA	2871		1866
HOCK					
Conrad	58	GER	5292		1896

Key: a = 1st part of year; b = 2nd part of year;
c = death certificate copy; c/o = child of

NAME	AGE OR YOB.	BIRTH PLACE	CERT. NO	ID	DEATH YEAR
John	30	GER	1112		1869
Lizzie	14	HI	502		1901
Ruth	<1	CA	3121		1902
HOCKER					
Alonzo C. (soldier)			302		1902
Henry	62	GER	H4		1882
Robt. M.	24	CA	5838a		1895
HOCKIN					
John Milnes					Dec 1898
HOCKING					
Florence	35	AUS	5874		1896
T./Florence, c/o		SF	5551		1896
HOCKLEY					
Edward W. (soldier)			1459		1901
HODAPP					
Regina	77	GER	1053a		1871
HODDE					
Glenn, Jr.	1	CA	2481		1894
Henry	<1	SF	2706a		1872
HODEL					
George	61	SWT	8790		1903
HODES					
August	45	GER	7129		1868
HODGDON					
George J.	34	CA	939b		1895
HODGE					
Alice					Feb 1899
Cathrine C.	5	SF	8384		1868
Cathrine L.	2	SF	4565b		1870
Chris	22	CA	H65		1885
Frances Lucille	6	SF	7809		1903
John	86	IRE	1410		1869
Joseph	29	SF	2859		1900
Margaret L.	<1	SF	2859		1866

NAME	AGE OR YOB.	BIRTH PLACE	CERT. NO	ID	DEATH YEAR
Mary L.	7	SF	1054		1868
Michael	68	IRE	4762		1902
Newton D.	60	MI	2134		1903
Toe	47	CHN	3452		1894
William (soldier)			6939		1900
HODGES					
John	31	IRE	4381		1867
Lorraine	<1	SF	3300		1894
Milton	2	SF	174		1903
Nettie	32	IL	6252		1902
Robert Leslie	27	CAN	5028a		1896
HODGHTON					
Ann	59	SCT	1031		1868
HODGKINS					
E.	30	NY	423		1865
Harriett	<1	SF	1120		1869
Sophia A.	32	AUT	274		1903
Thomas J.	5	SF	1308		1869
William	38	SF	3963		1870
HODGKINSON					
James Johnson	29	NY	1970		1903
HODGSDON					
Ione	19	CAM	893		1901
HODLEY					
Francis	19	CA	5813		1867
HODNETT					
Margaret	34	SF	1622		1894
HOE					
Ah	33	CHN	3090a		1872
Chung Ge	50	CHN	2027b		1895
Come	27	CHN	508b		1871
He	19	CHN	1086		1866
Lay			3323c		1904
Moe 1	<1	SF	3216		1895

NAME	AGE OR YOB.	BIRTH PLACE	CERT. NO	ID	DEATH YEAR
Moe 2	<1	SF	3217		1895
Quon Moy	<1	CA	6280	Feb	1901
Sam	24	CHN	4330b		1870
Tong	22	CHN	1209a		1871
Wah Keh				Jul	1898
Yep	30	CHN	1268b		1872
Ying	21	CHN	5913		1896
HOEBER					
Katharine Elizabeth	72	MO	4558		1903
HOECKELE					
Edward	12	SF	8874		1903
HOECKER					
Dora	1874	SF	3236c		1904
HOEE					
Godfrey	37	GER	1160		1870
HOEFER					
Heinrich L.G.	2	SF	4594b		1870
John F.	38	SF	5513		1903
Joseph, c/o		SF	6304		1896
HOEFNIESTER					
William	<1	SF	7419		1903
HOEFT					
Gustave	Abt	GER	1160		1903
HOEG					
George	59		4298		1867
HOEGER					
Herman	67	GER	1501b		1895
HOEHEN					
——	<1	SF	3504b		1870
HOEHNSBEIN					
——	27	GER	H76		1885
HOELSCHER					
Antoinette Henrietta	26	GER	1250		1869
Fannie E.	38	MA	4403		1901

NAME	AGE OR YOB.	BIRTH PLACE	CERT. NO	ID	DEATH YEAR
George	73	GER	6054		1902
HOELSCHU					
Antoinette Henrietta	26	GER	1238		1869
HOEPER					
John F.	1875	SF	3322c		1904
HOEPPERGER					
Josephine	12	SF	2226		1902
HOERR					
John				Apr	1899
HOERTKORN					
Chas,	52	GER	H181		1889
HOERTZ					
Henry/Edith, c/o		SF	6207		1901
HOESCH					
Henry	73	GER	7046		1902
Iga	43	CA	1097		1894
HOETZEL					
Joseph	70	GER	723		1902
Louise	60	GER	6679a		1895
HOEVEN					
Rosalia A.	1	CA	5005		1867
HOEY					
——		SF	1359		1869
Edward	1	SF	1407		1866
Eliza	54	IRL	H62		1884
Ellen Purcell	60	IRE	2163		1902
Etta	8	CA	8821		1868
James/Catherine, c/o		CA	832		1901
John	35	IRE	4746		1867
Laurence	44	NY	7796		1900
Lawrence	35	IRL	2460		1901
Michael F.		SF	408		1901
Thomas	70	IRL	3873	Nov	1901
Tic Su				Dec	1899

Key: a = 1st part of year; b = 2nd part of year;
c = death certificate copy; c/o = child of

NAME	AGE OR YOB.	BIRTH PLACE	CERT. NO	ID	DEATH YEAR
William	39	CA	409		1901
HOFER					
Christy	46	OH	892		1901
John	<1	SF	1965b		1895
HOFF					
August A./Gertrude, c/o		SF	3926		1902
Emilie	<1	SF	4876		1896
Herman	62	NOR	3339		1902
John W.	87	GER	2418		1900
Lena	66	GER	938		1903
Mabel	<1	SF	2139		1894
Mattie				Jun	1899
William C.	66	NY	776b		1872
HOFFMAN					
——	<1	SF	4205a		1895
Alfred	4	VI	3255		1866
August	33	GER	H136		1886
Augustus	61	GER	5010a		1895
Carl Henry	62	GER	2846		1903
Catherine	1	SF	2991		1866
Catherine	63	FRA	626		1903
Charles	70	GER	8149		1900
Charles P. (soldier)			7754		1901
Charles S.	35	IL	7779		1904
Elijah				Jul	1898
Eliza	37	NY	1842a		1872
Elizabeth	44	GER	4349b		1870
Elizabeth	35	IRE	4308		1867
Elizabeth	38	ENG	5066		1904
Emma	<1	SF	1355		1869
Eunice L.	57	NS	5125		1904
Flora	6	SF	9700		1868
Fred	34	GER	2495		1873
Fredericka	38	GER	4159		1903
George	6	SF	1534a		1871

NAME	AGE OR YOB.	BIRTH PLACE	CERT. NO	ID	DEATH YEAR
Hannah	47	ENG	5611		1902
Hannah	<1	CA	2326		1902
Harold Edwin	14	SF	4668		1901
Harold Joseph	6	SF	5526		1902
Henry	54	GER	7919		1903
Henry H.	64	GER	5960		1902
Henry W.	78	GER	6784		1903
James	39	NJ	4465		1904
Jennie	3	SF	1264		1869
John				Oct	1898
John				Jun	1899
John D. G.				Mar	1899
John Joseph	1	SF	764		1903
John, c/o	<1	SF	3340a		1872
Josephine	45	GER	1901		1866
Josephine	58	GER	8158		1904
Julius C. (soldier)			7444		1904
Lena Mrs.	35	PA	5987		1902
Leon L.	35	NY	311		1902
Lily May	1	SF	1394b		1871
Lizzie	69	IRL	8742		1900
Lizzie P.	32	ME	1633		1866
Lorenz	59	GER	700		1894
Louis/Louise, c/o		SF	4188		1896
Marcella	35	SF	1284		1900
Mary L.	40	RI	5184		1903
Mildred	1904	SF	3321c		1904
Minna	45	GER	450		1866
Minna	<1	SF	8047		1868
Morris	47	RUS	6811a		1895
Newton	65	NY	8644		1903
Oscar/Florence, c/o	<1	CA	7460		1904
Rachael	47	NY	1868		1901
Rachel				Aug	1899
Regina	69	GER	3448		1902
Rena C.	17	MN	3631a		1895

Key: a = 1st part of year; b = 2nd part of year;
c = death certificate copy; c/o = child of

NAME	AGE OR YOB.	BIRTH PLACE	CERT. NO	ID	DEATH YEAR
Robert				Oct	1899
Robert B. (soldier)			6177		1900
Roselle	71	PRU	1168		1869
Ruth	1		6574		1904
Sarah Ann	23	CA	6887		1900
Seligman				Jan	1899
Viola M.	<1	SF	1826		1900
Warren L.	15	MA	210a		1871
William	7	SF	1265		1869
William				Mar	1900
William A.	49	WI	5850		1903
HOFFMANN					
Albert	54	GER	2006		1902
Alex O.			2719		1866
Alphonso	37	FRA	3503		1896
Augusta	22	CA	2274b		1895
Bernard	1878	PA	2644c		1904
Clarisse Francoise	80	FRA	3630		1896
Ernst				Dec	1898
Fritz Johannes	21	CT	6886		1904
Julia	<1	SF	505b		1895
Mary W.	76	MD	6070		1896
Regina	1830	GER	468c		1904
Sophie	52	GER	5489a		1895
HOFFMASTER					
Nathan (soldier)			3681		1900
HOFFMEYER					
Irene V.	<1	SF	4784a		1895
Volmer A. H.	51	DEN	9080		1901
HOFFNER					
Johannah	54	IRE	1838		1903
HOFFOSE					
Eugene	16	SF	6560a		1895
HOFFSCHNEIDER					
J. M.				Oct	1899

NAME	AGE OR YOB.	BIRTH PLACE	CERT. NO	ID	DEATH YEAR
Wm.	<1	SF	1450		1866
HOFMAN					
Anna Christine	<1	SF	8299		1901
Emelia	1875	SF	2130c		1904
Emil	48	GER	6633		1904
Heinrich	3	SF	2104		1866
Robert	<1	SF	1561b		1872
HOFMANN					
Conrad	43	GER	6287		1896
George F.	31	GER	6069		1867
Mathias	50	GER	433		1870
Richard Henry	49	PA	6114	Jan	1901
Sarah E.	78	PA	3912	Dec	1901
Wilhelmina				Oct	1898
HOFMEIER					
Peter	38	GER	1632		1903
HOFNER					
Peter A.	<1	CA	1425b		1872
HOG					
Herman				Feb	1899
HOGAN					
——			8217		1868
Amalia Dobriner	48	GER	6499		1902
Ann	72	IRL	4119		1900
Ann	67	IRE	3591		1902
Bessie, Mrs.	52	IRL	2527		1901
Bille, c/o	<1	CA	4807		1895
Bridget	31	IRL	864b		1872
Catherine	67	IRL	3065		1895
Catherine Ann	1	SF	1299		1869
Cathrine	2	SF	6283		1867
Charles R.				Oct	1899
Dan	49	IRL	3009		1895
Daniel	45	IRL	1367b		1871
Daniel	40	IRL	5009a		1895

Key: a = 1st part of year; b = 2nd part of year;
c = death certificate copy; c/o = child of

NAME	AGE OR YOB.	BIRTH PLACE	CERT. NO	ID	DEATH YEAR	NAME	AGE OR YOB.	BIRTH PLACE	CERT. NO	ID	DEATH YEAR
Daniel	<1	SF	707		1900	Mary				Oct	1898
Dennis				Dec	1898	Mary Ann	64	ENG	4684		1903
Dennis				Jan	1900	Mary Antonia, Sister	64	IRE	6518		1904
Edward	38	IRL	7938		1900	Mary Ellen	3	SF	1290		1869
Eileen Concilia	3	SF	7630		1902	Mary Ellen	<1	SF	3815		1900
Eliha	2	SF	782		1866	Mary, c/o	<1	SF	734		1894
Elizabeth Frances	4	SF	5734		1867	Mary, Mrs.	50	IRL	5020a		1895
Emily	83	IRL	5941a		1895	Maurice	66	IRL	9251		1901
George Francis	1	SF	1113b		1871	Michael	75	IRL	3309		1895
Hannah	23	IRL	808		1894	Michael				Feb	1900
Henry Joseph	1	CA	6561		1902	P. J.	77	IRE	7439		1903
J. M.	69	OH	275b		1895	Patrick				Nov	1899
James	37	IRL	262b		1872	Pierce C.	34	IRE	1447		1903
James	1	SF	1390		1869	Robert E.	28	SF	1070b		1895
James	24	SF	3536		1896	Sebastin B.	24	CA	1353		1894
Jane		SF	793		1866	Sweyn Gustanus				Jan	1899
Joanna	44	IRE	8028		1903	T. D./S. M., c/o				Oct	1899
John	53	IRE	2858		1866	Tho's., c/o		SF	863b		1872
John	<1	SF	8084		1868	Thomas	29	ENG	1534		1870
John	22	NY	1170		1869	Thomas				Feb	1899
John	40	IRE	1242		1869	Thomas Garven Francis	59	IRL	3666	Nov	1901
John				Nov	1898	Thomas P.	4	SF	6421		1867
John Francis	1	SF	547		1870	Thomas P.	30	IL	3415		1903
John R.	25	IL	8229		1901	William	40		966b		1871
John T.	36	SF	3757		1896	William	32	NH	5708		1904
Joseph I.	38	SF	4996		1903	William A.	3	SF	2396		1866
Katherine	50	IRE	9011		1903	William A. (soldier)			5694	Jan	1901
Louis	36	CA	1411		1900	William S.	1	SF	6394		1867
Maggie L.	11	SF	4411		1896	Wm. Eugene	<1	SF	2855a		1872
Margaret	51	IRL	1503b		1871	**HOGARTY**					
Margaret E.	2	SF	7752		1868	James D.	73	OH	5973	Jan	1901
Martin				Nov	1898	**HOGEBOOM**					
Mary		SF	1802b		1872	Louise E.	31	NY	955a		1871
Mary	13	CA	686		1902						
Mary	33	IRL	5134a		1895	**HOGG**					
Mary	42	IRL	6559a		1895	Annie	39	CAN	2777		1895

Key: a = 1st part of year; b = 2nd part of year;
c = death certificate copy; c/o = child of

NAME	AGE OR YOB.	BIRTH PLACE	CERT. NO	ID	DEATH YEAR	NAME	AGE OR YOB.	BIRTH PLACE	CERT. NO	ID	DEATH YEAR
Samuel P.	75	MD	5999		1904	Katherine	19	CA	1384b		1895
William	32	USA	6630		1896	**Hoɪ**					
William				Nov	1899	Chung				Nov	1898
Hoggs						Gu	54	CHN	6457		1896
George F.	1	SF	4712		1867	**Hoɪe**					
Hogin						Ah	30	CHN	822b		1871
Jacob James	1	NY	9107		1868	Four	44	CHN	4324		1902
Hogrefe						Gee	32	CHN	1431		1869
Fritz	32	GER	5421		1903	**Hoɪg**					
Hogstrom						George	1	SF	6393	Feb	1901
Anna L.				Dec	1899	**Hoɪle**					
Hogue						Henry	22	GER	1319		1869
John E./Helen, c/o		SF	1550		1895	**Hoɪlt**					
Walter H.				Jan	1900	Anna B.	63	NY	6892		1868
Hoh						**Hoistendahl**					
Lee	50	CHN	6090		1902	Alfred Martin	<1	SF	2800		1873
Hohendorf						**Hoitt**					
Elvina	72	GER	3894		1896	Barton E.	27	NH	8460		1868
Hohener						**Hok**					
Samuel	44	SWT	1276		1869	La	37	CHN	1697b		1871
Hohenschild						**Hoke**					
Louis	39	GER	4361		1867	Max (soldier)			3046	Oct	1901
Maria	35	CHI	709b		1872	**Hoky**					
Hohenstein						Jane				Feb	1899
Richard				Nov	1899	**Holahan**					
Hohenthal						Martha J.	14	CA	383		1870
Henrietta	68	GER	1934		1901	Patrick	26	IRE	5879		1867
Hohler						Richard				Jan	1900
Nicolaus	49	SWT	2553a		1872	**Holan**					
Hohlfeld						Michael	38	IRE	5883		1867
Julius (soldier)			5490	Jan	1901	**Holand**					
Hohn						Sidney B.	<1	SF	7920		1903
Joseph Michael	3	SF	7860		1901						

NAME	AGE OR YOB.	BIRTH PLACE	CERT. NO	ID	DEATH YEAR	NAME	AGE OR YOB.	BIRTH PLACE	CERT. NO	ID	DEATH YEAR
HOLAWORTH						HOLDEN					
Mary	47	ENG	8903		1900	——			8280		1868
HOLBECK						——		SF	1360		1869
Matt	29	GER	3993		1903	Augustus	8	SF	1177		1869
HOLBRITTER						Cathrine	40	IRE	8283		1868
Ona V.	28	WV	4088	Dec	1901	Edward	62	IRE	2272		1903
						Edward J.	39	CA	4962		1902
HOLBROM						Flora M.	33	OH	1769		1902
Joseph H. (soldier)			97		1900	Helen Gertrude	4	SF	6472		1902
HOLBROOK						James J.	48	WI	7487		1901
Amelia M.	30	CA	3323		1900	John M.	37	SF	8872		1901
Angeline E.				Aug	1898	John T.	1836	NH	2953c		1904
Charles				Jun	1899	Lizzie	50	ME	5126		1904
David E./Grace, c/o	<1	SF	1836		1900	Margaret	75	IRE	7366		1902
Edward	63	MA	4835		1867	Mario S. (soldier)	24	PA	2068		1870
Ellisha	63	MA	H159		1887	Mary Jane	16	SF	3102		1870
George V. I.	29	CAN	3979a		1895	Mary M.	71	MA	904		1903
Henry C.	59	MA	9231		1901	Nancy				Aug	1898
Herbert	24	SF	6702		1900	Nicholas	27	CA	H43		1883
James H.				May	1899	Peter	36	CA	7000		1900
Maud A.	<1	SF	1673b		1895	Robert	49	MA	63		1902
Rufus K.				May	1899	Thomas				Feb	1899
HOLBROW						Vincent Harrold	1	SF	3048		1903
Henry E.	52	ENG	8399		1901	W.	28	CA	141b		1895
HOLCOMB						William B.	7	SF	1726		1866
Eddie W.	<1	SF	3987		1867	Wilson F.	43	CA	2553		1901
Emelie	41	LA	1171a		1871	HOLDER					
Emilie	<1	SF	2946		1866	Daniel J.	1824	CAN	3237c		1904
Helen Mary	32	POR	1167		1900	Myrtle C.	<1	SF	2306		1894
Samuel	35	MO	504		1866	HOLDREDGE					
HOLCOMBE						Eliza	90	NY	2465b		1895
Atkinson	76	NJ	2606		1900	Sterling M.	64	NY	359		1902
Sarah A.	92	MO	2984		1900	HOLDRIDGE					
Stephen	<1	SF	57b		1895	Mary				Mar	1899
Walter G.	37	CA	1626		1902	Sadie J.	17	SF	2663		1894

Key: a = 1st part of year; b = 2nd part of year; c = death certificate copy; c/o = child of

NAME	AGE OR YOB.	BIRTH PLACE	CERT. NO	ID	DEATH YEAR
HOLDSWORTH					
Henry Lee	38	CA	7327		1903
HOLEHAN					
Elizabeth	59	IRL	5612		1896
HOLES					
John	62	ENG	310b		1871
HOLESWORTH					
Joseph A.				Dec	1898
HOLGERSON					
Edward Harol	2	SF	6575		1904
HOLHOOK					
Sand E./Grace, c/o		SF	1694		1900
HOLIDAY					
James	2	SF	2194		1873
HOLJE					
Emil	35	SF	3388		1902
Herman		SF	4512b		1870
J. B.	<1	SF	7285		1868
HOLJES					
J. H./H., c/o		SF	1274		1894
HOLLA					
Christiana Charlotte	77	NY	5454		1904
HOLLADAY					
Charles				Apr	1899
HOLLAHAN					
Henry W.	<1	SF	1084b		1872
HOLLAND					
——			1963		1870
——			7360		1868
Alexander F.				Feb	1899
Amanda	34	WI	8562		1901
Andrew				Mar	1899
August K.	31	POL	5401		1904

NAME	AGE OR YOB.	BIRTH PLACE	CERT. NO	ID	DEATH YEAR
Bertrum John	<1	SF	8921		1901
Carrie T.				May	1899
Catherine	49	IRL	4902		1896
D. T./Susan, c/o	1904	CA	1901		1904
D. T./Susan, c/o			1901		1904
Daniel J.				Jan	1899
Edith Mabel	<1	SF	6627		1903
Edward	50	ENG	1795		1900
Elijah			7576		1902
Elizabeth	38	DC	7008	Feb	1901
Ellen	1	OR	1139		1870
Ellen	61	IRL	4188	Dec	1901
Ellen, Mrs.	71	IRL	3076		1894
Eva	<1	SF	1271		1901
Frank P. (soldier)			2069		1901
George				Dec	1899
Hannah	41	IRL	558b		1871
Harry				Jul	1898
Horatio	58	MA	4352a		1895
Jacob	1867		3066c		1904
James	30	TN	8954		1868
James	70	ENG	2907		1900
James				Jan	1899
John	7	MA	2991a		1872
John	49	ENG	H54		1884
John	64	IRE	7671		1902
John	60	IRE	331		1902
John				Feb	1899
John	37	ENG	919a		1871
John C.	13	CA	1054		1868
John M.	67	IRE	6439		1902
Joseph				Dec	1899
Jullia	33	IRE	6948		1868
Leo				Jul	1898
Louisa Caroline	53	ENG	7672		1902
Mabel B.	1	TX	8423		1903

NAME	AGE OR YOB.	BIRTH PLACE	CERT. NO	ID	DEATH YEAR	NAME	AGE OR YOB.	BIRTH PLACE	CERT. NO	ID	DEATH YEAR
Madeline	22	CA	7555		1904	Henry J. (soldier)			8686		1901
Marie Elizabeth	77	GER	4626		1902	Sylvester S. (soldier)			1854		1901
Mary	1	SF	803b		1872	**HOLLIDAY**					
Mary A. C.					Nov 1898	Benjamin C.	25	CA	154		1901
Mary Jane	1828	IRE	676c		1904	Grace E.				Jul	1899
Michael N.	63	IRL	2840		1873	H./C., c/o	<1	SF	3712		1895
Micheel					Dec 1899	Isaac				Nov	1898
Nathaniel	82	PA	587		1894	Laura	17	SF	4974		1896
Patrick	68	MA	2884		1895	Mary E.	73	NY	8873		1901
Patrick	26	IRL	6844a		1895	Thos.				Mar	1900
Patrick I.	1	SF	9536		1868	**HOLLIET**					
Philip					Mar 1900	William H.				Apr	1899
Sarah	52	PA	6255a		1895	**HOLLING**					
Sarah	2	SF	1399		1869	Chas. H.	71	GER	7328		1903
W.	51	GER	4311a		1895	Louisa Wachsmuth	47	OH	11		1902
William J.	33	MA	2982		1902	Wilhelm	60	GER	6599		1903
William/Fanny, c/o		SF	7503		1900	**HOLLINGS**					
Winnie	60	IRL	3814		1900	Amy	32	ENG	H200		1889
HOLLANDER						Behrend	27	GER	818b		1871
Frederick					Apr 1899	Caroline	64	GER	6567		1903
HOLLASTIN						Claus Henry	<1	SF	1764b		1871
William	35	RI	850		1866	Nicholas	1854	GER	1964c		1904
HOLLDORF						William	38	PRU	1517		1870
Henry B.	36	GER	6161	Jan	1901	**HOLLINGSHEAD**					
HOLLENBACH						Catherine	61	NY	6427		1867
Arthur (soldier)			6936		1900	**HOLLINGSWORTH**					
HOLLENBAUGH						Earl Preston	6	CA	1442		1902
Newton					Mar 1900	Thomas L. (soldier)			342		1901
HOLLENBECK						Wm.				Jan	1900
Frank	7	SF	8116		1868	**HOLLIS**					
HOLLERAN						Alfred	36	ENG	1333		1866
Anna	<1	SF	3251		1902	Geo. H	32	NY	H89		1885
HOLLEY						George Christopher	30	CA	9617		1901
Elizabeth					Apr 1899	Magnus				Dec	1899

Key: a = 1st part of year; b = 2nd part of year;
c = death certificate copy; c/o = child of

NAME	AGE OR YOB.	BIRTH PLACE	CERT. NO	ID	DEATH YEAR	NAME	AGE OR YOB.	BIRTH PLACE	CERT. NO	ID	DEATH YEAR
Melvin J.	19	ME	H66		1885	**HOLMAN**					
William	55	IA	6845a		1895	Alexandrini	31	NY	4685		1903
						Annie E.	40	LA	4474		1901
HOLLISTER						Charlotte M.	82	NY	8071		1904
Charles	29	OH	7569		1901	Emanuel (soldier)			3047	Oct	1901
Leon				Apr	1899	Gladys	2	SF	5571		1902
HOLLMAN						Margaret	55	IRE	8947		1903
Harry			3068		1902	Mary	45	IRE	7496		1868
Lydia Alice	20	CA	8658		1900	Thomas G.	40	TN	367		1865
HOLLORON						Thomas S.	2	SF	4579		1867
Johanna	72	IRE	4422		1902	**HOLMBERG**					
HOLLOWAY						Alfred	52	FIN	5376		1902
Charles	1	CA	830		1902	Edith O.	1	SF	552		1894
J. W.				Jan	1900	John	49	FIN	5544		1904
John/Mary Ellen, c/o	1904	SF	1139		1904	**HOLMES**					
John/Mary, c/o	1	SF	2956		1903	Albert	1	CA	3371		1903
Josephine Ellen	20	CA	1185		1894	Alfred				Feb	1900
Maggie	3	SF	5812		1903	Alice	36	IRL	1336b		1872
Maude Alice	6	SF	5604		1903	Avis F.	1825	MA	1046c		1904
William Henry	79	NY	5255		1904	Benjamin				Dec	1898
HOLLUB						Beulah J.	2	SF	3414a		1872
Edgar L.	8	SF	2072		1870	Charles	57	MA	1213b		1871
HOLLUT						Charles				Jul	1898
Susannah				Feb	1900	Charles H.	65	LA	7900		1903
HOLLY						Charles R.	8	SF	2275		1866
Martha J.	62	IL	5847	Jan	1901	Daniel	1883	VA	1707c		1904
HOLM						David	83	MA	8161		1868
Catherine	73	IRL	2918		1901	Edward K.	52	MA	7429		1904
Catherine Lorraine	7	SF	3268	Nov	1901	Edwin H.	40	SF	201		1902
Charles/Amy, c/o	1	SF	6662		1904	Elizabeth	35	NY	3074a		1872
Frederick	15	CA	1491		1894	Ellis H.				Mar	1899
John C.				Aug	1898	Ensign K.	54	ME	H28		1883
Neils	40	DEN	404b		1871	Eugene A.	30	ME	1173		1869
Ora	33	ENG	29		1901	Fannie	<1	SF	8918		1901
Otto			7577		1902	Fanny	<1	SF	9450		1901

Key: a = 1st part of year; b = 2nd part of year;
c = death certificate copy; c/o = child of

NAME	AGE OR YOB.	BIRTH PLACE	CERT. NO	ID	DEATH YEAR
Felix	<1	SF	6347		1904
Fred, c/o	<1	SF	1250		1869
George A.	76	CT	906b		1895
George F. (civilian)			7219		1900
George Warren	77	MA	7830		1904
Henry	65		2016		1903
Henry J.	32	ENG	8851		1868
Howard	1	SF	77		1903
Isabella T.	<1	SF	3877		1870
J.	64	DEN	5424a		1895
James	35	IRE	4658		1867
Jno.	53	PA	4517a		1895
Katie	42	SF	8625		1901
Laura Etta					Nov 1899
Lawrence	37	NOR	H124		1886
Lilian May	<1	SF	6444		1867
Lucy Jane					Oct 1899
M. P./Regina, c/o	1	SF	4445		1903
Marcus					Mar 1900
Margaret	1820	IRE	3294c		1904
Margaret Banks	32	SF	9474		1901
Margaret J.	<1	SF	2144		1866
Maria					Mar 1900
Maria F.	21	MA	1448		1869
Maria Gertrude					Feb 1899
Mary A.					Dec 1899
Mary Ann	46	ENG	8702		1904
Mary Elizabeth	41	CA	5916		1902
Mary J.	78	SCT	6811		1903
Michael	48	IRE	1244		1869
Minna A.	13	SF	113a		1871
Peter J.	40	GER	1044b		1872
Ralph	68	IRL	3656a		1895
Richard T.	44	MA	897		1866
Robert	<1	SF	1247		1901
Robert Taylor	64	GA	237		1902

NAME	AGE OR YOB.	BIRTH PLACE	CERT. NO	ID	DEATH YEAR
S. A.	62	USA	3077		1894
Samuel B.	50	NY	2256		1901
Sarah A. B.	58	MO	5847		1904
Sarah H.	45	MA	1227		1869
Silva Etta	3	SF	932a		1871
Simon					Dec 1898
Stanley	<1		8136		1904
Thomas	30	SF	4829		1904
W. H.	62	ME	3827a		1895
William Madison	41	KY	3637		1903
Wm. J.	50	IRL	H127		1886
HOLMES-COOK					
Catherine M.	55	IRE	6625		1902
HOLMGREN					
Harvey B.					Aug 1898
Hugh	39	SWE	2198b		1895
Joe	39	SWE	2198b		1895
HOLMGREW					
James A. L.	28	CAN	277b		1895
HOLMQUIST					
Niles Rudolph	65	SWE	9541		1901
HOLMS					
Hans	34	DEN	1135b		1872
HOLMSTROM					
Annie	2	SF	6446a		1895
Oscar	35	SWE	3179		1902
HOLOHAN					
Ellen	82	IRL	433		1901
John (soldier)	UN		3094c		1904
HOLOMON					
John (soldier)			8069		1900
HOLONOUS					
Mary	<1	SF	1118a		1871

NAME	AGE OR YOB.	BIRTH PLACE	CERT. NO	ID	DEATH YEAR	NAME	AGE OR YOB.	BIRTH PLACE	CERT. NO	ID	DEATH YEAR
HOLSCHER						Sarah P.	81	NH	6409		1896
Margaret	1826	IRE	827c		1904	T./F., c/o				May	1899
						William				Jul	1898
HOLST						William				Jan	1899
Betty, Mrs.	49	DEN	3297		1894	William H.	63	NH	5731		1904
Edward G.	<1	SF	3243		1870	Wm. A. (soldier)			7752		1901
Lillie E.				Jan	1900						
Margaret A.	19	SF	5455		1904	**HOLTHAUS**					
William	65	DEN	531		1901	Joseph F.	34	OH	7022		1900
HOLSTE						**HOLTINGER**					
Frederick	77	GER	3667		1903	———		SF	1097		1869
HOLSTEAD						**HOLTMANN**					
John Edward	35	SWE	8265		1901	Ben	29	GER	361b		1895
HOLSTEIN						**HOLTMEIER**					
August	63	SWE	3354		1896	Eliza A.	2	SF	8168		1868
HOLSTROM						**HOLTMUER**					
Alfred	42	FIN	6519		1904	Henry	1829	PRU	2214c		1904
August	<1	SF	7855		1900	**HOLTON**					
						Charles	36	MN	1440		1901
HOLSWORTH						Charlotte	70	NY	4339		1903
Harry J.	21	ENG	5092		1904	Margarita	24	CA	1281b		1895
HOLT						**HOLTUM**					
Anna	1853	MA	3472c		1904	Mary Jane	68	VT	2918		1903
Annie			6117		1867	**HOLTURN**					
Claude	20	OR	334		1903	Carrie				Mar	1899
Ewing	<1	SF	6407		1902	**HOLTZ**					
Fred C.	19	TX	1662		1902	Adela	<1	SF	394b		1872
G. A. Capt.	43	CT	H193		1889	Augusta	71	GER	7420		1903
Helen	2	CA	4158		1903	George	1887	CA	1667c		1904
James R.				Oct	1899	Johannie	69	GER	5397a		1895
James W.	69	ME	2561		1895	John Doe	47	GER	5092		1902
John	<1	CA	1372		1869						
Julian	7	CA	7645		1903	**HOLVARSON**					
Marie	29	NY	5958a		1895	Henry				Jun	1899
Marjorie	<1	SF	4121		1900	**HOLVERSON**					
Mary	50	IRE	969		1866	Elsie C.	1	CA	203		1900

NAME	AGE OR YOB.	BIRTH PLACE	CERT. NO	ID	DEATH YEAR	NAME	AGE OR YOB.	BIRTH PLACE	CERT. NO	ID	DEATH YEAR
Holz						Sing	50	CHN	3854a		1895
Caroline	63	GER	5562		1903	Sue	52	CHN	4911		1902
Louis	60	GER	H139		1886	Tin	49	CHN	2096		1902
Holze						Toy					Nov 1899
Martin	1	SF	986		1866	Toy Wah					May 1899
						Tu Lin	51	CHN	4408		1903
Holzhciser						Wah Shuck	34	CHN	6486a		1895
Peter	60	GER	4686		1903	Yoke	65	CHN	5980		1903
Holzheiser						Homan					
Phillipina	44	GER	2392b		1895	John	49	GER	3054		1866
Holzhutor						Homans					
Reinhold	58	GER	9229		1901	Isabella	<1	SF	3161		1866
Hom						Homer					
Bing Kin	41	CHN	1056		1894	John Wesley	43	MA	9545		1868
Bock Hof	28	CHN	4247a		1895	Lillie	11	MN	762		1870
Bok Yin	23	CA	8499		1904	Homieur					
Bon Yon	45	CHN	3242		1894	Henry Max.	11	SF	1098		1870
Chew Fong	35	CHN	5880a		1895	Hon					
Chin	52	CHN	4188		1900	Ah	50	CHN	739b		1871
Chong	46	CHN	8101		1903	Ah	32	CHN	1152		1869
Dong Bo	1859	CHN	3095c		1904	Ference	5	NY	1086		1869
Fong Lue	7	SF	1010		1894	Lyn	27	CHN	5311		1867
Fung Wah	55	CHN	6435		1904	Vir	37	CHN	2510a		1872
Him Mow	51	CHN	2989		1895	Wing	43	CHN	5001		1896
Jun	58	CHN	6327a		1895	Honan					
Li Tug	44	CHN	4576a		1895	James Francis	<1	SF	1831a		1872
Ling	1	SF	381		1903						
Ling Ouce	45	CHN	3865a		1895	Honar					
Mo Sung	42	CHN	3398		1896	Charles F.	25	CA	2791		1900
Moon Goon	35	CHN	6653		1902	Honauer					
Mun Law	47	CHN	529		1900	Joseph	68	SWT	3296		Nov 1901
My Min	39	CHN	8827		1900	Honchan					
Oive Jon	40	CHN	6366a		1895	Winglee	38	CHN	H165		1887
Quong	40	CHN	3072		1873	Honda					
Quong	60	CHN	7836		1903	Yasaku	30	JPN	4459		1896
Sen					Aug 1899						

NAME	AGE OR YOB.	BIRTH PLACE	CERT. NO	ID	DEATH YEAR	NAME	AGE OR YOB.	BIRTH PLACE	CERT. NO	ID	DEATH YEAR
HONE						Mark Gam	1842	CHN	3366c		1904
John	74	IRL	5106a		1896	Puck Chang				Jan	1899
						Qoon	44	CHN	7043		1904
HONEN						Song Kit	42	CHN	6564		1896
Andrew				Jan	1899	Sonny	34	CHN	9657		1868
						Sue				Nov	1899
HONETTE						Tan Chack	32	CHN	1390		1894
Caroline	27	COL	1412		1870	Toc	49	CHN	1218		1870
HONEY						Tom Mong	1844	CHN	3380c		1904
Theresa	53	ENG	H199		1889	Toy				Aug	1898
HONG						Ye	1845	CHN	2616		1904
Ah	20	CHN	911		1870	Yee Hing	28	CHN	7365		1904
Ah	27	CHN	913		1870						
Ah	32	CHN	1131		1870	**HONGER**					
Ah	32	CHN	1672a		1871	Albert	50	OH	1091		1900
Ah	46	CHN	1069		1869	**HONGO**					
Ah	10	SF	5928a		1895	E.	1870	JPN	2141c		1904
Ah Fi				Mar	1899						
Ah Sing	39	CHN	4180		1902	**HONIED**					
Ah Wing	41	CHN	5227		1901	Reginald H.				Mar	1900
Ah Wing				Dec	1899	**HONIGSBERGER**					
Bang				Nov	1898	Henry				May	1899
Chin Yue	35	CHN	7321		1900	Lewis	84	BAV	3139		1900
Chong	34	CHN	1258		1870	Margret A.	31	CA	4181		1902
Chong	46	CHN	2472		1902	**HONN**					
Chow Chun				Oct	1898	Chum	21	CHN	1227		1869
Fang				Dec	1899	Lum	30	CHN	1014		1866
Fong Man	39	CHN	8090		1904	**HONNER**					
Gum Sing	65	CHN	3201		1902	James Lord	1828	MA	2853c		1904
Hen Doo	42	CHN	910		1894	**HONORINE**					
Hen Hay				Jun	1899	——	<1	SF	4973		1896
Joe	22	CHN	H3		1882	**HONS**					
Ki Chew	26	CHN	5958		1904	Julius	27	GER	8390		1900
Koon	49	CHN	5361		1903	Nelson/Mary, c/o				Jan	1899
Kue	28	CHN	5027a		1896	**HONSDAY**					
Li Yung	2	SF	2605		1900	Edward	36	FRA	67		1865
Lum	42	CHN	2559		1902						

Key: a = 1st part of year; b = 2nd part of year;
c = death certificate copy; c/o = child of

NAME	AGE OR YOB.	BIRTH PLACE	CERT. NO	ID	DEATH YEAR
HONSON					
George W.			1306		1903
HONZA					
John W. (soldier)	27	IA	4311		1903
HOO					
Ah	16	CHN	343a		1871
Ah	42	CHN	1155b		1872
Chum Me	35	CHN	3500b		1870
Chung	38	CHN	2116		1902
Jibg				May	1899
Jung Gee	32	CHN	6600		1903
King Sheri				Oct	1898
Mang	<1	SF	1588		1902
Sing	48	CHN	4236		1896
Ting	20	CHN	1416		1869
Wah	3	CA	2482		1903
HOOD					
Annie	37	SF	549		1894
Charles H.	15	CA	7967		1904
Edward	4	SF	6191		1867
Edward Elbridge	57	NH	5547		1902
Ernest	1	SF	929b		1871
George J.	57	OH	1115		1900
Georgianna				Dec	1898
Martha Ann	38	IRL	H95		1885
Wm A.	60		6142		1900
HOOE					
Isabell	35	CA	7396		1902
HOOFSCHMIDT					
Eliza	<1	SF	9820		1868
HOOGS					
Agnes	63	IRE	6253		1902
Elizabeth G.				Mar	1899
Octavian	58	MA	2432		1866
W.	<1	SF	4027		1870
HOOK					
Ann	37	AUT	2942		1873
George W.	34	KY	9712		1868
J. H./T., c/o		SF	6328		1895
James	35	ENG	6390a		1895
Lou	40	CHN	1243		1869
Martin M.	53	DEN	6752		1904
Rosina Florence	50	NY	3094		1900
HOOKER					
Albert	<1	SF	1048		1900
R. C., Capt.	50	VA	2063		1900
HOON					
Fong Moon	36	CHN	484b		1872
Gue		CHN	563b		1872
HOONG					
Ah	35	CHN	6225		1867
HOONY					
Hoony Young/Pung Shee, c/o		SF	195		1904
HOOPER					
——			3722		1867
Arthur Appleton				Aug	1898
Eliza	<1	SF	4845a		1895
Elizabeth	64	IRL	3774		1896
Franklin Perry	1836	ME	115c		1904
George E.	6	CHL	9907		1868
George F.	75	VA	1109		1901
Helen	5	AUT	1016		1868
Henry Otis	71	MA	3247		1894
John	33	ENG	1108		1869
John				Oct	1898
Louisa M.	35	ENG	5118		1867
Martha S.				Jan	1900
Mary Campbell	54	ME	8207		1900

NAME	AGE OR YOB.	BIRTH PLACE	CERT. NO	ID	DEATH YEAR
Mary Eleanor	70	OH	515		1903
Querita Marjory	<1	SF	2889		1900
Richard	3	AUT	1108		1869
Robert N. (soldier)			249		1902
Thomas B.	63	KY	4225		1902
Thomas Carlton	2	CA	1891		1903
William	63	MA	242a		1871
William	48	ENG	1248		1901
William	1832	ENG	600c		1904
William B.	66	VA	428		1903
William Horace				Oct	1898
HOOPES					
Thomas C.	81	PA	6768		1900
HOOPS					
Henry	8	NJ	H8		1882
John C.				Oct	1899
Mary A.				Jul	1898
HOORMAN					
H.				Nov	1899
HOOS					
Stephen	45	GER	179b		1871
HOOTEN					
James Rolla	1879	CA	3400c		1904
HOOTMAN					
William	66	PA	3760		1896
HOOTON					
Joseph	56	ENG	1241		1903
HOOTS					
Raymond Henry	1	SF	4646		1902
HOOVER					
Edward			7657		1902
John C.				Feb	1900
Mary	32	CA	1053		1901
HOP					
Ah	22	CHN	1811a		1872
Ah	29	CHN	1451		1869
Ga Wey	43	CHN	717		1900
Sea				Jan	1899
HOPE					
Chas. L.				Mar	1900
John	20	MA	8690		1868
Sarah	71	ENG	7471		1903
Thomas B.	40	MD	3515		1870
William	48	ENG	2627		1900
HOPF					
Kate	39	IRE	2473		1902
HOPKIND					
Samuel O.	41	VA	5301		1867
HOPKINS					
——			4331		1867
Alfred B.	4	SF	1770		1903
Christopher J.	<1	SF	6652		1896
Debra	42	IRL	2790		1873
E. B.	1859		2074c		1904
Elizabeth	27	IRL	128b		1872
Estelle F.	7	SF	8477		1868
Florence Margaret	79	ENG	3507		1902
Ford (soldier)			8792		1901
Frederick V.	57	VT	6175		1896
H.	24	CA	H56		1884
Harry	1864	IN	1540c		1904
Herbert A.				Dec	1899
James	<1	SF	127b		1872
James Robert	<1	SF	8266		1901
John W.	1	SF	2492		1866
Joseph	50		7013		1902
L. B.	74	OH	5986a		1895
Lizzie A.	29	SF	5096		1867

Key: a = 1st part of year; b = 2nd part of year; c = death certificate copy; c/o = child of

NAME	AGE OR YOB.	BIRTH PLACE	CERT. NO	ID	DEATH YEAR	NAME	AGE OR YOB.	BIRTH PLACE	CERT. NO	ID	DEATH YEAR
Margaret	54	PA	3473		1903	James	69	NY	3702		1900
Maria	28	IRE	4574		1867	John Edward					Dec 1899
Mary H.	56	MA	2273		1903	Margaret		NY	775		1870
Mary Jane	5	SF	2716		1866	Mildred	1885	CA	1459c		1904
Meta Ruth	<1	SF	6325		1902	Rhode	6	SF	9941		1868
Michael	40	IRL	1603		1870	Theodore	50	GER	6102a		1895
Oscar C. (soldier)			2452		1900						
Peter	67	NY	2235		1903	**H**OPPERSBERGER					
Peter C.	72	OH	8012		1903	Julius	<1	SF	1046		1868
Rosa	23	ENG	323a		1871						
Samuel J.	60	MA	1221		1869	**H**OPPI					
Thomas					Jul 1899	Rudolph	2	SF	3125		1894
Thomas J.					Aug 1898						
W. L.	39	NY	2291a		1872	**H**OPPS					
William Augustus	34	CA	8500		1904	Alice C.	2	SF	588a		1870
						Alice Laura	<1	SF	2554		1873
HOPKINSON						Charles E.					Nov 1898
Delilah	65	OH	2889		1894	Elinor D.	<1	SF	5228		1901
Emerson B.					Oct 1899	Elizabeth	1	SF	708		1903
						F. H.					Feb 1900
HOPLINS						Isabel V.	40	SF	5106		1903
J. W.	45	TN	6762a		1895	Wm./E., c/o					Jun 1899
HOPP						**H**OPSON					
Otto	1	SF	144		1870	Joseph H. (soldier)	24	TN	1130		1900
Sophia	24	GER	5657a		1895	**H**OPWOOD					
HOPPE						Wm. R.					Feb 1900
Elizabeth T.					Feb 1900	**H**OR					
Ferdinand	75	GER	1035		1894	Chu	7	SF	3966		1896
H.	30	GER	1538b		1871	Pong	34	CHN	2496		1901
Jacob D.	42	CA	3248		1894	Young Sang	29	CA	6805Feb		1901
Otto	40	GER	2139b		1895	**H**ORABIE					
HOPPER						May	3	SF	1378		1870
——			8554		1868	**H**ORABIN					
Edward E.	4	CHL	1000		1868	Lucy	42	ENG	H5		1882
Emma	32	IRL	2724		1873	**H**ORAN					
Garrett	76	NY	5312		1903	——			4284		1867
Garrett D.	73	NJ	5000		1904	——			4834		1867

Key: a = 1st part of year; b = 2nd part of year; c = death certificate copy; c/o = child of

NAME	AGE OR YOB.	BIRTH PLACE	CERT. NO	ID	DEATH YEAR
Arthur H.	1	SF	2601		1866
Edward	65	IRE	7742		1902
Ellen J.				Feb	1899
Emma				Feb	1900
Francis				Apr	1899
George				Feb	1900
J.	50	IRL	321b		1895
James	51	IRL	4204a		1895
James (soldier)			7121		1900
James D.	65	CAN	8446		1903
John C.	44	IRL	1066a		1871
John H.	56	MA	3019		1900
John J.	23	NJ	7871		1900
John M.	48	MA	6535		1896
Kerrian				Oct	1898
Margaret	54	IRE	1770		1902
Margarett	<1	SF	1080		1869
Mary	76	IRL	5487a		1895
Mary D.	50	IRE	7788		1902
Patrick J.	52	ENG	4242	Dec	1901
Robert (soldier)			5054		1901
Susan	55	IRL	3453		1894
Thomas	44	IRE	5917		1902
Thomas				May	1899
William	48	IRL	1847		1870
William F.				Aug	1898
HORATH					
Mary	3	CA	8250		1900
HORCH					
Charles	42	GER	H150		1887
HORD					
John H.	62	VA	511a		1871
HORDER					
John	57	SWT	6147		1867

NAME	AGE OR YOB.	BIRTH PLACE	CERT. NO	ID	DEATH YEAR
HORELE					
Henry	39	GER	1525		1870
HOREN					
Andrew				Mar	1899
Frank				Nov	1898
John A.			7160		1901
HOREST					
Charles				Dec	1899
HORGAN					
Ambrose	47	IRE	1351		1902
Ann	33	IRL	3353		1870
David	32	IRL	3194		1895
Ethan A.	<1	SF	889		1894
Hannah	30	IRE	8834		1868
John	34	MA	1381		1866
John	28	IRE	5877		1867
John E.	<1	SF	273a		1871
Mary	60	IRL	6341	Feb	1901
HORHUMEL					
Toh G.	29	GER	1592b		1871
HORIA					
Motokichi	30	JPN	6487		1904
HORIGAN					
Daniel	55	IRE	385		1902
Daniel				Nov	1899
HORIN					
Thomas B.				Jul	1899
HORISTO					
Faure	21	FRA	1130		1869
HORKONS					
Patrick				Feb	1899
HORLOCK					
Ellen Elizabeth				Oct	1899

Key: a = 1st part of year; b = 2nd part of year; c = death certificate copy; c/o = child of

NAME	AGE OR YOB.	BIRTH PLACE	CERT. NO	ID	DEATH YEAR	NAME	AGE OR YOB.	BIRTH PLACE	CERT. NO	ID	DEATH YEAR
HORMANN						**HORNER**					
Wm.	60	GER	6091		1902	Drla W,	43	ENG	H120		1886
						John	30	ENG	4709		1904
HORN						William	41	NY	400		1900
Alexander	31	CA	2662		1894						
Ann	1834	IRE	449c		1904	**HORNET**					
Annie	39	SF	7891		1904	Michael	26	IRE	7553		1868
Barney, c/o		SF	2876		1873	**HORNFELDT**					
Bernard	66	NY	5358		1901	Max	58	GER	4875		1902
Charles A.				Feb	1900						
Charles H.	1	SF	3096		1870	**HORNG**					
Elizabeth Agnes	33	IRL	2885		1873	Nathan				Jun	1899
F. William	25	GER	3382		1870	Yo Kim				Aug	1898
Frank J.	1836	GER	2518c		1904	**HORNICH**					
Franz				Jun	1899	Pauline				Oct	1899
Harry	30	MO	4970		1904	**HORNING**					
Hazel				Jun	1899	Frank C.	63	GER	1439		1894
Jno. H. (soldier)			8681		1903	John				Dec	1899
Joan Frances	44	ENG	3094		1903	**HORNLEIN**					
Joseph P.				Mar	1899	Alvin E.				Feb	1900
Katharine				Feb	1900	**HORNUNG**					
Margaret	1854	IRE	1768c		1904	Gustav	79	GER	7025		1900
Marion Hazel	6	CA	5254		1901	Terese	10	CA	1162		1869
Mary A. Veronica	39	SF	6440		1902						
Robert George	53	OH	5440		1902	**HORR**					
Salomon Leib	70	AUS	5563		1903	Herbert G. (soldier)			6891		1900
Samuel M. (soldier)			7318		1901	William	52	MA	1214a		1871
Sarah B.				Feb	1900	Yaugh	44	CHN	3176		1870
Thomas Ludervick	71	CT	3874	Nov	1901	**HORRICK**					
Viola	1	SF	362b		1895	Rosa	58	IRL	3591		1900
William B.				May	1899	**HORSCH**					
HORNE						John	<1	SF	1087		1866
Charles W.	35	CAN	2035		1894	**HORST**					
James	50	ENG	2877c		1904	———	<1	SF	1172		1869
HORNELL						Emma	1	SF	3438		1867
Ellinor H.	55	NY	478		1903	John	62	GER	6196		1900

Key: a = 1st part of year; b = 2nd part of year;
c = death certificate copy; c/o = child of

NAME	AGE OR YOB.	BIRTH PLACE	CERT. NO	ID	DEATH YEAR	NAME	AGE OR YOB.	BIRTH PLACE	CERT. NO	ID	DEATH YEAR
HORSTMAN						**HORWEGE**					
Alice Mai				Jan	1899	Jacob	38	GER	4524		1867
Herman J.	1874	CA	3266c		1904	**HORWOOD**					
HORSTMANN						Robert	50	ENG	3129		1895
Brunhilde	<1	SF	1818		1894	**HOSCK**					
Henry F.	36	SF	4132	Dec	1901	Thomas				Jan	1900
John C.	27	GER	133		1865	**HOSFORD**					
Margaritha C.	64	GER	5741		1896	Fannie	64	IRL	759		1870
Marie	70	SWT	4759		1896	**HOSHIGUMA**					
Wm. J.	52	PA	3077a		1872	Sadamasa	29	JPN	9298		1901
HORSTMEYER						**HOSIE**					
William	59	GER	2333		1900	David	53	SCT	1241		1900
HORT						David Wellington	25	SF	742		1902
Emily Abigail	80	CAN	1909		1902	**HOSKIN**					
HORTON						Elmer/Ollie, c/o	1	SF	1328		1903
Annie	55	IRL	3353		1896	**HOSKINSON**					
Charles E.	1	SF	3578		1867	Walter (soldier)			7129		1900
Clement St.				May	1899	**HOSMAN**					
Elizabeth	29	CA	4369	Dec	1901	Horace B.	53	VT	1399b		1872
Elizabeth Taylor				Mar	1900	**HOSMER**					
Geo R. (soldier)			7756		1901	Lyman Mason	52	NY	4473		1901
Grace I.	1	SF	1799a		1872	**HOSSACK**					
Gray	<1	SF	8945		1903	Louise	71	SCT	6901		1902
Lewis (soldier)			250		1902	**HOSSOCK**					
Mariana	51	CT	2983		1902	Chas. Davidsen	67	SCT	6391a		1895
Minnie Elizabeth	30	WI	3076		1900	**HOST**					
Ray				Jun	1899	George	44	GER	2a		1872
Reginald	<1	SF	7312		1902	**HOSTETLER**					
Rena Gillespie	28	CA	1897		1901	Philip Augustus	<1	CA	1208		1900
William	67	KY	709		1903	**HOTALING**					
HORTUNG						Anson P.				Feb	1899
Wm. (sailor)			6524		1900	Anson P.				Feb	1900
HORVALT											
John Bell	50	SCT	6419		1900						

Key: a = 1st part of year; b = 2nd part of year;
c = death certificate copy; c/o = child of

NAME	AGE OR YOB.	BIRTH PLACE	CERT. NO	ID	DEATH YEAR	NAME	AGE OR YOB.	BIRTH PLACE	CERT. NO	ID	DEATH YEAR
HOTCHKISS						**HOUE**					
Charles B.					Aug 1899	Ah	24	CHN	573b		1872
Charles W.	40	NB	3579		1870	**HOUGE**					
HOTELL						Hamilton	51	IRL	9297		1901
John V.					Mar 1899	**HOUGEN**					
HOTSEN						Frederick		SF	1765		1870
Markus	47	GER	860b		1872	**HOUGH**					
HOTSI						James M. G.	3	SF	9144		1868
Catherine	19	TUR	3449		1894	John H.	32	PA	6331		1867
HOTSUTA						Martin	75	IRL	4460		1896
Linsaburo	25	JPN	3841		1902	Mary	40	NY	849b		1872
HOTTE						Susan Emelia	58	NY	4848		1901
William F.	62	GER	5791		1902	**HOUGHTON**					
HOTTENDORF						B. G.	54	CAN	43		1870
Peter Wm.	35	GER	5884		1867	Charles .					Oct 1899
HOTTNA						Frederick	15	CA	3792		1896
Mary Ellen					Jun 1899	Harry Bertram	43	MA	4		1901
HOTTON						James Franklin	75	MA	5391		1903
P. H.	50	MA	H37		1883	James Putnam	29	ENG	149b		1872
HOTZ						John	26	ENG	H117		1886
Otto					Jan 1900	Joseph					Jul 1899
HOTZEL						Samuel	59	IRE	4375		1867
Annette					Oct 1898	**HOUI**					
HOU						Yen Len	46	CHN	4150		1900
Chang Su	44	CHN	4386b		1870	**HOUIE**					
Hung	24	CHN	1147		1869	Sam	44	CHN	6663		1904
HOUARD						**HOUKER**					
Paul G.	60	FRA	5142		1901	John F.					Dec 1899
HOUCH						**HOULAN**					
W. S.					Mar 1900	Mary	62	IRE	7751		1868
HOUCK						**HOULEHAN**					
——			1026		1868	Thomas	24	MA	6751		1896
						HOULTON					
						Mary Ann					Jul 1899

Key: a = 1st part of year; b = 2nd part of year;
c = death certificate copy; c/o = child of

NAME	AGE OR YOB.	BIRTH PLACE	CERT. NO	ID	DEATH YEAR	NAME	AGE OR YOB.	BIRTH PLACE	CERT. NO	ID	DEATH YEAR
Samule W.	67	OH	1770		1894	Elizabeth	76	GER	521		1902
						Henry	62	GER	7780		1868
HOUN						Wilber (soldier)			770		1901
Ah	30	CHN	2052		1870						
						HOUSKEN					
HOUPEN						Oscar Lawrence	30	CA	1139		1901
Edward	4	NY	2274		1894						
						HOUSL					
HOUPIN						Joseph	34	GER	275		1903
Edward	62	FRA	5629		1903						
						HOUSMA					
HOURIE						Hans	63	HOL	3619		1867
Aggie	23	FRA	H188		1889						
						HOUSMAN					
HOURIGAN						Catherine C.	4	CA	6987		1902
Margaret	1834	IRE	143c		1904	Ellen	35	IRL	1766b		1871
T. J./Kate, c/o		SF	6233		1904	Mary	35	ME	1977		1902
HOURIHAN						**HOUSTON**					
John J.	<1	SF	3367		1902	A. H.	43	MD	1159		1869
Marie Virginia	3	SF	7342		1902	Carter	61	NH	6436		1904
						Edward J.	18	CA	4629a		1895
HOUSE						Emma	76	SCT	5778		1904
Frank E.				Mar	1900	Frank K.	49	MA	5484a		1895
Jonathan	61	PA	2086		1866	George	60		5501	Jan	1901
Josephine	45	OH	4669		1901	H. H.	28	ME	1144		1866
Wm. E. (soldier)			6399		1900	James T.	45	PA	2303		1902
						John	49	NY	78		1903
HOUSEE						Katherine	9	SF	4972		1896
Johanna E.	15	GER	1443		1869	Martha	79	IRL	367a		1871
						Robert	45	SCT	1271		1869
HOUSEHOLDER						Robert	60	AUT	6562		1902
Ed E. (soldier)			7119		1900	Wm.	<1	SF	1604		1894
HOUSEMAN						**HOUT**					
Belle				Oct	1898	Wm. S.	30	WV	H144		1887
Joseph D.	33	VA	622b		1895						
						HOVELER					
HOUSEMANN						John Simon				Dec	1898
Harvey P.				Nov	1899						
						HOVEY					
HOUSEN						Fred M.	<1	SF	8046		1904
William Van	1829	NY	1474c		1904						
HOUSER											
Bert			5019		1903						

Key: a = 1st part of year; b = 2nd part of year;
c = death certificate copy; c/o = child of

NAME	AGE OR YOB.	BIRTH PLACE	CERT. NO	ID	DEATH YEAR
Frederick A.	50	MA	182b		1895
Geo. W.				Feb	1900
George Dana	59	NY	984		1900
Maggie L. Rabbitt	57	ME	8159		1904
HOVINGTON					
Margaret	69	MD	2161c		1904
HOW					
Ah	17	CHN	1449a		1871
Ah	18	CHN	5090		1867
Ah	26	CHN	9133		1868
Ah	26	CHN	9152		1868
Ann (alias Lewis)	30	IRL	399b		1872
Chou	35	CHN	921a		1871
Chung	22	CHN	581b		1871
Com	30	CHN	907		1870
Cook	17	CA	8904		1900
Huy Gung	44	CHN	6332a		1895
Ing	53	CHN	2458a		1872
James			6746	Feb	1901
Man Song				Nov	1899
Moon Yup See	35	CHN	4000a		1895
Quan	1849	CHN	1751c		1904
Tock Chung	43	CHN	554		1901
Ton Chung	63	CHN	1313		1894
Wah Lung	22	CHN	901b		1872
Wong	37	CHN	482b		1871
HOW`					
Sen Cheup	65	CHN	8826		1900
HOWARD					
——	<1		9721		1868
Andrew	27	IRL	H7		1882
Andrew/Agnes, c/o		SF	2060		1900
Andrew/Megan, c/o				Jan	1899
Annie	<1	SF	984b		1895
Annie				Aug	1899

NAME	AGE OR YOB.	BIRTH PLACE	CERT. NO	ID	DEATH YEAR
Arnold	38	PRU	5303		1867
Benj. C.	39	MA	1278		1870
Bernice				Jan	1899
Bridget	76	IRL	3397		1896
Bridget				Dec	1898
C. F.	30	IL	6017		1896
C./Annie, c/o		SF	6048		1896
Dawn	35	TN	3874		1902
E. H.	48	NY	7299		1868
E./M., c/o				Dec	1899
Edith	38	CA	3094	Oct	1901
Edward H.	40	NY	7325		1868
Elizabeth				Feb	1899
Ellen	96	IRE	7185		1903
Eugene Burdett	4	TX	7123		1903
Fannie	58	KY	381		1901
Florence E.	<1	SF	3078		1894
Frances	35	NV	2352		1900
Frank				Dec	1898
Garrett	54	IRL	979		1894
Gayle E. (soldier)	23	IN	4639		1901
Geo. D.	6	SF	5912		1867
George	64	ENG	2936	Oct	1901
George H.	37	NY	5118		1903
Gertrude	2	SF	9788		1868
Guy				Nov	1899
I. J.				Feb	1900
Irvin	77	ENG	6576		1904
J. M.			1082c		1904
Jack	<1	SF	9129		1901
Jacob	50		9527		1868
James	35	IRL	1209b		1871
James	28	MA	2022		1866
James	69	IRE	4182		1902
James	36	IRL	6445a		1895
James	50	IRL	7654		1900

Key: a = 1st part of year; b = 2nd part of year;
c = death certificate copy; c/o = child of

NAME	AGE OR YOB.	BIRTH PLACE	CERT. NO	ID	DEATH YEAR	NAME	AGE OR YOB.	BIRTH PLACE	CERT. NO	ID	DEATH YEAR
John	45	IRL	2912a		1872	Thomas	19	SF	3085		1895
John	70	NY	2274		1903	Thomas	26	ENG	451a		1871
John (soldier)			2074		1901	Wallace	<1	SF	5034		1902
John C. (soldier)			2070		1901	Wilfred	<1	SF	5736		1902
Kate				Apr	1899	William	1822	NY	80c		1904
Leah				May	1899	William				Mar	1899
Leon	5	SF	3500	Nov	1901	Willie A.		SF	561a		1870
Lleen Louise Alice	<1	MA	1481		1894	**HOWARTH**					
Lottie	39	IN	4475		1901	Joseph M.	34	ENG	8697		1901
Lulu Dietz	42	CA	4460		1901	**HOWE**					
Mable E.	1	SF	1951		1866	——			9035		1868
Maggie	<1	SF	2591		1866	A. K.	37	NY	1803a		1872
Mary				Feb	1900	Alfred	<1	CA	6618		1900
Mary	61	IRL	6701		1900	Amelia	37	FRA	2792		1900
Mary, Mrs.	70	IRL	2262		1900	Andrew J.				Aug	1899
Mary/Geo., c/o				Aug	1899	Basil	<1	CA	7418		1900
Michael	22	IRL	2447b		1895	Bessie A.	1840	MA	2897c		1904
Michael E.	40	IRL	3503b		1870	Camilla C.				Dec	1899
Morris	14	SF	899		1894	Catharine				Dec	1898
Neill (soldier)			6823		1900	Charles	47	NY	264b		1872
Nellie A.	39	CA	2495		1901	Daniel T.	42	MO	5737		1902
Noah P.	68	NH	2675		1900	Edward B.	49	CA	2371		1903
Ralph				Apr	1899	Elizabeth	88	VA	5572		1896
Rebecca A.	68	NY	4483		1896	Ellen	73	IRE	6287		1904
Richard	38	PA	5310		1867	Fannie E.	44	ME	2931		1900
Robert	23	NY	213		1865	G. E./Ida, c/o	<1	SF	2304		1902
Robert	1	SF	38		1903	G. O. Fred	64	GER	528		1900
Robert A.	<1	SF	5865a		1895	George W.				May	1899
Rolland E.	21	MN	844		1902	George W. (soldier)			8744		1900
Rudolph				Mar	1899	Hannah A.	<1	SF	3244		1870
S.	71	MA	4459		1901	Harriet	66	MA	6882		1902
Squire J.	70	MA	6704		1903	Henry (soldier)			222		1902
Stella	19		4262		1902	Henry Langley				Oct	1898
Stephen	22	MI	1463		1866	J. Milton	73	NY	7596		1903
Stephen A.	64	MO	5344		1896	Jane	1	CA	7308		1868
Thomas	50	NY	1572		1894						

Key: a = 1st part of year; b = 2nd part of year;
c = death certificate copy; c/o = child of

NAME	AGE OR YOB.	BIRTH PLACE	CERT. NO	ID	DEATH YEAR
Jas. Eagan				Jun	1899
John	<1	SF	1805a		1872
John	70	PA	H64		1885
Leonard Wales				Feb	1899
Lewis	45	NH	117		1865
Lillie M.				Dec	1898
Margaret				Dec	1899
Nonie				Nov	1899
Oliver E.	<1	SF	1056		1868
Parthonia				Nov	1898
Quan Bow				Jul	1898
Roy Lawrence	1	CA	8		1903
Samuel	81	NH	3026		1902
Sylvia	<1	SF	5663	Jan	1901
Tersa A.	1	SF	6573		1868
Thomas P. A. (soldier)			5696	Jan	1901
Thos./Loreta, c/o		SF	149		1900
Victor				Feb	1899
William	24	NY	7900		1868
William Joseph	19	SF	386		1902
William T.	27	CA	6254		1902
Wm. G./Mary E., c/o		SF	6214		1900

HOWELL

NAME	AGE OR YOB.	BIRTH PLACE	CERT. NO	ID	DEATH YEAR
Anne Maria	1	SF	2119		1866
Catherine	63	SCT	6112	Jan	1901
Catherine				Nov	1898
Elizabeth	78	ENG	3637	Nov	1901
Ellen J.	55	OH	4897		1903
Emma Isabel	<1	SF	1295		1869
Evan J.	29	PA	1771		1903
Gertude	1878	CA	2705c		1904
Henry B.	58	NY	H197		1889
Irene M.				Jul	1899
James			3959		1902
John	62	IRE	1424		1903
John W.	49	NY	1182b		1872

NAME	AGE OR YOB.	BIRTH PLACE	CERT. NO	ID	DEATH YEAR
Josiah	71	ENG	8128		1901
Leverett				Oct	1899
Martin	50	WV	4834		1903
Minerva Anne	1	AR	1252		1869
Samuel F. (soldier)			6935		1900
William	1843	WAL	2413c		1904

HOWER

NAME	AGE OR YOB.	BIRTH PLACE	CERT. NO	ID	DEATH YEAR
Charlott Marjann	8	SF	2432		1894

HOWES

NAME	AGE OR YOB.	BIRTH PLACE	CERT. NO	ID	DEATH YEAR
Clarissa A.				Oct	1898
Egbert P.	41	NY	5998		1867
James	47	MA	526b		1895
John	75	MA	5313		1896
Mary G.	68	MA	1091		1869
Peter Sears	60	MA	1257		1866

HOWKINS

NAME	AGE OR YOB.	BIRTH PLACE	CERT. NO	ID	DEATH YEAR
Arthur	2	SF	6783	Feb	1901

HOWLAND

NAME	AGE OR YOB.	BIRTH PLACE	CERT. NO	ID	DEATH YEAR
Amanda J.	74	NB	3906		1900
Cornelia M.				Nov	1898
E.				Dec	1899
Geo. L.	3	CA	5944		1867
Harry A.	<1	SF	1420		1869
Nettie E.	3	SF	1096		1869
Olive Jane	42	NY	2975		1866
Oscar L.				Aug	1898
Susan B.	24	NY	5107a		1895

HOWLEY

NAME	AGE OR YOB.	BIRTH PLACE	CERT. NO	ID	DEATH YEAR
Bartholomew (soldier)			3048	Oct	1901
Patrick	32	IRL	4407	Dec	1901

HOWLIN

NAME	AGE OR YOB.	BIRTH PLACE	CERT. NO	ID	DEATH YEAR
Charles H.		SF	1579b		1871

HOWSE

NAME	AGE OR YOB.	BIRTH PLACE	CERT. NO	ID	DEATH YEAR
Isabella	60	IRL	3589		1870

NAME	AGE OR YOB.	BIRTH PLACE	CERT. NO	ID	DEATH YEAR	NAME	AGE OR YOB.	BIRTH PLACE	CERT. NO	ID	DEATH YEAR
HOWVEN						Julia B.	21	NY	1182		1869
Charles	1	SF	1265		1866	Lucius	41	CT	1816		1870
HOY						HOYTE					
Ah	33	CHN	4017		1867	Dalbert	22	NY	8236		1868
Chun	1832	CHN	962c		1904	Grace	4	SF	1003		1868
Isaac	55	VA	1327b		1871	HOYTS					
Linn	10	CHN	1025		1870	Frank				Jul	1899
Mary E.	57	DE	4045		1896	HOZAK					
Nicholas I.	<1	SF	830		1866	George B. (soldier)			7755		1901
Quan Ah	21	CHN	623		1866	HRATA					
Sar Bran	36	CHN	235b		1895	Maria	84	ITA	1848		1894
Sun	38	CHN	2936		1873	HU					
Suy	59	CHN	8232		1901	Ah	22	CHN	374		1870
Yok				Nov	1899	Ling	27	CHN	2338		1866
HOYASHI						Ming				Jan	1900
Toshetaro/Matsui, c/o	1904	SF	1140		1904	Sow	46	CHN	8818		1903
HOYER						Yen				Oct	1899
Alfred	<1	SF	1596		1870	HUANT					
HOYLE						Matilde	67	FRA	6340	Feb	1901
Henry Schroder	1	SF	3323		1873	HUAT					
James W.	1	SF	9522		1868	Napoleon/Annie, c/o		SF	576		1900
HOYNE						HUB					
Thomas J.	17	SF	3152		1902	Meriam	73	PA	7294		1902
HOYT						Peter	70	GER	2134		1902
Andrew I.	48	VT	6449		1867	HUBACEK					
Betsey J.	77	CT	2919		1903	Mathew	50	BOH	5623a		1895
Charles F.	62	NY	6101a		1895	HUBACHEK					
Elizabeth H.	23	MA	367b		1871	Hazel E.				Feb	1900
H., c/o	<1	SF	3411		1867	HUBAN					
Helen Louise				Feb	1900	Martin	10	MA	7251		1868
Henry H.	<1	SF	1183		1869	HUBARD					
James T., c/o	<1	SF	2978a		1872	John C.	56	VA	1997		1873
Jennie	60	OH	2573		1900						
John P.	69	MA	7679		1900						

Key: a = 1st part of year; b = 2nd part of year;
c = death certificate copy; c/o = child of

NAME	AGE OR YOB.	BIRTH PLACE	CERT. NO	ID	DEATH YEAR	NAME	AGE OR YOB.	BIRTH PLACE	CERT. NO	ID	DEATH YEAR
HUBAUGH						HUBBS					
Edgar			7578		1902	Harry B.	6	SF	2540		1873
HUBBARD						HUBENTHAL					
Alice E.	47	CA	3935		1903	Louis				Dec	1898
Benjamin				Feb	1900	HUBER					
Carrie W.	3	SF	8140		1868	Arthur	76	GER	2435		1902
Charles J.	23	CT	1578		1866	Charles	30	MO	365		1870
Chester W. (soldier)			5329		1901	Charles A.				Oct	1898
Dimon	50	ME	2464b		1895	Edward A.	74	PA	7431		1900
Edgar L.	Abt	USA	2772		1903	Frances Elizabeth	24	MO	898b		1872
Edward L.	<1	SF	4797		1867	Frank	35	MO	1545a		1871
Fannie V.	70	VA	5314		1896	Frank	15	SF	3191	Nov	1901
Frances J.	75	ME	1985		1900	Frantz H.	40	GER	9457		1868
Henrietta A.	<1	SF	3182		1873	Hans				Nov	1899
Henry	42	CT	1448		1866	Henry	66	GER	5959a		1895
Henry Francis	56	CT	8350		1904	John	85	GER	8391		1903
Hilda/William, c/o	1	SF	6610		1904	John	58	GER	3629a		1895
James F.	52	NY	596a		1871	Joseph	84	GER	1345		1869
Lorenzo	61	NY	1770b		1871	Louis	1	SF	6933		1868
May	40	AUS	H122		1886	Louise Josephine	<1	SF	2734		1900
Timothy W.	64	NY	7780		1904	Nettie Rebecca	2	SF	489b		1871
Willie S. P.	2	SF	6900		1868	HUBERD					
HUBBELL						Mary E.	1	SF	3212a		1872
Eveline	1	SF	8864		1868	HUBERT					
HUBBERD						Constant	50	FRA	201		1865
Edward J.	72	CAN	238		1902	Emile	28	IL	1870b		1895
John (soldier)			864		1901	Jeanne				Jun	1899
HUBBERT						Mrs. D. S.				Mar	1899
Catherine				Mar	1899	Numa	52	LA	1992		1873
George S.	35	KS	6819		1902	HUBIA					
Harry Edmond	1865	CA	1785c		1904	Louis	47	NY	7618		1904
Nathanial C.				Aug	1898	HUBIE					
Thomas E.	2	SF	2862		1895	Gertrude A.				Jul	1898
Willis H.	44	KS	5545		1904						

NAME	AGE OR YOB.	BIRTH PLACE	CERT. NO	ID	DEATH YEAR	NAME	AGE OR YOB.	BIRTH PLACE	CERT. NO	ID	DEATH YEAR
HUBLON						George A.	58	MA	7303		1868
Peter N.	41	CA	8206		1901	George B.	<1	SF	1362		1866
						James	59	IRE	1116		1903
HUBLOW						James	76	ENG	1713		1894
John F.	53	HOL	1307		1869	John Morris	56	NJ	6044		1903
						Joseph	35	SCT	518		1870
HUBNER						Mary C.	69	NY	9274		1901
Emil	40	GER	1235b		1895	Phineas	69	NY	785b		1872
						Sophie	67	ENG	5207a		1896
HUCK											
Alice	4	SF	312		1902	**HUDSPETH**					
Anna Maria	2	SF	6041		1867	Nellie	32	MA	4991a		1895
						William	37	MO	6634		1904
HUCKS											
Sarah	46	ENG	2394		1866	**HUE**					
						Ah	50	CHN	1370		1870
HUCKSON						Ah	39	CHN	9886		1868
Eliza A.	1853	ENG	727c		1904	Ah	32	CHN	9898		1868
						Ah Chow				Oct	1899
HUCKT						Ah Gue	41	CHN	2403b		1895
Henry	38	GER	H44		1883	Lee	20	HI	135		1865
						Lung	35	CHN	2732		1903
HUDDLESON											
Nathaniel				Dec	1898	**HUEGES**					
						James G.	19	NY	628		1870
HUDDLESTON											
Julia	41	SF	9163		1901	**HUELLMANTEL**					
						Bernard	79	GER	7831		1904
HUDDLESTONE											
James	33	NY	4209b		1870	**HUEN**					
						Chan	48	CHN	459		1866
HUDDY											
Katherine	55	IRL	5630	Jan	1901	**HUENERT**					
Margaret	38	NY	4133	Dec	1901	August F.	47	GER	190a		1871
William	63	IRL	2845		1895						
						HUESMAN					
HUDGIN						William N. (soldier)			279		1901
J.D.	77	PA	691		1901						
						HUESSON					
HUDSON						Henry	24	IN	7964		1868
Balfour	17	IN	5096a		1895						
Catherine A.	38	NY	1345		1866	**HUESTIS**					
Charles Newton	31	OH	3243		1903	Wilber F.	60	VA	2776		1895
Chas. W.	29	NY	H182		1889						
Elizabeth	55	NY	4189	Dec	1901						

Key: a = 1st part of year; b = 2nd part of year;
c = death certificate copy; c/o = child of

NAME	AGE OR YOB.	BIRTH PLACE	CERT. NO	ID	DEATH YEAR	NAME	AGE OR YOB.	BIRTH PLACE	CERT. NO	ID	DEATH YEAR
HUEY						**HUGG**					
Charles W. (soldier)			475		1901	Ellen M.	52	PA	621		1902
HUFF						**HUGGINS**					
Charles H. (soldier)			3079		1903	George	54	ENG	7019		1903
Eugenia A.	66	NY	4798		1904	Mary	27	IRL	567a		1870
Frank B. (soldier)			7319		1901	**HUGH**					
George W.	9	NY	750b		1895	Edward				Dec	1898
Harry S.	45	SF	4917		1904	**HUGHES**					
Jennie	24	CA	8275		1904	——			5289		1867
Louis A. (soldier)			2700		1900	Agnes B.	22	IRE	4820		1867
Malissa B.	54	IA	5424		1896	Amelia J.	45	MA	2534		1900
Margaret	72	GER	4436		1901	Anne	70	IRL	1345b		1871
W. B., c/o		SF	1303b		1872	Annie	57	AUt	7863		1904
William B.		SF	522		1870	Bertha	54	NY	6348		1904
HUFFAM						Bridget	54	IRL	1551		1900
Everett Roy	1	SF	3632		1900	Catherine	34	IRE	5542		1867
Walter	47	ENG	5548		1902	Charles	48	NY	508		1870
Walter/Kate, c/o	<1	SF	3655		1895	Clarence Boyd				May	1899
HUFFARCE						Constance	40	ENG	2932		1900
Rose	52	IL	988		1903	Dilys	12	SF	4723		1902
HUFFSCHMIDT						Edward	40	IRL	3782		1870
William F.	<1	SF	1766b		1872	Elizabeth B.	39	NY	4196b		1870
HUFSCHMIDT						Ellen	<1	SF	5709a		1895
Frederick	62	GER	6764Feb	1901		Ellen				May	1899
Henry	<1	SF	1306b		1872	Ellen R.	20	MA	7455		1901
HUFSEHMIDT						Ellis	79	WAL	3859		1900
——			6682		1868	Esther	70	NY	213b		1895
HUG						Francis J.	53	MD	6558		1868
Adolph A. (soldier)			1971		1900	Francis T.	44	IRL	2422		1873
Lee How	52	CHN	562a		1870	Francis V.	32	SF	4632		1904
HUGBERG						Frank (soldier)			1458		1901
Ole				Jan	1900	Genevieve				Jun	1899
HUGES						George A.	13	CA	5722a		1895
——		SF	917		1870	George V.	44	CA	8492		1900
						George W.	36	NJ	2892a		1872

              Key: a = 1st part of year; b = 2nd part of year;
c = death certificate copy; c/o = child of

NAME	AGE OR YOB.	BIRTH PLACE	CERT. NO	ID	DEATH YEAR	NAME	AGE OR YOB.	BIRTH PLACE	CERT. NO	ID	DEATH YEAR
Georgie N.	35	NY	2978		1894	Julia	39	CA	5127		1904
Gertrude M.	1	SF	6008	Jan	1901	Julia	52	IRL	7840		1901
Harrison/Edith, c/o				Jul	1898	Julia A.	41	NY	704		1866
Harry H. (soldier)			4554		1901	Kate	59	IRL	1502b		1895
Harry Morgan				Feb	1899	Kate E.	6	SF	614a		1871
Helen	<1	SF	1142		1894	Katherine I.	32	NY	3252		1902
Helia				Dec	1898	Lacy	35	IRL	1119		1870
Henry	10	SF	3562		1903	Lawrence	1893	SF	851c		1904
Henry	54	IRL	1976		1894	Lizzie	43	CT	2508b		1895
Isabell	38	SF	4647		1902	Maggie M.	38	CA	991		1902
James	64	ENG	3514		1900	Mamie	24	CA	106		1901
James E.	51	NY	5839a		1895	Margaret	34	CA	6654		1902
James E.				Mar	1900	Margaret	<1	SF	5940a		1895
James Gomiru	6	SF	302b		1872	Margaret C.				Dec	1899
James W.	49	NY	1486		1870	Marguerite	1	SF	5848		1904
Jane	<1	SF	872b		1872	Mary	<1	SF	4584		1867
Jane	80	WAL	2379		1902	Mary	72	IRE	728		1903
Jas. F.	54	CA	H194		1889	Mary	75	IRL	2785		1901
Jennie	1	SF	1714b		1872	Mary Catherine	1	SF	8564		1900
Jno. J.	34	NJ	4088a		1895	Mary Elizabeth	<1	SF	2199b		1895
Jno. W.	76	NC	5485a		1895	Mary Ellen	1	SF	2083		1866
John	45	IRL	H151		1887	Mary Wynne	70	IRE	7622		1903
John	68	IRE	1161		1866	Matthew	1	SF	1030		1868
John	66	IRE	7704		1902	Matthew E.	51	IRL	3005a		1872
John			7161		1901	Michael	22	IRE	4246		1867
John				Oct	1898	Michael				Jul	1898
John (soldier)			7162		1901	Michael H.	5	CA	607		1866
John A.	1	CA	3416		1903	Michael/Hanna, c/o	<1	SF	6045		1903
John J.	34	IRL	136b		1871	Nelson B.	45	IL	6851		1868
John J.	1	SF	5298		1867	Nora	<1	SF	1480		1901
John J.	<1	SF	8427		1868	Parmer (soldier)		IL	7320		1901
John J.				Feb	1900	Patrick	35	IRE	719		1866
John M.	53	WAL	1234b		1895	Patrick M.	61		4799		1904
Joseph	32	NY	6216		1896	Peter	42	LA	3087		1866
Joseph A.	<1	SF	8383		1901	Peter	30	IRE	4613		1867
Joseph B.	19	SF	3669		1896	Peter	<1	SF	8036		1868

Key: a = 1st part of year; b = 2nd part of year;
c = death certificate copy; c/o = child of

NAME	AGE OR YOB.	BIRTH PLACE	CERT. NO	ID	DEATH YEAR	NAME	AGE OR YOB.	BIRTH PLACE	CERT. NO	ID	DEATH YEAR
Peter J.	25	SF	6915		1904	Lena V.	28	MO	7684		1868
Rebecca B.	52	ENG	2599		1873	William E.	45	NY	2233		1873
Rienzi J.	66	NY	6407		1904	**HUGHSTON**					
Robert H.	21	KY	7197		1900	George				Jan	1900
Rose	50	IRE	4192		1903						
Samuel Frederick	1864	PA	564c		1904	**HUGNET**					
Sarah	60	IRL	6328		1900	Edmond A.	<1	SF	4318		1867
Sarah Ann	1	SF	714b		1872	**HUGOL**					
Sarah H.				Jul	1898	Aimee	76	FRA	8515		1901
Sarah J.				Apr	1899	**HUGOT**					
Stephen M.	61	WAL	4800		1904	Victor				Jun	1899
Thomas	40	WI	2198		1903	**HUGUS**					
Thomas	55	ENG	3875	Nov	1901	John W.	65	PA	2645		1901
Thomas A.	51	WAL	1302		1869	**HUH**					
William	50	NY	3699		1870	Ah	34	CHN	3479a		1872
William	<1	CA	1368		1871	**HUHN**					
William	55	IRL	2354a		1872	Samuel	32	PRU	6634		1868
William	45	WAL	5525		1867	**HUHS**					
William	44	IRE	8644		1904	Matilda	46	IRL	7706		1901
William	1839	ENG	3096c		1904	**HUICHMAN**					
William	27	NY	1023		1902	Charles Henry	83	NY	2026		1901
William	<1	SF	5935	Jan	1901	**HUIE**					
William D.				Feb	1900	Bock Quai	48	CHN	3180		1902
William T.	3	SF	3997		1870	Chong Bow	36	CHN	2117		1902
William T.	16	MA	1878		1866	Dai See	58	CHN	4866		1903
William/Elizabeth, c/o	1	CA	8439		1904	Goey	61	CHN	5945		1903
Wm.	60	RI	2630		1895	Suey Song	31	CHN	7076		1902
Wm., Capt.				Jul	1898	**HULACHER**					
HUGHEY						John/Emma L., c/o		SF	8445		1901
Jas.	45	IRL	H15		1882	**HULDAGRAVES**					
HUGHS						——	<1	SF	4997		1896
Charles H.	<1	SF	972		1866	**HULGAN**					
Elizabeth	30	MA	3193		1895	James C.				Dec	1899
HUGHSON											
Lena	2	HI	2097		1866						

NAME	AGE OR YOB.	BIRTH PLACE	CERT. NO	ID	DEATH YEAR
HULING					
Maria	<1	SF	7631		1902
HULL					
Charles	<1	SF	6981		1868
Charles F.	<1	SF	7738		1868
Jacob P. (soldier)			6257		1900
Jerome	<1	SF	8139		1900
Lion				Feb	1899
HULLO					
Joseph (soldier)			433		1902
HULME					
Charles (soldier)			4900		1901
George	50	NJ	222		1870
James S.	56	NJ	279b		1895
HULPIN					
John	35	IRL	508a		1871
HULSBERG					
Lenora	45	GER	6650		1903
HULSE					
Samuel D.				Jan	1899
HULSEBERG					
Frederick (soldier)			2506		1900
HULT					
George				Mar	1900
HULTBERG					
Augusta	32	SWE	6582		1896
HULTON					
Anthony				Mar	1899
HULTZ					
Andrew Thomas	<1	SF	3070a		1872
HUM					
Ah	29	CHN	348		1870
Ah	23	CHN	2713a		1872

NAME	AGE OR YOB.	BIRTH PLACE	CERT. NO	ID	DEATH YEAR
Ah Yep	36	CHN	4878		1896
Chun	25	CHN	992		1870
Chung Hui	54	CHN	5732		1904
Gin	39	CHN	5510		1904
Hum Y./Hum L., c/o			3203		1904
Jane	1829	CHN	2455c		1904
Lee	38	CHN	6243		1867
Mue	40	CHN	3306		1903
Qui	30	CHN	5580		1904
Si We	40	CHN	6049		1896
Yick	45	CHN	5786	Jan	1901
HUMAN					
Bones				Aug	1899
Bones				Aug	1899
HUMBER					
Robert C., Jr. (soldier)		CA	295		1903
HUMBERT					
Charles	35	FRA	789b		1872
Minnie Louise	52	OH	382		1901
William B.	56	PA	7588		1902
HUMBURG					
Mary	54	NY	3151		1895
HUME					
Charles W.	<1	SF	3191		1870
Emma E.	<1	SF	5424		1867
Lydia C.	27	OH	4574		1904
Myrtle Annie F.	1901	SF	2954c		1904
HUMMEL					
Charles	1847	PA	2266c		1904
John	74	GER	2961		1900
Joseph Aloys	<1	SF	242		1901
Mary Elizabeth	4	MO	1367		1869
Valentine	36	GER	3672a		1895

NAME	AGE OR YOB.	BIRTH PLACE	CERT. NO	ID	DEATH YEAR
HUMMELL					
Hannah	43	GER	284a		1871
John W.	40	GER	3579	Nov	1901
HUMMELTENBERG					
Nellie O.	58	SWE	6785		1903
HUMMER					
Chas. E. (soldier)			6822		1900
HUMMITZSCH					
Wm.	42	GER	309b		1872
HUMPHREY					
Clara Somerset				Jul	1898
George W.	52	NJ	3687		1903
Gertrude	<1	SF	6138	Jan	1901
Nellie	19	CA	5677		1903
Paul O. (soldier)			8565		1904
Peter A. (soldier)			2220		1903
Renney (soldier)			8068		1900
William E.	2	SF	1392		1870
HUMPHREYS					
David T.	73	WAL	7312		1904
Geo. W	45		H119		1886
Robert	69	IRE	6949		1904
HUMPHRIES					
Jac	1855	ENG	1769c		1904
William (soldier)			6938		1900
HUMUSEL					
——			6352		1867
HUN					
Chin	34	CHN	5494		1867
Tu				Dec	1899
Young Tie				Aug	1899
HUNCKE					
Adelheid H.	33	GER	4371b		1870

NAME	AGE OR YOB.	BIRTH PLACE	CERT. NO	ID	DEATH YEAR
HUND					
John B.	42	GER	6128		1896
HUNDLEY					
Geraldine Catherine	<1	SF	6578a		1895
HUNDON					
Sarah V.	75	ME	3605		1903
HUNDRUP					
Jens Peter	56	DEN	3727		1900
HUNDT					
Elenore E.	<1	SF	6205a		1895
Frederick				Jul	1898
HUNE					
Yung Sun	39	CHN	3278a		1872
HUNG					
Ah	30	CHN	292		1870
Ah	31	CHN	774b		1871
Ah	23	CHN	135a		1871
Ah	33	CHN	900b		1872
Ah	45	CHN	1156b		1872
Ah	29	CHN	5252		1867
Ah Song	24	CHN	2088		1870
Chin	22	CHN	2056		1870
Chun	16	CHN	1188b		1872
Chung	25	CHN	2165		1873
Gong	65	CHN	2735		1900
Hong	1852	CHN	1220c		1904
J.		CHN	567b		1872
Lieng Hee	50	CHN	3119	Oct	1901
Liis				Aug	1898
Loo	23	CHN	4408b		1870
Pock	24	CHN	947b		1871
Pon	1868	CHN	1189c		1904
Sie	55	CHN	7368		1901
Tom	1849	CHN	3256c		1904

Key: a = 1st part of year; b = 2nd part of year;
c = death certificate copy; c/o = child of

NAME	AGE OR YOB.	BIRTH PLACE	CERT. NO	ID	DEATH YEAR	NAME	AGE OR YOB.	BIRTH PLACE	CERT. NO	ID	DEATH YEAR
Hungenrt						Albert H.	<1	SF	711		1866
Theodore	41	GER	7078		1868	Amos O.	32	ME	5197		1867
						Andrew	59	IRL	2315		1873
Hungerford						Arthur (soldier)			1283		1902
Ella	26	WI	7304		1903	Arthur S.				Feb	1900
Hungnrt						Asa	43	IN	383a		1871
Theodore	41	GER	7078		1868	Augusta Maria	<1		1965b		1872
Hungton						Catherina	51	IRL	5989		1896
John E.		SF	1970		1870	Charles Edward	<1	SF	8082		1868
Huning						Charles H.	23	MA	2612		1866
Carl	36	GER	8123		1900	D.A.	62	MA	4129		1896
Hunke						Edgar L.	18	SF	941		1900
Frank	28	GER	257		1870	Edward	56	ENG	3545	Nov	1901
Hunken						Edward M.	45	ME	1980b		1895
Gertrude	<1	SF	1798		1894	Edward R.	17	NV	4313a		1895
						Edwin	21	MA	H155		1887
Hunker						Elizabeth	84	GER	9036		1903
Annie M.	46	GER	3477		1902	Florence A.	3	SF	237a		1871
Hunkin						Francis E.	<1	SF	2270		1866
Veda M.	<1	SF	3453		1896	Frank	72	KY	3781		1902
Hunksinger						George E. P.	60	MA	6255		1902
Pearl			H39		1883	George Washington	84	NY	1061		1903
Hunn						Graham				Dec	1899
Bernhard	65	GER	1270		1900	Harry	<1	SF	3924		1870
John				Mar	1899	Henry	<1	SF	8320		1868
Hunner						Isabela	<1	SF	2032		1866
Maria	2	SF	1299		1894	J. D.	45	CAN	687		1902
Hunsaker						J., c/o		SF	5038		1895
John Walter	1850	TX	3050c		1904	James S.	73	ME	3929		1900
						Jane				Jan	1899
Hunshan						Jane E.	73	ENG	4449a		1895
Edsel/Annie, c/o				Jan	1899	John	34	ENG	676		1866
Hunt						John	64	IRE	6916		1904
———			4696		1867	John L.	61	MA	4366		1896
———			5350		1867	John T.	36	PA	1455		1869
———			7699		1868	John/Kitty, c/o		SF	8606		1900

Key: *a = 1st part of year; b = 2nd part of year;
c = death certificate copy; c/o = child of*

NAME	AGE OR YOB.	BIRTH PLACE	CERT. NO	ID	DEATH YEAR	NAME	AGE OR YOB.	BIRTH PLACE	CERT. NO	ID	DEATH YEAR
Jonathan Page				Aug	1899	George	40	ENG	4507		1867
Julia E.	32	ME	129		1870	George	56	SCT	3535a		1895
Lorah C.	5	GER	3424		1867	Harry Elmer	28	CA	95		1902
Marcus	81	IRE	4710		1904	J. J.				Aug	1899
Margaret	61	IRL	2557		1900	James	5	SF	326		1870
Maria G.	<1	SF	1201		1866	James	41	IRL	1422a		1871
Mary	1	CA	2687		1903	James G.	53	NS	6208	Feb	1901
Mary Jane	60	NY	3353		1900	Jno. B.	24	RI	4248a		1895
Mary R.	34	NY	3740		1870	Joan N. G.				Jun	1899
Mattie, Mrs.	54	CA	2145		1900	John C. (sodier)			3049	Oct	1901
Minnie T.				Dec	1898	Joseph Burns	1844		2592c		1904
Nellie	36	MI	688		1902	Julia A.	68	NY	1191b		1895
Patrick	40	IRE	1106		1869	Leslie L./Emily, c/o	1	SF	963		1903
Robert	52	ENG	1425		1901	Luther	36	VA	8537		1903
Robert Menzo	74	NY	482		1902	Mary D.		SF	3043		1870
Thomas	<1	CA	2650		1895	P. S.				May	1899
Una	1	CA	1504		1903	S. L.	<1	SF	3046		1866
William	43	MD	1882b		1872	Samuel	34	SCT	8862		1868
William	59	IRL	H105		1886	Samuel R.	35	CAN	4159	Dec	1901
William B.	1837	ENG	565c		1904	Sarah Moss				May	1899
Huntaman						William	<1	SF	2026a		1872
Hannah, Mrs.	65	IRL	1029		1901	William	60		4687		1903
						William H.	49	SCT	2403		1866
Hunter						William W.	1878	NV	1990c		1904
Alexander	39	NY	1219		1866	Wm.				Jun	1899
Ameila	32	WAL	8912		1868	Wm. (soldier)			8793		1901
Andry Joseph	1904	SF	3097c		1904	Wm. E. (soldier)			3545		1900
Anna	37	CAN	6753		1904	**Hunthausen**					
Arthur	10	CA	280		1902	Ernst	28	PRU	1052		1868
Bruce	1	SF	8881		1900	**Huntinglen**					
Clara Louise	40	CA	6312		1904	Hurbert	<1	SF	5167		1867
Edward (soldier)			276		1901	**Huntington**					
Edward, Capt.			7707		1901	Almah M.	2	CA	H160		1887
Elizabeth Caroline				Apr	1899	Bella	61	ENG	4089	Dec	1901
Estelle Mary	8	SF	3546	Nov	1901	Charles A.	1812	VT	1934c		1904
Frank			7658		1902						

Key: a = 1st part of year; b = 2nd part of year;
c = death certificate copy; c/o = child of

NAME	AGE OR YOB.	BIRTH PLACE	CERT. NO	ID	DEATH YEAR
George	71	NY	5647		1904
James Pticher	35	NY	4437		1901
John A.	70		7345		1904
Mary Sophia, Mrs.	56	OH	9079		1901
Ray					Oct 1898
HUNTLEY					
Charles	1904	SF	2075c		1904
Charles D. (soldier)			943		1901
Wm.	47	VT	3866a		1895
HUNTON					
Lewis	28	ENG	3341		1866
HUNTRESS					
Temperance	60	NH	4334		1867
HUNTT					
Mary Elizabeth	45	SF	1589		1902
HUNZIKER					
Theodore Gottlieb A.	43	SWT	495		1903
HUPEL					
Aloysius	73	GER	5283		1903
HUPERO					
Josephine	41	SF	7673		1902
HUPERS					
Monitz					Dec 1899
HUPFELD					
Wilhelmina	58	NY	2864		1901
HUPPER					
Katherina	66	GER	8023		1900
HUPPERT					
Philip	28	CA	8249		1900
Philip					Aug 1899
HUPPMAN					
Ada	1867	CA	1902c		1904

NAME	AGE OR YOB.	BIRTH PLACE	CERT. NO	ID	DEATH YEAR
HURALGO					
Rose	<1	SF	455		1870
HURBY					
Horace	47	SC	99		1865
HURCHMAN					
Augustus Felix					Jan 1899
HURD					
Burt D./Clara F., c/o	<1	SF	3215		1895
Charles A.	24	AR	8259		1903
Charles E.	28	SF	3300		1900
Elsie May	35	CAN	8852		1904
James T.	73	KY	6350		1903
Jesse P.	32	CA	6988		1902
Jethro Hansen	67	ME	6208		1896
John Hiram	32	IA	746		1903
Joseph M.	62	NY	6915		1903
Marion Brunton	1	SF	2753		1903
Sarah A.	48	NY	3075a		1872
HURDEN					
George D.	45	ENG	33c		1904
HURLBERT					
Gustavus G.	56	MA	5914		1896
Sarah	<1	SF	5220		1902
HURLBRICK					
Ernest	35	GER	H80		1885
HURLBURT					
Mary	<1	SF	3517		1867
HURLBUT					
——			3083		1866
Charles M.	1862	PA	543c		1904
HURLEY					
——			2411		1866
Albert	<1	SF	2614		1894
Alexander	1904	CA	3324c		1904

Key: a = 1st part of year; b = 2nd part of year;
c = death certificate copy; c/o = child of

NAME	AGE OR YOB.	BIRTH PLACE	CERT. NO	ID	DEATH YEAR	NAME	AGE OR YOB.	BIRTH PLACE	CERT. NO	ID	DEATH YEAR
Anne	24	MA	3665		1867	Johanna				Jun	1899
Beatrice	6	CA	4345		1896	John	60	IRL	996b		1872
Bridget	57	IRL	2353		1894	John	<1	SF	2487		1873
Catherine	80	IRL	3953a		1895	John	45	IRE	7524		1903
Charles	1	SF	777b		1871	John	35	WAL	7921		1903
Charles	33	MA	905		1902	John	31	CA	1762b		1895
Charles J.	<1	SF	3890		1867	John	55	IRL	1399		1894
Cornelius	1	SF	4563b		1870	John				Aug	1899
Cornelius	32	IRE	2075		1903	John				Dec	1899
Daniel	23		5089		1867	John Francis	<1	SF	928		1900
Daniel	<1	SF	2261		1900	John I.	7	SF	8625		1868
Daniel	80	IRL	3021	Oct	1901	John J.	8	SF	5128		1904
Daniel				Feb	1900	John James	3	CA	8319		1900
Daniel/Annie, c/o	<1	SF	2135		1902	John W.	19	NV	4226		1902
Daniel/Margareth, c/o		SF	5122		1896	Julia	<1	SF	5038		1903
Dennis	<1	CA	615		1866	Julia	63	IRL	1501		1900
Dennis	82	IRE	2800		1903	Lawrence				Feb	1900
Dennis L.	5	CA	1204		1869	Lenora V.				Mar	1899
Elizabeth	13	IRL	897b		1871	Lizzey	<1	SF	4019		1867
Elizabeth				Nov	1898	Loretta				Oct	1899
Ellen	70	IRL	H41		1883	Margaret A.	13	SF	3751		1867
Ellen	<1	SF	6494		1868	Margaret D.	62	IRE	6664		1904
Ellen Elizabeth	<1	SF	583b		1872	Mark	79	IRL	809		1894
Florence	<1	SF	6234		1904	Mary	55	IRE	1453		1869
Hannah	40	IRL	975b		1871	Mary	41	IRE	8891		1903
J. D.	35		3969	Dec	1901	Mary	<1	SF	2377		1901
James	<1	SF	66		1870	Mary E.				Jun	1899
James	72	IRE	5292		1904	Michael	88	IRE	2773		1903
James	48	IRE	2757		1902	Michael	78	IRE	5605		1904
James F.	75	MA	665		1902	Michael	83	IRE	2642		1903
Jas./Mary, c/o				Mar	1899	Michael	44	IRL	7976		1900
Jeremiah	35	IRE	3976		1867	Michael J.	1858	CA	3238c		1904
Jeremiah				Feb	1900	Michael J.			3792		1902
Jeremiah T. (soldier)			597		1900	Michael M.	60	IRE	2819		1902
Johanna	21	SF	2297		1873	Michael P.	36	MA	768a		1871
Johanna	1851	IRE	379c		1904	Nellie	23	MA	H22		1882

Key: a = 1st part of year; b = 2nd part of year;
c = death certificate copy; c/o = child of

NAME	AGE OR YOB.	BIRTH PLACE	CERT. NO	ID	DEATH YEAR	NAME	AGE OR YOB.	BIRTH PLACE	CERT. NO	ID	DEATH YEAR
Nellie	36	CA	4844		1902	Jose	1	SF	8580		1868
Nellie Frances	19	SF	204		1901	**HURTHERE**					
Patrick	38	IRE	7728		1903	Helene	3	SF	6006	Jan	1901
Patrick	67	IRL	5204		1901	Leonie	10	SF	666		1902
Patrick	30	SF	1840		1900						
Sarah Gertrude	2	SF	3802		1903	**HURTON**					
Timothy	35	SF	2227		1902	Declan	<1	SF	2376		1901
William	<1	SF	3996		1867	**HUSBAND**					
						James A.	32	CAN	1095		1866
HURLY						Mary	<1	SF	3101a		1872
Caroline M.	<1	SF	3371		1870						
Charles J.	32	NY	8238		1868	**HUSBANDS**					
Mary		NY	6568		1868	Mary	36	IRL	1253b		1872
Timothy G.		CA	6162	Jan	1901	**HUSCH**					
						Pearl	3	SF	6305	Feb	1901
HURNEBERG											
Fredrick W.				Jan	1899	**HUSDON**					
						Mary				Aug	1899
HURNNEKINS											
John A. C. (soldier)			281		1901	**HUSHSPRING**					
						Hannah	99	POL	6638		1900
HURRELL											
Henry	47	ENG	3130		1895	**HUSING**					
						Fred	46	GER	1137b		1895
HURRELMANN						Henry/Ereka, c/o		SF	9061		1901
——	<1	SF	3817		1870	John	40	GER	2410		1873
						Mary Jane	31	SF	1136b		1895
HURSON						Rathys	54	GER	3298		1894
Ellen	56	IRE	1772		1903						
Joseph	<1	SF	3632		1896	**HUSON**					
						Charles L.	37	BC	2774		1903
HURST											
Aaron C. (soldier)			2065		1901	**HUSSELIER**					
Ellen	70	IRL	4310		1901	Jno. R.	<1	SF	4364a		1895
Frank	59	GER	4711		1904						
Harry	35	NY	H104		1886	**HUSSEN**					
James	53	IRE	1139		1903	Ellen				Jan	1900
John J. (soldier)			5051		1901	**HUSSENOT**					
Mabel	4	SF	379b		1895	Emilie	1903	SF	116c		1904
HURTADO						**HUSSEY**					
Hermania	<1	SF	3767		1867	Andrew	69	IRE	1606		1903

NAME	AGE OR YOB.	BIRTH PLACE	CERT. NO	ID	DEATH YEAR
Arthur C.	1	SF	669		1901
Bridget	78	IRL	5629	Jan	1901
Ellen	60	IRE	3726		1903
Hanna J.				Dec	1898
James	39	NY	3084		1895
Marie C.				Jul	1898
Mary A.	80	IRL	6619	Feb	1901
Michael	68	IRE	8221		1904
Patrick	44	IRL	3431a		1872
Patrick J.	50	NY	3879		1896
Rose Lillian	1	SF	2827		1903
Simon	88	IRE	5612		1902
Wm. H. (soldier)			6829		1900
Wurza Beatrice	2	SF	1609b		1872
HUSSMAN					
Rudolph	45	GER	3271		1902
HUSSMANN					
John/Kate, c/o				Jul	1899
HUSSON					
Elizabeth	74	IRL	3913	Dec	1901
Francois				Aug	1899
James	35	IRL	2699a		1872
HUSTED					
Harold Robert	2	CA	359		1903
HUSTEDT					
John	38	GER	6163	Jan	1901
HUSTENDAHL					
Julia		SF	1167b		1871
HUSTIN					
John	81	IRL	8093		1900
HUSTON					
——		SF	1362		1869
Arthur	27	ENG	5529	Jan	1901
Gertrude				Oct	1899

NAME	AGE OR YOB.	BIRTH PLACE	CERT. NO	ID	DEATH YEAR
John	65	IRL	2466b		1895
Minna Della	28	KS	6873		1903
Robert B. (soldier)			876		1900
Wm. D./Jannett, c/o	1904	SF	2854		1904
HUTCH					
Eben	47	MA	372a		1871
Mary				Aug	1899
HUTCHINGS					
Adrian	40	MA	6019		1903
Edward	23	NJ	360		1902
Mary	30	IRE	2694		1866
HUTCHINS					
Alfred L. (soldier)			2071		1901
C. B.				May	1899
Charles	<1	SF	1004b		1872
Charles E.				Dec	1898
George		SF	606		1866
George B.	53	ME	67b		1871
Henry				Dec	1899
Joseph A.				Dec	1898
Lemuel W.	1833	ME	2706c		1904
Lillie E.	42	CA	4111	Dec	1901
Lulu	31	CA	6780		1904
Thomas Boyd	56	CAN	2559		1903
HUTCHINSON					
Alden Vivian	<1	SF	845		1902
Andrew	65	IRL	8650		1900
Charles	9	SF	1349		1869
Charles A.	22	ME	1204		1869
Christopher J.	48	RI	6960		1902
Daniel				Aug	1898
De Forest (soldier)			6824		1900
Elma L.	58	OH	2972		1895
Ernest	13	CA	1413b		1871
James	31	NY	938a		1871

NAME	AGE OR YOB.	BIRTH PLACE	CERT. NO	ID	DEATH YEAR
Jane B.	72	WAL	3197		1900
John F.	42	IRE	6644		1868
John I.	5	SF	7167		1868
John Jennings				Oct	1898
Joseph C.				Dec	1898
Laura Stonefield	3	SF	1266		1869
Maria	32	ENG	1476b		1872
Mary Eubonia	34	NY	1273		1869
O. M.		PA	H154		1887
Patrick	50	IRL	6514		1900
Sarah West, Mrs.	70	PA	2433		1901
Stephen	69	MA	1948b		1895
Thomas	34	NY	9378		1868
William	<1	SF	7492		1868
William	78	SCT	6765	Feb	1901
William				Mar	1899
William G.	1825	ENG	3473c		1904
William J.	1	SF	8847		1868

HUTCHISON

NAME	AGE OR YOB.	BIRTH PLACE	CERT. NO	ID	DEATH YEAR
Alonzo/Annie, c/o	<1	CA	1335		1902
Dorothy Mason	1868	MA	81c		1904
Edmond S.	1870	SCT	1460c		1904
J. W.	1867	KY	2617c		1904
Jane P.	21	SCT	4677		1867
Kate E.	48	CA	6080		1902
William J.	41	PA	6942		1903

HUTH

NAME	AGE OR YOB.	BIRTH PLACE	CERT. NO	ID	DEATH YEAR
C. C.	63	GER	1839		1870
Jacob (soldier)			5489	Jan	1901

HUTSLAR

NAME	AGE OR YOB.	BIRTH PLACE	CERT. NO	ID	DEATH YEAR
Samuel W. (soldier)			6747	Feb	1901

HUTTE

NAME	AGE OR YOB.	BIRTH PLACE	CERT. NO	ID	DEATH YEAR
Arthur D.	<1	SF	8397		1904
Irene N.	2	SF	6069		1904
Mary A.	60	CAN	7862		1904

HUTTER

NAME	AGE OR YOB.	BIRTH PLACE	CERT. NO	ID	DEATH YEAR
Rosa	36	GER	5294		1901

HUTTON

NAME	AGE OR YOB.	BIRTH PLACE	CERT. NO	ID	DEATH YEAR
Caroline A.				Nov	1899
Corrinne	1878	CA	2519c		1904
Fred A.	36	SF	6351		1903
James B.	1871	CA	469c		1904
James W.				Oct	1898
John	76	NB	6408		1902
Margaret Cleary	79	SCT	3326		1895
Samuel J./Lizzie, c/o	<1	SF	1396		1900
William	44	SCT	992		1902
Wm. H./Margaret J., c/o	1	SF	4659		1904

HUTTORI

NAME	AGE OR YOB.	BIRTH PLACE	CERT. NO	ID	DEATH YEAR
Chinsuki				Jan	1900

HUTTS

NAME	AGE OR YOB.	BIRTH PLACE	CERT. NO	ID	DEATH YEAR
Janet	1		6806		1904

HUTTUNA

NAME	AGE OR YOB.	BIRTH PLACE	CERT. NO	ID	DEATH YEAR
Adolf (soldier)			2165		1901

HUTZ

NAME	AGE OR YOB.	BIRTH PLACE	CERT. NO	ID	DEATH YEAR
Diedrich H. Geo.	5	SF	5736		1867

HUWE

NAME	AGE OR YOB.	BIRTH PLACE	CERT. NO	ID	DEATH YEAR
Emma	<1	SF	926b		1872
Wendelin	65	GER	2048		1903

HUWYLER

NAME	AGE OR YOB.	BIRTH PLACE	CERT. NO	ID	DEATH YEAR
Jacob	49	SWT	6820		1902

HUXTABLE

NAME	AGE OR YOB.	BIRTH PLACE	CERT. NO	ID	DEATH YEAR
Alethea M.				Jul	1899

HUY

NAME	AGE OR YOB.	BIRTH PLACE	CERT. NO	ID	DEATH YEAR
Henry	50	GER	7769		1868

HUYBRECHT

NAME	AGE OR YOB.	BIRTH PLACE	CERT. NO	ID	DEATH YEAR
Henry L.				Jan	1899

HUYLAND

NAME	AGE OR YOB.	BIRTH PLACE	CERT. NO	ID	DEATH YEAR
Thor	50	NY	H169		1887

NAME	AGE OR YOB.	BIRTH PLACE	CERT. NO	ID	DEATH YEAR	NAME	AGE OR YOB.	BIRTH PLACE	CERT. NO	ID	DEATH YEAR
HYAMS						HYLAN					
——	<1	SF	3683		1867	Edward (soldier)			7221		1900
George S. S.	66	ENG	5613		1896	HYLAND					
Pauline	59	GER	766		1901	Dennis	15	MA	2971		1866
HYATT						Emma Matilda	26	SF	8786		1904
Charles	25	MS	8476		1903	J. Amos				Oct	1898
Emily	28	PA	320b		1871	James				Jul	1898
Helen	22	CA	8823		1868	John T.	1	SF	4088b		1870
Mary A.	3	CA	754b		1872	Joseph B.	56	IRL	H114		1886
HYDE						Mary	34	IRL	3956		1870
——		SF	1245		1869	Mary	45	IRL	3114a		1872
Annie	40	IRL	6679		1896	Mary	6	MA	1557		1866
Charlotte P.	<1	SF	4610a		1895	Mary Ann	43	IRE	7542		1903
Frank Gale	30	NY	5787		1903	Michael	<1	SF	6737		1868
Henry H.	44	MA	4676		1867	Michael C.	55	IRL	504b		1895
Honora	32	IRL	2126a		1872	Morgan	50	IRL	463a		1871
James T.	41	IRE	1592		1866	Thomas	<1	SF	2458		1866
Jane O.	70	NH	3246		1894	William	40	IRE	1150		1869
Marietta Butler				Dec	1898	Wm./Bridget, c/o		CA	3351		1900
Mary				Feb	1900	HYLLIER					
Nancy J.	71	MA	399b		1895	Frank	13	CA	5216		1867
Oliver	87	MA	434		1901	HYLTON					
Patrick James	2	NV	1069		1869	Isa G. (soldier)			4899		1901
Richard	52	NY	8160		1904	William	<1	SF	1202		1869
Sarah Abbie	67	CT	2702		1903	HYMAN					
Veronica	37	NJ	3959a		1895	Abraham	62	POL	780b		1895
William	32	MA	1370b		1872	Annie	16	SF	636		1894
Wm F./Martha C., c/o	1	SF	4312		1903	Carrie	1870	LA	1083c		1904
Wm.	25	ENG	5966		1867	Helena	52	GER	1871b		1895
HYDELEFF						Henry	42	PRU	494a		1871
Edgar	<1		2837		1866	Isaac				Feb	1899
HYDEN						Jay				Dec	1899
Luna D.	66	MS	8447		1903	Lilly				Jan	1900
Rose	42	OH	7254		1902	Rachael	82	GER	3731		1902
						Sarah	61	POL	8645		1903

Key: a = 1st part of year; b = 2nd part of year; c = death certificate copy; c/o = child of

NAME	AGE OR YOB.	BIRTH PLACE	CERT. NO	ID	DEATH YEAR	NAME	AGE OR YOB.	BIRTH PLACE	CERT. NO	ID	DEATH YEAR
HYMES						**HYSLOP**					
Pompy (soldier)			8146		1901	William	70	SF	6812a		1895
Rachel	104	PRU	7789		1902						
Sarah	61	NB	H149		1887	**IACANO**					
						Guiseppina	1903	SF	1338c		1904
HYNE											
Frederick N.	29	AUS	2100		1901	**IAGGI**					
						Emile	36	SWT	6288		1904
HYNER											
Frederick (soldier)			1317		1902	**IAN**					
John	41	IRL	H170		1887	Fannie Charlotte	44	SF	3978		1902
						Hebert	63	FRA	3020		1866
HYNES											
——			2048		1866	**IBERG**					
Aileen	1	SF	2305		1902	Lizzie	24	SF	1086b		1895
Bridget	77	IRL	768b		1872						
Bridget	1839	IRE	2645c		1904	**IBURG**					
David J.	39	IRE	1385		1869	Wm. M.	63	GER	6590		1896
Henry	1	SF	1043b		1871						
John		SF	1426		1869	**ICANBERRY**					
John	67	IRL	4343		1896	Dora	30	CA	5851		1903
John	72	IRL	2008		1901						
John				Dec	1898	**ICARD**					
John Henry	1	SF	1135		1869	Edward				May	1899
Kate	20	NY	3534a		1895	**ICE**					
Lloyd A.	1893	SF	1965c		1904	Haim	45	CHN	928		1901
Loretta	1904	SF	278c		1904						
Mary	48	IRL	4285		1901	**ICHIRO**					
Mary				Dec	1898	Hishi Moto				Jun	1899
Michael	60	IRE	2445		1903						
Michael				Nov	1899	**ICKETHEMIR**					
Michael P.	45		1196b		1871	——			7234		1868
William	40	PRU	1388		1869						
						IDDINGS					
HYPPOLITE						Henry A.	56	OH	6209	Feb	1901
Lacoste	22	FRA	1647a		1871						
						IDE					
HYSHAM						John	61	MA	1375		1869
Vetri R.				Aug	1898	M.	45	JPN	2101		1894
						IDEN					
						Diederich	55	GER	2436		1902
						IDINGTON					
						Alexander	28	CAN	946a		1871

NAME	AGE OR YOB.	BIRTH PLACE	CERT. NO	ID	DEATH YEAR	NAME	AGE OR YOB.	BIRTH PLACE	CERT. NO	ID	DEATH YEAR
IFFERT						ILG					
Leonard	66	GER	2901		1901	Alma	8	CA	5572		1902
IGEL						ILLCH					
Ludwig	55	GER	4328		1867	Dr. A.	27	NY	I6		1885
IGNACE						ILLIDGE					
Francois Emile	42	FRA	6373		1902	George Jacques	62	AUT	313		1902
IGNATIUS						ILLING					
Max			8054		1903	Fritz	54	GER	7061	Feb	1901
IGO						ILLINGWORTH					
James	25	IRE	8930		1868	Robert William	43	ENG	8417		1904
James	55	IRE	3153		1902	ILMAINEN					
Mary				Mar	1900	A. A.	38	FIN	5606		1904
IH						ILS					
Gee	40	CHN	5511		1904	Emilie	12	SF	1141c		1904
IHMELS						Josephine M.	<1	SF	125a		1871
Carl	40	GER	2700		1866	ILSE					
IHNEN						L./S., c/o	<1	SF	2532		1894
Isabella	48	IRL	1997b		1895	Louise	38	GER	5669		1902
IHRIE						ILTIS					
Mary Ann	66	NC	2690		1901	Willie (soldier)			69		1901
IIOHAN						IMAI					
Martin	50	HOL	1448		1903	Kiyoshi	26	JPN	2304		1903
IKEBE						IMANISHI					
Takeo	23	JPN	6		1901	J.	38	JPN	7991		1901
IKEDA						IMANUEL					
Gosaku	20	JPN	7461		1904	Herman			9173		1868
Miyo	22	JPN	359		1901	IMARSURA					
IKEN						Iwakichi	39	JPN	4046	Dec	1901
Frederick	65	GER	I5		1885	IMBERT					
IKI						Ferdinand	58	FRA	4867a		1895
Tsuji	<1	SF	4020		1900	IMBESCHEID					
IKULA						Bertha				Jun	1899
Goraku	19	JPN	3729		1900						

Key: a = 1st part of year; b = 2nd part of year; c = death certificate copy; c/o = child of

NAME	AGE OR YOB.	BIRTH PLACE	CERT. NO	ID	DEATH YEAR	NAME	AGE OR YOB.	BIRTH PLACE	CERT. NO	ID	DEATH YEAR
IMDORF						Elisabeth	1	SF	6152		1902
Joachim	69	GER	3253		1902	**IMSICK**					
IMELLI						Melvin	1	SF	7570		1903
Max	59	GER	5771		1902	Theodor F.				May	1899
IMES						William				Oct	1898
Benjamin	56	MD	7473		1902	**IMWOOD**					
Charles F.	73	NY	5920a		1895	Allen	45	ENG	2035		1866
IMGLIS						**INA**					
Charles	1862	NY	3098c		1904	Yung	46	CHN	1366		1869
IMHAUS						**INABA**					
Celesto	74	BEL	7144		1904	Masahisa	27	JPN	4046		1902
Jules H. L.	57	PRU	1114b		1872	**INANA**					
IMLAY						Kimo				Apr	1899
Belle	30	UT	6611		1904	**INCARDONO**					
IMMACULATA						Guiseppe	65	ITA	4408	Dec	1901
——	<1	SF	6068		1903	**INCELL**					
IMMIN						Harry W.	36	CA	5861		1896
C.	45		2847		1903	**IND**					
IMOHL						Mary	56	IRE	3606		1903
Joseph	61	GER	1336		1902	**INDA**					
Theresa	72	GER	1534		1902	Luz	33	MEX	1512		1866
IMOTO						**INDERBITSAN**					
Fugigusu	27	JPN	3030		1903	Ediom J. (soldier)			283		1901
IMPASTATO						**INDERCOME**					
Concetta	1900	LA	2878c		1904	Joseph	<1	SF	5745		1896
IMPERIALE						**INDERMILLEHOM**					
Carlo	41	ITA	4532		1901	Frederick	80	SWT	1024		1902
IMSAND						**INDERSTROTH**					
Celestine	<1	SF	7313		1902	Theo	53	GER	1661		1894
Joseph I.				Aug	1899	**INDIAN**					
Louise	<1	CA	4450a		1895	Ignatia	15	SF	1692		1866
IMSARD						Lena	14	CA	4392		1867
Anna	<1	SF	5941		1902	Nellie	18	CA	794		1866

Key: a = 1st part of year; b = 2nd part of year;
c = death certificate copy; c/o = child of

NAME	AGE OR YOB.	BIRTH PLACE	CERT. NO	ID	DEATH YEAR	NAME	AGE OR YOB.	BIRTH PLACE	CERT. NO	ID	DEATH YEAR
Nellie	20	CA	4258		1867	**INGENTHORN**					
						John M.				Oct	1899
INDIAN BOY											
Antonio	17	CA	4021		1867	**INGERSOLL**					
Dick	14	CA	1602		1866	Agnes	24	ENG	6696		1868
						Annie F.	66	MA	1361		1901
INDIG						Curtis H.			7659		1902
Louis	60	GER	5760		1896	William	<1	SF	3299		1902
Sarah	22	CA	I4		1885						
						INGERSON					
INDORF						Alice H.	11	SF	3780a		1895
Ernst A.	<1	SF	7657		1868	Edward B.				Jul	1898
INEZ											
Francisco	33	POR	7850		1868	**INGERTELA**					
Manuel	45	POR	6408		1867	Albert	41	FIN	8366		1900
ING						**INGHAM**					
Ah Gar	25	CHN	2412		1873	Francis A.	26	NY	9594		1868
Lei	25	CHN	3147		1870	Mamie	33	CO	7145		1904
						Richard	74	CT	1369		1902
INGALLS						Thomas L. (soldier)			6474		1900
George P.	31	ME	1318		1869						
William A.			3902		1902	**INGLANDER**					
						Bernard	<1	SF	2563a		1872
INGAM											
Elmer (soldier)			9566		1901	**INGLE**					
						Conley A. (soldier)			6831		1900
INGARGIOLA						Joesph	45		3638		1903
Gertrude	<1	SF	3301		1894						
Laurence	23	LA	662b		1872	**INGLIS**					
						Jane	72	ENG	1795		1901
INGARIOULA						Lillian	27	NV	1502		1900
Kate	37	PA	6870Feb		1901						
						INGOLS					
INGE						George H.	41	MA	7084		1868
Samuel W.	81	NC	7812		1868	Levi	73	MA	1289a		1871
INGELL						**INGRAHAM**					
George Percy	4	SF	1219		1901	——		SF	1191		1869
INGELS						Frederick	40	SF	963		1870
Ella	44	IA	2305		1903	James A.	32	MA	1757		1866
M./A., c/o		SF	6197		1895	Maud	1	SF	2740		1873

Key: a = 1st part of year; b = 2nd part of year; c = death certificate copy; c/o = child of

NAME	AGE OR YOB.	BIRTH PLACE	CERT. NO	ID	DEATH YEAR	NAME	AGE OR YOB.	BIRTH PLACE	CERT. NO	ID	DEATH YEAR
INGRAM						**INTERMAN**					
Fred W.	13	ENG	1451		1869	Henry	28	GER	2988		1873
Joseph E.	<1	SF	1371		1869	**INWOOD**					
Nelda				Jun	1899	George	88	ENG	8283		1901
Oscar V.	5	CA	2688		1903	Susan	70	ENG	2569a		1872
Sarah Louise	4	CA	I1		1882	William G.				Mar	1899
William	42	IRL	3187		1870	**IOEDICKE**					
William				Mar	1899	Hermann	35	GER	735		1870
INGRE						**IRAZOGUE**					
Louisa E.	50	AL	3143a		1872	Ramon	<1	SF	3552		1870
INGROERRSEN						**IRAZOQUI**					
Ole	25	DEN	4230a		1895	Francois	70	FRA	4826a		1895
INGUGLIA						**IREDALE**					
G. B.,/I. M., c/o				Mar	1899	Alfred S.				Dec	1899
Glayds Otelia	1	CA	3936		1903	John Jackson	30	ENG	1216		1869
INGWERSEN						**IRELAND**					
Chas./Anna, c/o		SF	834		1901	Albert	34	OH	7102		1902
INLAN						G./T., c/o	<1	SF	4630		1895
Wm.	84	NJ	4058a		1895	Liliy	<1	SF	2031		1900
INMAN						Thomas	49	ENG	7310		1868
Albert Masoh	45	MA	6813		1868	**IRELARRY**					
INNIS						Jean	60	FRA	387		1902
James (soldier)			7321		1901	**IRENBERGER**					
John	40	IRL	3093		1870	Dick R. (soldier)			8433		1900
INNS						**IRENE**					
Charles	50	ENG	5014		1901	Emelio	32	ITA	6774		1896
INOLA						**IRENE?**					
James	<1	SF	1383		1869	Josephine	<1	SF	2408		1902
INOUYE						**IRIASTE**					
Forakichi	28	JPN	8624		1903	Jiaute	36	CHN	4377		1867
Fuji	17	JPN	2736		1900	**IRIBARNE**					
Hideyoshi	16	JPN	2733		1903	Emelia	19	FRA	2742a		1872
INSBACH						Marie	19	FRA	3210a		1872
Alois	42	SWT	839		1900						

Key: a = 1st part of year; b = 2nd part of year;
c = death certificate copy; c/o = child of

NAME	AGE OR YOB.	BIRTH PLACE	CERT. NO	ID	DEATH YEAR
IRINA					
E./G., c/o		SF	2157		1894
IRISH					
Jonathan Rumsey	79	NY	206		1901
IRLAN					
Samuel	6	SF	5314		1867
IRM					
Carp	37	CHN	181a		1871
IRONMONGER					
Edna C.					Nov 1898
IRONS					
Mary A.	44	ENG	2244a		1872
IRONSIDES					
Sterling	35	ENG	2907		1895
IRVIN					
George W.	<1	SF	9366		1868
James	52	ENG	5908		1867
Jno	56	NB	1684		1894
Robt J.	47	IN	17		1886
William	42	IRL	1286b		1871
William B.	34	IA	2535		1903
IRVINE					
Abraham	51	IRE	8177		1868
Albert					Mar 1900
Chappille (twins)			8692		1868
David	36	IRL	3818		1896
Elizabeth	38	IRE	7229		1904
Emily	1862	ENG	2646c		1904
Frank Nutt	20	SF	8376		1904
Henry	45	CA	2049		1903
Irene	1891	SF	1493c		1904
James	65	NY	3705		1902
Joseph M.	<1	SF	5487		1867
Margaret	<1	SF	9753		1868
Thomas Frederick	7	SF	2195		1902
West	1837	PA	895c		1904
William L.	55	IRE	8328		1903
IRVING					
Andrew Kerr					Mar 1899
Caroline K.	63	NS	5801a		1895
David Wilfred	1903	SF	3204c		1904
Geo. W., Capt.					Dec 1899
Henry P.	77	VA	19		1887
Inez	<1	CA	2306		1902
Maria					Apr 1899
Walter					Jun 1899
Washington	<1	SF	1274		1869
Washington	66	MD	1698		1901
IRWIN					
Ann	77	NB	1673a		1871
Ann	77	NB	1673b		1871
Christopher	27	NY	6639a		1895
David Hanson	29	IRL	2140b		1895
Ellen	33	IRE	1030		1868
Fanny A.	60	IRL	1763b		1895
George W.	62	IRL	1574		1894
James	47	IRE	382		1903
James	75	IRL	4290		1901
James					Oct 1898
James B.	1878	SF	544c		1904
James Gilman	<1	SF	1306		1869
John	69	IRL	2632		1895
Julia	51	NY	7504		1904
Mariah	20	MA	8345		1868
Mary Ann	32	POL	1961		1866
Mary F.	55	IRL	4252		1896
Mary J.					Apr 1899
Pelig R	53	MA	13		1885
Robert	46	IRL	2646		1873

NAME	AGE OR YOB.	BIRTH PLACE	CERT. NO	ID	DEATH YEAR
Samuel	50	PA	5471		1902
Samuel Rutherford	52	PA	2908		1900
Sarah	28	NY	3352		1894
Thos,	24	IRL	I2		1883
William	1829	IRE	2454c		1904
ISAAC					
Albert	1	SF	9466		1868
Alice	83	ENG	3817		1896
Isador	24	PRU	1268		1869
John/Edith, c/o		SF	1766		1901
Lisa	10	SF	3021a		1872
Louis	26	POL	1171		1869
Solomon	65	BAV	6500		1902
William					Oct 1898
ISAACK					
Charles	1	SF	2970		1873
ISAACS					
——	<1	SF	3986		1870
Abbiegail	29	CA	3526		1903
Abraham/Fannie, c/o	1	SF	5169		1904
Albert	65	RUS	4771a		1895
Bella	1	SF	4409		1903
Benjamin	81	ENG	7680		1900
Bertha	25	CA	7994		1903
Caroline	38	GER	438		1866
Charles H.	25	CA	818b		1895
Emile	46	GER	1874b		1895
Esther Annie	1	CA	2871		1902
Genevive Agnes	3	SF	2833		1902
Hannah J.	53	PA	1387b		1895
Hulda	49	PRU	1686b		1871
Johanna, Mrs.	66	PRU	6433a		1895
John					Jul 1899
Joshua Laura	75	POL	3474		1903
Katie	62	MA	4481		1904

NAME	AGE OR YOB.	BIRTH PLACE	CERT. NO	ID	DEATH YEAR
Michael	76	GER	2009		1901
Minnie	69	GER	648		1901
Morris	1829	GER	3149c		1904
Nellie					Apr 1899
P. J.	28	ENG	1368		1869
Samuel	25	NY	I10		1889
Samuel	<1	SF	4945		1902
Samuel	61	GER	2885		1895
Sarah		SF	1410b		1872
Sim	64	ENG	5137a		1896
William	31	SF	8501		1904
William/Bertha, c/o	<1	SF	3218		1895
William/Minnie, c/o	<1	SF	1809		1902
Williams C.	<1	SF	6237		1903
ISAACSON					
Theodore	<1	SF	239		1902
ISACKSEN					
Christian	53	NOR	3170		1895
ISACSOHN					
Wolf	39	PRU	1218		1869
ISACSON					
Alfred	26	SWE	5942a		1895
ISADORE					
Isaac	62	RUS	1623		1894
ISAI					
Guadulope	22	SF	2580		1873
ISAIA					
Louisa	1	SF	4912		1902
ISAKSON					
Axel	23	FIN	6408		1904
ISELIN					
Albert					Jan 1899
Beartha	1	SF	1460b		1895

NAME	AGE OR YOB.	BIRTH PLACE	CERT. NO	ID	DEATH YEAR
ISENBERG					
Ernst George Otto	58	GER	3027		1902
ISENNEGGER					
Louis (soldier)			7774		1902
ISHEHARA					
Kamelaro				Jan	1900
ISHIHATA					
Tokumatsu	47	JPN	4253		1903
ISHII					
Yura	30	JPN	5524		1896
ISHIKAWA					
Chuzo	24	JPN	4482		1904
Fukumatsu	31	JPN	4425		1901
ISHIMIYU					
Yukia	<1	SF	8711		1903
ISHIYAMA					
Kanjiro	18	JPN	3111		1895
ISNARD					
Theophile	1874	FRA	3356c		1904
ISOLA					
Genoveffa	22	CA	6069		1903
Giacomo	<1	SF	5447		1867
James	<1	SF	8909		1868
Johannah	1	SF	719b		1871
John M.				Oct	1899
Joseph	<1	SF	1132b		1871
Louisa	4	SF	1268		1869
Patterina				Jan	1900
ISOMATO					
Yokichi	23	JPN	335		1903
ISOZAKI					
Shinshichi	40	JPN	4159		1902

NAME	AGE OR YOB.	BIRTH PLACE	CERT. NO	ID	DEATH YEAR
ISRA					
Josephine	1	SF	2213		1866
ISRAEL					
——			3036		1870
Charlotte	1857	SWT	3267c		1904
Earntine	27	PRU	3040		1870
Fannie	2	SF	5772		1902
G. L.	40		520a		1871
Geo. O.	2	CA	1869a		1972
Gustav, c/o		SF	3012		1895
Henry Clay				May	1899
Jacob	23	PA	7156		1903
Jacob M./Celia, c/o		SF	8735		1903
Jake/Celia, c/o		SF	5359		1901
Joseph				Nov	1898
Martha May	1	SF	6915		1868
ISRAELSKY					
Abraham				Jul	1899
Albert	25	GER	3252		1895
Esther	1851	GER	3176c		1904
Flora	70	FRA	6620	Feb	1901
William	21	SF	6413	Feb	1901
ISSLEITER					
Fred	35	GER	I8		1886
ISSOBY					
Caroline	40	FRA	2551		1873
ISSOLA					
Paoli	27	ITA	1125		1869
ISTEL					
Sohpia	78	ALS	144c		1904
ITEN					
Alfred	1864	SWT	1293c		1904
ITGEN					
Carl Herman	56	GER	9176		1901

Key: a = 1st part of year; b = 2nd part of year;
c = death certificate copy; c/o = child of

NAME	AGE OR YOB.	BIRTH PLACE	CERT. NO	ID	DEATH YEAR	NAME	AGE OR YOB.	BIRTH PLACE	CERT. NO	ID	DEATH YEAR
ITJEN						IVERSON					
Johannah	68	GER	3931		1900	Andrew (soldier)			7624		1900
ITO						Anna L.	<1	SF	908b		1872
Riketi	18	JPN	3688		1903	Charles	24	CA	1370		1902
ITOW						Charles Julian	1	SF	6722		1903
Maye		JPN	9220		1900	George W.	36	CA	2203		1900
S. I./Maye, c/o		SF	8221		1900	Jensine	1868	GER	2142c		1904
ITTNER						Peter	70	DEN	8330		1904
Emil	1902	SF	2037c		1904	IVES					
Paul/Augusta, c/o				Feb	1899	Abijah				Jul	1899
IUAI						Butler	40	MI	1777b		1871
Soo Shee	1860	CHN	1391c		1904	Chas. W.	42	NY	5815		1902
IUAKI						Frances T.	18	SF	6563		1902
Fuku	19	JPN	385		1901	IVINS					
IUERREN						Earnest B. D.	17	CA	8874		1901
Mary	1875	MA	627c		1904	IVISON					
IVANCEVICH						Ann Marie	2	CA	1533		1866
George	38	AUS	4688		1903	IVORY					
IVANCIH						——		SF	1245		1869
Giacomo	32	AUS	7157		1903	John Oscar	73	PA	6887		1903
IVANOVCH						Sarah	68	MA	1407		1903
Baseleo	38	RUS	3614		1867	IVY					
IVANOVICH						Minne E.	18	ME	3860		1870
John M.	32	AUS	361		1902	IWAKICHI					
IVANOVITCH						Miska	29	JPN	2347		1902
Nipolaus	50	SER	2529		1901	IWAMOTO					
IVERS						Seitaro	16	JPN	7124		1903
Ellen	48	MA	276		1903	IWATARO					
IVERSEN						Aoki				Oct	1899
Caroline	1854	CA	1619c		1904	IZUANAI					
Elsie K.	<1	SF	4637		1896	——	21	JPN	329		1870
Wilhelm Mark	7	CA	483		1902	IZZO					
						Benneditto	1859	ITA	1966c		1904

NAME	AGE OR YOB.	BIRTH PLACE	CERT. NO	ID	DEATH YEAR
JA					
Chuen	42	CHN	1623a		1871
Tu Ying	55	CHN	6018		1896
JACINTHO					
Jose	50	AZO	1892		1894
JACINTO					
John	3	CA	1074		1869
JACK					
——	1	SF	5293		1904
Ah	40	CHN	1438b		1895
Chock	37	CHN	1203		1894
Gon Sing		CHN	1136c		1904
He	42	CHN	4418		1867
How	41	CHN	J29		1885
Indian	85	CA	6406a		1895
Josephine	<1	SF	3186		1894
Robert Augustus					Jul 1898
William	86	IRE	6529		1902
Wong	1883	CA	1509c		1904
JACKARD					
William	45	ENG	3143		1870
JACKINS					
Franck C.	1	SF	1083		1866
JACKLIN					
Jno. H.	<1	SF	3632a		1895
Thomas/Mary, c/o	<1	SF	2509		1895
JACKMAN					
Anna Ida	2	WA	1275		1866
Arlington D. (soldier)			4704		1901
Geo.	35		J55		1889
Jelrict Blood	77	VT	960		1900
Margaret	70	IRL	8268		1901
Margaret					Nov 1898
Samuel C. (soldier)			823		1900

NAME	AGE OR YOB.	BIRTH PLACE	CERT. NO	ID	DEATH YEAR
JACKS					
Samuel E.	50	PA	4384		1867
JACKSON					
——			2004		1870
——			3708		1867
A./M., c/o					Oct 1899
Aham W.	85	MA	6304		1900
Alexander B.	67	PA	7821		1900
Andrew	52	AL	6789		1902
Anna	32	LA	3046		1873
Annie Amelia	1819	ENG	82c		1904
Augusta E.	1877	CA	1541c		1904
Catherine W.					Apr 1899
Charles	55	ME	3442		1900
Charles (soldier)			5187		1901
Charlotte Louise	1904	SF	1903c		1904
Chauncy T. (soldier)	25	PA	4703		1901
Clara	60	MD	4240		1903
Clarence					Oct 1899
Clyde Parker	1900	CA	828c		1904
Cyril F.	<1	SF	7491		1900
Delia	90	ENG	7930		1900
Eddie	<1	SF	5275		1896
Edward J.	75	ENG	7846		1900
Edward P.					Feb 1900
Elizabeth	25	CA	4207a		1895
Ellen					Aug 1898
Emma E.	3	SF	4848		1896
Fanny					Nov 1899
Francis	19	LA	2060		1870
Francis B.	47	OH	6591		1868
Frank	26	DEN	J22		1884
Frank	31	SF	8260		1903
Fred H.	47	ENG	3761		1896
Frederick C.			3903		1902

Key: a = 1st part of year; b = 2nd part of year;
c = death certificate copy; c/o = child of

NAME	AGE OR YOB.	BIRTH PLACE	CERT. NO	ID	DEATH YEAR	NAME	AGE OR YOB.	BIRTH PLACE	CERT. NO	ID	DEATH YEAR
Geo. L. (soldier)			62		1900	John C.				Dec	1898
George				Apr	1899	John Mason				Oct	1899
George H.	<1	SF	7832		1904	John Putnam	67	OH	1831		1900
George Hiram	53	MA	2838		1894	Josephine				Dec	1898
George S.	43	CA	9451		1901	Julia E.	48	AUS	194		1900
George W.	<1	SF	311		1900	Landon (soldier)	23	TN	6323	Feb	1901
Glen H. (soldier)			3685		1900	Lillie	<1	CA	6646		1900
H.				Dec	1899	Lizzie A.	22	NB	1172		1869
Hannah	66	POL	7539		1904	Logan B. (soldier)			285		1901
Hannah	41	POL	2834		1902	Louis	7	CA	J33		1886
Harold	<1	SF	537		1900	Louisa E.				Feb	1899
Harold				Nov	1899	Louisou	13	NY	3443		1867
Harriet	1	SF	3168		1903	Loyd	1904	SF	3357c		1904
Henry	59	VA	3861		1900	Lucy Ann	78	OH	621		1894
Isadore Gilbert	69	POL	1727		1902	Lucy S.	2	SF	1192		1869
J. F. Ernest				Jan	1900	Lulu C.	26	SF	4864		1896
J. J.			J40		1886	Magie	35	IRL	2403		1894
J. T.				Feb	1900	Margaret C.	74	OH	5606a		1895
J.D.	33	CAN	4439b		1870	Martin	64	DEN	8728		1904
Jacob Green	84	VT	7820		1901	Martin	64	NY	1621b		1895
James	29	SCT	823b		1872	Mary	1	SF	3730		1867
James			J43		1886	Mary	<1	SF	2404		1894
James	47	OH	1354		1869	Mary	38	ENG	3477	Nov	1901
James	31	SWE	4974a		1895	Mary				May	1899
James	26	SF	6814a		1895	Mary A.	2	SF	5808		1896
James	1904	CA	2593c		1904	Mary H.				Aug	1898
James J.	54	IRE	8071		1868	Matilda A.	62		6255		1896
James/Maud, c/o		SF	3095		1900	Milo (soldier)			1464		1901
Jane	51	SCT	1859b		1872	Nathan Lee	45	MO	6254		1904
Jas. A.	60	ENG	4046		1896	Patrick (soldier)			9567		1901
Jeanette	46	GER	4059a		1895	Phillip	1	CA	867		1903
Jennie	24	CAN	6390		1903	R.W.	28	ME	J53		1889
Jno. H.	25	SF	1576		1894	Ramona	32	CA	6186	Jan	1901
Joanna	36	CHI	1777		1870	Richard R.	87	NY	2263		1901
John	32	IRL	991		1870	Romeo (soldier)			7757		1901
John A.	58	OH	481		1900	Stephen				Jan	1899

NAME	AGE OR YOB.	BIRTH PLACE	CERT. NO	ID	DEATH YEAR	NAME	AGE OR YOB.	BIRTH PLACE	CERT. NO	ID	DEATH YEAR
Theodore A.	64	PA	4997		1903	A.				Dec	1898
Thomas Wilburn	39	CA	1371		1902	Adelaide E.	42	CA	1707		1902
Virginia	24	CA	4086		1900	Augusta	33	GER	3593		1900
Walter S.	32	JAM	1707b		1895	Baron	53	ENG	4254		1903
William				Apr	1899	Bertha	62	GER	3787		1900
William	1902	SF	1461c		1904	C. E.	48	GER	J16		1883
William (soldier)			7775		1902	Charles	39	FRA	9080		1868
William B.				Feb	1900	Charles B.(soldier)			3389		1900
William F.	60	SC	8913		1868	Clark	47	NY	2811		1873
William H.	53	ENG	3106		1870	Ephiram	52	NY	1734		1901
William L. G.				Mar	1899	Ester				Feb	1899
William Lewis	20	IL	31		1901	Eugene	<1	SF	3122		1902
William N.	73	SWE	3227		1902	Eva	<1	SF	5773		1902
JACMIN						Frank (soldier)			1259		1900
Victor	49	FRA	8854		1868	Frederick G.				Feb	1900
						George	27	ENG	5273		1867
JACOB						George	3	SF	4347		1896
Elias	64	GER	2196		1902	George	34	GER	1165a		1871
Ellis	3	SF	3971		1867	George M.	14	CA	9531		1901
Florence	1	SF	8604		1904	Hannah	56	POL	2341a		1872
Louisa	68	BAV	8140		1903	Harry	39	GER	4386a		1895
Lulu	1871	CA	703c		1904	Harry (soldier)			2176		1900
Phebe	3	SF	8777		1868	Haufman/Hanchen, c/o		SF	8670		1901
Samuel	59	GER	8682		1903	Henrietta	<1	SF	660b		1872
Theodore Emanuel	27	SF	7181		1900	Henry	40	PRU	3713		1870
JACOBAIN						Henry	46	NY	547		1866
Johanna C.	<1	SF	2913		1866	Henry	16	NY	891b		1895
JACOBE						Henry W.	82	GER	6886		1900
Albert	59	GER	2869		1903	Hyme/Stella, c/o	1	SF	449		1903
Florence May	<1	SF	6469a		1895	Isidor	71	GER	4999		1902
JACOBI						J. M.	42	IL	4522		1903
Hannah	72	GER	1990		1901	Jacob	68	GER	6065	Jan	1901
Hinrich	43	GER	5107		1903	Jacob G.	16	NY	1480		1866
JACOBS						Jens P.	1831	GER	2826c		1904
——			1802		1870	John	1857	AZO	1620c		1904
——		SF	903		1870	Joseph				Oct	1898

Key: a = 1st part of year; b = 2nd part of year;
c = death certificate copy; c/o = child of

NAME	AGE OR YOB.	BIRTH PLACE	CERT. NO	ID	DEATH YEAR	NAME	AGE OR YOB.	BIRTH PLACE	CERT. NO	ID	DEATH YEAR
Joseph Warren				Dec	1898	Fred	44	NOR	2703		1903
Julia	3	SF	7384		1868	Frida	1	SF	202b		1872
Leah	1	SF	7425		1868	Frieda Alberta				Jan	1899
Lee	50	NY	6520		1904	George	40	DEN	3915		1903
Mabel Irene	<1	SF	2819		1894	Henriette Amelia	23	SF	7186		1903
Mark	84	RUS	6115		1902	J. J.	43	NOR	1262		1902
Mark J.	78	ENG	2187		1894	Mary	3	CA	8384		1901
Martin	50	GER	6515		1868	Maurice	<1	SF	1676b		1895
Mary Anne				Jan	1899	Peter C.	75	GER	3580	Nov	1901
Mary E.	42	MA	2691		1901	Rudolph/Orphina, c/o	<1	SF	7400		1904
Morris				Feb	1899	Simon				Jun	1899
Morris, c/o		SF	2416		1873	Walter				Jun	1899
N. B.	39	VA	1434		1869	**JACOBSON**					
Nathan	44	CA	6752		1902	___			6318		1867
Pauline	60	GER	5678		1903	Albert	43	SWE	2354		1900
Pauline	67	PRU	3974		1900	Anna R.				Mar	1899
Pauline	<1	SF	5752	Jan	1901	Augusta W.	1	SF	1372		1869
Percy T. (soldier)	28	MI	6988	Feb	1901	Carls A.	36	DEN	1470		1866
Pierre	46	CA	6235		1904	Charles	75	GER	7980		1903
Rachael	63	PRU	1217		1902	Charles	35	GER	7096		1901
Ruth	14	SF	8853		1904	Chas.	33	DEN	5552		1896
Simon	50	NY	2528		1902	Conrad	25	NOR	7802		1904
Simon L.	54	GER	8598		1901	Ellie	26	SF	810		1894
Solomon		SF	1437b		1872	Elliott A.	22	NV	2238		1894
Solomon	71	POL	964		1903	Harold				Oct	1899
Thomas	81	ENG	5453	Jan	1901	Harris	55	NY	2442		1894
William (soldier)			5415	Jan	1901	Harris	52	NY	2533		1894
JACOBSEN						Hayward	55	SWE	6950		1904
Andrew Christian Theodore	77	GER	331		1900	Henrietta	67	SWE	6676		1902
Andrew J.	5	SF	4643		1901	I. M.	54	GER	J6		1882
Anton				Nov	1898	Jacob	60	GER	J31		1885
Bernard	1857	NOR	1311c		1904	John	49	GER	1551		1870
Charles	1840	NOR	3239c		1904	John	1836	GER	2414c		1904
Ester	8	CA	7521		1904	John	25	SWE	3355		1894
Felix Edwin	<1	CA	1259b		1895	Lawrentzen	26	DEN	9720		1868
Frank				Jul	1898	Leontine				Aug	1898

Key: a = 1st part of year; b = 2nd part of year;
c = death certificate copy; c/o = child of

NAME	AGE OR YOB.	BIRTH PLACE	CERT. NO	ID	DEATH YEAR
Margaret	38	POL	7573		1868
Mary	1856	FIN	1202c		1904
Mary Elizabeth	66	DEN	7414		1900
Mary, Mrs.	85	GER	J32		1885
Peter Elmer				Jan	1899
Rapsssel	<1	SF	203		1870
Rosalia				Jan	1899
Sigmund	75	GER	7759		1903
JACOBUS					
Clara Frances	36	CA	2984		1902
JACOBY					
Abraham	<1	SF	1423		1869
Henrietta	46	GER	4016		1896
Henry	78	GER	7216		1902
Jacob	75	GER	1612		1901
Jenny	56	GER	8267		1901
Julius S./Ida, c/o	<1	SF	1341		1900
Pauline				Nov	1898
William	29	OH	1987		1873
JACOT					
Geo/Katherine, c/o				Dec	1898
JACQUAY					
D. M.				Dec	1899
JACQUE					
John	48	FRA	2589		1894
JACQUENOT					
Louisa	<1	SF	5723a		1895
Madeline	2	SF	7570		1901
JACQUES					
Albert	25	BEL	750		1901
Caroline G.	14	ENG	7b		1895
Henry	44	FRA	710b		1895
Morley	33	FRA	147		1865

NAME	AGE OR YOB.	BIRTH PLACE	CERT. NO	ID	DEATH YEAR
JACQUOT					
Annie	63	NS	5490		1903
Ernest				Feb	1900
JACUE					
Jose	42	SPA	4020		1902
JADAROLA					
Louis S	60	ITA	7347		1903
JADOT					
Clemence	26	FRA	517		1870
JAECK					
Margarethe S.				May	1899
Minnie	40	GER	3157		1894
JAEGER					
George M.	73	GER	2902		1901
Henry	29	SF	2324		1894
M./M., c/o	<1	SF	2002		1894
JAENICKE					
Lulu	20	SF	6164	Jan	1901
JAENSEN					
Lars Peter	37	SWE	658a		1871
JAFFA					
——	5	SF	867		1870
Myer E./Adele, c/o	1	CA	8687		1904
JAFFE					
——			5053		1867
JAFFEE					
S.	32	PRU	7854		1868
JAGER					
Fredrick	31	GER	3882		1870
JAGGI					
John	32	SWT	4733		1896
JAGHEL					
Ann Emily	40	MD	4083b		1870

Key: a = 1st part of year; b = 2nd part of year; c = death certificate copy; c/o = child of

NAME	AGE OR YOB.	BIRTH PLACE	CERT. NO	ID	DEATH YEAR
JAGOE					
Robert	2	MA	7730		1868
JAGON					
Otto				Feb	1899
JAHN					
Frederick	45	CA	3927		1902
Herman, Jr.	37	NJ	6626		1902
Theresa				Oct	1899
JAHNCKE					
A. E.	24	RI	1763b		1872
Ida Silliann	2	SF	3282		1873
JAHNS					
Emilie	43	DEN	6682		1903
JAI					
Taw				Mar	1899
JAIMISON					
William J.	66	ME	2530		1901
JAJOC					
——			6569		1868
JAKADA					
H.	25	JPN	3828a		1895
JAKE					
Ah	29	CHN	3745		1870
Mon	<1	SF	5083		1867
Wey	34	CHN	1635		1870
JAKEWAY					
May	40	CT	8534		1901
JAKSAP					
Johan (soldier)			3050	Oct	1901
JAKSHA					
Anna	1860	AUS	1542c		1904
JALUMSTEINOLO					
Estella	29	CA	6577		1904

NAME	AGE OR YOB.	BIRTH PLACE	CERT. NO	ID	DEATH YEAR
JAMELOT					
Louis F.	60	FRA	5117		1867
JAMES					
——	<1	SF	388		1902
——	<1	SF	6812		1903
——	<1	SF	4684		1902
A. L.	35		2925		1895
A. R./Louise, c/o				Aug	1898
Adelaide M.	34	SF	2622		1902
Alfred W. (soldier)			3051	Oct	1901
Arthur W. (soldier)			4790		1901
Carl	31	CA	8424		1903
Caroline	77	NY	383		1903
Carrie L.	7	WA	1362		1869
Charles A.	64	RI	4079a		1895
Edward E.	<1	SF	4536		1867
Eliza J.	30	MD	3470b		1870
Eveline	<1	SF	7907		1901
Francis W.	56	MA	6482	Feb	1901
Frank	22	KY	3835		1903
Fred D. (soldier)			3548		1900
George F.	53	NY	1228		1869
George H.C.	31	NY	962		1870
Gertrude	50	ENG	1079		1901
Hans	<1	SF	8313		1903
Harriet C.	3	CA	690b		1871
Jennie L.	61	MO	5377		1902
Jos., c/o		SF	2576		1873
Joseph V.				Nov	1899
L. E./Elizabeth, c/o	1904	CA	2415		1904
Marks	<1	SF	3350a		1872
Mary S.	69	WAL	8733		1900
Mary T.				Oct	1899
Mary, Mrs.	34	NY	5838		1902
Oscar	36	PRU	359a		1871

Key: a = 1st part of year; b = 2nd part of year; c = death certificate copy; c/o = child of

NAME	AGE OR YOB.	BIRTH PLACE	CERT. NO	ID	DEATH YEAR	NAME	AGE OR YOB.	BIRTH PLACE	CERT. NO	ID	DEATH YEAR
Peter	<1	SF	2509		1866	Mary	35	NY	5317a		1895
Raphael	1	CA	8666		1904	Mary Elizabeth	1862	CA	677c		1904
Richard/Margarite, c/o		SF	7323		1900	Wallace T.	42	MI	4313		1903
Ruth	1	SF	5129		1904						
Thomas	1	SF	1199		1903	**JAN**					
Vincent	<1	SF	3028		1902	Ah	39	CHN	J44		1886
William	40	SWA	1035a		1871	Ah Me	48	CHN	1771		1900
William	41	AUS	4426		1901	Ah Sing	40	CHN	6989		1902
William P.				May	1899	Chu Pong				Dec	1898
Wm. H. (soldier)			9352		1901	Ka	25	CHN	9961		1868
						Shee				Feb	1900
JAMESON						Shung	53	CHN	649		1901
Clyde J. (soldier)			5055		1901	Tan Chun				Feb	1900
Grace	11	SF	8961		1868	Wang	49	CHN	6906		1900
Jeff	51	AR	8474		1900	Wing Chong			3358c		1904
John H.	3	SF	9212		1868	Woo Tez	1869	CHN	3346c		1904
Noah	38	IRE	8293		1904						
William	44	NOR	2680a		1872	**JANCH**					
						Anna				Oct	1899
JAMIESON						**JANCOVICH**					
Andrew	49	SCT	1289b		1872	Luca	77	AUT	4345	Dec	1901
Anna Amanda	16	CO	4235		1900						
Buchan Thom	54	SCT	7105		1903	**JANDER**					
Jane	86	IRE	5215		1904	Walter	2	CA	4451a		1895
John/Agnes, c/o		SF	7769		1901	**JANDIN**					
						Albert R.	<1	SF	7317		1868
JAMINEZ						Mary E.	59	NY	8744		1901
Juanita	1879	SF	1203c		1904	**JANE**					
						Catherine	1	SF	439		1870
JAMISKI						Jane				Nov	1898
Casimir (soldier)			2221		1903	John Crisp Coleman	1	SF	488		1903
						Luc			2391		1866
JAMISON						Mary	<1	SF	1137		1869
C. G.	61	ME	5506a		1895						
Eliza	79	IRE	6294		1902	**JANES**					
Ellen Bates	49	IA	6414	Feb	1901	Adderson M.	56	VT	7597		1903
Helen F.	1	SF	1084		1900	Anna E.	39	NY	1203		1869
James J.	42	CA	8765		1900	Catharine M.	2	SF	1426		1869
John	61	IRL	2599a		1872						
John	51	EIN	7369		1868						

NAME	AGE OR YOB.	BIRTH PLACE	CERT. NO	ID	DEATH YEAR
Charles M.	49	SF	5564		1903
Joseph L.	42	VT	1014		1868
JANETSKY					
Julius/Josephine, c/o	1904	SF	1597		1904
JANG					
Kar John	52	CHN	2121		1901
Kong	53	CHN	4206a		1895
Lin Gum	45	CHN	3793		1896
Loy Sing	40	CHN	6943		1903
Mun				Feb	1900
Quon Hang	37	CHN	7009	Feb	1901
Shing	70	CHN	1567		1903
Wang Toy				Jul	1899
JANIOT					
J. Eugene	38	FRA	2541a		1872
JANISCH					
Frederick	57	GER	8141		1903
JANKE					
Minnie	33	CA	6352		1902
William August	59	GER	3416		1902
JANNING					
Axel Thurs	36	SWE	5860a		1895
JANSEN					
Aaen	30	NOR	3351a		1872
Abraham	37	FIN	J26		1885
Albert H.				Feb	1900
Carl	1	SF	2587a		1872
Chr. R.	32	RUS	2886		1873
Eidici L.	1	SF	1639		1870
Erik	17	CA	6461		1900
Grandalupe	42	MEX	294		1870
Henry	30	RUS	J13		1883
Herbert William	5	SF	6990		1902
Josephine	22	NOR	4845		1902

NAME	AGE OR YOB.	BIRTH PLACE	CERT. NO	ID	DEATH YEAR
Lewis J. (soldier)			6997		1900
Lurena	21	CA	6639		1900
Mary B.	62	IRL	4593a		1895
Otto Gustave	43	NOR	5648		1904
Peter	41	GER	334b		1871
Sine	77	DEN	4123		1900
Thomas Nicholas	9	SF	7295		1902
JANSON					
John G.	4	SF	3584		1870
Lillie				Nov	1899
Richard	42	PRU	8520		1868
William F.	58	RUS	1481		1902
JANSSEN					
Alixe Sallie		SF	2029b		1895
JANSSON					
Charlotte	52	SWE	6000a		1895
JANTZEN					
Caroline				Oct	1898
Catherine B.	30	GER	1100		1869
JANUCA					
Michael	<1	SF	3458	Nov	1901
JAO					
Fong Youn	46	CHN	510		1902
JAP					
Mow Soo	43	CHN	1501		1894
On Nou	34	CHN	1605		1894
JAQUENOT					
George				Apr	1899
JAQUES					
Samuel B.	66	NJ	6313		1904
JAQUIN					
Geo. A.	31	CT	1150		1869
JAQUISH					
Cynthia Anna	62	LA	400b		1895

Key: *a = 1st part of year; b = 2nd part of year;*
c = death certificate copy; c/o = child of

NAME	AGE OR YOB.	BIRTH PLACE	CERT. NO	ID	DEATH YEAR	NAME	AGE OR YOB.	BIRTH PLACE	CERT. NO	ID	DEATH YEAR
JARBOE						**JASPER**					
John R. Jr.	10	SF	2997a		1872	John Francis	<1	SF	1364		1869
JARDINE						**JASPERSON**					
Alexander				Apr	1899	Lizzie C.	<1	SF	527b		1895
Charles C.	21	WA	8301		1901	**JASS**					
JARECKI						Emilie A.S.	<1	SF	5087a		1895
——		SF	1376		1869	**JAUHERS**					
Jessie	38	PRU	1379		1869	Olympe	38	FRA	314		1902
JARMAN						**JAUME**					
Hugh George	3	SF	2741		1894	Dominique	77	FRA	7025		1903
JARON						**JAUNAND**					
Rose	69	FRA	6355a		1895	Henry	40	FRA	8		1900
JARONI						**JAUNDA**					
John	43	SCT	1356		1869	Minnie N.	<1	CA	2803		1895
JARRATH						**JAUNET**					
Frederika	30	GER	8802		1868	Louis	57	LA	6141		1903
JARRETT						**JAUREQUEBERY**					
Esther E.	33	IN	5294		1904	Bernard	78	FRA	5086a		1895
Joseph				Nov	1898	**JAUSSAND**					
JARTEROIS						Benjamin A.		SF	4488b		1870
Clarence E.	1884	NE	2642c		1904	**JAUSSI**					
JARUS						Phillippe			6199		1903
David Sydney	<1	SF	2118		1902	**JAVIER**					
JARVIS						Rosie	<1	CA	100b		1895
Constance				Jul	1899	**JAVON**					
Joe A. (soldier)			824		1900	August	68	FRA	3457		1894
Lulir Hazel				Jul	1899	**JAWBONE**					
Mark	74	RUS	1296		1900	Andrew	22	CA	2984		1903
William	39	ENG	351b		1872	**JAY**					
JASAMO						Man Fong	60	CHN	8520		1900
Gauddalupe	19	MEX	1797		1866	Pock				Dec	1899
JASON						Shire	40	CHN	1847		1900
Margaret	28	ENG	3781a		1895	Sue	<1	SF	2492		1900

Key: a = 1st part of year; b = 2nd part of year;
c = death certificate copy; c/o = child of

NAME	AGE OR YOB.	BIRTH PLACE	CERT. NO	ID	DEATH YEAR
Wai Geet	32	CHN	450		1902
JAYEL					
John	52	IRL	2727a		1872
JAYMOT					
Marthe	27	FRA	3195		1895
JEA					
Man Tong	31	CHN	724		1902
JEALOUS					
George	40	ENG	2960a		1872
JEAN					
Joseph (soldier)	24		8261		1903
Louis	abt		8164		1901
JEANNERET					
Arnold	35	SWT	1218		1902
JEANNIN					
August				Mar	1899
Eugenie	56	BEL	6349		1904
Marie A.	72	FRA	6744		1900
JEANS					
Earl				Feb	1900
JEANSELINE					
Pierre				Jun	1899
JED					
Chew Jang	53	CHN	7981		1903
JEDER					
Robert	24	GER	5a		1871
JEE					
Ban	54	CHN	8892		1903
Clong You	54	CHN	1623		1900
Jung Yien	49	CHN	5598		1896
JEFFCOAT					
Cyril	25	ENG	707		1901

NAME	AGE OR YOB.	BIRTH PLACE	CERT. NO	ID	DEATH YEAR
JEFFERS					
Adam J.	39	NS	J4		1882
Ann	60	IRL	6294		1900
Ellen C.	44	DE	7781		1904
James B.	<1	SF	4677a		1895
James D.	52	NS	420		1902
Lizzie A.	<1	SF	3213a		1872
Milo Sidney	61	NY	695		1900
Patrick				Mar	1899
William				Feb	1900
William M.	22	CA	1452		1900
William M.	22	CA	1452		1900
JEFFERSON					
Elena	28	CAN	644b		1872
John W.				Jul	1898
Richard (soldier)			6942		1900
Thomas	41	DC	1037		1868
William H.	60	NY	8598		1900
William S.				Nov	1898
JEFFERY					
David S.	46	CA	1252		1900
Edwin L.				May	1899
Samuel C.	13	UT	2737		1900
Sarah A.	9	UT	4189a		1895
Thomas	58	ENG	403		1900
JEFFORDS					
Mary Ellen	72	IRE	5726		1903
JEFFRES					
Sarah Jane Taggart	72	ME	7892		1904
JEFFRESS					
A. M./Georgie, c/o		SF	5447		1896
Caroline				Jan	1899
Claude	<1	SF	1115a		1871
Georgie Ella	28	SF	5525		1896
Sue L.	29	NC	853a		1871

NAME	AGE OR YOB.	BIRTH PLACE	CERT. NO	ID	DEATH YEAR	NAME	AGE OR YOB.	BIRTH PLACE	CERT. NO	ID	DEATH YEAR
						Bark	1878	CHN	1760c		1904
JEFFREY						For Fouy	26	CHN	1396b		1872
Edwin	50	ENG	7760		1903						
Emily Louise					Jul 1899	**JENANCIO**					
R. H.	62	NY	5309		1867	Joseph W.	61	POR	4038b		1870
JEFFREYS						**JENETT**					
Albert	32	CA	3782		1902	Cavalier Hamilton					Oct 1898
JEFFRIES						**JENINI**					
Ellwood Pennell	1898	CA	2440c		1904	P./M., c/o		SF	1655b		1872
William T.	67	ENG	3368		1902	**JENKEL**					
JEGHERS						John Rudolph	1	SF	4313		1901
Augustus	1859	OR	1935c		1904	**JENKINE**					
JEHL						Andrew B.	65	MO	1014		1868
John	1856	GER	1807c		1904	**JENKINS**					
JEHLY						Adeline M.					Aug 1899
Albert					Apr 1899	Albert Leslie	2	SF	3832		1900
JEIDE						Annie					Jun 1899
Friedrich Phillip	1	SF	2957		1903	B. T.	69	NY	2742		1894
JELAWITZ						Benjamin P.	1830	VT	3325c		1904
Max	57	RUS	4591		1896	Chas. E.	30	ENG	J35		1886
JELINSKI						Daniel P. (soldier)			4702		1901
Aaron	34	NY	7693		1904	Elijah	6	CA	1155		1869
JELLIS						Elizabeth	78	IRL	4314		1901
Aggie					Aug 1898	Ellwood Alexander					Mar 1899
Jennie					Oct 1898	Frederick W. (soldier)			7163		1901
JELLISON						Freidrich Valentine	3	CA	6902		1902
Arthur M.					Jul 1898	George W.	48	MO	8849		1903
JEMET						Harry	<1	SF	4913		1902
Philip	4	SF	1060		1894	Ignacio S.	38	MD	1122		1869
JEMISON						Isabella	1	SF	406		1903
Caroline	58	ENG	8262		1903	James	65		2758		1902
JEN						James H. (soldier)			2385		1903
Ah Len	38	CHN	1011b		1895	John	46	DC	6753		1868
Ar Pon	53	CHN	2646		1901	John J. (soldier)	51	PA	1627b		1871
						John Joseph	<1	SF	5961		1902
						Julia M.	<1	SF	1171		1870

NAME	AGE OR YOB.	BIRTH PLACE	CERT. NO	ID	DEATH YEAR
Katie	14	BC	8448		1903
Louisa Rachel	2	SF	1848b		1872
Lydia M.	69	MA	3153		1895
Maria	75	IRL	2402		1894
Mary	44	IRL	1778		1870
Mary					Nov 1898
Mary C.	<1	JPN	1214b		1895
Mary E.	84	OH	6781		1904
Minnie B.	34	CA	1428		1894
Nellie	23	CA	6577		Feb 1901
Ormond C.					Jan 1899
Ormond Courtland					Jan 1899
Paul (soldier)			7776		1902
Reuben F.	47	MA	9993		1868
Russ	60	ENG	2878		1866
Sarah	1871	CA	9c		1904
Thomas	51	MD	2869a		1872
Will D.	51	IL	6014		1902
Wm. H.	42	MA	J1		1882
JENKS					
Chancellor	74	PA	4766		1903
Mildred R.					Feb 1900
Sarah	42	MA	6654		1896
JENNER					
Ellen	45	IRE	811		1866
Frederick	50	ENG	5220a		1896
JENNESS					
Maud P.	<1	SF	1263b		1872
JENNETTI					
Lizzie	33	NJ	7529		1901
JENNINGS					
——	<1	SF	3801		1870
——			1605		1866
——			1031		1868
——		SF	1256		1869
Annie	1834	IRE	2647c		1904
Barbara	60	IRE	6734		1902
Charles Augustus	1879	SF	567c		1904
Edward J. (civilian employee)			9353		1901
Ellen	60	NY	6564		1902
Emma F.	55	MA	7706		1900
Etty	19	ME	963b		1871
Geo S.					Feb 1900
George					Feb 1900
George, c/o					Aug 1899
Gilbert	1	SF	9024		1868
James H.	<1	SF	5342		1867
Jno.	54	ENG	4936a		1895
Jo. H.	<1	SF	8500		1868
John	62	IRL	430		1870
John	73	IRE	6916		1903
John J. (soldier)			2079		1901
John Thomas					Jan 1899
Julia					Dec 1899
Mahala S.		MA	1091		1869
Mary	2	SF	1367		1869
Mary	70	IRL	867b		1895
Nancy P.					Jun 1899
Patrick	53	IRE	2077		1902
Pauline	62	NY	6997		1903
Raymond	<1	CA	6349		1900
Susan	28	IRE	1362		1869
Thomas					Jul 1899
Thomas	62	IRL	1461b		1895
Walter	24	NY	7886		1901
William	5	SF	1302b		1872
William M.	40	NY	529b		1871
JENNIURNES					
Fred M. (soldier)			6557		1900

NAME	AGE OR YOB.	BIRTH PLACE	CERT. NO	ID	DEATH YEAR
JENNY					
Augustus Desire	50	NY	5074		1903
(Indian girl)	13	AK	442a		1871
Levy				Dec	1898
JENS					
Emma	8	SF	5015		1901
Portia Cordelia	1	SF	1810b		1895
JENSEN					
Agnethia H.				Nov	1899
Alfred/Pauline, c/o	<1	CA	7112		1904
Anna	27	DEN	5962		1902
Antoine	40	DEN	5375a		1895
Asmus	36	GER	1539b		1871
Caroline F. E.	2	SF	1155		1869
Cath	25	GER	6619a		1895
Charles P.	24	CA	3631		1902
Charles Peter	<1	SF	1132		1869
Christian J.	42	DEN	4575		1904
Christina				Feb	1899
Edward John				Oct	1898
Ellen	50	IRL	4658a		1895
Ellen	<1	SF	4912		1901
Flora				Oct	1899
Gladys E.				Apr	1899
Gottfried/M., c/o				Feb	1899
Helen	35	GER	195b		1895
Johanna				Nov	1899
John	1884	NY	2310c		1904
John Edward				Jul	1898
Josie				Mar	1899
Julia				Nov	1899
Kathereen	1873	IA	2520c		1904
Lauritz (soldier)			7164		1901
Lawrence	37	SF	965		1903
Louise	56	GER	4971		1904
Maria	63	DEN	4461		1901
Maria W.	1	SF	2010		1866
Moritz C. (soldier)			7531		1900
Neils T.	50	DEN	5188a		1896
Sophie Hospelle	3	SF	106		1900
Thomas	70	DEN	87		1900
JENSON					
George M.	<1	SF	7743		1902
JENTSEN					
L.	36	DEN	1126b		1895
JENTZSCH					
Rosina				Oct	1898
JEONG					
On		CHN	6415	Feb	1901
Woo	25	CHN	J15		1883
Yee	56	CHN	1629c		1904
Yuen	20	CHN	7126		1903
JEP					
We Ap	45	CHN	1012b		1895
Wo	45	CHN	6660		1900
JEPHSON					
Mary	47	IRL	3716		1896
JEPSEN					
John Hanson	55	GER	8626		1901
JEPSON					
L./M., c/o				Mar	1899
JER					
Sin	53	CHN	7893		1904
JEREMIAH					
	1	CHN	3957		1903
JERG					
Herman Patrick				Feb	1900
JERGENS					
George	10	SF	6651		1903

Key: a = 1st part of year; b = 2nd part of year;
c = death certificate copy; c/o = child of

NAME	AGE OR YOB.	BIRTH PLACE	CERT. NO	ID	DEATH YEAR	NAME	AGE OR YOB.	BIRTH PLACE	CERT. NO	ID	DEATH YEAR
						Mathias	76	GER	2863		1895
JEROME						Waldemar	2	SF	3458		1894
Alphonse	24	FRA	J9		1883						
Clara E.	51	IN	1481		1901	**JESSET**					
Edith Merritt	1	CA	2801		1903	Emily J.	2	SF	2444		1866
Edward Baker	57	IL	5177		1902						
Eliza	25	NS	2056		1873	**JESSICA**					
Francis	<1	CA	8263		1903	Emil (soldier)			6941		1900
Frederick	76	ENG	708		1900	**JESSON**					
Hazel	2	SF	6612		1904	Catherine					Aug 1898
James L.	39	WI	7803		1904	**JESSUP**					
Manuel	44	LA	3110a		1872	Thomas C.					May 1899
Moses	50	NY	4521b		1870	**JESTER**					
Vincent	<1	SF	8142		1903	William	35	MA	1237		1866
JERRTZKI						**JESTON**					
Mendel	72	RUS	5059a		1896	A.			1353b		1872
JERRY						**JET**					
Jerry, Mrs.					Mar 1900	Sie	42	CHN	4487		1867
JERVIL						**JEW**					
Silas H.	50	ME	6517		1868	Bing Foo	`846	CHN	2618c		1904
						Bo	59	CHN	4942		1904
JESLEI						Dong Ling	63	CHN	8807		1904
John W.					Feb 1900	Doo Goey	31	CHN	567		1903
JESS						Fook	27	CHN	6141		1904
James	78	IRE	8091		1904	Gen	53	CHN	3828	Nov	1901
John	38	GER	6958		1900	Gow	78	CHN	2985		1900
William Allen	74	NS	8161		1904	Gum	49	CHN	1569		1903
JESSE						Gwan	55	CHN	3766		1903
George R.	70	VA	85		1901	Ho	57	CHN	3715		1903
						Jick Wong	39	CHN	2125		1900
JESSEN						Joon Teu	49	CHN	1568		1903
Boye Theodor	27	SF	2582		1902	Loui Shee	30	ENG	8538		1903
Charles	4	GER	1064		1869	Man Way	49	CHN	2793		1900
Elizabeth P.	42	CA	6521		1904	Mock	52	CHN	6996		1903
Frederick	60	GER	3632		1902	Mon Gee Shee	54	CHN	3010		1903
Gus	28	SF	4374		1902	Mon Lau Shee	27	CA	6972		1903
John	62	DEN	2229		1900						

    Key: a = 1st part of year; b = 2nd part of year;
c = death certificate copy; c/o = child of

NAME	AGE OR YOB.	BIRTH PLACE	CERT. NO	ID	DEATH YEAR	NAME	AGE OR YOB.	BIRTH PLACE	CERT. NO	ID	DEATH YEAR
Ning Coey	64	CHN	6723		1903	**JEY**					
Quock Fon	56	CHN	6173		1904	Ang Hang	62	CHN	7552		1900
Shen	61	CHN	4874		1904						
Sin Tong	43	CHN	4231a		1895	**JHUN**					
Som	45	CHN	4017		1896	Chun					Oct 1898
Tze Gun	58	CHN	2985		1902	**JIEGENFUSS**					
Yoke Charm	36	CHN	3225		Nov 1901	Mamie Crowley	29	SF	4915a		1895
Yon	40	CHN	1164		1902	**JIEW**					
						Quong Leenlis	60	CHN	2003		1894
JEWELL											
Barnard	22	SF	6273		1896	**JILECK**					
Francis P.	2	SF	3064		1873	Frances Ellen	<1	SF	3140		1900
Godfrey	66	ENG	6020		1903	Frank J.	57	OH	4972		1904
J. W.	63	KY	5667		1896						
Jno.	38	IRL	J21		1884	**JILLSON**					
Lydia E.	72	MA	3479		Nov 1901	Clara E.	<1	SF	2462a		1872
William	41	ENG	3327a		1872	**JILSON**					
						George P.	<1	SF	1195b		1871
JEWETT						**JIM**					
Adela	39	MEX	227		1870	——	18	SIN	378b		1871
Albert	1	CA	4505		1901	Ah	30	CHN	1826a		1872
Charles	65	MEX	8331		1904	Ah	25	CHN	8771		1868
Edward Merrill					Aug 1898	Kie	55	CHN	1441		1894
Frank C.	20	CA	4217		1903	Lee	26	CHN	J34		1886
Harry P.					Mar 1900	Sing	52	CHN	3836		1903
J. W.	34	NY	3056		1870	Suck	37	CHN	2273		1873
Laffayett M.	78	MA	5630		1903						
Lyman					Apr 1899	**JIMENEZ**					
Maria H.	63	MEX	4477		1867	Guillermo					Dec 1899
Miles	44	ME	627		1870	**JIMENO**					
Philo D.	64	VT	5694		1902	Jose Manuel	40	ECU	3289		1866
Thomas M.					Aug 1898	**JIMINEZ**					
JEWITT						Louisa	1874	MEX	1462c		1904
Acenath	74	ME	8485		1901	Nicholas					Mar 1899
Alfred	23	IL	6846a		1895	**JIN**					
JEWN						Jen Ton			2743c		1904
Hin Sing	72	CHN	6409		1904	Jew Git	1850	CHN	2076c		1904
						Loon Yee	43	CHN	5584		1903

NAME	AGE OR YOB.	BIRTH PLACE	CERT. NO	ID	DEATH YEAR	NAME	AGE OR YOB.	BIRTH PLACE	CERT. NO	ID	DEATH YEAR
Loy	1835	CHN	1968c		1904	**JOE**					
Nuey	49	CHN	3755		1903	Ah	28	CHN	7113		1868
Yit Len	65	CHN	2529		1902	Ak Gim	46	CHN	4557		1896
						Chas./Ahseen, c/o	<1	SF	6856		1902
JING						Shee	37	CHN	677		1903
Dat	35	CHN	1836a		1872	Suey Yorke	4	CA	6518		1900
Sam	35	CHN	3519		1900						
						JOEL					
JINS						Albert	47	GER	J12		1883
Yo Pak				Feb	1900	James Lewis	24	SF	7047		1902
						Mary	<1	SF	1300		1869
JO						Pauline/Otto, c/o	1	CA	3393		1903
Ah	36	CHN	3444a		1872	Pauline/Otto, c/o	1	CA	3394		1903
Ka Wing	46	CHN	5850	Jan	1901	Sarah E.	<1	SF	3662		1870
JOACHIM						**JOELL**					
——	1	SF	5362		1896	Bertram H.	1	SF	2707		1894
James	<1	SF	4344	Dec	1901	**JOENSUN**					
						Katri	22	FIN	699		1902
JOAQUINA											
Lauriana	66	AZO	1236b		1895	**JOERG**					
						Alfred August	1	SF	6416	Feb	1901
JOAST											
John , c/o		SF	2607a		1872	**JOHANNES**					
						Margaret	50	GER	7612		1901
JOB											
Jane				Oct	1898	**JOHANNESSEN**					
Ruby Louise				Apr	1899	R./S., c/o		SF	1275		1894
JOBBLING						**JOHANNING**					
Arthur				Jun	1899	Louis W.	36	OH	3135a		1872
JOBMANN						**JOHANNSEN**					
Minnie	65	GER	7376		1903	Isabelle				Oct	1899
						Julius (soldier)			1973		1900
JOBSON						Willet Peter	<1	SF	854a		1871
Charles F.	47	TN	3196		1866						
Ellen	33		1960b		1872	**JOHANNSING**					
M., Mrs.	32	AUS	2027		1901	Louis	58	GER	7983		1868
JOCHUM						**JOHANSEN**					
Barbara	63	BAV	4568		1867	Anna G.				Mar	1899
						Carl	1867	NOR	896c		1904
JOCZ											
Helen Wanda	1	CA	34		1902						
Henry Edmund	5	CA	4724		1903						

Key: a = 1st part of year; b = 2nd part of year;
c = death certificate copy; c/o = child of

NAME	AGE OR YOB.	BIRTH PLACE	CERT. NO	ID	DEATH YEAR	NAME	AGE OR YOB.	BIRTH PLACE	CERT. NO	ID	DEATH YEAR
Ch			2062		1902	How Jung				Dec	1899
Christine	48	DEN	168		1900	Joseph	1	SF	1799		1903
Elmer Clyde				Mar	1899	Joseph	<1	SF	8426		1903
Emanuel	33	NOR	1863		1902	Marie	42	GER	5085a		1895
Hans C.	27	DEN	1084		1869	Ton	25	CHN	2081		1870
Herbert A.	1	CA	4506		1901	**JOHNATON**					
J.	57	DEN	507b		1895	John P.	73	PA	915		1900
Jens	43	DEN	9177		1901	**JOHNBAYSS**					
Johan Bernhard	19	SF	3656		1896	John, c/o	<1	SF	2672		1873
Julius	41	SWE	2828		1903	**JOHNCOCK**					
Thos	37	GER	J11		1883	Nettie	18	MI	3478		1902
JOHANSON						**JOHNNPSON**					
Athilde	24	SWE	2914		1894	K. H. O.		SF	1060		1869
August	43	SWE	7744		1902	**JOHNS**					
Christina	26	NOR	8029		1903	Asa T. (soldier)			7961		1901
Frans A.	34	SWE	7585		1900	Benedict	1	SF	1351		1866
Hanna				Jul	1899	Clara J.	46	OH	7440		1903
Jurgon	40	SWE	1318b		1871	Florence	1	SF	7833		1904
Tiro	1881	FIN	2485c		1904	John Francis	62	ENG	7483		1904
JOHANSSEN						John H.				Dec	1898
Julia	39	CA	3731		1900	Lucy Ann				Jun	1899
JOHANSSON						Raymond H., Rev.	59	ENG	6153		1902
Arne	30	NOR	J51		1889	Richard	52	ENG	3703		1900
Gustaf Adolf	26	FIN	5257		1903	Thomas James				Nov	1899
JOHN						Vyoyan A. E.	48	ENG	6241a		1895
——	<1	SF	5839		1902	**JOHNSEN**					
——	1	SF	2896		1903	Arthur M.				Oct	1898
Andrew	<1	SF	4047	Dec	1901	Birger	35	NOR	8565		1903
August	44	PRU	3557		1867	Hakon	55	NOR	4160	Dec	1901
Cheu	40	CHN	2689a		1872	James A.	1	SF	175		1903
Dr. L.		GER	J38		1886	John				Nov	1898
G. M.	25	FIN	1100b		1871	Ole				Jun	1899
Hardin	45	ENG	2389		1873	Rebecka Elizabeth	80	NOR	7489		1901
Henry	47	GER	1259b		1871						
Ho	35	CHN	4508		1867						

 Key: *a = 1st part of year; b = 2nd part of year;*
c = death certificate copy; c/o = child of

NAME	AGE OR YOB.	BIRTH PLACE	CERT. NO	ID	DEATH YEAR	NAME	AGE OR YOB.	BIRTH PLACE	CERT. NO	ID	DEATH YEAR
JOHNSON						Amelia	37	NOR	1416b		1895
——			1782		1866	Andreas Sigfred	<1	SF	3732		1902
——			7934		1868	Andreu	<1	SF	3420		1867
——			1058		1869	Andrew	43	NOR	7187		1903
——		SF	1365		1869	Andrew	53	FIN	506b		1895
——		SF	1377		1869	Andrew	63	SWE	6380		1896
A.	31	DEN	3448		1867	Andrew	abt		386		1901
A. M.	60	MO	7623		1903	Andrew	53	FIN	503		1901
A. S.	56	SWE	2903		1901	Andrew				Jul	1898
A., c/o	<1	SF	163b		1872	Andrew	50	SWE	6726	Feb	1901
A./A., c/o		SF	1964		1894	Andrew G.				Jul	1898
A.L.	31	IL	1138		1869	Andrew/A., c/o				Jun	1899
Aaron	40	SWE	4183		1902	Andrew/Laura, c/o	<1	SF	6991		1902
Abbie	1	SF	5421		1902	Ann	5	SF	3338		1873
Adaline E.	58	MI	3704		1900	Ann	17	IRE	3840		1867
Adam	35	SWE	1009		1868	Ann C.	<1	SF	3489a		1872
Al				Feb	1900	Anna	77	SWE	5585		1903
Albert	20	IN	1097		1869	Anna	45	IRL	5987a		1895
Albert	89	ME	3201		1903	Anna Johanna	<1	SF	608b		1872
Albert	36	SWE	4409a		1895	Annie	<1	SF	1332b		1872
Albert	26	SWE	5241a		1895	Annie	59	IRE	3031		1903
Albert Conrad	<1	SF	55		1900	Annie	50	OH	3633		1900
Albert Rollins	<1	CA	620		1894	Annie C. M.	30	SF	1423		1900
Alex	45	WIN	3356		1894	Annie E.	1843	MO	1104c		1904
Alexander				Mar	1899	Anthony	59	NOR	4700		1896
Alfred	57	MD	3877		1867	Anton/Martha, c/o		SF	8810		1901
Alfred	53	SWE	2327		1903	Arthur E.	1865	SCT	1339c		1904
Alfred R.	<1	SF	5378		1902	Arvily				Oct	1899
Alice	30	IA	4737		1904	Ashael C.	1	SF	2091		1866
Allen R.	14	SF	5491		1903	August	21	SWE	514a		1871
Alonzo L. (soldier)			4705		1901	August	35	SWE	J18		1883
Aloysius				Apr	1899	August	29	CA	3143		1903
Aloysius				Jul	1899	August Hilmer	<1	SF	1564		1902
Alvira Mildred	2	SF	5472		1902	Augusta	<1	SF	1048b		1872
Amanda Christina	30	SWE	5527		1902	Augusta A.	51	SWE	6256a		1895
Amelia	<1	SF	4993a		1895	Augusta N.	39	SWE	3697		1896

Key: a = 1st part of year; b = 2nd part of year;
c = death certificate copy; c/o = child of

NAME	AGE OR YOB.	BIRTH PLACE	CERT. NO	ID	DEATH YEAR	NAME	AGE OR YOB.	BIRTH PLACE	CERT. NO	ID	DEATH YEAR
Axel (soldier)	24	IL	6435	Feb	1901	Charles	40		2222b		1895
Axil				Jul	1899	Charles	32	SWE	5755a		1895
B.F./Mary, c/o		SF	4849		1896	Charles	35	SWE	726b		1895
Bendix O.	28	SF	7001		1900	Charles	25	SWE	3158		1894
Benj./Anna, c/o	<1	SF	4274		1896	Charles				Aug	1899
Benjamin C. (soldier)			223		1902	Charles				Oct	1899
Bertha Estella				Feb	1899	Charles	43	FIN	5849		1904
Blanche	<1	SF	5849	Jan	1901	Charles	50	FIN	5884		1904
Bridget	28	IRL	2722		1873	Charles A.		SF	3000		1870
C.	27	SWE	7768		1901	Charles E.	60	ENG	860b		1871
C. E./S., c/o		SF	2426		1873	Charles Henry	<1	SF	1355		1869
C. O./K. E., c/o		SF	8376		1900	Charles J.	31	SWE	8150		1900
Carl	1	CA	7453		1900	Charles N.	39	SF	5426		1896
Carl				Jun	1899	Charles Oscar	37	MO	336		1900
Carl	52	SWE	8627		1901	Charles Wm.				Aug	1899
Carl (soldier)			6834		1900	Charlotte Ervin	67	MD	1062		1894
Carl M. (soldier)			2222		1903	Chas.	39	NOR	J23		1884
Carl Victor	1862	SWE	3474c		1904	Chas.	55	GER	5505a		1895
Carla Martin				Apr	1899	Chas.	38	DEN	6889		1895
Caroline	41	NOR	6456	Feb	1901	Chas.	68	SWE	1400		1901
Caroline Moore	75	AR	9232		1901	Chas. (soldier)			7802		1902
Carrie L.	55	VT	6562a		1895	Chas. E. (soldier)			6404		1900
Catherine	35	SCT	784b		1871	Chas./Johanna, c/o	<1	SF	4021		1902
Catherine	71	IRE	1728		1902	Chas/J., c/o				Mar	1899
Catherine M.	65	MA	4863		1896	Chris	68	DEN	6665		1904
Catherine Vivian	5	SF	3975		1900	Christian	37	NOR	807		1900
Charles	38	GER	616		1870	Christine	35	SWE	3864		1896
Charles	35	NOR	941		1870	Christine				Feb	1900
Charles	24	SWE	1361b		1871	Clara B.	5	SF	3200		1866
Charles	24	NJ	2836a		1872	Clara B.	43	IL	4517		1896
Charles	34	SWE	2992		1873	Clara Josephine	15	SF	3455		1894
Charles	42	FIN	J45		1887	Clara L.	7	SF	5178		1902
Charles	25	SWE	6647		1868	Cordelia A.				Nov	1898
Charles	30	RUS	7174		1868	Daniel	36	SCT	572b		1895
Charles	32	IL	1329		1903	David L.			3904		1902
Charles	40	ENG	6786		1903	E. Richard	66	WV	1078		1900

Key: a = 1st part of year; b = 2nd part of year;
c = death certificate copy; c/o = child of

NAME	AGE OR YOB.	BIRTH PLACE	CERT. NO	ID	DEATH YEAR	NAME	AGE OR YOB.	BIRTH PLACE	CERT. NO	ID	DEATH YEAR
Earle Gordon	4	SF	3733		1902	F. (soldier)			5699	Jan	1901
Edgar J.				May	1899	Fanny	34	CA	3655		1896
Edmund C. (soldier)			7547		1901	Florence G.				Dec	1898
Edward	36	SWE	6961		1902	Florida	25	CA	1059		1894
Edward	27	SF	1503		1902	Frank	59	GER	2120		1894
Edward	39	GER	3928		1902	Frank	<1	CA	6989	Feb	1901
Edward	<1	SF	5813		1903	Frank				Mar	1899
Edward				Oct	1899	Frank C.	2	SF	725b		1871
Edward	37	NOR	7251		1901	Frank Irving	1884	CA	2038c		1904
Edwin L.	44	WI	1586		1900	Frank W. (soldier)			7322		1901
Edwin Van Weber	<1	SF	588		1894	Frans	51	SWE	515c		1904
Eleanor	20	SF	663b		1895	Fred	45	MA	3606a		1895
Elias	23	SWE	9829		1868	Fred	35	SWE	6546		1900
Elison Carl	70	IA	5295		1902	Fred	21	IN	2537		1900
Eliza	32	MA	644		1866	Fred S.			7579		1902
Ella	<1	SF	645		1902	Frederic	32	FIN	499b		1871
Ella	<1	SF	2102		1894	Frederick	32	CA	7790		1902
Ellen	76	IRE	3029		1902	Frederick	58	DEN	6621	Feb	1901
Elsie	61	FRA	516		1903	Frederick				Jul	1899
Elsie Amanda	1903	SF	251c		1904	Frederick				Feb	1900
Emily	69	CT	1350		1869	G. Oscar	1872	CA	1105c		1904
Emily	<1	SF	1458		1894	Geo.	21	CA	J52		1889
Emily	68	NY	8208		1901	Geo. A.	54	MD	1519		1894
Emily	37	SWE	3095	Oct	1901	George	28	GRE	5329		1902
Emily Jane	70	ME	4090	Dec	1901	George	70	ME	1742		1901
Emma	1882	SWE	546c		1904	George				Nov	1899
Emma	54	IL	3118		1900	George				Feb	1900
Emma Louisa	4	SF	9252		1901	George	24	PA	1538a		1871
Ernest Victor	1	SF	8630		1900	George C.	61	NOR	3136a		1872
Estella	13	SF	2028b		1895	George W.	41	MD	2383a		1872
Esther	<1	SF	1249		1901	George W.	50	NY	9172		1868
Ethel Jeanette				Aug	1899	George W.	49	NY	8312		1904
Eugane	14		1057		1868	George W.		SF	4300b		1870
Eva	<1	SF	1834b		1895	Georgia McVeigh	53	VA	5726		1896
Eva C.	<1	SF	4903		1896	Gertrude	1897	CA	1936c		1904
Exel (soldier)			3728	Nov	1901	Gladys A.	2	SF	4670		1901

Key: a = 1st part of year; b = 2nd part of year;
c = death certificate copy; c/o = child of

NAME	AGE OR YOB.	BIRTH PLACE	CERT. NO	ID	DEATH YEAR	NAME	AGE OR YOB.	BIRTH PLACE	CERT. NO	ID	DEATH YEAR
Godfrey	41	SWE	2170		1903	Henry R.	51	PA	1174		1870
Gustaf	35	RUS	3096		1900	Henry Schuyler	<1	SF	794b		1872
Gustave	41	SWE	7474		1902	Herman	<1	SF	8022		1901
H. J.	53	NOR	3116		1866	Hillard T.				Dec	1899
Halldor	22	CAN	3232		1900	Hiram W.	28	TN	4466		1867
Hanna	36	SWE	5422		1903	Hulda	28	SWE	1998b		1895
Hannah	32	SWE	2829		1903	Ida	18	MO	1628a		1871
Hannah	82	SWE	6307	Feb	1901	Ida	<1	SF	8811		1901
Hannah	<1	SF	1669		1901	Ida M.	36	IL	2830		1900
Harold	<1	SF	6019		1896	Imogene E.				Jan	1899
Harold				Mar	1899	Ina Josephine	<1	SF	2961		1873
Harriet	38	CA	8727		1904	Isaac	28	FIN	8264		1903
Harriet, c/o	<1	SF	1877b		1872	Isaac				Aug	1899
Harriett Lorraine	<1	CA	418b		1895	J.	34	SWE	7431		1868
Harry	1	SF	841		1894	J.	42	SWE	3377		1894
Harry	56	CA	2265		1900	J. E.	52	ENG	301a		1871
Harry	16	IL	2317		1900	J. E.	26	SWE	6212a		1895
Harry	41	NOR	6871	Feb	1901	J. G. (soldier)			6945		1900
Harry				Feb	1900	J. H.	11		1046		1868
Harry P.	50	SWE	1887		1900	J. Kelly	<1	CA	8024		1904
Harry W.	24	NY	2007		1902	Jacob	39	FIN	4722		1867
Hattie Bell	38	CA	6214		1902	Jacob	43	SWE	5213		1903
Hattie Hoadley	44	OH	3518		1900	Jacob E.	34	RUS	1225		1894
Hattie S.	39	IL	2183b		1895	Jacob P.	23	ME	3831		1870
Hattie S.	27	CA	687b		1895	James	38	MD	1436		1870
Hazel	4	CA	6021a		1895	James	62	MD	629b		1872
Hector	<1	SF	4161	Dec	1901	James	61	IRL	1221b		1872
Helen Jeanette	39	MI	8286		1900	James	60	POR	J58		1889
Henry	2	SF	572a		1870	James	35		5087a		1896
Henry	56	FIN	1538b		1872	James A.	65	AR	5833		1896
Henry	24	NOR	J2		1882	James Charles	<1	SF	2164		1902
Henry	35	GER	J30		1885	James Howard	38	CA	8222		1904
Henry	35	GER	J41		1886	James J.	30	SF	1685		1894
Henry	56	MA	1252		1869	James P.	56	DEN	3665		1900
Henry	57	NOR	183b		1895	James W. (soldier)			4701		1901
Henry E.	44	ENG	8252		1904	James/Mary, c/o				Apr	1899

Key: a = 1st part of year; b = 2nd part of year;
c = death certificate copy; c/o = child of

NAME	AGE OR YOB.	BIRTH PLACE	CERT. NO	ID	DEATH YEAR
Jane	20	CA	6585		1902
Jane, Mrs.	58	IRL	2006		1900
Janey				Apr	1899
Jasper	<1	CA	2380a		1872
Jennie	37	MD	3534a		1872
Jennie	20	SWE	1967b		1895
Jennie	<1	SF	582b		1895
Jeremiah	52	SWE	J46		1887
Jno.	<1	CA	J54		1889
Johannis				Feb	1899
John	40	SWE	1823		1870
John	46	NOR	2251a		1872
John	32	DEN	2293		1873
John	24	SWE	1030		1868
John	30	IRE	1188		1869
John	1834	NOR	920c		1904
John	24	IL	4423		1902
John	41	SWE	7936		1903
John	43	DEN	4556		1896
John	58	SWE	1318		1894
John				Mar	1899
John A.				Dec	1899
John Albert	33	SWE	6015		1902
John C.	50	SWE	6342	Feb	1901
John E./Julia E., c/o		SF	3154		1902
John F.	34	SWE	9178		1901
John Henry	30	IL	5885		1904
John R.	29	CA	7154		1900
John/Julia, c/o	<1	SF	1551		1895
Jonas				Dec	1899
Joseph	<1	SF	2899		1866
Joseph	46	HOL	1067		1869
Joseph	<1	SF	5604	Jan	1901
Joseph				Jul	1898
Joseph				Dec	1899
Joseph C.	1	SF	4551b		1870

NAME	AGE OR YOB.	BIRTH PLACE	CERT. NO	ID	DEATH YEAR
Joseph E.	49	ENG	3734		1902
Joseph H	35	FIN	4914		1902
Joseph H.	<1	SF	2886		1895
Joseph M.	82	MD	450b		1895
Josephine	25	CA	3070	Oct	1901
Joshua W.				Mar	1900
Josiah G.				Mar	1899
Julia	41	WI	952b		1895
Julia				Nov	1899
Julius A.	28	SWE	1350		1900
Katherine Elizabeth	30	CA	8755		1900
Katie				Nov	1898
L. A.	40	SWE	6487		1896
Lars P.				Jul	1899
Lavinia M.	59	NC	5130		1904
Lawrence	22	BEL	J19		1884
Lena	52	SWE	6142		1904
Leo Andrew	4	SF	9		1903
Lillian May	13	IL	2372		1903
Louis	35	DEN	J10		1883
Louis	27	SWE	1891		1894
Louisa	31	CA	5145		1901
Louisa Christina	1866	SWE	1494c		1904
Lucretia				Nov	1899
Luther A.				Dec	1898
Lyman B.	48	CA	4152		1900
Maggie	5	SF	1078		1869
Margaret	62	IRL	5659a		1895
Margaret	40	ENG	6608		1896
Margaret	80	ENG	3354		1900
Margaret				Apr	1899
Margaret				May	1899
Margaret				Nov	1899
Margaret C.	36	CA	2010b		1895
Margaretta	63	GER	8236		1903
Maria	<1	SF	949b		1872

Key: *a = 1st part of year; b = 2nd part of year;*
c = death certificate copy; c/o = child of

NAME	AGE OR YOB.	BIRTH PLACE	CERT. NO	ID	DEATH YEAR	NAME	AGE OR YOB.	BIRTH PLACE	CERT. NO	ID	DEATH YEAR
Maria	50	NOR	4951		1903	Nellie	30	IL	6725		1896
Marie, c/o		SF	2254		1895	Nels	37	SWE	5170		1904
Martin	38	NOR	4022		1902	Nels				May	1899
Martin	44	SWE	6486		1903	Nels P.				Mar	1900
Martin	43	NOR	9253		1901	Nicholas B.	62	NB	8092		1904
Martin (soldier)			6833		1900	Nick P. (soldier)			6298		1904
Martin Ludwig	57	NOR	96		1902	Nicol	75	NOR	3346		1903
Mary	4	SF	1399		1869	Nicolena				Feb	1900
Mary	45	NY	3607		1903	O. B. (soldier)			3052	Oct	1901
Mary	60	SWE	4835		1903	O./A., c/o		SF	490		1895
Mary	8	SF	4625		1901	Olaf	50	SWE	5001		1904
Mary	64	IRL	1552		1900	Olaf	41	NOR	6031		1904
Mary A.	53	IL	868		1903	Olaf	36	NOR	5597		1896
Mary A.	45	IRL	7369		1901	Ole	41	NOR	7175		1868
Mary Agnes	<1	SF	1989		1873	Ole (soldier)			6402		1900
Mary Ann	18	RI	7662		1868	Olif	1	CA	4368		1896
Mary Ann	36	CAN	7525		1903	Olif	4	SF	1869		1901
Mary E.	1869	MA	1183c		1904	Olof G.	1	CA	1622b		1895
Mary E.	28	MA	4263		1902	Oscar	37	FIN	4376		1901
Mary E.	70	IN	8762		1903	Oscar E.				Feb	1900
Mary Gustava				Mar	1900	Oscar F.			7619		1902
Mary Louise	30	SF	5546		1904	Oscar Stephanus	51	SWE	646b		1895
Mary Teresr	1	CA	7113		1904	Ostrid				Mar	1899
Mary Vashti	18	OR	8166		1900	Otto F. (soldier)			6944		1900
Matilda	37	SWE	463b		1872	Otto W.			3712		1902
Matilda	38	SWE	6147		1896	P. A.	26	SWE	J56		1889
Matt B.	73	DEN	175		1902	Paul	35	NY	1505		1903
Matthew Fontaine	55	AR	1		1900	Permela	55	ME	6238		1903
Max	27	NOR	4898		1903	Peter	63	DEN	2787		1873
May	30	CA	4275		1896	Peter	41	NOR	J27		1885
Michael	<1	SF	8736		1903	Peter	52	SWE	3340		1902
Milton Foster	<1	SF	3829	Nov	1901	Peter	47	NOR	3584		1896
Minnie	28	CT	9321		1901	Peter	72	NOR	2437		1901
Morris				Feb	1899	Peter				Mar	1899
Morris M.	24	SWE	2239		1894	Peter A.	52	SWE	8905		1900
Neils Alfred				Jan	1899	Peter L.	55	SWE	3353		1894

Key: a = 1st part of year; b = 2nd part of year;
c = death certificate copy; c/o = child of

NAME	AGE OR YOB.	BIRTH PLACE	CERT. NO	ID	DEATH YEAR	NAME	AGE OR YOB.	BIRTH PLACE	CERT. NO	ID	DEATH YEAR
Pher. A.	45	SWE	2036		1894	Theodore Lord	33	CA	8165		1900
Phoebe J.	<1	CA	7084		1904	Thomas	73	IRE	5035		1902
Rasmus (soldier)			7165		1901	Thomas	<1	SF	6279		1900
Richard (soldier)			1318		1902	Thomas	36	ENG	9299		1901
Richard O.	27	WAL	9949		1868	Thomas	1860	DEN	1428c		1904
Robert	18	USA	518b		1872	Thomas		SWE	1157c		1904
Robert	<1	SF	1286		1869	Thomas (soldier)			4700		1901
Robert	39	CA	5330		1902	Thomas A.				Dec	1899
Robert	40	IRE	3341		1902	Thomas A./Belle, c/o	1904	SF	2780		1904
Robert	<1	SF	8791		1903	Thos./JB, c/o		SF	5943		1895
Robert L.			4491		1901	Tina	23	SWE	8102		1903
Robert, c/o	<1	SF	2030a		1872	——v		SF	523		1870
Rosie				Dec	1898	Victor	46	FIN	6368	Feb	1901
Roy Axel	1	SF	709b		1895	Victoria Ann	<1	SF	1071a		1871
S./L., c/o	<1	SF	114		1895	Virginia E.	72	NY	3837		1903
Sadie Gustava	12	SF	7262		1904	W. E.	60		5702		1903
Samuel	74	ENG	4576		1904	Wallace E. (soldier)			8503		1901
Samuel A.	14	IRL	6213a		1895	Walter (soldier)			5188		1901
Samuel S.			662b		1871	Walter Cutting	1	SF	8992		1901
Sarah A.	42	ME	1322b		1872	William	38	SWE	60a		1871
Sarah D.	65	ME	2354		1894	William	<1	CA	318b		1872
Sarah Logan	75	IRE	5423		1903	William	74	ENG	3427		1867
Sarah/James, c/o	<1	SF	4130		1896	William	31	NOR	1079		1869
Sarah/James, c/o	<1	SF	4131		1896	William	50	IRE	8093		1904
Simon	63	NOR	743		1902	William				Jun	1899
Sivert E.	1	SF	1064		1869	William				Nov	1899
Sophie	37	GER	1442		1869	William				May	1899
Sophie	29	FIN	7920		1900	William (soldier)			9568		1901
Sophie Christina	1835	DEN	2077c		1904	William A.	39	CA	2518		1903
Stire (soldier)			3453c		1904	William E.	55	SWE	5607		1904
Swan	1842	SWE	2378c		1904	William F. (soldier)			3422	Nov	1901
Swan	37	SWE	6829	Feb	1901	William H.	34	PA	8195		1868
Sydney	45		8872		1904	William J.			3961		1902
Thelma	1904	SF	1403c		1904	William Leslie	6	CA	6334		1904
Theodore	1860	OH	118c		1904	William N. P.	10	SF	6522		1904
Theodore	1		6951		1904	William O.	11	SF	3084		1870

Key: a = 1st part of year; b = 2nd part of year;
c = death certificate copy; c/o = child of

NAME	AGE OR YOB.	BIRTH PLACE	CERT. NO	ID	DEATH YEAR	NAME	AGE OR YOB.	BIRTH PLACE	CERT. NO	ID	DEATH YEAR
William W.	49	IRL	2149		1873	Elizabeth				Aug	1898
William W.			3960		1902	Ellen O.	<1	SF	4843		1867
William W.	49	NY	7781		1903	Emma T.				Oct	1898
William/Edith, c/o	<1	CA	4795		1902	Evelyn	<1	SF	7060		1903
William/Ethel, c/o		SF	1362		1901	Francis Herbert	32	CA	3254		1902
Willie R.	2	SF	2653		1895	Frank B. (soldier)			6324		1900
Winnie (soldier)			3686		1900	Frederick	46	VA	34		1870
Wm	60		6124		1904	Geo. W.	<1	SF	3510a		1872
Wm.	46	NY	1887b		1872	George	49	NY	7637		1868
Wm.	58	IRL	4594a		1895	Halford E.	2	CA	7188		1903
Wm. C.	55	IRL	J57		1889	Harriet	41	CA	6070		1904
Wm. J.	<1	SF	3128		1894	Harry				Jul	1899
Wm./Emma, c/o	1	SF	5067		1904	Henry	31	SWE	1450		1869
Wm./Mary, c/o		SF	8806		1900	Henry				Oct	1899
						Henry A. (soldier)			2078		1901
JOHNSTON						Henry W. (soldier)			6403		1900
——		SF	4415b		1870	Horace Morrison	6	CA	1269		1869
——			6807		1868	J. Dale	82	IRL	281b		1895
A./E., c/o	<1	SF	3981		1895	James	32	CVE	3365a		1872
Alexander	45	RUS	6154		1867	James	35	SCT	1660		1866
Alexander	<1	SF	5179		1902	James	26	NOR	4523		1867
Alice				Jan	1899	James	1	SF	6635		1904
Alice A.	53	MO	3668		1903	James G.	47	IRL	J49		1887
Alpha				Jan	1900	James/Maggie , c/o	<1	SF	1427		1900
Andrew	38	PA	9813		1868	John	51	ENG	2696		1873
Andrew	51	ENG	5003		1896	John	24	SF	359		1865
Ann	32	CA	6076a		1895	John	60	CAN	2113		1903
August	41	SWE	1349		1903	John A.	22	OH	771		1866
Bridget	50	IRL	5205		1901	John Edward	3	MA	2485a		1872
Catherine				Aug	1898	John H.	41	MD	7219		1868
Catherine				Jan	1900	Joseph	43	SWE	1466b		1871
Catherine E.	<1	SF	1677b		1895	Josie	49	OH	6636		1904
Cecelia Theresa	<1	SF	1113		1869	Julia F.	1866	PA	3359c		1904
Charles C.	46	ME	2756		1873	Louis W.	73	PA	315		1903
Christopher	35	SWE	J50		1887	Mabel Alice	24	CAN	5424		1903
Donald M.	38	TN	3649		1870	Margaret	40	IRL	3090		1873
Elizabeth	56	WAL	2228		1900						

Key: a = 1st part of year; b = 2nd part of year;
c = death certificate copy; c/o = child of

NAME	AGE OR YOB.	BIRTH PLACE	CERT. NO	ID	DEATH YEAR
Margaret	2	SF	1444		1869
Margaret	34	MA	3696		1896
Margaret	74	IRL	6420		1900
Margaret	24	SF	1453		1900
Margaret	24	SF	1453		1900
Mary	<1	SF	2542a		1872
Mary , c/o	<1	SF	1249		1869
Mary Ann	70	IRE	3994		1903
Mary Elizabeth	36	PA	6890		1895
Mary Ella	1	SF	7213		1868
Mary, Mrs.	78	ENG	6075a		1895
Milton	<1	SF	1067		1900
Patrick	<1	SF	7514		1868
Patrick				Mar	1899
Robert Francis				Dec	1898
Sam	60	MD	6095		1867
Samuel P.	33	SWE	1849		1866
Sarah	23	NJ	1088b		1872
Sophia	79	NH	5015		1867
Taylor (soldier)			7323		1901
W. P.	50	PA	6233		1896
Walter	<1	SF	3979		1902
William	<1	SF	1518		1866
William	35	NY	3599		1867
William	30	MD	6077		1867
William	<1	SF	7838		1868
William	60	PA	5514		1903
William	1904	SF	2898c		1904
William D.	48	NY	2924		1895
William G.	25	SF	6460		1896
William H.	43	NY	646		1902
William W.	3	SF	9210		1868
JOHNSTONE					
Charles H.	72	SCT	1140		1903
Emma	27	CA	919		1903
Lizzie	27	VA	8528		1904
Margaret	43	MA	7901		1903
Sarah	32	IRL	176b		1871
Wm. or John	43	AUT	5990		1896
JOHNSTONS					
Edward	72	IRE	1372		1869
JOHUM					
Frank H.	26	NY	6329		1900
JOICE					
——			6223		1867
Francis	32	IRE	1028		1868
Joseph	28	IRL	2437a		1872
Richard	4	SF	1308		1869
Thomas	91	IRE	1337		1902
JOIE					
Ah	34	CHN	9038		1868
JOINER					
Frederick Edwin	<1	CA	5446		1896
Miles (soldier)			284		1901
Richmond				Aug	1898
JOINET					
Alexander V.	34	SF	5159		1902
JOLET					
Joseph A.				Feb	1900
JOLEZZI					
Maria	54	ITA	5052a		1895
JOLIDUE					
Elsie, Mrs.	58	FRA	5658a		1895
JOLIFFE					
Johanna O.				Mar	1900
JOLLY					
Eleanore	91	IRL	4699a		1895
Emile A.	60	FRA	2759		1902
S. C.	34	DC	2989		1866

Key: a = 1st part of year; b = 2nd part of year; c = death certificate copy; c/o = child of

NAME	AGE OR YOB.	BIRTH PLACE	CERT. NO	ID	DEATH YEAR	NAME	AGE OR YOB.	BIRTH PLACE	CERT. NO	ID	DEATH YEAR
JOLY						Bertha	<1	SF	4644		1901
Joseph M.	28	FRA	1122		1869	Blanche				Oct	1898
JON						Bridget	<1	SF	3482b		1870
Sing Wing				Feb	1900	Burgher R. (soldier)			5491	Jan	1901
JONAS						C. A.	55	MA	7595		1868
Amelia	5	SF	312b		1872	Carmelita Alice	<1	SF	4963		1902
Isaac A.	70	ENG	J5		1882	Carrie Katie	<1	SF	1064b		1872
John	65	GER	986b		1895	Catherine J.	48	MO	387		1901
Simon				Jul	1898	Cathrine	42	GER	3549		1870
JONATHAN						Charles A.	44	CA	6702		1902
——	<1	SF	646		1894	Charles E.				Oct	1898
JONE						Charles E.	30	OH	2296		1900
D.			J48		1887	Charles R.	48	SF	5608		1904
Duck				Dec	1899	Cornelia	34	MI	602a		1871
JONES						Cyrus Winship	70	MA	645b		1895
——	<1	SF	3645		1870	Daisey P.	<1	SF	9679		1868
——	<1	SF	107a		1871	Daniel				Jan	1900
——		SF	1106		1869	Daniel Edward	64	OH	12		1902
Abbey A.	50	NY	7010	Feb	1901	David	41	ENG	1459		1870
Abbott	35	NY	3076a		1872	David	68	ENG	3639		1903
Aileen	2	SF	4633		1904	David R.	83	WAL	1633		1903
Albert E./Mary, c/o		SF	2204		1900	David W.		CA	1091		1869
Albert William	52	ENG	2342		1903	David, c/o	<1	SF	2107a		1872
Ann Jane	84	MA	7611		1901	Davie	1851	ENG	1142c		1904
Anna M.	<1	SF	3030		1902	Deborah W.	75	NY	1372		1902
Anne				Jun	1899	Dela, c/o				Aug	1899
Annie	<1	SF	6530		1902	Douglas A.	35	OR	2831		1900
Annie	<1	SF	7314		1902	Ed	52	ENG	J28		1885
Annie	<1	SF	1142		1901	Edith	4	SF	124		1900
Annie E.	60	LA	7992		1901	Edna M.	<1	SF	4035		1896
Anset G./C. L., c/o		CA	1680		1900	Edward	81	LA	7993		1901
Arthur Denby	17	ENG	7837		1903	Edward	29	NY	2352		1866
Arthur Howel	35	WAL	7014		1902	Edward (civilian)			1017		1901
Arthur W.	33	NV	6071		1904	Edward (soldier)			6832		1900
Bernice Jeffreys	<1	SF	1986		1900	Edward (soldier)			7960		1901
						Eliza	65	IRE	6652		1903

Key: a = 1st part of year; b = 2nd part of year;
c = death certificate copy; c/o = child of

NAME	AGE OR YOB.	BIRTH PLACE	CERT. NO	ID	DEATH YEAR	NAME	AGE OR YOB.	BIRTH PLACE	CERT. NO	ID	DEATH YEAR
Eliza	47	IRL	3399		1896	George N.				May	1899
Eliza Jane	68	IL	2208		1901	George W.	70	MO	4103		1903
Elizabeth	<1	SF	1654b		1871	Gertrude	1	CA	5531	Jan	1901
Elizabeth	49	ENG	1098		1894	Gertrude Estella	12	NV	1187		1894
Elizabeth				Jun	1899	Grace	<1	SF	8458		1900
Elizabeth J.	52	ENG	3479		1902	Grace M.	4	SF	6726		1896
Ellen	32	IRL	1560b		1871	Griffith	26	WAL	3967		1896
Ellen	80	IRL	570b		1895	Guy	<1	SF	2001		1866
Emma	47	NB	1481		1903	Guy				Feb	1900
Emma O.	2	CA	4739		1867	H. B.	29	LA	7297		1900
Emma Oakley				Apr	1899	Harold	1904	SF	351c		1904
Ethel	23	OR	5362		1903	Harry	35		4689		1903
Evan L.	<1	SF	6143		1904	Harry (soldier)			5797		1904
Eve L.	1	MI	1300		1869	Harry A.				Feb	1900
F. C.				Dec	1899	Harry J.	30	SF	844		1903
Fanny, c/o		SF	5002		1896	Harry Paul	36	IL	2820		1902
Francis Paul	18	CA	8875		1901	Hattie				Feb	1899
Frank	26	CA	J3		1882	Hazel	16	CA	9254		1901
Frank	55		9035		1901	Helen	51	VT	8300		1901
Frank LeB		SF	1745		1870	Helena Melvina	<1	SF	2483		1894
Frank Preston	<1	SF	8163		1901	Henry	69	ENG	8850		1903
Fred	25	ENG	6737a		1895	Henry	3	SF	7745		1902
Fred	<1	SF	5381		1896	Henry	65	USA	1694		1903
Fred A.			3822		1902	Henry B.	36	IRL	4427		1896
Frederick	<1	SF	7315		1902	Henry Gates	51	CAN	5974	Jan	1901
Frederick (soldier)	21	NY	4355	Dec	1901	Herbert	<1	MN	6350		1867
G. H. J.	55	ENG	6254		1896	Horatio Nelson	62	NB	7995		1903
G. M.	70	MA	1429		1869	Hugh	29	WAL	812a		1871
George	2	SF	3443b		1870	Hum	1829	CHN	2455c		1904
George	36	ENG	9384		1868	I. W.				Mar	1899
George	1904	SF	3009c		1904	Ira (soldier)			6943		1900
George A.	54	NY	8030		1903	Irene L.	15	NV	7928		1901
George C.	1837	CAN	1543c		1904	Isaac	48	ENG	1233		1869
George F.				Jul	1898	Isaih	31	CA	2536		1900
George H.	58	NY	7370		1901	Isidora	60	MEX	5061		1902
George J.	66	NB	5790	Jan	1901	Ivon	<1	CA	2028		1902

Key: a = 1st part of year; b = 2nd part of year;
c = death certificate copy; c/o = child of

NAME	AGE OR YOB.	BIRTH PLACE	CERT. NO	ID	DEATH YEAR	NAME	AGE OR YOB.	BIRTH PLACE	CERT. NO	ID	DEATH YEAR
J. C.	67	ENG	6208		1903	Larry				Feb	1900
J. H.	23	IA	1025		1868	Leander (soldier)			7223		1900
J. P./C., c/o		CA	2037		1873	Lenora J.	58	ME	6457	Feb	1901
Jabez	40	ME	6461		1868	Lewis E.				Mar	1900
James				Jan	1899	Lilian C.	43	NY	2741		1895
James (soldier)			3053	Oct	1901	Lillie B., Mrs.	36	NY	1272		1901
James D.				Feb	1900	Louisa	39	ENG	2530		1902
James E.	36	SF	6447	a	1895	Louise	1	SF	8605		1904
James M.	69	KY	7681		1903	Lucil C.	43	NY	5875		1903
James P.	60	KY	9543		1901	Manuela	90	MEX	9549		1868
Jennie E			4886		1902	Maraday E.				Mar	1900
Jesse H./Edith, c/o		SF	1143		1901	Margaret	<1	CA	3020		1900
Jesse Hayden	49	KY	4484		1896	Margaret	80	WAL	5096		1901
Joel Benjamin	59	ENG	1141		1903	Margaret	68	IRL	1870		1901
John	25	IRL	1094		1870	Margaret A.	<1	SF	1451		1869
John	<1	CA	1242b		1871	Margaret J.	79	PA	1885		1902
John	26	NY	407 a		1871	Margaret W.				Jun	1899
John	56	NH	1252a		1871	Martha J.	1	CA	1355		1894
John	<1	SF	3308a		1872	Martin	1	SF	1038		1903
John	54	ENG	5868		1867	Mary	<1	SF	2537		1873
John	<1	SF	1051		1868	Mary	<1	SF	2562		1873
John	63	IA	8599		1903	Mary		SF	1128		1866
John	72	WAL	9037		1903	Mary	55	OH	5402		1904
John	75	NJ	879		1894	Mary	70	WAL	5363		1903
John	62	WAL	8167		1900	Mary	<1	SF	811		1894
John	60	IRL	4134	Dec	1901	Mary Ann				Nov	1899
John	40	ENG	2827		1873	Mary E.				Nov	1899
John E.	55	WAL	5247a		1896	Mary F.		SF	4524b		1870
John H.	28	ENG	2008		1902	Mary Faustina	1	SF	6733		1904
John H.				Jul	1899	Mary G.	31	MA	7412		1902
John W.	<1	SF	362		1902	Mary Joseph A., Sister	31	CA	4975		1896
John W.				Feb	1899	Mary, c/o				Dec	1898
John/Sadie, c/o				Dec	1898	Mary, c/o	<1	SF	2979a		1872
Joseph M.	<1	SF	815 b		1872	Maud Harriet	25	CA	4452		1902
Josephine	<1	SF	3216		1870	Maurice				Dec	1898
L. G.	50		J42		1886	Michael	67	NJ	1552		1901

Key: a = 1st part of year; b = 2nd part of year;
c = death certificate copy; c/o = child of

NAME	AGE OR YOB.	BIRTH PLACE	CERT. NO	ID	DEATH YEAR	NAME	AGE OR YOB.	BIRTH PLACE	CERT. NO	ID	DEATH YEAR
Michael Purcel				Aug	1899	Thomas E.	65	NY	2080		1894
Milton	<1		7918		1904	Thomas J.	32	ME	3556		1867
Nimrod W.	81	VA	1644		1894	Thos./Mgt., c/o				Nov	1898
O. G.	38	WAL	1043		1868	Van Cullen	1859	NJ	2744c		1904
Oliver	54	DC	2322a		1872	Victor	73	PRU	7099		1900
Olliver	221	TN	4369		1896	Walter	20	SF	3657		1896
Oscar R.				Dec	1898	Webster/Jean, c/o	<1	SF	6410		1904
P. C.	50	MA	5701		1867	William	56	IRL	J36		1886
Peter	27	CA	7338		1900	William	37	SCT	1118		1869
Philip	48	ENG	151		1900	William	64	CAN	2703		1902
R. C./M. G., c/o		SF	1715		1894	William	15	SF	3355		1896
Reuben	48	VA	1965a		1872	William (soldier)			7758		1901
Richard	50	NY	1837		1902	William Andrew	26	SF	8906		1900
Richard	59	ENG	326		1901	William C.	57	MA	6049		1867
Richard F.	<1	SF	3856		1870	William C.	29	CA	5695		1902
Richard M.	40	SF	4340		1903	William H.				Feb	1900
Robert	62	WAL	6627		1902	William Jos.	<1	SF	2393		1873
Robert	<1	SF	5603Jan		1901	William L.	51	ENG	4533		1901
Robert L.	37	ENG	532		1901	William R.	53	MO	5256		1904
Rose Marie	<1	SF	4915		1902	William Saunder				Aug	1899
Rose Mary	1	SF	1672		1903	William W.	33	WAL	2051		1866
S. A. D.	42	CA	8703		1904	William W.				Apr	1899
Samuel (soldier)			6401		1900	Winfield S.	56	DC	5942		1902
Samuel H.				Jun	1899	Winifred	23	LA	1436		1869
Samuel S.	34	ME	1140		1869	Wm.	30	WAL	J24		1885
Sandy	75	LA	3740		1867	Wm.				Feb	1900
Sarah	1	SF	9140		1868	Wm. H.	26	WAL	J20		1884
Sarah A.	<1	SF	166		1870	Wm. H./Florence L., c/o	1	SF	3345		1903
Sarah R.				Oct	1899	Wm. R.	54	MO	6333a		1895
Sarah Russell	34	IL	5395		1867	**JONG**					
Septimus Arthur	43	ENG	5633Jan		1901	Shew	48	CHN	4255		1903
Stephen J. (soldier)			3054Oct		1901	**JONGENEEL**					
Thomas	64	WAL	1457b		1871	A. W. M.	53	POL	280b		1895
Thomas	39	CT	7995		1900	**JONN**					
Thomas				Dec	1899	Yet Kin				Feb	1900
Thomas D.	1855	SF	3401c		1904						

NAME	AGE OR YOB.	BIRTH PLACE	CERT. NO	ID	DEATH YEAR
JONSEN					
Hans P.	34	DEN	4453		1902
JOONE					
James	40	NY	8952		1868
JOONG					
Mon Wong Shee	73	CHN	3275		1903
Mon Young Shee	54	CHN	3563		1903
JOOST					
Anna C.	39	GER	1090		1903
F.	42	GER	1443		1869
Frederich H.	35	GER	2135		1903
Henry	47	GER	4002		1900
John/Kate, c/o	1	CA	1015		1903
Josephine	50	NY	1440		1894
JORDAN					
——	<1	SF	1229		1869
Abbie F.					Aug 1898
Albert B.					Feb 1900
Anita	19	SF	8055		1903
Ann	26	NY	8755		1868
Anna					Jul 1898
Caroline	65	LA	1170		1869
Catharine	25	MA	1648b		1871
Catherine	66	IRL	4850		1901
Charles	55		2132a		1872
Charles Frank	11	SF	4612		1896
Conrad	55	GER	5297		1901
Dennis	73	IRE	2343		1903
Eliza	77	ENG	9099		1901
Eliza J.	32	MO	1792a		1872
Ella	22	CA	4880		1896
Eojenio	1903	SF	2311c		1904
Florence J.					May 1899
Frank	<1	SF	8255		1868
George	22	TX	1514b		1872
George	34	ME	1104		1869
Grace	<1	SF	616b		1872
Ira	20	CA	7217		1902
James	38	ME	3706		1902
James H./Mary, c/o		SF	5360		1901
James Harry	1	SF	2985		1903
John	55	IRL	2964a		1872
John F.	45	IRL	J47		1887
John M.	28	CT	4334b		1870
Letty A.	30	NV	282b		1895
Louisa	<1	SF	7497		1868
Maria	69	GER	1201		1901
Marie	27	SF	2050		1903
Martha	53	ENG	728		1901
Martin	41	IRE	6209		1903
Mary	37	CA	2870		1903
Mary Anne	25	LA	977b		1871
Maud A.	<1	SF	6710a		1895
Michael	67	IRL	8235		1900
Roy E.	25	KS	7734		1900
Wendell	63	GER	4949		1901
William	27		2413		1903
William M.	70	IRL	3256		1900
JORDON					
Henry	36	ENG	J14		1883
John (soldier)			4706		1901
JOREY					
Joseph	<1	SF	2326		1873
Lillie	23	ENG	2092		1873
JORGENSEN					
Andrew Bent	26	DEN	3417		1903
Annie Elizabeth	31	SF	1018		1900
Annie Teresa	<1	SF	3051		1900
Cecilie	30	GER	3910		1896
Charles J.					Feb 1900

Key: a = 1st part of year; b = 2nd part of year; c = death certificate copy; c/o = child of

NAME	AGE OR YOB.	BIRTH PLACE	CERT. NO	ID	DEATH YEAR	NAME	AGE OR YOB.	BIRTH PLACE	CERT. NO	ID	DEATH YEAR
Charles T.	48	MN	6937	Feb	1901	Aloysius	<1	SF	542		1902
Christine				Nov	1899	Anita	1	SF	729		1903
Emil	56	DEN	7520		1902	Annie	2	AUT	3333		1866
Lawrence				Oct	1898	Antone	68	CPV	8235		1901
Mamie	34	MA	8667		1904	B.	<1	SF	104b		1872
Mangins				Oct	1898	Caroline	50	GER	3506		1896
Maren				Nov	1899	Charles				Apr	1899
Peder or Peter	18	NOR	7494		1903	Charles D.	40	IN	4409	Dec	1901
Peter/Dorothy, c/o	<1	CA	1101		1901	Emma	61	GER	4341		1903
JORICK						Eva				Apr	1899
Ah	40	CHN	5125		1867	Felicia	1	SF	1275		1870
JORIS						Francis	24	WIS	1037		1868
Lucie	3	SF	1219		1869	Frank	68	SCT	8804		1900
JOROVICH						Harris				Aug	1899
Peter	39	AUT	4452a		1895	Henri	65	FRA	81a		1871
						J.	<1	SF	1251a		1871
JORSKY						John	<1	SF	4237		1867
Adam	79	RUS	5393		1901	John	35	CPV	4560a		1895
JORST						John	<1	SF	3730		1900
Fabian				Mar	1899	Joseph				Feb	1899
JORY						Joseph				Jan	1899
Polly Ann	60	OH	5379		1902	Joseph/Daisy, c/o	<1	SF	8425		1903
JOSE						Kanaka	23	HI	2313		1873
Emmanuel				Nov	1899	Laurence	<1	SF	4671		1901
Francis	4	SF	1347		1869	Leir	62	PRU	J17		1883
Nathaniel T.	38	ME	5302		1867	Louie	8	SF	4538b		1870
JOSEPH						Manuel, c/o		CA	771b		1872
——	1	SF	731		1870	Mary	46	POR	146		1902
——	1	SF	317a		1871	Mary				Aug	1898
——	1	SF	5649		1904	Michael	80	POL	2221		1873
——	1	SF	213		1903	Michael J.	67	ENG	265		1900
——	<1	CA	2955		1902	Patrick	<1	SF	64		1902
——		SF	3668	Nov	1901	Peter	49	NY	641a		1871
Agusta	20	NY	107		1901	Thomas	<1	CA	1966		1901
Alfred H.	55	SC	6288		1896	Valentine V.	<1	SF	1061		1894
						Vincent	<1	CA	6148		1896

NAME	AGE OR YOB.	BIRTH PLACE	CERT. NO	ID	DEATH YEAR	NAME	AGE OR YOB.	BIRTH PLACE	CERT. NO	ID	DEATH YEAR
Wilfred	<1	CA	7674		1902	**JOSSMAN**					
William	<1	CA	7937		1903	Albert L. (soldier)			2547		1902
William Nathaniel	63	WIN	7263		1904						
						JOSSYLYN					
JOSEPHI						Percy Ed	3	SF	1248		1869
Isaac S.	40	ENG	27b		1871						
						JOST					
JOSEPHINE						Charles	<1	SF	6498		1868
——	1	SF	791		1903	Christian	53	GER	4237		1896
Mary	<1	SF	9436		1868	Frank	1	SF	4729		1867
Mary	<1	SF	1315		1869	Susanna	31	SF	4353a		1895
Mary				Jun	1899						
						JOTA					
JOSEPHS						Ahikanoshike				May	1899
John	28	WIS	9109		1868						
						JOU					
JOSEPHSON						Kun	49	CHN	1569		1903
Ernestine				Mar	1900						
J. S.				Dec	1899	**JOUANNEAU**					
Joseph L.	35	GER	1145		1869	Geannet	12	FRA	6628		1903
JOSEPHUS						**JOUANOW**					
——	<1	CA	6149		1896	Jean Baptiste	58	FRA	2871		1903
JOSLIN						**JOUBERT**					
Charles Allen	62	MA	4507		1901	Martin	43	FRA	815		1901
Silas B.	70	CT	2380		1900						
						JOUETT					
JOSLYN						Cavalier Hamilton				Oct	1898
Charles S.	64	NY	3995		1903						
Elise Gertrude	50	NY	8031		1903	**JOUGLARD**					
						Fernand/Mary, c/o	<1	CA	3667		1901
JOSSELIN											
Charles	44	FRA	3359		1870	**JOULDIN**					
						J.	50		8712		1903
JOSSELYN											
Albert B.	1	SF	1543		1866	**JOUNG**					
Edgar LeRoy	<1	SF	1281		1869	——			3065		1870
Henry M.	27	MA	464		1866	H. F./C., c/o		SF	6461		1896
J. H.	83	MA	2446		1903	**JOURDEN**					
Lockwood H.				Dec	1898	John Albert				Jul	1899
Maria				Feb	1900	Lucy H.	48	LA	224		1900
						JOURNEAY					
						Albert				Nov	1898

Key: a = 1st part of year; b = 2nd part of year; c = death certificate copy; c/o = child of

NAME	AGE OR YOB.	BIRTH PLACE	CERT. NO	ID	DEATH YEAR
JOUS					
Ah	30	CHN	310		1870
JOUSSE					
Victor	59	FRA	3524a		1872
JOUVENTINE					
Francois, Mrs.	93	FRA	5130		1902
JOVANOVICH					
Stane	22	AUS	6314		1904
JOVIER					
Annie Elizabeth	<1	SF	2899a		1872
JOVOVICH					
John	26	AUT	J25		1885
Sposo/Kate , c/o	1	SF	1971		1903
Vladimir	42	AUS	7397		1902
JOVOVICK					
Lazar					Oct 1899
JOW					
Chung Chow	49	CHN	1568		1903
Dock		CHN	6417		Feb 1901
Loy	54	CHN	2781		1902
Sing Quong	36	CHN	2199		1903
Tung	47	CHN	6510		1896
JOY					
Earl Raymond	<1	SF	6944		1903
Harry E.	30	NH	5081		1902
Hartford	59	ME	94 b		1872
Horace Edgar					Oct 1898
James F.	45	DEN	J39		1886
Mabel	<1	CA	3342		1902
Nettie	57	VT	5186a		1896
Samuel A.	64	ME	1299		1902
JOYCE					
Catherine	71	IRL	3043		1895
Cecil L.	<1	SF	5067a		1895
Charles					Feb 1900
Edmond	23	SF	5237		1903
James	58	IRL	1050		1900
John	30	IRE	4012		1867
Joseph	39	SWT	5492		1903
Katie	33	CA	30		1901
Mary	60	IRE	4767		1903
Mary E.	2	SF	3076		1870
Michael	49	IRE	7693		1868
Michael	60	IRL	3311		1895
Thomas	63	IRL	835		1901
JOYES					
James J.	65	IRL	1699		1894
JOYNER					
Benjamin Edward	6	SF	7922		1903
Peter	4	SF	8207		1901
Sarah J	43	IRE	4916		1902
Thos.	1	SF	3376		1894
William A.	6	CT	616		1866
JSINE					
Gu	45	CHN	3617		1867
JU					
Hui Lee	42	CHN	J37		1886
Kue	50	CHN	2740		1894
JU KAY					
Chew Kee	36	CHN	5925		1903
JUAIN					
Margaret T.	44	NY	3501		Nov 1901
JUAREZ					
Maria Isabel	80	MEX	3909a		1895
Micaela	31	CA	473a		1871
Roy Darrel	1900	CA	2162c		1904
JUDAH					
Benj. W.	43	VA	1174		1869

Key: a = 1st part of year; b = 2nd part of year;
c = death certificate copy; c/o = child of

NAME	AGE OR YOB.	BIRTH PLACE	CERT. NO	ID	DEATH YEAR
Maria B.				Oct	1899
JUDD					
——		CA	1992		1870
Emily E.				Aug	1898
J. W. /Elizabeth, c/o	1904	SF	1904		1904
Wilhelmina	67	GER	5792		1902
William	46	ENG	6503		1868
JUDDBOVITCH					
Recky	8	SF	8377		1904
JUDE					
Bridget	40	IRL	2948		1895
Friedrich Phillip	1	SF	2957		1903
Patrick	65	IRE	144		1903
JUDELE					
Adele	1872	CA	3268c		1904
JUDELG					
George/Sarah , c/o	<1	SF	761		1902
JUDGE					
——			1039		1868
Annie E.				Oct	1898
Austin	16	CA	1307a		1871
B. J./R., c/o				Nov	1898
Frank W.	58	IRL	7862		1901
James				Jan	1900
John	61	IRL	7051		1900
John J.	1848	IRE	2815c		1904
Kate G.	22	NV	1062		1903
JUDKINS					
Edith May	19	ME	4809a		1895
William/Emma, c/o	1	CA	79		1903
JUDNIC					
Joseph	<1	SF	6529a		1895
Rosalia	<1	SF	5187a		1896

NAME	AGE OR YOB.	BIRTH PLACE	CERT. NO	ID	DEATH YEAR
JUDNICK					
Annie	1904	SF	352c		1904
JUDSON					
Augustus	76	NY	3494		1900
Harry C.	49	NY	2623		1894
Marie D.				Feb	1900
Mary E.	48	NY	3013		1895
Willet P.	8	NY	897b		1872
JUDWICH					
Mary Rosa	1	WA	214		1903
JUDY					
Joseph M. (soldier)			1402		1900
Oscar M.	44	KS	1172		1900
JUE					
Fook	48	CHN	6321		1903
Lee	26	CHN	6561a		1895
Lung Sud	40	CHN	1575		1894
Quon	55	CHN	3766		1903
Sing				Feb	1900
Yat Yuen	41	CHN	3727		1903
JUELL					
Anna	16	MN	6350		1904
JUEY					
Wing				Jul	1898
JUG					
Ah	26	CHN	412b		1871
JUGEL					
Ernest	1850	GER	1158c		1904
JUGLAS					
Jean Baptiste	49	FRA	1439		1866
JUIKAI					
Maukichi	20	JPN	3876	Nov	1901
JUIN					
Ah	28	CHN	154b		1871

NAME	AGE OR YOB.	BIRTH PLACE	CERT. NO	ID	DEATH YEAR
Juio					
Joan	<1	SF	5605		1867
Julian					
Fauny					Dec 1898
Lena	18	MN	7472		1903
Lydia Mary	2	SF	2302		1873
Philippe Clement	63	FRA	1411b		1872
Julien					
Ambroise		SF	3160		1873
Julke					
Chas	20	GER	J8		1883
Jullard					
Edward	70	ENG	2381		1900
Jullien					
Jules	64	FRA	2076		1903
Julsch					
Mary	61	OH	9		1900
Jun					
Chuck Wing	53	CHN	678		1903
Fook	52	CHN	6064	Jan	1901
Hip	<1	SF	985b		1895
Uh	44	CHN	1354		1894
Junc					
Hong	34	CHN	5515		1903
Juncas					
Louis Cannon					Oct 1899
Jundell					
Robert	<1	SF	1197		1894
June					
Yoke	27	CHN	2704		1903
Jung					
Ah Ho	22	CHN	1010b		1895
Ah You	66	CHN	7145		1902

NAME	AGE OR YOB.	BIRTH PLACE	CERT. NO	ID	DEATH YEAR
Bing Ken	62	CHN	2872		1903
Carl	63	GER	4140		1903
Chin	1865	CHN	1780c		1904
Chong	54	CHN	8047		1904
Den Quon	53	CHN	986		1900
Dip Young	54	CHN	1862		1903
Harry	61	PRU	4097		1902
Jack					Mar 1899
Jring	45	CHN	6407a		1895
Katherine	52	IRE	2447		1903
Lou	35	CHN	384b		1872
Lung	1844	CHN	2901c		1904
Mary	<1	SF	2390a		1872
Mon Tzang Shee	23	CA	2620		1903
Nicholas	1849	FRA	3177c		1904
Now	1902	CA	2521c		1904
Poey	39	CHN	5632		1896
Poo	45	CHN	8683		1903
Sing	60	CHN	6782		1900
Wai Fron	50	CHN	6846		1904
Yet	38	CHN	5988		1902
Yet Den					Nov 1898
Yow	20	SF	3803		1903
Jungblut					
O. A./W., c/o	<1	SF	5807		1896
O./M. (twin ?), c/o					Jan 1899
O./M. (twin ?), c/o					Jan 1899
Jungers					
John	34	FRA	7218		1902
Jungs					
Peter	33	RUS	1109		1869
Juniel					
William	56	GER	1575b		1895
Junior					
Manuel J.	28	SCT	4163b		1870

Key: *a = 1st part of year; b = 2nd part of year; c = death certificate copy; c/o = child of*

NAME	AGE OR YOB.	BIRTH PLACE	CERT. NO	ID	DEATH YEAR	NAME	AGE OR YOB.	BIRTH PLACE	CERT. NO	ID	DEATH YEAR
Mary	<1	SF	1402		1869	Peter	3	SF	1315		1869
JUNK						**JURIENS**					
Chow Kan				Oct	1898	John	32	RUS	J7		1883
Sing Yuen				Dec	1898	**JURMAN**					
Wah Quai				Nov	1898	Eskel L.	3	SF	2297b		1895
JUNKAI						**JURSO**					
B.	43	JPN	9082		1901	John	68	GER	8367		1900
JUNKER						**JUST**					
Louis	60	GER	6734		1904	Elizabeth				Jul	1899
JUNKIN						Herman	36	HAN	7852		1868
Mary B.	43	NB	2055		1894	Sophia	40	GER	855b		1871
JUPERTINO						**JUSTI**					
Joseph	4	SF	2718		1873	Mary				Jun	1899
JURD						**JUSTICE**					
Charley (soldier)	23	KS	6436	Feb	1901	Charles William	32	CA	2430b		1895
JUREY						**JUSTIS**					
Cornelius	23	SF	360		1901	Mary	1	SF	934b		1871
Lily	<1	CA	2896a		1872	**JUSTOU**					
JURGENS						Alixandr	43	FRA	8616		1868
Carolina				Oct	1899	**JUZIX**					
J. T.				Nov	1898	Henri	4	SF	7894		1904
N./H., c/o		SF	1036		1894	Henry/Emma, c/o		SF	4690		1903
Richard D., Jr.	18	SF	942		1900	Leoni	1	SF	2958		1903
Wm.	57	GER	6720		1900	Leopold	30	SF	1773		1903
JURGENSEN						Leopold	62	FRA	6176		1896
Ellis Margareta	1	CA	7496		1903	Louise	69	GER	3547	Nov	1901
George/Louise, c/o		SF	1678		1895	**JWAAL**					
Gottfried G. W.	<1	SF	892b		1895	S.	44		1649		1900
JURGINS						**KA**					
Wm./L., c/o				Jul	1898	Pumo	30	HI	1102		1869
JURI						**KAACH**					
Amelia	1	SF	1621b		1871	Rudolph	68	SWT	3369	Nov	1901
Andrea	<1	SF	1223a		1871						
Jennie	30	SF	4544a		1895						

Key: a = 1st part of year; b = 2nd part of year;
c = death certificate copy; c/o = child of

NAME	AGE OR YOB.	BIRTH PLACE	CERT. NO	ID	DEATH YEAR	NAME	AGE OR YOB.	BIRTH PLACE	CERT. NO	ID	DEATH YEAR
KAAIHNE						**KAFFKE**					
David	28	HI	4875		1904	Henrietta	73	GER	3877	Nov	1901
KABAYASHI						Martin	71	GER	8565		1900
I.	51	JPN	401	b	1895	**KAFKA**					
KABISH						Clotildee A. C.	<1	SF	5218		1867
Max				Jul	1899	**KAFKE**					
KACH						Joseph	<1	SF	3673	a	1895
Laura	<1	SF	3508		1902	**KAFORD**					
KACHELE						J./T., c/o	<1	CA	3845		1895
Sophia	44	GER	966	a	1871	**KAFOURY**					
KACK						Alias	<1	SF	6081		1902
Sun Sea	61	CHN	6020		1896	George/Emma, c/o		SF	5138		1903
KADESS						George/Emma, c/o		SF	5139		1903
——	37	RUS	1015		1868	George/Emma, c/o		SF	5140		1903
KADO						**KAGEYAMA**					
Takasuki	23	JPN	421		1902	Matahichi	23	JPN	5376		1903
KAECHELE						**KAGL**					
Michael John	65	GER	3789		1900	Henry L. B.	70	GER	9497		1901
KAEDING						**KAHER**					
Francis	57	IRL	3504	b	1870	Daniel				Jan	1899
Gustin L.	44	SWE	6463		1896	Daniel J.	1	SF	8269		1901
KAEHLER						Ignatius	1900	SF	1683	c	1904
Fredrick	3	SF	2784		1866	Mary C.	25	SF	1695		1903
KAEINTZ						Mary D.	31	SF	4765		1904
Jacob	47	GER	8396		1900	Olinda	1	SF	5754		1903
KAELIN						**KAHL**					
C./A., c/o		SF	588		1895	Eliza	1	SF	2043		1866
KAELL						Mary	49	IRL	3538		1896
Gideon (civ, employ.)			9354		1901	**KAHLEART**					
KAENJI						Fred	30	GER	4868	a	1895
Takeoka				Nov	1899	**KAHLER**					
KAETING						John H.	32	PA	556		1894
Owen		SF	4405	b	1870	**KAHLKE**					
						Alfred				Jan	1899

Key: a = 1st part of year; b = 2nd part of year;
c = death certificate copy; c/o = child of

NAME	AGE OR YOB.	BIRTH PLACE	CERT. NO	ID	DEATH YEAR
J./M., c/o		SF	4391		1895
Kahman					
August	43	MO	2474		1902
Lloyd	7	SF	5918		1902
Kahn					
Abraham	40	FRA	9485		1868
Elizabeth	32	GER	3182		1866
Ernestine				Aug	1899
Fannie	69	GER	2654		1895
Hannah	11	SF	2873a		1872
Henrietta	60	AUT	4146		1896
Henry L.	<1	SF	2927		1895
Jacob	<1	SF	3426b		1870
Jacob	4	CA	908		1870
Jennette	62	GER	7023		1900
Jonas	45	GER	5189		1904
Joseph	22	GER	5943		1902
Joseph				Oct	1899
Kate E.	64	MA	196b		1895
Leon	<1	SF	2175a		1872
Louise	55	GER	8094		1900
Lucile	1	SF	3868a		1895
Max	49	LA	8659		1900
Sophie	59	GER	2077		1903
Kahron					
Fritz	7	MO	553b		1895
Kahrs					
Alma B.	24	CA	2266		1900
Claus H.	30	GER	4519b		1870
Kahrstrom					
Axel Frederick	25	SWE	3613		1896
Kaier					
Fred	48	GER	4428		1896

NAME	AGE OR YOB.	BIRTH PLACE	CERT. NO	ID	DEATH YEAR
Kaighin					
Charles J.	48	UT	2306		1903
John Carroll	1	SF	145		1903
Kain					
Charles W.				Aug	1899
Edith	<1	SF	1554		1901
Kaio					
George	25	HI	1989		1866
Kaiser					
Alma Martha Lee	16	CA	336		1903
August	40	GER	6724		1903
Celestin Pierre	34	FRA	3914	Dec	1901
Charles	70	GER	2807		1901
Chas L.	30	OH	K55		1885
Chas. A. (soldier)			7532		1900
Ernst Max	41	GER	8418		1904
Esther				Jan	1899
F./A., c/o				Apr	1899
Frederick	59	GER	K87		1887
Frederick W.	31	MA	4639		1896
Henry	16	PRU	604b		1871
Herman	58	GER	7371		1901
Johanna	37	GER	7522		1868
John	1841	GER	1340c		1904
John Lockwood	24	CA	7667		1903
Lena	<1	SF	1443		1902
Louis	50	GER	3425a		1872
Otto				Jul	1899
Richard				Mar	1899
Kaistens					
Chas. P.	46	GER	K82		1887
Kako					
Edmond K.	22	SAN	8399		1868

Key: a = 1st part of year; b = 2nd part of year;
c = death certificate copy; c/o = child of

NAME	AGE OR YOB.	BIRTH PLACE	CERT. NO	ID	DEATH YEAR	NAME	AGE OR YOB.	BIRTH PLACE	CERT. NO	ID	DEATH YEAR
KAKUJIRA						KALLSTROM					
Yamamoto	45	JPN	8351		1904	Rosanna	66	IRE	8729		1904
KALALUR						KALLUM					
James		SF	4229b		1870	John	20	GER	2625		1866
KALAR						KALMUK					
Ralph	1904	SF	1828c		1904	Moritz	75	GER	7838		1903
KALB						KALNING					
Richard	63	GER	8713		1903	Aug/Kate, c/o	1904	CA	2185		1904
KALBER						KALNUCK					
Ottilie				Jan	1899	Johanna	<1	SF	3413		1867
KALBIN						KALTENBACH					
Carl	50	PRU	3416b		1870	William	25	GER	2141b		1895
KALBY						KALTENBUM					
Reinhard/G., c/o				Nov	1898	E. H., Mr.	abt	IL	1670		1901
KALIS						KALTENMAYER					
Minnie	64	GER	8673		1901	Maria	68	GER	1606b		1895
KALISHCHER						KALTER					
Bertha	59	RUS	4102		1896	Max	24	GER	60b		1872
KALISHER						KALTHOFF					
Lena	63	GER	5627		1904	Amelia A. Mrs.	72	GER	5093		1902
KALISKY						Bernard H.	41	SF	2794		1900
Louis	59	RUS	7475		1902	Emanuel	16	CA	3064a		1872
KALISRI						KAMA					
Delphine Augusta	1	SF	5609		1904	Wemura	40	JPN	600		1903
KALLEBACH						KAMENA					
Jake				Nov	1898	Margarita				Dec	1898
KALLENBERG						KAMENZIND					
Theodore	70	SWT	7044		1904	Philip	13	CA	1025		1902
KALLMASS						KAMIKA					
Joseph	62	GER	4132		1896	N.	1904	CA	829c		1904
KALLOCK						KAMILADE					
Adoniram (soldier)			224		1902	Aileen	<1	SF	3548	Nov	1901

Key: a = 1st part of year; b = 2nd part of year;
c = death certificate copy; c/o = child of

NAME	AGE OR YOB.	BIRTH PLACE	CERT. NO	ID	DEATH YEAR
KAMINSKY					
Simon	35	PRU	1248		1866
KAMLADE					
Edna M.	<1	SF	1663		1902
Fred/C., c/o				Aug	1899
M./Q., c/o		SF	5971		1895
Mary	31	SF	1634		1903
Milton	5	SF	246		1901
KAMLER					
Hannah	78	POL	7273		1901
KAMLODE					
Amelia	<1	SF	1646		1894
KAMMEN					
Fredrick	24	NOR	1799		1866
KAMMERER					
Fred G.	32	MD	8072		1904
KAMP					
August	21	GER	1409a		1871
George Lester (Little Jim)	17	CA	8969		1901
Josephine	45	MA	1936		1902
KAMPEHL					
Louisa A.	30	FRA	149a		1871
KAMPF					
Peter	31	SWT	K57		1885
KAMPFER					
Jacob	65		5380		1902
KAMPL					
Elsie	<1	MI	5137		1903
KAMPMEYER					
Hinrich	17	GER	2782		1902
KAMPS					
Catherine	65	GER	7077		1902
George W.	35	SF	315		1902
William T.	4	SF	460		1870
KAMYSAKI					
Z.	22	JPN	5631		1903
KAN					
Ah	30	CHN	3855		1870
Lee Young	40	CHN	5694		1867
Yee	21	CHN	1224		1870
KANADA					
Jimpo	24	JPN	7571		1903
KANADY					
Catharine	5	SF	3347		1873
Charles A.				Jul	1898
KANAKA					
——	40	PAN	1419b		1872
Bill	32	HI	6129		1867
Jack	60		1711b		1872
Jack A.	30	HI	6355		1867
(KANAKA)					
Solomon	19	HI	7000		1868
KANAKER					
Kalua		SAN	3075		1866
KANAMEZO					
Matashira				Nov	1898
KANARY					
Jasper D.	30	CA	6021		1896
KANE					
——	35	IRL	114		1870
——			1009		1868
Agnes	1	SF	3354a		1872
Anna	75	IRL	1983b		1895
Anne	28	IRL	3446b		1870
Annie L.	18	SF	3261		1895
Catherine	63	IRE	6523		1904
Charles I.	1	SF	6343		1867

Key: a = 1st part of year; b = 2nd part of year;
c = death certificate copy; c/o = child of

NAME	AGE OR YOB.	BIRTH PLACE	CERT. NO	ID	DEATH YEAR	NAME	AGE OR YOB.	BIRTH PLACE	CERT. NO	ID	DEATH YEAR
Christopher	60	IRE	4867		1903	John F./Mary Elizabeth, c/o	<1	SF	1915		1901
Cornelius	56	IRL	K2		1882	John H.	24	IRE	3769		1867
Daniel	26	IRL	1913b		1872	John J. (general prisoner)			3620	Nov	1901
Dennis Carlton	<1	SF	2558		1900	John Joseph	1	SF	1708		1902
Edward				Oct	1898	Joseph				Jan	1899
Edwin O.	<1	SF	4262		1867	Julia	7	SF	6938	Feb	1901
Eliza Jane				Feb	1900	Kate	36	ENG	3123		1902
Elizabeth	41	IRE	920		1903	L.W./Annie, c/o		SF	4398		1902
Ellen	30	IRE	5823		1867	Louis Desharst	<1	SF	7102		1868
Eugene	63	IRE	7343		1902	Margaret	91	IRL	4846a		1895
Frank	23	SF	7158		1903	Margaret				Mar	1899
Grace Josephine	5	SF	7015		1902	Margarit Ann	<1	SF	1767		1866
Grace Woods, c/o	<1	CA	3052		1900	Mary	1	CA	804b		1871
Gregory	35		2738		1900	Mary	86	IRE	2269		1902
Helen	32	IRE	4314		1903	Mary	75	IRL	2315b		1895
Isabella	50	IRL	4346	Dec	1901	Mary	54	IRL	908b		1895
J. F. Ernest				Jan	1900	Mary	<1	SF	2708		1894
James	35	IRE	1116		1869	Mary	64	IRL	867		1900
James	25	IRL	3580a		1895	Mary	62	IRE	2275		1903
James	11	SF	4772a		1895	Mary A.				Jul	1899
James				Dec	1899	Mary Ann	1	SF	2350a		1872
James C.				Nov	1899	Mary Ellen	1	SF	3163		1870
James H.	40	MA	K18		1883	Mary Josephine	18	SF	4338a		1895
James T.	36	CA	3633		1902	Michael	47	IRL	956b		1871
James, c/o		SF	1512b		1872	Michael	35	IRE	7358		1868
Jennie	24	IRE	3841		1867	Michael	2	SF	1365		1869
Jno.	46	IRL	5135a		1895	Michael	56	IRL	1624		1900
Joe	27	IL	5131		1904	Michael				Dec	1899
Johanna	71	IRE	8769		1904	Michael (soldier)			7166		1901
John	1	SF	964b		1871	Michael E. (soldier)			4707		1901
John	3	MD	8855		1868	Nellie	1	SF	2344		1903
John	58	IRE	4648		1902	Nellie	15	SF	647		1894
John	48	IRE	5613		1902	Norah				Feb	1899
John				Jan	1899	Robert John	15	SF	512b		1872
John				Mar	1900	Rodger P.	35	IRL	1446a		1871
John F.	69	NJ	7566		1900	Rosanna	<1	SF	377		1870

Key: a = 1st part of year; b = 2nd part of year;
c = death certificate copy; c/o = child of

NAME	AGE OR YOB.	BIRTH PLACE	CERT. NO	ID	DEATH YEAR	NAME	AGE OR YOB.	BIRTH PLACE	CERT. NO	ID	DEATH YEAR
Sarah Ann	3	NY	1064		1869	**KAPLAN**					
Stephen	2	SF	1995		1870	Abraham				Jul	1898
Thomas (soldier)			4710		1901	Edgar W.				Nov	1899
Thomas Edward	41	SF	3559		1902	Heiman	79	GER	963		1902
Thomas J.				May	1899	Jacob	35	POL	9038		1903
Thomasina	23	IRE	9904		1868	**KAPLER**					
Thos.				Nov	1899	Joseph G.	<1	SF	1535		1902
____ (twins)	<1	SF	5713		1867	**KAPP**					
William Francis				Mar	1899	Kathleen	21	CA	4047		1902
Winifred				Dec	1899	**KAPPELAR**					
KANEIN						Caroline Antonetta	1	SF	4918		1904
Edward B.	27	IL	5946		1903	**KAPPELER**					
KANEJUKI						Jacob	55	SWT	6280		1900
Kameji	43	JPN	4818		1902	**KAPPKE**					
KANETZ						Henry J.	68	GER	2188		1894
Rosalie	52	HUN	796b		1872	Maria E. W.	5	SF	5816		1867
KANEY						Veronica R.	2	SF	1210		1869
Thomas S.	1877	ENG	1047c		1904	**KAPPLER**					
KANGAS						Kathleen	55	IRL	453b		1895
Robert	61	SWE	1363		1901	**KAR**					
KANGER						Ah	40	CHN	1420		1869
Chas.				Mar	1900	**KARATAI**					
KANJA						Louise	65	FRA	8151		1900
Edmund	1876	GER	165c		1904	**KARBE**					
KANKKUNEN						Adolf	39	GER	4950		1901
George John	1902	FIN	2215c		1904	**KARG**					
KANNGIESSEN						Peter	42	GER	397		1865
J., c/o	<1	SF	2243		1873	**KARKA**					
KANTZ						Libidiy	<1	SF	5137a		1895
Anna Marie				Jul	1898	**KARL**					
KANZEE						Fred. A. A.	43	GER	1554		1870
Robert	2	NY	7798		1868	Margaret	28	NY	2320		1873
KANZELMEIER						Thomas S. (coxwain USN)			9355		1901
Arthur	<1	SF	1564a		1871						

Key: a = 1st part of year; b = 2nd part of year; c = death certificate copy; c/o = child of

NAME	AGE OR YOB.	BIRTH PLACE	CERT. NO	ID	DEATH YEAR	NAME	AGE OR YOB.	BIRTH PLACE	CERT. NO	ID	DEATH YEAR
KARLES						**KARSKI**					
——		SF	8479		1868	Tessie	24	SF	8547		1900
KARLHOFER						**KARSTENS**					
——			7575		1868	Henry	52	GER	4112	Dec	1901
KARLSON						**KARSTON**					
John				Jan	1899	Henry	50		3786	Nov	1901
Mathilda	21	FIN	601		1902	**KARTSCHOKE**					
N. P.	27	SWE	3159		1894	Edward	78	GER	147		1902
KARNER						**KASAMATSU**					
Anton				Jul	1899	S.	27	JPN	8679		1900
KARNES						**KASE**					
John	31	SF	3527	Nov	1901	Elizabeth A.	63	PA	4755		1901
KARNEY						**KASELAU**					
——			7557		1868	John C.	76	GER	8209		1900
William	<1	SF	3981		1867	**KASHERAROFF**					
KARNHEIM						William G.				Feb	1900
Minna	74	GER	3504a		1872	**KASHIWAGI**					
KARP						T.	22	JPN	678c		1904
Carl	<1	SF	7159		1903	**KASHOU**					
Ernest Brune	4	SF	1839		1903	Israel	86	OH	35		1902
John Henry	41	GER	3937		1903	**KASKEL**					
Max				Nov	1898	Frank	7	LA	954b		1895
KARPE						**KASLIN**					
Estelle D.	32	NY	6917		1903	Peter	29	IRL	2609a		1872
KARPER						**KASPER**					
——	<1	SF	1146		1869	Bartholome	74	SWT	8294		1904
KARR						**KASSER**					
Carrie D.	19	MI	5502	Jan	1901	Bella	1	SF	4662		1896
John	12	CA	K86		1887	Marian	3	CA	4412		1896
John	64	NY	7849		1904	**KAST**					
Lovina	<1	SF	5148		1901	Mary T. A.	27	FRA	2295		1866
Lucy	60	NY	4073		1896	Max	48	GER	1319b		1895
KARSCHELITZ						Walburga	89	GER	7313		1904
Felix	1843	GER	897c		1904						

Key: a = 1st part of year; b = 2nd part of year; c = death certificate copy; c/o = child of

NAME	AGE OR YOB.	BIRTH PLACE	CERT. NO	ID	DEATH YEAR
KASTENS					
Rebecca A.	52	MA	8876		1901
KASTIANA					
Jas.	35	ITA	K63		1886
KASTOR					
John, c/o	<1	SF	3219a		1872
KATAYAMA					
Hirokichi	23	JPN	5959		1904
KATE					
K.	29	JPN	1732		1900
KATELHOT					
William	50	GER	2042		1873
KATENHAMP					
F. C.	30	GER	1023		1866
KATHER					
L. A.	48	GER	K51		1885
KATHRINER					
Felix	26	SWT	696		1900
KATING					
Patrick	56	IRE	4598		1867
KATO					
Kiyokusu	41	JPN	840		1900
KATON					
Louise	32	CA	2051		1902
KATOW					
Masanosuka	30	JPN	146		1903
KATTELMANN					
Johanna	40	CA	1607b		1895
KATTERMAN					
Fred	35	MO	1765b		1895
KATZ					
Fred A.					Aug 1899
Frederick	1889	SF	1992c		1904

NAME	AGE OR YOB.	BIRTH PLACE	CERT. NO	ID	DEATH YEAR
Gottlieb	1855	GER	1381c		1904
Louisa	73	GER	4634		1904
Malke	1	SF	905		1903
Rebecca Levy	26	SF	2653		1900
KATZBON					
S./E., c/o					Nov 1898
KATZLON					
Katherine					Mar 1900
KATZMAIEN					
Christian	32	GER	2878		1873
KATZS					
Mamie	<1	SF	6198a		1895
KAU					
Ah	20	CHN	465		1870
Ak Kin					May 1899
KAUCHER					
John	56	OH	6586		1902
KAUCK					
Emma	8	CA	2437		1902
KAUFFMAN					
A./E., c/o	<1	SF	622		1894
Elise	35	GER	7264		1904
James F. (soldier)			1469		1901
KAUFFMANN					
John A.	14	SF	6727		1896
KAUFMAN					
F., c/o		SF	230b		1872
Fredrick	33	GER	4325b		1870
George C. (soldier)			8428		1901
Henry Louis	43	GER	8168		1900
Louise	43	CA	8276		1904
Mary	75	GER	4292		1903
Morris	42	PRU	2106a		1872
William August	<1	SF	530		1900

Key: a = 1st part of year; b = 2nd part of year;
c = death certificate copy; c/o = child of

NAME	AGE OR YOB.	BIRTH PLACE	CERT. NO	ID	DEATH YEAR
KAUFMANN					
Aqusta C.	1	SF	3903		1870
Charles	30	GER	8463		1901
Elise	35	SWT	6351		1904
Isaac	41	GER	7522		1904
Jonas	64	GER	361		1901
Nellie C.	2	SF	8736		1868
Sebastian					Aug 1898
Sig/Bettie, c/o	1	SF	2017		1903
W./B., c/o	<1	SF	4041		1895
Walter					Jan 1899
KAUGER					
Emily	5	NY	1184		1869
KAUM					
Lu	40	CHN	2800a		1872
KAUMERER					
Eugene					Mar 1899
KAUNANAIN					
Mary	43	IRE	1075		1869
KAUS					
Cris					Aug 1899
John/Lizzie, c/o	<1	SF	451		1902
Lizzie B.	31	GER	452		1902
KAUSTEINER					
Carlton Evert	5	CA	2937	Oct	1901
KAUTI					
Jacob	19	FIN	2497		1901
KAVANAGH					
Cathrine	<1	SF	4934		1867
Cecilia	<1	SF	6787		1903
Elizabeth	85	IRL	5660a		1895
George H.	1864	CA	980c		1904
James	21	ENG	58		1870
John	73	IRL	3044		1895

NAME	AGE OR YOB.	BIRTH PLACE	CERT. NO	ID	DEATH YEAR
John		SF	704b		1871
Joseph	53	IRE	8329		1903
Martin J.					Dec 1899
Maurice	76	IRE	4264		1902
Michael	41	IRL	3061a		1872
Robbie	1	SF	5402a		1895
William	<1	SF	8180		1903
William Francis	38	NY	602		1902
KAVANAH					
——			7669		1868
KAVANAUGH					
Elizabeth	60	IRL	4236		1900
M., c/o					Dec 1899
Margaret	48	IRL	1814a		1872
Nellie	22	CA	4672		1901
Walter					Aug 1899
KAVANEY					
Richard/Eliz., c/o	<1	SF	6139		1901
Theodore Leroy	<1	SF	6210	Feb	1901
KAVENAUGH					
George W.	<1	SF	1175b		1872
KAVENS					
Mchael I.	<1	SF	8155		1868
KAVENY					
Anna M.	46	ENG	4801		1904
KAVINAGH					
Chailot	35	SF	5197a		1895
KAVNAGH					
Lizzie	1	SF	7632		1902
KAWABATA					
T.	28	JAP	4193		1903
KAWAGACHI					
Jack	68	JPN	5504	Jan	1901

Key: a = 1st part of year; b = 2nd part of year;
c = death certificate copy; c/o = child of

NAME	AGE OR YOB.	BIRTH PLACE	CERT. NO	ID	DEATH YEAR	NAME	AGE OR YOB.	BIRTH PLACE	CERT. NO	ID	DEATH YEAR
KAWAHARA						**KEAINS**					
Yaozo	28	JPN	4606		1904	John	35	IRL	K77		1886
KAWAKA						**KEAMP**					
Aimatsu	36	JPN	2514		1901	Wm.				Feb	1900
KAWALKOWSHI						**KEAN**					
Joseph	<1	SF	2648		1902	John	10	SF	1051		1868
KAWALKOWSKA						Michael	45	IRE	4416		1867
Anna Frances	45	POL	964		1902	Peter H. (soldier)			9356		1901
KAWAMOTO						Thomas L.	70	SCT	3895		1896
Tomaichiro	30	JPN	8992		1903	William				Aug	1899
KAWASAKA						**KEANE**					
Sechicusu				Jul	1898	Ann		SF	5636	Jan	1901
KAY						Daniel	58	ENG	8645		1904
Samuel	55	ENG	K95		1889	Dennis D.	56	IRL	1427		1901
KAYANO						Edward J.	27	SF	3916		1903
Jendo	31	JPN	5871		1902	Eleonor	73	IRE	1176		1869
KAYE						Emily A.	1	SF	1297		1869
Philip L.	1851	GER	450c		1904	James				Feb	1899
KAYER						Joanna	79	IRL	622		1900
Thomas E.	31	ENG	5512		1904	Josephine V.	5	SF	4023		1903
KAYSER						Laurence J.	1	SF	791		1900
Christian F. (soldier)			947		1901	Margaret	55	IRL	3705		1900
Elmer Charles	1	SF	7011		1904	Margaret J.	25	CA	5471		1903
George W.	1882	MN	3240c		1904	Mary A.	1	SF	8825		1904
Ruby	4	SF	1370		1900	Patrick	29	IRL	1116		1900
KAYSSER						Patrick	50	IRL	7994		1901
Oscar	29	GER	3595		1900	Peter	1865	IRE	2379c		1904
KEACH						Teresa	54	IRE	7709		1904
Louisa A.	52	CAN	1308		1900	Theodosia Jane	53	NY	6583		1900
KEAFE						**KEANELEY**					
Thomas	<1	SF	1318a		1871	David	14	NV	1758b		1872
KEAGH						**KEANEY**					
Martin	32	IRE	5280		1867	Susan	76	IRL	398b		1871
						Thomas	50	MA	1666b		1871

NAME	AGE OR YOB.	BIRTH PLACE	CERT. NO	ID	DEATH YEAR	NAME	AGE OR YOB.	BIRTH PLACE	CERT. NO	ID	DEATH YEAR
KEANY						John		SF	1197		1869
Mary	61	MI	2502		1902	John	82	IRE	2704		1902
Mary	19	SF	5538		1903	John	54	IRE	3735		1902
						John B.	31	MA	5403		1904
KEARCE						Julia E.	27	SF	1893		1894
Mary Ann	4	SF	3496b		1870	Lizzie	49	NY	1679b		1895
						Mary J.	38	AUS	5634	Jan	1901
KEAREN						Mary Jane	16	LA	1297		1869
Simon/Catherine, c/o		SF	7361		1900	Mary M.	<1	CA	7155		1868
						Michael	40	IRE	1128		1869
KEARNAN						Michael	52	IRE	4483		1904
Patrick	32	IRE	6008		1867	Patrick	79	IRE	9715		1868
						Peter	28	IRE	1032		1868
KEARNEN						Peter Joseph	62	IRL	985		1900
Chas. A., c/o	<1	SF	3259a		1872	Philip	79	IRE	3810		1902
						Rose Elinore	24	SF	8084		1903
KEARNES						Thomas F.				May	1899
Michael	32	IRE	5155		1867	William	64	IRE	176		1902
						William	36	MA	2480b		1895
KEARNEY						Wm.	38	IRL	780		1870
Agnes	41	IRL	K92		1889						
Ann	79	IRE	7675		1902	**KEARNS**					
Annie				Nov	1898	Agnes	28	SF	6568		1903
Annie Mary	39	CAN	5107a		1896	Ann	55	IRL	5317		1896
Bridget	33	IRL	406b		1871	Ann	75	IRL	1642b		1895
C./B., c/o				May	1899	Annie	65	IRE	1886		1902
Catharine	13	CA	1591b		1872	Bernard	42	IRL	1046b		1872
Catherine	42	IRL	2159		1894	Bernard	69	IRE	7146		1902
Daniel B.	27	CA	6456		1903	Bernard				Jun	1899
Edward T.	36	KY	1373b		1895	Chris				Jan	1899
Ellen				Dec	1899	Edith	1	CA	4725		1903
Francis P.	<1	SF	4048	Dec	1901	Guy				Jul	1899
Frank	42	MA	1026		1902	Harriet				Jan	1899
Fredrick	45	NY	1027		1868	John	27	IRL	3175a		1872
James		SF	1347b		1872	John	1	SF	1101		1866
James	3	SF	1090		1869	John	<1	SF	5772		1896
James	64	IRL	4594		1901	Margaret	<1	SF	99b		1871
James P.	56	IRL	6369	Feb	1901						
Johanna	45	IRE	762		1902						
John	60	IRL	988		1870						

Key: a = 1st part of year; b = 2nd part of year;
c = death certificate copy; c/o = child of

NAME	AGE OR YOB.	BIRTH PLACE	CERT. NO	ID	DEATH YEAR	NAME	AGE OR YOB.	BIRTH PLACE	CERT. NO	ID	DEATH YEAR
Margaret	32	IRE	8633		1868	John	65	IRE	5313		1903
Morris	40	IRL	K93		1889	John	30	DC	3585		1903
Thomas				Aug	1899	Joseph	27	LA	4342		1903
						Katherine	78	IRE	435		1901
KEARNY						Margaret	45	IRE	5493		1903
Ann	40	IRL	992 b		1872	Mary Ann	65	ENG	813		1894
Barney				Jan	1899	Mary I.	54	IRE	5632		1903
Catherine	<1	SF	2769		1900	Mary Jane	65	IRE	1800		1903
Celia	24	IRL	3066		1870	Michael	35	IRE	7381		1868
John	<1	SF	1664		1902	Michael	40	IRE	1452		1869
Louis	<1	CA	2676		1895	Minnie	24	IN	3830	Nov	1901
Walter	60	IRE	1409		1869	Peter	65	IRE	6851		1903
						Robert	63	NY	4367a		1895
KEARON						Robert				Nov	1898
Helen Minnie	3	CA	3536a		1895	William				Mar	1899
						Wm/Frances, c/o		SF	7887		1901
KEARSE											
Joseph	2	SF	5088a		1896	**KECK**					
Maggie	34	SF	6281	Feb	1901	Francis B. (soldier)			7445		1904
						George				Jul	1898
KEASER						Louis	33	GER	K94		1889
Antone	<1	SF	5696		1902	Susie	25	SF	1914		1901
KEAST						**KEDDIE**					
Alfred				Jun	1899	Robert	17	SCT	177		1902
Thomas E.				Jul	1899	**KEDON**					
KEASTEN						Annie	44	GER	36		1902
Afvina F.	3	AUT	8149		1868	Martin	68	IRL	1836b		1895
KEATING						Peter	9	SF	4577		1867
	35	NY	1715		1870	**KEE**					
Annie	50	IRL	2674		1895	Ah	24	CHN	5540		1867
Bridget	71	IRL	6051		1896	Ah	10	CHN	9002		1868
Catherine	46	IRL	2485		1894	Ah	35	CHN	1304		1869
Charles M.				Oct	1898	Ah	30	CHN	452a		1871
Clara B.	6	SF	685		1900	G.	52	CHN	3097a		1872
Cornelius	47	IRE	4876		1904	Leon	42	CHN	492		1870
Cornelius	70	IRL	1530		1900	Mup Ah	34	CHN	K11		1882
Edward H.	64	IRL	4212		1896						
Honora	1871	IRE	3241c		1904						

Key: a = 1st part of year; b = 2nd part of year; c = death certificate copy; c/o = child of

NAME	AGE OR YOB.	BIRTH PLACE	CERT. NO	ID	DEATH YEAR	NAME	AGE OR YOB.	BIRTH PLACE	CERT. NO	ID	DEATH YEAR
Quong	46	CHN	1243b		1871	Thomas	35	SF	27		1900
Sin	46	CHN	2287a		1872	Walter Cooper	35	CA	2575		1902
Sue	28	CHN	462b		1872	William	55		1615		1901
Sun	9	SF	1250		1869	William (soldier)			1855		1901
Ung Teck	33	CHN	2153a		1872						
Ying	48	CHN	6778		1868	**KEEFER**					
You	46	CHN	1465b		1871	Adam J.	57	PA	3344	Nov	1901
KEEBLER						**KEEFFE**					
Henry	6	CT	2988		1866	Catherine O.	34	NY	2870		1866
						Cornelius	40	IRL	661b		1871
KEEFA											
Dorce	42	CHN	365a		1871	**KEEGAN**					
						Bridget	55	IRE	5257		1904
KEEFE						Cathrine F.	<1	SF	3428b		1870
Catherine	29	GER	1279		1869	Delia	30	MA	4476		1901
Catherine	60	ME	4079		1903	Edward	1855	NY	2456c		1904
Cathryn G.	1	CA	3748		1903	Edward A.	<1	CA	2986		1902
Clara Viola				Nov	1898	Francis	<1	CA	3048a		1872
Daniel	48	NY	6154		1902	Henry P.				May	1899
David/Margaret, c/o	<1	SF	6857		1902	James	65	IRE	7430		1904
David/Margaret, c/o	<1	SF	7619		1904	James				Apr	1899
Edward A.	28	SF	5586		1903	James				Nov	1899
Hannah	73	IRE	3124		1902	James	40		880		1902
Hanorah				Oct	1898	James/Kate, c/o		CA	2806		1901
James	<1	SF	6052		1896	John	33	IRL	2023		1873
James B.	49	IRE	7238		1902	John	57	IRL	4307		1896
Joseph	13	SF	6666		1904	John R.	4	SF	8825		1868
Lillien Gertrude	19	SF	8253		1904	John/Mary, c/o				Dec	1898
Margaret	27	IRE	8344		1868	Mary	2	SF	221b		1872
Margaret	31		7045		1904	Mary Jane	56	NJ	611		1901
Mary	70	IRL	7824		1900	Mary, c/o	<1	CA	5507		1895
Mary Ag.	<1	SF	174		1865	Michael			5020		1903
Mathew				Mar	1899	Michael				Jul	1899
Michael				Mar	1900	Peter				Oct	1899
Ralph/Mary, c/o	1	SF	1863		1903	William	32	IRL	4191b		1870
Robert D.				Dec	1899						
						KEEHAN					
Thomas	30	CA	4613		1896	Martha J.				Feb	1900

NAME	AGE OR YOB.	BIRTH PLACE	CERT. NO	ID	DEATH YEAR
KEEL					
J./C., c/o	<1	SF	468		1895
KEELE					
Emma Jane	67	VA	3978		1900
KEELER					
Chas. I./Louise, c/o		SF	828		1900
Daniel				Dec	1899
Hubert D.				Feb	1900
James Edward	42	IL	884		1900
Lewis	1865	OH	3360c		1904
Mary E.	48	WI	4047		1896
Nancy	86	OH	2775		1903
W.H.				Aug	1899
KEELEY					
Anna	1	SF	1030		1866
Annie M.	62	ENG	4366a		1895
John	30	NY	998		1866
Julia				Oct	1898
Mary	45	IRL	2820a		1872
KEELY					
Eugenia, Mrs.	27	SF	735		1894
James	56	IRE	3994		1902
James J.	44	IRL	4354a		1895
Marguerite	<1	SF	1037		1894
Maud Doreen	1	SF	1425		1903
Thomas	19	SF	5412a		1895
KEEN					
James F. (soldier)	25		4490		1901
John	<1	SF	334b		1872
Yid	50	CHN	1835		1870
KEENAN					
Alexander	71	IRL	4162	Dec	1901
Anna				Oct	1898
Annie	2	SF	4291b		1870

NAME	AGE OR YOB.	BIRTH PLACE	CERT. NO	ID	DEATH YEAR
Bernard R.				Jul	1898
Bridget	40	IRL	2629		1873
Bridget	75	IRE	5816		1902
Daniel	24	IRL	2384		1873
Edward Dougherty	<1	IRL	1839a		1872
Elizabeth	57	IRE	1070		1902
Ellen		SF	1909		1870
Frank	36	IRL	658b		1872
Henry	45	IRL	557		1894
James				Dec	1898
James				Feb	1899
Jane	84	SCT	581		1901
John	42	IRL	895b		1871
John	26	ENG	1004		1868
John C.	38	IRE	1221		1869
Joseph	1904	SF	1159c		1904
Joseph	13	SF	7316		1902
Katie	21	CA	6655		1896
Lizzie	9	SF	389		1902
Mary	21	IRE	8789		1868
Mary	42	IRE	8606		1904
Mary Jane	21	IRL	4810a		1895
Michael	39	ENG	808		1902
Patrick	57	IRL	4100		1896
Thomas	49	IRL	K73		1886
Thomas				Jan	1899
William	30	SCT	555		1894
KEENE					
Henry, Jr.				Mar	1900
Sam	42	CHN	1986		1866
Thomas	36	CHI	1126b		1872
KEENEY					
Chas W.	62	CT	6653		1903
Joseph	2	SF	3189		1873

Key: a = 1st part of year; b = 2nd part of year; c = death certificate copy; c/o = child of

NAME	AGE OR YOB.	BIRTH PLACE	CERT. NO	ID	DEATH YEAR
KEEP					
George	18	MA	6707		1868
Sarah	53	PA	7377		1903
KEESING					
Leo				Jan	1899
Myrtle Cecil				Dec	1898
KEET					
Ah	27	CHN	2855		1866
KEFOE					
John J.				Mar	1900
KEHELAR					
James	1	SF	8030		1868
KEHELY					
Timothy	41	IRE	1942		1866
KEHILL					
Michael				Aug	1898
KEHLENBECK					
John				Jun	1899
KEHMM					
Josephine H.				Aug	1899
KEHOE					
Bryan				Dec	1898
Caroline Elizabeth	<1	SF	2032		1873
Catherine				Nov	1898
Catherine	45	IRL	1008a		1871
Edward	22	NY	1301b		1871
Ella				Jan	1899
George M.	1	SF	201		1870
James (soldier)			225		1902
James H.	31	SF	5988a		1895
Jno. P.	4	SF	5930		1867
John	30	IRL	2182		1873
John				Mar	1899
John W.	45	IRL	1982b		1895

NAME	AGE OR YOB.	BIRTH PLACE	CERT. NO	ID	DEATH YEAR
Margaret	62	IRE	5141		1903
Martin Wm.	<1	SF	6527		1868
Mary Ann	<1	SF	2253		1866
Michael	34	IRL	1891b		1872
Patrick	50	IRL	1835b		1895
Peter J.	63	IRE	6637		1904
Thomas				Jan	1899
Thomas E.				Oct	1899
Wm.				Mar	1900
KEHOR					
Vincent Henry	9	SF	7540		1904
KEHRER					
Edna Marie	8	CA	2503		1902
Henrietta	51	GER	7572		1903
KEI					
Fook	22	CHN	1817b		1872
KEIASBERG					
Philip	27	GER	K85		1887
KEIE					
P. G./Genevieve, c/o	<1	SF	4267		1901
KEIFFER					
Charles				Nov	1899
KEIGE					
Elizabeth	<1	SF	895b		1872
KEIGHARY					
Hugh	33	IRE	6918		1903
KEIGHTLEY					
Mary	79	IRL	652		1900
KEIL					
Frederick C.	54	DEN	7314		1904
Walter David	5	SF	7655		1901
KEILLENG					
Annie L.	1	SF	8546		1868

NAME	AGE OR YOB.	BIRTH PLACE	CERT. NO	ID	DEATH YEAR
KEILY					
Joanna	1839	IRE	1106c		1904
KEIN					
Edward	27	IRE	1285		1869
KEINERT					
Aug	35	GER	K21		1883
KEIPFLER					
Maggie Fulton	3	SF	1415b		1872
KEIRNS					
Julia	57	IRL	59b		1895
Thomas F.	33	CA	7401		1904
KEISER					
Otto Fred	<1	SF	4339a		1895
KEITH					
Benj R.	66	NB	119		1903
E. D./R. E., c/o				Dec	1899
Eldridge G.	67	MA	4167b		1870
Samuel D.	67	MA	5276		1896
Walter S. (soldier)			4711		1901
Wm. R.	75	ME	2184b		1895
KEITHLY					
Harrison	66	MO	5026		1904
KEIZ					
Elsa M.	7	SF	7504		1900
KEKOW					
Theresa				Apr	1899
KELBY					
Chas.	53	NY	K89		1887
KELEHAR					
William	<1	SF	1404		1869
KELEHER					
Emmet	3	SF	3548		1867
Mourth	44	IRL	1272b		1871

NAME	AGE OR YOB.	BIRTH PLACE	CERT. NO	ID	DEATH YEAR
KELFER					
Bridget	65	IRL	4785a		1895
KELLAR					
James A. (soldier)			1131		1900
KELLEGHAN					
Patrick	65	IRE	6613		1904
KELLEGHER					
John				Jul	1898
KELLEHAR					
Margaret	1	SF	2883a		1872
KELLEHER					
Anna	<1	SF	3692	Nov	1901
Catherine Mary	<1	SF	4601		1903
Corneliuis	<1	SF	5486		1896
Ellen	22	IRL	1948		1870
Ellen	58	IRL	4646		1901
Francis				Feb	1899
Helen	<1	SF	4678a		1895
James Peter	1	SF	3418		1903
Jeremiah	25	IRE	7603		1868
Jno. T.	3	SF	2158		1894
Jno., c/o		SF	3349		1873
John	76	IRE	869		1903
John W.	27	SF	5915		1896
Josephine	20	CA	2307		1903
Julia	31	IRL	4243	Dec	1901
Kathleen	5	SF	1791		1902
Loretta A.				Dec	1898
Margaret	76	IRE	4296		1902
Mary	58	IRL	1520		1894
Mary	<1	SF	5487		1896
Matthew				Mar	1900
Michael				Oct	1898
Michael / May, c/o				Feb	1900
Michael, Jr.	38	SF	3640		1903

Key: a = 1st part of year; b = 2nd part of year; c = death certificate copy; c/o = child of

NAME	AGE OR YOB.	BIRTH PLACE	CERT. NO	ID	DEATH YEAR	NAME	AGE OR YOB.	BIRTH PLACE	CERT. NO	ID	DEATH YEAR
Michael/Mary, c/o	1	SF	6952		1904	Joseph P.	1	OR	728		1866
Nellie				Mar	1900	Levi	39	PRU	9752		1868
Thomas	34	SF	3594		1900	Magdalena				Oct	1898
Timothy	42	IRL	K12		1882	Marguerite	28	CA	1225		1900
William	66	IRE	1696		1903	Martin B.	1843	OH	229c		1904
KELLEHR						Mary	<1	SF	622		1902
Matthew Melvin	4	SF	8826		1904	Michael	20	AUT	1002		1868
KELLEN						Morice				Apr	1899
Francis				Jan	1899	Robert M. (soldier)			948		1901
Mich	74	GER	2446		1873	Rose				Feb	1900
Raymond Francis				Jan	1899	Sara	75	PRU	1275b		1872
KELLENBERGER						William J. (soldier)			7324		1901
Chas. L.	58	IL	2136		1903	**KELLERAN**					
KELLENG						Isaac S.	41	ME	6711a		1895
Charles	<1	SF	879		1866	**KELLERMAN**					
KELLER						August				Apr	1899
Alexander	57	GER	1570		1903	**KELLETT**					
Alma				Nov	1898	Mary	93	IRL	1282b		1895
Amanda M.				Feb	1899	Richard C.				Jan	1899
Caroline E.	33	LA	5316		1896	Robert J.	28	IRL	2568		1873
Charles			1307		1903	**KELLETTE**					
Charles	45	GER	5348		1904	Maza	38	CA	6727	Feb	1901
Cornelius	34	IRL	756b		1872	**KELLEY**					
Elizabeth	65	IRE	4412		1867	——	<1	SF	3521		1870
Elizabeth M.	69	FRA	5190a		1896	——			4767		1867
Emma				Feb	1899	——	<1	SF	1213		1869
Frederic C.	35	WI	5031a		1896	——	1	CA	1259		1869
Isabel R.				Aug	1899	——		SF	1376		1869
Jacob	60	SWT	1100b		1872	Agnes				May	1899
John	52	FRA	396b		1871	Alexander				Oct	1899
John	52	IRL	5315		1896	Alice Anna	40	MA	330a		1871
John	58	IRL	3142	Oct	1901	Ambrose	34	PA	1370		1869
John	14	HI	8698		1901	Catharine	44	IRL	1790a		1872
John	1865	IRE	2955c		1904	Catherine	<1	SF	2361		1866
Joseph Anton	25	CA	187		1903	Catherine	62	IRE	3504		1903

Key: a = 1st part of year; b = 2nd part of year;
c = death certificate copy; c/o = child of

NAME	AGE OR YOB.	BIRTH PLACE	CERT. NO	ID	DEATH YEAR
Charles A.	38	MA	3404	Nov	1901
Charles H.	4	CA	1184		1870
D. B.	53	NY	4693		1867
Daniel	2	SF	2625a		1872
Dora		SF	530		1866
Edward J. (soldier)			4713		1901
Ellen	<1	SF	1533b		1871
Ellen	<1	SF	1073		1869
Ellen				Jan	1899
George W.	21	OH	1025		1868
George W.	67	NH	4190	Dec	1901
Gertrude	22	CA	7346		1904
Hiram Francis	52	NY	5446		1903
Howard Dow	1902	CA	2186c		1904
Hubert Wood	1888	CA	323c		1904
James	8	SF	1023		1868
James B.	<1	SF	2116		1866
James Joseph	64	IRE	7676		1902
Jane	76	IRL	1023b		1872
John	50	IRL	3245a		1872
John	45	IRL	K22		1883
John	45	IRE	8767		1868
John	66	IRL	6705	Feb	1901
John Francis	<1	SF	166b		1871
John P.	<1	SF	9375		1868
Jonathan C.	38	MA	1420		1870
Jos. V.	44	OH	K54		1885
Joseph	<1	SF	1284		1869
Katie	33	PA	3406		1872
Katie	33	KY	2536		1903
Maggie				Jan	1899
Marssella	74	IRE	4938		1867
Mary	60	CAN	4952		1903
Mary Ann	32	PA	1669		1870
Mary Ann	4	MA	1067		1869
Mary Ellen	<1	SF	1808		1866
Mary Jane	34	MA	1871		1901
Michael, c/o	<1	SF	2976a		1872
Minnie A.	28	KY	4868		1903
Patrick	30	IRE	741		1866
Peter	56	MA	6352		1903
Rollin /Elizabeth, c/o	<1	SF	3813		1901
Sarah	1	SF	1316		1866
Seth				Aug	1899
Simon	70	NY	1318		1900
Susan	58	MA	156		1901
Thomas	1	SF	5496		1902
Thos. J.	<1	SF	1607		1894
Timothy	3	SF	8722		1868
William (soldier)			5056		1901
William H.	1	CA	836		1866

KELLICK

NAME	AGE OR YOB.	BIRTH PLACE	CERT. NO	ID	DEATH YEAR
John John (soldier)			6712		1904

KELLIE

NAME	AGE OR YOB.	BIRTH PLACE	CERT. NO	ID	DEATH YEAR
Charles	8	SF	6578	Feb	1901

KELLIGHER

NAME	AGE OR YOB.	BIRTH PLACE	CERT. NO	ID	DEATH YEAR
Ann Maria	32	IRL	1266a		1871

KELLING

NAME	AGE OR YOB.	BIRTH PLACE	CERT. NO	ID	DEATH YEAR
Lizzie Loretta	34	SF	4851		1901
Paul F.	29	SF	4256		1903
Santos Ponzi de	54	CHL	5755		1903

KELLNER

NAME	AGE OR YOB.	BIRTH PLACE	CERT. NO	ID	DEATH YEAR
Clifton W.				May	1899
Heymann	<1	SF	6100		1867
Mary Ellen	29	SF	4561		1901
Sadie	1904	SF	2143c		1904

KELLOG

NAME	AGE OR YOB.	BIRTH PLACE	CERT. NO	ID	DEATH YEAR
Francis D.	35	NY	1046		1868
Geo. F.				Oct	1898
John G.	55	NY	7		1901

San Francisco Deaths 1865 - 1905:
Abstracts from Surviving Civil Records

Volume 2: E - K

NAME	AGE OR YOB.	BIRTH PLACE	CERT. NO	ID	DEATH YEAR
KELLOGG					
Calvin W.	72	MI	5588a		1895
Charles A.	79	NY	5394		1901
Charles H.				Oct	1898
Charlotte R.	60	NH	2468b		1895
D.M.	49	NY	1018b		1871
Dwight	43	NY	1253		1869
Hurley B. (soldier)			4792		1901
Isabella	37	NY	4004		1870
Lorenzo	50	NY	3557		1870
Maria	39	MI	2059		1866
Martin	75	CT	1274		1903
Mary E.	60	IL	650		1901
Orphe				Dec	1899
Orrin J.	72	NY	3838		1903
KELLS					
Mary	85	IRL	3174		1900
Ralph				Jan	1899
KELLSTER					
Elizabeth	33	IRE	2141		1866
KELLUNE					
Wm. C.	50	PA	1245b		1872
KELLY					
——		SF	3098		1870
——	<1	SF	3819		1870
——			3166		1866
——			5648		1867
Abbie Catherine	1	SF	1717		1894
Agnes	1	SF	8480		1868
Albert Joseph	<1	SF	45b		1871
Alice	<1	SF	6423		1867
Alice	22	NV	5392		1903
Alice	50	IRE	7305		1903
Angelette	51	MA	3728		1903
Ann	71	IRL	890		1900
Ann	1833	IRE	1740c		1904
Anna Augusta	1894	SF	2457c		1904
Anna Elizabeth	60	NY	2448		1903
Anna R.	36	OH	5680		1904
Anne	75	IRE	1330		1903
Annie	29	IRL	407		1870
Annie	35	IRL	2181		1873
Annie	35	IRL	2443		1894
Annie E.	1	CA	821		1870
Annie, Mrs.	66	IRE	6353		1902
Archibald E.	2	MT	3698		1896
Archibald H.	90	IRL	3302		1894
B. J.	17	MA	K50		1885
Bernard	<1	SF	2755a		1872
Bernard	46	IRL	1406b		1872
Bernard M.	72	NY	2165		1902
Bernard/Mary, c/o		SF	881		1902
Bruce	13	CA	3449		1902
Bryan	74	IRL	1220		1901
Catharine	1	SF	1151		1870
Catharine	48	IRL	1104b		1871
Catharine	35	IRL	2060a		1872
Catherine	<1	SF	1214		1869
Catherine	64	IRE	8193		1904
Catherine	55	IRE	2560		1902
Catherine	69	IRE	6278		1903
Catherine	78	IRL	1843		1900
Catherine				Aug	1898
Cathrine I.	<1	SF	1580		1870
Cecile Lillian	6	SF	6326		1902
Cecilia M.	82	IRE	3389		1902
Charles	30	SF	1091		1903
Charles	31	IRE	8398		1904
Charles	44	CA	6352		1904
Charles	<1	SF	1012		1894
Charles (soldier)	36	VT	3175		1900

Key: a = 1st part of year; b = 2nd part of year; c = death certificate copy; c/o = child of

NAME	AGE OR YOB.	BIRTH PLACE	CERT. NO	ID	DEATH YEAR	NAME	AGE OR YOB.	BIRTH PLACE	CERT. NO	ID	DEATH YEAR
Charles A. (soldier)	24	WY	1596		1901	Emma C.				Aug	1899
Charles E.	71	MO	8085		1903	Eugene	60	IRE	5190		1904
Charles M.	54	CAN	7589		1904	Eveline Maria	15	SF	528b		1872
Chas.	52	NY	K6		1882	Fannie				Dec	1898
Chas./Ellen Raines, c/o					1899	Fanny	5	ME	1214		1869
Constance Johanna	2	SF	5132		1904	Francis				Nov	1898
Cornelius	2	SF	1628b		1871	Francis A.				Nov	1898
Cornelius	74	NJ	4141		1903	Francis J. E.	37	CAN	3255		1902
David L.				Mar	1899	Francis, c/o		SF	801b		1872
Dennis	89	IRL	758b		1872	Frank				Aug	1898
Dennis (soldier)			4043		1900	Frank (alias Buckley)	19	IRL	1559a		1871
Dennis H.	70	NJ	7523		1904	Frank E.	1840	MA	1184c		1904
Edith Agnes	13	SF	929		1900	George	27	WIN	1391		1894
Edward	38	IRL	1372a		1871	George				Nov	1899
Edward	45	IRE	2460		1866	George I.	1	SF	9354		1868
Edward	73	IRE	7462		1904	George P.	<1	SF	2067		1894
Edward H.	<1	SF	8223		1868	Gerald E.	1875	SF	3361c		1904
Edward Stephen	35	SF	3608		1903	Gertrude	1876	CA	34c		1904
Edward T., Jr.	<1	SF	4506		1901	Grace Agnes	3	SF	1355b		1895
Eliza	77	NF	3476b		1870	Gracie	<1	SF	2769		1901
Eliza	75	IRL	4905		1896	Hannah				Nov	1899
Elizabeth	<1	CA	6582a		1895	Hanora				Jan	1899
Elizabeth	72	IRE	4315		1903	Harriet M.				Jul	1899
Ellen	45	IRL	2541		1873	Harry E.	26	SF	2336		1901
Ellen	<1	SF	2786		1866	Hazel Beatrice	3	SF	1140		1900
Ellen	32	IRE	4602		1867	Helen	1	SF	4711		1867
Ellen	30	IRE	7860		1868	Henry	64	ME	7296		1902
Ellen	80	IRE	4766		1904	Henry J. S. De Paul	15	SF	8166		1868
Ellen	1825	IRE	83c		1904	Henry W.	55	CT	3096	Oct	1901
Ellen	54	IRE	5670		1902	Hilda Catherine	1902	SF	2054c		1904
Ellen	18	SF	3155		1902	Hugh	45	IRE	7315		1904
Ellen	53	IRL	6632		1896	Irene Frances	8	SF	7061		1903
Ellen				Jul	1898	J Wells			6406		1867
Ellen F.	57	IRL	2362		1901	J.	45		4428		1903
Emeline Hillman	30	ENG	6786		1900	J.T.M./Isabella, c/o		SF	2142		1895
Emily Agnes	1	SF	1234a		1871	James	30	IRL	1384b		1871

NAME	AGE OR YOB.	BIRTH PLACE	CERT. NO	ID	DEATH YEAR	NAME	AGE OR YOB.	BIRTH PLACE	CERT. NO	ID	DEATH YEAR
James	53	IRL	3269a		1872	John	62	IRE	8265		1903
James	4	SF	6162		1867	John	55	IRL	4937a		1895
James	38	IRE	6960		1868	John	18	SF	1680b		1895
James	63	IRE	4257		1903	John	72	IRL	3196		1895
James	1851	IRE	704c		1904	John	30	IRL	2101		1901
James	63	IRE	1838		1902	John	35	IRL	8354		1901
James	<1	SF	1271		1900	John					Aug 1898
James	65	IRL	3790		1900	John					Aug 1899
James	31	NY	4004		1900	John					Dec 1899
James	27	CA	1573		1900	John					Jan 1899
James					Mar 1900	John					Oct 1899
James					Apr 1899	John	5	SF	3419		1903
James	48	IRE	4484		1904	John	30	ENG	4691		1903
James (soldier)			6178		1900	John	1839	IRE	3269c		1904
James (soldier)			7168		1901	John G.	43	IRE	3461		1867
James A.	4	SF	5121		1867	John (soldier)			1627		1902
James F.					Nov 1898	John (soldier)			1497		1901
James M.	15	SF	159b		1895	John A.	<1	PAN	1316		1869
James William	1	SF	1057		1870	John A.	1839	NY	1107c		1904
James/Mary, c/o		SF	362		1901	John A.	19	CA	5633		1903
Jane	67	IRL	4315		1901	John F.	36	SF	4508		1901
Janes	1869	IRE	547c		1904	John F.					Nov 1898
Jas. F. (soldier)			9357		1901	John G.	69	IRE	7497		1903
Jennie					Dec 1898	John G./Mary A., c/o		SF	9083		1901
Jessie					Feb 1900	John H.	3	SF	1179		1869
Jno.	85	IRL	6302a		1895	John H.					Mar 1899
Jno.	74	IRL	3208		1894	John Henry	40	SF	3833		1900
Jno. J.	49	NY	K61		1886	John J.			408c		1904
Jno. P.	29	NY	K53		1885	John Joseph	<1	CA	7114		1904
Johanna	35	IRL	622		1870	John Joseph	29	SF	531		1900
Johannah E.	10	SF	1065		1870	John N.	21	CA	K16		1882
John	<1	SF	936		1866	John P.	43	SF	7968		1904
John	28	IRE	7847		1868	John P.	1875	NV	3099c		1904
John	37	IRE	9718		1868	John W.	39	CA	6725		1903
John	44	IRE	1240		1869	John/Mary, c/o					Dec 1898
John	71	IRE	5075		1903	John/Mary, c/o	<1	CA	5221		1902

NAME	AGE OR YOB.	BIRTH PLACE	CERT. NO	ID	DEATH YEAR	NAME	AGE OR YOB.	BIRTH PLACE	CERT. NO	ID	DEATH YEAR
John/Mary, c/o	<1	CA	5222		1902	Margaret	<1	SF	484		1870
Joseph	<1	SF	3819		1896	Margaret	38	IRL	446b		1871
Joseph A.	41	NY	2097		1900	Margaret	<1	SF	1929a		1872
Joseph A.	32	SF	5147		1901	Margaret	66	IRE	4323		1867
Joseph Edmond	<1	SF	8780		1900	Margaret	26	NY	2161		1894
Joseph F.				Dec	1899	Margaret	60	ENG	7031	Feb	1901
Joseph H.	<1	SF	6002		1867	Margaret C.				Nov	1899
Joseph Palito	<1	SF	113b		1872	Margaret F.	58	IRE	3736		1902
Joseph/Ellen				Apr	1899	Margaret T. W.				Jul	1899
Josephine	<1	SF	9123		1868	Margarett	7	SF	1301		1869
Josephine				Aug	1898	Mari Ann	<1	SF	6569		1903
Josephine Louisa	3	ME	1222		1869	Martha	<1	CA	814		1894
Josie				May	1899	Martha	28	SF	5790		1896
Josie Delia	40	IRL	1030		1901	Martin	79	IRL	1152		1900
Julia	22	IRL	536		1870	Martin Arther	2	SF	1269		1869
Julia	40	IRE	1271		1869	Mary	2	SF	3326		1870
Julia	79	IRL	1716		1894	Mary	79	IRL	3355		1870
Julia A.	25	SF	1782		1894	Mary	35	IRL	2504		1873
Julia Ann	6	SF	1672b		1871	Mary	<1	SF	5290		1867
Kate	50	IRL	1104		1900	Mary	85	IRE	7557		1903
Katie M.	33	SF	6032		1904	Mary	27	SF	6411		1904
Kieran F.	<1	SF	7894		1868	Mary	70	IRL	5802a		1895
Kitty				Dec	1899	Mary	46	IRL	5773		1896
Lawrence	54	MA	8614		1904	Mary	66	IRL	6506		1900
Lawrence				Nov	1899	Mary	76	IRL	1865		1900
Lewis	23	IRE	6578		1868	Mary	37	IRL	1866		1900
Lillie Manning	29	SF	6532		1903	Mary				Apr	1899
Lizzie	78	IRL	6071		1896	Mary				Jan	1899
Louis Edward	28	CA	3141		1900	Mary	64	IRE	3300		1902
Luke	87	IRL	8564		1901	Mary	44	IRE	2830		1903
M. C./A., c/o	<1	CA	5221		1896	Mary	31	NY	5185		1903
M./L., c/o	<1	CA	7267		1901	Mary Ann	<1	SF	50b		1872
Maagaret E.				Mar	1899	Mary Ann	<1	SF	1236		1869
Maggie	37	MA	2357b		1895	Mary Ann	70	NY	3753	Nov	1901
Malachy	70	IRL	4370		1896	Mary Ann				Jul	1899
Mamie	14	CA	K74		1886	Mary Anna	14	SF	1342		1870

Key: a = 1st part of year; b = 2nd part of year;
c = death certificate copy; c/o = child of

NAME	AGE OR YOB.	BIRTH PLACE	CERT. NO	ID	DEATH YEAR	NAME	AGE OR YOB.	BIRTH PLACE	CERT. NO	ID	DEATH YEAR
Mary C.	<1	SF	1558		1866	Minnie	31	CA	1428		1901
Mary E.	<1	SF	9338		1868	Morris	55	IRE	8194		1904
Mary E.	45	MO	2534		1894	Muriel C.	1	CA	6953		1904
Mary E.				Aug	1899	Murley	1851	IRE	705 c		1904
Mary Elizabeth	43	WI	3609		1903	Nellie	28	NJ	4994a		1895
Mary Ellen	8	SF	1336		1871	Nora	<1	SF	8025		1904
Mary J.	3	SF	869		1870	Ora D.				Feb	1900
Mary J.	<1	SF	187		1870	P./B., c/o	<1	SF	3266		1873
Mary Jane	<1	SF	3978		1870	P./K., c/o				May	1899
Mary O.	<1	SF	3742		1870	Patrick	39	IRL	582 a		1870
Mary Teresa	6	SF	1244		1869	Patrick	34	IRL	K59		1886
Mary/Selby Arthur, c/o	<1	CA	2475		1902	Patrick	63	IRE	870		1903
Mathew	37	IRL	K96		1889	Patrick	1	SF	8770		1904
Matthew B.	72	IRL	7078Feb		1901	Patrick	1849	IRE	1905c		1904
Michael			1968 b		1872	Patrick	38	IRL	7939		1900
Michael	49	IRE	7919		1904	Patrick	45	IRL	6305		1900
Michael	67	IRE	6093		1902	Patrick				Mar	1899
Michael	34	NY	6279		1903	Patrick	40	IRL	1547a		1871
Michael	75	IRE	6762		1903	Patrick C.	42	IRL	1964a		1872
Michael	56	IRE	8143		1903	Patrick C.	40	IRE	451 c		1904
Michael	62	IRL	6193		1896	Patrick F.	45	IRE	5516		1903
Michael				Apr	1899	Patrick J.	56	IRE	5381		1902
Michael				May	1899	Patrick Martin	58	IRE	5404		1904
Michael				Nov	1899	Paul	29	CA	1106		1902
Michael	34	IRL	765a		1871	Peter	1853		647c		1904
Michael	6	SF	3677		1870	Peter	47	IRL	3539		1896
Michael Francis				Jun	1899	Peter	64	IRL	6649		1900
Michael J.	45	MA	3181		1902	Peter				Nov	1899
Michael J.	34	CA	1300		1901	Peter	9	SF	6640		1902
Michael Jos.	1	SF	3610		1903	Peter J.	60	IRL	4904		1896
Michael L.				Dec	1899	Peter Joseph	37	IRL	504		1900
Michael L.	53	IRL	7268		1901	Phillipena	56	GER	2878		1901
Mike	45	IRL	K43		1885	R. R.	45	IRE	1840		1903
Mike	50	IRL	3327		1895	Rebecca				Jan	1899
Milton J.	78	NY	8566		1903	Richard				Dec	1898
Minnie	20	CA	1910		1902	Robert	46	IRL	6659		1900

Key: *a = 1st part of year; b = 2nd part of year;*
c = death certificate copy; c/o = child of

NAME	AGE OR YOB.	BIRTH PLACE	CERT. NO	ID	DEATH YEAR
Robert	<1	SF	9202		1901
Robert E.	4	SF	3755		1870
Robert Lloyd	2	SF	5981		1903
Rosanna	60	IRL	2915		1894
Rose	21	OR	1771		1902
Rose	72	IRL	2241		1894
Rose Cecilia	1	SF	598b		1872
Ruth Gertrude				Dec	1898
S/Lottie, c/o	<1	SF	6487		1903
Samuel Colter	86	IRL	8024		1901
Sarah Agnes	<1	SF	1300		1869
Sarah E.	<1	SF	1026		1870
Sarah Frances	37	CA	2998	Oct	1901
Sarah Jane	56	IRL	322b		1895
Sarah, c/o	<1	SF	2913a		1872
Stephen				Nov	1898
Susie E.	1860	DC	1853c		1904
T. J., Mrs.	abt	IRE	7448		1902
Thomas	7	SF	645b		1871
Thomas	<1	SF	584		1866
Thomas	6	SF	2830		1866
Thomas	40	IRE	7093		1868
Thomas	29	NY	1437		1869
Thomas	25	IRE	1991		1903
Thomas	45	PA	8332		1904
Thomas	34	CA	5989		1902
Thomas	55	IRL	5703		1896
Thomas	27	NV	7847		1900
Thomas	48	IOM	2575		1900
Thomas				Mar	1900
Thomas				Mar	1900
Thomas	72	IRE	3343		1902
Thomas	40	IRL	3747		1870
Thomas (marine)			7169		1901
Thomas F.	28	SF	6680	Feb	1901
Thomas J.	29	SF	7189		1903

NAME	AGE OR YOB.	BIRTH PLACE	CERT. NO	ID	DEATH YEAR
Thomas J.	<1	SF	4881		1896
Thomas Micheal	2	SF	1302		1869
Thomas P. (soldier)			5700	Jan	1901
Thomas W.	<1	SF	883		1900
Thomas William	<1	SF	973b		1872
Thos.	35	ENG	6522a		1895
Timothy	67	IRL	2438		1901
Timothy J.				Aug	1898
Timothy/Elizabeth, c/o		SF	3863		1900
William	36	IRE	2342		1866
William	42	IRE	9612		1868
William	25	SF	7016		1902
William	1	CA	846		1902
William				Aug	1899
William				Dec	1899
William	abt		8059		1901
William Downes	46	ENG	8895		1901
William H.	40	SF	7421		1903
William J. (soldier)			2082		1901
William James	47	MD	5497		1902
William P.	<1	SF	122		1902
William R.				May	1899
William Thomas	11	SF	4485		1896
Winifred G.	33	NY	8948		1903
Wm. A.	20	SF	4274a		1895
Wm. M.	42	OH	K67		1886

KELROE

NAME	AGE OR YOB.	BIRTH PLACE	CERT. NO	ID	DEATH YEAR
Andrew				Aug	1899

KELSEY

NAME	AGE OR YOB.	BIRTH PLACE	CERT. NO	ID	DEATH YEAR
George W.	44	OH	6105		1896
H. B., c/o		SF	3292		1873
Lymance J.				Mar	1900
R. C., Mrs.	60	VT	6344	Feb	1901

KELSH

NAME	AGE OR YOB.	BIRTH PLACE	CERT. NO	ID	DEATH YEAR
William D. (soldier)			7167		1901

Key: a = 1st part of year; b = 2nd part of year;
c = death certificate copy; c/o = child of

NAME	AGE OR YOB.	BIRTH PLACE	CERT. NO	ID	DEATH YEAR	NAME	AGE OR YOB.	BIRTH PLACE	CERT. NO	ID	DEATH YEAR
KELSHAW						J. W.	68	IRL	2977	Oct	1901
Tillie	55	ENG	5223		1902	Mamie, c/o	<1	CA	3862		1900
KELSO						Margret		SF	468		1866
John T.				Apr	1899	Nellie Agnes	34	MA	845		1903
KELTING						Richard	62	GER	5531a		1895
Jacob	54	GER	K88		1887	Richard F.	50	OH	K84		1887
Maria	1	GER	3849	Nov	1901	Walter	7	SF	8162		1904
KELTON						Warren J.		SF	1854		1870
Charles L.	3	SF	6236		1896	**KEMPE**					
Clarence O.	34	OR	4375		1902	Conrad	45		4439		1901
S. B.	50	VT	1942b		1872	Mariem	75	PRU	1022b		1871
Violet	<1	SF	6360		1896	**KEMPER**					
KELTY						George	<1	SF	1359b		1872
Mary	50	IRE	1287		1869	Oran A.(soldier)			3053		1900
William/Louise, c/o	<1	CA	1107		1902	**KEMPINSKY**					
KELVEK						Hermann	55	GER	451b		1895
Frank	<1	SF	6813		1903	**KEMPL**					
KEM						Adele	50	FRA	4602		1903
William B.	3	SF	5455	Jan	1901	**KEMPNER**					
KEMBALL						Jetta	79	GER	5068a		1895
F. Adelaide	34	MA	2754		1866	**KEMPSON**					
Fanny K.	21	RI	1670		1870	Harry				Feb	1900
KEMBECK						**KEMPTNER**					
Mary Jane	41	MA	6488		1896	Jacob	35	GER	1551a		1871
KEMBLE						**KEN**					
John	<1	SF	3091		1873	Sum	22	CHN	6858		1902
William R.	47	NY	2787		1901	**KENADAY**					
KEMMERLING						Rowell	<1	SF	4320		1867
Elizabeth L.	16	SF	2223b		1895	**KENADY**					
KEMP						Martin	61	IRL	9618		1901
Alice				Aug	1898	Mary		SF	2920		1873
Charles	50	MA	1846a		1872	Patrick	35	IRE	4294		1867
Hattie	1871	OR	280c		1904	**KENALLY**					
Henry/Nellie, c/o		SF	593		1900	Sarah		IRL	1841		1870

Key: *a = 1st part of year; b = 2nd part of year;*
c = death certificate copy; c/o = child of

NAME	AGE OR YOB.	BIRTH PLACE	CERT. NO	ID	DEATH YEAR	NAME	AGE OR YOB.	BIRTH PLACE	CERT. NO	ID	DEATH YEAR
KENDAL						**KENEALLY**					
Martin	78	IN	6370	Feb	1901	Florence	<1	SF	8471		1900
						Nicholas	43	IRL	7613		1901
KENDALL											
Alva	18	CA	119		1870	**KENEALY**					
Arthur				Nov	1898	Eliza	48	IRL	5792	Jan	1901
Belle				Jul	1898	Ellen				Jul	1899
Charles I.	40	NY	7729		1903	Thomas J.	36	CT	1188		1902
Emma G.	1862	CA	3433c		1904	W. J./M., c/o	<1	SF	4233		1895
Frank H.	51	ME	8772		1900	W. J./M., c/o		SF	3014		1895
George	44	NH	7082		1868	**KENEDY**					
Haneplin (soldier)			7225		1900	Louis R. O.	<1	SF	1276		1870
Hattie	8	SF	5021a		1895	William	29	IRL	4573b		1870
John T.				Jul	1898	William	44	IRE	1505		1866
Joseph H.	1847	OH	1877c		1904						
Mary A.				May	1899	**KENEFICK**					
Mary E.	56	IN	3031		1902	Jullia A.	24	SF	5062		1902
Neal (soldier)	22	KY	4586		1901	**KENELY**					
Richard Bowden	1836	ENG	1005c		1904	――		SF	3229		1870
Robert/Catherine, c/o		SF	5793		1901	**KENGLA**					
Sabina	67	IRE	8001		1904	L. A./E. R., c/o		SF	5970		1895
Sophroma	89	NY	969b		1895	Louis A.	43	DC	6649		1904
Thomas	59	ENG	3336		1866	**KENIN**					
Thomas	<1	SF	1320		1894	Ann	45	IRE	3299		1866
Valentine	40	CA	3586		1903	**KENISON**					
Valentine T.	6	SF	8086		1901	Asa H.				Nov	1899
KENDRICK						**KENISTON**					
Catherine	3	SF	1201		1869	Mary E.	24	SF	4614		1896
Julia Elizabeth	1	SF	3202		1903	**KENITZER**					
May	5	SF	1608b		1895	Jeannette	69	GER	3080		1894
Robert Marcus	1904	SF	2554c		1904	**KENKEN**					
Thomas	60	IRE	2030		1903	Christ	46	GER	1452		1869
Thomas J.	1868	SF	1544c		1904	**KENNA**					
KENDRIGAN						――			1039		1868
Patrick	44	IRL	9300		1901	Anthony	<1	SF	3417		1902
						Edna				Mar	1899

Key: a = 1st part of year; b = 2nd part of year; c = death certificate copy; c/o = child of

NAME	AGE OR YOB.	BIRTH PLACE	CERT. NO	ID	DEATH YEAR	NAME	AGE OR YOB.	BIRTH PLACE	CERT. NO	ID	DEATH YEAR
James M.	32	IRE	7743		1868	Alma					Aug 1898
John	56	IRL	836		1901	Andrew	38	CA	4293		1903
Maggie	24	CA	3834		1900	Anna Jane	81	MD	6954		1904
Mamie E.	58	CA	157		1901	Anna Jane	81	MD	6322		1903
Margaret	63	ENG	3412b		1870	Annie					Oct 1898
William M.				Mar	1900	Annie E.	1	SF	802b		1871
KENNADY						B. E./Mary E., c/o	1	SF	731		1903
Cellie	<1	SF	4964		1867	Bartholomew	1836	IRE	1854c		1904
Mary Ellen	<1	SF	5563		1867	Bernard	88	IRE	2776		1903
Mary F.	2	SF	1448		1869	Bridget	70	IRL	5248a		1896
KENNAN						Bridget A.	68	IRL	9544		1901
Alex S./Laura, c/o	1	SF	4160		1903	C. F.,Mrs., c/o	<1	SF	6728		1901
KENNARD						Caroline I.	56	ME	8095		1900
Eugene	<1	SF	8848		1900	Cathe	46	IRL	K33		1884
Geo Wesley	72	MD	6852		1903	Catherine	22	IRL	3413a		1872
						Catherine	2	NV	9792		1868
KENNEALLY						Catherine					May 1899
B., Mrs.	65	IRL	4207		1900	Catherine E.	3	SF	1134		1869
John				Feb	1899	Cathrine P.	3	SF	4994		1867
Patrick	78	IRE	3480		1902	Cecelia	1	SF	85		1865
KENNEALY						Cecila	15	SF	8073		1904
Honora	44	IRL	2616a		1872	Charles	<1	SF	1578		1870
Julia A.	<1	SF	7786		1868	Charles	1844	NY	43c		1904
KENNEDAY						Charles	<1	SF	2802		1902
Annie	60	CT	1950		1903	Charles					Aug 1898
KENNEDY						Christina V.					Mar 1899
——	<1	SF	1315		1869	D. W.	34	PA	K41		1884
A.	46	IRL	674		1894	Daniel					Oct 1899
Agnes	<1	SF	4071		1896	Delia	38	IRL	2030b		1895
Alfred	58	IRE	1864		1902	Delia	60	IRL	4003		1900
Alfred				Mar	1900	Dennis					Jan 1899
Alfred J.		SF	2019		1870	Edward	32	NY	10b		1871
Alice C.	1	SF	1673		1903	Edward	29	CA	5526		1896
Alice Jane	1	SF	9161		1868	Eliza	68	IRE	4577		1904
Allen				Nov	1899	Elizabeth	27	CAN	463		1901
						Elizabeth A.	30	MA	4819		1867

Key: a = 1st part of year; b = 2nd part of year;
c = death certificate copy; c/o = child of

NAME	AGE OR YOB.	BIRTH PLACE	CERT. NO	ID	DEATH YEAR	NAME	AGE OR YOB.	BIRTH PLACE	CERT. NO	ID	DEATH YEAR
Ellen	65	IRL	6308	Feb	1901	John (soldier)			4708		1901
Fanny H.	3	SF	1275		1869	John C.	80	PA	3549	Nov	1901
Frances J.	7	SF	1890a		1872	John Doe				Jun	1899
Frank	62	IRL	6581a		1895	John E.	60	NY	9084		1901
Genevieve	8	SF	809		1902	John H.	2	SF	1140		1869
Geo. P.	37	SWE	2753		1894	John Joseph	68	IRL	8331		1901
George	44	NY	3867a		1895	John P.	35	IRE	2348		1902
George (soldier)			286		1901	John T. (soldier)			6444		1900
George Aloysius	1890	SF	196c		1904	John T./J., c/o				Jan	1899
Georgina	<1	SF	4785		1867	John/Hannah, c/o	<1	SF	3297		1901
Hattie				Jan	1899	Joseph	48	CT	1006		1902
Henry A.	45	NB	3233		1900	Julia	29	SF	2011b		1895
Henry E.	1	SF	1033b		1872	Julia	59	IRL	8289		1900
Hugh	40	IRL	1147b		1871	Julia M.	26	CA	8183		1900
Hugh		SF	1109		1869	Katie Ann	3	SF	1947b		1872
Hugh	33	IRL	4519		1896	Kitty	21	SF	5198a		1895
Hugh				Dec	1899	L./N.Wilson, c/o				Jan	1899
Hugh				Mar	1899	Lawrence	<1	SF	844b		1872
James	30	IRL	2820		1895	Lena S.	50	PA	8056		1903
James	87	IRL	3977		1900	Lilly	2	SF	1434		1869
James	87	IRL	4914		1901	Lucy E.	26	NY	2044		1866
James				Feb	1900	M.	72	IRL	K52		1885
James G.	52	IL	1605b		1895	Maggie				Dec	1898
Jane	55	IRL	5653		1896	Margaret	<1	SF	8761		1868
Jane	52	IRL	2709		1894	Margaret	45	PA	7783		1900
Jno.	40	VT	K4		1882	Margaret	54	SCT	1068		1900
Jno. Francis	<1	SF	2616		1894	Margaret	40		2337		1900
John	42	IRL	3156		1873	Margaret	11	SF	1261b		1895
John	46	NY	7446		1868	Margaret L.	74	PA	3143		1894
John	<1	SF	8321		1868	Martin	65	IRL	3479		1896
John	<1	SF	8338		1868	Mary	44	IRL	3762		1896
John	3	SF	1408		1869	Mary				Jan	1899
John	75	IRL	4702		1896	Mary				Mar	1899
John	63	IRL	953		1900	Mary A.	54	MI	3344		1902
John	1829	IRE	2619c		1904	Mary Agnes	1	SF	1091		1869
John (marine)			8427		1901	Mary Ann				Jul	1899

Key: a = 1st part of year; b = 2nd part of year;
c = death certificate copy; c/o = child of

NAME	AGE OR YOB.	BIRTH PLACE	CERT. NO	ID	DEATH YEAR
Mary C.	33	IRE	1275		1869
Mary I.	3	SF	1027		1870
Mary J.	28	CA	5834		1896
Mary J. or Fay	<1	AL	1071		1902
Mary Michael, Sister				Oct	1898
Michael	26	NJ	K90		1887
Michael J.	30	IRE	3630		1867
Michael/Mary, c/o	<1	CA	7941		1904
Neil				Dec	1898
Nellie	33	CA	2705		1902
Nicholas	30	IRL	2004a		1872
Patrick	34	IRL	4092b		1870
Patrick	22	IRL	2016		1894
Paul	40	SF	5697		1902
Richard	57	IRL	331b		1872
Robert S.	23	IL	4918		1903
Thomas				Nov	1898
Thomas Joseph				Jul	1898
Thomas/Pansy, c/o	1	SF	2415		1903
Thos. F.	8	CA	K9		1882
Thos. W.	34	SF	2004		1894
W. H.				Mar	1899
William	51	NY	2787a		1872
William	37	IRE	1318		1869
William G. (soldier)			7224		1900
KENNELEY					
William	1852	IRE	1770c		1904
KENNELLY					
Dennis	58	IRL	6371Feb		1901
Edward J.	38	SF	7551		1902
KENNELY					
Michael F.	1	SF	3222		1866
KENNENA					
Bernhard	65	GER	K7		1882

NAME	AGE OR YOB.	BIRTH PLACE	CERT. NO	ID	DEATH YEAR
KENNERSON					
Caroline	70	ME	4846		1902
William				Mar	1900
KENNEY					
——			7337		1868
A.	41	AK	6368a		1895
Annie	<1	SF	1639		1866
Annie	50	IRL	6991		1900
Arthur/Mathilda, c/o	<1	SF	3667		1900
Bridget	61	IRL	1667		1870
Bridget	95	IRL	1144		1901
Catherine				Feb	1900
Catherine/Joseph, c/o		SF	2337		1901
Edwd.	44	IRL	K32		1884
Ellen	55	NJ	1080		1901
Ellen L.	53	IRE	8648		1868
Francis W.	2	SF	3194		1870
George G.	51	CA	1482		1901
James	34	IRE	1016		1866
James	67	IRL	4372		1896
James	72	IRL	2448b		1895
James H.	8	SF	5507		1867
Jane	77	IRE	6070		1903
John	60	IRL	7821		1901
John Deagon	2	SF	1202		1901
John J./Suev, c/o		CA	3495		1900
Joseph	60	IRL	3516		1896
Joseph Francis				Dec	1898
Joseph W.	43	NY	3022a		1872
Katherine Frances	41	NY	4683		1904
Loretta				Oct	1899
Luke	51	IRE	5814		1903
Margaret	50	IRL	5921a		1895
Mary	37	IRE	3983		1867
Mary	33	SF	1609		1894

Key: a = 1st part of year; b = 2nd part of year;
c = death certificate copy; c/o = child of

NAME	AGE OR YOB.	BIRTH PLACE	CERT. NO	ID	DEATH YEAR	NAME	AGE OR YOB.	BIRTH PLACE	CERT. NO	ID	DEATH YEAR
Mary H.	73	ME	2628		1901	Joseph H.	2	SF	2582		1901
Mary Jane	73	IRL	245		1900	Katie M.	<1	SF	9181		1868
Patrick	36	IRL	1575		1870	Lewis Tesse	<1	SF	1164		1869
Peter	<1	SF	2651		1900	Maggie	19	IRL	1518b		1872
Susie Van Arslale	22	CA	4377		1901	Margaret	65	IRL	709		1900
Thomas	1852	MN	2019c		1904	Margaret W.				Feb	1899
Thomas P.	<1	SF	4684		1867	Mary	50	IRE	3882		1903
William H.	3	SF	9336		1868	Mary	<1	SF	2926		1895
						Mary E.	<1	SF	1449		1869
KENNIFF						Mathew	68	IRL	5635	Jan	1901
Rose	12	SF	870		1900	Melvina	38	NY	4468		1867
						Patrick	1861	IRE	1160c		1904
KENNISON						Patrick	70	IRL	393		1900
Mary				Jan	1899	Peter F.	34	MA	2298		1866
						S. K.			1416		1869
KENNY						Thomas	27	IRE	1165		1866
——			7540		1868	W. B. J.	56	IRE	1103		1869
Ann	12	MA	8180		1868	William	3	SF	4374		1903
Bartholemew	17	SF	1113		1894	William C.	1836	NY	751c		1904
Catherine	8	IRL	3298	Nov	1901	William Fox				Nov	1898
Catherine				Aug	1898						
Edward	60	IRE	8032		1903	**KENOYER**					
Edward I.	46	IRE	9878		1868	Al/Emma, c/o	<1	SF	1401		1901
Frederick W.	5	CT	1372		1869	**KENSCHER**					
Genevieve	1	SF	215		1903	Adelia	1	SF	2057		1866
Gertrude	6	SF	2835		1902						
Honora Mary	<1	SF	1404		1900	**KENT**					
James	78	IRE	3881		1903	——			1266		1870
James/Mary, c/o		SF	5108		1896	Cathrine	58	SCT	7186		1868
Jas. J.	38	IRL	K40		1884	Chearles F. (soldier)			3549		1900
Johanna	65	IRE	80		1903	Edwin				Jun	1899
John	35	IRE	6412		1867	Fanny	45	PA	3360		1894
John				Oct	1898	Isabella	26	ENG	369b		1872
John				Oct	1898	Jane M.	33	NJ	1407		1869
John				Mar	1899	Josephine				Mar	1899
John C.	32	SF	152		1900	Joshua	20	ENG	3512		1870
John F.	33	CA	4371		1896	K. C., c/o		SF	250b		1872
John J.			2872		1902						

Key: a = 1st part of year; b = 2nd part of year; c = death certificate copy; c/o = child of

NAME	AGE OR YOB.	BIRTH PLACE	CERT. NO	ID	DEATH YEAR
Mabel Charlotte	20	ENG	363b		1895
Sarah	2	PA	1279		1869
W. F.	40		6591		1904
William S. (soldier)			1882		1900
KENTARO					
Suzaki				Dec	1899
KENTFIELD					
George	75	NY	6859		1902
Harriet	75	ENG	1872		1900
Martha	65	NY	5494		1903
KENTZEL					
Mary	46	MO	5209a		1896
KENTZELL					
Robert W.	32	SF	7654		1901
KENTZELMEIER					
Fred	55	GER	K36		1884
KENUCAN					
Charles P.	24	CA	3765		1902
KENVILL					
Kate	33	IRE	2197		1902
KENWAY					
Delia	29	IRL	1837		1900
KENWOOD					
Charles	54	WI	7431		1904
KENWORTHY					
Mary Elizabeth	72	NY	3523		1902
KENY					
Fong Nong	54	CHN	2238a		1872
KENYON					
Alice	31	CA	553		1900
Catherine				Nov	1899
John	43	NY	283b		1895
William P.	51		1164		1869

NAME	AGE OR YOB.	BIRTH PLACE	CERT. NO	ID	DEATH YEAR
KEOCH					
Took Som	31	CHN	390		1902
KEOGAN					
Larry/Lizzie, c/o	<1	SF	2166		1902
Peter	85	IRE	4768		1903
KEOGH					
Annie T.	27	CA	1810		1902
Harry				Feb	1900
Johana	38	IRE	7320		1868
Mary	4	SF	6264		1867
Michael W.	63	ENG	1604b		1895
Ruth	1	SF	98		1903
Thomas J.	44	CAN	1524		1903
Wm. H.	36	CAN	2081		1894
KEOHRN					
H. M.	<1	SF	807		1866
KEON					
Michael	42	IRE	4694		1867
KEONEK					
Duck	42	CHN	1614		1901
KEONKE					
Wilhelm	1	SF	1711		1870
KEOUGH					
Frank	1	SF	3911a		1895
Henry	40	IRE	1449		1869
Jno. Frank	3	SF	3801a		1895
Millard Hall	17	CA	3729		1903
Patrick	27	IRE	9738		1868
Thomas	2	SF	3660		1867
KEOWN					
Caroline Mary M.				Jul	1898
KEP					
Ah	22	CHN	448a		1871

Key: a = 1st part of year; b = 2nd part of year;
c = death certificate copy; c/o = child of

NAME	AGE OR YOB.	BIRTH PLACE	CERT. NO	ID	DEATH YEAR
KEPFLER					
Louis	1871	SF	2745c		1904
KEPLER					
Fred	42	NJ	1283b		1895
KEPNER					
Edgar S.				Feb	1900
KEPO					
Leonora	33	FRA	1312		1869
KEPP					
George A.			1308		1903
KEPPEL					
Walter D. P.	35	ENG	3328		1895
KEPPLE					
Daniel	29	IRE	4944		1904
KERATY					
Mary	1	SF	8468		1904
KERBAUGH					
Marion Lorenza	4	CA	7750		1900
KERBY					
Everette (soldier)			1974		1900
KERGAN					
John Depew	1838	ON	2458c		1904
KERGER					
Pauline A. A.	67	GER	2734		1903
KERLEN					
George B.				Jan	1899
KERLIN					
Charles C.	3	SF	1769b		1872
Walter	28	SF	1536		1902
KERN					
C. P. Louise	22	SF	2795		1900
Caroline Fannie	1849	NZD	706c		1904
Henry	55	GER	K23		1883

NAME	AGE OR YOB.	BIRTH PLACE	CERT. NO	ID	DEATH YEAR
Julius	44	MO	8620		1900
Patrick	38	IRL	1224		1900
KERNAGHAM					
John	46	IRL	K91		1887
KERNAN					
Francis	59	IRL	1439		1870
James	53	IRL	788		1901
Peter	36	IRE	7476		1902
Thomas B.	38	KY	247		1901
Wm.P.	6	NY	1375		1869
KERNAU					
Frances Grima Emma	<1	SF	1203		1869
KERNELE					
——	<1	SF	3727		1870
KERNER					
George	42	GER	K97		1889
Jacob				Jan	1899
KERNET					
Margaret	23	IRE	834		1866
KERNIN					
——			6267		1867
KERNS					
Mary Ann	1	SF	592b		1871
Patk	44	IRL	K34		1884
KERNY					
Maggie	50	IRE	6094		1902
Mary	<1	SF	1267b		1871
KERR					
Alice M.	1	SF	1801		1903
Andrew	70	IRL	8023		1901
Andrew T.	1	SF	3592		1867
Anna Maria	<1	SF	9770		1868
Benjamin M. (soldier)			4791		1901
Charles	69	IRE	7284		1868

Key: a = 1st part of year; b = 2nd part of year;
c = death certificate copy; c/o = child of

NAME	AGE OR YOB.	BIRTH PLACE	CERT. NO	ID	DEATH YEAR
David	55	IRL	2121		1894
Edd	27	MI	6315		1902
Edmund D.	21	CA	6071		1903
Edward	56	SCT	K5		1882
Elizabeth I.	4	SF	9411		1868
George P.				Dec	1898
Isabella	68	IRE	2097		1902
James	1862	SCT	252c		1904
James A.				Nov	1899
Jennings	39	NC	4024		1903
John	63	SCT	5681		1904
John	64	MO	3481		1902
Joseph M.	28	CA	2155		1903
Margaret	74	IRL	4241b		1870
Oliver	37	NY	2416		1903
Robert C. (soldier)			5057		1901
Robert H.	42	CAN	6280		1903
Robert/Margaret, c/o		SF	2701		1900
Samuel	40		6703		1868
Sarah	18	KS	K17		1882
Susan	69	SCT	4943		1904
Thomas	<1	SEA	9389		1868
Thomas P.				Jan	1899
Virginia F.	<1	SF	1625		1866
William	<1	SF	8785		1868
William	69	IRL	4018		1896
William				Dec	1899
William I.	2	SF	9438		1868

KERRELL

NAME	AGE OR YOB.	BIRTH PLACE	CERT. NO	ID	DEATH YEAR
Albert Daws A	62	ENG	1635		1903

KERRIGAN

NAME	AGE OR YOB.	BIRTH PLACE	CERT. NO	ID	DEATH YEAR
Ambrose				Nov	1898
Bernard	79	IRL	7921		1900
Bridget	48	IRL	3356		1896
Catherine	2	SF	1129		1869
Elizabeth	64	IRE	1242		1903
Ellen	63	IRL	6194		1896
Emma	<1	SF	9233		1868
Eugene	38	IRE	7872		1903
James	77	IRE	6428		1903
Jho. J.	44	NY	2461		1894
John	<1	SF	2664		1873
John	34	IRE	1414		1869
John	90	IRL	489		1900
John M.	1	SF	2897		1903
John M.				Feb	1900
Loretta Frances	<1	SF	4534		1901
Marguerite Violet	<1	SF	7598		1903
Maria	88	IRL	9100		1901
Mary				Jul	1898
Matthew H.	30	CA	4700a		1895
Owen	41	IRE	151		1865
Patrick G.	42	IRL	4043b		1870
Thomas	<1	CA	4640		1896
Thomas Joseph	<1	SF	3192	Nov	1901
William M.	15	SF	2098		1900
William Milton	<1	SF	3415		1900

KERRIN

NAME	AGE OR YOB.	BIRTH PLACE	CERT. NO	ID	DEATH YEAR
Hugh				Dec	1899

KERRINS

NAME	AGE OR YOB.	BIRTH PLACE	CERT. NO	ID	DEATH YEAR
Mary				Jan	1899

KERRISON

NAME	AGE OR YOB.	BIRTH PLACE	CERT. NO	ID	DEATH YEAR
Ann	40	ME	1717		1903
Geo. E.				Jul	1899
Maggie	38	NJ	3129		1894

KERRWITH

NAME	AGE OR YOB.	BIRTH PLACE	CERT. NO	ID	DEATH YEAR
Edward	<1	SF	5129		1867

KERSCH

NAME	AGE OR YOB.	BIRTH PLACE	CERT. NO	ID	DEATH YEAR
Franz	80	GER	2160		1894

Key: a = 1st part of year; b = 2nd part of year; c = death certificate copy; c/o = child of

NAME	AGE OR YOB.	BIRTH PLACE	CERT. NO	ID	DEATH YEAR	NAME	AGE OR YOB.	BIRTH PLACE	CERT. NO	ID	DEATH YEAR
KERSHON						KESPRINGAES					
Max Howard	29	CO	9675		1901	Alice	42	FRA	1262b		1872
KERSKY						KESSELER					
Isidore	37	PRU	6091		1867	Francis/Marie C., c/o	<1	SF	6903		1902
KERSTEN						Joseph				Dec	1899
Louis A.	32	AUS	4003a		1895	KESSING					
KERSTON						Jno. A.	5	SF	3982a		1895
Joseph	51	AUS	9736		1868	Robt. H.	<1	SF	1826b		1872
KERSTTLE						KESSLER					
Anthony	45	MA	1373		1869	Anna	15	SF	2666		1902
KERTELL						Anna	35	GER	5697a		1895
Rudolph	7	CA	6035	Jan	1901	Frank (soldier)			3055	Oct	1901
KERVAN						Fred	48	GER	1709		1900
Thomas Lawrence	72	NY	5093		1904	Lucy	8	SF	1950		1900
KERVIN						Mabel	14	SF	3910a		1895
Bridget	<1	SF	4594		1867	KESTENMANCHER					
Patrick				Jul	1899	Frederick				Feb	1900
Roy	7	SF	6214a		1895	KESTER					
KERWIN						Harril B.	4	CA	6		1865
Catherine	55	IRL	6258	Feb	1901	J. H.				Aug	1898
Cathrine	<1	SF	1022		1868	KESTNO					
Dorothy	1	CA	6828		1904	Herman	23	SCT	K15		1882
Eliza	85	IRE	5405		1904	KETCHENER					
Hugh, c/o		SF	1682b		1872	Max	45	GER	4726		1903
John P.	50	IRE	1084		1869	KETCHIN					
Margaret	66	IRE	4919		1903	Henry	31		2803		1873
Martin	40	IRL	K8		1882	KETCHUM					
Thomas	55	IRE	120		1903	Adelia P., Mrs., Dr.	80	VT	8060		1901
KERZ						KETTECHER					
Walter F.	4	SF	6143		1900	L.	27	AUT	K75		1886
KESKALDIE						KETTLE					
George	33	GER	3764		1867	John J.	1890	SF	1496c		1904
KESKINEN						Mary	41	IRE	6000		1904
Eustaf	50	FIN	5539		1903						

Key: a = 1st part of year; b = 2nd part of year;
c = death certificate copy; c/o = child of

NAME	AGE OR YOB.	BIRTH PLACE	CERT. NO	ID	DEATH YEAR
KETTLEWELL					
Anna D.				Feb	1900
KETTLINELL					
Charles P.	6	IA	2771		1866
KETTNANER					
Antone				Nov	1899
KETTNER					
Albert	66	GER	4515		1904
KEVELL					
Sarah	56	ENG	6665		1900
KEVINS					
James	61	IRE	4824		1867
KEW					
Ah	27	CHN	3454b		1870
Ah	28	CHN	841		1866
Hong	<1	SF	3038a		1872
KEWELL					
Charles	71	ENG	7011	Feb	1901
KEWIN					
William B.	69	ENG	1318b		1895
KEWLEY					
Phillip	52	ENG	2796		1900
KEY					
Margaret	23	VA	1301b		1895
T. W., Mrs.	42	MO	5503	Jan	1901
KEYER					
C. J., c/o	<1	SF	1049b		1872
John	50	LA	3866		1896
KEYES					
Cathrine	26	IRE	2252		1866
George D.		SF	1784		1870
George O.	39	MA	3839		1903
James	23	CA	542		1903

NAME	AGE OR YOB.	BIRTH PLACE	CERT. NO	ID	DEATH YEAR
Laura Ervilla	16	MA	275b		1872
Mary Anna	22	NY	3376		1873
KEYS					
Douglas	80	NY	7255		1902
George				Oct	1898
James	62	IRE	7761		1903
John	21	ENG	769a		1871
John	60	IRE	965		1902
John				Jan	1899
Lovenia M.	1	CA	408		1903
Maxwell				Dec	1899
O. F., c/o		SF	2456a		1872
Orsen H.	74	NH	6285	Feb	1901
KEYSER					
Charles				Feb	1899
Margaret	49	MO	265b		1871
Myron N.	26	WI	K19		1883
KEZAR					
Abner H.	63	ME	6763		1903
KFURY					
Mary	<1	SF	6343a		1895
KI					
Long	31	CHN	557b		1871
Pang	49	CHN	5634		1867
KIAESEL					
Annie Mary	1	SF	2332a		1872
KIBBEY					
Frank L.	27	IL	4071	Dec	1901
KIBISH					
Hedwego Elizabeth	<1	CA	2007		1900
KIDD					
Anna	45	IRL	726a		1871
Dollie	42	SF	2484		1894
Geo. A.				Mar	1900

Key: a = 1st part of year; b = 2nd part of year;
c = death certificate copy; c/o = child of

NAME	AGE OR YOB.	BIRTH PLACE	CERT. NO	ID	DEATH YEAR
George W.	49	PA	8279		1900
George Washington	33	CA	1072		1902
"Hans" Emily	63	ENG	3538a		1895
Hugh A.	27	CA	1243		1903
James E.	37	OR	264b		1895
Katie				Dec	1899
Mary L.	70	ENG	4558		1896
Phoebe A., Mrs.	70	TN	1967		1901
Rosey (Sonia Pierce)	27	IN	5345a		1895
William Hutchinson	69	OH	6289		1904
KIDNEY					
Bridget				Dec	1898
John	60	IRL	1051		1900
John T. (soldier)			1496		1901
KIDO					
Katie				Dec	1899
KIDWELL					
Katie K.	23	PA	455b		1871
KIE					
Ah	<1	SF	3666		1870
Lun	35	CHN	1080b		1871
Ming	22	CHN	1722b		1872
KIEFE					
Timothy	36	IRL	K48		1885
KIEFER					
Barha				Jan	1899
Bernard	34	FRA	1098		1869
D. E.	50	GER	58b		1895
Theodore				Feb	1900
KIEHL					
Daniel	49	PA	5050		1904
Emilia	35	PRU	507b		1872
KIEHT					
Jacob	84	GER	6166		1900

NAME	AGE OR YOB.	BIRTH PLACE	CERT. NO	ID	DEATH YEAR
KIEL					
Frane				Feb	1900
Frederick	56	GER	4047		1903
Henry	46	GER	K69		1886
KIELBERG					
Carl E.	57	DEN	7208		1903
Nielsine Christina				Feb	1899
KIELIORT					
Pauline	64	GER	3983a		1895
KIELY					
Ellen	<1	SF	3674a		1895
Johanna	27	ME	1153		1869
Michael M.				Feb	1900
KIEMAN					
Wm. Bernard	1	SF	859b		1872
KIEMEYER					
Frank J. H.	37	GER	584		1902
KIENNAN					
Mary	72	IRL	442b		1872
KIENY					
Leonard	33	FRA	1320b		1895
KIEP					
John H./Jennie F., c/o		SF	4593		1901
KIERESAKE					
Wilhelmina	46	GER	4870		1867
KIERMAN					
——		SF	2867		1866
Francis James	<1	SF	1724		1901
Rossanna	2	CA	1529		1870
Thomas				Feb	1899
KIERNAN					
Annie	70	IRL	7668		1900
Bartholomew	34	CA	6125		1904
Bessie	1	SF	3095		1903

Key: *a = 1st part of year; b = 2nd part of year;*
c = death certificate copy; c/o = child of

NAME	AGE OR YOB.	BIRTH PLACE	CERT. NO	ID	DEATH YEAR
Bridget	61	IRE	1636		1903
Charles				Feb	1899
Clare	<1	CA	187		1901
Edward (soldier)			6509		1900
Elizabeth	66	IRE	6985		1868
Frances J				Feb	1899
Francis Michael	32	SF	7938		1903
Henry	2	MA	1074		1869
James	37	IRL	2531		1901
John James		SF	3021		1870
John Patrick				Oct	1898
Mary Alice	5	SF	8599		1900
Mary Ann	<1	CA	2647		1901
Mary Jane		SF	4566b		1870
Mary Jane	2	SF	36		1865
Mary Louise	64	IRE	8771		1904
Myrtle	7	SF	7491		1901
Patrick	35	IRL	3418b		1870
Philip	49	IRE	1103		1869
Willie R.				Feb	1899
KIERNEN					
Margaret Agnes	1	SF	1293		1869
KIERSKI					
William	66	GER	496		1903
KIERULFF					
Thomas Nightingale	1	CA	5133		1904
KIESTER					
Melville				Feb	1900
KIETZMANN					
Fredrick	62	GER	5002		1904
KIFURY					
Joseph	1	OR	5448a		1895
KIGARICE					
Francis H. (soldier)	29	OH	1466		1901

NAME	AGE OR YOB.	BIRTH PLACE	CERT. NO	ID	DEATH YEAR
KIGHTMAN					
John	5	SF	321		1865
KIHAHA					
John	28	HI	9912		1868
KIHM					
Ulrich	37	SWT	517b		1871
KIKUCHI					
Micao	<1	CA	3911		1896
KIKUMOSKA					
Ichimura	24	JPN	980		1901
KILBORN					
Alden D.	57	MI	5298		1901
August Henry	1	CA	7419		1900
James	28	IRL	804b		1872
KILBURN					
Cora	15	CA	K56		1885
Floyd L.	<1	SF	916		1900
KILCLINE					
Joseph	36	CA	5134		1904
Joseph Lantry	4	SF	1968		1901
Maria	42	MA	5000		1902
KILDALE					
James	45	NOR	9952		1868
KILDAY					
——	<1	SF	3497b		1870
Bridget	70	IRL	4427		1901
Edward	38	IRE	1224		1869
Isabella	2	SF	8117		1868
James R.	44	CA	3299	Nov	1901
Patrick J.	62	IRE	8772		1904
Walter P.	1	SF	981b		1872
William	70	IRE	7367		1902
William J.	1861	MA	3100c		1904
William J.	43	MA	7160		1903

Key: a = 1st part of year; b = 2nd part of year;
c = death certificate copy; c/o = child of

NAME	AGE OR YOB.	BIRTH PLACE	CERT. NO	ID	DEATH YEAR	NAME	AGE OR YOB.	BIRTH PLACE	CERT. NO	ID	DEATH YEAR
KILDE						**KILKENNEY**					
Martin Anderson	34	NOR	1273b		1872	Annie	36	IRE	7886		1903
KILDISH						**KILKENNY**					
Charles (soldier)			8795		1901	Alice	<1	SF	1261		1894
						Francis				Apr	1899
KILDUFF						Mary	6	SF	4315a		1895
George	1	SF	4712		1904	Susan	44	IRE	8469		1904
Martin	43	CA	1504b		1895	**KILL**					
Mary Elizabeth	1867	CA	568c		1904	Emelia	20	OR	1873b		1872
Robert P.	1884	SF	3362c		1904						
KILEY						**KILLAVARY**					
——			1818		1866	Levina	43	IRL	6507	Feb	1901
Delia	25	IRE	8650		1868	**KILLCARE**					
Frances Josephine	35	CA	1147		1902	James	45	IRE	4427		1867
KILGALLON						**KILLCLINE**					
Ethel Marie	3	SF	4769		1903	Eliza	29	CA	5229		1901
James	<1	SF	6583		1896						
James	35	IRL	8653		1901	**KILLEEN**					
						Albert	<1	SF	683		1894
KILGORE						James				Jan	1899
Arthur B. S.				Jan	1899	John Joseph	1872	SF	1429c		1904
KILGROY						Joseph	3	SF	4727		1903
Mary				May	1899	Mary Agnes	47	IRL	3829a		1895
						Michael	1851	IRE	970c		1904
KILHAM						**KILLELAY**					
Frank B.	6	SF	1108		1869	Peter	70	IRL	2103		1873
KILHILL						**KILLELEA**					
John Ramsy	<1	SF	1090		1869	Annie M.	55	IRE	3875		1902
KILIAN						**KILLELIA**					
Margaret	44	WAL	4216b		1870	Joseph A.	<1	SF	174a		1871
KILK						Thos./Mary, c/o	<1	SF	4168		1895
Rose	34	SCT	1565		1900	**KILLEN**					
KILKALLY						Ellen				Jan	1899
Julia	<1	SF	6583a		1895	Francis	81	SCT	K14		1882
KILKELLY						Margaret E.	31	SF	8057		1903
Mary	48	IRE	3524		1902						

Key: a = 1st part of year; b = 2nd part of year; c = death certificate copy; c/o = child of

NAME	AGE OR YOB.	BIRTH PLACE	CERT. NO	ID	DEATH YEAR	NAME	AGE OR YOB.	BIRTH PLACE	CERT. NO	ID	DEATH YEAR
KILLEY						**KILLROY**					
Chas. W.				Oct	1899	John/Delia, c/o		SF	8273		1900
Robert	35	IRE	1291		1869	Maggie Ellen				Apr	1899
KILLGOUR						Mary Ellen	<1	SF	6565		1896
James	52	CAN	5936		1896	**KILLSING**					
KILLIAN						Michael	80	IRL	2652		1900
John A. (soldier)			7533		1900	**KILLYN**					
Richard	<1	SF	1180		1869	Frederick G.				Jun	1899
William	26	IRE	9956		1868	**KILPATRICK**					
KILLILEA						Elizabeth Sol	54	GER	6782		1904
Beatrice M.	1883	CA	2267c		1904	George	70	IRE	1108		1902
Rose	54	IRL	2204a		1872	Mary	68	IRL	6830Feb		1901
Thomas	32	CA	5517		1903	Robt.	<1	SCT	6359		1896
KILLILEN						William (soldier)			7170		1901
Mary	42	IRL	675b		1871	**KILPECK**					
KILLIN						Rose	76	IRL	1614		1900
Frederick G.				Jul	1899	**KILROY**					
KILLINGER						Patrick	67	IRE	7037		1903
John Andrew	71	GER	4379		1901	**KIM**					
KILLION						Ah	<1	SF	574		1871
Bridget	59	IRE	6703		1902	Ah	22	CHN	2753a		1872
Hanora				Jun	1899	Ho	19	CHN	1913a		1872
Michael F.	<1	SF	9523		1868	John C.	51	SWT	2198		1902
KILLIVAN						Lim	37	CHN	K80		1887
Rudolph	33	PRU	2757a		1872	Lun Boing	19	KOR	6994		1904
KILLOUGH						Nora May	<1	SF	2513		1873
Rollie B. (soldier)			2166		1901	Zo	27	CHN	894a		1871
KILLPACK						Zu				Oct	1899
Ellen	26	NY	K39		1884	**KIMANS**					
Jane Ann	28	WAL	4344		1901	Edward H. (soldier)			6835		1900
KILLPATRICK						**KIMBALL**					
Andrew				May	1899	Charles Henry	35	IN	7530		1901
William	32	IRL	400a		1871	Charles Stokes	70	NJ	7402		1903
						Ezra D.	30	MA	1099		1869

Key: a = 1st part of year; b = 2nd part of year;
c = death certificate copy; c/o = child of

NAME	AGE OR YOB.	BIRTH PLACE	CERT. NO	ID	DEATH YEAR
Fred L.	35	SF	4611		1901
Helen F.	64	IL	3011		1903
Isabella	68	NY	2562		1895
Jennie/Charles, c/o	<1	SF	3537		1896
Kimball R.	<1	SF	120		1865
Lillian				Mar	1900
Maria M.	85	MEX	2287		1902
Mary B.	65	ME	651		1901
Moses Coombs	74	ME	2735		1903
Phineas B.	<1	SF	4859		1867
KIMBATT					
Lillian				Mar	1900
KIMBLE					
Alonzo C.				May	1899
Anna Barbara	43	OH	5850		1904
Chas.	<1	CA	K101		1889
Katie	47	NY	2200		1894
KIMI					
Imai	1885	JPN	84c		1904
KIMMEL					
Catharine	61	GER	1799b		1872
KIMMENS					
Joseph	45	NY	2870		1873
KIMON					
Cathrine	40	PE	3671		1870
KIMPTON					
Clarence	1892	UT	2797c		1904
KIMURA					
Frank Kinzaburo	25	JPN	186		1901
Shioya	37	JPN	5374		1904
Toyoda/Kita, c/o		SF	4325		1902
Toyota/Kita, c/o	1	SF	4343		1903
Ushich	1858	JPN	971c		1904

NAME	AGE OR YOB.	BIRTH PLACE	CERT. NO	ID	DEATH YEAR
KIN					
___		SF	1288		1869
Ah	21	CHN	1771		1866
Gun				Jun	1899
Lin Lip	49	CHN	4589		1867
Two	21	CHN	1319		1869
Zenkei	1879	KOR	1096c		1904
KINAMOTO					
Fromasa	48	JPN	4410a		1895
KINCADE					
Thomas (soldier)	23	WV	3788		1900
KINCAID					
Charley (soldier)			5799		1904
Earle W.	20	SF	790		1900
Elizabeth	2	SCT	1231		1869
William				Aug	1899
KINCAIDE					
Mary E.	4	HI	1224		1869
KINCER					
Harvey	50	KY	2890		1900
KINCHELOE					
Julius	30	VA	1043		1868
KIND					
Henry (soldier)			4709		1901
Richard C. T.	65	GER	6256		1896
KINDANE					
Elizabeth	55	MI	1173		1894
KINDBERG					
Augustus	33	SWE	856		1870
KINDBLED					
F./G., c/o				Oct	1898
KINDELON					
Edward F.				Aug	1899

Key: a = 1st part of year; b = 2nd part of year;
c = death certificate copy; c/o = child of

NAME	AGE OR YOB.	BIRTH PLACE	CERT. NO	ID	DEATH YEAR	NAME	AGE OR YOB.	BIRTH PLACE	CERT. NO	ID	DEATH YEAR
KINDER						Burk				Dec	1899
Cecelia C.	58	GER	4701		1896	Casia				May	1899
John Charles	62	GER	6330		1900	Catherine	3	SF	394		1865
						Catherine				Oct	1899
KINDLEBERGER						Catherine Anna	5	SF	2941		1866
Charles J.	10	OH	2232a		1872	Charles A. E. (soldier)	42	MD	6437	Feb	1901
KINDRED						Charles B. (marine)			8426		1901
Ellis (soldier)			1468		1901	Charles E. (soldier)			7446		1904
KINDU						Chas. (soldier)			7226		1900
Ernst	38	GER	3281		1894	Chas. C.	1	CA	1429		1894
KINE						Chen	38	CHN	9456		1868
Pon, c/o		SF	2824a		1872	Chen Ah	41	CHN	K72		1886
KINEMANN						Chew	42	CHN	5972a		1895
Sophia	1	SF	1368		1869	Choy	25	CHN	3037a		1872
KINEMIN						Christopher	26	SCT	784		1870
Maria L.	4	SF	207		1870	Chung	54	CHN	6473		1902
						Daniel/Sarah, c/o		SF	7278		1903
KINEY						Dolores	<1	SF	6072		1904
Henry	42	IRE	403		1865	Doney				Mar	1900
KING						Dwight C.	71	MA	1738b		1895
——	4	SF	1017		1868	Effidera	4	SF	1021		1868
Addie E.	24	SF	180		1900	Effie B.	20	IL	701		1894
Adella	45	PA	4151a		1895	Eliza	58	SCT	5382		1902
Agnes	18	MA	2583		1895	Elizabeth A.	4	SF	6991		1868
Agnes	77	NB	1407		1900	Ella J.	37	CA	5146		1901
Ah	38	CHN	3160		1870	Ella L.	1	SF	7152		1868
Ah		SF	2091		1870	Fannie M.	23	NY	2045a		1872
Ah	27	CHN	K44		1885	Frank	35	ENG	1375		1869
Ah	44	CHN	4576		1867	Frank E.				Mar	1900
Alicia A.	16	SF	6537a		1895	Frank J.	43	CA	6614		1904
Ann	80	IRL	2566		1894	Genevieve	<1	SF	5397		1896
Annie Elizabeth	69	RI	1263		1902	George	36	MO	1136a		1871
Annie Lawrence	10	SCT	5422		1902	George	34	MA	1049		1868
Annie M.				Oct	1899	George	28	SF	3865		1896
Arthur John	<1	CA	2031b		1895	George L.	23	ENG	577		1866
Bartholomew	56	IRE	7501		1902	George R.	65	PA	6524		1904

Key: a = 1st part of year; b = 2nd part of year; c = death certificate copy; c/o = child of

NAME	AGE OR YOB.	BIRTH PLACE	CERT. NO	ID	DEATH YEAR	NAME	AGE OR YOB.	BIRTH PLACE	CERT. NO	ID	DEATH YEAR
George T., c/o (twins)		SF	956		1866	Julia	1	SF	8607		1904
George Wiliam	52	KY	5702		1896	Julia				Feb	1900
Geraldine	<1	SF	5485		1896	Lee	42	CHN	762a		1871
Hanorah	60	IRE	5982		1903	Leona	<1	CA	2119		1902
Henry				May	1899	Leroy J.	<1	SF	3686		1902
Henry L.				Jan	1899	Lillie	<1	SF	1270		1869
Hugh	69	IRE	1084		1869	Loriston J.	52	NY	670		1901
Jacob A.	50	OH	5568		1867	Louis	<1	SF	1392		1869
James	<1	SF	1238b		1895	Louis Joseph				Feb	1900
James	44	IRL	2742		1895	Luke	66	IRL	2565		1894
James	87	VA	6235		1900	Lyda	18	SF	5991		1902
James G./Carrie J., c/o	<1	SF	4559		1903	Lyda/James, c/o	<1	SF	5990		1902
James J.	1836	ENG	2338c		1904	Mamie	12	CA	K66		1886
James T.	27	MO	8583		1904	Manuel J.	1	SF	3372		1903
Jeremiah	68	NY	4684		1904	Margaret	55	IRE	1749		1902
Jessie				Jul	1898	Margaret Tanered	65	IRL	2200b		1895
Joesph	<1	SF	2240		1873	Marguerite	23	NY	4964		1902
Johanna	60	IRE	6973		1903	Maria	47	IRE	2502		1903
John	60	CHN	1793a		1872	Mark	abt		8166		1901
John	<1	SF	189b		1872	Martha	34	CA	4161		1903
John	21	ENG	1110b		1895	Martin	60	ITA	4586b		1870
John				Mar	1899	Martin/Delia, c/o	1904	SF	569		1904
John				Mar	1899	Mary	<1	SF	4777		1867
John Samuel	1856	MA	2312c		1904	Mary Alice	6	SF	7273		1868
John W.	50		6945		1903	Mary Elizabeth	<1	SF	1932b		1872
John Walter	4	SF	6386		1900	Mary Josephine	<1	SF	3279		1873
John/Mary, c/o		SF	2895		1902	Matilda	1868	SF	1143c		1904
Joseph			K65		1886	Matilda S.				May	1899
Joseph	27	POR	2950		1866	Maud	5	SF	9677		1868
Joseph	65	IRE	2308		1903	Moon	62	CHN	4016a		1895
Joseph Francis	<1	SF	1187		1901	O. Key	31	WV	8330		1903
Josephine	53	CAN	6510		1903	Patrick	36	IRL	1432b		1871
Josephine	<1	SF	2318		1900	Patrick	54	IRL	1319		1894
Josie E.	64	NY	6955		1904	Patrick				May	1899
Juan	19	CA	9369		1868	Patrick Edward	32	MA	1399		1869
Julia	46	IRL	K29		1884	Paul	28	NY	6224		1900

NAME	AGE OR YOB.	BIRTH PLACE	CERT. NO	ID	DEATH YEAR
Philip				Oct	1898
Qui	3	SF	299		1865
Quon	42	CHN	1620b		1871
Rhoda J.	53	NY	966b		1872
Richard	75	NS	3357		1894
Richard	48	NY	5349		1904
Robert W.	62	ENG	4788		1896
Rose	24	CA	2643		1903
Ruth	32	IL	8684		1903
Sarah	81	PRU	4284a		1895
Sophia F.	<1	SF	3999		1870
Stewart (soldier)			368		1900
T. T.	50	PA	K25		1883
Theresa	44	MA	2031		1903
Thomas	<1	SF	477a		1871
Thomas	30	IRE	4617		1867
Thomas	45	USA	7887		1903
Thomas	64	IRL	5791	Jan	1901
Thomas	3	SF	1408		1869
Thomas	65	IRL	3209		1894
Thomas	74	ENG	6429		1903
Thomas	76	MA	6291a		1895
Thomas Francis				Oct	1899
Thomas Mercer	55	IRL	1418b		1872
Toie	43	CHN	2819a		1872
Victor Owyang	8	SF	6904		1902
Wee	44	CHN	347a		1871
William				Nov	1898
William	58	ENG	4104		1903
William D.				Mar	1899
William E. (soldier)			2080		1901
William F.	1876	CA	85c		1904
William G.	1	SF	730		1903
William Henry	4	SF	1435		1869
William R.	<1	SF	2063		1866
William R.	68	VT	7843		1901

NAME	AGE OR YOB.	BIRTH PLACE	CERT. NO	ID	DEATH YEAR
William W.				Jul	1898
Wm F.	24	DC	2745a		1872
Wm. J.	10	SF	3378		1894
Wm. V.	30	SF	284b		1895
Wong Loy	35	CHN	6050a		1895
KINGBY					
Alice	1	SF	1461		1903
John	1	SF	1506		1903
KINGERY					
William H. (soldier)			7325		1901
KINGJOHN					
Wibe Claude	35	SWE	19b		1871
KINGON					
Andrew/Lizzie, c/o				Feb	1900
KINGSBURG					
Geo. F.	31	NH	2884		1866
KINGSBURY					
Albert	37	MA	1349		1866
Chester				Oct	1899
Eleanor	26	SF	8353		1901
George W.	29	MA	3712		1867
Helen S.	70	NY	2470		1900
Jas. T.	60	OH	K26		1883
Kate	34	CA	1426		1900
Lola	2	SF	4863		1867
Mary	74	IRE	7161		1902
Thos. P.	70	DC	2871		1894
Willard/Clara, c/o	<1	SF	3915		1901
Wm. de L./Clara J., c/o	1	CA	3730		1903
KINGSHOTT					
Matilda	58	ENG	5189a		1896
KINGSLEY					
Alfred M.				Nov	1899
Charles H.	43	ENG	2293		1901

Key: a = 1st part of year; b = 2nd part of year;
c = death certificate copy; c/o = child of

NAME	AGE OR YOB.	BIRTH PLACE	CERT. NO	ID	DEATH YEAR	NAME	AGE OR YOB.	BIRTH PLACE	CERT. NO	ID	DEATH YEAR
Edward E.	1	SF	659		1870	**KINNEAR**					
Elisha	50	MA	436b		1872	Gracie				Oct	1898
Elizabeth	32	CA	3764		1902	John Sidney	50	NS	3433	Nov	1901
James Cook				Mar	1899	**KINNEARS**					
John L.	33	ME	1178		1869	Hugh	59	IRL	6462		1896
Nellie A.	2	SF	2438		1866	**KINNEBLOCK**					
Peter	64	NJ	5878	Jan	1901	Frederick	2	CA	75		1865
S. W.		SF	2187a		1872	William L.	7	CA	72		1865
William J.	42	CA	8320		1900	**KINNERSON**					
William M.	62	PA	3244		1903	Homer E.	35	SF	3633		1896
KINGSTON						**KINNEY**					
Anna Thresa	1	SF	1418		1869	Elizabeth	1834	IRE	1545c		1904
Georgie				Apr	1899	George	36	NY	7675		1901
Gerome F.	<1	SF	6244		1867	George C.	21	IN	661		1901
James E.	1872	SF	2538c		1904	I., c/o	<1	SF	1883a		1872
John				Aug	1899	John	7	SF	1849		1870
Leo				Jan	1899	Joseph P.	31	MA	6448a		1895
Margaret/William, c/o		SF	8446		1901	Katherine	<1	SF	841a		1871
Mary A.	38	MA	2210		1901	**KINON**					
Samuel Joseph	1866	SF	353c		1904	Maru	43	IRE	184		1865
KINKEAD						**KINOSHITA**					
William				May	1899	Eiji	23	JPN	575		1902
KINKELING						Shataro	25	JPN	1233		1901
Bertha A./Charles, c/o	<1	SF	3405		1901	**KINQUINST**					
KINKIVONI						Pierre J.	65	BEL	1729		1900
Man				Jan	1899	**KINSELL**					
KINKLE						Harry/Eliza Jane, c/o		SF	2205		1900
Guy				Mar	1899	William J. (soldier)			7786		1901
KINLLEYN						**KINSELLA**					
Alice	<1		8232		1868	Catherine	18	SF	8632		1904
KINNARY						John	62	IRL	6437		1900
John	45	IRL	K60		1886	Patrick	85	IRL	8405		1901
KINNE						William H.	36	MA	5208a		1896
Robert J.	17	SF	5136a		1895						

Key: a = 1st part of year; b = 2nd part of year;
c = death certificate copy; c/o = child of

NAME	AGE OR YOB.	BIRTH PLACE	CERT. NO	ID	DEATH YEAR	NAME	AGE OR YOB.	BIRTH PLACE	CERT. NO	ID	DEATH YEAR
KINSEY						**KIRAKICHI**					
Easter	70	IRL	531		1870	Hirano	25	JPN	6282		1900
Isabella R.	68	IL	7839		1903	**KIRBY**					
KINSLEY						Beatrice				Jul	1899
Arthur J.	19	CO	4582		1903	Charles	45	IRL	1103		1900
KINSLOW						Daniel				Dec	1898
Thomas (soldier)	30	KY	1073		1902	Ed/Annie, Mrs., c/o		SF	5097		1901
KINSMAN						Edward H.	5	SF	2418		1873
Eugenia R.	56	IL	6366		1900	Joseph	37	ENG	1205		1869
Laura	6	SF	1290		1869	Joseph Yorke	<1	CA	7295		1904
Mary Sophia	31	CT	1309b		1872	Maria	25	IRL	2240		1894
KINSON						Ora Bruce	42	CA	2276b		1895
George W.	37	MA	536b		1872	Patrick E. , c/o				Nov	1899
KINSPEL						Susan Mary	80	IRL	8699		1901
Bertha	1874	GER	1027c		1904	Thomas		SF	2061		1870
KINTZELE						Thomas	<1	SF	5322		1867
Theodore	70	GER	6197		1900	Thomas	31	IRL	1723b		1895
KINUCAN						Thomas	26	NY	1084		1869
Susan	<1	SF	190b		1872	Thomas J.	52	ENG	2504		1902
KINZER						Walter M.	31	NE	765		1894
H. G.	22	MO	57b		1872	William P.	43	IRE	5329		1904
KIOJAN						William Wayt	1881	VA	1906c		1904
Frederick	33		1957b		1872	**KIRCH**					
KIP						John	47	GER	K70		1886
Lee Hi	1849	CHN	1499c		1904	**KIRCHER**					
William Ingraham	35	SF	2270		1902	Anna Maria	3	SF	1613		1901
KIPHEN						**KIRCHHOFF**					
Hans	<1	SF	3537a		1895	Theodor				Mar	1899
KIPP						**KIRCHMER**					
Jacob	34	GER	1943		1866	George F.	<1	SF	847		1902
Matthew R.	44	SF	1608		1894	**KIRCHNER**					
KIPPS						Adolph Frederick J.	40	GER	5749		1896
						Charles R./Dora, c/o		SF	7190		1902
Alfred K.	68	ENG	3202		1902	Henry G. J.				Dec	1899

Key: a = 1st part of year; b = 2nd part of year;
c = death certificate copy; c/o = child of

NAME	AGE OR YOB.	BIRTH PLACE	CERT. NO	ID	DEATH YEAR
Henry Gustave	29	SF	2309		1903
Kenneth Keith	4	SF	2327		1902
Odilia		FRA	2006		1870
Rosalie D.	<1	SF	2909		1900
KIRCHUER					
Fredericka	56	GER	1298b		1872
KIRK					
Agnes	82	SCT	1583		1866
Charles	<1	SF	38		1865
Edward	42	MA	177		1870
Ellen	70	IRE	979		1866
Emily	73	MO	3611		1903
George Ross	7	CA	510		1866
Isabella Jane	64	NY	2916		1902
Joseph				Oct	1898
Marion	71	CAN	971		1900
Michael	76	IRE	8875		1903
Patrick Alfred	66	ENG	552b		1895
Rosanna	5	SF	1423		1902
Terese Graffam				Oct	1899
William C. (soldier)	33	TN	6681	Feb	1901
William Easton				Jan	1899
KIRKBRIDE					
Otto F.	24	OH	6482		1902
KIRKENDALL					
James				May	1899
Mary Ann				Feb	1899
KIRKETERP					
Wm. Christian	38	SF	3737		1902
KIRKINDALL					
James				Jul	1899
KIRKLAND					
Emma H.	<1	SF	1509		1866
Henry (soldier)			9358		1901

NAME	AGE OR YOB.	BIRTH PLACE	CERT. NO	ID	DEATH YEAR
Robert McGin	1824	MO	898c		1904
KIRKLIN					
John	41	WI	7620		1904
KIRKNESS					
Rupert	<1	CAN	3489b		1870
KIRKPATRICK					
Frank E. Pierson	41	MA	2938	Oct	1901
James	75	ENG	2382		1900
John		SF	1264		1866
John	44	IRE	1241		1869
Katherine	50	IRL	7206		1900
Mary	35	SCT	3949		1867
Roger	1904	CA	86c		1904
KIRKWOOD					
William J.	44	USA	5207		1901
KIRLIN					
Rebecca				Jan	1899
KIRMAN					
Richard	70	ENG	6234		1896
KIRMANE					
John				Dec	1898
KIRNAN					
Bridget	30	IRL	316b		1871
KIRRANE					
Michael	27	IRL	6540		1896
KIRSCH					
Elizabeth	55	GER	2171		1903
KIRSCHBERG					
Sigmund/Aurelia, c/o	1	SF	8730		1904
William	78	GER	235		1900
KIRSCHBRAUM					
Ethel	15	CA	6215		1902

Key: a = 1st part of year; b = 2nd part of year;
c = death certificate copy; c/o = child of

NAME	AGE OR YOB.	BIRTH PLACE	CERT. NO	ID	DEATH YEAR	NAME	AGE OR YOB.	BIRTH PLACE	CERT. NO	ID	DEATH YEAR
KIRSCHNER						KISSINGER					
Heinan	74	GER	5032a		1896	Joseph (soldier)			7228		1900
KIRVIN						KISSLING					
Mary	<1	SF	433b		1872	Adolphe L.	33	SWT	4211b		1870
KIRWAN						KISSON					
James	62	IRE	3307		1903	Mary Ann	<1	NY	404		1865
John Francis	11	CT	1694b		1871	KISTEUMACHER					
KIRWEN						Julius	27	GER	3470		1900
Jane	72	ENG	2667		1902	KISZLER					
KIRWIN						Anna M.	47	GER	2692a		1872
Andrew	48	IRL	2650		1900	Annie	41	SF	5216		1904
James	37	IRL	1552		1870	Henry				Jul	1899
Mary Josephine	1	SF	2293a		1872	KIT					
Patrick	62	IRL	6120		1900	Lee Ah	26	CHN	2487a		1872
Thomas	28	IRL	1302		1870	KITADANI					
KISHI						F.	32	JPN	2275b		1895
Tome	27	JPN	2271		1902	KITCHEN					
KISHIMOTO						Chauncy A. (soldier)			2081		1901
Yoshio	<1	SF	5423		1902	Dora				Oct	1899
KISING						Geo. (soldier)			9359		1901
Susan L.	19	MA	7823		1868	George Albert	33	CAN	1340b		1895
KISKADDEN						Zades (soldier)			6946		1900
Jas. H.	60	MA	K27		1883	KITT					
KISKEY						Ye Bou	25	CHN	859b		1871
Martin	50	FIN	K81		1887	KITTERMAN					
KISPERT						Hannah	44	IRL	8724		1900
Christopher	38	BAV	7590		1868	KITTLE					
KISSELER						Nicholas Gosman	35	SF	3482		1902
Francis H.				Mar	1900	Richard			1309		1903
KISSELL						KITTLEBECKER					
Violet Annie	1903	SF	490c		1904	Henry	64	PRU	1109		1870
KISSICK						KITTLER					
Edwyne R.				Oct	1899	Franke	5	SF	3916	Dec	1901

Key: a = 1st part of year; b = 2nd part of year;
c = death certificate copy; c/o = child of

NAME	AGE OR YOB.	BIRTH PLACE	CERT. NO	ID	DEATH YEAR
Mary E.	<1	SF	6235		1896
Roman	44	GER	4965		1902
William	18	SF	6833		1903
William	50	GER	3444		1900
KITTO					
John	44	ENG	2986		1900
KITTREDGE					
A.G./Grace L., c/o	<1	SF	6704		1902
Harriet W.	71	MA	1357b		1871
Isabelle Holmes	1831	MA	679c		1904
KITTRIDGE					
Isabella G.	3	SF	3228		1866
Lucy A.	<1	SF	701		1866
KITTTLAR					
Teresa					Feb 1900
KITZ					
Gertrude	84	GER	8331		1903
KITZENBERGER					
August	32	GER	1276		1869
KIVI					
Alma	16	SF	2770		1900
KIYAMA					
Sakumatsu	23	JPN	1972		1903
KIZZLER					
Jacob Conrad	12	PER	2043a		1872
KLAHN					
Herman					Jun 1899
KLAIBER					
Rosina					Dec 1898
KLAINCLAUS					
Edward	<1	SF	2399		1866
KLAMEN					
Adam					Dec 1899

NAME	AGE OR YOB.	BIRTH PLACE	CERT. NO	ID	DEATH YEAR
KLANER					
Anna	55	GER	6864		1895
KLANGER					
August	67	GER	517		1903
KLAPPERICH					
Louis Henry	7	SF	1515b		1871
KLAPPROTT					
Carrie	43	IA	2136		1902
KLARE					
Dorothea	67	GER	4454		1902
KLASS					
Philip	46	GER	6807		1904
KLATTER					
Robert	40	HOL	4847		1902
KLAUENBERG					
Herman	36	GER	6525		1904
KLAUSEN					
Ernest	24	GER	5562a		1895
KLAUSS					
——	40		7633		1902
KLEBSCH					
Nellie	29	NV	5866a		1895
KLECHNER					
Philip					Feb 1900
KLEE					
John W.	1	SF	8184		1900
KLEEBAUER					
Frederick C.	63	GER	2706		1902
Henry/Minnie, c/o	<1	SF	453		1902
KLEEBAUGH					
Lorenzo Fletes					Jul 1899
KLEECK					
Robert Van	1904	CA	2350c		1904

Key: a = 1st part of year; b = 2nd part of year;
c = death certificate copy; c/o = child of

NAME	AGE OR YOB.	BIRTH PLACE	CERT. NO	ID	DEATH YEAR	NAME	AGE OR YOB.	BIRTH PLACE	CERT. NO	ID	DEATH YEAR
KLEHM						**KLEINE**					
Elsie	5	SF	8348		1900	Frederick H.				Jun	1899
KLEIBER						**KLEINER**					
Emma	1	SF	1872		1901	Emma	<1	SF	1273		1869
Paul/Sophie, c/o				Jan	1899	**KLEINHANS**					
KLEIBRINK						John	67	NJ	7571		1901
Conrad	40	PRU	36		1870	**KLEINMANN**					
KLEIN						Joseph	<1	SF	6939	Feb	1901
——			1870		1870	Maria	39	RUS	3976		1900
Adolph Diedrich	64	GER	3888a		1895	**KLEIS**					
Anne Coxon	82	ENG	6430		1903	Sarah A.	1852	WI	2798c		1904
Anton	42	GER	8024		1900	**KLEIST**					
Benjamin	48	DE	1185		1869	Anna	37	GER	3749		1903
Charles	43	ENG	6210		1903	C. L.	30	GER	K71		1886
Dorothy F.				Mar	1899	**KLEMEN**					
Emil	9	LA	1216		1869	Mary	<1	SF	5382		1896
Emilie C.	<1	SF	7757		1868	**KLEMM**					
Frederick	45	GER	1407		1869	Mary	45	GER	501		1870
H.	32	GER	741a		1871	**KLEMSCHMIDT**					
Herman Hugo	27	GER	K46		1885	Albert (soldier)			7131		1900
J./P., c/o	<1	SF	3249		1894	**KLENCK**					
Jacob	64	GER	2531		1902	Margaret	65	IRE	8792		1903
Jacob				Dec	1898	**KLENTZER**					
Jacob				Feb	1899	Herman	73	GER	7986		1900
Jacob (soldier)			7326		1901	**KLENZ**					
Knecht Gustav	52	GER	3582a		1895	Fred Paul				Jan	1899
Mark	66	FRA	1173		1900	**KLERCK**					
Mary E	29	IN	7046		1904	Claus	42	GER	2770a		1872
R./T., c/o				Jun	1899	**KLESOW**					
Theodore				Jan	1899	Frank	7	CA	K64		1886
KLEINBERG						**KLEVESAHL**					
Flx	35		8674		1901	Sophie	60	GER	6488		1903
KLEINCLAUS											
Barbara	86	FRA	3657a		1895						

Key: a = 1st part of year; b = 2nd part of year; c = death certificate copy; c/o = child of

NAME	AGE OR YOB.	BIRTH PLACE	CERT. NO	ID	DEATH YEAR	NAME	AGE OR YOB.	BIRTH PLACE	CERT. NO	ID	DEATH YEAR
KLEVISAHTE						Regina	64	GER	8828		1900
Henry	<1	SF	1276		1869	William	7	SF	108a		1871
KLEWISCH						KLINESCHMIDT					
A. M., Mrs.				Dec	1898	Wilhelmina	1833	GER	3402c		1904
KLICK						KLING					
Paul W.				Mar	1900	Clarence B.	1879	MO	3270c		1904
						Emily C.	73	SWE	4337a		1895
KLIDER						Freddie	1	SF	123		1902
A. F.			7171		1901	George (soldier)			2453		1900
KLIEHN						Hans Lauritzen	1863	GER	728c		1904
Joseph	26	PRU	7355		1868	J./C., c/o		SF	1099		1894
KLIEN						KLINGBERG					
Victor	52	FRA	2759a		1872	Thomas	57	SWE	1839		1902
KLINDT						KLINGE					
Henry	69	GER	6350		1900	Regina	74	BAV	543		1903
Theresa K.	32	DEN	4945		1904	Wm	61	GER	7902		1900
KLINE						KLINGELHOFER					
Adolph M.	59	AUT	3717		1896	Mamie C.	21	CA	8949		1903
Albert A. S.	<1	SF	8499		1903	KLINGENSMITH					
Bertha		SF	4292b		1870	Charles				Jul	1899
Carrie	37	NY	2738		1902						
Catharine	48	PA	1399		1869	KLINGER					
Elza (soldier)			5416	Jan	1901	Augustus J.				Feb	1900
F/A., c/o				Jun	1899	KLINGFELT					
Francis				Dec	1899	Alfred	36	SWE	6563a		1895
Harry	<1	SF	4791		1903	KLINGLER					
Irwin D.	66	PA	1377		1900	Julia				Jan	1899
James W.				Feb	1900	Marie Louisa				Jul	1898
John Doe	60		3995		1902	KLINGMANN					
Katie	1	SF	4033b		1870	George	67	GER	2314b		1895
Lewis (soldier)			7803		1902	KLINGNER					
Louis	70	BAV	3581a		1895	Margaret				Dec	1898
Mae	28	NV	5704		1896						
Mary	37	AUS	4792		1903	KLINGSHUME					
Michael				Dec	1898	Peter J.	1866	SWE	776c		1904

NAME	AGE OR YOB.	BIRTH PLACE	CERT. NO	ID	DEATH YEAR	NAME	AGE OR YOB.	BIRTH PLACE	CERT. NO	ID	DEATH YEAR
KLINHAMMER						**KLOPPENBURG**					
Harry	31	GER	1968b		1895	Adaline Dougall	33	SF	8043		1901
KLINK						Dora	67	GER	5709		1904
Nathaniel B.	72	NY	6408a		1895	Jno. Leo	<1	SF	452b		1895
KLINKE						**KLOPPENBURZ**					
Frederick (soldier)			1032		1900	Catherine	74	GER	7269		1901
KLINKER						**KLOPPER**					
Anna M. E.	40	ENG	7920		1904	John				May	1899
KLINTZING						**KLOPSTOCK`**					
Peter	27	GER	1007		1868	Lion	<1	SF	2687a		1872
KLIPPEL						**KLOS**					
Valentine				Nov	1898	William/Alice, c/o		SF	543		1902
KLIPSTEIN						**KLOSE**					
Robert E. F.	1869	IA	1907c		1904	Ida	27	GER	6973		1904
William E. E.	29	IA	6290		1904	**KLOSS**					
KLIVESAHL						John	52	GER	K37		1884
Ernst William	74	GER	518		1903	John (twin ?), c/o				Aug	1898
KLOADT						John (twin ?), c/o				Aug	1898
Hermann				Dec	1899	Mary				Jul	1898
KLOCK						**KLOTZ**					
George W.				Jun	1899	Charles August	66	GER	7668		1903
KLOCKENBAUM						Francisco				Aug	1898
Joseph	37	GER	2788		1901	Jacob	50	GER	6956		1904
KLOCKENKEMPER						John Yost	53	MD	8539		1903
Henry J. (soldier)			949		1901	**KLUBER**					
KLOMAN						Joseph	3	SF	3162	Nov	1901
Edward A.			1310		1903	**KLUETSCH**					
KLOOS						Christian	50	GER	5727		1903
Jacob	7	SF	3481a		1872	**KLUGE**					
KLOPENSTINE						Emil G.	60	RUS	3996		1903
Joseph	76	OH	3917	Dec	1901	**KLUMPKE**					
KLOPF						Bernardina	67	GER	2987		1902
Mary	24	GER	5427		1896	Geo Frederick	<1	SF	1258		1869

NAME	AGE OR YOB.	BIRTH PLACE	CERT. NO	ID	DEATH YEAR
KLUMPP					
Fredrick	<1	SF	8396		1868
KLUN					
Max	20	GER	5919		1902
KLUNDGIN					
Peter	64	HOL	4869a		1895
KLUNDGREN					
Jennie	62	FRA	4991		1901
KLUSMANN					
Charles E.	33	GER	3876		1902
KLUTE					
Frederika	45	GER	1188		1901
KLUTO					
Adelheid	<1	SF	143b		1895
KNABE					
Peter	53	GER	2846		1895
KNACK					
Charles John	28	SF	5614		1896
John	<1	SF	1281		1869
KNACKSTEDT					
Bertha	6	SF	7517		1868
Minna	<1	SF	3604		1867
KNAGGS					
John	90	IRL	8197		1900
KNAKE					
Wilhelm	33	GER	4659a		1895
KNAPP					
——		SF	1371		1869
Alrina S.	79	ME	1647		1894
Aurelia Ann	1828	NY	1638c		1904
Baby	<1	SF	890		1894
Charles A.	32	NY	211a		1871
Charles S.	23	MI	2959		1903

NAME	AGE OR YOB.	BIRTH PLACE	CERT. NO	ID	DEATH YEAR
Elijah	74	NH	6729	Feb	1901
Ernest				Mar	1900
Frederick	35	GER	K78		1887
George R.	30	MO	8640		1900
James Lester	1	SF	1426		1901
Jesse C.	42	CA	2933		1900
Leah	40	NY	1254a		1871
Mary	74	BAV	6109		1903
Mary Esther	1	SF	3318		1902
Oliver S.	72	VT	6579	Feb	1901
Richard C.	<1	OR	7359		1868
Stephen Horton	73	NY	5835		1896
Wellington A.	87	NY	8633		1904
KNARSTON					
Alice L.	1870	SF	3403c		1904
John H.	39	ENG	2908		1895
KNAUER					
Ferdinand	73	GER	4805		1903
KNAUFF					
Oscar	1	CA	2051		1903
Rudolph/Josephine, c/o	<1	SF	5094		1902
KNAUL					
Katie	24	SF	4848		1902
KNEASS					
Mary				Aug	1898
KNEBEL					
Thomas (soldier)			9569		1901
KNEE					
Daniel Joseph	1904	SF	601c		1904
Tuck	42	CHN	1508b		1872
KNEISCH					
Jacob	59	GER	1646		1901
KNELEY					
James	<1	SF	8778		1868

Key: a = 1st part of year; b = 2nd part of year;
c = death certificate copy; c/o = child of

NAME	AGE OR YOB.	BIRTH PLACE	CERT. NO	ID	DEATH YEAR
KNELL					
Alphon	45	WI	1192b		1895
Elizabeth	1880	OH	3178c		1904
H./D., c/o	<1	SF	4098		1895
Herbert	1904	SF	2245c		1904
Jacob	61	GER	962		1900
Paulina	11	SF	179a		1871
KNIBB					
Henry	61	ENG	2985c		1904
Wilhelmina	40	GER	8350		1868
KNICK					
George W.	75	OH	3596		1900
KNICKMEYER					
Henry	26	GER	2703		1900
KNIE					
Ah	24	CHN	1906a		1872
KNIEF					
Elizabeth	83	GER	4345		1901
Henry				Oct	1899
KNIERR					
Byron Francis	10	SF	765		1903
KNIFRE					
Robert James	1	SF	857a		1871
KNIGHT					
——		SF	654		1870
——	<1	SF	1195		1869
Anna Louisa	1	SF	6365		1867
Annie	54	ENG	1606		1894
Beatrice	31	NY	276b		1871
Charles T. S.	1863	CA	2986c		1904
Daniel	39	VT	4066b		1870
David (soldier)			8875		1900
E. H.	71	VT	1665		1902
Earl				Mar	1899
Eliza	23	NY	1164		1870
Elizabeth	66	MD	4611a		1895
Ephraim C.	25	MN	1981b		1895
Ethan	33	CA	4998		1903
Ethes	66	MO	204		1900
Frank	44	NH	2405		1894
George	50	ME	102b		1872
George	1	SF	1108		1869
George E.	23	NV	3324		1900
George W.	40	ME	6344		1867
Hiram D.	53	MD	4326		1902
James H.				Feb	1900
Laura	<1	SF	1389		1869
Morton W. (soldier)			296		1903
Patrick	33	IRL	6580	Feb	1901
Samuel	45	CT	1232		1866
Silas P. Jr.	25	MA	172b		1871
Thomas	82	VT	8661		1903
Thomas C.				Feb	1899
Thomas W. D.	26	RI	9528		1868
Vollie (soldier)			7804		1902
William A.				Jun	1899
KNIGSLEY					
May				Aug	1898
KNIL					
Louis	60	GER	8579		1900
KNILL					
Ernst G. N.	47	DEN	1139b		1895
KNIN					
Emilie				Jan	1899
KNIPE					
Frederick Augustus	1833	MA	1006c		1904
KNIPPEN					
Addison E. (soldier)			2538		1900

Key: a = 1st part of year; b = 2nd part of year;
c = death certificate copy; c/o = child of

NAME	AGE OR YOB.	BIRTH PLACE	CERT. NO	ID	DEATH YEAR	NAME	AGE OR YOB.	BIRTH PLACE	CERT. NO	ID	DEATH YEAR
KNITSCH						**KNOPH**					
Henry	76	GER	1718		1903	Marvin E.	41	IL	6022a		1895
KNITTER						**KNOPP**					
John J. (soldier)			9570		1901	Russell (soldier)			1401		1900
KNITTLE						**KNOPPEL**					
Albert (soldier)			7578		1900	Charles William	3	SF	544		1902
KNITZEN						**KNORP**					
James Thos.	1	SF	2107		1873	John				Jul	1899
KNOBLAU						Kate	<1	SF	3767		1870
Ellena C.	1	SF	384		1903	**KNORR**					
KNOBLOCH						John	57	GER	2096a		1872
Barbara Ruth	<1	SF	3032		1902	**KNOTT**					
Gretchen	10	CA	6283Feb		1901	Jessie Craib	71	SCT	2760		1902
Jacob	68	GER	5810		1896	John	59	NY	6239		1903
KNOBLOCK						Maggie E.	68		5513		1904
Jacob	45	PA	8118		1903	**KNOUSE**					
KNODRE						Frank				Jan	1899
Henry				Oct	1898	**KNOW**					
KNOECHEL						Emma	64	PA	4607		1904
Chas. F.	63	GER	8329		1900	**KNOWER**					
KNOEDLER						Leoni M.	39	NY	6295		1902
Alexander				Dec	1898	**KNOWES**					
Marguerite	38	SCT	4806		1903	Audley R.	<1	SF	2127		1866
KNOLL						**KNOWLAND**					
Charles G.	62	GER	118		1870	Hollis Russell	3	SF	1372		1869
KNOP						Thomas				Jan	1899
August	58	GER	6282Feb		1901	**KNOWLES**					
Elfert	64	GER	5840		1902	Barton H.	40	ME	4441		1896
Franklin August				Jul	1898	Chas. P.	29	RI	K98		1889
Henry	1830	GER	470c		1904	Harriet	<1	SF	3078		1902
KNOPF						Lulu	32	CA	8567		1903
Lizzie	1881	SF	2746c		1904	Lyman P.	1	SF	770b		1871
						Mary A.	62	NY	4232a		1895
						Mary Anne	31	CA	5721		1896

Key: a = 1st part of year; b = 2nd part of year;
c = death certificate copy; c/o = child of

NAME	AGE OR YOB.	BIRTH PLACE	CERT. NO	ID	DEATH YEAR	NAME	AGE OR YOB.	BIRTH PLACE	CERT. NO	ID	DEATH YEAR
Nellie C.	22	CA	7316		1904	Freddie Martin	5	SF	7147		1902
Samuel	1	SF	332		1865	Mary	33	FRA	1535		1901
Sarah	1834	IRE	921c		1904	Nancy Matilda	36	SF	5131		1902
Sheman A.	54	MA	1357		1894	Peter/Marie, c/o	1904	SF	2855		1904
KNOWLS						**KNUDSON**					
Irwin	43	RI	1282		1869	Christian	45	NOR	K24		1883
KNOWLTON						**KNUNBERG**					
Alfred E.	2	SF	1027		1868	William	1	SF	287		1865
Elizabeth R.	1850	ME	3150c		1904	**KNUPFER**					
Fredrick H.	35	CAN	2777		1903	Karl George	21	SF	5896		1896
Harvey D.	26	SF	1052		1900	**KNUR**					
William	75	NY	1991		1901	E.	<1	SF	3402a		1872
KNOX						Edward	80	AUS	8449		1903
——			2796		1866	**KNUS**					
Charles Cole	67	NY	4732a		1895	Henry	24	SWE	7481		1900
Elmer	1	SF	1607		1903	Maria Matilda	22	FIN	385		1900
Emilie				Mar	1899	**KNUTSEN**					
George N. (soldier)			7130		1900	Cornelius/Magna, c/o		SF	3234		1900
Henry Cannon	20	NY	3195a		1872	Helga M.				Aug	1899
Isreal W.	67	MA	3993a		1895	**KNUTTE**					
Jennie	19	CAN	3140a		1872	Christ	55	SWT	3615		1902
John	43		1301		1901	Ester L.	5	SF	2836		1902
Joseph (soldier)			9571		1901	**KNUTZEN**					
Richard F., c/o	<1	SF	3166a		1872	Axel Albert	<1	DEN	3614		1896
Ruth				May	1899	**KO**					
Wm./Forne Addie , c/o	<1	CA	4612		1901	?	27	CHN	1902b		1872
Wm./Forni Addie , c/o	<1	CA	4440		1901	Hyn		CHN	2795a		1872
KNUCKLES						Lum	42	CHN	363		1902
William (soldier)			4712		1901	**KOALVIG**					
KNUDSEN						Elizabeth	36	NOR	5157		1901
Catherine	24	DEN	6284Feb		1901	**KOBAYASHI**					
Charles	42	NOR	2493		1900	Taro	1	SF	39		1903
Charles Tobey	50	NOR	6622Feb		1901	**KOBER**					
Chas.	42	NOR	K62		1886	Henry	1867	WI	1204c		1904
Frank	40	SWE	2057b		1895						

Key: a = 1st part of year; b = 2nd part of year;
c = death certificate copy; c/o = child of

NAME	AGE OR YOB.	BIRTH PLACE	CERT. NO	ID	DEATH YEAR
KOBICKE					
Henriette	28	SF	7505		1904
Robert C.	34	SF	4194		1903
KOBOLDT					
Charles	57	GER	5549		1902
KOBRO					
Fredrick	41	DEN	257		1865
KOBYLANSKIE					
Charlotte	71	WAL	3177		1866
KOCH					
Adolph F.	1882	SF	707c		1904
Alfua				Mar	1900
Appolonia				Aug	1898
August	59	GER	6343	Feb	1901
Caroline	45	NY	7047		1904
Catherine	85	ALS	2898		1903
Charles	73	GER	2897		1902
Charles Frederick	24	CA	7079	Feb	1901
Christine				Nov	1898
Elizabeth	90	GER	5605	Jan	1901
Emil	32	GER	K35		1884
Ethel M.				Oct	1899
Henry (soldier)			1467		1901
Herman	40	GER	585a		1870
Herman	36	GER	4124		1900
Hilda	36	SF	1483		1901
Joesph	64	GER	3912		1896
John	83	SWT	3325		1900
John/Maria, c/o				Dec	1898
Joseph P.	<1	SF	6669a		1895
Katharina	53	GER	8714		1903
Marie Wilhelmine	29	GER	3480		1896
Ola	<1	SF	8540		1903
Peter				Jan	1899
Philip				Dec	1899

NAME	AGE OR YOB.	BIRTH PLACE	CERT. NO	ID	DEATH YEAR
Richard				Aug	1899
Simon	73	GER	9179		1901
Theodore	42	GER	5258		1903
W. L.	62	GER	5124a		1896
William	62	GER	5004		1896
William	40	GER	4153		1900
William	82	GER	4645		1901
KOCHLAND					
Isidor	18	SF	1634		1870
KOCHLER					
Auguste	81	GER	4167a		1895
KOCK					
Claus	63	GER	5881a		1895
Guie Shing	38	CHN	4505		1903
Shee	33	CHN	5206		1901
William G.				Feb	1900
KODFORD					
Martin F.	<1	CA	1027		1902
KOEBELIN					
Laurence	62	GER	1641b		1895
KOEGEL					
Christopher C.(soldier)			287		1901
Frank A.	71	GER	5395		1901
George Dewey				Feb	1899
Jane	76	IRE	5841		1902
Louis	46	LA	590a		1871
Matilda	38	CA	3443		1900
KOEHLER					
Charles	54	GER	7940		1900
Edgar F. (soldier)			7579		1900
George B. (soldier)			3056	Oct	1901
Henry	20	GER	K49		1885
Henry				Mar	1899
William/Katie, c/o	<1	SF	1504		1902

Key: a = 1st part of year; b = 2nd part of year;
c = death certificate copy; c/o = child of

NAME	AGE OR YOB.	BIRTH PLACE	CERT. NO	ID	DEATH YEAR	NAME	AGE OR YOB.	BIRTH PLACE	CERT. NO	ID	DEATH YEAR
Wm. G.	65	GER	2539c		1904	Magdalena	46	GER	545		1902
						Otto	33	SF	4135	Dec	1901
KOELCH											
Thomas			1438		1866	**KOEPF**					
						John	15	SF	6578		1904
KOELLING											
Charles	42	GER	6367a		1895	**KOERBER**					
						——		SF	1364		1869
KOELZER											
Anthony				Feb	1900	**KOERDELL**					
Charles L.				Dec	1899	Frederick	19	MEX	8713		1900
KOENIG						**KOESEL**					
Albert	1	CA	2865		1901	George T.	1881	SF	2555c		1904
Albert	34	GER	8352		1901						
Anton	<1	SF	3420b		1870	**KOESLER**					
Anton	<1	SF	3425b		1870	Rita Dorothea	<1	SF	554		1894
George	34	BAV	7777		1868	**KOESTER**					
George	70	GER	7864		1904	Sophie Ungermann	64	GER	7422		1903
Helene	4	SF	5722		1896						
Julia				Dec	1898	**KOFFOD**					
Louis	7	SF	4441		1901	Carl C.	27	DEN	1357		1869
Louis	50	GER	227		1901	**KOFKA**					
Louis				Jul	1899	Ida				Aug	1898
Marie E.	4	SF	3934		1900	**KOFOD**					
William	60	GER	1013		1894	Hans P.	32	DEN	6699a		1895
						Martin/Eleanor, c/o		SF	4992		1901
KOENIGSBERG						**KOFOURI**					
Rubin	23	ENG	3379		1894	Katrina	<1	CA	1031b		1895
KOENIGSBERGER						**KOHEN**					
Philip	54	GER	1000		1900	Solomon				Jul	1898
KOENING						**KOHL**					
Elizabeth	66	GER	1482		1903	Adolph	1870	GER	1123c		1904
						Edith Dumlap	26	PA	7490		1901
KOENITZER											
Otto M.	34	GER	9514		1901	**KOHLAR**					
						Joseph Francis	6	SF	1422		1869
KOEPEN											
Emma	<1	SF	4950		1867	**KOHLBERG**					
						Helena	68	GER	1331b		1872
KOEPER						J./E., c/o	<1	SF	1063		1894
Frederico	70	GER	4999		1903						

Key: a = 1st part of year; b = 2nd part of year;
c = death certificate copy; c/o = child of

NAME	AGE OR YOB.	BIRTH PLACE	CERT. NO	ID	DEATH YEAR
KOHLE					
Louisa	21	SWT	703		1866
KOHLER					
Adolf	75	GER	3358		1894
Agnes	53	GER	8103		1903
Alexander	36	RUS	8866		1900
Ambrose	<1	SF	1204		1869
Caroline L.	45	CA	4115		1902
Catharine	53	GER	5809		1896
Cathrine L.	5	SF	581		1866
Charles	35	SF	3539a		1895
Charles H.	<1	SF	5235		1867
Chas.	58	GER	K83		1887
Chas. J.	15	CT	K1		1882
Francis M.	<1	SF	1413		1869
Freda	4	SF	3219		1895
Geo. H.	25	CA	K102		1889
Guido	1882	OH	1063c		1904
Henry J.	33	NY	6364		1902
Joseph Jerome	<1	SF	6637		1900
Louisa Florence	<1	SF	1543a		1871
KOHLMAN					
Chas.	50	GER	4435		1867
John P.	59	GER	1915		1866
KOHLMANN					
Pauline	24	FRA	9051		1868
KOHLMOOS					
Cora Doretta	1	SF	6409		1902
Henrich	72	GER	1923b		1872
KOHLY					
Johann G.	25	SWT	2608		1866
KOHN					
Abraham	31	IL	2310		1903
Alice Mathilda	47	GER	3581		1900
Amelia	14	SF	4002		1870
Diedrich/Julia, c/o		SF	8779		1900
Frederika	62	GER	1503		1900
Henry	<1	SF	5222		1867
Henry				Jan	1899
Henry A.	49	GER	6483	Feb	1901
Henry Lincoln	<1	SF	2075		1866
Herrman, Jr.	24	SF	3980		1902
Jacob				Feb	1900
Josphine	4	SF	5153		1867
Rose	40	NY	2602		1901
Simon	<1	SF	6946		1868
Walter Braden	23	SF	6587		1902
KOHNKE					
Margarethe	86	GER	2649		1902
KOHRAN					
R. A. W.	36	GER	1913b		1895
KOHRN					
Otto A.	<1	SF	275a		1871
KOHSMASKI					
Frank	56	GER	1351		1900
KOI					
Ah	45	CHN	540b		1871
KOK					
Tau	20	CHN	718		1870
KOLB					
Christian/Lizzie, c/o		SF	8759		1900
George	76	GER	7059	Feb	1901
Mary I.	64	GER	144b		1895
KOLBERER					
Margareta	67	GER	56		1900
KOLBERG					
Esther Brond	39	NY	937		1902

Key: a = 1st part of year; b = 2nd part of year; c = death certificate copy; c/o = child of

NAME	AGE OR YOB.	BIRTH PLACE	CERT. NO	ID	DEATH YEAR	NAME	AGE OR YOB.	BIRTH PLACE	CERT. NO	ID	DEATH YEAR
KOLDENSTRODT						**KOMOTO**					
Dora C.	<1	SF	1552		1894	George	23	JPN	2199		1902
KOLGER						**KOMPF**					
Susan	32	SWT	8309		1868	Louis	51	GER	K10		1882
KOLLE						**KOMULA**					
James Henry	1850	ENG	2620c		1904	Axle/Mary, c/o		SF	953		1895
KOLLN						Mary	37	FIN	2837		1902
John	1842	GER	1495c		1904	**KOMULE**					
KOLLSTER						Axel G.	73	FIN	4105		1903
John	35	GER	700		1902	**KON**					
KOLMER						Choy	23	CHN	1190		1869
Peter	38	GER	1178		1903	Duck	41	CHN	4917		1902
KOLSHORN						Shew	58	CHN	2208		1873
William	55	GER	6872		1868	**KONCAL**					
KOLSKY						James	32	GER	3811		1902
Mary Rachel	1	SF	1360		1869	**KONDWORTH**					
KOLVEK						William R.	29	NY	1266		1869
Joe	<1	SF	5879Jan		1901	**KONEMAN**					
Joseph/Susie, c/o		SF	5553		1896	August	38	PRU	1196		1869
KOLVICH						**KONG**					
Susan	35	AUS	2896		1902	Chan	29	CHN	6		1870
KOM						Ese	<1	SF	1553		1894
Ah	28	CHN	8517		1868	He	58	CHN	7117		1868
KOMAI						Hon	29	CHN	3346		1873
Tadao	1	SF	2932		1902	Hoo	63	CHN	376b		1872
KOMAICH						Jack	40	CHN	1237b		1895
John	21	AUT	873		1901	Lee Hung	27	CHN	7810		1868
KOMINAMI						Ling	48	CHN	4048		1902
Kusutaro	35	JPN	8477		1903	Ny Chick	30	CHN	K47		1885
KOMMAYER						Pook	60	CHN	8647		1903
Franz	50	GER	6609		1896	Sing	34	CHN	6050		1896
						Sue Yung	4	SF	6806Feb		1901
KOMMER						Yim Conn	45	CHN	755b		1871
Emanuel	73	GER	8763		1903	Yuen	42	CHN	1104a		1871

Key: a = 1st part of year; b = 2nd part of year;
c = death certificate copy; c/o = child of

NAME	AGE OR YOB.	BIRTH PLACE	CERT. NO	ID	DEATH YEAR	NAME	AGE OR YOB.	BIRTH PLACE	CERT. NO	ID	DEATH YEAR
Yuen	40	CHN	2987		1900	Koue See	34	CHN	775b		1872
KONIG						**KOONS**					
Charles F.	53	GER	1526		1900	Ephrim B	68	NY	7086		1904
Louis/Ida, c/o		SF	5683		1896	Mary E.	64	IA	1440		1900
KONIGSBERG						**KOONTZ**					
Mary Louise	33	MA	7085		1904	Adrian R.	34	IL	7579		1904
KONINATZKY						Howard M. (soldier)			1856		1901
Anna	1	CA	3033		1866	Lizzie				Mar	1900
KONISHI						Spencer S. (soldier)			7759		1901
Otozi	18	JPN	6394	Feb	1901	**KOONZ**					
KONK						William			4492		1901
Ching	32	CHN	1949		1900	**KOOPMAN**					
KONKIN						Elizabeth	1837	IRE	1247c		1904
William				Oct	1898	George J.				Aug	1898
KONO						Henry	47	GER	2805		1873
Kashikioki	30	JPN	4496a		1895	John	44	GER	3158		1873
KONOPINSKI						T. Henrick	5	SF	115		1865
Ladislaus Sigismund	<1	SF	1812b		1895	Thomas Edward	32	SF	1462b		1895
KONRAD						**KOOPMANN**					
Hermann				Jan	1899	George	<1	SF	1530b		1872
KONZIE						**KOOPS**					
Albert M.			5831		1867	Anna Marie	55	GER	6315		1904
KOO						Lucas Paul	30	HOL	6391		1903
Hen				Oct	1899	**KOPF**					
Jin	40	CHN	5284		1903	Henry Vincent	1904	SF	2856c		1904
KOOFMAN						**KOPLAN**					
James T.	44	GER	4422		1867	Birdie	10	SF	5259		1903
KOOISTRA						**KOPMANN**					
Gretta	31	HOL	603		1902	Sophie	28	GER	3933		1900
KOON						**KOPP**					
A. Hubbell	52	NY	147b		1872	——	30	GER	45		1865
Ah	30	CHN	602		1866	Catherine				Nov	1899
Ia		SF	3159		1866	Charles				Jul	1899
						Francis	52	FRA	1134		1869

NAME	AGE OR YOB.	BIRTH PLACE	CERT. NO	ID	DEATH YEAR	NAME	AGE OR YOB.	BIRTH PLACE	CERT. NO	ID	DEATH YEAR
Fredericka	66	GER	544		1903	**KORCHHOFFER**					
Joseph	70	GER	3276		1903	Louise/Dr. F., c/o	<1	SF	5750		1896
Leonhard	77	GER	7810		1903						
Louise	44	GER	8459		1900	**KORDT**					
Michael	38	GER	4295		1902	Mary	31	FL	1356		1894
Otto				Mar	1900	**KORE**					
William	1	SF	8208		1903	Freida, c/o	<1	SF	5224		1902
William				Feb	1900	**KORKER**					
KOPPE						Anna	32	CA	661		1894
August Ferdinand	70	GER	3226	Nov	1901	**KORLICK**					
KOPPEL						Sarah	67	IRL	1662		1900
Joseph C.	66	GEr	2805		1894	**KORN**					
Meyer	70	GER	1408		1903	Adam	62	PRU	328		1870
Moses	70	GER	2137		1903	Alexander	54	GER	664b		1895
KOPPELL						**KORNARENS**					
Gustave Wm.	53	RUS	8840		1901	Louis	52	NY	8541		1903
KOPPEN						**KORNFELD**					
Harold	<1	SF	5454	Jan	1901	Charles	77	HUN	766		1903
KOPPER						**KORNFIELD**					
——		SF	1153		1869	A./Gussie, c/o	1	SF	519		1903
						Helen	1877	HUN	2827c		1904
KOPPIKUS						May				Feb	1900
Harry	30	CA	5295		1904	**KORNMAN**					
John	51	KY	7650		1900	Esther	56	RUS	6588		1902
Mary A.	49	CA	40		1903	**KORNS**					
KORB						Kattie S.	51	NY	1204		1894
Auguste	46	FRA	178		1902	Thomas	23	IRE	1263		1869
Geo. F.	33	SF	2486		1894	**KORPMANN**					
Jno. H.	36	SF	3359		1894	Henry	2	SF	1009		1868
Louisa M.	71	GER	926b		1871	**KORSBERG**					
William A.	5	SF	3587		1903	Oscar William	22	SWE	6412		1904
KORBEL						**KORSGREN**					
Joseph				Feb	1900	Daniel G.	1871	SWE	1064c		1904
Maria	81	BOH	3749a		1895						

NAME	AGE OR YOB.	BIRTH PLACE	CERT. NO	ID	DEATH YEAR	NAME	AGE OR YOB.	BIRTH PLACE	CERT. NO	ID	DEATH YEAR
						Thobald	1838	DEN	3404c		1904
KORTICK						Walter E.				Jan	1899
Frank	70	AUT	8486		1901						
Rosalyn	1	SF	2297		1900	**KOSTMEYER**					
						Valentine	34	GER	1196		1869
KORTS											
Christian Henry	33	GER	1295b		1872	**KOTANI**					
George H.		SF	1890		1870	Mankichi	45	JPN	4049		1902
Henry Edwin	1	SF	2702		1900	Yataro	22	JPN	4516		1904
Susie	30	SF	2209		1901	**KOTE**					
KORVER						Paul	43	GER	6395	Feb	1901
Emma	6	SF	819		1870	**KOTGIAN**					
KOSCH						W.	51	AUT	3012		1894
Soloma Philomina	5	SF	9130		1901	**KOTH**					
						Hung Un	36	CHN	7929		1901
KOSCHNITSKI						**KOTOKU**					
Albert	49	GER	3607a		1895	Manzura	36	JPN	5960		1904
KOSHER						**KOTONA**					
Will	44	GER	4411a		1895	Bertha	<1	SF	546		1902
KOSHLAND						**KOTROZOS**					
Henry	40	GER	4638		1896	George	52	GRE	1364		1901
KOSKER						**KOTTA**					
Anna	32	CA	661		1894	Amaglia	<1	SF	4184		1902
KOSKY						Guadalupe				Dec	1899
Katie	33	CA	4509		1901	Mr./Mrs., c/o				Jul	1899
KOSSMAN						**KOTTCHOFF**					
Anthony	43	GER	6735		1904	Carl F.				Nov	1899
KOSTER						**KOTTEMANN**					
Alma Henrietta				Jan	1899	Frederick	<1	SF	3718		1896
Anna	32	CA	661		1894	**KOTTINGER**					
Eliza	<1	SF	1242		1869	Eleanor	3	CA	3878	Nov	1901
Emilda	1	SF	3804		1903	**KOUCK**					
Frederick	4	CA	4635		1904	Mon Ho Shee	67	CHN	3480	Nov	1901
Harry W. P.	1	CA	9150		1901						
Henry	56	GER	1244		1903	**KOUGH**					
Jno. N.	46	GER	K68		1886	Ka Fe	3	CO	5006		1867
Mary A.M.	37	GER	7573		1903						

NAME	AGE OR YOB.	BIRTH PLACE	CERT. NO	ID	DEATH YEAR	NAME	AGE OR YOB.	BIRTH PLACE	CERT. NO	ID	DEATH YEAR
KOVARY						**KOZMINSKY**					
Joseph	26	HUN	945		1894	Harris	56	POL	6104		1896
KOW						**KRABLER**					
A.	4	SF	1070		1869	Frank A.					Apr 1899
Ah	28	CHN	189		1870	**KRACKE**					
Ah	47	CHN	1355a		1871	Annie	34	NY	2603		1895
Ah	27	CHN	1571a		1871	**KRAFFT**					
Ah	36	CHN	1093b		1872	Ferdinand	59	BEL	2510b		1895
Ah	20	CHN	6339		1867	**KRAFT**					
Ah	18	CHN	8489		1868	Hugo C. (soldier)			8429		1901
Ah	35	CHN	1171		1869	John D.	35		1322		1869
Ah	32	CHN	2061a		1872	**KRAGEMORE**					
Ah	40	CHN	1130		1869	Serena	60	NOR	6174		1903
Back Sir	45	CHN	2675		1895	**KRAGEN**					
Chong Lan	62	CHN	5789		1896	Bertha	59	GER	895		1901
Chung	35	CHN	4715a		1895	Philip	<1	SF	1290		1869
He	46	CHN	837b		1871	**KRAGER**					
Kong	42	CHN	1047		1868	Annie	1	SF	1006		1868
Man	43	CHN	1832		1870	Mary	69	IRL	5089a		1896
Tong	49	CHN	4162		1903	**KRAGGE**					
Wong	40	CHN	2802a		1872	John	47	GER	3595		1896
Young Go	65	CHN	7147		1900	**KRAHENBUHL**					
KOWALSKI						Emilie					Jun 1899
Christine	1846	SWT	3434c		1904	**KRAHN**					
KOWALSKY						Lulu	12	SF	7762		1903
Fanny	39	POL	996		1870	**KRAHNER**					
KOWER						Ernest	51	GER	504		1901
——		SF	634		1870	**KRAKANER**					
KOWINATZKY						Morris					Nov 1899
Alfred	40	PRU	6391		1867	**KRALL**					
KOY						Henry	33	NY	1977		1894
Chu Ah	23	CHN	1086		1869	**KRALLMANN**					
KOZMINSKI						Henry			3713		1902
Florence	1	SF	2528a		1872						

Key: a = 1st part of year; b = 2nd part of year;
c = death certificate copy; c/o = child of

NAME	AGE OR YOB.	BIRTH PLACE	CERT. NO	ID	DEATH YEAR	NAME	AGE OR YOB.	BIRTH PLACE	CERT. NO	ID	DEATH YEAR
KRAMBICK						**KRANSGRILS**					
Louis	55	PRU	9610		1868	Cathrine	43	GER	8564		1868
KRAMEN						**KRANZ**					
Anthony Thomas	<1	SF	2077		1873	Henry J. (soldier)			7962		1901
KRAMER						**KRASKY**					
Alice	2	SF	3375		1873	Theodor R.	76	GER	4446		1903
Barbara Deroge	1822	GER	324c		1904	**KRATGENSTEIN**					
Bertha	52	GER	5920		1902	C.		SF	854		1870
Francis	74	GER	614b		1895	**KRATZ**					
Frank H.	22	CA	K99		1889	Carolus	78	GER	2803		1902
Franz	28	HOL	K42		1885	**KRATZENSTIEN**					
Frederick	37	GER	1373		1869	C.	<1	SF	4550		1867
Gustave Bernard	79	GER	6905		1902	**KRATZENSTIRO**					
Hannah	65	IRL	682		1894	G. L.	<1	SF	1785b		1872
Hanora	64	IRE	6327		1902	**KRATZMAN**					
Henry					Dec 1898	Mary J.	39	IRL	6497a		1895
Henry	1850	RUS	1312c		1904	**KRAUGRILL**					
Henry Frederick	46	GER	4953		1903	Margaret	35	SF	7306		1903
Herman W. (soldier)			1465		1901	**KRAUS**					
Isaac	28	TN	3256		1902	Aaron	37	SF	160b		1895
Jno. W.	59	BEL	K76		1886	Babetta	76	FRA	1483		1903
Joseph	28	SF	285b		1895	David Wolf	43	HUN	1127		1901
Leon B.	43	WI	8542		1903	Ernestina E.	11	SF	64b		1872
Louis	59	GER	5851		1904	Henry	35	GER	K38		1884
Mary	36	GER	K103		1889	Henry	32	CA	1442		1894
Peter	45	PRU	3071		1866	Hetty	<1	SF	710a		1871
Rose	10	SF	1385		1869	Joseph	41	GER	1124		1869
Samuel	60	GER	3319		1902	Julia	58	AUS	6533		1903
Sophie Electa	1	SF	1324		1869	Robt	13	SF	4442		1901
KRANDKILL						**KRAUSCH**					
——			5405		1867	Katherine	57	GER	7995		1901
KRANE						**KRAUSE**					
Harry	28	NS	1188		1894	Appalonia	50	GER	5789a		1895
KRANSGRELL						Charles					Jun 1899
George	<1	SF	8724		1868						

NAME	AGE OR YOB.	BIRTH PLACE	CERT. NO	ID	DEATH YEAR
Henry	<1	CA	K30		1884
Julius G. (soldier)			6713		1904
Lester A.	1	SF	3932		1900
Myrtle	6	WA	5599		1896
Phillip F.	36	CT	323b		1895
KRAUSS					
David	64	HUN	3850	Nov	1901
George				Feb	1899
KRAUT					
Emiel	1	SF	3452		1903
KRAYENBUHL					
Maurice G.				Nov	1899
KRAZOR					
August Ferdinand	11	SF	3387a		1872
KREAMER					
Anthony	31	GER	9959		1868
KREANERT					
Jos. (soldier)			9360		1901
KREBS					
Fritz	49	SWT	789		1900
Herman	64	GER	4244	Dec	1901
Marie	62	GER	7432		1900
KRECEK					
Joseph	31	AUS	4327		1902
KRECHER					
Catherine				Oct	1899
KREFT					
Catharina				Oct	1899
John W./Franaziska, c/o		SF	4976		1896
John/Francisca, c/o		SF	4913		1901
Wm. A.	1	SF	1643		1900
KREGER					
August (soldier)			3057	Oct	1901

NAME	AGE OR YOB.	BIRTH PLACE	CERT. NO	ID	DEATH YEAR
KREINHOFF					
Henrich	28	HAN	7238		1868
KREINS					
Conrad	65	HOL	7599		1900
KREISS					
Lauretta Louisa	64	GER	3540		1896
KREISSE					
F.	49	GER	1496b		1871
KREITZER					
Adolph M. (soldier)			7227		1900
August	37	SWT	3345	Nov	1901
KREITZKANNER					
Agnes				May	1899
KREKER					
Jacob	73	GER	8447		1901
KRELING					
Frederick William	80	GER	6898		1900
Martin				Aug	1898
KREMBSER					
August I.				Jul	1898
KREMSER					
Paul				Mar	1899
KRENEE					
Richard	<1	SF	1907		1866
KRENJENDORFF					
John Fergus	50	GER	2934		1866
KRENTZBERGER					
M./R., c/o				Aug	1899
KRENZ					
Emil A., Jr.	26	SF	2960		1903
Oswald	61	GER	7062		1903
Otto M.	54	GER	332		1902

Key: a = 1st part of year; b = 2nd part of year;
c = death certificate copy; c/o = child of

NAME	AGE OR YOB.	BIRTH PLACE	CERT. NO	ID	DEATH YEAR	NAME	AGE OR YOB.	BIRTH PLACE	CERT. NO	ID	DEATH YEAR
KREONKE						**KRIBEL**					
——			1710		1870	Adam	30	BAV	7500		1868
KRESHEL						**KRICKAW**					
Martha Ellen	49	MA	8489		1900	Peter	61	GER	4770		1903
KRESIN						**KRIE**					
John T. (marine)			4390		1903	Adolph	30	GER	4048		1903
						Ah	55	CHN	1248b		1872
KRESLER						**KRIEG**					
Annie	34	CA	6281		1900	Anton	14	SF	8427		1903
Elmer	28	MO	4036		1896	Nellie	30	CA	3257		1902
KRESS						Oswald	4	SF	8209		1903
Henry Charles	19	CA	613b		1895	Peter	50		2249		1902
KRETSHMAN						Raymond Anton	1	SF	1446b		1895
Alfred	53	GER	1447		1870						
John	67	GER	688b		1895	**KRIEGER**					
						Lucielle M.	2	SF	1553		1901
KRETZ											
Anna M.	76	SWT	5605		1903	**KRIETE**					
						——		SF	139a		1870
KRETZSCHMAR						Emily	27	SF	4101		1896
Max	45	GER	4726		1903						
						KRIGBAUN					
KREUDER						Amilee	31	CA	407		1900
Phillip L.	27	KS	6974		1903						
						KRIGER					
KREUGER						Berki	28	GER	6536a		1895
Joseph	34	GER	4455b		1870						
						KRILL					
KREUL						Wm. H.	2	CA	5318a		1895
Philip Otto	21	GER	4258		1903						
						KRING					
KREUTZER						Louis S. (soldier)			7784		1901
Ida					Nov 1898						
Lizabeta	46	ITA	7431		1902	**KRISKE**					
						Ernst L.	57	GER	5349		1902
KREUZER											
Louis/Minna, c/o	<1	SF	2933		1902	**KRISSELDROFFER**					
Rosie	23	SWT	4535		1901	Annie	53	GER	3420		1903
						KRISTEN					
KREYE						Joseph	28	GER	6683		1903
John L.	51	GER	520		1903						

Key: a = 1st part of year; b = 2nd part of year;
c = death certificate copy; c/o = child of

NAME	AGE OR YOB.	BIRTH PLACE	CERT. NO	ID	DEATH YEAR
KRISTIANSEN					
Gardeman	22	NOR	4462		1901
KRISTIN					
Emile	28	FRA	1454		1900
KRISTU					
Emile	28	FRA	1454		1900
KRITIKI					
Agatha	42	AK	4974		1904
KRIZ					
Louis Daniel	38	AUT	2633		1895
KROEGER					
George	49	GER	3067		1895
KROENCKE					
August H./Louise M., c/o	1	SF	1802		1903
KROENKE					
Walter H. H.	<1	SF	1952		1894
KROFF					
John E.				Jan	1899
KROGER					
August	73	GER	2138		1903
Christoffer	31	NOR	6565		1902
Claus F.	62	GER	7317		1902
Julius	24	CA	816		1901
Louisa	67	GER	5906		1904
Maud Gertrude	26	SF	2052		1903
KROGH					
Caroline F.	60	NY	1973		1903
Marcus				Mar	1899
KROHN					
Andreas	22	GER	1516a		1871
Arthur C.	<1	SF	1537		1902
August John			3069		1902
Fred H.	54	GER	1974		1903
Fritz	27	GER	7452		1868

NAME	AGE OR YOB.	BIRTH PLACE	CERT. NO	ID	DEATH YEAR
Gustave A.	23	SF	1987		1900
Henry	23	GER	1205		1869
KRON					
Oscar J.				Nov	1899
KRONBERGER					
Herman/Rose, c/o		SF	7614		1901
KRONCHE					
Justina				Feb	1899
KRONE					
Susan	1	SF	2620		1873
KRONENBERG					
Barbara	54	GER	8165		1901
Vencentoria	85	GER	6121a		1895
KRONENBERGER					
Anna	37	GER	2754		1903
Joseph	1	SF	1637		1903
KRONER					
George W. (civilian)			451		1901
KRONHOHN					
John Albert	<1	SF	875b		1872
KRONHOLN					
Gustaf F.				Dec	1898
KRONI					
——		SF	1442		1869
KRONING					
Ditrich	31	GER	4364b		1870
KROPLIN					
Henrietta	52	DEN	3597		1900
KROPP					
Charles	44	NY	1053		1900
Henry W.	25	SF	3071	Oct	1901
KROSBERG					
Edward	66	SWE	6544	Feb	1901

Key: *a = 1st part of year; b = 2nd part of year;*
c = death certificate copy; c/o = child of

NAME	AGE OR YOB.	BIRTH PLACE	CERT. NO	ID	DEATH YEAR
KROTOSZYNER					
Robert E.	<1	SF	6230		1902
KROU					
Pauline	15	NY	4072		1896
KROUE					
Cathrine	<1	SF	1036		1868
KROUHOLM					
Catherine Sophia	31	FIN	515b		1872
KROUSE					
Samuel				Oct	1899
KRUCIUS					
Mary	74	GER	1001		1900
KRUECKEL					
Peter Frank	51	GER	2078		1903
KRUEGER					
Charles	1828	RUS	1084c		1904
George/Daisy, c/o	1904	CA	1786		1904
Gustav A.			7172		1901
William (soldier)			288		1901
KRUG					
Christiana	75	GER	3767		1903
Fritz	48	GER	5565		1903
Joseph P.	68	GER	2623		1902
KRUGE					
——			9200		1868
KRUGER					
Albert R. (soldier)			7963		1901
Anna	21	GER	1264		1870
Anna E.	67	GER	6175		1903
August	31	PRU	824a		1871
Carl	38	CHI	1948		1900
Charles	45	GER	3658		1902
Charles J. (soldier)			771		1901
Clara				Jan	1899
Fred				Mar	1900
Henry/Minnie, c/o	<1	SF	246		1900
Johan	<1	SF	2469b		1895
Louis	55	GER	3541		1896
Minnie	26	CA	2311		1903
William	10	SF	4796		1902
William	60	GER	8734		1900
KRUKAN					
Nicholas J.	63	DEN	2692		1901
KRULL					
John F.	70	GER	1893b		1895
KRUMBECK					
Diedrick				Aug	1899
Minna	61	GER	4378		1901
KRUMBERG					
Wilhelm	40	GER	3925		1896
KRUMMACKER					
W B	49	GER	660		1894
KRUSA					
William	50	GER	727b		1895
KRUSCHEWSKY					
August Herman	60	GER	1590		1902
KRUSE					
Dina	20	NE	4877		1904
Earnest/Mary, c/o		SF	1339		1895
Ernest A.	<1	SF	231a		1871
Frank H.				Dec	1898
Henry				Jul	1898
Henry F.	67	GER	3453		1903
Henry, Sr.	62	GER	2109a		1872
Jno. Henry	<1	SF	1645		1894
Martin				Nov	1899
Mary	1868	NJ	2216c		1904
Mary, c/o	<1	SF	2684a		1872

Key: *a = 1st part of year; b = 2nd part of year;*
c = death certificate copy; c/o = child of

NAME	AGE OR YOB.	BIRTH PLACE	CERT. NO	ID	DEATH YEAR	NAME	AGE OR YOB.	BIRTH PLACE	CERT. NO	ID	DEATH YEAR
Wm. H.				Jan	1899	**KUCHMEISTER**					
						Anna Maria	3	SF	380a		1871
KRUTMEYER						Mary	28	SF	4523		1903
Gustaf B.				Jan	1899						
						KUCICH					
KRUTZMANN						Jerome	61	AUS	2961		1903
W. S.	65	DEN	3066		1895						
						KUCK					
KRYER						Diedrich	47	GER	812		1894
Catharine	30	SC	K58		1885	Ernest	16	SF	5813a		1895
KRYNSKI						**KUE**					
Lucas	83	POL	3502	Nov	1901	Ah		CHN	K79		1887
						Ah	19	CHN	9800		1868
KRZYZANOWSKI						Ah	1852	CHN	719c		1904
Palagia Maria	43	POL	5425		1903	Lee	1903	SF	452c		1904
						Toy	18	CHN	1090c		1904
KU						Wong Fong	30	CHN	3482b		1870
Sun	9	SF	1233		1869						
						KUECHLER					
KUA						Gottlobe	1835	GER	777c		1904
Arthur	24	HI	3567		1896						
						KUEHLING					
KUANS						Henry Anton Gustave	68	GER	5634		1903
Frank	11	CA	K100		1889						
						KUEHN					
KUBACH						Becky				Aug	1898
Louis	57	GER	7572		1901						
						KUEHNE					
KUBER						Dorothy	62	GER	6833	Feb	1901
Charles	4	SF	2615		1894	Gustave	28	GER	236		1903
						Gustave R.W.	1	SF	7621		1904
KUBLLUSY											
Benjamin	24	SWE	1316		1869	**KUEHNIS**					
						Charles G.	47	GER	6584		1900
KUBO											
K.	1887	JPN	2707c		1904	**KUEN**					
						Man	43	CHN	426		1865
KUCH											
Geo.	45	GER	K28		1883	**KUENNE**					
Maria	39	GER	3714		1867	Gafried	25	SWT	551		1866
KUCHIN											
P./B., c/o	<1	SF	4152		1895	**KUESTER**					
						Josephine	66	GER	1592b		1895
KUCHLKEN											
Joseph	56	GER	9036		1901						

NAME	AGE OR YOB.	BIRTH PLACE	CERT. NO	ID	DEATH YEAR	NAME	AGE OR YOB.	BIRTH PLACE	CERT. NO	ID	DEATH YEAR
KUEY						Jno. R.	27	GER	1931		1894
Ng	1855	CHN	2464c		1904	John N.	<1	SF	6022		1896
						Lenore	<1	SF	1260		1894
KUGELEN						**KUHLMEYER**					
Geo./Louise, c/o					Feb 1900	Louisa	62	GER	2781		1894
KUGELER						**KUHLO**					
Regina	87	GER	5447a		1895	Geo.	21	GER	K31		1884
KUGELMAN						**KUHLS**					
Adolph	29	GER	1406b		1871	Edward	66	GER	914		1901
KUGENER						Mary Elizabeth	47	NY	6610		1896
Pauline	<1	SF	5138a		1896	**KUHN**					
KUGH						Anna	54	GER	4583		1903
Harry W.			3793		1902	Edward/Mary, c/o		SF	5753		1901
KUGLER						Fred	16	SF	3748a		1895
Louis (soldier)			7785		1901	Hellmuch Edward	<1	SF	7127		1903
Othniel	<1	CA	1260b		1895	Herman	26	SF	7219		1902
KUHE						Joseph/Margaret, c/o	1904	SF	1878		1904
John	5	SF	1982		1873	Joseph/Margaret, c/o	1904	SF	1879		1904
KUHIRTZ						Max	61	GER	1145		1894
Chas. H.	<1	SF	1365		1869	W. F. H.	21	SF	6242a		1895
KUHKLKE						William	18	SF	4811		1896
Hermann	41	GER	3503	Nov	1901	**KUHNELL**					
KUHL						Maria Caro E.	62	GER	1981		1873
Catharine	3	SF	2389a		1872	**KUHNERT**					
F. G.	39	PA	K13		1882	Otto Conrad	<1	SF	1840		1894
Katherina E.	<1	SF	3011a		1872	**KUHR**					
KUHLAND						Claus				Jul	1898
William	60	GER	2887		1895	**KUIE**					
KUHLEMANN						Ah	45	CHN	2985a		1872
Wm./Louisa, c/o	1904	SF	1578		1904	Ma	1859	CHN	2441c		1904
KUHLENKAMP						**KUK**					
Henry	4	SF	4005		1896	Laes	36	CHN	292		1865
KUHLMANN						**KUKAR**					
Esther	66	GER	7985		1900	John		SF	3738		1902

Key: a = 1st part of year; b = 2nd part of year;
c = death certificate copy; c/o = child of

NAME	AGE OR YOB.	BIRTH PLACE	CERT. NO	ID	DEATH YEAR	NAME	AGE OR YOB.	BIRTH PLACE	CERT. NO	ID	DEATH YEAR
Maria	35	AUS	7865		1904	Tai	26	CHN	1064		1903
KUKEYA						**KUMAKICHI**					
S.	24	JPN	6372	Feb	1901	Iki	26	JPN	5532	Jan	1901
KUKIZA						**KUMMER**					
Michael	63	AUT	4443		1901	Gustave A.	68	GER	3877		1902
KUKULJICA						**KUMMEROW**					
Carolina	40	AUS	1063		1903	Henry	52	GER	8819		1903
KULIACHA						**KUMMOTO**					
Nicholas	20	AUT	8061		1901	S.				Jul	1899
KULL						**KUMP**					
Louise				Aug	1898	Joseph				Nov	1899
KULLMAN						**KUMPF**					
Herman	69	GER	4264		1900	Jacob	25	GER	6887		1904
KULLMANN						**KUN**					
August	51	FRA	5068		1904	Ah	2	SF	4689		1867
Edward	1	SF	337		1903	**KUNAST**					
Jacques	40	FRA	4833		1896	Henry				Jan	1899
KULPER						**KUNATH**					
Adolph	33	GER	K3		1882	Erwin				Oct	1898
Fred	1903	CA	3295c		1904	**KUNAUER**					
KULSTRUM						Jennie	1857	IRE	3037c		1904
Alex	29	FIN	6239		1900	**KUNE**					
KUM						A.	26	CHN	692b		1871
Ah	20	CHN	101a		1871	Mark	36	CHN	1157		1869
Ah	25	CHN	648b		1872	**KUNG**					
Ah	47	CHN	1445		1869	Ah	30	CHN	2976		1866
Ching Ye	36	CHN	1447		1869	Chong	63	CHN	4849		1902
Chun				Mar	1900	Li	31	CHN	2236a		1872
Gow	20	CHN	760a		1871	Moey				Oct	1899
Kuo Yung	20	CHN	478b		1871	Sah Jung	31	CHN	6611		1896
Oge	<1	SF	9291		1868	Yit/Son Shee, c/o	2	SF	7705		1902
Sing	16	CHN	K20		1883	**KUNHARDT**					
Sum	34	CHN	679b		1871	Ada Elizabeth, Mrs.	23	NY	6753		1902
Sy	22	CHN	114b		1871						

Key: a = 1st part of year; b = 2nd part of year;
c = death certificate copy; c/o = child of

NAME	AGE OR YOB.	BIRTH PLACE	CERT. NO	ID	DEATH YEAR	NAME	AGE OR YOB.	BIRTH PLACE	CERT. NO	ID	DEATH YEAR
						Therese	68	GER	7368		1902
KUNI											
Chue	26	CHN	3883		1870	**KURLEIH**					
						Anton/Molly, c/o		SF	1764		1895
KUNITZ											
Andrew	43	GER	1573a		1871	**KURNAN**					
						Bridget	61	IRE	1636		1903
KUNKEL											
David	29	MO	338		1903	**KURNMER**					
						Harry H.				Jan	1899
KUNST											
Annie	39	OH	6531		1902	**KURNON**					
August				Apr	1899	John L.	36	IRL	4134b		1870
KUNTZ						**KURNZAR**					
Andrew L.	27		5076		1903	Paul				Dec	1898
Barbara	77	GER	2665		1894						
Francis H.	61	NJ	2312		1903	**KUROZANA**					
						Swen Ichi				Feb	1899
KUNTZE											
Richard Daniel	56	GER	4208a		1895	**KURPINSKY**					
						Hazel A.	2	CA	889		1903
KUNZE						Mary E.	18	SF	627		1903
Johanna	71	GER	3970	Dec	1901						
John C.	68	GER	1401		1870	**KURTH**					
P. G. G./Maria, c/o	<1	SF	4213		1901	W.	74	GER	4901a		1895
KUPFER						**KURTOVICH**					
Genevieve	71	FRA	5811		1896	Chris	29	AUS	4847		1904
KURANO						**KURTZ**					
Kuniharu	1873	JPN	2339c		1904	Edward			6227		1903
						Miriam Sallie	69	AUS	1811		1902
KURAYA						**KURZ**					
Ichitaro	24	JPN	874		1901	Paulina	6	SF	2782		1894
KURIN						**KUSABA**					
Michael/Aliverda, c/o	<1	SF	3022		1901	Jusaku				Feb	1899
KURIYAMA						**KUSCHHOFERE&**					
D.				Aug	1898	Ursula	35	SWT	3918	Dec	1901
KURLANDZIK						**KUSICK**					
Minnie	46	GER	5160		1902	Vincent/Vincentia, c/o		CA	938		1902
KURLBAUM						**KUSS**					
Jesse Jason				Aug	1898	Rosina M.	69	GER	4318		1901

Key: a = 1st part of year; b = 2nd part of year;
c = death certificate copy; c/o = child of

NAME	AGE OR YOB.	BIRTH PLACE	CERT. NO	ID	DEATH YEAR	NAME	AGE OR YOB.	BIRTH PLACE	CERT. NO	ID	DEATH YEAR
KUSTER						KWANG					
A./M., c/o	<1	SF	5840		1895	Ho	50	CHN	4900a		1895
KUSTINBORDER						Lun Lo	29	CHN	1856b		1895
Wm.				Feb	1900	KWOK					
KUTCHERA						Cow				Mar	1899
Barbara	1	SF	2200		1903	KWON					
KUTH						Jung	49	CHN	5573		1902
James	79	MA	7191		1902	KWONG					
KUTNER						Quan Yow				Nov	1898
Adolph	65	POL	1424		1902	Wong	38	CHN	6037a		1895
Leopold				Aug	1899	KWY					
KUTOCH						Ling	32	CHN	3111a		1872
John	25	AUS	9568		1868	KY					
KUTSCHER						Ling				Nov	1898
Elizabeth P.	55	AUS	4376		1902	KYBURZ					
KUTSCHINSKY						Mary Ann	1834	SWT	2594c		1904
Frank (soldier)			1470		1901	KYE					
KUTTBERT						Ah	45	CHN	8160		1868
H.	24	SWE	647b		1872	KYGER					
KUTTER						David				Jan	1899
Carl Edward	66	GER	5679		1903	Miles E.				Jan	1899
KUTTNER						KYLBURG					
Chas. A.	55	GER	4453a		1895	Ida Fredricka	30	SWE	6257a		1895
Naphthaly	73	PRU	7599		1903	KYLE					
KUTZ						James	49	IRL	337b		1895
Gabriel M.	59	GER	1533b		1895	Mary	8	SF	1004		1870
KUWAHARA						KYMAN					
Masa	1	SF	587		1903	Michael (soldier)			3058	Oct	1901
KVATZ						KYNE					
John	78	GER	1695		1900	Frank C.				Jan	1899
KWAN						John	48	IRL	153		1900
Ah Sue	45	CHN	4292		1901	Pat	38	IRL	6238		1900
Choy				Jan	1899						

Key: a = 1st part of year; b = 2nd part of year;
c = death certificate copy; c/o = child of

NAME	AGE OR YOB.	BIRTH PLACE	CERT. NO	ID	DEATH YEAR	NAME	AGE OR YOB.	BIRTH PLACE	CERT. NO	ID	DEATH YEAR
KYRAGGEN											
Marie	1	CA	K45		1885						
KYSELA											
Henry J. (soldier)			5813	Jan	1901						
KYSER											
Albert R.	<1	SF	8114		1904						

Key: a = 1st part of year; b = 2nd part of year; c = death certificate copy; c/o = child of

Publications from the California Genealogical Society and Library

To order publications from the California Genealogical Society and Library visit the society's website at *CaliforniaAncestors.org*.

San Francisco Probates 1906-1942: Register of Actions, Volumes 1-2, is an index, for the first time in print, to the 179 Registers of Action for Probate cases, each containing 500 pages, dating from the 1906 earthquake and fire through March 27, 1942. Included are 108,998 names representing over 85,500 probates and guardianship proceedings. Vernon A. Deubler, comp., pub. 2010, softbound, 8 1/2 x 11 format, 487 pp. (vol. I), 480 pp.(vol. II). ISBN 978-0-9785694-7-1 (vol. I, A-K); ISBN 978-0-9785694-8-8 (vol. II, L-M); LOC 2010926283.

San Francisco Deaths 1865-1905: Abstracts from Surviving Civil Records, Volumes 1-4, is an index, unsurpassed for accuracy and completeness, to over 96,000 civil records known to have survived the 1906 earthquake and fire. Barbara Close and Vernon A. Deubler, comp., pub. 2010, softbound, 8 1/2 x 11 format. ISBN 978-0-9785694-1-9 (vol. I, A-D); ISBN 978-0-9785694-2-6 (vol. II, E-K); ISBN 978-0-9785694-3-3 (vol. III, L-P); ISBN 978-0-9785694-4-0 (vol. IV, Q-Z); LOC 2009940489.

Raking the Ashes is a "must have" for researching San Francisco ancestors, providing invaluable guidance on which records were lost in the 1906 San Francisco earthquake and fire, which records survived, and where to find the surviving records. Nancy Peterson, pub. 2006, softbound, 8 1/2 x 11" format, 222 pp. ISBN 978-0-9672409-8-5; LOC 2006920734.

A Most Dreadful Earthquake, based on the previously unpublished correspondence of a young San Francisco woman describing the aftermath of the 1906 San Francisco earthquake and fire, graphically describes the sights of the city and gives details of everyday life in the chaos of those first days. Dorothy Fowler, Pub. 2006, Softbound, 5 1/2 x 8 1/4" format, 174pp. ISBN 978-0-9672409-7-8; LOC 2005935823.

San Francisco, California: Columbarium Records 1847-1980 is an index listing nearly 6,000 names found in previously unpublished records of San Francisco's Odd Fellows Columbarium. Vernon A. Deubler, comp., pub. 2003, softbound, 8 1/2 x 11 format, 130 pp. ISBN 978-0-9672409-4-7; LOC 2003112862.

San Francisco, California: I.O.O.F. Crematory Records is an index to approximately 10,000 previously unpublished cremation records of the Independent Order of Odd Fellows, dating primarily from 1895 to 1911. Records providing each person's birthplace, date of death and age, place and cause of death, and indication of obituaries are available. Barbara Ross Close, comp., pub. 2001, softbound, 8 1/2 x 11" format, 413 pp. ISBN 978-0-9672409-2-3; LOC 2001093990.

California Surname Index: Biographies From Selected Histories provides an integrated index to more than 18,000 biographical sketches of early Californians named in 42 historical works on the shelves of the California Genealogical Society's George R. Dorman Collection. Barbara Ross Close, comp., pub. 2000, hard-bound, 8 1/2 x 11" format, 325 pp. ISBN 978-0-9672409-1-6; LOC 9976177.

San Francisco Probate Index 1880-1906: A Partial Reconstruction contains more than 10,000 names in pre-1906 San Francisco records, compiled and indexed, from a variety of sources. Kathleen C. Beals, comp., pub. 1996, softbound, 8 1/2 x 11" format, 239 pp. ISBN 978-0-9672409-9-2; LOC 97179094.

Index to San Francisco Marriage Returns 1850-1858 presents a compilation of some of San Francisco's earliest marriage returns, indexed alphabetically and chronologically. Kathleen C. Beals, comp., pub. 1992, softbound, 8 1/2 x 11" format, 109 pp. ISBN 978-0-9785694-0-2; LOC 97179098.

Order Form for a Copy of a Death Record

To order a photocopy of an original record as it appears in the old ledgers, use the Lookups feature on the society's website, CaliforniaAncestors.org. Generally the original record contains more information than is included in this book.

If you would prefer to place your order by regular mail, please make a copy of this form and fill in the blanks, or write a letter and be sure to provide the surname, given name, any certificate number and ID, and the year of death for each record requested. The current fee at publication is $10 per record and will be honored through 2012. For fees after 2012, please check the society's website under Lookups or call 510- 663-1358. Please send your request(s), with a *check or money order payable to the California Genealogical Society, to:

California Genealogical Society
2201 Broadway, LL2
Oakland, CA 94612-3031.

* Requests from outside the United States: Please order through the society's website, CaliforniaAncestors.org, using PayPal. For written requests, include a foreign draft, drawn on a financial institution in the United States, made payable in United States currency.

Records Requested

	Surname	Given Name	Certificate No.	ID	Death Year	Fee
1.	_____	_____	_____	_____	_____	$_____.____
2.	_____	_____	_____	_____	_____	$_____.____
3.	_____	_____	_____	_____	_____	$_____.____
4.	_____	_____	_____	_____	_____	$_____.____

Total payment $_____.____

Contact Information

_____
Your Name

_____
Address Line 1

_____
Address Line 2

_____
City/State/Zip

_____
Telephone

_____
Email Address (optional)

www.ingramcontent.com/pod-product-compliance
Lightning Source LLC
Chambersburg PA
CBHW081426270326
41932CB00019B/3107